Interpersonal Communication

Interpersonal Communication

Everyday Encounters

edition

8

Julia T. Wood

Lineberger Distinguished Professor of Humanities Emerita
Caroline H. and Thomas S. Royster Distinguished
  Professor of Graduate Education Emerita

THE UNIVERSITY OF NORTH CAROLINA AT CHAPEL HILL

CENGAGE
Learning·

Australia • Brazil • Japan • Korea • Mexico • Singapore • Spain • United Kingdom • United States

CENGAGE
Learning

Interpersonal Communication: Everyday Encounters, Eighth Edition
Julia T. Wood

Product Director: Monica Eckman

Senior Product Manager: Nicole Morinon

Senior Content Developer:
Sue Gleason Wade

Senior Media Developer: Jessica Badiner

Associate Content Developer:
Karolina Kiwak

Product Assistant: Colin Solan

Marketing Director: Stacey Purviance

Content Project Manager: Dan Saabye

Art Director: Linda May

Manufacturing Planner: Doug Bertke

IP Analyst: Ann Hoffman

IP Project Manager: Farah Fard

Production Service: Lumina Datamatics, Inc.

Text and Cover Designer: Rokusek Design

Cover Image: All Cover Photos by
Shutterstock

Compositor: Lumina Datamatics, Inc.

Library of Congress Control Number: 2014938884

ISBN-13: 978-1-285-44583-0

Cengage Learning
20 Channel Center Street
Boston, MA 02210
USA

Cengage Learning is a leading provider of customized learning solutions with office locations around the globe, including Singapore, the United Kingdom, Australia, Mexico, Brazil and Japan. Locate your local office at **international.cengage.com/region.**

Cengage Learning products are represented in Canada by Nelson Education, Ltd.

For your course and learning solutions, visit **www.cengage.com.**

Purchase any of our products at your local college store or at our preferred online store **www.cengagebrain.com.**

Instructors: Please visit **login.cengage.com** and log in to access instructor-specific resources.

Printed in Canada
Print Number: 01   Print Year: 2014

For my niece, Michelle, whose wit, imagination, and daring inspire me

BRIEF CONTENTS

PART ONE The Fabric of Interpersonal Communication

PART TWO Weaving Communication into Relationships

CONTENTS

chapter FOUR
THE WORLD OF WORDS   103

chapter FIVE
THE WORLD BEYOND WORDS   133

X
Contents

PART TWO Weaving
Communication into Relationships

chapter SEVEN
EMOTIONS AND COMMUNICATION 189

chapter EIGHT
COMMUNICATION CLIMATE: THE FOUNDATION OF PERSONAL RELATIONSHIPS 217

chapter **TEN**

FRIENDSHIPS IN OUR LIVES 281

chapter **ELEVEN**

COMMITTED ROMANTIC
RELATIONSHIPS 307

chapter **TWELVE**

COMMUNICATION IN FAMILIES **334**

COMMUNICATION IN EVERYDAY LIFE

I wrote this book to introduce students to knowledge and skills that will allow them to live fuller, more satisfying lives than they could without competence in interpersonal communication. To achieve that goal, *Interpersonal Communication: Everyday Encounters* is distinct in three ways. First, it gives prominence to theories, research, and practical skills from the field of communication and supplements these with scholarship from other fields. Second, this book gives strong attention to three issues that are vital in the 21st century: social diversity, social media, and workplace contexts. Finally, this book offers unique pedagogical features that encourage personal learning. Throughout the book, I encourage students to engage theory and concepts personally and to apply theoretical and practical information to their lives.

In writing this book, I've focused on communication research and theory and complemented them with work from other fields. Interpersonal communication is a well-established intellectual area, complete with a base of knowledge, theories, and research developed by communication scholars. The maturation of interpersonal communication as an intellectual discipline is evident in the substantial original research published in academic journals and scholarly books. Consistent with this scholarly growth, *Interpersonal Communication: Everyday Encounters* features current research on communication. For example, Chapter 2 discusses communication strategies that we use to present our face and, if it's threatened, to protect it. Chapter 6, which focuses on listening, invites students to consider research showing that social media increasingly interfere with mindful, attentive listening; Chapter 11 discusses ways that social media facilitate and sometimes constrain interpersonal communication and offers information on long-distance romantic relationships, which are increasingly common. And Chapter 12 highlights family communication patterns that influence how parents and children interact and what they can talk about.

Scholarship in other fields can enhance understanding of communication. For this reason, *Interpersonal Communication: Everyday Encounters* incorporates research from other fields. For example, research in psychology deepens our understanding of the role of attributions in interpersonal perception. Ongoing work in anthropology, sociology, philosophy, psychology, and other disciplines enriches insight into differences in communication that are influenced by gender, economic class, sexual orientation, ethnicity, and race.

Attention to Significant Social Trends

Interpersonal Communication: Everyday Encounters speaks to the context of students' lives today. I have given attention to the social trends, issues, and concerns that characterize the 21st century in Western culture.

Social Diversity The United States, like many other countries, is enriched by a cornucopia of people, heritages, customs, and ways of interacting. *Interpersonal Communication: Everyday Encounters* reflects and addresses social diversity by weaving it into the basic fabric of interpersonal communication.

Truly incorporating diversity into this book entails more than adding an isolated chapter on the topic or tacking paragraphs about gender or race onto conventional coverage of topics. To achieve a more organic approach to diversity, I weave discussion of race, ethnicity, economic class, gender, age, religion, and sexual orientation into the book as a whole. This approach allows students to appreciate the relevance of diversity to all aspects of interpersonal communication. For example, in exploring personal identity, I examine race, gender, socioeconomic class, and sexual orientation as the core facets of identity. You'll also find numerous examples of ways in which diversity affects communication in the contemporary workplace, which is populated by people from different cultures and social communities. Chapters 4 and 5, which cover verbal and nonverbal communication, respectively, feature examples of communication in non-Western cultures. Chapter 11, on romantic relationships, discusses research on interracial, gay, and lesbian romance; and Chapter 12, on family communication, includes research on a range of families, including ones that are not white, middle-class, and heterosexual.

To discourage stereotyped thinking about groups of people, I rely on qualifying adjectives. For instance, when citing research about differences between Hispanic and European American communication patterns, I refer to "most Hispanics" and what is "typical of European Americans." My intent is to remind students that generalizations are limited and may not apply to every member of a group.

To further weave diversity into this book, I include "Communication in Everyday Life" features that emphasize connections between communication and diversity.

Social Media   Another defining feature of our era is the pervasive presence of social media in our lives. We use e-mail and texting to stay in touch with friends and family. We join online support groups. We blog, check Facebook, Skype, text, and instant message (IM). We participate in online religious and political discussions. We meet people, make friends, network, flirt, and date—all online. As with social diversity, this topic is better covered by integrating it organically into all chapters rather than by relegating it to a separate chapter.

Every chapter in this edition includes a main section, immediately before the chapter's summary "Guidelines for" section, in which I discuss how social media pertain to the chapter's content. In addition, this edition includes "Communication in Everyday Life" features that highlight social media. Finally, I have integrated technology into the text itself. I suggest a number of websites and online sources for students who want to learn more about particular topics in "Communication in Everyday Life."

Ethics   Ethical issues are much in the news. We hear reports about insider trading in the stock market, politicians who take bribes, and public officials who have affairs and engage in sexting. Yet, ethical issues are not confined to the public realm. They also surface in interpersonal life; in fact, they infuse interpersonal interaction. We are frequently confronted with ethical choices: Do we tell a "white lie" when a friend asks us how we like a very expensive new hairstyle she has or do we tell her that we don't think it's flattering? Do we exaggerate our attractiveness when creating our profile for an online dating site? Do we pretend to be listening when we are really not? Do we judge people from other cultures by the norms and standards of our own culture? These are just a few of the ethical considerations that arise in our everyday encounters. To underline the ethical character of interpersonal communication, I call attention to such issues both in the chapter content and in the "Thinking Critically" exercises at the end of each chapter.

Coverage of Timely Topics

Interpersonal Communication: Everyday Encounters provides coverage of topics and issues that have increased importance in this era. There is a **full chapter on friendships**, because so many of my students tell me that friendships are essential to them in the face of the growing number of broken marriages and geographically dispersed families. Social media make it possible for friends to stay in touch with each other across distances that separate them. The chapter on romantic relationships addresses some of the **"dark side" issues** in intimate relationships such as abuse and violence between intimates. This chapter also discusses using communication to negotiate safer sex in an era where hooking up is not uncommon and sexually transmitted diseases are a danger.

Students are also increasingly career-focused. They want to know how what they are studying pertains to the world of work and how it will help them succeed in that world. This edition of *Interpersonal Communication: Everyday Encounters* gives **prominence to connections between interpersonal communication concepts and skills and the workplace** in four ways. First, I include research about on-the-job communication within each chapter. Second, I call attention to particularly interesting connections between interpersonal communication and careers by highlighting them in "Communication in Everyday Life—Workplace" boxes. Third, at the end of each chapter, I include a workplace application. Finally, for instructors who want fuller coverage of on-the-job communication, I have prepared a chapter on organizational communication that can be bundled with this text as a part of our customization program; contact your sales representative for details.

Changes in the Eighth Edition

Interpersonal Communication: Everyday Encounters has evolved in response to feedback from instructors and students as well as new research in communication and kindred disciplines.

I have made several significant content changes in this edition:

- This edition weaves cultural diversity more thoroughly into the book. Specifically, Chapter 2, which covers identity, discusses cultural influences on self-presentation. Chapter 3, which focuses on perception, highlights research showing that people from different cultures actually perceive visual phenomena differently—Westerners are more likely to be deceived by optical illusions than are people whose physical environments have fewer box shapes (for instance, rooms in homes). My discussion of conflict (Chapter 9) now includes information about cultural influences, on how people manage conflict and the extent to which they help one another maintain or save face in conflict situations.

- As noted earlier, this edition provides stronger and more integrated attention to social media. Every chapter includes a section that discusses connections between chapter themes and social media. In addition, every chapter includes one or more "Communication in Everyday Life" features that highlight social media.

- The text gives enhanced attention to ethics. In addition to coverage of ethical choices woven throughout the text, a Thinking Critically question focused specifically on ethics appears at the end of each chapter.

- Chapter 2, Communication and Personal Identity, includes a new section on how we express, or perform, our identities. In highlighting our human ability to choose how to perform our identities, this new material provides a useful complement to existing coverage of ways that others and culture shape identity.

- I've revised Chapter 12, Communication in Families, to be more relevant to contemporary students. I have added discussion of family communication patterns that reflect the degrees of openness and hierarchy in different families, and I have included material on cultural influences on family interaction. I have added material on difficult conversations, such as telling parents of an unplanned pregnancy or the intention to drop out of school, or helping parents transition to retirement communities. This new material should help students think about and manage issues that face or will face them and their families.

- I have included findings from more than 125 new sources that reflect the latest research related to interpersonal communication. Attention to current research ensures that *Interpersonal Communication: Everyday Encounters* remains grounded in strong scholarship while also being accessible to students.

Pedagogy for Personal Learning

In addition to this book's distinct conceptual emphases, I've adopted a **conversational and personal tone** to encourage students to feel they are full participants in a dialogue. I use contractions, as people do in everyday conversations. Also, I include examples of everyday interactions so that abstract ideas are clarified in practical ways. In my writing, I share with students some of the communication challenges and encounters that have surfaced in my life. The conversational writing style aims to prompt students to think of their own examples and applications of material presented in the book. As students do this, they interact personally with the concepts, principles, and skills presented in this book.

My voice is not the only one that students will encounter in this book. All chapters are enhanced by a second personal learning feature— **student commentaries** that were written by students in interpersonal communication classes at my university and other colleges and universities around the nation. Their experiences, insights, and concerns broaden the conversation to include a wide range of perspectives. The student commentaries also encourage active learning through observation, comparison, and analysis. As students read the commentaries, they observe others and compare and contrast others' experiences and perspectives with their own. If students wish to write their own commentaries for future editions of this book, I invite them to send those to me at Cengage.

In particular, this edition's pedagogy is built on a strengthened learning architecture, based on skill building, application, and critical thinking, reflected and integrated carefully in **MindTap**—a personalized teaching experience with assignments that guide students to analyze, apply, and improve thinking, allowing instructors to measure skills and outcomes with ease. At MindTap students are able to use dynamic technological resources, including interactive videos and simulations; find high-value gradable activities; and practice in an engaging, personalized online environment.

Each chapter now previews the chapter content for students with an easily reviewed set of **Learning Objectives** paired with a chapter outline. Each Learning Objective has been carefully matched with one or more activities that will demonstrate its mastery.

The **photo program** now includes more stills from popular media, with thought-provoking captions.

"Everyday Skills" now cover most Learning Objectives and emphasize that they are all about skill building. They may be answered in the book or online, in MindTap.

"Communication in Everyday Life" features— with the subcategories "Diversity," "Insight, "Social Media," and "Workplace"—highlight interesting research and examples of interpersonal communication in real life. These items encourage students to observe how principles and concepts actually work in concrete situations, to witness the application of theory and concepts to particular cases, and to compare their own experiences and values with those presented in the "Communication in Everyday Life" features. The features now include a new "Social Media" subcategory; I have renamed the "Career" subcategory "Workplace" to reflect the

fact that not all work need be considered a "career"; and I often conclude with a suggestion for applying the boxed material via reflection, action, or visiting an online site, to which students can provide written responses in MindTap.

An unparalleled collection of skill-building, application, and critical thinking activities appears at chapter's end and online in MindTap, beginning with the highly engaging "Continuing the Conversation" video situations. Chapter-end features have been revised and reorganized to provide a logical learning sequence for all activities, building up to progressively more challenging levels of practice and application. The levels move from the simplest review ("Chapter Summary" and "Key Concepts") to the most challenging application ("Thinking Critically").

High-value, gradable versions of all activities are incorporated in MindTap, and MindTap is cued in the text wherever appropriate, to remind students that they may take activities there interactively. End-of-chapter highlights:

"Continuing the Conversation," a short case study that continues the conversation of the chapter by allowing students to see how the theories and principles that they just read about show up in everyday life, appears first, as a warm-up activity. Video is available for students in MindTap.

"Assessing Yourself" self-assessment quizzes in most chapters allow students to apply chapter concepts at the most basic level: themselves.

"Everyday Skills" emphasize the next level of application: skill building with author support. "Everyday Skills" icons in the book's margins point students to these skill-building application exercises at the end of the chapter. In MindTap these exercises may be taken exactly where they are referenced in the text.

"Engaging with Ideas" reflections and **"Thinking Critically"** activities allow students to reflect and write in more depth—in MindTap—by considering questions about personal, on-the-job, and ethical applications.

Additional Resources for Instructors

Accompanying *Interpersonal Communication: Everyday Encounters* is an Instructor Companion Website where you will find an Instructor's Resource Manual, Cengage Learning Testing Powered by Cognero, and PowerPoint presentations.

The extensive **Instructor's Resource Manual**, coauthored by Narissra Punyanunt-Carter of Texas Tech University and me, supplements the textbook. The manual discusses philosophical and pragmatic considerations involved in teaching the introductory course in interpersonal communication. It also includes suggestions for course emphases, sample syllabi, exercises, and films appropriate for each chapter, journal items, and panel ideas.

Cengage Learning Testing Powered by Cognero is a flexible, online system that allows you to

- Author, edit, and manage test bank content from multiple Cengage Learning solutions.
- multiple test versions in an instant.
- Deliver tests from your LMS, your class-room, or wherever you want.

The **Microsoft® PowerPoint® presentations** are predesigned for use with the book and fully customizable.

Acknowledgments

Although my name is the only one that appears as the author of this book, many people have contributed to it. I am especially indebted to my product manager at Cengage, Nicole Morinon. From the start, she was a full partner in this project. Her interest and insights greatly enhanced the content of this book, and her amazing sense of humor and fun made working on it a joy.

Also essential to this book were members of the publishing team who transformed my manuscript into the final book you are holding. Specifically, I thank Sue Gleason Wade, my awesome senior content developer; Karolina Kiwak, associate content developer; Stacey Purviance, marketing director; Dan Saabye, content project manager; Jessica Badiner, senior media developer; Colin Solan, product assistant; Daniel Nighting, copyeditor; Linda May, art director; Ann Hoffman, IP analyst; and Sumathy Kumaran, project manager.

In addition to the editorial and production teams at Cengage, I am grateful to the survey respondents and reviewers who gave me valuable feedback that I used in preparing this edition: Erica Cooper, Roanoke College; Karen Daas, University of Texas at San Antonio; Tina Harris, University of Georgia; Stacy Kuntzman, University of North Carolina at Charlotte; Dianna Laurent, Southeastern Louisiana University; Matt Sanders, Utah State University; Kristi Schaller, University of Georgia; Neeley Silberman, Saint Mary's College; Brent Sleasman, Gannon University; Jason Stone, Oklahoma State University, Oklahoma City; and Judith Vogel, Des Moines Area Community College.

Finally, I am indebted to family and friends who enrich my life. At the top of that list is Robbie (Robert) Cox, my partner in love, life, adventure, and dreams for 40 years. He cheers with me when writing is going well and bolsters my confidence when it isn't. He provides a critical ear when I want a sounding board and privacy when I am immersed in a project. And he is an ongoing source of experience in interpersonal communication. Along with Robbie, I am fortunate to have the love and support of my sister Carolyn and my close friends, Todd, Sue, and LindaBecker. And, of course, always, I appreciate the love and patience of the four-footed members of my family: our dog, Cassidy, and our cats, Rigby and Rowdy. Unlike my two-footed friends, these three keep me company when I am writing at 2:00 or 3:00 in the morning.

Julia T Wood

October 2014

ABOUT THE AUTHOR

Julia Wood joined the faculty at the University of North Carolina at Chapel Hill when she was 24. During her 37 years on the faculty, she taught classes and conducted research on personal relationships and on gender, communication, and culture. She was named the Lineberger Distinguished Professor of Humanities and the Caroline H. and Thomas S. Royster Distinguished Professor of Graduate Education.

She has published 25 books and 100 articles and book chapters. In addition, she has presented more than 100 papers at professional conferences and campuses around the United States. She has received 14 awards honoring her teaching and 16 awards recognizing her scholarship.

Professor Wood lives with her partner, Robert Cox, who is a Professor Emeritus of Communication Studies at the University of North Carolina at Chapel Hill. Sharing their home are their dog, Cassidy, and two cats, Rigby and Rowdy.

Professor Wood continues to write and conduct research. In addition, she tutors ESL students in reading, volunteers at her local animal shelter, and enjoys travel and conversation with friends, family members, and former students.

INTRODUCTION

STARTING THE CONVERSATION

When I was 20 years old, something happened that changed the rest of my life: I took my first interpersonal communication class. A new world of meaning opened up for me as I learned about the power of communication to enhance or harm our relationships. The more courses I took, the more fascinated I became, so I decided to make a career of studying and teaching interpersonal communication. I wrote *Interpersonal Communication: Everyday Encounters* because I wanted to awaken you, as my first course awakened me, to the power of interpersonal communication to enrich us and the relationships in our lives.

In the opening pages of this book, I'll introduce you to the field of interpersonal communication, to myself, to the features of this book, and to some of the special concerns and issues that surround interpersonal communication in this era.

THE FIELD OF COMMUNICATION

The field of communication has a long and distinguished intellectual history. It dates back to ancient Greece, where great philosophers such as Aristotle and Plato taught rhetoric, or public speaking, as a necessary skill for participation in civic life. In the 2,000 years since the communication field originated, it has expanded to encompass many kinds of interaction, including group discussion, family communication, health communication, oral traditions, organizational communication, and interpersonal communication.

Interpersonal communication is one of the most popular and vibrant areas in the discipline. Student demand for courses in interpersonal communication is consistently strong. Faculty respond by offering more classes, including advanced ones, that help students learn to interact effectively in their everyday interpersonal encounters.

Reflecting the intellectual maturity of the field, communication theory and research offer rich insight into the impact of interpersonal communication on individual identity and on personal, social, and professional relationships. Because interpersonal communication is central to our lives, it naturally intersects with other disciplines that are concerned with human behavior. Thus, research in communication contributes to and draws from work in such fields as psychology, business, sociology, anthropology, and counseling. The interdisciplinary mingling of ideas enriches the overall perspective on human interaction that you will find in *Interpersonal Communication: Everyday Encounters*.

A PERSONAL INTRODUCTION

When I was an undergraduate, most of the books I read seemed distant and impersonal. I never had the feeling a real human being had written them, and authors never introduced themselves except by stating their titles. Certainly, that's no way to begin a book about interpersonal communication! I'd like to introduce myself personally to you and explain my reasons for writing this book.

As I've already mentioned, I became fascinated by interpersonal communication when I was an undergraduate student. Today, I'm more excited than ever about the study and practice of interpersonal communication. It has been exciting to watch and participate in the growth of research on interpersonal communication and to observe how strong scholarship has facilitated applications to people's everyday lives.

Although research and writing occupy a great deal of my time, I have other interests as well. For instance, I tutor English as a second language (ESL) citizens in English, and I invest in caring for animals that have been abused or abandoned. I also cherish my relationships with my partner, Robbie, and close friends and family. My interaction with these people continuously enlarges my appreciation of the vital role of interpersonal communication in our everyday lives.

In describing myself to you, I can also tell you that I am European American, southern, middle class, middle aged, and heterosexual and that I strive to live in ways that are consistent with my spiritual values. Each facet of my identity shapes how I communicate, just as your age, race, class, gender, spirituality, and sexual orientation shape your communication. For instance, I don't know what it is like to be a man, to be in a same-sex romantic relationship, or to live in poverty. However, that doesn't mean that I, or you, can't learn to understand and respect the experiences of people who differ—sometimes radically—from us.

All of us are limited by our own identities and the experiences and understandings they have—and have not—given us. Yet this doesn't mean we have to be completely uninformed about those who differ from us. In fact, the more we interact with a range of people, the more we discover important

> ## Communication in Everyday Life
>
> # DIVERSITY
>
> ### A Kaleidoscopic Culture
>
> The face of America is changing. We have always been a country of many races and ethnicities, and it's only going to become more so in years ahead. By 2043, the Census predicts that there will be no majority racial or ethnic group in the United States; by 2018, there will be no single racial or ethnic majority group of people under 18 years old (Cooper, 2013). Between 2005 and 2050, demographics in the United States are projected to change substantially (Yen, 2012).
>
> | | 2005 | 2050 |
> |-------------------|------|------|
> | African American | 13% | 13% |
> | Asian | 5% | 9% |
> | Caucasian | 67% | 47% |
> | Hispanic | 14% | 29% |
>
> The Census also predicts that there will be more older Americans in the years to come. Currently 1 in 7 Americans is 65 or older; by 2060, that should grow to 1 in 5 (Cooper, 2013).
>
> To learn more about changing demographics in the United States, go to http://www.census.gov. Read information in the "People" category under "Estimates and Projections."

similarities as well as interesting differences. Learning about both is essential for ethical, effective participation in our pluralistic world.

Living and Learning in a Diverse World

In our era, it is essential to learn about and respect perspectives that differ from our own and from those of the communities in which we were raised. It's very likely that you will have friends and neighbors of different ethnic backgrounds from your own. It's even more likely—almost guaranteed—that you will work with people of diverse ages, races, ethnicities, sexual orientations, and spiritual commitments. You may date people of many races and religious backgrounds, and if you have children, it's very likely they will do the same. Personal effectiveness in our era requires skill in communicating well with a range of people.

Interacting with people who differ from us not only teaches us about them; it also prompts insights about ourselves. Westerners can see their competitive attitude toward athletics in a new light if they consider the Japanese preference for tied or very close scores in sporting events so that neither side loses face. It is difficult to understand what whiteness is if you interact only with whites; it's hard to recognize the character of heterosexuality if you know only straight people. Thus, learning about people in other cultures and people who are outside of what the culture defines as mainstream inevitably teaches us about the mainstream as well.

The diversity of our society offers both opportunities and challenges. Exploring variations in gender, race, class, cultural heritage, sexual orientation, age, physical and mental ability, and spiritual belief can enhance our appreciation of the range of human behavior and the options open to us as people and as communicators. At the same time, diversity can complicate interaction because people may

---

Communication in Everyday Life

DIVERSITY

About Vocabulary in this Book

Because social diversity is woven into this book, it's important to think carefully about the language used to refer to social groups. Drawing on research, I present generalizations about various groups. Whenever possible, I cite research done by members of the groups we are discussing so we understand groups from the perspectives of insiders. But the generalizations are only that: generalizations. They are not universal truths that apply to all members of a group. There are always exceptions to generalizations. As you read, you may discover that you are a living exception to some of the generalizations about groups to which you belong. If so, you may want to reflect on the reasons you depart from group tendencies.

Generalizations should not be used to stereotype members of particular groups. For instance, in Chapter 4 you will read about gendered speech communities. You will learn how women and men typically—but not always, not in every case—differ in their communication styles. You will also learn about communication patterns in some traditional African American communities. The general patterns you read about don't describe every woman, man, or African American. Any of us may depart from the usual patterns of our groups, because of individual differences and because we belong to multiple groups.

The key point to keep in mind as you read is this: Generalizations are both important and limited. They are important because they inform us of broad patterns that can be useful starting points in our efforts to understand and interact with others. At the same time, generalizations are limited because they do not necessarily tell us about any single individual who belongs to a group. Thus, it's important to qualify generalizations. You'll notice that I use words such as *usually*, *typically*, and *in general*. These are to remind us that there are exceptions to generalizations, so we can never assume that a generalization applies to a specific person.

communicate in dissimilar ways and misunderstand one another, as Yih-Tang Lin notes in her commentary.

> When I first came here to school, I was amazed at how big the rooms in dormitories are, so I remarked on this. All of the Americans had a laugh at that and thought I was joking. In my country, individuals have very little space, and houses are tight together. The first time an American disagreed with me, I felt angry that he would make me lose face. We don't ever contradict another person directly. I have had many miscommunications in this country.

Students today recognize the importance of understanding a range of cultures. A survey of students who entered colleges and universities in the fall of 2009 showed that 49.4% believe that it is essential or very important to improve their understanding of other countries and cultures. That's an increase from the 42.7% who believed this in 2004 ("This Year's Freshmen," 2010).

Students are correct in thinking that contact with diversity enriches them. Recent studies show that students who encounter diversity score higher on critical thinking than students who do not, and white students show the most benefit (Berrett, 2012).

In this book, we will consider many ways in which diversity intersects with communication. For instance, we'll see how the same gestures mean very different things in different cultures, and we'll discover that women and men, in general, rely on both similar and distinct types of communication to create closeness. We'll also learn that race and ethnicity influence how people interact. And, as the Communication in Everyday Life: Social Media feature shows, we will learn how

age differences affect interpersonal communication. Weaving diversity into how we think about interpersonal communication enlarges understandings of communication and the range of people and perspectives it involves. Cherrie, a student in one of my courses, makes this point effectively in her commentary.

Communication in Everyday Life

SOCIAL MEDIA

What's Digitally Polite?

Is it polite to leave a voice message when someone doesn't answer the phone? How about sending an email to tell someone you left a voice mail—is that polite? Should you open emails with "hello" and close with "bye"? It turns out that whether you think those are polite courtesies or not may depend on your age.

Younger people are rewriting the rules of etiquette to fit an era saturated by social media. When you are sending dozens or even hundreds of messages a day, "hello" and "goodbye" become superfluous. So do emails or texts that say "thank you"—no need for those. If you call someone who doesn't answer their cell phone, they'll see that you called and should call or text you back to talk, so there's no need to leave a voice message (Bilton, 2013).

People who aren't digital natives, however, often operate by the rules that regulated communication as they were growing up. To them, it *is* polite to start messages with "hello" and end them with "goodbye"; in fact, it's impolite not to do so. And, to them, you should leave a message if the person you called doesn't answer—it's only polite to let her or him know why you called.

Communicating via social media, like communicating face to face, is most effective when we adapt our communication to the people with whom we are interacting. If you're calling a 60-year-old, it's probably fine to leave a voice message that you wouldn't leave when calling a 20-year-old.

This isn't the first time that new technologies have presented etiquette puzzles. When the telephone was invented in the 1870s, people weren't sure how to answer the phone. Many picked up the phone and said nothing, waiting for the caller to start the conversation. Alexander Graham Bell, who had invented the phone, proposed "Ahoy" as the proper greeting (Bilton, 2013).

I am Hispanic, and I am tired of classes and books that ignore my people. Last year, I took a course in family life, and all we talked about was Western, middle-class white families. Their ways are not my ways. A course on family should be about many kinds of families. I took a course in great literature, and there was only one author who was not Western and only three who were women. It's not true that only white men write great literature.

Cherrie

Cherrie and others who were not born and raised in the United States also have much to teach students who are native citizens of the United States, as Carl's commentary reveals.

At first, I was really put off by the two students in our class who were from China. Like when we talked about conflict and they just didn't get it—I mean, that's the way it seemed to me when they said they tried to avoid it. But the more I listened to them, the more I saw that they were really saying there are ways for people to work around differences without having to attack each other or make the other person look bad. It's really different than how I was brought up—you know, stand your ground, muster your arguments, win! I'm still not sure I really get their perspective, but it does make me think about whether I always need to be so fast to try to beat the next guy.

Carl

Like many of us, Carl's first inclination is to view ways other than his own as inferior. But Carl moved beyond that starting point. He worked to consider his Chinese classmates' perspectives on conflict on their terms, in the context of their culture. In turn, they enlarged Carl's perspective on ways to deal with conflict. Like Carl, most of us will not always find it easy to appreciate or respect ways that are different from our own. Yet the struggle is worthwhile because it can enrich us personally and enable us to participate more effectively in a world characterized by many perspectives on life and communication.

INTRODUCTION TO FEATURES OF THIS BOOK

Woven into this book are four features that I think will make it more interesting to you and more helpful as a resource for understanding and improving your own interpersonal communication.

First, I've written this book in a **conversational tone** so that you can connect with the ideas in the pages that follow. Like you, I am interested in interpersonal communication, and I am continually trying to figure out how to be more effective in my everyday encounters with others. In this book, I share some of my experiences and some of the perspectives and skills that enhance my interactions.

Second, in each chapter I feature **comments from students** such as Cherrie, Carl, and Yih-Tang Lin. Because students teach me so much, I've included many of their comments in the chapters that follow. These are taken from journals they've kept in interpersonal communication classes taught by me and by instructors at other schools. In reading their commentaries, you'll discover that some of these students seem much like you and that others seem quite different. It's likely that you'll agree with some of the students' comments, disagree with others, and want to think still further about others. However you respond to their ideas, I suspect that, like me, you will find them interesting, insightful, and often challenging.

Third, each chapter includes several "Communication in Everyday Life" features that extend chapter coverage by **spotlighting interesting research and news items** about interpersonal communication. When this information is particularly relevant to cultural diversity, social media, or the workplace, I call that to your attention with special titles for each of those themes.

Fourth, this book emphasizes **personal learning**. Most of us, especially students, are familiar with impersonal learning, which occurs when someone else tells or shows us something. In other words, we receive knowledge passively.

Personal learning, in contrast, occurs when we interact with subject matter. Rather than just receiving information, we do something active—we reflect, observe, assess ourselves, discuss, debate, engage in action, or reflect on and write about ideas; we experiment with principles and skills; we contrast, compare, and analyze. All of these activities involve us in generating and testing knowledge rather than just receiving it. The personal learning approach assumes that effective learning involves some kind of experience and some dialogue with the self (reflection, application) or others.

Several specific end-of-chapter and online features in this book foster personal learning. First is a feature titled "Continuing the Conversation." These are short case studies that allow you to see, on the web, how concepts, theories, and principles discussed in the chapter show up in real-life interactions. Second, in most chapters you will find an "Assessing Yourself" quiz whose answers will be revealed if you take it online. Third, you'll find several "Everyday Skills" that give you an opportunity to extend and apply material discussed in the text to your own life by doing something or engaging in dialogue with yourself or others. Some of the "Everyday Skills" show you how to develop a particular communication skill; others ask you to reflect on ideas we've discussed to observe communication principles and patterns in your everyday encounters. Fourth, there are "Engaging with Ideas" features that ask you to reflect on one question that requires personal learning, as well as two other questions that focus on the workplace and ethics. Finally, there are "Thinking Critically" questions for you to reflect on and write about in more depth.

I hope this book will enhance your appreciation of the power of interpersonal communication in our relationships. I also hope it will motivate you to apply the principles and skills presented here in your everyday life.

Julia T Wood

© bikeriderlondon/Shutterstock.com

A FIRST LOOK AT INTERPERSONAL COMMUNICATION

Topics covered in this chapter

Define Interpersonal Communication

Models of Interpersonal Communication

Principles of Interpersonal Communication

Social Media in Everyday Life

Guidelines for Interpersonal Communication Competence

After studying this chapter, you should be able to . . .

Give examples of the three types of relationships in Buber's view of communication.

Identify the key features that define interpersonal communication.

Distinguish content and relationship levels of meaning.

Apply the transactional model of interpersonal communication to a specific interaction.

List the range of needs that people try to meet in a particular interaction.

Recognize eight principles behind effective interpersonal communication.

Explain how the definition of interpersonal communication and its features apply to social media.

Apply the guidelines discussed in this chapter to assess communication competence in a particular interaction.

You've been interviewing for 2 months, and so far you haven't gotten a single job offer. After another interview that didn't go well, you text a friend. Instead of a terse response, your friend texts back to suggest getting together for lunch. Over pizza, you disclose that you're starting to worry that you won't ever get hired because the economy is so bad. Your friend listens closely and lets you know he understands how you feel and he isn't judging you. Then he tells you about other people he knows who also haven't yet gotten job offers. All of a sudden, you don't feel so alone. Your friend reminds you how worried you felt last term when you were struggling with your physics course and then made a B on the final. As you listen to him, your sagging confidence begins to recover.

Before leaving, he tells you about a virtual interview website that allows you to practice interviewing skills, and he works with you to communicate more effectively in interviews. By the time you leave, you feel hopeful again.

Interpersonal communication is central to our everyday lives. We count on others to care about what is happening in our lives and to help us celebrate good moments and deal with problems and disappointments. In addition, we need others to encourage our personal and professional growth. Friends and romantic partners who believe in us enable us to overcome self-defeating patterns and help us become the people we want to be. Coworkers who give us advice and feedback help us increase our effectiveness on the job. And sometimes we just want to hang out with people we like, trust, and have fun with.

In the workplace, interpersonal communication is critically important. A 2010 national survey of employers reported that 89% of employers consider that college students should focus on learning to communicate effectively orally and in writing in order to be successful professionally (Rhodes, 2010). Similarly, in 2012 employers said that key qualities for job applicants were interpersonal skill, oral communication skill, and adaptability (Selingo, 2012). A very recent poll (Hart Research, 2013) found that 93% of employers think a job candidate's demonstrated capacity to think critically and communicate clearly is more important than their undergraduate major.

Leaders of organizations such as FedEx and GlaxoSmithKline list communication as a vital skill for their employees (O'Hair & Eadie, 2009). The pivotal role of communication in health care (see first Communication in Everyday Life: Workplace) makes it unsurprising that an increasing number of medical schools base admissions, in part, on applicants' communication skills, especially their ability to communicate empathy to patients (Rosenbaum, 2011).

In this chapter, we take a first look at interpersonal communication. We start by defining interpersonal communication and providing a model of how it works. Then we consider how interpersonal communication meets important human needs. Next, we discuss principles of effective interpersonal communication and consider how social media affect interpersonal communication. To close the chapter, we identify guidelines for achieving competence in interpersonal communication.

DEFINING INTERPERSONAL COMMUNICATION

When asked to distinguish interpersonal communication from communication in general, many people say that interpersonal communication involves fewer people, often just two. According to this definition, an exchange between a homeowner and a plumber would be interpersonal, but a conversation involving parents and four children would not. Although interpersonal communication often involves only two or three people, this isn't a useful definition.

Perhaps you are thinking that intimate contexts define interpersonal communication. Using this standard, we would say that a couple on a first date in a romantic restaurant engages in more interpersonal communication than an established couple in a shopping mall. Again, this context is not the key.

The best way to define interpersonal communication is by focusing on what happens between people, not where they are or how many are present. For starters, then, we can say that interpersonal communication is a distinct type of interaction between people.

A Communication Continuum

We can begin to understand the unique character of interpersonal communication by tracing the meaning of the word *interpersonal*. It is derived from the prefix *inter-*, meaning "between," and the word *person*; interpersonal communication literally occurs between people. In one sense, all communication happens between people, yet many interactions don't involve us personally. Communication exists on a continuum from impersonal to interpersonal (see Figure 1.1).

Much of our communication is not really personal. Sometimes we don't acknowledge others as people at all but treat them as objects; they bag our groceries, direct us around highway construction, and so forth. In other instances, we do acknowledge people, yet we interact with them on a surface level and often in terms of their social roles rather than personally. For instance, I often run into neighbors when I'm walking my dog, Cassie. We engage in small talk about weather and home projects. Through this kind of interaction, we acknowledge each other as people, but we don't get really personal. With a select few people, we communicate in deeply intimate ways. These distinctions are captured in poetic terms by the philosopher Martin Buber (1970), who distinguished among three levels of communication: I–It, I–You, and I–Thou.

I–It Communication   In an I–It relationship, we treat others very impersonally, almost as objects. In **I–It communication**, we do not acknowledge the humanity of other people; we may not even affirm their existence. Sometimes we do not treat salespeople, servers in restaurants, and clerical staff as people but only as instruments to take our orders and deliver what we want. In the extreme form of I–It relationships, others are not even acknowledged. When a homeless person asks for money for food, some people look away as if the person weren't there. In dysfunctional families, parents may ignore children and refuse to speak to them, thereby treating the children as things—as "its"—not as unique individuals. Students on large campuses may also feel they are treated as "its," not as people. Jason, a sophomore in one of my classes, makes this point.

Impersonal   Interpersonal

It   You   Thou

Cengage Learning

Figure 1.1

The Communication Continuum

> **JASON**
>
> At this school, I get treated like a number a lot of the time. When I go to see my adviser, he asks what my identification number is—not what my name is. Most of my professors don't know my name. In high school, all the teachers called on us by name. It felt more human there. Sometimes I feel like an "it" on this campus.

I-You Communication   The second level Buber identified is **I–You communication**, which accounts for the majority of our interactions. People acknowledge one another as more than objects, but they don't fully engage each other as unique individuals. For example, suppose you go shopping, and a salesclerk asks, "May I help you?" It's unlikely you will have a deep conversation with the clerk, but you might treat him or her as more than an object (Wood, 2006a). Perhaps you say, "I'm just browsing today. You know how it is at the end of the month—no money." The clerk might laugh and commiserate about how money gets tight by the end of the month. In this interaction, the clerk doesn't treat you as a faceless shopper, and you don't treat the clerk as just an agent of the store.

I–You relationships may also be more personal than interactions with salesclerks. For instance, we talk with others in classes, on the job, and on sports teams in ways that are somewhat personal. The same is true of interaction in Internet forums, where people meet to share ideas and common interests. Interaction is still guided by our roles as peers, as members of a class or team, and as people who have common interests. Yet we do affirm the existence of others and recognize them as individuals within those roles. Teachers and students often have I–You relationships. In the workplace, most of us have many I–You relationships that are pleasant and functional.

I-Thou Communication
The rarest kind of relationship involves **I–Thou communication**. Buber regarded this as the highest form of human dialogue because each person affirms the other as cherished and unique. When we interact on an I–Thou level, we meet others in their wholeness and individuality. Instead of dealing with them as occupants of

> **Communication in Everyday Life**
>
> ## INSIGHT
>
> ### Poor Interpersonal Communication as the Number One Cause of Divorce
>
> According to a nationwide poll, a majority of people perceive communication problems as the number one reason marriages fail (Roper poll, 1999). Poll results showed that, regardless of age, race, sex, or income level, Americans reported that communication problems are the most common cause of divorce; 53% of those who were polled said that ineffective communication was the principal reason for divorce. Compare this with the frequency with which people named other causes of divorce: money problems, 29%; interference from family members, 7%; sexual problems, 5%; previous relationships, 3%; and children, 3%. This finding is consistent with the long-standing insight of marital therapists that good communication is essential to satisfying marriages (Scarf, 2008).

social roles, we see them as unique human beings whom we know and accept in their totality. In I–Thou communication, we open ourselves fully, trusting others to accept us as we are, with our virtues and vices, hopes and fears, and strengths and weaknesses.

Buber believed that only in I–Thou relationships do we become fully human, which for him meant that we discard the guises and defenses we use most of the time and allow ourselves to be completely genuine (Stewart, 1986). Much of our communication involves what Buber called "seeming," in which we're preoccupied with our image and careful to manage how we present ourselves. In I–Thou relationships, however, we engage in "being," through which we reveal who we really are and how we really feel. I–Thou relationships are not common because we can't afford to reveal ourselves totally to everyone all the time. Thus, I–Thou relationships and the communication in them are rare and special.

Features of Interpersonal Communication

Building on Buber's poetic description, we can define **interpersonal communication** as a selective, systemic process that allows people to reflect and build personal knowledge of one another and create shared meanings. We'll discuss the key terms in this definition.

Selective   First, as we noted earlier, we don't communicate intimately with the majority of people we encounter. In some cases, we neither want nor need to communicate with others even at the I–You level. For instance, if we get a phone call from a pollster, we may only respond to the questions and not engage the caller in any personal way. We invest the effort and take the risks of opening ourselves fully with only a few people. As Buber realized, most of our communication occurs on I–It or I–You levels. This is fine because I–Thou relationships take more time, energy, and courage than we are willing to offer to everyone.

Systemic   Interpersonal communication is also **systemic**, which means that it takes place within various systems, or contexts, that influence what happens and the meanings we attribute to interaction. The communication between you and me right now is embedded in multiple systems, including the interpersonal communication course you are taking, our academic institutions, and American society. Each of these systems influences what we expect of each other, what I write, and how you interpret what you read. Communication between me and Chinese students taking a class in interpersonal communication would reflect the context of Chinese culture.

Consider an example of the systemic character of communication. Suppose Ian gives Mia a solid gold pendant and says, "I wanted to show how much I care about you." What do his words mean? That depends in large part on the systems within which he and Mia interact. If Ian and Mia have just started dating, an expensive gift means one thing; if they have been married for 20 years, it means something different. On the other hand, if they don't have an established relationship, and Mia is engaged to Manuel, Ian's gift may have yet another meaning. What if Ian argued with Mia the previous day? Then, perhaps, the gift is to apologize more than to show love. If Ian is rich, a solid gold pendant may be less impressive than if he is short on cash. Systems that affect what this communication means include Mia's and Ian's relationship, their socioeconomic classes, cultural norms for gift giving, and Mia's and Ian's personal histories. All these contexts affect their interaction and its meaning.

Everyday Skills To practice identifying types of relationships, complete the activity "Communicating in Your Relationships" at the end of the chapter or online.

Because interpersonal communication is systemic, situation, time, people, culture, personal histories, and so forth interact to affect meanings. We can't just add up the various parts of a system to understand their impact on communication. Instead, we have to recognize that all parts of a system interact; each part affects all others. In other words, elements of communication systems are interdependent; each element is tied to all the other elements.

All systems include **noise**, which is anything that distorts communication or interferes with people's understandings of one another. Noise in communication systems is inevitable, but we can be aware that it exists and try to compensate for the difficulties it causes.

There are four kinds of noise. *Physiological noise* is distraction caused by hunger, fatigue, headaches, medications, and other factors that affect how we feel and think. *Physical noise* is interference in our environments, such as noises made by others, overly dim or bright lights, spam and pop-up ads, extreme temperatures, and crowded conditions. *Psychological noise* refers to qualities in us that affect how we communicate and how we interpret others. For instance, if you are preoccupied with a problem, you may be inattentive at a team meeting. Likewise, prejudice and defensive feelings can interfere with communication. Our needs may also affect how we interpret others. For example, if we really need affirmation of our professional competence, we may be predisposed to perceive others as communicating more praise for our work than they really do. Finally, *semantic noise* exists when words themselves are not mutually understood. Authors sometimes create semantic noise by using jargon or unnecessarily technical language. For instance, to discuss noise, I could write, "Communication can be egregiously obstructed by phenomena extrinsic to an exchange that actuate misrepresentations and symbolic incongruities." Although that sentence may be accurate, it's filled with semantic noise. Similarly, the abbreviations typical in texts and tweets may not be understood by people who use social media infrequently.

I wish professors would learn about semantic noise. I really try to pay attention in class and to learn, but the way some faculty talk makes it impossible to understand what they mean, especially if English is a second language. I wish they would remember that we're not specialists like they are, so we don't know all the technical words.

CARMELLA

Some noise is more than one type. Listening to your favorite music on your iPod while walking across campus creates both physical noise and psychological noise. Social media can be so distracting that people have accidents. One survey found that 1,000 people visited emergency rooms in a single year because they tripped, fell, or walked into something while using a cell phone to talk or text (Richtel, 2010). This is particularly worrisome when we realize that people between the ages of 8 and 18 spend more than 7 hours a day using electronic devices (Lewin, 2010a).

In summary, when we say that communication is systemic, we mean three things. First, all communication occurs within multiple systems that affect meanings. Second, all parts and all systems of communication are interdependent, so they affect one another. Finally, all communication systems have noise, which can be physiological, physical, psychological, or semantic.

Process Interpersonal communication is an ongoing, continuous **process**. This means, first, that communication evolves over time, becoming more personal as people interact. Friendships and romantic relationships gain depth and significance over the course of time, and they may also decline in quality over time. Relationships on the job also evolve over time. Ellen may mentor Craig when he starts working at her firm, but over time they may become equal colleagues. Because relationships are dynamic, they don't stay the same but continually change just as we do.

JANA My daughter is my best friend, but it wasn't always that way. As a child, she was very shy and dependent. She was a sullen teenager who resented everything I said and did. Now that she's 22, we've become really good friends. But even now, our relationship has all of the echoes of who we were with each other at different times in our lives.

An ongoing process also has no discrete beginnings and endings. Suppose a friend stops by and confides in you about a troubling personal problem. When did that communication begin? Although it may seem to have started when the friend came by, earlier interactions may have led the friend to feel that it was safe to talk to you and that you would care about the problem. We can't be sure, then, when this communication began. Similarly, we don't know where it will end. Perhaps it ends when the friend leaves, but perhaps it doesn't. Maybe your response to the problem helps your friend see new options. Maybe what you learn changes how you feel toward your friend. Because communication is ongoing, we can never be sure when it begins or ends.

Because interpersonal interaction is a process, what happens between people is linked to both past and future. In our earlier example, the meaning of Ian's gift reflects prior interactions between him and Cheryl, and their interaction about the gift will affect future interactions. All our communication occurs in three temporal dimensions: past, which affects what happens now; present, which reflects the past and sets the stage for the future; and future, which is molded by what occurs in this moment and past ones (Dixson & Duck, 1993; Wood, 2006a). How couples handle early arguments affects how they deal with later ones. Yesterday's email response from a friend influences what we write today and, in turn, what our friend may write back tomorrow. In communication, past, present, and future are always interwoven.

The ongoing quality of interpersonal communication also suggests that we can't stop the process, nor can we edit or unsay what has been said. In this sense, communication is irreversible: We can't take it back. This implies that we have an ethical responsibility to recognize the irreversibility of communication and to communicate carefully.

Personal Knowledge Interpersonal communication fosters personal knowledge and insights. To connect as unique individuals, we have to get to know others personally and understand their thoughts and feelings. With family members whom you have known all of your life, you understand some of their worries, concerns, and personal issues in ways that new acquaintances cannot. Longtime friends have a history of shared experiences and knowledge that allows them to interact more deeply than casual friends can.

Walt (Bryan Cranston) and Jesse's (Aaron Paul) relationship during the course of Emmy award–winning drama *Breaking Bad* changed dramatically from teacher–student to feuding partners in crime.

AMC/Photofest

Just as every person is unique, so is every interpersonal relationship. Each develops its own distinctive patterns and rhythms and even special vocabulary that are not part of other interpersonal relationships (Nicholson, 2006). In the process of becoming close, people work out personal roles and rules for interaction, and these may deviate from general social rules and roles (Duck, 2006; Dainton, 2006; Wood, 2006a). With one friend, you might play pickup basketball and get together for films. With a different, equally close friend, you might talk openly about feelings.

As our relationships with others deepen, we build trust and learn how to communicate in ways that make each other feel comfortable and safe. The personal knowledge we gain over time in relationships encourages us to know and be known: We share secrets, fears, and experiences that we don't tell to just anyone. This is part of what Buber meant by "being" with others. Personal knowledge is a process, one that grows and builds on itself over time as people communicate interpersonally. Sometimes, we may even feel that our closest friends know us better than we know ourselves, as Lizelle explains.

> **LIZELLE**
>
> What I like best about long-term relationships is all the layers that develop. I know the friends I've had since high school in so many ways. I know what they did and felt and dreamed in high school, and I know them as they are now. They have the same kind of in-depth knowledge of me. We tell each other everything, so it sometimes seems that my deepest friends know me better than I know myself.

Sharing personal information and experiences means that interpersonal communication involves ethical choices. We can use our knowledge to protect people we care about. We can also use it to hurt those people, for example by attacking vulnerabilities others have revealed to us. Ethical communicators choose not to exploit or treat casually personal information about others.

Meaning Creating   The heart of interpersonal communication is shared meanings between people. We don't merely exchange words when we communicate. Instead, we create meanings as we figure out what each other's words and behaviors stand for, represent, or imply. Meanings grow out of histories of interaction between unique persons. For example, my partner, Robbie, and I are both continually overcommitted, and we each worry about the pace of the other's life. Often, one of us says to the other, "*bistari, bistari.*" This phrase will mean nothing to you unless you know enough Nepalese to translate it as meaning, "Go slowly, go gradually." When one of us says, "*bistari, bistari,*" we not only suggest slowing down but also remind each other of our special time living and trekking in Nepal.

Like Robbie and me, most close friends and romantic partners develop vocabularies that have meaning only to them. People who work together also develop meanings that grow out of their interactions over time and the shared field in which they work.

You may have noticed that I refer to *meanings*, not just one meaning. This is because interpersonal communication involves two levels of meaning (Rogers, 2008; Watzlawick, Beavin, & Jackson, 1967). The first level, called the

content meaning, deals with literal, or denotative, meaning. If a parent says to a 5-year-old child, "Clean your room now," the content meaning is that the room is to be cleaned immediately.

The second level is the **relationship meaning**. This refers to what communication expresses about relationships between communicators. The relationship meaning of "Clean your room now" is that the parent has the right to order the child; the parent and child have an unequal power relationship. If the parent says, "Would you mind cleaning your room?" the relationship meaning reflects a more equal relationship. Suppose a friend says, "You're the only person I can talk to about this," and then discloses something that is worrying him. The content level includes the actual issue itself and the information that you're the only one with whom he will discuss this issue. But what has he told you on the relationship level? He has communicated that he trusts you, he considers you special, and he probably expects you to care about his troubles.

ANI My father needs to learn about relationship meanings. Whenever I call home, he asks me if anything's wrong. Then he asks what the news is. If I don't have news to report, he can't understand why I'm calling. Then Mom gets on the phone, and we talk for a while about stuff—nothing important, just stuff. I don't call to tell them big news. I just want to touch base and feel connected.

Cultures vary in how much they emphasize content- and relationship-level meanings. In high-context cultures, great emphasis is put on holistic understanding of meanings based on a collective understanding of context. Words themselves have little meaning until placed in the context of culture, relationships, and people. Some cultures are low-context, which means that communicators do not assume a great deal of shared, collective knowledge. Because a high level of collective knowledge is not assumed, the content level of meaning is given great priority. Words and literal meaning are emphasized and specifics are provided in conversation. The United States is a low-context culture, whereas many Asian cultures are high-context, which means that collective knowledge is assumed. In high-context cultures, less emphasis is given to content-level meaning and to providing specifics because communicators can assume that others share their collective knowledge. For example, in a low-context culture, a person might say to a coworker, "Let's get together to talk about our project. We can meet in my office at 2 today and you can bring the draft. I'll order some coffee for us." In a high-context culture, the message might be "Let's meet at 2 to discuss our project." In the high-context culture, the communicator assumes that the coworker will share cultural understandings about where to meet, what to bring, and whether there will be a beverage (Lim, 2002).

Scholars have identified three general dimensions of relationship-level meanings. The first dimension is responsiveness, and it refers to how aware of others and involved with them we are. Perhaps you can remember a conversation you had with someone who shuffled papers and glanced at a clock or kept looking at a computer screen while you were talking. If so, you probably felt she wasn't interested in you or what you were saying. In Western culture, low responsiveness is communicated on the relationship level of meaning when people don't look at us, or when they are preoccupied with something other than talking with us. Higher responsiveness is communicated

Everyday Skills To practice distinguishing between content and relationship levels of meaning, complete the activity "Levels of Meaning" at the end of the chapter or online.

MindTap™

by eye contact, nodding, and feedback that indicates involvement (Richmond & McCroskey, 2000).

A second dimension of relationship meaning is liking, or affection. This concerns the degree of positive or negative feeling that is communicated. Although liking may seem synonymous with responsiveness, the two are actually distinct. We may be responsive to people we don't like but to whom we must pay attention. We may also be responsive by glaring or scowling, which indicate we are attentive to the other person but we are not affectionate. Also, realize that we are sometimes preoccupied and unresponsive to people about whom we care. We communicate that we like or dislike others by what we actually say as well as by tone of voice, facial expressions, how close we sit to them, and so forth.

Power, or control, is the third dimension of relationship meaning. This refers to the power balance between communicators. Friends and romantic partners sometimes engage in covert power struggles on the relationship level. One person suggests going to a particular movie and then to dinner at the pizza parlor. The other responds by saying she doesn't want to see that movie and isn't in the mood for pizza. They could be arguing on the content level about their different preferences for the evening. If arguments over what to do or eat are recurrent, however, chances are the couple is negotiating power—who gets to decide where to go and what to do. In many relationships, power is imbalanced: teacher–student, parent–child, coach–athlete. Usually both people in relationships like these recognize that one has more power, but sometimes the person who has less power challenges the person who has more. For instance, a student may question a teacher's authority, and a player may argue with a coach's instructions.

Thus far, we have seen that communication exists on a continuum, ranging from impersonal to interpersonal. We've also defined interpersonal communication as a selective, systemic process that allows people to build personal knowledge of one another and to create meanings. Meanings, we have seen, reflect histories of all interactions and involve both content and relationship levels. To further clarify the nature of interpersonal communication we'll first discuss three efforts to model the communication process.

MODELS OF INTERPERSONAL COMMUNICATION

A **model** is a representation of a phenomenon such as an airplane, a house, or human communication. Models show how a phenomenon works. Early models of interpersonal communication were simplistic, so we will discuss them very briefly. We'll look more closely at a current model that offers sophisticated insight into the process of interpersonal communication.

Linear Models

The first model of interpersonal communication (Laswell, 1948) depicted communication as a linear, or one-way, process in which one person acts on another person. This was a verbal model that consisted of five questions describing a sequence of acts that make up communication:

Who?
Says what?
In what channel?
To whom?
With what effect?

A year later, Claude Shannon and Warren Weaver (1949) offered a revised model that added the feature of noise. Earlier in this chapter, we noted that noise is anything that interferes with communication. Noise might be spam in online communication, regional accents, or background conversations in the workplace. (Figure 1.2 shows Shannon and Weaver's model.)

These early **linear models** had serious shortcomings. They portrayed communication as flowing in only one direction—from a sender to a passive receiver. This implies that listeners never send messages and that they absorb only passively what speakers say. But this isn't how communication really occurs. Listeners nod, frown, smile, look bored or interested, and so forth, and they actively work to make sense of others' messages. Linear models also erred by representing communication as a sequence of actions in which one step (listening) follows an earlier step (talking). In actual interaction, however, speaking and listening often occur simultaneously or they overlap. On the job, coworkers exchange ideas, and each listens and responds as one person speaks; those who are speaking are also listening for cues from others. Online, as we compose our messages, instant messages (IMs) pop up on our screens. At any moment in the process of interpersonal communication, participants are simultaneously sending and receiving messages and adapting to one another.

Figure **1.2**

The Linear Model of Communication

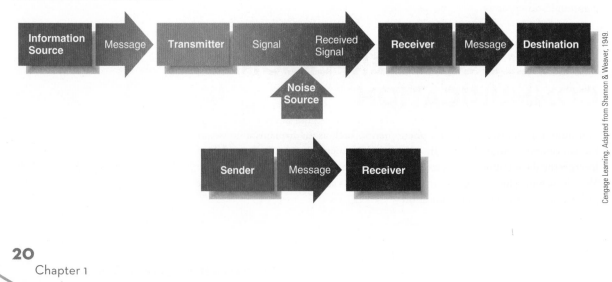

Cengage Learning. Adapted from Shannon & Weaver, 1949.

Interactive Models

Interactive models portrayed communication as a process in which listeners give **feedback**, which is a response to a message. In addition, interactive models recognize that communicators create and interpret messages within personal fields of experience (see Figure 1.3). The more communicators' fields of experience overlap, the better they can understand each other. When fields of experience don't overlap enough, misunderstandings may occur. Madison's commentary gives an example of this type of misunderstanding.

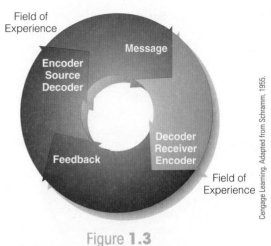

Figure **1.3**

The Interactive Model of Communication

> I studied abroad last year. For the first couple of weeks that I was in Germany, I thought Germans were the rudest people I'd ever met. They aren't friendly with small talk and saying hello; they push and bump into others and don't apologize. After I got to know some Germans, I realized they are very nice, but they have different social norms than Americans—especially Americans from the South!
>
> **MADISON**

Although the interactive model is an improvement over the linear model, it still portrays communication as a sequential process in which one person is a sender and another is a receiver. In reality, everyone who is involved in communication both sends and receives messages. Interactive models also fail to capture the dynamic nature of interpersonal communication and the ways it changes over time. For example, two people communicate more openly after months of exchanging email messages than they did the first time they met in a chat room. Two coworkers communicate more easily and effectively after months of working together on a project team.

Transactional Models

The **transactional model** of interpersonal communication is more accurate because it emphasizes the dynamism of interpersonal communication and the multiple roles people assume during the process. In addition, this model includes the feature of time to call our attention to the fact that messages, noise, and fields of experience vary over time (see Figure 1.4).

The transactional model recognizes that noise is present throughout interpersonal communication. In addition, this model includes the feature of time to remind us that people's communication varies over time. Each communicator's field of experience, and the shared field of experience between communicators, changes over time. As we encounter new people and have new experiences that broaden our outlooks, we change how we interact with others. As we get to know others over time, relationships may become more informal and intimate. For example, people who meet online sometimes decide to get together face to face, and a serious friendship or romance may develop.

The transactional model also makes it clear that communication occurs within systems that affect what and how people communicate and what meanings are

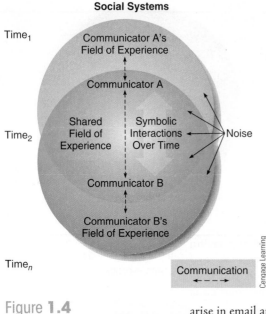

Social Systems

Time₁

Communicator A's Field of Experience

Communicator A

Shared Field of Experience | Symbolic Interactions Over Time

Time₂

Noise

Communicator B

Communicator B's Field of Experience

Timeₙ

Communication

Cengage Learning

Figure **1.4**

The Transactional Model of Communication

Figure **1.5**

Maslow's Hierarchy of Needs

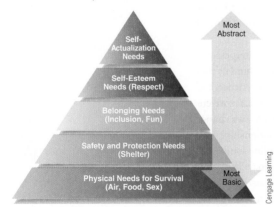

Self-Actualization Needs

Self-Esteem Needs (Respect)

Belonging Needs (Inclusion, Fun)

Safety and Protection Needs (Shelter)

Physical Needs for Survival (Air, Food, Sex)

Most Abstract

Most Basic

Cengage Learning

created. Those systems, or contexts, include the shared systems of both communicators (shared social networking sites, campus, town, workplace, religion, social groups, or culture) and the personal systems of each person (family, religious association, friends).

Finally, we should emphasize that the transactional model doesn't label one person a sender and the other a receiver. Instead, both people are defined as communicators who participate equally and often simultaneously in the communication process. This means that, at a given moment in communication, you may be sending a message (speaking or nodding your head), receiving a message, or doing both at the same time (interpreting what someone says while nodding to show you are interested).

The transactional nature of interpersonal communication implies that communicators share responsibility for effectiveness. People often say, "You didn't express yourself clearly," or "You misunderstood me," as if understanding rested with a single person. In reality, responsibility for good communication is shared. One person cannot make communication successful, nor is one person totally responsible for problems. Misunderstandings often arise in email and online communication because feedback tends to be delayed, a problem that instant messaging can decrease. Another limitation of online communication is the inability to convey inflection and nonverbal behaviors, such as winks, that tell another person we are joking. Sometimes we add emoticons—such as :) or :(—to signal emotions online. Because interpersonal communication is an ongoing, transactional process, all participants share responsibility for its effectiveness.

Now that we have defined and modeled interpersonal communication, let's consider important human needs that it helps us meet.

The Interpersonal Imperative

Have you ever thought about why you communicate? Psychologist William Schutz (1966) developed interpersonal needs theory, which asserts that we create and sustain relationships to meet three basic needs. The first need is for affection, the desire to give and receive love and liking. The second need is for inclusion, the desire to be social and to be included in groups. The third need is for control, which is a desire to influence the people and events in our lives.

Expanding on Schutz's ideas, Abraham Maslow (1968) proposed that we communicate to meet a range of human needs. According to Maslow, basic needs must be satisfied before we can focus on those that are more abstract (see Figure 1.5).

Physical Needs

At the most basic level, humans need to survive, and communication helps us meet this need. Babies cry to alert others when they are hungry or in pain or danger. Beyond survival, children need interaction if they are to thrive. As we grow older, we continue to rely on communication to survive and to thrive. Good communication between doctors and patients is related to effective treatment and to patients' physical health (Fleishman, Sherbourne, & Crystal, 2000). Our effectiveness in communicating affects what jobs we get and how much we earn to pay for medical care, food, leisure activities, and housing.

Furthermore, researchers have amassed impressive evidence to document the close link between physical health and relationships with others (Cacioppo & Patrick, 2009). College students who are in committed relationships have fewer mental health problems and are less likely to be obese (Braithwaite, Delevi, & Fincham, 2010), cancer patients who are married live longer than single cancer patients ("Cancer," 2009), and people who lack close emotional connections with others are more likely to develop dementia than are people who have strong relationships (Beekman, Deege, Jonker, & Schoevers, Stek, Tjalling, van Tilburg, 2012; Brody, 2013). So important is the connection between meaningful interpersonal relationships and health that doctors John Cacioppo and William Patrick (2009) assert that "social isolation has an impact on health comparable to the effect of high blood pressure, lack of exercise, obesity, or smoking" (p. 5). Given this information, it is unsurprising that people who have strong social connections live almost 4 years longer than people with weaker social ties (Holt-Lunstad, Smith, & Layton, 2010).

We also rely on communication to manage our practical needs and preferences. We describe exactly where we want a tattoo; we negotiate for a lower price at a consignment shop; we explain our housing preferences to a realtor; and we talk with a personal trainer to develop a workout program that helps us meet our goals.

Safety Needs

We also meet safety needs through communication. If your roof is leaking or if termites have invaded your apartment, you must talk with the property manager or owner to get the problem solved so that you have safe shelter. If someone is threatening you, you need to talk with authorities to gain protection. If you take the car keys from a friend who has been drinking and say, "I'll drive you home," you may save a life. We go online to research symptoms we have and to learn about medical conditions affecting friends or family members. After the tragic shootings at Virginia Tech, many campuses around the country developed plans for email alerts and sirens to warn students of any dangers.

CHLOE

My mom is a worrier, and she was really concerned when I decided to come to this big school instead of the one near home. She calls me like five times a day just to ask what I'm doing and if I'm okay. I get on her case about that a lot, but I really like knowing she stays in touch and always has my back.

Communication also helps protect us from dangers and harm. When foods are determined to be unsafe, news media inform the public. Workers persuade managers to do something about unsafe working conditions, and professionals communicate with each other to do their jobs. Residents in communities with toxic waste dumps rely on social networks to organize and then communicate with officials and media to call attention to environmental toxins that endanger their safety.

Belonging Needs

The third level in Maslow's hierarchy is belonging, or social, needs. All of us want to feel that we fit in our work and social groups. We want others' company, acceptance, and affirmation, and we want to give companionship, acceptance, and affirmation to others. The painful feeling of being excluded or rejected is often described as being "frozen out" or getting the "cold shoulder." It turns out, the cold sensation is not just metaphorical, but is real. Researchers Hans Ijezerman and Justin Saddlemyer (2012) found that our body temperature drops when we feel excluded.

The connection between belonging needs and health is well established. People who are deprived of human interaction over a long time may fail to develop a concept of themselves as humans. The "Communication in Everyday Life: Diversity" feature summarizes two dramatic cases of social isolation. The first case is that of Victor, a wild boy found in France in 1800; the second case is that of Ramu, or "*Ghadya ka Bacha,*" the "wolf boy" (Gerstein, 1998; Shattuck, 1994). Doctors who examined Ramu concluded that he was a feral child, which means he was raised in the wild with little or no human contact. As a result, he did not have a sense of himself as a person or a human being. His self-concept and self-esteem were shaped by those with whom he interacted, presumably wolves.

Two other cases are documented by sociologist Kingsley Davis (1940, 1947). Anna and Isabelle, two girls who were not related to one another, received minimal human contact and care during the first 6 years of their lives. Authorities who discovered the children reported that both girls lived in dark, dank attics. Anna and Isabelle were so undeveloped intellectually that they behaved like 6-month-olds. Anna was startlingly apathetic and unresponsive to others. She did not progress well despite care, contact, and nutrition. She died 4 years after she was discovered. Isabelle fared better. When she was found, she communicated by grunts and gestures and was responsive to human interaction. After 2 years in systematic therapy, Isabelle's intelligence approached normal levels for her age.

How do we explain the difference between these two isolated children and what happened to them? There was one major difference. Anna was left alone all the time and had no human contact. Food was periodically put in her room, but nobody talked to her or played with her. Isabelle, on the other hand, shared her space with her mother, who was deaf and mute. The family had renounced both of them and sequestered them in an attic.

Although Isabelle didn't have the advantage of normal family interaction, she did have contact with a mother. Because the mother was deaf and mute, she couldn't teach Isabelle to speak, but she did teach Isabelle to interact with gestures and sounds that both of them understood. Thus, Isabelle suffered less extreme deprivation than Anna.

Self-Esteem Needs

Moving up Maslow's hierarchy, we find self-esteem needs, which involve valuing and respecting ourselves and being valued and respected by others. As we will see in Chapter 2, communication is the primary way we figure out who we are and who we can be. We gain our first sense of self from others who communicate how they see us. Parents and other family members tell children they are pretty or plain, smart or slow, good or bad, helpful or difficult. As family members communicate their perceptions, children begin to form images of themselves.

This process continues throughout life as we see ourselves reflected in others' eyes. In elementary school, our teachers and peers influence our perceptions of how smart we are, how good we are at soccer, and how attractive we are. Later, friends and romantic partners reflect their views of us as loving or unloving, generous or selfish, open or closed, and trustworthy or untrustworthy. In professional life, our coworkers and supervisors communicate in ways that suggest how much they respect us and our abilities. Through all the stages of our lives, our self-esteem is shaped by how others communicate with us.

Communication in Everyday Life

DIVERSITY

Missing Socialization

Most of us take socialization for granted. We are born into families, and they socialize us as members of the human world of meaning and action. But what if there were no humans around to socialize you? Would you still be human? The question of what it means to be human is at the heart of two extraordinary stories of "wild children" who appear to have grown up without human contact (Douthwaite, 2002; Gerstein, 1998; Shattuck, 1994).

The first case took place in 1800. One day, French hunters found a strange creature in the woods. They were unsure what the creature was—perhaps a wild pig or monkey, they thought. The hunters tied the creature to a pole and brought it out of the woods for villagers to see. Quickly, it was determined that the creature was a human boy—filthy, naked, mute, and wild, but human nonetheless. When scientists were consulted, they said the boy was severely mentally disabled and unteachable. However, Jean-Marc Gaspard Itard disagreed. He was a young doctor who devoted many years to trying to socialize the wild boy, whom he named Victor. Itard was not successful, perhaps because Victor had missed human socialization during a critical developmental period early in life. The story of Victor is portrayed in François Truffaut's film *The Wild Child*.

A second case occurred in India in the middle of the 20th century. A young, naked, starving boy found his way to the hospital at Balrampur, India. He showed no ability to interact with people and had heavy calluses as though he moved on all fours. In addition, there were scars on the boy's neck as though he had been dragged by animals. The boy, named Ramu by the hospital staff, spent most of his time playing with a stuffed animal, as a wild animal might in its lair. He showed no interest in communicating; indeed, he seemed to feel no connection with other people. Ramu howled when he smelled raw meat in the hospital kitchen more than 100 yards from his room—far too great a distance for the human sense of smell to detect a scent. Ramu also didn't eat like a human; he tore meat apart and lapped milk from a container. Most of the doctors and scientists who examined Ramu concluded that he was a "wolf boy"—"*Ghadya ka Bacha*" in the Hindi language—who had grown up in the wild and had been socialized by wolves.

🅜 MindTap· Would you say Ramu was a wolf, a boy, or something else?

Self-Actualization Needs

According to Maslow, the most abstract human need is self-actualization. Maslow (1954/1970) defined *self-actualization* as fully developing and using our unique "talents, capacities, potentialities" (p. 150). To achieve this, we need to refine talents that we have and cultivate new potentials in ourselves. As humans, we seek more than survival, safety, belonging, and esteem. We also thrive on growth. Each of us wants to cultivate new dimensions of mind, heart, and spirit. We seek to enlarge our perspectives, engage in challenging and different experiences, learn new skills, and test ourselves in unfamiliar territories.

Communication fosters our personal growth. Therapists can be powerful resources in helping us identify our potentials. Friends, family, coworkers, and teachers can help us recognize promise in ourselves that we otherwise might not see. Adam recalls how such a person affected him in his first job.

ADAM

Mr. Bentley really helped me when I had my first job. It wasn't much—just serving at a sandwich shop—but he mentored me. He noticed I was awkward interacting with people, and he said I could learn social skills. He showed me how to be more effective—how to make customers feel comfortable, how to notice subtle cues that they needed something. Before that job, I'd thought of myself as kind of an introvert, somebody not very good with people. But Mr. Bentley saw a possibility in me that I hadn't seen in myself, and, as a result, I developed social skills and confidence that I never had before.

Another way in which we seek personal growth is by experimenting with new versions of ourselves. For this, too, we rely on communication. Sometimes we talk with friends about ways we want to grow or with coworkers about ways we want to advance professionally. At other times, we try out new styles of identity without telling anyone what we're doing. Some people experiment with their identities online where visual cues won't expose their real race, sex, age, or other characteristics. Lashelle's commentary stresses the importance of feedback from others in actualizing our potential.

LASHELLE

A person who changed my life was Mrs. Dickenson, my high school history teacher. She thought I was really smart, and she helped me see myself that way. I'd never considered myself all that intelligent, and I sure

hadn't thought I would go to college, but Mrs. Dickenson helped me to see a whole new image of who I could be. She stayed after school a lot of days to talk to me about my future and to help me get ready for the SAT. If it weren't for her, I wouldn't be in college now.

Others also help us self-actualize through inspiration and teaching. Mother Teresa was well known for inspiring others to be generous, compassionate, and giving. She had the ability to see the best in others and to help them see it in themselves. Mohandas Gandhi embodied the principle of nonviolent resistance so gracefully and effectively that he inspired thousands of Indians to define themselves as nonviolent resisters. Years later, in the United States, the Reverend Martin Luther King Jr. followed Gandhi's example with his nonviolent resistance of racism. Spiritual leaders such as Buddha, Confucius, Jesus, Moses, and Muhammad also inspire people to grow personally. As we interact with teachers and leaders who inspire us, we may come to understand their visions of the world and of themselves, and we may weave them into our own self-concepts.

Participating Effectively in a Diverse Society

In our era, the likelihood of meeting the needs Maslow discussed depends on our ability to participate effectively in a very diverse social world. Western culture includes people of different ethnicities, genders, social classes, sexual orientations, ages, spiritual commitments, and abilities. The United States is becoming increasingly diverse. In 2009, almost 49% of births in the United States were minorities, and 48.3% of children under 5 years old were minorities (Nasser & Overberg, 2010). In 2010 Caucasians made up 64% of the population, but by 2050 there will be no majority race in the United States (Cooper, 2012; Yen, 2012).

In a recent survey of first-year students at colleges and universities, nearly half said that learning about other cultures is essential or very important (Hoover, 2010). Research also shows that exposure to students from a range of backgrounds is one of the best predictors of whether first-year college students return for a second year (Berrett, 2011).

Most of us realize that we expand intellectually and personally when we engage people who differ in background, ethnicity, age, and so forth. Dante notes the importance of this type of communication.

DANTE

My friend Bobby is about as different from me as a person could get. He's black; I'm white. He's from a big city; I grew up on a farm. He's liberal politically; I'm conservative. That's what I like about Bobby—he doesn't see a lot of things the way I do. When we talk, we often start out at different points, but we listen to each other and each of us learns other ways of looking at things.

Understanding and interacting with diverse people is also critical to success in professional life. Today's and tomorrow's employers think it is very important for employees to be able to interact effectively with different kinds of people. Job applicants who can do this have a keen advantage.

Understanding and adapting to social diversity is critical to professional success and even to professional competence. Doctors, for instance, need to realize that some Hispanic patients are reassured by eye contact, whereas some patients from traditional Asian backgrounds are uneasy when looked at directly. Social workers need to understand that many people of Spanish and Asian heritage have extended families that are much larger than most Caucasian families.

In summary, interpersonal communication meets human needs ranging from survival to self-actualization and growth through encounters with a diversity of people. Of course, our ability to meet our needs depends on the effectiveness of our interpersonal communication. That is why the final sections of this chapter identify principles that enhance effectiveness.

PRINCIPLES OF INTERPERSONAL COMMUNICATION

There are eight basic principles for effectiveness in interpersonal communication.

Principle 1: We Cannot *Not* Communicate

A key principle to keep in mind is that we cannot avoid communicating when we are with others because they interpret what we do and say as well as what we don't do and don't say. Even if we choose to be silent, we're communicating. What we mean by silence and how others interpret it depend on cultural backgrounds.

Because Westerners typically are more verbal than many other cultural groups, they are likely to regard silence as a signal of anger, disinterest, or lack of knowledge. Some Native Americans and members of many Eastern cultures might interpret silence as thoughtfulness or respect. Either way, silence communicates.

Even when we don't intend to communicate, we do so. We may be unaware of a grimace that gives away our disapproval or an eye roll that shows we dislike someone, but we are communicating nonetheless. Unconscious communication often occurs on the relationship level of meaning as we express feelings about others through subtle, often nonverbal communication. Regardless of whether we aim to communicate and whether others understand our intentions, we continuously, unavoidably communicate.

Principle 2: Interpersonal Communication Is Irreversible

Perhaps you have been in a heated argument in which you lost your temper and said something you later regretted. It could be that you hurt someone or revealed something about yourself that you meant to keep private. Later, you might have tried to repair the damage by apologizing, explaining what you said, or denying what you revealed. But you couldn't erase your communication; you couldn't unsay what you had said.

You may have had similar experiences when communicating by email or posting on Facebook. Perhaps you read a message that made you angry, and you dashed off a barbed reply, sent it, and then wished you could unsend it. Perhaps you posted a picture of yourself when you were not sober, and your parents saw it. The fact that communication is irreversible reminds us that what we say and do matters. It has impact. Once we say something to another person, our words become part of the relationship. Remembering this principle keeps us aware of the importance of choosing when to speak and what to say—or not to say!

Principle 3: Interpersonal Communication Involves Ethical Choices

Ethics is the branch of philosophy that focuses on moral principles and codes of conduct. Ethical issues concern right and wrong. Because interpersonal communication is irreversible and affects others, it always has ethical implications. What we say and do affects others: how they feel, how they perceive themselves, how they think about themselves, and how they think about others. Thus, responsible people think carefully about ethical implications of their communication.

Our everyday lives are filled with ethical choices. Should you not tell someone something that might make him less willing to do what you want? If you read a message on your social network that makes you angry, do you fire off a nasty reply, assuming that you will never meet the person and so won't face any consequences? Do you judge another person's communication from your own individual perspective and experience? Or do you try to understand her communication on her terms and from her perspective? In work settings, should you avoid giving negative feedback because it could hurt others' feelings even if it might help them advance? In these and many other instances, we face ethical choices. Throughout this book, we note ethical issues that arise when we interact with others. As you read, consider what kinds of choices you make and what moral principles guide your choices.

Principle 4: People Construct Meanings in Interpersonal Communication

The significance of communication doesn't lie in words and nonverbal behaviors. Instead, meaning arises out of how we interpret communication. This calls our attention to the fact that humans use symbols, which sets us apart from other creatures.

As we will see in Chapter 4, **symbols**, such as words, have no inherent or true meanings. Instead, we must interpret them. What does it mean if someone says, "You're sick"? To interpret the comment, you must consider the context (a counseling session, a professional meeting, after a daredevil stunt), who said it (a psychiatrist, a supervisor, a subordinate, a friend, an enemy), and the words themselves, which may mean various things (a medical diagnosis, a challenge to your professional competence, a compliment on your zaniness, disapproval).

In close relationships, partners gradually coordinate meanings so that they share understandings of issues and feelings important to their connection. When a relationship begins, one person may regard confrontation as healthy, and the other may avoid arguments. Over time, partners come to share meanings for conflict—what it is, how to handle it, and whether it threatens the relationship or is a path to growth.

The meanings we attribute to conflict are shaped by cultural backgrounds. Because standing up for your own ideas is emphasized in the United States, many people who were born and raised in this country value confrontation more than do many Asians who were raised in traditional Asian families. Conflict means different things to each group.

Even one person's meanings vary over time and in response to experiences and moods. If you're in a good mood, a playful gibe might strike you as funny or as an invitation to banter. The same remark might hurt or anger you if you're feeling down. The meaning of the gibe, like all communication, is not preset or absolute. Meanings are created by people as they communicate in specific contexts.

Principle 5: Metacommunication Affects Meanings

The word *metacommunication* comes from the prefix *meta*, meaning "about," and the root word *communication*. Thus, **metacommunication** is communication about

communication. For example, during a conversation with your friend Pat, you notice that Pat's body seems tense and her voice is sharp. You might say, "You seem really stressed in our conversation." Your statement is metacommunication because it communicates about Pat's nonverbal communication.

We can use words to talk about other words or nonverbal behaviors. If an argument between Joe and Marc gets out of hand, and Joe makes a nasty personal attack, Joe might later say, "I didn't really mean what I just said. I was just so angry it came out." This metacommunication may soften the hurt caused by the attack. If Joe and Marc then have a productive conversation about their differences, Marc might conclude by saying, "This has really been a good talk. I think we understand each other a lot better now." This comment verbally metacommunicates about the conversation that preceded it.

Metacommunication can increase understanding. For instance, teachers sometimes say, "The next point is really important." This comment signals students to pay special attention to what follows. A parent might tell a child, "What I said may sound harsh, but I'm only telling you because I care about you." The comment tells the child how to interpret a critical message. A manager tells a subordinate to take a comment seriously by saying, "I really mean what I said. I'm not kidding." On the other hand, if we're not really sure what we think about an issue, and we want to try out a stance, we might say, "I'm thinking this through as I go, and I'm not really wedded to this position, but what I tend to believe right now is . . . ." This preface to your statement tells listeners not to assume that what you say is set in stone.

We can also metacommunicate to check on understanding: "Was I clear?" "Do you see why I feel like I do?" "Can you see why I'm confused about the problem?" Questions such as these allow you to find out whether another person understands what you intend to communicate. You may also metacommunicate to find out whether you understand what another person expresses to you. "What I think you meant is that you are worried. Is that right?" "If I follow what you said, you feel trapped between what you want to do and what your parents want you to do. Is that what you were telling me?" You may even say, "I don't understand what you just told me. Can you say it another way?" This question metacommunicates by letting the other person know you did not grasp her message and that you want to understand.

Effective metacommunication also helps friends and romantic partners express how they feel about their interactions. Linda Acitelli (1988, 1993) has studied what happens when partners in a relationship talk to each other about how they perceive and feel about their interaction. She reports that women and men alike find metacommunication helpful if there is a conflict or problem that must be addressed. Both sexes seem to appreciate knowing how the other feels about their differences; they are also eager to learn how to communicate to resolve those differences. During a conflict, one person might say, "I feel like we're both being really stubborn. Do you think we could each back off a little from our positions?" This expresses discontent with how communication is proceeding and offers an alternative. After conflict, one partner might say, "This really cleared the air between us. I feel a lot better now."

> I never feel like an argument is really over and settled until Andy and I have said that we feel better for having thrashed out whatever was the problem. It's like I want closure, and the fight isn't really behind us until we both say, "I'm glad we talked," or something to say what we went through led us to a better place.
>
> TARA

Acitelli also found that women are more likely than men to appreciate metacommunication when there is no conflict or immediate problem to be resolved. For example, while curled up on a sofa and watching TV, a woman might say to her male partner, "I really feel comfortable snuggling with you." This statement comments on the relationship and the nonverbal communication

MindTap

Everyday Skills To practice metacommunication, complete the activity "Improve Your Metacommunication" at the end of the chapter or online.

between the couple. According to Acitelli and others (Wood, 1997, 1998), men generally find talk about relationships unnecessary unless there is an immediate problem to be addressed. Understanding this gender difference in preferences for metacommunication may help you interpret members of the other sex more accurately.

Principle 6: Interpersonal Communication Develops and Sustains Relationships

Interpersonal communication is the primary way we build, refine, and transform relationships. Partners talk to work out expectations and understandings of their interaction, appropriate and inappropriate topics and styles of communicating, and the nature of the relationship itself. Is it a friendship or a romantic relationship? How much and in what ways can we count on each other? How do we handle disagreements—by confronting them, ignoring them, or using indirect strategies to restore harmony? What are the bottom lines, the "thou shalt not" rules for what counts as unforgivable betrayal? What counts as caring—words, deeds, both? Because communication has no intrinsic meanings, we must generate our own in the course of interaction.

Communication also allows us to construct or reconstruct individual and joint histories. For instance, when people fall in love, they often redefine former loves as "mere infatuations" or "puppy love," but definitely not the real thing. When something goes wrong in a relationship, partners may work together to define what happened in a way that allows them to continue. Marriage counselors report that couples routinely work out face-saving explanations for affairs so that they can stay together in the aftermath of infidelity (Scarf, 1987). Partners often talk about past events and experiences that challenged them and ones that were joyous. The process of reliving the past reminds partners how long they have been together and how much they have shared. As partners communicate thoughts and feelings, they generate shared meanings for themselves, their interaction, and their relationship.

Communication is also the primary means by which people construct a future for themselves and their relationships. For intimates, talking about a vision of a shared future is one of the most powerful ties that link people (Dixson & Duck, 1993; Wood, 2006a). Romantic couples often dream together by talking about the family they plan and how they'll be in 20 years. Likewise, friends discuss plans for the future and promise reunions if they must move apart, and work colleagues talk about advancement and challenges down the road. Communication allows us to express and share dreams, imaginings, and memories, and to weave all of these into shared understandings of a continuing relationship.

KAREN

I love talking about the future with my fiancé. Sometimes, we talk for hours about the kind of house we'll have and what our children will be like and how we'll juggle two careers and a family. I know everything won't work out exactly like we think now, but talking about it makes me feel so close to Dave and like our future is real.

Principle 7: Interpersonal Communication Is Not a Panacea

As we have seen, we communicate to satisfy many of our needs and to create relationships with others. Yet it would be a mistake to think communication is a cure-all. Many problems can't be solved by talk alone. Communication by itself won't end hunger, abuses of human rights around the globe, racism, intimate partner violence, or physical diseases. Nor can words alone bridge irreconcilable differences between people or erase the hurt of betrayal. Although good communication may increase understanding and help us solve problems, it will not fix everything. We should also realize that the idea of talking things through is distinctly Western. Not all societies think it's wise or useful to communicate about relationships or to talk extensively about feelings. Just as interpersonal communication has many strengths and values, it also has limits, and its effectiveness is shaped by cultural contexts.

Principle 8: Interpersonal Communication Effectiveness Can Be Learned

It is a mistake to think that effective communicators are born, that some people have a natural talent and others don't. Although some people have extraordinary talent in athletics or writing, those who don't can learn to be competent athletes and writers. Likewise, some people have an aptitude for communicating, but all of us can become competent communicators. This book and the course you are taking should sharpen your understandings of how interpersonal communication works and should help you learn skills that will enhance your effectiveness in relating to others.

SOCIAL MEDIA IN EVERYDAY LIFE

As in every chapter, we will explore how social media are relevant to the ideas presented in the foregoing pages. Consider what the definition of interpersonal communication implies for communication via social media. When we talk with people face to face (f2f), we are aware of their immediate physical context, which is not the case with much online and digital interaction. We may not know who else is present and what else is happening around a person we text. When the systems within which communication occurs are unknown to us, it's more difficult to interpret others. Also, because nonverbal communication is restricted online and especially digitally, we may miss out on meaning, particularly on the relationship level.

Our definition of interpersonal communication also emphasizes process—changes in communication that happen over time. Think about how online and digital communication have evolved in the course of the past two

decades. When email first emerged, most people treated it much like letter writing: An email started with "Dear" or "Hello" and ended with a closing such as "Thank you" or "Sincerely." As email became more popular and as all of us were flooded with email messages, the opening and closing courtesies largely disappeared. As email traffic continued to increase, abbreviations started being used: BRB (be right back), LOL (laughing out loud), and so forth. Texting brought more innovation in use of symbols. Vowels are often dropped, single letters serve for some words (u for you, r for are), and phrases are more acceptable than complete sentences. The rules of grammar, syntax, and spelling have been loosened for digital natives who are accustomed to the autocorrect function that is standard on most phones and computers.

Our definition of interpersonal communication also highlights meanings, which are at the heart of our interaction via social media. We blog and tweet to tell others what issues and events mean to us; we follow others' blogs and tweets to learn what they think. Emerging norms for using social media also challenge some long-standing meanings. For example, having dinner with others traditionally has meant interacting in a focused and continuous way with the people at the table; attending a meeting has meant being mentally present in the meeting. Yet people increasingly send or check texts during meals and meetings, which may mean they are partially present in multiple spaces, yet not fully present in any one.

We also discussed human needs that we satisfy through communication, and these are met by interaction on social media just as they are met by f2f interaction. For example, Facebook and other social networking sites are a major source for satisfying our needs for belonging. You might take a moment to reflect on the extent to which you rely on digital and online communication to meet physical, safety, belonging, self-esteem, and self-actualization needs and to participate effectively in a diverse society.

Consider also how the eight principles of interpersonal communication apply to online and digital interaction. For instance, the principle that we cannot *not* communicate implies that just as texting friends is communication, so is *not* texting them. When we don't answer others' texts, they may interpret this as meaning we are angry or uninterested in them. Or consider the principle that interpersonal communication is irreversible. Have you ever sent a text or tweet and then regretted it but been unable to call it back? Have you ever wished you could erase some of your electronic footprints—embarrassing photos you posted years ago or flames that you regret? Our online and digital communication is irreversible, just as our face-to-face communication is.

A third principle is that interpersonal communication involves ethical choices. Important ethical issues infuse the online and digital world. Is it ethical to misrepresent yourself or your goals when creating your profile for an online dating site? Is exaggerating just a little (saying you are 5'10" when you are really 5'8") unethical? What about flaming or cyberbullying and cyberstalking? How does the anonymity of much online communication affect the ethical (or unethical) choices people make? These are critical questions to keep in mind as you communicate interpersonally using social media. Continue this discussion by thinking about how the remaining five principles we discussed apply to interaction via social media.

Everyday Skills To understand your reasons for using social media, complete the activity "Your Use of Social Media" at the end of this chapter or online.

GUIDELINES FOR INTERPERSONAL COMMUNICATION COMPETENCE

Sometimes we handle interactions well, and other times we don't. What are the differences between effective and ineffective communication? Scholars define **interpersonal communication competence** as the ability to communicate effectively, appropriately, and ethically. Effectiveness involves achieving the goals we have for specific interactions. In different situations, your goals might be to explain an idea, to comfort a friend, to stand up for your position, to negotiate a raise, or to persuade someone to change behaviors. The more effectively you communicate, the more likely you are to be competent in achieving your goals.

Competence also emphasizes appropriateness. This means that competent communication is adapted to particular situations and people. Language that is appropriate at a party with friends may not be appropriate in a job interview. Appropriateness also involves contexts. It may be appropriate to kiss an intimate in a private setting but not in a classroom. Similarly, many people choose not to argue in front of others but prefer to engage in conflict when they are alone.

Five skills are closely tied to competence in interpersonal communication: (1) developing a range of communication skills, (2) adapting communication appropriately, (3) engaging in dual perspective, (4) monitoring communication, and (5) committing to ethical interpersonal communication. We'll discuss each of these skills now.

Develop a Range of Skills

No single style of communication is best in all circumstances, with all people, or for pursuing all goals. Because what is effective varies, we need to have a broad repertoire of communication behaviors. Consider the different skills needed for interpersonal communication competence in several situations.

To comfort someone, we need to be soothing and compassionate. To negotiate a good deal on a car, we need to be assertive and firm. To engage constructively in conflict, we need to listen and build a supportive climate. To support a friend who is depressed, we need to affirm that person, demonstrate that we care, and encourage the friend to talk about his or her problems. To build good work relationships, we need to communicate supportively, express our ideas clearly, and listen well. Because no single set of skills composes interpersonal communication competence, we need to learn a range of communicative abilities.

Adapt Communication Appropriately

The ability to communicate in a range of ways doesn't make us competent unless we also know which kinds of communication to use in specific interactions. For instance, knowing how to be both assertive and deferential isn't useful unless we can figure out when each style of communication is appropriate. Although there is no neat formula for adapting communication appropriately, it's generally important to consider personal goals, context, and the people with whom we communicate.

Your goals for communication are a primary guideline for selecting appropriate behaviors. If your purpose in a conversation is to give emotional support to someone, then it isn't effective to talk at length about your own experiences. On the other hand, if you want someone to understand you better, talking in depth about your life may be highly effective. If your goal is to win an argument and get your way, it may be competent to assert your point of view, point out flaws in your partner's ideas, and refuse to compromise. If you want to work through conflict in a way that doesn't harm a relationship, however, other communication choices might be more constructive.

MARY MARGARET For most of my life, I wasn't at all assertive, even when I should have been. Last spring, though, I was so tired of having people walk all over me that I signed up for a workshop on assertiveness training. I learned how to assert myself, and I was really proud of how much more I would stand up for myself. The problem was that I did it all the time, regardless of whether something really mattered enough to be assertive. Just like I was always passive before, now I'm always assertive. I need to figure out a better way to balance my behaviors.

Context is another influence on decisions of when, how, and about what to communicate. It is appropriate to ask your doctor about symptoms during an office exam, but it isn't appropriate to do so when you see the doctor in a social situation. When a friend is feeling low, that's not a good time to criticize, although at another time criticism might be constructive. Sometimes in-person communication is more appropriate than texting or emailing. When communicating online, it's useful to compensate for the lack of nonverbal cues by adding emoticons and expressing warmth explicitly.

Remembering Buber's discussion of the I–Thou relationship, we know it is important to adapt what we say and how we say it to particular people. As we have seen, interpersonal communication increases our knowledge of others. Thus, the more interpersonal the relationship, the more we can adapt our communication to unique partners. Abstract communicative goals, such as supporting others, call for distinct behaviors in regard to specific people. What feels supportive to one friend may not to another. One of my closest friends withdraws if I challenge her ideas, yet another friend relishes challenges and the discussions they prompt. What is effective in talking with them varies. We have to learn what our intimates need, what upsets and pleases them, and how they interpret various kinds of communication. Scholars use the term **person-centeredness** to refer to the ability to adapt messages effectively to particular people (Bernstein, 1974; Burleson, 1987). Appropriately adapted communication, then, is sensitive to goals, contexts, and other people.

Engage in Dual Perspective

Central to competent interpersonal communication is the ability to engage in **dual perspective**, which is understanding both our own and another person's perspective, beliefs, thoughts, or feelings (Phillips & Wood, 1983). When we adopt dual perspective, we understand how someone else thinks and feels about issues. To meet another person in genuine dialogue, we must be able to realize how that person views himself or herself, the situation, and his or her own thoughts and feelings. We may personally see things much differently, and we may want to express our perceptions. Yet we also need to understand and respect the other person's perspective.

Research (Tomasello, 2009) shows that the tendency to try to understand and help others may be innate in humans. Infants as young as 14 months old offer to pick up an object dropped by an adult not related to them (Wade, 2009). This innate tendency to reach out to others thrives when it is nurtured by adults around a child.

People who cannot take the perspectives of others are egocentric. They impose their perceptions on others and interpret others' experiences through their own eyes. Consider an example. Roberto complains that he is having trouble writing a report for his supervisor. His coworker Raymond responds, "All you have to do is outline the plan and provide the rationale. That's a snap." "But," says Roberto, "I've always had trouble writing. I just go blank when I sit down to write." Raymond says, "That's silly. Anyone can do this. It just took me an hour or so to do my report." Raymond has failed to understand how Roberto perceives writing. If you have trouble writing, then composing a report isn't a snap, but Raymond can't get beyond his own comfort with writing to understand Roberto's different perspective.

> Sometimes it's very difficult for me to understand my daughter. She likes music that sounds terrible to me, and I don't like the way she dresses sometimes. For a long time, I judged her by my own values about music and dress, but that really pushed us apart. She kept saying, "I'm not you. Why can't you look at it from my point of view?" Finally, I heard her, and now we both try to understand each other's point of view. It isn't always easy, but you can't have a relationship on just one person's terms.

ASHA

As Asha says, engaging in dual perspective isn't necessarily easy, because all of us naturally see things from our own points of view and in terms of our own experiences. Parents often have trouble understanding the perspectives of children, particularly teenagers (Fox & Frankel, 2005). Yet we can improve our ability to engage in dual perspective (Greene & Burleson, 2003). Three guidelines can help you increase your ability to take the perspective of others.

+ First, be aware of the tendency to see things only from your own perspective, and resist that inclination.
+ Second, listen closely to how others express their thoughts and feelings, so you gain clues of what things mean to them and how they feel.
+ Third, ask others to explain how they feel, what something means to them, or how they view a situation. Asking questions and probing for details communicates on the relationship level that you are interested and that you want to understand.

Making a commitment to engage in dual perspective and practicing the three guidelines just discussed will enhance your ability to recognize and respond to others' perspectives.

Monitor Your Communication

The fourth ability that affects interpersonal communication competence is **monitoring**, which is the capacity to observe and regulate your own communication. Most of us do this much of the time without even thinking about it. Before bringing up a touchy topic, you remind yourself not to get defensive and not to get pulled into counterproductive arguing. During the discussion, Chris says something that upsets you. You think of a really good zinger but stop yourself from saying it because you don't want to hurt Chris. In each instance, you monitored your communication.

Monitoring occurs both before and during interaction. Often, before conversations we indicate to ourselves what we do and don't want to say. During communication, we stay alert and edit our thoughts before expressing them. Online communication offers us especially effective ways to monitor our communication. We can save messages, reread them to see if they express what we really intend, and edit them before sending or posting. Our ability to monitor allows us to adapt communication in advance and gauge our effectiveness as we interact.

Of course, we don't monitor all the time. When we are with people who understand us or when we are talking about unimportant topics, we don't necessarily need to monitor communication with great care. Sometimes, however, not monitoring can result in communication that hurts others or that leads us to regard ourselves negatively. In some cases, failure to monitor results from getting caught up in the dynamics of interaction. We simply forget to keep a watchful eye on ourselves, and so we say or do things we later regret. In addition, some people have poorly developed monitoring skills. They have a limited awareness of how they come across to others. Communication competence involves learning to attend to feedback from others and to monitor the impact of our communication as we interact with them.

Commit to Ethical Communication

The final requirement for interpersonal competence is commitment to ethical communication. This commitment requires that you invest energy in communicating ethically with others as unique human beings both f2f and on social media. This implies that you can't treat another person as merely a member of some group, such as men, coworkers, or customers. Responding to another as a unique and valuable person also means you can't dismiss the other person's feelings as wrong, inappropriate, or silly. Instead, you must honor the person and the feelings he or she expresses, even if you feel differently.

A commitment to ethical communication also requires you to respect yourself and your ideas and feelings. Just as you must honor those of others, you must respect yourself and your own perspective. Finally, ethical communicators are committed to the integrity of the communication process itself. They realize that it is interactive and always evolving, and they are willing to deal with that complexity. In addition, they are sensitive to multiple levels of meaning and to the irreversibility of communication. Commitment, then, is vital to relationships, other people, ourselves, and communication.

In sum, interpersonal communication competence is the ability to communicate in ways that are effective and appropriate. The five requirements for competence are (1) developing a range of communication skills; (2) adapting them appropriately to goals, others, and situations; (3) engaging in dual perspective; (4) monitoring communication and its impact; and (5) committing to ethical interpersonal communication. Consider which aspects of communication competence you would most like to improve, and make a contract with yourself to work on them during this course.

CHAPTER SUMMARY

In this chapter, we launched our study of interpersonal communication. We began by defining interpersonal communication and considering different models of the process. We then saw that communicating with others allows us to meet basic needs for survival and safety as well as more abstract human needs for inclusion, esteem, self-actualization, and effective participation in a socially diverse world.

We discussed eight principles of interpersonal communication. First, it is impossible not to communicate. Whether or not we intend to send certain messages and whether or not others understand our meanings, communication always occurs when people are together. Second, communication is irreversible because we cannot unsay or undo what passes between ourselves and others. Third, interpersonal communication always has ethical implications. Fourth, meanings reside not in words alone but rather in how we interpret them. Fifth, metacommunication affects meanings in interpersonal interaction. Sixth, we use communication to develop and sustain relationships. In fact, communication is essential to relationships because it is in the process of interacting with others that we develop expectations, understandings, and rules to guide relationships. Seventh, although communication is powerful and important, it is not a cure-all. Eighth, effectiveness in interpersonal communication can be learned through committed study and practice of principles and skills. We noted that the foundations of communication discussed in the chapter are relevant to digital and online communication. We also discussed how the foregoing ideas are relevant to digital communication.

Competent interpersonal communicators interact in ways that are effective, appropriate, and ethical. This means that we should adapt our ways of communicating to specific goals, situations, and others. Effectiveness and appropriateness require us to recognize and respect differences that reflect personal and cultural backgrounds. Guidelines for doing this include developing a range of communication skills, adapting communication sensitively, engaging in dual perspective, monitoring our own communication, and committing to effective and ethical interpersonal communication. In later chapters, we focus on developing the skills that enhance interpersonal communication competence.

Key Concepts

Practice defining the chapter's terms by using online flashcards.

FLASHCARDS...

content meaning 18
dual perspective 36
ethics 2
feedback 21
I–It communication 12
interactive model 21
interpersonal communication 14

interpersonal communication competence 3
I–Thou communication 13
I–You communication 13
linear model 20
metacommunication 30
model 19
monitoring 40

noise 15
person-centeredness 40
process 17
relationship meaning 18
symbol 30
systemic 14
transactional model 21

Continuing the Conversation

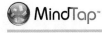

Jason Harris © 2001 Wadsworth

When you've watched the video online, critique and analyze this encounter based on the principles you learned in this chapter. Then compare your work with the author's suggested responses. Online, even more videos will let you continue the conversation with your instructor.

> Your supervisor asks you to mentor a new employee, Toya. After 2 weeks, you perceive that the new person is responsible and punctual, and takes initiative. At the same time, you realize that Toya is careless about details. You've also noticed that she seems insecure and wants a lot of affirmation and praise. You want to give her honest feedback so she can improve her performance, yet you are afraid she will react defensively. You ask her to meet with you to discuss her first 2 weeks.

You: How are you liking the job?

PRACTICE...

Toya: I like it a lot, and I'm trying to do my best. Nobody has said anything, so I guess I'm okay.

You: I've noticed how responsible you are.

Toya: Thanks. So I guess I'm doing okay?

You: What if someone suggested that there are ways you can improve?

Toya: What do you mean? Nobody's said anything to me.

1. What would you say next to Toya? How would you meet your ethical responsibilities as her mentor and also adapt to her interpersonal needs for reassurance?
2. What is your ethical responsibility to Toya, your supervisor, and the company? Reflect thoughtfully about potential tensions among these responsibilities.
3. How would your communication differ if you acted according to a linear or transactional model of communication?

Assessing Yourself

Begin the process of applying this chapter's concepts by taking a self-assessment quiz here or online—where you will find out what the results mean.

Purpose: To allow you to assess how satisfied you are with your ability to communicate in different situations.

Instructions: Listed below are 10 interpersonal communication situations. Imagine that you are involved in each situation. Then, indicate how confident you are that you could communicate competently using the following scale.

PRACTICE...

5 Very satisfied that I could communicate competently

4 Somewhat satisfied that I could communicate competently

3 Not sure how effectively I could communicate

2 Somewhat dissatisfied with my ability to communicate effectively

1 Very dissatisfied with my ability to communicate effectively

_____ 1. Someone asks you personal questions that you feel uncomfortable answering. You'd like to tell the person that you don't want to answer, but you don't want to hurt the person's feelings.

_____ 2. You think a friend of yours is starting to drink more alcohol than is healthy. You want to bring up the topic with your friend, but you don't want to create a barrier in the friendship.

_____ 3. You really care about the person you've been dating recently, but neither of you has ever put your feelings in words. You'd like to express how you feel but aren't sure how your partner will respond.

_____ 4. During a heated discussion about social issues, the person with whom you are talking says, "Why won't you hear me out fairly??!"

_____ 5. A friend shares his creative writing with you and asks if you think he has any talent. You don't think the writing is very good, and you need to respond to his request for an opinion.

_____ 6. Your roommate's habits are really getting on your nerves. You want to tell your roommate you're bothered, but you don't want to cause hurt.

_____ 7. A classmate asks you for notes for the classes he missed. You agree but then discover he has missed nearly half of the classes and expects you to bail him out. You feel that's exploitive.

_____ 8. You go to a party and discover that you don't know anyone there.

_____ 9. The person you have been dating declares "I love you." You care about the person but your feelings are not love, at least not yet. The person expects some response from you.

_____ 10. A person that you care about comes to you whenever he has problems he wants to discuss, and you give him attention and advice. When you want to talk about your problems, however, he doesn't seem to have time. You want the friendship to continue, but you don't like feeling that it's one-way.

_____ TOTAL (Add up the numbers you placed in each blank. Make sure that your total is between 10 and 50).

Everyday Skills

Build your communication skills further by completing the following activities here or online.

1. Communicating in Your Relationships

Consider how Buber's theory of communication applies to your life. For each of the three types of relationship (I–It, I–You, I–Thou) identify one person with whom you share that relationship.

I–It:

_____

_____

I–You:

_____

_____

I–Thou:

_____

_____

How does communication differ in the relationships? What ethical obligations do you feel in each type of relationship? What don't you say in I–It and I–You relationships that you do say in I–Thou relationships? How do different levels of communication affect the closeness you feel with others? Which of these three kinds of relationship can be created or sustained using social media?

2. Levels of Meaning

For the next 48 hours, observe others communicating on the relationship level of meaning.

Record examples of the following:

- Communicating responsiveness
- Communicating lack of responsiveness
- Expressing liking
- Expressing disliking
- Expressing superiority
- Expressing subordination
- Expressing equality

What do your observations tell you about the relationship issues being negotiated and expressed in your relationships?

3. Improve Your Metacommunication

For each of the scenarios described here, write out one verbal or nonverbal metacommunication that would be appropriate to express your feelings about what has been said or to clarify understanding.

a. You are arguing with a person who seems more interested in winning the argument than in working things through so that both of you are satisfied. You want to change how the argument is proceeding.

Metacommunication:

_____

_____

_____

b. Your manager at work routinely gives you orders instead of making requests. You resent it when she says to you, "Take over the front room," "Clean up the storeroom now," and "I want you in early tomorrow." You want to change how your manager expresses expectations for your performance.

Metacommunication:

_____

_____

_____

c. Lately, someone who used to be a close friend seems to be avoiding you. When you do see the friend, he seems eager to cut the conversation short. He doesn't meet your eyes and doesn't tell you anything about his life anymore. You want to know what is going on and how to interpret his communication.

Metacommunication:

_____

_____

_____

d. You have just spent 10 minutes telling your father why you want to study abroad next year. Earlier, your father said that studying abroad was just an extravagance, but you've tried to explain why it will broaden your education and your marketability when you look for a job next year. You aren't sure your father has understood your points.

Metacommunication:

_____

_____

_____

4. Your Use of Social Media

Review the emails, texts, and tweets that you have sent in the past 12 hours. Identify which of the six needs that interpersonal communication meets motivated each of your social media messages. Do you use social media to meet some needs more than other needs?

Message	Need(s)
_____	_____
_____	_____
_____	_____

 MindTap   **DO...** Additional interactive discussions, online quizzes, and activities that your instructor may assign for a grade.

Engaging with Ideas

Reflect and write about the ideas in this chapter by considering questions about personal, workplace, and ethical applications, here or online.

Personal Application List the six needs that interpersonal communication helps us meet. By each need, list one example of communication you have engaged in to meet that need. Compare your answers to those of your classmates.

Workplace Application Interview a professional in the field you plan to enter. Ask him or her to explain the communication skills needed for success and

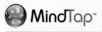

REFLECT ON...

advancement in the field. Which skills do you already have? Which ones do you need to develop or improve? Write out a personal action plan for using this book and the course it accompanies to enhance your effectiveness in interpersonal communication.

Ethical Application Consider the ethical implications of the interactive and the transactional models of interpersonal communication. How do our ethical responsibilities to others differ when we conceive of communication as interactive versus transactional?

Thinking Critically

Think and write critically about the ideas in this chapter, here or online.

1. Visit the placement office on your campus, and read descriptions of job openings. Record the number of job descriptions that call for communication skills. Share your findings with others in your class.
2. Identify a relationship of yours that has become closer over time. Describe the earliest stage of the relationship. Was it an I–It or an I–You relationship at that time? During that early stage of the relationship, what did you talk about? Were

REFLECT ON...

there topics or kinds of talk you avoided? Now, describe the current relationship. What do you now talk about? Can you identify differences over time in your own and the other person's shared fields of experience?
3. The National Communication Association provides information on careers for people with backgrounds in communication. Learn about these by visiting their website. [[http://www.natcom.org/CommunicationCareerPaths/]]

COMMUNICATION AND PERSONAL IDENTITY

Topics covered in this chapter

What Is the Self?

Presenting and Negotiating Identity

Social Media and Personal Identity

Guidelines for Enriching the Self

After studying this chapter, you should be able to . . .

Name forms of communication that shape self-concept.

Recognize examples of face presentation in a particular interaction.

Identify identities that social media idealize.

Apply the guidelines in this chapter to set a personal goal.

Madison signs onto Facebook to catch up on what's happening with her friends. Sarah, who was Madison's best friend in high school, <Going to hang out with totally awesome new guy I met.> Madison comments back <Enjoy!> and wishes she had a new guy in her life. Scrolling down, she checks posts from other friends. One says he was just selected to be the sports editor for the school paper. Another announces that her friends surprised her with a birthday party. A third comments that she is having a super vacation in the Bahamas.

Madison gets out of Facebook and slumps back on her bed. "Why is my life so dull?" she wonders. "I'm not having a great vacation; my friends don't surprise me on my birthday; I wasn't selected to be editor or anything else." Compared to her friends, Madison feels she and her life are boring.

Have you read posts like those Madison read? If so, it seems everyone else is living a perfect life—dream job offers, amazing adventures and opportunities, success at work, good grades, loads of friends, and romantic interests. Do you, like Madison, ever wonder why your life isn't as totally fantastic as everyone else's? If so, quit worrying; their lives are probably not nearly as rosy as their postings suggest. Most people choose to present themselves positively online. They announce their accomplishments and post about the good, exciting things happening in their lives. They are less likely to comment on boredom and unhappy aspects of their lives.

In this chapter, we explore the self, or personal identity. Who are you? How did you develop your identity? What choices do you make about the identity, or identities, that you present to others, both face to face and online? How can you improve your self-concept? These are the questions this chapter addresses.

WHAT IS THE SELF?

Cultures vary in how they view the self and even in when they believe social identity begins. In some societies, the self does not start at birth—and certainly not prior to birth (Morgan, 1996). The Arunta people of Central Australia regard a premature infant as a nonperson, an animal that mistakenly has entered the body of the pregnant woman. In Ghana, a newborn is a nonperson until it has lived for 7 days. If the child doesn't live that long, members of the society believe that it was a spirit child, not a human being. Parents in Ghana do not mourn a baby who dies before the seventh day because their society has taught them that such a being was a mistake and that they should be glad it is gone. The Tallensi people of Africa traditionally have not regarded twins as human until they have lived for a full month.

In Western culture, we believe that a person exists at birth, but what is the self that exists? Although you have a general sense of what the word means, we want a more precise definition to guide our discussion. The **self** arises in communication and is a multidimensional process of internalizing and acting from social perspectives. Although this is a complicated way to describe the self, it directs our attention to some important propositions about this very complicated concept.

The Self Arises in Communication with Others

Babies aren't born with clear understandings of who they are. Instead, we develop a self in the process of communicating with others. Interaction with others usually begins in the family as we learn how our parents, siblings, and other relatives view us. Later, as we interact with peers and teachers, we gain additional perspectives on ourselves. Still later, when we take jobs, we learn how coworkers, supervisors, customers, and clients see us as employees. We also tune in to media, which give us additional perspectives on ourselves and where we fit in the social world. We internalize many of the perspectives on our identity, and they become part of who we are and how we see ourselves.

We develop selves by internalizing two kinds of perspectives that are communicated to us: the perspectives of particular others and the perspective of the generalized other (Mead, 1934). Let's look at these two perspectives that help us define ourselves and guide how we think, act, and feel.

Particular Others

The first perspectives that affect us are those of **particular others**, who are specific people who are important in our lives. For infants and children, particular others usually include family members and caregivers. Later in life, particular others include peers, teachers, friends, coaches, romantic partners, coworkers, and other individuals who are especially important in our lives. As babies interact with particular others in their world, they learn how others see them. This is the beginning of a self-concept. Notice that the self starts from outside—with particular others' views of and communication with us.

For most of us, family members are the first major influence on how we see ourselves (Bergen & Braithwaite, 2009). Mothers, fathers, siblings, and often daycare providers are particular others who are significant to most infants. In addition, some families include aunts, uncles, grandparents, and others who live together. Hispanics and African Americans, in general, have larger extended families than do most European Americans; children in large families often have more family members who affect how they see themselves. In other cultures, too, the extended family is very important. Many Indian and other Asian families include grandparents, aunts, uncles, and even second and third cousins who live together in the same household (Ferrante, 2013).

Family members and other individuals who matter to us communicate their views of us through direct definitions, reflected appraisals, scripts, and attachment styles. If parents communicate to children that they are special and cherished, the children are likely to see themselves as worthy of love. On the other hand, children whose parents communicate that they are not wanted or loved may come to think of themselves as unlovable.

Direct Definition　As the term implies, **direct definition** is communication that tells us explicitly who we are by labeling us and our behaviors. Family members, as well as peers, teachers, and other individuals, define us by telling us who we are or are expected to be. Positive direct definitions enhance our self-esteem: "You're smart," "You're strong," "You're great at soccer." Negative direct definitions can damage children's self-esteem: "You're a troublemaker," "You're stupid," "You're impossible." Negative messages can demolish a child's sense of self-worth. Andrew Vachss (1994), who fights for children's rights, believes that emotional abuse is just as damaging as other forms of abuse.

Important individuals in our lives often provide us with direct definitions of our racial and ethnic identities. In cultures with a majority race, members of minority races often make special efforts to teach children to take pride in the strength and traditions of their racial and ethnic group. Thus, the ethnic training in many African American families stresses both positive identification with black heritage and awareness of prejudice on the part of people who are not black.

ANTHONY My brother and I are identical twins. We worked really hard to distinguish ourselves by not dressing alike and doing different sports. But some of our peers in high school addressed both of us as "twin." The way they defined us disconfirmed our sense of ourselves as individuals.

Direct definition also takes place as specific people respond to children's behaviors. If a child clowns around, and parents respond by saying, "What a cut-up; you really are funny," the child learns to see herself or himself as funny. If a child dusts furniture and receives praise ("You're a good cleaner"), helpfulness is reinforced as part of the child's self-concept. From direct definition, children learn what others value in them, and this shapes what they come to value in themselves. I still have vivid memories of being shamed for receiving a B in reading on my first-grade report card. Just as intensely, I recall the excessive praise heaped on me when I won a reading contest in fourth grade. By then, I had learned that reading was highly valued in my family. Through explicit labels and responses to our behaviors, family members and others who matter to us provide direct definitions of who we are and—just as important—who we are supposed to be.

Direct definitions can boost or impair children's self-esteem. Especially important is responding with enthusiasm to a child's accomplishments. When a baby learns to walk, she or he will show a look of delight at this new achievement. For that feeling to be complete, however, a child needs positive responses from others. Family members need to smile and say, "Wow, you did it!" If a child's early accomplishments are noticed and praised, she or he progressively gains self-confidence and undertakes increasingly difficult challenges. On the other hand, if the child's achievements are not noted and affirmed, the child is a candidate for low self-expectations.

Reflected Appraisal **Reflected appraisal** is our perception of another's view of us. How we think others appraise us affects how we see ourselves. This concept

is similar to the *looking-glass self*, based on Charles Cooley's poetic comment, "Each to each a looking glass/Reflects the other that doth pass" (1961, p. 5). Others are mirrors for us—the views of ourselves that we see in them (our mirrors) influence how we perceive ourselves. If others communicate even indirectly that they think we are smart, we are likely to reflect that appraisal in how we act and think about ourselves. If family members indicate that they see us as dumb or unlikable, we may reflect their appraisals by seeing ourselves in those ways.

Did your parents ever look disappointed when you acted a certain way? Did they ever smile with pride when you did something they valued? If so, you know how effectively others' appraisals can communicate that they regard our behaviors as unacceptable. Parents, especially fathers, encourage in children what they perceive to be gender-appropriate behaviors, fostering more independence, competitiveness, and aggression in sons and more emotional expressiveness and gentleness in daughters (Bryant & Check, 2000; Fivush, Brotman, Buckner, & Goodman, 2000; Galvin, 2006). Did your parents encourage you to conform to gender roles? Many parents reward daughters for acting feminine and criticize any feminine behaviors in sons. The converse is less true: While parents, especially fathers, encourage masculinity in sons, they are less critical of masculine behaviors in daughters. Heterosexual fathers are particularly clear in encouraging sons to be heterosexual (Solebello & Elliott, 2011).

For years, mothers have been regarded as essential to children's development. Yet mothers are only half the picture. Fathers play important roles in children's development, and the roles they play tend to be distinct from those of mothers (Bianchi, Robinson, & Milkie, 2006; Galvin, 2006; Gray & Anderson, 2010).

Fathers seem more likely than mothers to challenge and stretch children to achieve. Many fathers urge children to take initiative, to tolerate risks, and to experiment with unfamiliar activities and situations. Fathers tend to play more roughly than mothers, and this encourages development of courage and resilience. Additionally, fathers especially seem prepared to help their sons and daughters develop confidence, autonomy, and high expectations of themselves.

Peers also express their appraisals of us. When we accept them, peers' reflected appraisals affect how we see ourselves. The importance of peers' reflected appraisals is illustrated by this amusing example. Jeremy Bem was raised by parents who were committed to nonsexist child rearing. When Jeremy put barrettes in his hair, his parents expressed neither surprise nor disapproval. But a different response greeted Jeremy when he wore his barrettes to nursery school. His male peers repeatedly told him that "only girls wear barrettes." Jeremy tried to tell them that wearing barrettes had nothing to do with being a boy or a girl, but his peers were adamant that he couldn't be a boy if he wore barrettes. Finally, in frustration, Jeremy pulled down his pants and declared that, because he had a penis, he was a boy. The other boys laughed at this and informed Jeremy, "Everybody has a penis; only girls wear barrettes" (Monkerud, 1990, p. 83).

Communication in Everyday Life

WORKPLACE

A New Job for Dad

The recession that began in 2008 has propelled changes in men's involvement in home life. Between 2008 and 2010, millions of Americans lost jobs, resulting in the highest percentage of unemployed men since 1948 when the labor bureau began keeping track (Brooks, 2010). Many of the men who lost jobs became stay-at-home dads, while their partners have become sole breadwinners. The shift from a high-powered career to picking children up from school and entertaining them was difficult for some men (Garcia, 2008). Laid off after 20 years in a Fortune 500 company, Andrew Emery says, "It was a big part of my identity; it's who you are. It took me a long time to fill in the blank when people asked me what I do" (Kershaw, 2009b, p. E6). Yet, after the initial adjustment, many men discovered opportunities and satisfaction in being full-time fathers. In fact, many of them are hoping to find reemployment in careers that enable them to spend more time with their children (Kershaw, 2009).

We don't have a record of how Jeremy and his barrettes fared after this incident, but it's likely that Jeremy, like all of us, was affected by his peers' reflected appraisals.

ANDERSON My grandmother never criticized me, even when she should have. Around her I always felt really good about myself. I knew that in her eyes I could do no wrong. That was a great gift.

As we interact with others and perceive their appraisals of us, we figure out how we measure up to other people. **Social comparison** is the process of assessing ourselves in relation to others to form judgments of our own talents, abilities, qualities, and so forth. Whereas reflected appraisals are based on how we think others view us, social comparisons are our own use of others as measuring sticks for ourselves. We gauge ourselves in relation to others in two ways.

First, we compare ourselves with others to decide whether we are like them or different from them. Are we the same sex, age, color, religion? Do we like the same music? Do we have similar backgrounds? Assessing similarity and difference allows us to decide with whom we fit. Research shows that most people are more comfortable with others who are like them, so we tend to gravitate toward those we regard as similar (Pettigrew, 1967; Whitbeck & Hoyt, 1994). However, this can deprive us of the perspectives of people whose experiences and beliefs differ from our own.

Second, we use social comparison to measure ourselves and our abilities in relation to others. Am I as good a guard as Hendrick? Do I play the guitar as well as Chris? Am I as smart as Serena? Am I as attractive as Leigh? Do we have as many friends as others on Facebook? Comparing ourselves to others is normal, and it helps us develop realistic self-concepts. However, we should be wary of using inappropriate standards of comparison. It isn't realistic to judge our attractiveness in relation to stars and models or our athletic ability in relation to professional players.

Reflected appraisals and direct definitions can elevate or lower our self-concepts. People elevate our self-concept when they admire our strengths and accomplishments and accept our weaknesses and problems without discounting us. When we're around these people, we feel more upbeat and positive about ourselves. But people who elevate our sense of self-worth aren't necessarily unconditionally positive in their communication. A true friend can recognize our weaknesses and help us overcome or reduce them. Instead of putting us down, a good friend believes in us and helps us believe in ourselves and our capacity to change.

We tend to feel less good about ourselves when we are around people who express negative evaluations of us and our self-worth. They call attention to our flaws, emphasize our problems, and put down our dreams and goals. When we're around such people, we tend to feel down about ourselves. Reflecting their perspectives, when we're around people who put us down, we're more aware of our weaknesses and are less confident of what we can accomplish.

Reflected appraisals and direct definitions are not confined to childhood but continue throughout our lives. Teachers who communicate that students are talented in a particular area encourage the students to see themselves that way. Later, as you enter professional life, you will encounter coworkers and bosses who reflect their appraisals of you: You're on the fast track, average, or not suited to your position. The appraisals of us that others communicate shape our sense of ourselves.

 MindTap™

Everyday Skills To practice reflected appraisal, complete the activity "Reflecting on Reflected Appraisals" at the end of the chapter or online.

One particularly powerful way in which direct definitions and reflected appraisals can affect our self-concept is through **self-fulfilling prophecies**, which occur when we internalize others' expectations or judgments about us and then behave in ways that are consistent with those expectations and judgments (Watzlawick, 2005). If you have done poorly in classes where teachers didn't seem to respect you, and you have done well with teachers who thought you were smart, then you know what a self-fulfilling prophecy is. The prophecies we act to fulfill usually are first communicated by others. However, because we internalize others' perspectives, we may allow their definitions and prophecies for us to become our own.

Many of us believe things about ourselves that are inaccurate. Sometimes, labels that were once true aren't any longer, but we continue to believe them. In other cases, the labels may never have been valid, but we believe them anyway. Unfortunately, children often are called "slow" or "stupid" when they have physiological difficulties, such as impaired vision or hearing, or when they are struggling with a second language. Even when the real source of difficulty is discovered, the children already may have internalized a destructive self-fulfilling prophecy.

> Since I was in first grade, my grandmother said I was fat and that I would never lose weight. Well, you can imagine what this did to my self-esteem. I felt there was nothing I could do about being fat. At one point, I weighed 181 pounds—pretty heavy for a girl who's 5 feet 5 inches tall. Then, I got with some other people who were overweight, and we convinced ourselves to shape up. I lost 50 pounds, but I still thought of myself as fat. That's only started to change lately as friends and my family comment on how slim I am. Guess I'm still seeing myself through others' eyes.

RENEE

Identity Scripts   Particular others also influence our identity by providing **identity scripts**, which are rules for living and identity (Berne, 1964; Harris, 1969). Like the scripts for plays, identity scripts define our roles, how we are to play them, and the basic elements in the plots of our lives. Think back to your childhood. Did you hear any of these scripts from family members: "We are responsible people," "Our family always helps those in need," "A good education is the key to success," "Look out for number one," or "Live by God's word"? These are examples of identity scripts people learn in families.

Many psychologists believe that the basic identity scripts for our lives are formed very early, probably by age 5. This means that fundamental understandings of who we are and how we are supposed to live are forged when we have almost no control. Adults have the power, and children often unconsciously internalize the scripts that others write. As adults, however, we have the capacity to review the identity scripts that were given to us and to challenge and change those that do not fit the selves we now choose to be.

Attachment Styles   Finally, particular others shape our identities through **attachment styles**, which are patterns of caregiving that teach us who we and others are and how to approach relationships. From extensive studies of interaction between parents and children, John Bowlby (1973, 1988) developed the theory

MindTap™

Everyday Skills To understand more about identity scripts, complete the activity "Reflecting on Your Identity Scripts" at the end of the chapter or online.

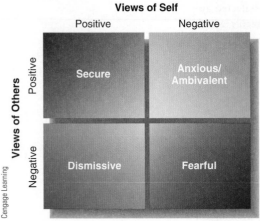

Figure **2.1**

Styles of Attachment

that we learn attachment styles in our earliest relationships. In these formative relationships, caregivers communicate how they see us, others, and relationships.

Most children form their first human bond with a parent—usually the mother, because women typically take primary responsibility for children. Clinicians who have studied attachment styles believe that the first bond is especially important because it forms expectations for later relationships (Ainsworth, Blehar, Waters, & Wall, 1978; Bartholomew & Horowitz, 1991; Guerrero, 2008; Trees, 2006). This first bond shapes how comfortable we feel getting close to others and how secure we feel in others' acceptance and commitment to us (Butzer & Campbell, 2008). Four distinct attachment styles have been identified, as shown in Figure 2.1.

A **secure attachment style** is facilitated when the caregiver responds in a consistently attentive and loving way to the child. In response, the child develops a positive sense of self-worth ("I am lovable") and a positive view of others ("People are loving and can be trusted"). People with secure attachment styles tend to be outgoing, affectionate, and able to handle the challenges and disappointments of close relationships without losing self-esteem. Equally important, people who have secure attachment styles usually are comfortable with themselves when they are not involved in close relationships. Their security enables them to engage in intimacy with others without depending on relationships for their self-worth. In a study of both different- and same-sex couples, Rachel Domingue and Debra Mollen (2009) found that couples in which both partners had secure attachment styles had the most mutually constructive communication.

A **fearful attachment style** is cultivated when the caregiver in the first bond is unavailable or communicates in negative, rejecting, or even abusive ways to the child. Children who are treated this way often infer that they are unworthy of love and that others are not loving or trustworthy. Thus, they learn to see themselves as unlovable and others as rejecting. Not surprisingly, people with a fearful attachment style tend to be apprehensive about relationships. Although they often want close bonds with others, they may fear others will not love them or that they are not lovable. Thus, as adults they may avoid others or feel insecure in relationships. Fearfully attached individuals also tend to feel less hope, disclose less, and experience less satisfaction with relationships than people with other attachment styles (Welch & Houser, 2010).

ZONDI In South Africa, where I was born, I learned that I was not important. Most daughters learn this. My name is Zondomini, which means "between happiness and sadness." The happiness is because a child was born. The sadness is because I am a girl, not a boy. I am struggling now to see myself as worthy.

A **dismissive attachment style** is also promoted by caregivers who are disinterested in, rejecting of, or unavailable to children. Yet people who develop this style do not accept the caregiver's view of them as unlovable. Instead, they typically dismiss others as unworthy. Consequently, children develop a positive view of themselves and a low regard for others and relationships. Those with a dismissive attachment style may view relationships as unnecessary or undesirable.

A final pattern is the **anxious/ambivalent attachment style** (also called preoccupied), which is the most complex of the four. Each of the other three styles results from a consistent pattern of treatment by a caregiver. The anxious/ambivalent style, however, is fostered by inconsistent treatment from the caregiver. Sometimes the caregiver is loving and attentive; at other times, the caregiver is indifferent or rejecting. The caregiver's communication is not only inconsistent but also unpredictable. He or she may respond positively to something a child does on Monday but react negatively to the same behavior on Tuesday. Naturally, this unpredictability can cause anxiety for the child who depends on the caregiver (Miller, 1993). Because children tend to assume that adults are always right, they believe themselves to be the source of any problem—that they are unlovable or deserve abuse. As a result, they may avoid or minimize attachments (Brenning, Soenens, Braet, & Bosmans, 2011).

> When I was little, my father was an alcoholic, but I didn't know that then. All I knew was that sometimes he loved me and played with me, and sometimes he would shout at me for nothing. Once he told me I was his sunshine, but later that same night he told me he wished I'd never been born. Even though now I understand the alcohol made him act that way, it's still hard to feel I'm okay.
>
> **NOREEN**

In adult life, people who have anxious/ambivalent attachment styles tend to be preoccupied with relationships. On one hand, they know others can be loving and affirming. On the other hand, they realize that others can hurt them and be unloving. Reflecting the pattern displayed by the caregiver, people with an anxious/ambivalent attachment style are often inconsistent themselves. One day, they invite affection; the next day, they rebuff it and deny needing or wanting closeness.

The likelihood of developing a particular attachment style is affected by socioeconomic class, as clinical psychiatrist Robert Karen reports (in Greenberg, 1997). Whereas nearly two-thirds of middle-class children in the United States are securely attached, the numbers are much lower for children from poor families that face serious hardships brought on by poverty: lack of adequate and nutritious food, poor shelter or homelessness, and inadequate medical care. These hardships can preoccupy and depress parents, making it difficult for them to be as consistently responsive and loving to children as parents who have more material resources (Greenberg, 1997).

The attachment style we learned in our first close relationship tends to persist (Bartholomew & Horowitz, 1991; Belsky & Pensky, 1988; Bowlby, 1988; Guerrero, 1996). However, this is not inevitable. We can modify our attachment styles by challenging the disconfirming self-perceptions communicated in our early years and by forming relationships that foster secure connections. Studies by Beth LePoire, Carolyn Shepard, and Ashley Duggan (1999) and Franz Neyer (2002) show that the influence of parental attachment style can be modified later in life. In other words, the people we choose to have relationships with affect our attachment styles.

Before we end this discussion, we should note that most of the research on attachment styles has been conducted in the United States. Would we find the same connections between attachment styles and relationship health in other cultures? That's the question recently posed by a research team (Friedman, Rholes, Simpson, Bond, Diaz-Loving, & Chan, 2010). They found that people who are highly anxious about attachments are more likely to have relationship problems in collectivist cultures such as Mexico and Hong Kong than in individualistic cultures such as the United States.

The Generalized Other

Particular others are not the only influence on our identity. It is also shaped by what Mead called the perspectives of the **generalized other**, by which he meant the general, or overall, society. Every society and social group has values, experiences, and understandings that are widely shared among members but may not be endorsed by those outside of the culture or group.

Research shows that media offer boys limited role models (Lamb, Brown, & Tappan, 2009). Interviews with nearly 700 boys aged 4 to 18 allowed the researchers to identify the media characters with whom the boys most identified. Two were dominant: (1) The superhero who is aggressive and often violent, has high-powered weapons, and is disrespectful, if not exploitative, of women—such as motorcycle club leader Jax Teller (Charlie Hunnam) of *Sons of Anarchy*. (2) The slacker who is amusing, doesn't like school or responsibility, and has no plans for his life.

Culture Every culture has values, norms, and ways of interacting that most members follow. People learn their culture's values in three ways. First, we learn them as we interact with others who have internalized cultural values. In some cultures, children see adult women deferring to adult men; in other cultures, they see adult women and men interacting as equals. In many Asian societies, families teach children to value cooperation and teamwork over competition and individual achievement (Yum, 2000) whereas competitiveness is more likely to be encouraged in Western children.

Second, we learn broadly shared social perspectives by participating in institutions that embody cultural values. For example, our judicial system reminds us that, as a society, we value laws and punish those who break them. In Western culture, the institution of marriage communicates society's view that when people marry, they become a single unit, which is why joint ownership of property is assumed for married couples. Cultural institutions inevitably reflect prevailing social prejudices. For instance, the United States may be a lawful society, but wealthy defendants often can buy better "justice" than poor ones can.

Third, we learn our culture's values through media, including traditional media such as TV and newspapers, online media, and social media. Mass media are woven into our everyday lives. Nearly all (98.9%) of American homes have at least one television, and the average American home has more televisions than people—3.3 televisions and fewer than 3 people per household, and at least one of those televisions is on 8 hours and 21 minutes a day (Media Trends Track, 2010; Vivian, 2011).

In addition, we rely on social media to connect with others, craft our identities, and find out what's happening. Across all ages, the average person spends 53 hours a week engaging with various media, and 38.5 of those hours are spent on social media (Kendall, 2011). Media don't just inform, educate, and allow social contact. They also communicate cultural values. Studies have also shown that men who watch music videos and pro wrestling are more likely to believe that forcing a partner to have sex is sometimes okay (Ensslin & Muse, 2011; Kilbourne, 2010; Yao, Mahood, & Linz, 2010).

Western culture emphasizes race, gender, sexual orientation, and socioeconomic class as central to personal identity, and it communicates definitions of each of these through institutions, media, and social interaction.

Race   In Western society, race is considered a primary aspect of personal identity. In the United States, the race that has been historically favored and privileged is Caucasian. Sociologist Charles Gallagher (2012) notes that it is easy to assume we are in a post-racial era in which racial discrimination no longer exists and race no longer matters. We see African Americans with blonde hair and white rappers with corn rows. We see an African American elected to the highest office in the land. Yet behind these images lurk persisting inequities that belie the idea that we live in a post-racial era (Higginbotham & Anderson, 2012).

In America today, race remains a consequential aspect of identity. Although much progress has been made toward racial equality, white privilege still exists today. Often, white children have access to better schools than children of other races do. The upper levels of government, education, and most businesses are dominated by white men, whereas people of color and women continue to fight overt and covert discrimination in admission, hiring, and advancement. Race also has implications for housing, health care, and life expectancy.

If my mama told me once, she told me a million times: "You got to work twice as hard to get half as far because you're black." I knew that my skin was a strike against me in this society since I can remember knowing anything. When I asked why blacks had to work harder, Mama said, "Because that's just how it is." I guess she was telling me that's how this society looks on African Americans.

DERRICK

SUE

The media call Asian Americans the "ideal minority." That's a stereotype that's really hard for some of us to live up to. I'm a good student, but I'm not excellent, especially not at math and computers, which people of my heritage are supposed to be naturally good at. So it's like I'm always not living up to the image of me that people have just because I'm Chinese American.

The meaning of race is socially constructed, which implies that it is not set, but open to change. America's history provides ample evidence of changes in meanings ascribed to race. The word *white* wasn't used to describe race or identity in the United States until Europeans arrived on the East Coast. Colonizers of the United States used the label *white* as a way to increase solidarity among European settlers, who actually had diverse ethnic backgrounds. Who was considered white varied. The first generations of Irish immigrants were not considered white (Negra, 2006; Painter, 2010). As they internalized the mainstream values of whites, they came to be regarded as white (Bates, 1994).

Beyond the borders of the United States, race is constructed in other ways. For example, South Africa recognized three major racial categories: white, colored, and black. Under apartheid, Japanese were classified as white, and Chinese were classified as colored.

Critical whiteness studies point out that whiteness has been so normalized in Western culture that many people think terms such as *ethnicity* and *race* refer only to people who are not white, as if white people have no race or ethnicity. Nonwhites are often identified by their race (black congressman, Indian student), but whites seldom are.

Gender   Gender is another important category in Western culture. Despite significant progress toward equal rights for the sexes, there are still inequities in expectations of women and men. Girls and women are expected to be caring, supportive of others, and cooperative, whereas boys and men are supposed to be more independent, self-assertive, and competitive. Consequently, women who assert themselves or compete sometimes experience social disapproval for violating gender prescriptions. Men who depart from broadly held social views of masculinity and who are gentle and caring risk being labeled "wimps."

ALLISON

When I was real young, I was outside playing in a little swimming pool one day. It was hot, and my brothers had their shirts off, so I took mine off, too. When my mother looked up and saw me, she went berserk. She told me to get my shirt back on and act like a lady. That's when I knew that girls have to hide and protect their bodies, but boys don't.

Sexual Orientation   A third aspect of identity that is salient in our culture is sexual orientation. Historically and, to a lesser extent, today, heterosexuality is viewed as the normal sexual orientation. Although bias against other sexual orientations has decreased, some people still regard lesbians, gays, bisexuals, transsexuals, transgenders, intersexuals, and genderqueer people as abnormal.

Broadly endorsed social perspectives are communicated through privileges given to heterosexuals but still denied to people with other sexual orientations. For example, a woman and a man who love each other can have their commitment recognized religiously and legally in any state in America, they can cover each other on insurance policies, and they can inherit from each other without paying taxes. Those rights are not yet guaranteed to all same-sex couples.

In 2013, the Supreme Court ruled that same-sex couples are entitled to the same federal rights as different-sex couples. Some religions now perform same-sex union ceremonies, an increasing number of states recognize same-sex marriages, and some organizations provide insurance and other benefits to same-sex partners of employees.

Communication in Everyday Life

DIVERSITY

David and Brenda

Imagine being born a boy but being raised as a girl. Imagine discovering at age 14 that your sex had been reassigned right after your birth and you were never told. That's exactly what happened to one person (Butler, 2004; Colapinto, 2000; McClellan, 2004).

David was born a physically normal male child. However, during his circumcision, doctors erred tragically and cut off most of his penis. The doctors decided that David could never be a normal male so they performed surgery to make him like a female anatomically, and they gave him estrogen treatments to enhance his femininity. The confused parents renamed their child Brenda and brought the child up as a girl. Brenda was never told she had been born a boy, but she resisted being treated as a girl. At age 14, Brenda learned of the botched circumcision.

Brenda decided to live as a male, took the name David, and ceased estrogen treatments. As an adult, David had strong relationships with family members and friends and, at age 25, he married a woman who already had children. However, he apparently was not completely comfortable with his identity or society's response to him, for in June of 2004, at the age of 38, David took his own life.

🔵 MindTap· What would you do if you were the parent of David/Brenda and the doctors informed you of the surgical calamity?

I'm gay, and many people think that gay is all I am. Once they find out I'm gay, nothing else about me seems relevant to them. They can't see all the ways in which we are alike and that we have more similarities than differences. They don't see that, once they find out I'm gay. They don't see that I am a student (just like them), that I am working my way through school (just like them), that I am Christian (just like them), that I worry about tests and papers (just like them), that I love basketball (just like them). All they see is that I am gay, and that is not like them.

DEL

Socioeconomic Class   A fourth important aspect of general social views of identity is socioeconomic class (Acker, 2013; Scott & Leonhardt, 2013). Even though the United States is less rigid than many societies with regard to class, the socioeconomic class we belong to affects everything from how much money we make to the schools we attend, the jobs open to us, the restaurants we patronize, and the cars we drive.

Socioeconomic class influences which needs we focus on in Maslow's hierarchy. For example, people with economic security have the resources and leisure time to focus on therapy, yoga, and spiritual development. These are not feasible for people who are a step away from poverty.

GENEVA I don't fit with most of the folks here. That hits me in the face every day. I walk across campus and see girls wearing shoes that cost more than all four pairs I own. I hear students talking about restaurants and trips that I can't afford. Last week, I heard a guy complaining about being too broke to get a GPS for his car. I don't own a car. I don't know how to relate to these people who have so much money. I do know they see the world differently than I do.

It's important to realize these aspects of identity. Race interacts with gender, so many women of color experience double oppression and devaluation in our culture. Socioeconomic class and sexual orientation also interact: Homophobia, or fear of homosexuals, is particularly pronounced in the working class, so a lesbian or gay person in a poor community may be socially ostracized (Langston, 2007). Socioeconomic class and gender also are interlinked; women are far more likely to live at the poverty level than men (Roux, 2001). Gender and race intersect, so black men have burdens and barriers not faced by white men. All facets of our identity interact.

We should also realize that social views (the perspective of the generalized other) are not fixed once and for all. Social perspectives are constructed in particular cultures at specific times. A society's values do not reflect divine law, absolute truth, or the natural order of things. The values that are endorsed by any society at a specific time reflect the prevailing values and prejudices of that era and place.

The constructed and arbitrary nature of social values becomes especially obvious when we consider how widely values differ from culture to culture. For example, in Sweden, Denmark, and Norway, same-sex marriages are given full legal recognition. Members of Japanese culture are expected to fit in with the group and not to stand out as individuals (Gudykunst & Lee, 2002), whereas individualism is a key value in Western cultures (Baxter, 2011). In some cultures, men tend to be emotional and dependent, and women tend to be assertive and emotionally controlled. In many countries south of the United States, race is emphasized less than in North America, and mixed-race marriages are more common and more accepted.

JEREMY My grandmother is always telling me how lucky I am to be at this school. She says that my granddaddy couldn't get into any school except a historically black one, and she couldn't get into that one. She remembers Jim Crow days and separate bathrooms and all of those things that have never been part of my life. Even though I still see a lot of racism and discrimination, talking with her makes me aware of how much less there is today than when she was my age.

Social meanings also vary across time within single cultures. For example, the frail, pale appearance considered feminine in the 1800s gave way to robust, fleshy ideals in the mid-1900s, as embodied by Marilyn Monroe. Today, much thinner and more toned bodies are the cultural ideal for women.

David Malan/The Image Bank/Getty Images

Social prescriptions for men have also varied. The rugged he-man who was the ideal in the 1800s and disposed of unsavory rustlers was supplanted by the savvy businessman whose money replaced muscle as a sign of manliness. Today, as our society struggles with changes in women, men, and families, the ideals of manhood are being revised yet again. Increasingly, men are involved in caring for children, and women in heterosexual relationships often earn more than their male partners.

Other socially constructed views are also variable. Just 10 or 15 years ago, most people regarded online relationships as poor substitutes for "real" relationships. In contrast, today many people meet and form relationships—sometimes lasting ones—through online interaction.

Each of us has an ethical responsibility to decide which social views we personally accept and will use as guides for our own behaviors, attitudes, and values. We also have an ethical responsibility to challenge social views and values that we consider harmful or wrong. By doing so, we participate in the ongoing process of refining who we are as a society.

My parents are pretty straitlaced and conservative. They brought me up to think homosexuals are sinners and whites are better than any other race. But I don't think like that now, and I've been speaking my mind when I'm home to visit my folks. At first, they got angry and said they didn't send me to college to get a bunch of crazy liberal ideas, but gradually they are coming around a little. I think I am changing how they think by voicing my views.

JENNIFER

We have seen that the self arises in communication. From interaction with family members, peers, and society, others tell us how they see us. We are also taught the prevailing values of our culture and of particular people who are significant in our lives. These perspectives become part of who we are. But this is only part of the story of identity. We now consider the ways in which we actively manage our identities.

PRESENTING AND NEGOTIATING IDENTITY

Have you ever been afraid of *losing face* in a situation? Have you ever done something to help another person *save face*? Have you ever put *your best face* forward or put on your *game face*? If so, you will probably be interested in the work of

Erving Goffman, a distinguished sociologist who devoted his career to studying how people present their faces in everyday interaction.

Goffman (1959, 1967) used theatrical metaphors to describe the process of self-presentation. He regarded social situations as stages on which people perform identities. We do this by presenting a **face**, which is the impression of self that we want others to accept when we are interacting in social situations. For example, in a job interview, you want the interviewer to see you as professional and knowledgeable about the job. To perform a face credibly, you must communicate in ways that embody the identity you are trying to present. This involves what Goffman called **impression management**, which is how we use communication in an effort to persuade others to believe in the face we present. In our example, you dress well, maintain good eye contact, and offer the interviewer examples from your past jobs that demonstrate that you are experienced and skilled.

But you do not have complete control over your face. Goffman stressed that interaction is always social, which means others are involved. Others respond to the face you present. The interviewer might confirm your face by complimenting you on your accomplishments and qualifications. Alternatively, the interviewer might challenge your face by saying, "It appears you had some problems when you got supervisory responsibility." Or the interviewer might directly reject your face by saying, "You are not qualified for this position."

Most of the time, people cooperate in helping one another maintain face because we don't want to be embarrassed or to embarrass others. In other words, we try to support others' projected identities and count on others to support ours.

Sometimes, however, we are unsure that our face will be confirmed. To manage this situation, we engage in preventive facework. For example, you might say to the interviewer, "I'm not wedded to this idea, but…." before offering an idea you think the interviewer may not agree with. At times, others threaten our face by challenging or rejecting it, as in the above example in which the interviewer notes the interviewee had some problems in a supervisory role. To deal with these, we may engage in restorative facework. You might provide an excuse for a problem the interviewer identifies: "I had just started the job and hadn't learned the ropes, which I know now." Or you might apologize and try to move the conversation to positive ground: "You're right. I should have handled a couple of issues differently. Fortunately, I learn from my mistakes, and I don't repeat them."

We've seen that presenting and negotiating face are social processes because they require others' responses to the face we present. Communication scholar Stella Ting-Toomey (2005, 2009) observes that face is social in another sense: Culture influences the faces we tend to prefer as well as the ways we deal with disagreements about face. In other words, the norms, values, beliefs, and traditions of our culture affect what we consider positive face and what we consider appropriate responses to the faces that others present.

In collectivist cultures, which prize group membership over individual identity, explicit rejections of another's face are rare because that creates conflict or tension among group members. If Maria, who was raised in a collectivist culture, doesn't accept the face that Leon, who was raised in an individualistic culture, presents, she is likely to avoid conflict and look for ways to help Leon find an acceptable face. In individualistic cultures, which value the individual over the group, direct challenges are more likely and more socially acceptable. Leon might directly challenge Maria's face by turning away or saying, "I'm not believing you." He might also leave it to Maria to revise her self-presentation.

Now that we have considered how identity develops and how we present ourselves in interaction, let's turn to a final chapter focus: ways that we can nurture a healthy self and facilitate its growth.

SOCIAL MEDIA AND PERSONAL IDENTITY

In this section, we'll discuss three of many ways that this chapter's focus on personal identity is pertinent to social media. First, consider the importance of social media in providing us with direct definitions and reflected appraisals. A 2013 survey ("The Social Scene") reports that nearly 30% of Americans 12 or older have a profile on at least one social networking site, and 60% of Americans 12 or older are heavy users of social networks. That implies we get and give a lot of appraisals through online and digital communication. When you post a photo on Facebook, others respond by saying, "You look great!" and "Very cool outfit." Knowing that others think you look attractive probably elevates your own sense of your attractiveness. But what if others' comments are less positive? "Have you gained weight?" "What did you do to your hair?" Those reflected appraisals are likely to make you feel less good about yourself.

Girls and women are more likely than boys to use social media as a venue for self-development. Teen girls use their blogs and pages on social networking sites to talk about issues such as pressures to be skinny, drink (or not), have sex (or not), and dress particular ways (Bodey, 2009; Bodey & Wood, 2009). As girls work out what they think and want to do in their online communities, they count on comments from others to clarify their own thinking and gain confidence in their ability to reject gender norms they find troubling.

Social networks can be—and too often are—used for **cyberbullying**, which includes text messages, comments, rumors, embarrassing pictures, videos, and fake profiles that are meant to hurt another person and are sent by email or posted on social networking sites. Direct definitions such as "Jeanie is a slut" or "Angie is fat" are very hurtful, regardless of whether they are true. According to a recent report (Burney, 2012), 43% of teenagers are subject to some form of cyberbullying. For LGBTQ teenagers the percentage is even higher: 53% (Burney, 2012). When asked why people were so cruel online, one young boy explained, "You can be as mean as you want on Facebook" (Hoffman, 2010, p. A12). Cyberbullying has no necessary stopping point. The schoolyard bully pretty much stays on the school yard. Thus, a victim can escape by going home or visiting a friend. Online bullying can follow the victim anywhere, 24/7. It is unremitting.

Second, social media are also key sources for social comparison, as was evident in the scenario that opened this chapter. We read others' updates and compare our accomplishments to theirs, our activities to theirs, our number of friends to theirs, and so on. On social networking sites, many, perhaps most, people emphasize what is positive in their lives and downplay or omit mention of what is not so positive.

This suggests that we might be wise to be cautious in comparing ourselves to the selves others present online. Third, social media are platforms for skilled facework. In fact, social media allow us more time to plan and sculpt our self-presentation than we have in most f2f encounters. We can edit, re-edit, and re-re-edit our profile until it is exactly the way we want it. We can choose only our best photos for posting, and we can modify them to make ourselves appear more attractive. Also, we can take time to compose new posts to our home page and to reply to friends' postings. This means that online communication has great potential for strategic manipulation and even misrepresentation. Of course, we can be strategic and manipulative in f2f encounters too, but we don't always have as much time to prepare our self-presentations, and we don't have the luxury of editing what we say.

GUIDELINES FOR ENRICHING THE SELF

In the final section of the chapter, we consider five guidelines for developing and maintaining a healthy identity.

Make a Firm Commitment to Personal Growth

The first guideline is the most difficult and the most important. You must make a firm commitment to cultivating personal growth. This isn't as easy as it might sound. A firm commitment involves more than saying, "I want to be less judgmental." Saying this sentence is simple. You have to invest energy and effort to bring about change. From the start, realize that changing how you think of yourself is a major project.

Because the self is a process, it is not formed in one fell swoop, and it cannot be changed in a single moment of decision. We must realize at the outset that there will be setbacks, and we can't let them derail our resolution to change. Last year, a student said she wanted to be more assertive, so she began to speak up more often in class. When a professor criticized one of her contributions, her resolution folded. Changing how we see ourselves is a long-term process, so we can't let setbacks undermine our commitment to change.

A second reason it is difficult to change self-concept is that the self resists change. Apparently, consistency itself is comforting. If you realize in advance that you may struggle against change, you'll be prepared for the tension that accompanies personal growth.

Gain and Use Knowledge to Support Personal Growth

Commitment alone is insufficient to bring about constructive changes in your self-concept. In addition, you need several types of knowledge. First, you need to understand how your identity was formed. In this chapter, we've seen that much of how we see ourselves results from socially constructed perspectives. Based on what you've learned, you can think critically about which social perspectives to accept and which to reject.

One social value I do not accept is that it's good to be as thin as a rail if you're female. A lot of my girlfriends are always dieting. Even when they get weak from not eating enough, they won't eat, because they'll gain weight. I know several girls who are bulimic, which is really dangerous, but they are more scared of gaining a pound than of dying. I refuse to buy into this social value. I'm not fat, but I'm not skinny either. I'm not as thin as models, and I'm not aiming to be. It's just stupid to go around hungry all the time because society has sick views of beauty for women.

In addition to reading this book and learning from your class, there are other resources to help you set and achieve personal goals. There are books and websites that focus on personal growth. Other people are another source of knowledge. Talking with others is a way to learn about relationships and what people want in them. Others can also provide useful feedback about your interpersonal skills and your progress in the process of change. Finally, others can serve as models. If someone you know is particularly skillful in supporting others, observe her or him carefully to identify particular communication skills. You may not want to imitate this person exactly, but observing will make you more aware of concrete skills involved in supporting others. You can then tailor some of the skills that others display to suit your personal style.

Second, you need information about yourself. How we view ourselves is one source of information, but often we don't have a sound understanding of how others see us and how they might see parts of ourselves that we keep private.

A number of years ago, Joseph Luft and Harry Ingham (Luft, 1969) created a model of different sorts of knowledge that affect self-development. They called the model the **Johari Window** (Figure 2.2), which is a combination of their first names, Joe and Harry. Four types of information are relevant to the self:

1. Open, or public, information is known both to us and to others. Your name, height, major, and tastes in music probably are open information that you share easily with others.
2. The blind area contains information that others know about us but we don't know about ourselves. For example, others may see that we are insecure even though we think we've hidden that well. Others may also recognize needs or feelings that we haven't acknowledged to ourselves.
3. Hidden information is what we know about ourselves but choose not to reveal to most others. You might not tell many people about your vulnerabilities or about traumas in your past because you consider this private information.
4. The unknown area is made up of information about ourselves that neither we nor others know. This consists of your untapped resources, your untried talents, and your reactions

Figure **2.2**

The Johari Window

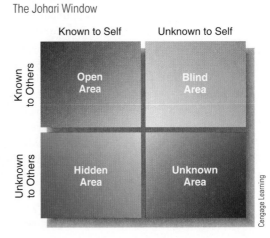

to experiences you've never had. You don't know how you will manage a crisis until you've been in one, and you can't tell what kind of parent you would be unless you've had a child.

It is important to gain access to information in our blind and unknown areas. One way to do this is to expand our experiences by entering unfamiliar situations, trying novel things, and experimenting with new kinds of communication. Another way to increase self-knowledge is to interact with others to learn how they see us. We can gain insight into ourselves by reflecting on their perceptions. Others are likely to offer us insights into ourselves only if we make it safe for them to do so. But a word of caution: Anonymous communication about you may not be useful. Social networking sites allow people to send anonymous comments to members' private mailboxes. Without the responsibility of owning their comments, some people post hurtful, even vicious comments such as "you're ugly" and "everyone knows you're a loser." Cyberbullying is cruel and as cowardly as face-to-face bullying.

Another way to learn how others see us is to open up to them. That leads us to the second guideline.

Self-Disclose when Appropriate

One way to get information about how others do and might see us is through **self-disclosure**, which is intentionally revealing information about ourselves to another person that she or he is unlikely to discover in other ways. For instance, you might disclose an embarrassing experience or a fear to a close friend.

Benefits of Self-Disclosure   Self-disclosure has notable benefits. First, it allows us to learn about ourselves (Greene, Derlega, & Mathews, 2006). Sometimes our thoughts and feelings become clearer to us in the process of disclosing them to others. In addition, we gain insight into ourselves by seeing how we handle others' feedback. Do we reflect on it seriously and use it to chart our growth?

Second, self-disclosing can be cathartic (Vilhauer, 2009). It can be very helpful to let go of a secret by sharing it with someone we can truly trust. We may feel unburdened and relieved to no longer be keeping something inside of us. This value of disclosure, however, is not always a sufficient reason to disclose. If the person to whom you disclose does not treat the information discreetly, you may regret having opened up.

Third, telling private information to others may provide affirmation of ourselves. For example, if you tell a close friend that you are gay or transsexual and the friend responds positively, you are validated. In addition, those to whom we disclose may respond in ways that give us new perspectives on who we are and what we've done. Others may perceive something we consider shameful in a different light. They may see a fear we have as reasonable.

Fourth, self-disclosure can be ethical. If you value honesty you may feel obligated to disclose information to others in order to maintain your self-respect. Both honesty and care for others require a person who has herpes to disclose that to her or his partner in advance of any contact that could infect the partner.

Finally, self-disclosure is often reciprocal so that when you disclose to a friend, the friend discloses something to you in return (Forgos, 2011). The process of mutual self-disclosure generally increases positive feelings between people, and it can enhance interpersonal relationships.

Risks of Self-Disclosure　Although self-disclosure has many potential values, it is not always advisable. Self-disclosure necessarily involves risks, such as the risk that others will not accept what we reveal or may like us less or reject us. There is also the possibility that others might use information we have disclosed against us. Finally, self-disclosure can hurt others. For example, a person who says she or he loves you may be hurt if you respond by disclosing that you don't feel the same way. Online disclosures are not secure so they may be read by others, and there is no guarantee of what they will do with information you divulge.

Appropriate self-disclosure minimizes these risks by proceeding slowly and in relationships in which trust has been established. It's wise to test the waters gradually with limited disclosures before making a major self-disclosure. Begin by revealing information that is personal but not highly intimate or damaging if exploited. Before disclosing further, observe how the other person responds to your communication and what she or he does with it. You might also pay attention to whether the other person reciprocates by disclosing personal information to you. Because self-disclosures involve risk, we need to be cautious about when and to whom we reveal ourselves.

Set Goals That Are Realistic and Fair

Efforts to change how we see ourselves work best when we set realistic and fair goals. In a culture that emphasizes perfectionism, it's easy to be trapped into expecting more than is humanly possible.

If you define your goal as becoming a totally perfect communicator in all situations, you are setting yourself up for failure. It's more reasonable and constructive to establish a series of realistic small goals that you can meet. You might focus on improving one of the skills of communication competence we discussed in Chapter 1. When you are satisfied with your ability in that skill, you can move on to a second one.

Remembering our discussion of social comparison, it's also important to choose reasonable people to compare yourself with. It isn't realistic to compare your ability at tennis to that of Serena or Venus Williams. It is reasonable to measure your tennis ability in relation to people who have talent and training similar to your own.

KENDRICK

I really got bummed out my freshman year. I had been the star on my high school basketball team, so I came to college expecting to be a star here, too. The first day of practice, I saw a lot of guys who were better than I was. They were incredible. I felt like nothing. When I got back to my room, I called my mom and told her I wasn't going to try out here. She told me I couldn't expect to compete with guys who had been on the team for a while and who had gotten coaching. She asked how I stacked up against just the other first-year players, and I said "Pretty good." She told me they were the ones to compare myself to.

Kendrick's reflection reminds us that we should be fair in judging ourselves. We often judge our abilities and set our goals with reference to unfair standards. For example, my friend Meg is a very accomplished writer, but she faults herself constantly for not doing as much volunteer work as her neighbor. Meg's neighbor doesn't work outside the home, so she has more time for volunteer work. It might be reasonable for Meg to acknowledge that she doesn't volunteer a great deal of time if she also recognizes her impressive achievements in writing. However, when judging her writing, she compares herself to writers of national stature. Meg's self-assessment is unfair to her because she compares herself with people who are extremely successful in particular spheres of life, yet she doesn't notice that her models are not especially impressive in other areas. As a result, she mistakenly feels that she is inadequate in most ways. We should be fair to ourselves by acknowledging our strengths and virtues as well as our limitations and aspects of ourselves we want to change.

TIMOTEO I've really struggled with my academic goals. It's very important to me and my whole family that I do well in school. I am the first in my family to go to college, so I must succeed. I've felt bad when I make Bs and Cs and others in my classes make As. For a long time, I said to myself, "I am not as smart as they are if they make better grades." But I work 35 hours a week to pay for school. Most of the others in my classes either don't have to work or work fewer hours than I do. They have more time to spend writing papers and studying for tests. I think better of my academic abilities when I compare myself to other students who work as much as I do. That is a more fair comparison than comparing myself to students who don't work.

MindTap

Everyday Skills To practice improving yourself, complete the activity "Setting Personal Goals" at the end of the chapter or online.

Being fair to yourself also requires you to accept that you are in process. Each of us is in process, always becoming. This implies several things. First, it means you need to accept who you are now as a starting point. You don't have to like or admire everything about yourself, but it is important to accept who you are now as a basis for going forward. The self that you are results from all the interactions, reflected appraisals, and social comparisons you have made during your life. You cannot change your past, but you do not have to let it define your future.

Accepting yourself as in-process also implies that you realize you can change. Who you are is not necessarily who you will be in 5 or 10 years. Don't let yourself be hindered by defeating, self-fulfilling prophecies or the false idea that you cannot change (Rusk & Rusk, 1988). You can change if you set realistic goals, make a genuine commitment, and then work for the changes you want.

According to psychiatrist Judith Orloff (2009), we are not generous with ourselves when it comes to compassion. Orloff says that many people are not self-compassionate because they think it's the same as being self-indulgent. But, says Orloff, we would be wise to accept our imperfections as a step in the life-long process of creating selves. Lack of care and understanding for oneself undermines the motivation to change and even the belief that change is possible. In contrast, self-compassion can motivate change because it starts with caring about and supporting yourself.

Seek Contexts That Support Personal Change

Just as it is easier to swim with the tide than against it, it is easier to change our views of ourselves when we have some support for our efforts. You can do a lot to create an environment that supports your growth by choosing contexts and people who help you realize your goals. First, think about settings. If you want to become more extroverted, put yourself in social situations rather than in libraries. But libraries are a better context than parties if your goal is to improve your academic performance.

> **ERIN**
>
> My first two years on campus I hung out with a party crowd. Mostly all we did was drinking, dancing, and hooking up. The summer after my sophomore year, I got a job tutoring kids who were failing high school. The other tutors were really cool people who were about something important. I wanted to be more like them—more about making positive change than about partying. When I got back to school, it was really hard to keep that vision of myself because the crowd I hung out with hadn't changed. So I did; I changed. I stopped going out with my old friends and started going to service organizations and meeting people and doing things with people who are more like the person I want to be.

Second, think about the people whose appraisals of you will help you move toward changes you desire. You can put yourself in supportive contexts by consciously choosing to be around people who believe in you and encourage your personal growth. It's equally important to steer clear of people who pull us down or say we can't change. In other words, people who reflect positive appraisals of us enhance our ability to improve.

Others aren't the only ones whose communication affects our self-concepts. We also communicate with ourselves, and our own messages influence our esteem. One of the most crippling kinds of self-talk we can engage in is **self-sabotage**. This involves telling ourselves we are no good, we can't do something, there's no point in trying to change, and so forth. We may be repeating judgments others have made of us, or we may be inventing our own negative self-fulfilling prophecies. Either way, self-sabotage defeats us because it undermines belief in ourselves. Self-sabotage is poisonous; it destroys our motivation to change and grow.

Recent research (Arroyo & Harwood, 2012; Martz, Petroff, Curtin, & Bassini, 2009) shines a light on a particularly common and damaging form of self-talk. Fat talk is conversation about body weight: "Look at me—I'm really fat." "My butt is huge." "My stomach is so huge." The majority of this fat talk is negative, shining a spotlight on how real people's bodies fall short of the ideals media presents. Given the negative nature of fat talk, it's not surprising that engaging in it predicts lower body satisfaction and higher depression. Conversely, people who are less satisfied with their bodies are more likely to engage in fat talk. In other words, it's a self-reinforcing and self-defeating cycle.

Positive self-talk builds motivation and belief in yourself. It is a useful strategy to interrupt and challenge negative messages from yourself and others. The next time you hear yourself saying, "I can't do this" or someone else says, "You'll never change," challenge the negative message with self-talk. Say out loud to yourself, "I can do it. I will change." Use positive self-talk to resist counterproductive communication about yourself.

Before leaving this discussion, we should make it clear that self-improvement is not facilitated solely by uncritical positive communication. None of us grows and improves when we listen only to praise, particularly if it is less than honest. True friends offer constructive criticism to encourage us to reach for better versions of ourselves.

In sum, to enhance who you are, find contexts that support growth and change. Seek out experiences and settings that foster belief in yourself and the changes you desire. Also, recognize people who affirm you and your ability to grow and those who put you down and criticize in nonconstructive ways so that you can choose to interact with people who assist you in achieving your goals for self-improvement.

CHAPTER SUMMARY

In this chapter, we explored the self as a process that evolves over the course of our lives. We saw that the self is not present at birth but develops as we interact with others. Through communication, we learn and import social perspectives—those of particular others and those of the generalized other, or society as a whole. Reflected appraisals, direct definitions, and social comparisons, whether they occur online or in f2f interaction, shape how we see ourselves and how we change over time. The perspective of the generalized other includes cultural perspectives and social views of aspects of identity, including race, gender, sexual preference, and class. Social views are not necessarily fixed or unchangeable. Like people before us, we can challenge and change those we consider unworthy.

The self is not simply the result of how particular others and our culture defines us. We take an active role in managing our self-presentation, both in f2f and online interaction. We decide what face we want to present in specific contexts and then put it forward to others who may affirm, challenge, or reject it. In interaction, we engage in the ongoing process of negotiating our own and others' faces.

Social media are important both for developing identity and for managing identity. Just as in f2f communication, online communication can provide direct definitions, reflected appraisals, and social comparisons that affect how we view ourselves. Also, facework, or managing self-presentation, is at least as relevant to our communication on social media as in f2f contexts.

The final section of the chapter focused on ways to improve ourselves. Guidelines for doing this are to make a firm commitment to personal growth, to acquire knowledge about desired changes and concrete skills, to self-disclose when appropriate, to set realistic goals, to assess ourselves fairly, and to create contexts that support the changes we seek. Transforming how we see ourselves is not easy, but it is within your reach. We can make amazing changes in who we are and how we feel about ourselves when we embrace our human capacity to make choices.

Key Concepts

Practice defining the chapter's terms by using online flashcards.

anxious/ambivalent
   attachment style 53
attachment style 51
cyberbullying 61
direct definition 47
dismissive attachment style 52
face 60

fearful attachment style 52
generalized other 54
identity script 51
impression management 60
Johari Window 63
particular others 47
reflected appraisal 48

FLASHCARDS...

secure attachment
   style 52
self 46
self-disclosure 64
self-fulfilling prophecy 51
self-sabotage 67
social comparison 50

Continuing the Conversation

Jason Harris © 2001 Wadsworth

When you've watched the video online, critique and analyze this encounter based on the principles you learned in this chapter. Then compare your work with the author's suggested responses. Online, even more videos will let you continue the conversation with your instructor.

Amy met Hailley at the beginning of the school year and was drawn to her because she seemed confident and positive. Over several months, they became good friends. Two months ago, Hailley started dating Dan. At first Hailley seemed happy with Dan, but then she started becoming less extroverted and a lot less positive. Often, when Amy suggests doing something together, Hailley says she can't because Dan doesn't like her not to be available to him. When Amy sees them together, she notices that Dan doesn't treat Hailley with respect. Amy is concerned that Hailley may be in a relationship that is verbally or physically abusive. She wants to help.

Amy: I'm just worried about you. I don't like the way he treats you.

PRACTICE...

Hailley: Because he called me clumsy? I am clumsy, and besides, if I do something stupid, I can't expect him not to notice.

Amy: But he doesn't show any respect for you at all.

Hailley: Well, he's a guy. He says what he's thinking. I know a lot of people's boyfriends are like that. Besides, I don't think there's anything wrong with Dan. I think I just have to stop doing things that make him mad.

1. Thinking about what you've read in this chapter, what might you say or do for Hailley?
2. How do social comparisons affect her view of the relationship with Dan?
3. Can you think of ways in which you might be a constructive looking-glass self for Hailley?
4. What could you do to help create a context that would foster positive change in Hailley's self-concept?
5. What would it mean to support Hailley right now? How could you express your support of her without endorsing her relationship with Dan?

Assessing Yourself

Begin the process of applying this chapter's concepts by taking a self-assessment quiz here or online—where you will find out what the results mean.

Purpose: To provide insight into how you and others perceive you.

Instructions: Fill out the form below by indicating how true of you each statement is.

Next, make a copy of the second form and ask someone you think **PRACTICE...** knows you well to fill out the second form. Write your name in the blank spaces on the second form. Compare your own and the other person's perceptions of you.

Your Form

Rate each item for how true it is of you. Use the following scale:

5 Very true or always true
4 Mostly true or usually true
3 Somewhat true or true in some situations
2 Mostly untrue or usually untrue
1 Untrue or never true

_____ 1. I am an optimistic person.

_____ 2. I am personally mature.

_____ 3. I am extroverted.

_____ 4. I am thoughtful about others and their feelings.

_____ 5. I am ambitious.

_____ 6. I am generally cheerful or upbeat.

_____ 7. I am moody.

_____ 8. I am a reliable friend.

_____ 9. I am unconventional in my beliefs.

_____ 10. I am assertive.

Form for Person Who Knows You Well

Rate each item for how true it is of _____. Use the following scale:

5 Very true or always true
4 Mostly true or usually true
3 Somewhat true or true in some situations
2 Mostly untrue or usually untrue
1 Untrue or never true

_____ 1. He/she is an optimistic person.

_____ 2. He/she is personally mature.

_____ 3. He/she is extroverted.

_____ 4. He/she is thoughtful about others and their feelings.

_____ 5. He/she is ambitious.

_____ 6. He/she is cheerful or upbeat.

_____ 7. He/she is moody.

_____ 8. He/she is a reliable friend.

_____ 9. He/she is unconventional in his/her beliefs.

_____ 10. He/she is assertive.

Everyday Skills

Build your communication skills further by completing the following activities here or online.

1. Reflecting on Reflected Appraisals

   To understand how reflected appraisals have influenced your self-concept, try this exercise.

   a. Below, list five words that describe how you see yourself. (Examples: *responsible, ambitious, introverted, clumsy, funny, intelligent, shy, athletic*)

   b. Next, identify the particular people who have been and are especially significant in your life. Try to think of at least five people who matter to you.

   c. Now, think about how these special people communicate with you about the traits you listed in step a. How did they express their appraisals of what you defined as important parts of yourself?

Words to Describe You	How Others Communicate This to You
_____	_____
_____	_____
_____	_____
_____	_____
_____	_____
_____	_____

   Can you trace how you see yourself to the appraisals reflected by particular others in your life?

2. Reflecting on Your Identity Scripts

   To take control of our own lives, we must first understand the influences that currently shape them. Identify identity scripts that your parents taught you.

   a. First, recall explicit messages your parents gave you about "who we are" and "who you are." Can you hear their voices telling you codes that you were expected to follow?

   b. Next, write down the scripts. Try to capture the language your parents used as they communicated the scripts to you.

   c. Now, review each script. Which ones make sense to you today? Are you following any that are not constructive for you today? Do you disagree with any of them?

   d. Finally, commit to changing scripts that aren't productive for you or that conflict with values you hold.

   We can rewrite scripts once we are adults. To do so, we must become aware of what our families have taught us and take responsibility for scripting our own lives.

3. Identifying Ideals in Online Media

   Select a popular website that you visit frequently. Record the focus of the articles and advertisements on the site. What do the articles and ads convey about what is valued in the United States? Identify themes and types of people that are emphasized.

   What cultural values about gender does the site communicate? What do articles convey about how women or men are regarded and what they are expected to be and to do? Ask the same questions about advertisements.

   How many ads aimed at women focus on being beautiful, looking young, losing weight, taking care of others, and attracting men? How many ads aimed at men emphasize strength, virility, success, and independence? What do you conclude about the ideals for men and women promoted by online media?

4. Setting Personal Goals

   Apply the guidelines in the last section of this chapter to set a personal goal for yourself. After deciding on the focus of your goal, use these prompts to make it useful and attainable.

   a. Is your goal specific enough to be realistic?

   b. Is your means of measuring the achievement of your goal reasonable (for instance, are your social comparisons fair)?

   c. Have you identified people and contexts that will support your effort to attain your goal?

MindTap **DO** ... Additional interactive discussions, online quizzes, and activities that your instructor may assign for a grade.

Engaging with Ideas

Reflect and write about the ideas in this chapter by considering questions about personal, workplace, and ethical applications, here or online.

Personal Application Apply what you learned in this chapter by setting one specific, fair, and realistic goal for improving your self-concept. Define contexts that will support you in making this change.

Workplace Application Identify an individual who is or was important to you in a job you hold or once held. Describe direct

definitions of you that this person expressed and your reflected appraisals. How did these affect your self-concept when you were on the job? How did these affect your self-concept in general?

Ethical Application Reflect on your online postings and any changes in your profile over the past 2 weeks. Have you exaggerated anything? Do your postings accurately reflect positive news and not-so-positive news about yourself? Is it unethical to exaggerate or to post only about positive aspects of your life?

Thinking Critically

Think and write critically about the ideas in this chapter, here or online.

1. Talk with one man and one woman who are at least 20 years older than you. Talk with one man and one woman who are at least 30 years older than you. In each conversation, ask them to explain how men and women were expected to behave when they were 20 years old. Ask them to describe how women and men were expected to act and dress. Ask them to explain what behaviors, goals, and attitudes were considered inappropriate for women and men when they were 20 years old. Compare their responses with views held by 20-year-olds today.

2. Discuss the idea of race with others in your class. You may want to reread the section on race and identity in this chapter. Given what you read in this chapter and your own experience, to what extent do you think race is a physical or genetic quality versus a social construction? Is race a useful way to classify people? Why or why not?

3. Think about a time when you tried to create some change in yourself and were not successful. Review what happened by applying the five principles for improving self-concept presented in the last section of this chapter. Now that you understand these principles, how might you be more effective if you wanted to create that same change in yourself today?

4. One way to engage the ideas we've discussed in this chapter is to talk with a classmate or friend about influences on your identity. Choose a person you feel comfortable talking with about somewhat personal information. Once you've decided on the person, ask him or her to share memories of scripts and direct definitions in the early years or his or her life. Ask how the person thinks those affected his or her self-concept, even today. Be prepared to share your own memories and their impact on you.

5. Watch the film *Catch Me if You Can*. It is based on the life of Frank Abagnale Jr. (played by Leonardo DiCaprio), whose early years in a dysfunctional family influenced him to become a very skillful impersonator and criminal. It is also the story of Carl Hanratty (played by Tom Hanks), a detective who tracks Abagnale and becomes a father figure and mentor to him. As you watch the film, apply concepts learned in this chapter. Here are some probes that will help you start applying the chapter material to the film:

   a. Identify Abagnale's attachment style.
   b. Point out examples of direct definition.
   c. Link Abagnale's success in impersonation to social comparisons.
   d. How did Hanratty support Abagnale's change of identity?

chapter THREE

PERCEPTION AND COMMUNICATION

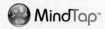

Topics covered in this chapter

The Process of Human Perception

Influences on Perception

Social Media and Perception

Guidelines for Improving Perception and Communication

After studying this chapter, you should be able to . . .

Recognize how perception is made up of means of selecting, organizing, and interpreting the world to create meaning.

Identify factors that affect individuals' perceptions.

List examples of the reciprocal relationship between your perceptions and social media.

Apply this chapter's guidelines to enhance your perceptions.

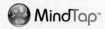

Cengage Learning

Figure 3.1

The Nine-Dot Problem

This chapter focuses on meaning, which is the heart of communication. To understand how humans create meanings for themselves and their activities, we need to understand the reciprocal relationship between perception and communication. As we will see, perception shapes the meaning we assign to others' communication and how we ourselves communicate. At the same time, communication influences how we perceive people and situations.

Before reading further, try to connect the nine dots in Figure 3.1 without lifting your pencil from the paper. You may use no more than four lines, the lines must be straight, and the lines must be connected to one another.

This chapter explores relationships between perception and communication. We'll first discuss the three-part process of perception. Next, we'll consider factors that affect our perceptions. Third, we'll apply material in this chapter to digital and online communication. Finally, we'll identify guidelines for improving perception so we can communicate more effectively.

Before we explore those topics, let's return to the nine-dot problem. Could you connect the dots? Most people have trouble solving the problem because they label the nine dots a square, and they try to connect the dots while staying within the boundaries of a square. However, it's impossible to connect the dots with four straight lines if you define the dots as a square. One solution (there are several) appears at the end of the chapter.

This exercise makes an important point about the relationship between words and human perception. If you label the dots with the word *square*, it's impossible to solve the problem. In everyday communication, our words affect how we perceive others, situations, events, behaviors, and ourselves. At the same time, our perceptions shape what things mean to us and hence the labels we use to name them. We communicate with others according to how we perceive and define them, and we may miss opportunities when our labels limit what we perceive. In the pages that follow, we will unravel the complex relationships between perception and communication.

THE PROCESS OF HUMAN PERCEPTION

Perception is the active process of creating meaning by selecting, organizing, and interpreting people, objects, events, situations, and other phenomena. Note that perception is defined as an active process. We do not passively receive what is "out there" in the external world. Instead, we actively work to make sense of ourselves, others, and interactions. To do so, we select only certain things to notice, and then we organize and interpret what we have selectively noticed. What anything means to us depends on the aspects of it we notice and on our organization and interpretation of those aspects. Thus, perception is not a simple matter of receiving external reality. Instead, we invest a lot of energy in constructing the meanings of phenomena.

Perception consists of three processes: selecting, organizing, and interpreting. These processes are continuous, so they blend into one another. They are also interactive, so each of them affects the other two. For example, what we select to perceive in a particular situation affects how we organize and interpret the situation. At the same time, how we organize and interpret a situation affects our subsequent selections of what to perceive in the situation.

Selection

Stop for a moment and notice what is going on around you right now. Is there music in the background? Is the room warm or cold, messy or neat, large or small, light or dark? Can you smell anything—food being cooked, the stale odor of last night's popcorn, traces of cologne? Can you hear muted sounds of activities outside? Now, think about what's happening inside you: Are you sleepy, hungry, comfortable? Do you have a headache or an itch anywhere? On what kind of paper is your book printed? Is the type large, small, easy to read? How do you like the size of the book, the colors used, the design of the pages? If you're reading an e-book, is the screen resolution good? How do the colors and print look?

Probably you weren't aware of most of these phenomena when you began reading the chapter. Instead, you focused on understanding the content in the book.

chameleonseye/Photos.com

You narrowed your attention to what you defined as important, and you were unaware of other aspects of the book and your surroundings. This is typical of how we live our lives. We can't attend to everything in our environment so we focus on what we decide is relevant to us in any given moment.

We select to attend to certain stimuli based on a number of factors. First, some qualities of phenomena draw attention. For instance, we notice things that **STAND OUT** because they are larger, more intense, or more unusual than other phenomena. So we're more likely to hear a loud voice than a soft one and to notice bright, flashy ads on the Internet than a black-and-white message. In the photo on this page, your eyes are probably drawn to the reddish-brown boots because they stand out from all of the other boots. Further, eyes aren't drawn to the soldier who isn't even visible as a whole person; eyes go to the boots instead.

Change also compels attention, which is why we may take for granted all the pleasant interactions with a friend and notice only the tense moments.

Recent research shows that we can override the tendency to focus on noisy or novel stimuli. We can use the prefrontal cortex, which is known as the brain's planning center, to focus our attention deliberately (Gallagher, 2009; Tierney, 2009). We rely on self-indication when we call particular phenomena to our attention. In fact, in many ways education is a process of learning to indicate to ourselves things we hadn't seen before. Right now, you're learning to be more conscious of the selectivity of your perceptions, so in the future you will notice this more on your own. In science courses, you learn to attend to molecular structures and chemical reactions. Look at the white vase in Figure 3.2. Look again at Figure 3.2, knowing that it is not a vase but profiles of two faces. Do you see the faces now?

What we select to notice is also influenced by who we are and what is going on within us. Our motives and needs affect what we see and don't see. If you have recently ended a romantic relationship, you're more likely to notice attractive people at a party than if you are committed to someone. Motives also explain the oasis phenomenon, in which thirsty people stranded in the desert see water although none really exists. In a series of experiments, researchers showed that people perceive objects they desire (water when thirsty, or money) as closer than objects they do not desire (Balcetis & Dunning, 2013).

Cultures also influence what we select to perceive. Assertiveness and competitiveness are encouraged and considered good in the United States, so we don't perceive it as unusual when people compete and try to surpass one another. By contrast, because some traditional Asian cultures emphasize group loyalty, cooperation, and face saving, competitiveness stands out as unusual and is judged negatively (Gudykunst & Lee, 2002). In Korea, age is an important aspect of identity: The older a person is, the more he or she is respected. Many Koreans also place priority on family relations. Consequently, Koreans are more likely than Westerners to perceive the ages and family roles of people with whom they communicate. The Korean language reflects the cultural value of age and family ties through its different word forms used for people of different ages and different family status. A student from Korea explained that elders are generally addressed more formally by putting *yuh* or *yo* at the end of a phrase. For instance, a teenager who wants to communicate that she or he is going somewhere might say *"gahsaeyuh"* or *"gahsaeyo"* ("Goodnight, sir") to an elder family member, but the more informal *"gahndah"* ("Later, guys") to friends (*gahndah* means "to go").

Figure 3.2

Perception

Cengage Learning

Organization

Once we have selected what to notice, we must make sense of it. We organize what we have noticed and attribute meaning to it. A useful theory for explaining how we organize experience is **constructivism**, which states that we organize and interpret experience by applying cognitive structures called *schemata* (Burleson & Rack, 2008). We rely on four schemata to make sense of interpersonal phenomena: prototypes, personal constructs, stereotypes, and scripts (Hewes, 1995; Kelly, 1955). (See Figure 3.3.)

Communication in Everyday Life

DIVERSITY

Which Line is Longer?

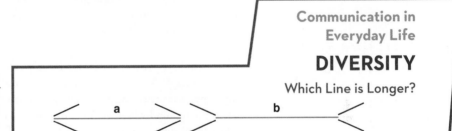

Is line *a* or line *b* in the figure longer? The lines are known as the **Müller-Lyer illusion**. The lines are actually identical in length, but they don't appear so to some people. If you are a Westerner, it's likely that you perceive line b as longer. However, if you are a San Forager of the Kalahari, you are likely to perceive the lines as equal in length.? Why the difference?

Researchers (Henrich & Norenzayan, 2010; Watters, 2013) have found that cultures shape not just our behaviors and values, but also our perceptions. Westerners live in a world with lots of carpentered corners—squared corners in rooms and buildings—so they learn to perceive lines in three dimensions. People who live in less industrialized cultures see fewer carpentered corners, and their perceptions are not trained to see lines as three dimensional. Of more than a dozen cultures studied, Americans emerge as the most likely to perceive line *b* as longer.

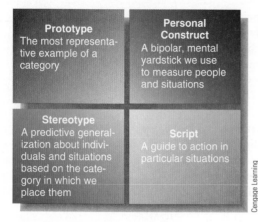

Prototype The most representative example of a category	**Personal Construct** A bipolar, mental yardstick we use to measure people and situations
Stereotype A predictive generalization about individuals and situations based on the category in which we place them	**Script** A guide to action in particular situations

Cengage Learning

Figure 3.3

Cognitive Schemata

Prototypes   A **prototype** defines the clearest or most representative example of some category (Fehr, 1993). For example, you probably have prototypes for categories such as teachers, supervisors, friends, and coworkers. Each of these categories is exemplified by a person who is the ideal; that's the prototype. For example, if Jane is the best friend you've ever known, then Jane is your prototype of a friend. The prototype (Jane) helps you decide who else fits in that particular category (friend). You get to know Burt, and then ask yourself how much he is like Jane. If you view him as a lot like her, then you would put Burt in the category Jane exemplifies: friend. Prototypes organize our perceptions by allowing us to place people and other phenomena in broad categories. We then consider how close they are to our prototype, or exemplar, of that category.

 DAMION

The person who is my ideal of a friend is my buddy Jackson. He stood by me when I got into a lot of trouble a couple of years ago. I got mixed up with some guys who used drugs, and I started using them too. Pretty soon the coach figured out what was going on, and he suspended me from the team. I felt like I was finished when he did that, and then I really got into drugs. But Jackson wouldn't give up on me, and he wouldn't let me give up either. He took me to a drug center and went there with me every day for 3 weeks. He never turned away when I was sick or even when I cried most of one night when I was getting off the drugs. He just stood by me. Once I was straight, Jackson went with me to see the coach about getting back on the team.

We also have prototypes of relationships (Fehr, 1993; Fehr & Russell, 1991; Hasserbrauck & Aaron, 2001). Most Americans' prototypes of romantic relationships emphasize trust, caring, honesty, friendship, and respect. Although passion may come to mind when we think of love, it seems less central to our prototype of love than companionship, caring, and a comfortable lifestyle. In addition, most Americans' prototype of enduring relationships reflects media's emphasis on acquisition of material goods and enjoyment of leisure (Bachen & Illouz, 1996).

Personal Constructs   A **personal construct** is a "mental yardstick" we use to measure a person or situation along a bipolar dimension of judgment (Kelly, 1955). Examples of personal constructs are intelligent–not intelligent, kind–not kind, responsible–not responsible, assertive–not assertive, and attractive–not attractive. We rely on personal constructs to size up people and other phenomena. How intelligent, kind, responsible, and attractive is this person? Whereas prototypes help us decide into which broad category a phenomenon fits, personal constructs let us make more detailed assessments of particular qualities of people and other phenomena.

 NAI LEE

One of the ways I look at people is by whether they are independent or related to others. That is one of the first judgments I make of others. In Korea, we are not so individualistic or independent as people in the

United States. We think of ourselves more as members of families and communities than as individuals. The emphasis on independent identity was the first thing I noticed when I came to this country, and it is still an important way I look at people.

The personal constructs we rely on shape our perceptions because we tend to perceive in terms of the constructs we use. Notice that we structure what we perceive and what it means by the constructs we choose to use. Thus, we may not notice qualities of people that aren't covered by the constructs we apply.

Stereotypes   A **stereotype** is a predictive generalization applied to a person or situation. Based on the category in which we place someone or something and how that person or thing measures up against the personal constructs we apply, we predict what he, she, or it will do. For instance, if you label someone as a liberal, you might stereotype her or him as likely to vote Democratic and support environmental protections. You may have stereotypes of fraternity and sorority members, military personnel, athletes, and people from other cultures. Stereotypes don't necessarily reflect the actual groups to which they refer. Instead, stereotypes are based on our perceptions of groups or on social perspectives that we've internalized.

> I had a lot of difficulty getting people to respect me in my summer internship at a radio station. I'm very career focused, and I worked hard to get that internship, but everyone there treated me like a ditzy college student. They acted like I took the job as kind of a light summer lark or something, but I took it to learn how radio stations actually work. No matter what I did, they didn't take me seriously because they put me in a category that had nothing to do with who I am or the work I was doing.

KATIE

Research shows that a majority of Americans of all races have racial stereotypes that lead them to have an unconscious preference for white people over black people. You read that correctly—black people as well as people of other races favor white people (Nosek & Hansen, 2008). Cultural critic Raina Kelley, who is African American, recounts a time when she assumed a black man at a party might be a criminal. She says, "Being black doesn't get me a pass on unconscious negative feelings about African Americans" (2009, p. 28).

Racial and ethnic stereotypes can lead us to not see differences among people we place in a particular category. The broad label *Asian* doesn't distinguish among people from varied cultures, including Japan, Malaysia, Nepal, and China. *Native American* is a very broad category that includes diverse indigenous North American tribes (Vickers, 1999). A student of mine, Winowa, believes that the term *Native American* leads people not to notice differences among tribes.

> People have a stereotype of Native Americans. People who are not Native American think we are all alike—how we look, how we act, what we believe, what our traditions are. But that isn't true. The Crow and Apache are as different as people from Kenya and New York. Some tribes have

WINOWA

In *The Crazy Ones*, Robin Williams plays Simon Roberts, the unorthodox head of an advertising agency. Roberts could be considered a negative prototype or anti-prototype of bosses.

CBS/Photofest

a history of aggression and violence; others have traditions of peace and harmony. We worship different spirits and have different tribal rituals and customs. All of these differences are lost when people stereotype us all into one group.

Stereotypes may be accurate or inaccurate. In some cases, we have incorrect understandings of a group, and in other cases individual members of a group don't conform to the group as a whole. Interestingly, Americans are often negatively stereotyped in other parts of the world. They may be perceived as arrogant or ethnocentric because they often cannot speak the native language of the cultures they visit and expect English to be spoken by others, they expect luxurious treatment, and they may expect American norms and preferences to be observed—for instance, serving salads before entrees, which is the norm in America but not in most of Europe. Yet Americans, like all groups, are diverse—some Americans can speak other languages and can do without luxury accommodations; some can't or won't. Although we need stereotypes to predict what will happen around us, they can be harmful if we forget that they are based not on objective reality but instead on perceptions.

Scripts   The final cognitive schema we use to organize perceptions is the **script**. A script is a guide to action. Scripts consist of sequences of activities that are expected of us and others in particular situations. They are based on our experiences and observations of interaction in various contexts. Many of our daily activities are governed by scripts, although we're typically not aware of them. We have a script for greeting casual acquaintances on campus ("Hey, what's up?" "Not much"). You also have scripts for managing conflict, talking with professors, dealing with clerks, and interacting with coworkers on the job.

Scripts are useful in guiding us through many of our interactions. However, they are not always accurate or constructive, so we shouldn't accept them uncritically. For instance, if your parents often engaged in bitter, destructive quarreling, you may have learned a script for conflict that can undermine relationships. If you grew up in a community that treated people of certain races negatively, you may want to assess that script critically before using it to direct your own activities.

The four cognitive schemata we have discussed interact with one another. A good example of this interaction comes from Dr. Jerome Groopman (2007), who has studied patterns in doctors' thinking that can result in misdiagnosis and mistreatment of patients. For instance, a man may stumble into an emergency room and mutter incoherently. If the doctor puts the man in the category of homeless (prototype) because he stumbles and mumbles, the doctor may then stereotype him as having drunk too much and follow a script of not testing the man and assuming he just needs to sleep off the intoxication. Conversely, if the doctor assumes the man is middle class and employed, the doctor might perceive the stumbling and mumbling as signs of a medical problem. Accordingly, the doctor would order tests to diagnose the problem.

Prototypes, personal constructs, stereotypes, and scripts are cognitive schemata that we use to organize our perceptions of people and phenomena. These cognitive schemata reflect the perspectives of particular others and the generalized other. As we interact with people, we internalize our culture's ways of classifying, measuring, and predicting phenomena and its norms for acting in various situations.

Interpretation

Even after we have selectively perceived phenomena and used cognitive schemata to organize our perceptions, what they mean to us is not clear. There are no intrinsic meanings in phenomena. Instead, we assign meaning by interpreting what we have noticed and organized. **Interpretation** is the subjective process of explaining our perceptions in ways that make sense to us. To interpret the meaning of another's actions, we construct explanations, or attributions, for them.

Attributions An **attribution** is an explanation of why something happened or why someone acts a certain way (Heider, 1958; Kelley, 1967; Manusov & Spitzberg, 2008). Attributions have four dimensions, as shown in Figure 3.4. The first is locus, which attributes a person's actions to internal factors ("He has no patience with people who are late") or external factors ("The traffic jam frustrated him"). The second dimension is stability, which explains actions as the

Everyday Skills To practice recognizing the cognitive structures called schemata, complete the activity "Be Aware of Your Schemata" at the end of the chapter or online.

Dimension

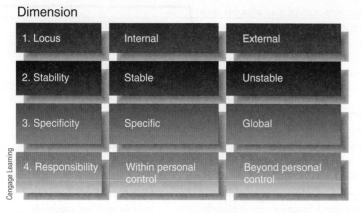

Dimension		
1. Locus	Internal	External
2. Stability	Stable	Unstable
3. Specificity	Specific	Global
4. Responsibility	Within personal control	Beyond personal control

Cengage Learning

Figure **3.4**

Dimensions of Attributions

result of stable factors that won't change over time ("She's a Type A personality") or unstable factors that may or will be different at another time ("She acted that way because she has a headache right now").

Specificity is the third dimension, and it explains behavior in terms of whether the behavior has global implications that apply in most or all situations ("He's a big spender") or specific implications that apply only in certain situations or under certain conditions ("He spends a lot of money on clothes."). At first it may seem that stability and specificity are the same, but they are distinct dimensions. Stability concerns time (whether the reason is temporary or enduring), whereas specificity concerns the breadth of the explanation (all situations, events, and places, or particular or limited situations and places). Here are examples of how we might combine these two dimensions to explain why Angela yelled at Fred:

- Stable and specific: She yelled at Fred (specific) because she is short-tempered (stable).
- Stable and global: She yells at everyone (global) because she is short-tempered (stable).
- Unstable and specific: She yelled at Fred (specific) because she was in a hurry that day (unstable).
- Unstable and global: She yells at everyone (global) when she is in a hurry (unstable).

The fourth dimension of attributions is responsibility. Do we hold a person responsible for a particular behavior? We're more likely to hold people responsible for behavior that we think they can control. If we attribute Angela's yelling to her lack of effort to control her temper, we're more likely to judge her harshly than if we attribute her yelling to lack of sleep during exam week (unstable) or to a medication she's taking (external) for a short time (unstable). How we account for others' actions affects our perceptions of them and our relationships with them. We can feel more or less positive toward others depending on our interpretation of why they act as they do.

Attributional Errors Researchers have identified two common errors people make in their attributions. The first is the **self-serving bias**. As the term implies, this is a bias toward ourselves and our interests. Research indicates that some people tend to construct attributions that serve our personal interests (Hamachek, 1992; Manusov & Spitzberg, 2008). For example, you might say that you did well on a test because you are a smart person (internal and stable) who is always responsible (global) and studies hard (personal control). We also attribute the victories of our athletic teams to internal, stable factors within the players' control, and we attribute our teams' losses to external, unstable factors which the teams could not control (Wann & Schrader, 2000).

When I do badly on a test or paper, I usually say either the professor was unfair or I had too much to do that week and couldn't study like I wanted to. But when my friends do badly on a test, I tend to think they're not good in that subject or they aren't disciplined or whatever.

The self-serving bias also works in a second way. We tend to avoid taking responsibility for negative actions and failures by attributing them to external, unstable, and specific factors that are beyond personal control (Schutz, 1999). To explain a failing grade on a test, you might say that you did poorly because the professor (external) put a lot of tricky questions on that test (unstable, specific factor), so all your studying didn't help (outside of personal control). In other words, our misconduct results from outside forces that we can't help, but all the good we do reflects our personal qualities and efforts. This self-serving bias can distort our perceptions, leading us to take excessive personal credit for what we do well and to abdicate responsibility for what we do poorly. When the self-serving bias shapes how we interpret our behaviors, we form an unrealistic image of ourselves and our activities.

There's an important qualification to the research on self-serving bias. Most of it was conducted on Westerners. When researchers decided to see whether the self-serving bias was equally prominent in other cultures, they discovered it was not. It is more pronounced in Western populations than in non-Western ones (Heine & Hamamura, 2007). Mexicans (Tropp & Wright, 2003), Native Americans (Fryberg & Markus, 2003), and Chileans (Heine & Raineri, 2009) are less likely to engage in self-serving bias, and some East Asians, whose cultures encourage modesty and humility, engage in self-effacing bias (Heine & Hamamura, 2007).

The second kind of attributional error is so common it is called the **fundamental attribution error**. This involves the dimension of locus. We tend to overestimate the internal causes of others' undesirable behaviors and underestimate the external causes. Conversely, we are likely to underestimate the internal causes of our own misdeeds and failures and overestimate the external causes (Schutz, 1999; Sedikides, Campbell, Reeder, & Elliott, 1998).

The fundamental attribution error was obvious in a legal case on which I consulted. A woman sued her employer for transferring her. She alleged that he did so because her supervisor was biased against women. Her supervisor denied being biased against women. He claimed that he transferred her because of her poor performance. Written records, such as yearly performance reviews, and the woman's own testimony revealed that she had not met all of her job responsibilities, and she had been told this repeatedly. Furthermore, her supervisor's record of hiring and promotions showed that nearly 50% of his hires and promotions over the past decade had been women and minorities.

At the trial, the plaintiff was asked whether it was possible that her performance had influenced her supervisor's decision to transfer her. "No, he did it because he doesn't want to work with women," she replied. Thus, she totally discounted external factors that could explain his decision and placed full responsibility on internal qualities (his alleged sex bias). When asked whether she thought her performance might have made her more expendable than others who worked in her former department, she said, "No, the only problems with my performance were due to interruptions and lack of cooperation from others." Thus, she rejected any personal

MindTap

Everyday Skills To practice guarding against the fundamental attribution error, complete the activity "Guard against the Fundamental Attribution Error" at the end of the chapter or online.

INSIGHT

Thinking Your Way to a Good Relationship

How we think about what our partners do and don't do has a lot to do with how happy we are in our relationships (Bradbury & Fincham, 1990; Fletcher & Fincham, 1991; Friesen, Fletcher, & Overall, 2005; Seligman, 2002). Partners in happy relationships tend to think in positive ways about each other. People attribute nice things a partner does to internal, stable, and global reasons. "He got the DVD for us because he is a good person who always does sweet things for us." Happy couples attribute unpleasant things a partner does to external, unstable, and specific factors. "She yelled at me because all the stress of the past few days made her not herself."

In contrast, unhappy couples tend to think negatively. They tend to attribute a partner's nice actions to external, unstable, and specific factors. "He got the DVD because he had some extra time this particular day." Negative actions are seen as stemming from internal, stable, and global factors. "She yelled at me because she is a nasty person who never shows any consideration to anybody else." Negative attributions fix pessimistic views and undermine motivation to improve a relationship. Whether positive or negative, attributions may be self-fulfilling prophecies.

Related research demonstrates that attributional patterns are linked to marital quality and forgiveness. We are less likely to forgive a partner if we attribute his or her transgression to personal irresponsibility (Fincham, 2000; Fincham, Paleari, & Regalia, 2002; Finkel, Rusbult, Kumashiro, & Hannon, 2002; McCullough & Hoyt, 2002).

responsibility for errors in her work and laid full responsibility on circumstances beyond her control. In court, I explained the fundamental attribution error to the jury and showed how it surfaced in the woman's testimony. The jury found in favor of the woman's supervisor.

We've seen that perception involves three interrelated processes. The first of these, selection, involves noticing and attending to only certain things. The second process is organization, whereby we use prototypes, personal constructs, stereotypes, and scripts to organize what we have selectively perceived. Finally, we engage in interpretation to make sense of the perceptions we have gathered and organized. Attributions are a primary way we explain what we and others do.

Although we've discussed selection, organization, and interpretation separately, in reality they may occur in a different order or simultaneously. Thus, our interpretations shape the cognitive schemata we use to organize experiences, and the ways we organize perceptions affect what we notice and interpret.

INFLUENCES ON PERCEPTION

Individuals differ in how they perceive situations and people. In this section, we consider some of the influences on our perceptions.

Physiology

One reason perceptions vary among people is that we differ in our sensory abilities and physiologies. If you are tired or stressed, you're likely to perceive things more negatively than you normally would. For instance, a playful insult from a coworker might anger you if you were feeling down but wouldn't bother you if you were feeling good. Each of us has our own biorhythm, which influences the times of day when we tend to be more and less perceptually alert.

Medical conditions are another physiological influence on perceptions. If you've ever taken drugs that affected your thinking, you know how dramatically they can alter perceptions. People may become severely depressed, paranoid, or uncharacteristically happy under the influence of hormones or drugs. Changes in our bodies caused by medical conditions may also affect what we selectively perceive. I have a back disorder that periodically limits my mobility. When my back is out of order, I am keenly aware of stairs and uneven ground that I barely notice when my back is working well.

Expectations

Our expectations also affect what we notice (Bargh, 1999). Imagine that a friend tells you she wants you to meet a "really cool guy. He's funny and considerate and so easy to talk to. I know you'll like him." It's likely that you'll expect to like the new person and will perceive the good qualities your friend has called to your attention. If instead your friend had said, "This guy is a real drag. He is totally self-centered and boring," then your expectations would be low and you would be less likely to notice any good qualities in the man.

The impact of expectations on perception explains the self-fulfilling prophecy we discussed in Chapter 2. A child who is told she is unlovable may notice rejecting, but not affirming, communication from others. An employee who is told he has leadership potential is likely to notice all his professional successes and strengths and to be less aware of his shortcomings.

Expectations influence perceptions in a range of communication situations. If you are told that a newly hired person is a "real team player," you're likely to notice the new employee's cooperative behaviors and be less aware of her competitive behaviors. If you hear that a campus group is "welcoming to new members and very friendly," you're more likely to perceive members of the group positively.

Age

Age is another factor that influences our perceptions. Compared with a person of 20, a 60-year-old has a more complex fund of experiences to draw on in perceiving situations and people. When I was 22 years old and in graduate school, I mentioned to my father that it was hard to get by on the salary from my teaching assistantship. He said that, during the early 1930s, he would have been very happy to have had enough money just to eat. Because my father had lived through the Great Depression, he had a broader perspective than I did on how hard life can be.

As we grow older and have more experiences, both pleasant and challenging, our perspective on many things changes. Issues that seem overwhelming to a teenager are often manageable to a 30-year-old, who has more experience meeting and dealing with life's challenges.

Culture

Throughout this chapter and the prior one, we've seen that we are influenced by culture**, which** is the totality of beliefs, values, understandings, practices, and ways of interpreting experience that are shared by a number of people. The influence of culture is so pervasive that it's hard to realize how powerfully it shapes our perceptions.

Consider a few aspects of modern American culture that influence our perceptions. American culture emphasizes technology and its offspring, speed. Most Americans expect things to happen fast, almost instantly. We text messages and send letters by email attachment, we jet across the country, and we microwave meals. In countries such as Nepal and Mexico, life often proceeds at a more leisurely pace, and people spend more time talking, relaxing, and engaging in low-key activity.

The United States is also a highly individualistic culture in which personal initiative is expected and rewarded (Baxter, 2011). In more collectivist cultures, identity is defined in terms of membership in a family rather than as an individual quality. Because families are more valued in collectivist cultures, elders are given greater respect and care than they often receive in the United States. More communal countries also have policies that reflect the value they place on families. In every developed country except the United States, new parents, including adoptive parents, are given at least 6 weeks of paid parental leave, and some countries provide a year's paid leave.

Many doctors and businesspeople in the United States now are encouraged to attend workshops that teach them about the cultural practices of immigrants from other countries. Without awareness of cultural differences, the risk of misperception and misunderstanding is high.

Social Location   We are affected not only by the culture as a whole but by particular social groups to which we belong (Hallstein, 2000; Haraway, 1988; Harding, 1991; Wood, 2005). A **standpoint** is a point of view that grows out of political awareness of the social location of a group—the material, social, and symbolic conditions common for members of a social group. People who belong to powerful, high-status social groups have a vested interest in preserving the system that gives them privileges; thus, they are unlikely to perceive its flaws and inequities. Conversely, those who belong to less-privileged groups are able to see inequities and discrimination (Collins, 1998; Harding, 1991).

MindTap

Cultural Values

To practice assessing the impact of cultural values on your perceptions, complete the activity "Cultural Values" at the end of the chapter or online.

Women and men tend to occupy different social locations in some ways. For instance, girls and women are more often in caregiving roles than boys and men. However, the caregiving we generally associate with women results less from any maternal instinct than from occupying the social role of caregiver (mother, older sister, babysitter), which teaches women to care for others, to notice who needs what, and to defer their own needs. Men who engage in caring for others often become nurturing, accommodative, and sensitive to others' needs as a consequence of being in the social role of caregiver.

JANICE

I was always a pretty independent person. Some people even thought I was kind of selfish, because I really would prioritize myself. Then I had my first baby, and I stayed home with him for a year. I really changed—and I mean in basic ways. I believed that my most important job was to be there for Timmy, and so my whole day focused on him. He was the person I thought about first, not myself. I learned to hear the slightest difference in his cries, so I could tell when he was hungry or needed his diapers changed or wanted company. When I went back to work after a year, a lot of my former colleagues said I was different—much more attentive and sensitive to what they said and more generous with my time than I had been. I guess I developed new patterns of communicating as a result of mothering.

Gender differences also are obvious in how much we invest in maintaining relationships. Socialized into the role of relationship expert, many women are expected by others and themselves to take care of relationships (Brehm, Miller, Perleman, & Campbell, 2001; Wood, 1993, 1994c, 1998, 2001, 2011b). It's often assumed they know when something is wrong and know how to resolve it.

Racial–ethnic groups are also social locations that shape our perceptions. Stan Gaines (1995), who studies minority groups in the United States, reports that African Americans and Latinos and Latinas tend to perceive family and extended community as more central to their identities than most European Americans do. Perceiving self as a part of larger social groups also is characteristic of many Asian cultures. Our membership in an overall culture, as well as our location in particular social groups, shapes how we perceive people, situations, events, and ourselves.

Louise Gubb/The Image Works

Roles   Our perceptions also are shaped by roles. Both the training we receive to fulfill a role and the actual demands of the role affect what we notice and how we interpret and evaluate the role. Professors often perceive classes in terms of how interested students seem, whether they appear to have read the material, and whether they're applying course material to their lives. Students have told me that they perceive classes in terms of time of day, number and difficulty of tests, whether papers are required, and whether the professor is interesting.

The professions people enter influence what they notice and how they think and act. Medical professionals are trained to be highly observant of physical symptoms; lawyers are trained in analytic thinking; human resources personnel are taught to be sensitive to others' emotions and life situations.

Social roles can also influence how we perceive communication about feelings. Professions that call for detachment and objectivity may encourage members not to express their emotions and to be uncomfortable when others do. We'll discuss the relationship between social roles and communication about emotions more fully in Chapter 7.

Cognitive Abilities

In addition to physiological, cultural, and social influences, perception is also shaped by cognitive abilities. How elaborately we think about situations and people, and our personal knowledge of others, affect how we perceive them.

Cognitive Complexity People differ in the number and type of cognitive schemata they use to perceive, organize, and interpret people and situations. **Cognitive complexity** refers to the number of personal constructs used (remember, these are bipolar dimensions of judgment), how abstract they are, and how elaborately they interact to shape perceptions. Most children have fairly simple cognitive systems: They rely on few personal constructs, focus more on concrete categories than abstract and psychological ones, and often are unaware of relationships between personal constructs.

In general, adults are more cognitively complex than children. However, adults have different degrees of cognitive complexity, and this affects perceptions. If you think of people only as nice or not nice, you have a limited range for perceiving others. Similarly, people who focus on concrete data tend to have less sophisticated understandings than people who also perceive psychological data. For example, you might notice that a person is attractive, tells jokes, and talks to others easily. These are concrete perceptions. At a more abstract, psychological level, you might reason that the concrete behaviors you observe reflect a secure, self-confident personality. This is a more sophisticated perception because it offers an explanation of why the person acts as she or he does.

What if you later find out that the person is very quiet in classes? Someone with low cognitive complexity would have difficulty integrating the new information into prior observations. Either the new information would be dismissed because it doesn't fit, or it would replace the former perception, and the person would be redefined as shy (Crockett, 1965; Delia, Clark, & Switzer, 1974). A more cognitively complex person would integrate all the information into a coherent account. Perhaps a cognitively complex person would conclude that the person is very confident in social situations but less secure in academic ones.

Person-Centeredness   Person-centeredness is related to cognitive complexity because it entails abstract thinking and use of a wide range of schemata. As discussed in Chapter 1, person-centeredness is the ability to perceive another as a unique individual. Our ability to perceive others as unique depends, first, on how well we make cognitive distinctions. People who are cognitively complex rely on more numerous and more abstract schemata to interpret others. Second, person-centered communicators use knowledge of particular others to guide their communication. Thus, they tailor vocabulary, nonverbal behaviors, and language to the experiences, values, and interests of others. The result is person-centered communication.

Recalling the discussion of I–Thou relationships in Chapter 1, you may remember that these are relationships in which people know and value each other as unique individuals. To do so, we must learn about another, and this entails much time and interaction. As we get to know another better, we gain insight into how she or he differs from others in a group ("Rob's not obsessive like other political activists I've known," "Ellen's more interested in people than most computer science majors"). The more we interact with another and the greater the variety of experiences we have together, the more insight we gain into the other's motives, feelings, and behaviors. As we come to understand others as individuals, we fine-tune our perceptions of them. Consequently, we're less likely to rely on stereotypes. This is why we often communicate more effectively with people we know well than with strangers or casual acquaintances.

> **STEVE**
>
> When I first started dating Sherry, I sent her red roses to let her know I thought she was special. That's the "lovers' flower," right? It turns out that was the only flower her father liked, and they had a million red roses at his funeral. Now they make Sherry sad because they remind her he's dead. I also took her chocolates once, then later found out she's allergic to chocolate. By now, I know what flowers and things she likes, but my experience shows that the general rules don't always apply to individuals.

Person-centeredness is not empathy. **Empathy** is the ability to feel with another person, to feel what she or he feels in a situation. Person-centeredness is a cognitive skill that allows us to connect as well as we can based on efforts to understand another (Muehlhoff, 2006). With commitment and effort, we can learn a lot about how others see the world, even if that differs from how we see it. This knowledge, along with cognitive complexity, allows us to be person-centered communicators.

When we take the perspective of another, we try to grasp what something means to that person. This involves suspending judgment at least temporarily. We can't appreciate someone else's perspective when we're imposing our evaluations of whether it is right or wrong, sensible or crazy. Instead, we must let go of our own perspective and perceptions long enough to enter the world of another person. Doing this allows us to understand issues from the other person's point of view so that we can communicate more effectively. At a later point in interaction, we may choose to express our own perspective or to disagree with the other. This is appropriate, but voicing our own views is not a substitute for the equally important skill of recognizing others' perspectives.

Self

A final influence on our perceptions is ourselves. Consider how differently people with the four attachment styles we discussed in Chapter 2 would perceive and approach close relationships. People with secure attachment styles assume that they are lovable and that others are trustworthy. Thus, they tend to perceive others and relationships in positive ways. In contrast, people with fearful attachment styles perceive themselves as unlovable and others as not loving. Consequently, they may perceive relationships as dangerous and potentially harmful. The dismissive attachment style inclines people to perceive themselves positively, others negatively, and close relationships as undesirable. People who have anxious/ambivalent attachment styles often are preoccupied with relationships and perceive others in unpredictable ways.

Each of us also tends to have an **implicit personality theory**, which is a collection of unspoken and sometimes unconscious assumptions about how various qualities fit together in human personalities. Most of us think certain qualities go together in people. For instance, you might think that people who are outgoing are also friendly, confident, and fun. The assumption that outgoing people are friendly, confident, and fun reflects your implicit personality theory of the qualities that accompany outgoingness.

In sum, physiology, culture and standpoint, social roles, cognitive abilities, and we ourselves affect what we perceive and how we interpret others and experiences. In the final section of the chapter, we'll consider ways to improve the accuracy of our perceptions.

SOCIAL MEDIA AND PERCEPTION

As in previous chapters, we now want to consider how ideas that we've discussed in the foregoing pages apply to digital and online communication. We'll focus on three connections between social media and perception.

First, our choices of social media shape our perceptions of events, issues, and people. If you follow Rush Limbaugh's tweets, you will get a conservative perspective on national and international issues and on the people involved in them. If you follow Rachel Maddow's tweets, you will get a much more liberal perspective on the same issues and people. Limbaugh frequently disparages feminists, by labeling them "feminazis"; Maddow identifies as a feminist and speaks favorably about feminist issues. Limbaugh sympathizes with corporate interests and tends to support lowering corporate taxes and boosting capitalism; Maddow is inclined to be distrustful of corporate interests, to think corporations should pay more taxes, and to favor reigning in some capitalist tendencies. Who's right? There is no objective answer to that question, but your views on such issues are shaped by the bloggers you follow.

Second, our cultural memberships influence the content of our digital and online communication. Try this experiment: Look at the social network profiles of people you know who belong to different ethnic groups. How often do their postings include boasting about individual accomplishments? How many of the photos posted show the individual with family members? How often are family members and family values mentioned? Now look at the profiles of women and men you know. To what extent does each sex tweet and post about relationship issues and sports? Are the trends that you note consistent with research we've discussed about Western and non-Western cultural values and feminine and masculine social communities?

Third, think about the relationship between social media and our perceptions and expectations of time. When you text someone, do you expect a reply almost immediately? Do you get frustrated if a friend doesn't reply for several hours or days? Are you irritated when your Internet connection goes down or is slow? Most of us would answer yes to each of these questions. In doing so, we reflect a sense of time that has been radically speeded up as a result of technologies of communication. A hundred years ago, people stayed in touch by writing letters and waiting weeks for replies. Fifty years ago, phones were landlines, and long-distance calls were rare since they were expensive. Forty years ago, most people didn't have personal computers, much less tablets and smartphones, and email didn't exist. As technologies of communication have evolved, they have altered how we perceive time, making what was once a short time to wait for a reply seem very long now.

Our interaction with social media has also altered our sense of space. The world seems smaller when we can see on a smartphone a protest occurring across the country or a tsunami across the world. With the aid of media, we are no longer confined to physical, material space for interaction. We can Skype with friends who are far away, participate in virtual meetings, conduct relationships online, and take classes at schools hundreds or even thousands of miles away. This means that we no longer perceive our physical location as an absolute limit on where we can be. These are just three of the many ways that our engagement with digital and online communication affects how we perceive ourselves and our world.

GUIDELINES FOR IMPROVING PERCEPTION AND COMMUNICATION

Because perception is central to interpersonal communication, it's important to form perceptions carefully and check their accuracy. Here, we discuss seven guidelines for improving the accuracy of perceptions and, ultimately, the quality of interpersonal communication.

MindTap

Everyday Skills To practice observing the distinct ways that social media represent issues and events, complete the activity "Virtual Worldviews" at the end of the chapter or online.

Recognize That All Perceptions Are Partial and Subjective

Our perceptions are always partial and subjective. They are partial because we cannot perceive everything; and they are subjective because they are shaped by our physiology, culture, standpoint, social roles, cognitive abilities, and personal experiences. A film you think is hilarious may be boring to your friend.

THALENA

So this girl I met a few weeks ago said she was having a party, and it would be lots of fun with some cool people. She asked if I wanted to come, so I said, "Sure—why not?" When I got there everybody was drinking—I mean seriously drinking. They were playing this weird music—sort of morbid—and they had the tape of *Rocky Horror Picture Show* going nonstop. They got so loud that the neighbors came over and told us to hold it down. In a couple of hours, most of the people there were totally wasted. That's not my idea of fun. That's not my idea of cool people.

The subjective and partial nature of perceptions has implications for interpersonal communication. One implication is that when you and another person disagree about something, neither of you is necessarily wrong. It's more likely that you have attended to different things and that there are differences in your personal, social, cultural, cognitive, and physiological resources for perceiving.

A second implication is that it's wise to remind ourselves that our perceptions are based at least as much on ourselves as on anything external to us. If you perceive another person as domineering, there's a chance that you are feeling insecure or out of your league. You may perceive a person as being aggressive whereas others see the person as assertive. Remembering that perceptions are partial and subjective curbs the tendency to think that our perceptions are the only valid ones or that they are based exclusively on what lies outside us.

Avoid Mind Reading

Mind reading is assuming we understand what another person thinks, feels, or perceives. When we mind read, we act as though we know what's on another person's mind, and this can get us into trouble. Marriage counselors and communication scholars say mind reading contributes to conflict between people (Dickson, 1995; Gottman, 1993). The danger of mind reading is that we may misinterpret others.

Consider a few examples. A supervisor notices that an employee is late for work several days in a row and assumes the employee isn't committed to the job. Gina is late meeting her friend Alex, who assumes she is late because Gina's still mad about

MindTap

Everyday Skills To practice catching yourself mind reading, complete the activity "Monitor Mind Reading" at the end of the chapter or online.

what happened. A friend doesn't return your text message so you think the friend is angry.

Mind reading also occurs when we say or think, "I know why you're upset" (has the person said she or he is upset? What makes you think you know why he or she is upset, if he or she actually is?) or "You don't care about me anymore" (maybe the other person is too preoccupied or worried to be as attentive as usual). We also mind read when we tell ourselves we know how somebody else will feel or react or what he or she will do. The truth is that we don't really know; we're only guessing. When we mind read, we impose our perspectives on others instead of allowing them to say what they think. This can cause misunderstandings and resentment because most of us prefer to speak for ourselves.

CONSUELA

Mind reading drives me crazy. My boyfriend does it all the time, and he's wrong as often as he's right. Last week, he got tickets to a concert because he "knew" I'd want to go. Maybe I would have if I hadn't already planned a trip that weekend, but he never checked on my schedule. A lot of times, when we're talking, he'll say something, then before I can answer, he says, "I know what you're thinking." Then, he proceeds to run through his ideas about what I'm thinking. Usually he's off base, and then we get into a sideline argument about why he keeps assuming what I think instead of asking me. I really wish he would ask me what I think.

Check Perceptions with Others

The third guideline follows directly from the first two. Because perceptions are subjective and partial, and because mind reading is an ineffective way to figure out what others think, we need to check our perceptions with others.

Perception checking is an important communication skill because it helps people arrive at mutual understandings of each other and their relationships. To check perceptions, you should first state what you have noticed. For example, a person might say to a coworker, "Lately, I've thought you were less talkative in team meetings." Then the person should check to see whether the other perceives the same thing: "Do you feel you've been less talkative?" Finally, it's appropriate to ask the other person to explain her or his behavior. In the example, the person might ask, "Why do you think you're less talkative?" (If the other person doesn't perceive that she or he is less talkative, the question might be, "It seems to me that you've been reading memos and not saying much during our team meetings lately. Am I wrong?")

When checking perceptions, it's important to use a tentative tone rather than a dogmatic or accusatory one. This minimizes defensiveness and encourages good discussion. Just let the other person know you've noticed something and would like him or her to clarify his or her perceptions of what is happening and what it means.

MindTap™

Everyday Skills To practice sensitivity to your own tendencies to confuse facts and inferences, complete the activity "Use Tentative Language" at the end of the chapter or online.

Distinguish between Facts and Inferences

Competent interpersonal communication also depends on distinguishing facts from inferences. A fact is based on observation. An inference involves an interpretation that goes beyond the facts. For example, suppose that a person is consistently late reporting to work and sometimes dozes off during discussions. Coworkers might think, "That person is lazy and unmotivated." The facts are that the person comes in late and sometimes falls asleep. Defining the person as lazy and unmotivated is an inference that goes beyond the facts. It's possible that the coworker is tired because he or she has a second job, has a sick child, or is taking medication that induces drowsiness.

It's easy to confuse facts and inferences because we sometimes treat the latter as the former. When we say, "That employee is lazy," we make a statement that sounds factual, and we may then perceive it as factual. To avoid this tendency, substitute more tentative words. For instance, "That employee seems unmotivated" or "That employee may be lazy" are more tentative statements that keep the speaker from treating an inference as a fact. We must make inferences to function in the world. Yet we risk misperceptions if we don't distinguish our inferences from facts.

Guard against the Self-Serving Bias

Because the self-serving bias can distort perceptions, particularly those of Westerners, we need to monitor it carefully. Observe yourself to see whether you attribute your failures or your adverse behaviors to factors beyond your control and whether you attribute your accomplishments to your own efforts. The self-serving bias also inclines us to notice what we do and to be less aware of what others do. Obviously, this can affect how we feel about others, as Janet illustrates in her comments.

JANET

For years, my husband and I have argued about housework. I am always criticizing him for not doing enough, and I have felt resentful about how much I do. He always says to me that he does a lot, but I just don't notice. After studying the self-serving bias in class, I did an "experiment" at home. I watched him for a week and kept a list of all the things he did. Sure enough, he was—is—doing a lot more than I thought. I never noticed that he sorted laundry or walked the dog four times a day or wiped the kitchen counters after we'd finished fixing dinner. I noticed everything I did but only the big things he did, like vacuuming. I simply wasn't seeing a lot of his contributions to keep our home in order.

Monitoring the self-serving bias also has implications for how we perceive others. Just as we tend to judge ourselves generously, we may also be inclined to judge others too harshly. Monitor your perceptions to see whether you attribute others' successes and admirable actions to external factors beyond their control and their shortcomings and blunders to internal factors they can (should) control. If you do this, substitute more generous explanations for others' behaviors, and notice how that affects your perceptions of them.

Guard against the Fundamental Attribution Error

We've also discussed a second error in interpretation: the fundamental attribution error. This occurs when we overestimate the internal causes of others' undesirable behavior and underestimate the external causes, and when we underestimate the internal causes of our own failings or bad behaviors and overestimate the external causes. We need to guard against this error because it distorts our perceptions of ourselves and others.

To reduce your chances of falling victim to the fundamental attribution error, prompt yourself to look for external causes of others' behaviors that you may not have thought of or appreciated. Instead of assuming that the unwanted behavior reflects another's motives or personality, ask yourself, "What factors in the person's situation might lead to this behavior?" You can ask the converse question to avoid underestimating internal influences on your own undesirable actions. Instead of letting yourself off the hook by explaining a misdeed as caused by circumstances you couldn't control, ask yourself, "What factor inside of me that is my responsibility influenced what I did?" Looking for external factors that influence others' communication and internal factors that influence your own communication checks our tendency to make fundamental attribution errors.

Monitor Labels

In giving names to our perceptions, we clarify them to ourselves. But just as words crystallize experiences, they can also freeze thought. Once we label our perceptions, we may respond to our own labels rather than to actual phenomena. If this happens, we may communicate in insensitive and inappropriate ways.

Consider this situation. Suppose you get together with five others in a study group, and a student named Andrea occupies a lot of group time by asking questions. Leaving the meeting, one person says, "Gee, Andrea is so selfish and immature! I'll never work with her again." Another person responds, "She's not really selfish. She's just insecure about her grades in this course, so she was hyper in the meeting." Chances are that these two people will treat Andrea differently

© Suzanne Tucker/Shutterstock.com

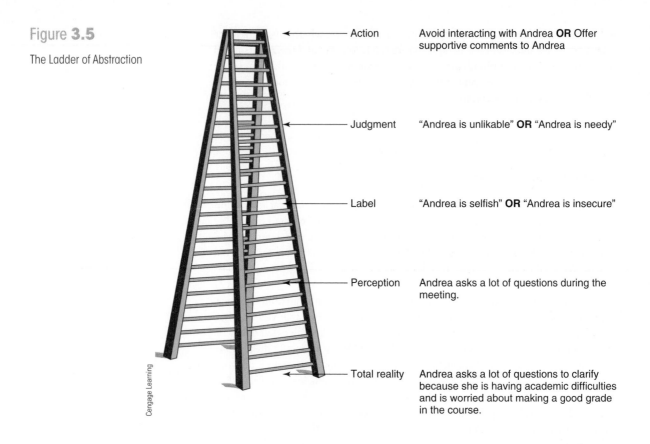

Figure **3.5**

The Ladder of Abstraction

Action — Avoid interacting with Andrea **OR** Offer supportive comments to Andrea

Judgment — "Andrea is unlikable" **OR** "Andrea is needy"

Label — "Andrea is selfish" **OR** "Andrea is insecure"

Perception — Andrea asks a lot of questions during the meeting.

Total reality — Andrea asks a lot of questions to clarify because she is having academic difficulties and is worried about making a good grade in the course.

Cengage Learning

depending on whether they've labeled her "selfish" or "insecure." Once the two people have labeled Andrea's behavior based on their subjective and partial perceptions, they may act toward Andrea based on their labels.

When we engage in interpersonal communication, we perceive only certain aspects of the total reality around us. Our perceptions are one step away from reality because they are always partial and subjective. We move a second step from reality when we label a perception. We move even further from the actual reality when we respond not to behaviors or our perceptions of them but instead to the label we impose. This process can be illustrated as a ladder of abstraction (see Figure 3.5), a concept emphasized by an early scholar of interpersonal communication (Hayakawa, 1962, 1964).

We should also monitor our labels to adapt our communication to particular people. Competent interpersonal communicators are sensitive to others and their preferences and choose their words accordingly. This is especially important when we are talking with or about identities. Most gays and lesbians reject the label *homosexual*, and they may resent hearing themselves labeled as such. Many people who have disabilities perceive the term *disabled people* as suggesting that they are disabled as people simply because they have some physical or mental condition. They prefer the term *person with disabilities* to the term *disabled person* (Braithwaite, 1996).

The U.S. Department of Labor surveyed 60,000 households to learn what identity labels different ethnic groups prefer. Not surprisingly, the survey revealed that members of various racial groups do not have uniform preferences. Among blacks, 44% wanted to be called *black*, 28% wanted to be called *African American*, 12% wanted to be called *Afro-American*, and 16% preferred other labels or had no preference. Nearly half of American Indians preferred to be called *American Indian*, yet 37% wanted to be called *Native American*. A majority of Hispanics wanted to be called *Hispanic*, not *Latino* or *Latina*. Whites overwhelmingly preferred to be called *white*; only 3% wanted to be called *European American* ("Politically Correct," 1995).

Is effective, sensitive communication possible when there are no universal guidelines for what to call people? Yes, if we are willing to invest thought and effort in our interactions. We begin by assuming that we may not know how others want to be labeled and that not all members of a group have the same preferences. Just because my friend Marsha wants to be called *black*, I shouldn't assume that others share that preference. It's appropriate to ask others how they identify themselves. Asking shows that we care about their preferences and want to respect them. This is the heart of person-centered communication.

Perceiving accurately is neither magic nor an ability that some people naturally possess. Instead, it is a communication skill that can be developed and practiced. Following the seven guidelines we have discussed will allow you to perceive more accurately.

CHAPTER SUMMARY

In this chapter, we've explored human perception, a process that involves selecting, organizing, and interpreting experiences. These three processes are not separate in practice; instead, each one affects the others. What we selectively notice affects what we interpret and evaluate. At the same time, our interpretations become a lens that influences what we notice in the world around us. Selection, interpretation, and evaluation interact continuously in the process of perception.

We have seen that perception is influenced by many factors. Our sensory capacities and our physiological condition affect what we notice and how astutely we recognize stimuli around us. In addition, our cultural backgrounds and standpoints in society shape how we see and interact with the world. Social roles, cognitive abilities, and who we are also influence perception. Thus, interpersonal perceptions reflect both what is inside of us and what is outside of us. The pervasiveness of digital and online communication, like f2f communication, both reflects and shapes our perceptions.

Understanding how perception works provides a foundation for improving our perceptual capacities. We discussed seven guidelines for improving the accuracy of perceptions:

1. Realize that all perceptions are subjective and partial, so there is no absolutely correct or best understanding of a situation or a person.
2. Because people perceive differently, we should avoid mind reading or assuming that we know what others perceive or what their actions mean.
3. It's a good idea to check perceptions, which involves stating how you perceive something and asking how another person does.
4. Distinguish facts from inferences.
5. Avoid the self-serving bias because it can lead us to perceive ourselves too charitably and to perceive others too harshly.
6. Guard against the fundamental attribution error, which can undermine the accuracy of our explanations of our own and others' communication.
7. Monitor the labels we use. This involves awareness that our labels reflect our perceptions of phenomena and sensitivity to the language others prefer, especially when we describe their identities. Just as we can't see how to solve the nine dots problem if we consider the dots a square, so we cannot see aspects of ourselves and others when our labels limit our perceptions. Figure 3.6 shows one solution to the nine-dot problem in Figure 3.1.

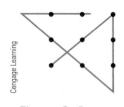

Figure **3.6**

One Solution to the Nine-Dot Problem

Key Concepts

Practice defining the chapter's terms by using online flashcards.

attribution 81
cognitive complexity 88
constructivism 77
culture 77
empathy 89
fundamental attribution
   error 83

implicit personality theory 90
inattention blindness 76
interpretation 81
mind reading 92
Müller-Lyer illusion 77
perception 75
personal construct 78

prototype 78
script 80
self-serving bias 82
standpoint 86
stereotype 79

Continuing the Conversation

Jason Harris © 2001 Wadsworth

When you've watched the video online, critique and analyze this encounter based on the principles you learned in this chapter. Then compare your work with the author's suggested responses. Online, even more videos will let you continue the conversation with your instructor.

Your friend Jim tells you about a problem he's having with his parents. According to Jim, his parents have unrealistic expectations of him. He tends to be an average student, but his parents are angry that his grades aren't better. When he went home last month, his father said this:

Jim's father: I'm not paying for you to go to school so you can party with your friends. You have a free ride, and you're still just pulling Cs. You just have to study harder.

Jim: I mean, I like to hang out with my friends, but that's got nothing to do with my grades. My dad's this brilliant guy, I mean, he just cruised through college, he thinks it's easy. I don't know how it was back then, but all my classes are hard. No matter how much studying I do I'm not gonna get all As. How do I convince them that I'm doing everything I can?

1. Both Jim and his parents make attributions to explain his grades. Describe the dimensions of Jim's attributions and those of his parents.
2. How might you assess the accuracy of Jim's attributions? What questions could you ask him to help you decide whether his perceptions are well founded or biased?
3. What constructs, prototypes, and scripts seem to operate in how Jim and his parents think about college life and being a student?
4. What could you say to Jim to help him and his parents reach a shared perspective on his academic work?

Everyday Skills

Build your communication skills further by completing the following activities here or online.

1. Be Aware of Your Schemata

   This chapter calls attention to how your perceptual processes affect your impressions of people.

Apply what you've learned to your everyday use of cognitive schemata. Pay attention to the cognitive schemata you use the next time you meet a new person. First, notice how you classify the person. Do you categorize her or him as a potential friend, date, coworker, or neighbor? Next, identify the constructs you use to assess the person. Do you focus on physical characteristics (attractive–not attractive), mental qualities (intelligent–not intelligent), psychological features (secure–not secure), or interpersonal qualities (friendly–not friendly)?

Next, ask whether you would rely on different constructs if you used a different prototype to classify the person. Now, note how you stereotype the person. What do you expect him or her to do based on the prototype and constructs you've applied? Finally, identify your script, or how you expect interaction to unfold between you.

2. Guard against the Fundamental Attribution Error

In each of the following scenarios, an internal attribution is made. Write out an alternative explanation based on external factors that might account for the other person's behavior.

a. The person you've been dating for a while is late to meet you. It is the third time this month you've had to wait, and you are angry that your date is so inconsiderate.

b. Your supervisor never makes time to talk with you. You are upset that he is excluding you from the network on the job.

c. You're talking with a friend about your anxiety about what you will do after you graduate. You notice that your friend seems uninterested and texts while you are talking. You think to yourself, "If you are so self-centered that you can't make time for me, I don't need you for a friend."

In each of the following scenarios, an external attribution is made for your actions. Write out an alternative explanation based on internal factors that could influence your behavior.

a. You are running late, so when a friend stops by to chat, you don't invite him in and don't encourage conversation. Your friend says, "You're being a real jerk." You think to yourself, "This has nothing to do with me. It has to do with the fact that I'm behind schedule for getting my project done."

b. During an argument with your roommate about who is going to do the grocery shopping, you get

really angry. Without thinking, you blurt out, "With all the weight you've gained, you should stop thinking about groceries." Your roommate looks hurt and leaves the room. Afterward, you think, "Well, I wouldn't have said that if she hadn't been so belligerent."

c. At work, your supervisor criticizes you for filling out forms carelessly. You dismiss the criticism because you think the supervisor requires too much senseless paperwork.

3. Cultural Values

How do values in Western culture affect your everyday perceptions and activities? See whether you can trace concrete implications of the five cultural values listed below.

Example: Competition—This value is evident in concrete practices such as competitive sports, grading policies, and attempts to have the last word in casual conversations.

Productivity

_____

Individualism

_____

Speed

_____

Youth

_____

Wealth

_____

Discuss with classmates the impact of cultural values on your day-to-day perceptions and activities.

4. Virtual Worldviews

To appreciate the distinct ways that social media represent issues and events, do these activities:

a. Select one current political issue (budget matters, international relations, voting rights, elections) or person (president, senator, candidate for office) that interests you.

b. Google the issue or person and visit the sites provided until you find at least one highly conservative and one highly liberal site. Identify differences in how the two sites represent the issue or person and what information and opinion relevant to the person or issue they present.

5. Monitor Mind Reading

Monitor your tendencies to mind read, especially in established relationships in which you feel you know the other person well. The next time you catch yourself mind reading, stop. Instead, tell the other person what you are noticing and invite her or him to explain how she or he perceives what's happening. First, find out whether the other person agrees with you about what you noticed. Whether or not the two of you agree, find out how the other person interprets and evaluates the issue.

Mind-Reading Example	Other's Perception	Other's Interpretation
_____	_____	_____
_____	_____	_____

6. Use Tentative Language

To become more sensitive to our tendencies to confuse facts and inferences, for the next 24 hours pay attention to the language you use to describe people and interactions. Listen for words such as _is_ and _are_ which imply factual information. Do you find instances in which tentative language would be more accurate?

Now, extend your observations to other people and the language they use. When you hear others say, "She is," "They are," or "He is," are they really making factual statements, or are they making inferences?

Engaging with Ideas

 MindTap™

Reflect and write about the ideas in this chapter by considering questions about personal, workplace, and ethical applications, here or online.

Personal Application Think about your interaction with social media. Do you let bright visual and noisy auditory stimuli control what you attend to? For instance, do you favor sites that have vivid images and colors?

Workplace Application Identify an example of the self-serving bias in a workplace. Describe how you engaged in self-serving bias to explain your own or a coworker's behavior, or how a coworker engaged in self-serving bias in explaining your or his/her behavior.

REFLECT ON...

Ethical Application Is it unethical to engage in the self-serving bias? Is doing so a kind of dishonesty, both with others and ourselves?

MindTap **DO...** Additional interactive discussions, online quizzes, and activities that your instructor may assign for a grade.

Thinking Critically

Think and write critically about the ideas in this chapter, here or online.

1. To understand how your social location influences your perceptions, visit a social group that is different from your own. If you are white, you might attend services at a black church or go to a public meeting of Native Americans on your campus. If you are Christian, you could go to a Jewish synagogue or a Buddhist temple. In the unfamiliar setting, what stands out to you? What verbal and nonverbal communications do you notice? Do they stand out because they are not present in your usual settings? What does your standpoint highlight and obscure?

2. Identify an example of the fundamental attribution error in your perceptions. Describe how you explained your own behavior and that of others. Then, revise your explanation in such a way that it no longer reflects the fundamental attribution error.

3. Conduct a survey to find out how students on your campus prefer to define their identities. Ask blacks whether they prefer *black*, *African American, Afro-American*, or another

REFLECT ON...

label. Ask whites how they identify their race. Ask Hispanic students what term they use to describe their ethnicity. Compare your findings to those of the U.S. Department of Labor discussed in the section "Monitor Labels." Do students on your campus reflect national preferences? Go beyond the findings discussed in this chapter to ask students from China, Japan, Korea, and other countries how they identify their ethnicities.

4. Use the ladder of abstraction to describe the relationships between perception, communication, and action in one interpersonal encounter in your life. First, describe the total situation as fully as you can (your descriptions won't be absolutely complete—that's impossible). Next, describe the behaviors and environmental cues you noticed. Then, identify the way you labeled what was happening and others who were present. Finally, describe how you acted in the situation. Now, consider alternative selective perceptions you might have made and how they might have influenced your labels and actions.

**THE WORLD
OF WORDS**

Topics Covered in this Chapter

The Symbolic Nature of Language

Principles of Verbal Communication

Symbolic Abilities

Speech Communities

Social Media and Verbal Communication

Guidelines for Improving Verbal Communication

After studying this chapter, you should be able to . . .

Recognize the ambiguity and abstractness of language in a particular interaction.

Identify key principles of verbal communication.

Apply chapter guidelines to identify examples of symbolic abilities in your own context.

Report on your own and others' expectations of gendered and other speech communities.

Become aware of specialized language used in social media.

Apply chapter guidelines to improve your verbal communication.

In 2004, the Viaduct de Millau opened in France and claimed the title of tallest bridge in the world. German newspapers noted that the viaduct "floated above the clouds" with "elegance and lightness." French newspapers described the viaduct as an "immense concrete giant" (Begley, 2009a). Both newspapers were praising the grand new structure, but they offer very different impressions. Perhaps the Germans saw the bridge in more feminine ways because the German word for bridge, *brücke*, is feminine. The French word for bridge, *pont*, is masculine, which may explain why French newspapers extolled the bridge's size and strength.

In this chapter, we build on Chapter 3's discussion of relationships between language and perception. Language or verbal communication shapes how we perceive the world (Gentner & Boroditsky, 2009). Language is also a primary means by which we present ourselves and build relationships with others. The chapter begins by defining symbols and symbolic abilities. We then discuss different speech communities to understand how distinct social groups use language. Third, we consider how symbolic abilities and speech communities are relevant to online and digital interaction. We close the chapter by discussing guidelines for effective use of verbal communication.

THE SYMBOLIC NATURE OF LANGUAGE

Words are **symbols**, which are arbitrary, ambiguous, abstract representations of other phenomena. For instance, your name is a symbol that represents you. The word *house* is a symbol that stands for a particular kind of building. *Love* is a symbol that represents certain intense feelings. All language is symbolic, but not all symbols are language. Art, music, and much nonverbal behavior are symbolic representations of feelings, thoughts, and experiences. To better understand symbols, we'll consider three characteristics of symbols: arbitrariness, ambiguity, and abstraction.

Symbols Are Arbitrary

Symbols are **arbitrary**, meaning that words are not intrinsically connected to what they represent. The word *book*, for example, has no necessary or natural connection to what you are reading now. Particular words, such as *book*, seem right because members of a particular society or social group agree to use them in particular ways, but they have no natural correspondence with their referents. All symbols are arbitrary because we could easily use other symbols as long as we all agreed that certain symbols would refer to certain things. The arbitrary nature of language becomes obvious—sometimes humorously so—when we discover that our words don't mean the same thing in another culture. The manufacturer of Dr. Pepper learned this lesson when marketing of the soft drink didn't work in the United Kingdom, where "I'm a pepper" means "I'm a prostitute" (Leaper, 1999).

Because language is arbitrary, the meanings of words can change over time. In the 1950s, *gay* meant "lighthearted" and "merry"; today it is generally understood to refer to people who prefer same-sex partners. Calling someone a *geek* or *nerd* used to be an insult, but today these terms often convey admiration of someone's technological expertise.

The arbitrary character of language allows us to invent new words. In the 1970s some people noticed that women were referred to as *Miss* or *Mrs.*, which indicate

LARRY, I'D LIKE YOU TO MEET SUSAN, MY…ERRR…MATE… UHHH…MY COMPANION…. YOU KNOW, MY PARTNER…ACTUALLY, MY CLOSEST FRIEND….ERRR, UH, MY LOVER…MY SOULMATE … MY SIGNIFICANT OTHER, IF YOU WILL…

OH, YOU'RE AN ITEM? GOING TOGETHER? A COUPLE? ROMANTICALLY INVOLVED? A MONOGAMOUS PAIR? DOMESTIC PARTNERS? IS THAT IT?

marital status, whereas men were referred to as *Mr.*, which does not connote marital status. The term *Ms.*, which can refer to a married or unmarried woman, was coined to correct this inequity. Some African Americans began using *disrespect*, which had been treated as a noun, as a verb to describe behaviors that demean someone. Now, the term *disrespect* and its abbreviated form, *dis*, are widely used. When cell phones became popular, we coined the term *land line* to refer to their predecessor.

The arbitrary quality of language also allows us to make up special words or to attach unconventional meanings to words. Most groups have some in-group terms that are understood only by its members. People who work together tend to share specialized vocabularies that aren't understood by outsiders. Families, too, often use terms that only family members understand. Paul Dickson, author of *Family Words* (2007), says that family nicknames are signs of intimacy. Dickson also reports that some families invent words that only they understand and that enhance feelings of closeness among family members (for example, *niblings* for nieces and nephews). Some of the words that families invent reflect special times or experiences. For instance, in his book, Dickson tells of a family that referred to historical markers on highways as *hysterical markers*, after the youngest child once mispronounced the word *historical*.

In the film *Mean Girls,* the ultra-popular group of girls nicknamed the Plastics used in-group terms such as "fetch" (cool) and "fugly."

Symbols Are Ambiguous

Symbols are **ambiguous** because what they mean isn't clear-cut. The term *affordable clothes* means different things to people who earn the minimum wage and to people who are affluent. A friend of mine learned that there are regional differences in the meanings of words while visiting me in North Carolina. At a restaurant, she ordered iced tea and nearly choked on her first sip. "Yuck—this is sweet!" she exclaimed. I explained that, in the South, tea has sugar dissolved in it, and you must specify "unsweetened tea" if you want tea without sugar.

In learning language, we learn not only words but also the meanings and values attributed to them by our society. In the United States, most children learn that *dogs* are four-footed creatures who are friends, members of the family, or are useful in guarding, herding, and so forth. In some other countries, children learn that dogs are four-footed creatures that, like other animals, are food for humans. Because symbols are ambiguous, there is no guarantee that people will agree on what words mean.

ETHAN

Last summer my manager told all of us we were supposed to be more personal with customers. It was part of branding our store as the "one that cares about you." We all tried to do that, but we had very different ideas about what it meant to "be more personal." I started asking each customer things like, "How is your day going? Did you find everything you wanted?" Another salesperson made it a point to make a personal comment like, "That's a beautiful sweater" or "Your son is so well behaved." Another salesperson began to share her own experiences with customers—like telling them about a problem she was having with her boyfriend and asking their advice. Still another person had this formal little speech that went something like, "It is my pleasure to help you because you are a guest in our store and I want you to be comfortable." After a few days, our manager called us in and spelled out what he meant by "be more personal"!

The ambiguity of language can lead to misunderstandings between friends and romantic partners. Martina tells her friend that he's not being attentive, meaning that she wants him to stop texting when she is talking with him. However, he interprets "more attentive" to mean she wants to get together more often to talk.

Ambiguity in language can also create confusion in the workplace. Telling your supervisor that you'd appreciate feedback on your job performance doesn't identify the kind of feedback you want or which aspects of your job performance you want your supervisor to assess. It would be more effective to say, "I would like you to give me your assessment of the thoroughness of my written reports."

Symbols Are Abstract

Finally, symbols are **abstract**, which means that they are not concrete or tangible. Words stand for ideas, people, events, objects, feelings, and so forth, but they are not the things they represent. In Chapter 3, we discussed the process of abstraction, whereby we move farther and farther away from concrete reality. As our symbols become increasingly abstract, the potential for confusion mushrooms. One way this happens is through overgeneralization. Couple counselor Aaron Beck (1988) reports that overly general language distorts how partners think about a relationship. They may make broad, negative statements, such as, "You are so negative." In most cases, such statements are overgeneralizations and hence not accurate. Yet, by symbolizing experience this way, partners frame how they think about it.

We can lessen the potential for misunderstanding by using less abstract language. It's clearer to say, "I wish you wouldn't interrupt when I'm talking" than to say, "Don't be so dominating." It's clearer to say, "On Fridays, men don't need to wear ties, and women don't need to wear heels" than to say, "Casual dress is okay on Fridays."

PRINCIPLES OF VERBAL COMMUNICATION

We've seen that language is arbitrary, ambiguous, and abstract. We're now ready to explore how language works. We'll discuss four principles of verbal communication.

Language and Culture Reflect Each Other

Communication reflects cultural history, values, and perspectives. It also creates or reproduces culture by naming and normalizing practices valued by the culture. Calendars name days that the culture considers important. Are Christmas, Thanksgiving, New Year's Day, and Passover recognized on your calendars? Are Kwanzaa, Saka, Elderly Day, and Ramadan on the calendars? Most Western calendars reflect the Judeo-Christian heritage of the mainstream culture.

To understand further how cultural values are woven into language, consider the cultural values that adages, or common sayings, express. What is meant by the American saying, "Every man for himself"? Does it reflect the idea that men, and not women, are the standard? Does it reflect individualism as a value? What is meant by "The early bird gets the worm"? Does it mean that initiative brings success?

Distinct values are expressed in adages from other cultures. What values are expressed in the Mexican proverb, "He who lives a hurried life will soon die"? How is this view of time different from dominant views of time in the United States? In Africa, two popular adages are "The child has no owner," and "It takes a whole village to raise a child," and in China a common saying is "No need to know the person, only the family" (Samovar & Porter, 2000). A Japanese adage states that "it is the nail that sticks out that gets hammered down" (Gudykunst & Lee, 2002). What values are expressed by these sayings? How are they different from mainstream Western values?

Many Asian languages include specific words to describe numerous particular relationships, such as "my paternal grandfather's sister," "my mother's uncle," or "my youngest son." These words reflect traditional Asian cultures' emphasis on family relationships (Ferrante, 2006). The English language has far fewer words to represent specific kinship bonds, which suggests that Western culture places less priority on ties beyond those in the immediate family.

Cultural differences in language use sometimes lead to difficulties in the workplace. In recent years, a growing number of Americans have traveled to China for employment opportunities. These Americans quickly discover that speaking their minds, as Americans are taught to do, is frowned upon in China. Further, the American tendency to use direct language is considered rude by the Chinese (Seligson, 2009).

Communication also changes cultures. A primary way in which communication changes cultural values and perspectives is by naming things in ways that alter understandings. For example, the term *date rape* was coined in the late 1980s. Although probably many women had been forced to have sex with their dates before that time, until the term was coined there was no way to describe such an occurrence as a violent and criminal act (Wood, 1992). Cultural understandings of other sexual activities have been similarly reformed by the coining of terms such as *sexual harassment* and *marital rape*, both of which characterize activities previously perceived as acceptable. As society has become more aware and accepting of gay and lesbian relationships, the terms *domestic partners* and *same-sex partners* have gained acceptance.

If I'd been in college 20 years ago, people would have just called me a freak or maybe a dyke. Now people—at least some people—accept the fact that I am trans. I don't think *trans* was even a word 20 years ago. I'm sure there were trans people back then, but it must have been hard not to have a way to say who you were.

VANESSA

Language is a primary tool that social movements use to change cultural life and meanings. In the 1960s, the civil rights movement in the United States relied on communication to transform public laws and, more gradually, public views of blacks. Powerful leaders, such as the Reverend Martin Luther King Jr. and Malcolm X, praised black Americans' heritage and identity. Language has also been influential in altering social views of persons with disabilities. Whereas *disabled person* was a commonly accepted phrase for many years, most people are now aware that this label can offend, and they know that the preferred phrase is *person with a disability* (Braithwaite, 1996). The environmental movement has made us aware of our "carbon footprint."

The Meanings of Language Are Subjective

Because symbols are abstract, ambiguous, and arbitrary, the meanings of words are never self-evident or absolute. Instead, we construct meanings in the process of interacting with others and through dialogues we carry on in our own heads. The process of constructing meaning is itself symbolic because we rely on words to think about what words and other things mean.

In an episode of *Modern Family,* Gloria interpreted the saying "dog eat dog world" literally and said, "That doesn't make any sense! Who wants to live in a world where dogs eat each other? Doggy-dog world is a beautiful world filled with little puppies!"

Words are layered with meanings. Although we're usually not conscious of the effort we invest to interpret words, we continuously engage in the process of constructing meanings. The word *home* evokes warm feelings in people who have loving, happy homes; the same word may prompt anxiety in people whose homes feature stress and violence.

Language Use Is Rule-Guided

Verbal communication is patterned by unspoken but broadly understood rules (Argyle & Henderson, 1985; Schiminoff, 1980). **Communication rules** are shared understandings of what communication means and what kinds of communication are appropriate in particular situations. For example, we understand that people take turns speaking, that flaming can get us kicked out of some chat rooms, and that we should speak softly in libraries. In the course of interacting with our families and others, we unconsciously absorb rules that guide how we communicate and how we interpret others' communication. According to Judi Miller (1993), children begin to understand and follow communication rules as early as 1 to 2 years of age.

Two kinds of rules govern communication (Cronen, Pearce, & Snavely, 1979; Pearce, Cronen, & Conklin, 1979). **Regulative rules** specify when, where, and with whom to talk about certain things. For instance, some families have a rule that people cannot argue at the dinner table. Families also teach us rules about when we can engage in conflict—for example, were you allowed to disagree with parents or elders, in general? Regulative rules vary across cultures and social groups, so what is acceptable in one context may be regarded as inappropriate elsewhere.

YUMIKO I try to teach my children to follow the customs of my native Japan, but they are learning to be American. I scold my daughter, who is 7 this year, for talking loudly and speaking when she has not been addressed, but she tells me all the other kids talk loudly and talk when they wish to talk. I tell her it is not polite to look directly at others, but she says everyone looks at others here. She communicates as an American, not a Japanese.

Constitutive rules specify how to interpret and perform different kinds of communication. We learn what counts as respect (listening, eye contact), friendliness (smiles or smiley emoticons in online communication), affection (kisses, hugs), and professionalism (punctuality, assertive communication). We also learn what communication is expected if we want to be perceived as a good friend (showing support, being loyal), a responsible employee (meeting deadlines, making confident oral presentations), and a desirable romantic partner (showing respect and trust, being faithful, sharing confidences). Like regulative rules, constitutive rules are shaped by cultures and social groups.

In high school my best friend was Chad. He was a better guitar player than I was, but he would frequently play rhythm with me so I would have a chance to shine. That was a way he showed he cared about me because he wouldn't play rhythm with other guys. He also didn't drink or smoke in my house, which was a way he showed he respected me and my family's house rules.

Everyday Skills To understand more about the regulative and constitutive rules that you follow in your communication, complete the activity "Communication Rules" at the end of the chapter or online.

We don't have to be aware of communication rules to follow them. For the most part, we're not conscious of the rules that guide how, when, where, and with whom we communicate about various things. We may not realize we have rules until one is broken, and we become aware that we had an expectation. A study by Victoria DeFrancisco (1991) revealed a clear pattern between spouses, in which husbands interrupted wives and were unresponsive to topics wives initiated. Both husbands and wives were unaware of the rules, but their communication nonetheless sustained the pattern. Becoming aware of communication rules empowers you to change those that don't promote good interaction.

My boyfriend and I had this really frustrating pattern about planning what to do. He'd say, "What do you want to do this weekend?" And I'd say, "I don't know. What do you want to do?" Then, he'd suggest two or three things and ask me which of them sounded good. I would say they were all fine with me, even if they weren't. And this would keep on forever. Both of us had a rule not to impose on the other, and it kept us from stating our preferences, so we just went in circles about any decision. Well, two weekends ago, I talked to him about rules, and he agreed we had one that was frustrating. So we invented a new rule that says each of us has to state what we want to do, but the other has to say if that is not okay. It's a lot less frustrating to figure out what we want to do since we agreed on this rule.

Punctuation Shapes Meaning

In writing, we use commas, periods, and semicolons to define where ideas stop and start and where pauses are needed. Similarly, in interpersonal communication, **punctuation** defines beginnings and endings of interaction episodes (Watzlawick, Beavin, & Jackson, 1967). To punctuate communication, we define when interaction begins and who starts it. When we don't agree on punctuation, misunderstandings may arise. If you've ever heard children arguing about who started a fight, you understand the importance of punctuation.

A common instance of conflicting punctuation is the demand–withdraw pattern (Bergner & Bergner, 1990; Caughlin & Vangelisti, 2000; Christensen & Heavey, 1990; Wegner, 2005). In this pattern, one person tries to create closeness with personal talk, and the other strives to maintain autonomy by avoiding intimate discussion (Figure 4.1).

Figure 4.1

The Demand–Withdraw Pattern

Cengage Learning

The more the first person pushes for personal talk ("Tell me what's going on in your life"), the further the second withdraws ("There's nothing to tell"). Each partner punctuates interaction as starting with the other's behavior. Thus, the demander thinks, "I pursue because you withdraw," and the withdrawer thinks, "I withdraw because you pursue." The demand–withdraw pattern also surfaces in parent–child interactions (Caughlin & Ramey, 2005). A parent tells a 17-year-old she should dress more modestly (the demand). The child responds by wearing a revealing top (withdrawal from parental control). Seeing the top, the parent tells the child that she cannot wear that top to school (intensified demand). The child responds by changing the top for one that is even more revealing, and then storming out the door (intensified withdrawal from parental control).

There is no objectively correct punctuation. Punctuation depends on subjective perceptions. When communicators don't agree on punctuation, they don't share meanings for what is happening between them. To break out of unconstructive cycles such as demand-withdraw, communicators need to realize that they may punctuate differently and should discuss how each of them experiences the pattern. It's also helpful to realize that because the cycle depends on each person's communication, either person can stop it by altering what she or he says.

HAL Punctuation helps me understand what happens with me and my girlfriend a lot of times. Sometimes, when we first get together, she's all steamed, and I can't figure out why. I'm like, what's going on? How can you be mad at me when we haven't even started talking? But she's steamed about something that happened the night before or even longer ago. For me, whatever argument we might have had is over—it ended when we separated the last time. But for her, it may not be over—we're still in that episode.

The meaning of verbal communication arises out of cultural teachings, subjective interpretations, communication rules, and punctuation. These four principles highlight the creativity involved in constructing meaning. We're now ready to probe how verbal communication affects us and our relationships.

SYMBOLIC ABILITIES

Our ability to use symbols allows us to live in a world of ideas and meanings. Instead of just reacting to our concrete environments, we think about them and sometimes transform them. Philosophers of language have identified five ways that symbolic abilities affect our lives (Cassirer, 1944; Langer, 1953, 1979). As we discuss each one, think about how it affects your life and relationships.

Language Defines Phenomena

The most basic symbolic ability is definition. We use symbols to define experiences, people, relationships, feelings, and thoughts (Pinker, 2008). As we saw in Chapter 3, the definitions we impose shape what things mean to us. Years ago, a linguist named Benjamin Whorf and an anthropologist named Edwin Sapir (Whorf, 1956) advanced the theory of **linguistic determinism**, which states that language determines what we can perceive and think (Hoijer, 1994). According to this theory, we cannot perceive or think about things for which we don't have names.

Over time, however, linguistic determinism has been discredited. Numerous examples show that members of a culture can perceive phenomena that have no specific names. For example, Geoff Nunberg (2003) notes that although Arabic does not have a single word for *compromise*, the language has many phrases that capture the idea of compromise. According to legend, when members of the Piegan Blackfoot, a Native American tribe, first saw a horse, they called it *elk-dog* because it was large and shaped somewhat like an elk and could carry a pack as their dogs did. They drew from familiar vocabulary to name an unfamiliar species.

DIVERSITY

Everything Has a Name!

Imagine being 27 years old and not having language. What would your world be like? Ildefonso called his 27 years without language the dark time in his life. He says that he couldn't understand the concept of time or how it passes. He had no concept of a birthday. He got to work on time by memorizing how the face of the clock looked when he was supposed to leave, but he did not comprehend the meaning of the minute and hour hands on the clock. He didn't even have a way to conceive of deafness and hearing (Words, 2013).

Twenty-four-year-old Susan Schaller (1991) was teaching reading to deaf students at a community college. She noticed that a man older than most of her students stood at the back of the classroom every day. When she approached him, she realized he was deaf and didn't know sign language. Schaller worked with Ildefonso for days without any progress. Finally, one day she was spelling *cat* in sign, and Ildefonso grasped that what she was doing with her hands (spelling *c-a-t*) meant a furry animal with whiskers. Ildefonso broke down crying. "Everything has a name!" is what he realized in that moment, and names, words, gave him access to the world.

Although linguistic determinism is no longer accepted by most scholars, there is acceptance of the less extreme claim that language reflects and shapes perception and thought. This notion helps us understand why some words and phrases can't be translated into other languages. The language of the Muskogee–Creek tribe includes a word that designates the unique kind of love between parents and children (Seay, 2004), and the Pacific Islanders' language, which is now disappearing, includes names for many species of fish that are unnamed in the languages of cultures less dependent on fish for survival (Nettle & Romaine, 2000).

Language Shapes Perceptions   When we label someone, we focus attention on particular aspects of that person and her or his activities, and we neglect or overlook other aspects of the person. We might define a person as an environmentalist, a teacher, a gourmet cook, our boss, or a father. Each definition directs our attention to certain aspects of the person. We might talk with the environmentalist about wilderness legislation, discuss class assignments with the teacher, swap recipes with the chef, restrict ourselves to work topics with the boss, and exchange stories about children with the father. We tend to perceive and interact with people according to how we define them.

Language Can Totalize   Totalizing occurs when we respond to a person as if one label (one we have chosen or accepted from others) totally represents who he or she is. We fix on one symbol to define someone and fail to recognize many other aspects of that person. Some people totalize gay men and lesbians as if sexual orientation were the only facet of their identities. Yet we don't totalize heterosexuals on the basis of their sexuality. Totalizing is not the same as stereotyping. When we stereotype someone, we define him or her in terms of characteristics of a group. When we totalize others, we negate most of who they are by focusing on a single aspect of their identity.

JAMAL

I know all about totalizing. A lot of people relate to me as black, like that's all I am. Sometimes in classes, teachers ask me to explain the "African American perspective" on something, but they don't ask me to explain my perspective as a premed major or a working student. I am an African American, but that's not all I am.

Language Shapes and Reflects Relationships   The symbols we use to define experiences in our relationships affect how we think and feel about those relationships. My colleagues and I asked romantic couples how they defined differences between themselves (Wood, Dendy, Dordek, Germany, & Varallo, 1994). We found that some people defined differences as positive forces that energize a relationship and keep it interesting. Others defined differences as problems or barriers to closeness. There was a direct connection between how partners defined differences and how they dealt with them. Partners who viewed differences as constructive approached them with curiosity, interest, and a hope for growth through discussion. Conversely, partners who labeled differences as problems tended to deny differences and to avoid talking about them.

The language we use to think about relationships affects what happens in them. Couples in satisfying relationships rely more on "we" language when discussing problems, whereas partners in distressed relationships rely more on "I" pronouns (Williams-Baucom, Atkins, Sevier, Eldridge, & Christensen, 2010). People who consistently use negative labels to describe their relationships heighten awareness of what they don't like (Cloven & Roloff, 1991). It's also been shown that partners who focus on good facets of their relationships are more conscious of virtues in partners and relationships and less bothered by imperfections (Bradbury & Fincham, 1990; Duck & Wood, 2006; Fletcher & Fincham, 1991; Seligman, 2002). This suggests that we might want to be mindful of the language we use when talking or thinking about our relationships.

Language Evaluates

Language isn't neutral or objective. It is laden with values. This is an intrinsic quality of language. It's difficult, if not impossible, to find words that are completely neutral or objective. Thus, the particular words that we use shape our perceptions and those of others.

KAREEM

My brother was killed in the Iraq war. The worst part is that he wasn't killed in battle, but by American troops who shot him by mistake. We were told he died as a result of "friendly fire." Friendly? What a horrible term for murder.

Language Reflects and Shapes Perceptions   We tend to describe people we like with language that accents their good qualities and downplays their flaws. The reverse is true of our descriptions of people we don't like. Restaurants use positive words to heighten the attractiveness of menu entrees. A dish described as "tender London broil gently sautéed in natural juices and topped with succulent mushrooms" sounds more appetizing than one described as "cow cooked in blood and topped with fungus."

Perhaps you've seen humorous illustrations of how we describe the same behaviors enacted by ourselves, by people we like, and by people we don't like. I am casual; you are messy; she's a slob. I am organized; you are methodical; he is obsessive–compulsive. I am assertive; you are aggressive; she's a bully. These examples reflect our tendency to use language that reflects our values and views.

In recent years, we have become more sensitive to different groups' preferences for names. The term *African American* emphasizes cultural heritage, whereas *black* focuses on skin color. People with roots in Spanish-speaking Caribbean countries usually refer to themselves as Latinas and Latinos, whereas people with roots in Mexico and Central and South America generally define themselves as Hispanic (Glascock, 1998).

Language Can Be Loaded   **Loaded language** refers to words that strongly slant perceptions and thus meanings. Terms such as *geezer* and *old fogey* incline us to regard older people with contempt or pity. Alternatives such as *senior citizen* and *older person* reflect more respectful attitudes.

MAYNARD

I'm as sensitive as the next guy, but I just can't keep up with what language offends what people anymore. When I was younger, *Negro* was an accepted term, then it was *black*, and now it's *African American*. Sometimes I forget and say *black* or even *Negro*, and I get accused of being racist. It used to be polite to call females *girls*, but now that offends a lot of the women I work with. Just this year, I heard that we aren't supposed to say *blind* or *disabled* anymore; we're supposed to say *visually impaired* and *differently abled*. I just can't keep up.

Many of us probably sympathize with Maynard, who was 54 years old when he took a course with me. It is hard to keep up with changes in language, and it's inevitable that we will occasionally irritate or offend someone unintentionally. Nonetheless, we should try to learn what terms hurt or offend others and avoid using them. It's also advisable for us to tell others when they've referred to us with a term that we don't prefer. As long as we speak assertively but not confrontationally, it's likely that others will respect our preferences for terminology that refers to us.

Language Can Degrade Others   Language can be used to degrade and dehumanize others. Children often taunt each other by name-calling. Beyond childhood, degrading language continues. One form of degrading language is **hate speech**, which is language that radically dehumanizes members of particular groups. A number of years ago, Brown University student Dennis Hann made national news because of the way he chose to celebrate turning 21. After drinking heavily, Hann went to a central quad on campus and spewed out curse words and epithets, including *niggers* and *faggots*. Hann was promptly and permanently expelled from Brown.

Unfortunately, Hann's actions were not an isolated incident. Around the nation, hate speech erupts both on and off campus. Malicious and abusive messages are scrawled on the cars and homes of minority citizens. Graffiti in bathrooms and on public buildings disparages gays, lesbians, and other groups. People post vicious gossip and hateful messages online (Lewin, 2010b), and numerous Internet hate groups target children as well as adults (Waltman, 2003).

Language is powerful. It shapes our perceptions and those of others. This implies that each of us has an ethical responsibility to recognize the impact of language, and to guard against engaging in uncivil speech ourselves as well as refusing to tolerate it from others.

Language Organizes Perceptions

We use symbols to organize our perceptions. As we saw in Chapter 3, we rely on cognitive schemata to classify and evaluate experiences. How we organize experiences affects what they mean to us. For example, your prototype of a friend affects how you judge particular friends. When we place someone in the category *friend*, the category influences how we interpret the person and his or her communication. An insult is likely to be viewed as teasing if made by a friend but a call to battle if made by an enemy. The words don't change, but their meaning varies depending on how we organize our perceptions of words and those who speak them.

Language Allows Abstract Thought   The organizational quality of language also allows us to think about abstract concepts, such as justice, integrity, and healthy family life. We use broad concepts to transcend specific, concrete activities and to enter the world of conceptual thought and ideals. Because we think abstractly, we don't have to consider every specific phenomenon individually. Instead, we can think in broad terms.

Language Can Stereotype   Our capacity to abstract can also distort thinking. A primary way this occurs is through stereotyping, which is thinking in broad generalizations about a whole class of people or experiences. Examples of stereotypes are "sorority women are preppy," "teachers are smart," "jocks are dumb," "feminists hate men," and "religious people are kind." Notice that stereotypes can be positive or negative. Each of these is a broad generalization that may apply to some or even most members of the group. Yet each of these stereotypes is not true of some members of the group, and each focuses on only one facet of identity instead of many.

Common to all stereotypes is classifying an experience or person based on general perceptions of some category. When we use group terms such as *athletes*, *African Americans*, *lesbians*, *men*, and *blue-collar workers*, we may see what members of each group have in common and may not perceive differences between individuals.

Stereotyping is related to totalizing because, when we stereotype someone, we may not perceive other aspects of the person, aspects not represented in the stereotype. For example, if we stereotype someone as a fraternity man, we may see only what he has in common with other members of fraternities. We may not notice his political stands, individual values, commitment to family, and so forth.

Clearly, we have to generalize. We simply cannot think about everything in our lives as a unique phenomenon. However, stereotypes can blind us to important differences between phenomena we lump together. Thus, it's important to reflect on stereotypes and to stay alert to differences between phenomena we place in any category. We should also remind ourselves that we place others in categories; the categories are our tools. They are not objective descriptions.

Language Allows Hypothetical Thought

Where do you hope to be 5 years from now? What is your fondest memory from childhood? Do you think your friend will text you in the next half hour? To answer these questions, you must think hypothetically, which means thinking about experiences and ideas that are not part of your concrete, present situation. Because we can think hypothetically, we can plan, dream, remember, set goals, consider alternative courses of action, and imagine possibilities.

We Can Think Beyond Immediate, Concrete Situations   Hypothetical thought is possible because we use symbols. When we symbolize, we name ideas so that we can hold them in our minds and reflect on them. We can contemplate things that currently have no real existence, and we can remember ourselves in the past and project ourselves into the future. Our ability to imagine possibilities that do not exist in the moment explains why we can set goals and work toward them. For example, you've invested many hours studying and writing papers because you imagine yourself as someone with a college degree. The degree is not real now, nor is the self that you will become once you have the degree. Yet the idea is sufficiently real to motivate you to work hard for many years.

We Live in Three Dimensions of Time   Hypothetical thought also allows us to live in more than just the present moment. We infuse our present lives with knowledge of our histories and plans for our futures. Both past and future affect our experience in the present. In the context of work, we often remember past interactions with a colleague and anticipate future ones, and both of these affect how we communicate in the present.

Close relationships rely on ideas of past and future. One of the strongest "glues" for intimacy is a history of shared experiences (Bellah, Madsen, Sullivan, Swindler, & Tipton, 1985; Bruess & Hoefs, 2006; Wood, 2006a). Just knowing that they have weathered rough times in the past helps partners get through trials in the present. Belief in a future also sustains intimacy. With people we don't expect to see again, we interact differently from the way we interact with people who are continuing parts of our lives. Talking about the future also knits intimates together because it makes real the idea that more shared time lies ahead (Acitelli, 1993; Wood, 2006a).

RACHAEL During the first week of my freshman year, I went to a mixer and got smashed. I'd never drunk in high school, so I didn't know what alcohol could do to me. I was a mess—throwing up, passing out. The next morning, I hated myself for how I'd been. But in the long run, I think it was good that it happened. Whenever I feel like having more to drink than I should, I just remember what I was like that night and how much I hated myself that way, and that stops me from having anything more to drink.

We Can Foster Personal Growth   Thinking hypothetically helps us grow personally. In Chapter 2, we noted that we need to accept ourselves as in process as a foundation for moving forward. This requires you to remember who you were at an earlier time, to appreciate progress you've made, and to keep an ideal image of the person you want to become to fuel continued self-improvement.

DUK-KYONG Sometimes, I get very discouraged that I do not yet know English perfectly and that there is much I still do not understand about customs in this country. It helps me to remember that, when I came here 2 years ago, I did not speak English at all, and I knew nothing about how people act here. Seeing how much progress I have made helps me not to be discouraged with what I do not know yet.

Communication in Everyday Life

WORKPLACE

Police Have New Tool for Detecting Lies

Lie detector tests base judgments of honesty on vocal pitch and rhythm, which the test assumes differ when people lie and when they tell the truth. But lie detector tests have not proven particularly reliable. Now law enforcement has a new tool for detecting deception: the detail in stories told by people being interrogated. New research indicates that when people lie, they develop a tight, bare-bones script and stick with it (Coldwell, Hiscock-Anisman, Memon, Colwell, Taylor, & Woods, 2009). They do not include details and comments on context because that just adds to what they have to remember. In contrast, when we tell a truthful story, we include 20% to 30% more detail (Carey, 2009). People who are giving honest accounts do not have a script. They also tend to recall details about context—what was happening at the time of the event, who was present—that are extraneous to the main story. The researchers explain that "if you're telling the truth, this mental reinstatement of contexts triggers more and more external details" (Carey, p. D4). In the summer of 2009 the researchers began training techniques for conducting and judging interrogations to San Diego Police.

> **MindTap** Test the research cited above by asking friends to give you a true description of something and a false one. Describe how detailed stories are when they are truthful and when they are not.

Language Allows Self-Reflection

Just as we use language to reflect on what goes on outside of us, we also use it to reflect on ourselves. According to Mead (1934), there are two aspects to the self. First, there is the *I*, which is the spontaneous, creative self. The *I* acts impulsively in response to inner needs and desires, regardless of social norms. The *Me* is the socially conscious part of the self that monitors and moderates the *I*'s impulses. The *Me* reflects on the *I* from the social perspectives of others. The *I* is impervious to social conventions and expectations, but the *Me* is keenly aware of them. In an argument, your *I* may want to hurl a biting insult at someone you don't like, but your *Me* censors that impulse and reminds you that it's impolite to put others down.

The *Me* reflects on the *I* by analyzing the *I*'s actions. This means we can think about who we want to be and set goals for becoming the self we desire. The *Me* can feel shame, pride, and regret for the *I*'s actions, an emotion that is possible because we self-reflect. We can control what we do in the present by casting ourselves forward in time to consider how we might later feel about our actions. Elyse makes this point in her commentary.

ELYSE

I volunteer at the homeless shelter. Sometimes, when I'm talking to the people who come there for food or to sleep, I feel like shaking them and telling them to get their lives in order. I get so frustrated with the ones who don't seem to make any effort to change their situations. But I know that everybody puts them down all the time—the last thing they need is to hear more of that from a college kid who never experienced real hardships. So I keep my frustration to myself. I guess that's the Me part of me controlling my I.

We Can Monitor Our Communication   Self-reflection also empowers us to monitor ourselves, a skill we discussed in Chapter 1. For instance, during a discussion with a friend, you might say to yourself, "Gee, I've been talking nonstop about me and my worries, and I haven't even asked how she's doing." Based on your monitoring, you might inquire about your friend's life. When interacting with people from different cultures, we monitor by reminding ourselves that they may have different values and communication rules from ours. Self-reflection allows us to monitor our communication and adjust it to be effective.

We Can Manage Our Image   As we noted in Chapter 2, we want to present a particular face in our interpersonal encounters (Ting-Toomey, 2009). Because we reflect on ourselves from others' perspectives, we are able to adapt our communication so that we appear positively in their eyes. When interviewing for a job, you may work to appear especially confident and hardworking. When talking with someone you'd like to get to know, you may be more attentive than you are in other circumstances. We continuously adjust our communication to fit particular situations and people.

We use symbols to define, classify, and evaluate experiences; to think hypothetically; and to self-reflect. Each of these abilities helps us create meaning in our personal and interpersonal lives. Each of them also carries with it ethical responsibilities for how we use communication and the impact it has on ourselves and others.

SPEECH COMMUNITIES

Although all humans use language, we don't all use it in the same way. As we have noted, we learn what particular words and language rituals mean in the process of interacting with particular others and the generalized other. It's not surprising that people from different social groups learn distinct ways of using language and interpreting others' language.

A **speech community** exists when people share norms about how to use talk and what purposes it serves (Labov, 1972). From Chapter 3, recall our discussion of social locations. Speech communities arise out of social locations—that is, people who share a social location tend to develop shared understandings of communication. Members of speech communities share perspectives on communication that outsiders do not have. This is one reason why misunderstandings often arise between members of different social groups.

Speech communities are defined not by countries or geographic locations but by shared understandings of how to communicate. In Western society, there are numerous speech communities. For example, African American scholars report that African Americans generally communicate more assertively (Hamlet, 2004; Johnson, 2000; Orbe & Harris, 2001; Ribeau, Baldwin, & Hecht, 1994) and place greater emphasis on verbal wit (Kelley, 1997) than most European Americans. Traditional Korean, Japanese, and some other South Asian cultures emphasize communication more as a means of building community than as a means of asserting individual selves (Diggs, 1998, 2001).

Gendered Speech Communities

Of the many speech communities that exist, gender has received particularly extensive study. Because we know more about it than about other speech communities, we'll explore gender as a specific speech community and the misunderstandings that surface between members of different speech communities. Researchers have investigated both the way in which women and men are socialized into some different understandings of how communication functions and the way their communication differs in practice.

Socialization into Gendered Speech Communities One of the earliest studies showed that children's games are a primary agent of gender socialization (Maltz & Borker, 1982). Since that landmark study, many other researchers have studied gender socialization in children's playgroups (Clark, 1998; Leaper, 1994, 1996; Martin et al., 2000; McGuffey & Rich, 2004). They report that much of children's play is sex segregated, and there are notable differences between the games the sexes tend to play. These differences seem to teach boys and girls some distinct rules for using communication and interpreting the communication of others.

Games that are traditionally favored by girls, such as playing house and school, involve few players, include talk to negotiate how to play (because there aren't clear-cut guidelines), and depend on cooperation and sensitivity between players. Baseball and war, which are typical boys' games, involve more players and have clear goals and rules, so less talk is needed to play. Most boys' games are highly competitive, both between teams and for individual status within teams. Interaction in games teaches boys and girls distinct understandings of why, when, and how to use talk.

Gendered Communication in Practice Research on women's and men's communication reveals that the communication rules learned in childhood play are carried forward into our adult interactions. For instance, women's talk generally is more expressive and focused on feelings and personal issues, whereas men's talk tends to be more instrumental and competitive (Johnson, 1989; Martin et al., 2000; Mulac, 2006; Wood, 1994b, 1994c, 1998).

Another general difference between the sexes involves what members of each sex tend to perceive as the primary foundation of close relationships. For most men, activities tend to be the primary foundation of close friendships and romantic relationships (Inman, 1996; Metts, 2006a, 2006b; Swain, 1989; Wood & Inman, 1993). Thus, men typically cement friendships by doing things together and for one another. For many women, communication is a primary foundation of intimacy (Becker, 1987; Braithwaite & Kellas, 2006; Metts, 2006a, 2006b; Riessman, 1990; Taylor, 2002).

It is important to realize that these general differences between men and women are matters of degree. They are not absolute dichotomies (MacNeil & Byers, 2005). Men sometimes use talk expressively, and women sometimes use talk instrumentally. Also, keep in mind that not all women follow rules of feminine communication communities, and not all men follow rules of masculine ones.

Misunderstandings between Gendered Speech Communities
Socialization in different gender communities accounts for some common misunderstandings between women and men. One such misunderstanding occurs when women and men discuss problems. Often, when a woman tells a man about something that is troubling her, he offers advice or a solution (Duck, 2006; Tannen, 1990; Wood, 1994c, 1996, 1998). His view of communication as primarily instrumental leads him to show support by doing something. Because feminine communities see communication as a way to build connections with others, however, women often want empathy and discussion of feelings to take place before turning to practical matters such as advice about solving a problem (Guerrero, Jones, & Boburka, 2006). Thus, women sometimes feel that men's practical responses to their concerns are uncaring and insensitive. On the other hand, men may feel frustrated when women offer empathy and support instead of advice for solving problems.

Another conundrum in interaction between men and women concerns different styles of listening. Socialized to be responsive and expressive, women tend to make listening noises such as "um hm," "yeah," and "I know what you mean" when others are talking (Tannen, 1990; Wood, 1996, 1998).

MindTap

EVERYDAY SKILLS To increase your awareness of the impact of socialization on verbal communication in gendered speech communities, complete the activity "Breaking the Rules of Gendered Communication" at the end of the chapter or online.

Blend Images/SuperStock

This is how they show that they are attentive and interested. Yet masculine communities don't emphasize using communication responsively, so men tend to make fewer listening noises when someone else is talking (Guerrero et al., 2006). Thus, women sometimes feel that men aren't listening to them because men don't symbolize their attention in the ways women have learned and expect. Notice that this does not mean that men don't listen well. Rather, the ways in which many men listen aren't perceived as listening by some women because women and men tend to have different regulative and constitutive rules for listening.

A common misunderstanding occurs when a woman says, "Let's talk about us." To many men, this often means trouble because they interpret the request as implying that there is a problem in the relationship. For women, however, this is not the only—or even the main—reason to talk about a relationship. Feminine speech communities regard talking as the primary way to create relationships and build closeness (Riessman, 1990). In general, women view talking about a relationship as a way to celebrate and increase intimacy. Socialized to use communication instrumentally, however, men may tend to think that talking about a relationship is useful only if there is some problem to be resolved (Acitelli, 1988, 1993). For many men, the preferred mode of enhancing closeness is to do things together. Suzie's commentary illustrates this gender difference.

SUZIE

My boyfriend and I have dated for 3 years, and we're pretty serious, so I wanted our anniversary to be really special. I suggested going out for a romantic dinner where we could talk about the relationship. Andy said that sounded dull, and he wanted to go to a concert where there would be zillions of people. At the time, I thought that meant he didn't care about us like I do, but maybe he feels close when we do things together instead of when we just are together.

Gender is just one example of many speech communities. Communication patterns vary among people from different social groups, even if they live in the same society (Johnson, 2000). Online communities also have particular communication patterns, which new members must learn if they are to participate effectively. Recognizing and respecting different speech communities increases our ability to participate competently in a diverse culture.

Social Media and Verbal Communication

How does what we have learned about verbal communication apply to online and digital interaction? One of the most obvious ways is our coining new words to describe experiences and modes of communication that are unique to social media. Some of the words we invented are variations on words and phrases that already existed: *buddy list, instant message, netiquette, cyberbullying, chat room.* Other words are wholly new, invented to describe what happens in cyberspace. For instance, *blog* (which was originally *web log*) refers to online journals. *Tweeting* refers to very short messages. Fifteen years ago, none of these words existed or were used in the ways they are now. What words can you add to the above examples of ones we have coined to reference interaction on social media?

A second way in which this chapter applies to digital and online communication is the rules that we discussed. What regulative rules have evolved to govern when, where, and with whom it is appropriate to communicate online and digitally? Are there people you do not text, but instead call or email? Are there people you do not email but always text? Are some disclosures not appropriate on Facebook?

Now think about constitutive rules that are generally followed for online and digital communication. What counts as rudeness in texting? What counts as supportive in Facebook comments? What counts as attentiveness online? How do you communicate friendliness or disinterest online?

GUIDELINES FOR IMPROVING VERBAL COMMUNICATION

Building on what we've learned about language, we will now consider guidelines for improving effectiveness in verbal communication.

Engage in Dual Perspective

A critical guideline for effective verbal communication is to engage in dual perspective. This involves being person-centered so that you recognize another's perspective and take it into account as you communicate. Effective interpersonal

 MindTap

Everyday Skills To increase your awareness of the specialized language used in social media, complete the activity "Translation Guide" at the end of the chapter or online.

communication is not a solo performance but a relationship between people. Awareness of others and their viewpoints should be reflected in how we speak. For instance, it's advisable to refrain from using a lot of idioms when talking with someone for whom English is a second language. Craig Naylor, CEO of a Japanese company, recounts an amusing example of confusion caused by idioms: "When I first came to Japan, I tried the idioms and spent 15 minutes explaining why this idea doesn't have a snowball's chance in hell" (Sanchanta, 2010, p. B6). Similarly, instead of giving advice when a woman tells him about a problem, a man who uses dual perspective might realize that empathy and supportive listening are likely to be more appreciated. The point is that competent communicators respect and adapt to the perspectives of those with whom they interact.

LUKE

For a long time, I've thought the guy in the apartment next to mine is totally weird. I've never been near a shotgun and don't approve of sports hunting, but he loves to hunt and that's always bothered me. For this assignment, I tried to understand where he's coming from so I asked him why he liked hunting so much. He told me that he learned to hunt with his dad. Hunting days were the only times he and his dad really talked, and his dad was really proud of him when he shot his first buck. He also told me that he's closest with the guys he hunts with. I still don't want to hunt, but now I get why it matters to him. It's not about killing animals, but about important time with his dad and other guys.

We don't need to abandon our own perspectives to accommodate those of others. In fact, it would be as unhealthy to stifle your own point of view as to ignore those of others. Dual perspective, as the term implies, consists of two perspectives. It requires honoring both our own point of view and another's. Most of us can accept and grow from differences, but we seldom feel affirmed if we are unheard or disregarded.

Own Your Feelings and Thoughts

We often use language in ways that obscure our responsibility for how we feel and what we think. For instance, we say, "You made me mad" or "You hurt me," as if what we feel had been caused by someone else. On a more subtle level, we sometimes blame others for our responses to what they say. "You're so demanding" really means that you are irritated by what someone else wants or expects. The irritation is *your* feeling.

Although how we interpret what others say may lead us to feel certain ways, others do not directly cause our responses. In certain contexts, others may powerfully influence our thoughts and feelings. Yet, even in extreme situations, we need to remember that we, not others, are responsible for our feelings. Telling others they make you feel some way denies your responsibility for your own feelings and is likely to arouse defensiveness, which doesn't facilitate healthy interpersonal relationships.

Effective communicators take responsibility for themselves by using language that owns their thoughts and feelings. They claim their feelings and do not blame

Table 4.1 *You* Language and *I* Language

YOU LANGUAGE	I LANGUAGE
"You make me nervous on the job."	"When you watch me work, I feel nervous."
"You hurt me."	"I feel hurt when you ignore what I say."
"You make me feel small."	"I feel small when you tell me that I'm selfish."
"You're so domineering."	"When you shout, I feel dominated."
"You humiliated me."	"I felt humiliated when you mentioned my problems in front of our friends."

others for what happens in themselves. To take responsibility for your own feelings, rely on *I* **language** rather than **you language**. *I* language owns thoughts and feelings and does not blame them on others. Table 4.1 gives examples of the difference.

There are two differences between *I* language and *you* language. First, *I* language accepts personal responsibility, whereas *you* language projects it onto another person. Second, *I* language is more descriptive than *you* language. *You* language tends to be accusatory and abstract. This is one of the reasons it's ineffective in promoting change. *I* language, on the other hand, provides concrete descriptions of behaviors we dislike without directly blaming the other person for how we feel.

Some people feel awkward when they first start using *I* language. This is natural because most of us have learned to rely on *you* language. With commitment and practice, however, you can learn to communicate with *I* language.

Once you feel comfortable using *I* language, you will find that it has many advantages. First, it is less likely than *you* language to make others defensive, so *I* language opens the doors for dialogue. In general, *you* language is particularly likely to arouse defensiveness or anger when it is used to express criticism or dissatisfaction. Yet *you* language may be acceptable or even appreciated when it conveys praise of another. For instance, in a recent study, Amy Bippus and Stacy Young (2005) found that some people reacted positively when they were targets of positive *you* language (e.g., "You make me feel wonderful.").

Second, *I* language is more honest. We misrepresent our responsibility when we say "You made me feel …" because others don't control how we feel. Finally, *I* language is more empowering than *you* language. When we say "You made me feel that," we give control of our emotions to others. This reduces our personal power and, by extension, our motivation to change what is happening. Using *I* language allows you to own your own feelings while explaining to others how you interpret their behaviors.

> I thought that the idea of *I* language was kind of silly, but I did the exercise assigned in class anyway. Surprise. I found out I was using a lot of *you* language, and it had the effect of letting me off the hook for what I felt and did. Like, I would say, "You pushed me to say that," when really I had control over whether to say it or not. But when I said, "You pushed me," I could dismiss what I said as not my fault.

MindTap

EVERYDAY SKILLS

To practice using *I* language and noticing *you* language, complete the activity "Using *I* Language" at the end of the chapter or online.

NEELY

Respect What Others Say about Their Feelings and Thoughts

Compassionate Eye Foundation/Digital Vision/Getty Images

Has anyone ever said to you, "You shouldn't feel that way"? If so, you know how infuriating it can be to be told that your feelings aren't valid, appropriate, or acceptable. It's equally destructive to be told our thoughts are wrong. We tend to feel hurt or disrespected when someone tells us our ideas or feelings are wrong. Effective communicators don't dispute or disparage what others say about what they feel and think. Even if you don't feel or think the same way, you can still respect another person as the expert on her or his own thoughts and emotions.

One of the most disconfirming forms of communication is speaking for others when they are able to speak for themselves. We shouldn't assume we understand how they feel or think. As we have seen, our distinct experiences and ways of interpreting life make each of us unique. We seldom, if ever, completely grasp what another person feels or thinks. Although it is supportive to engage in dual perspective, it isn't supportive to presume that we fully grasp what's happening in someone else and can speak for them.

It's particularly important not to assume we understand people from other cultures and distinct communities within our society. Recently, an Asian Indian woman in one of my classes commented on the discrimination she faces, and a white man in the class said, "I know what you mean. Prejudice really hurts." Although he meant to be supportive, his response angered the woman, who retorted, "You have no idea how I feel, and you have no right to act like you do until you've been female and nonwhite."

Respecting what others say about what they feel and think is a cornerstone of effective interpersonal communication. We also grow when we open ourselves to perspectives, feelings, and thoughts that differ from our own. If you don't understand what others say, ask them to elaborate. This shows you are interested and that you respect their expertise or experience. Inviting others to clarify, extend, or explain their communication enlarges understanding between people.

Communication in Everyday Life

DIVERSITY

Respecting Others' Experiences

Marsha Houston, an accomplished communication scholar, explains how claiming understanding can diminish a person. She writes that white women should never tell African American women that they understand black women's experiences. Here is Houston's (2004) explanation:

> I have heard this sentence completed in numerous, sometimes bizarre, ways, from "because sexism is just as bad as racism," to "because I watch 'The Cosby Show,'" to "because I'm also a member of a minority group. I'm Jewish . . . Italian . . . overweight." Similar experiences should not be confused with the same experience; my experience of prejudice is erased when you identify it as "the same" as yours (p. 124).

Strive for Accuracy and Clarity

Because symbols are arbitrary, abstract, and ambiguous, the potential for misunderstanding always exists. In addition, individual and cultural differences foster varying interpretations of words. Although we can't completely eliminate misunderstandings, we can minimize them.

Be Aware of Levels of Abstraction Misunderstanding is less likely when we are conscious of levels of abstraction. Much confusion results from language that is excessively abstract. For instance, suppose a professor says, "Your papers should demonstrate a sophisticated conceptual grasp of material and its pragmatic implications." Would you know how to write a paper to satisfy the professor? Probably not, because the language is abstract. Here's a more concrete description: "Your papers should include definitions of the concepts and specific examples that show how they apply in real life." With this more concrete statement, you would have a clear idea of what the professor expected.

Sometimes, however, abstract language is appropriate. As we have seen, abstract language allows us to generalize, which is necessary and useful. The goal is to use a level of abstraction that suits particular communication objectives and situations. Abstract words are appropriate when speakers and listeners have similar concrete knowledge about what is being discussed. For example, an established couple might talk about "lighthearted comedies" and "heavy movies" as shorthand ways to refer to two kinds of films. Because they have seen many movies together, they have shared referents for the abstract terms *lighthearted* and *heavy*, so confusion is unlikely. Similarly, long-term friends can say "Let's just hang out," and understand the activities implied by the abstract term *hang out*. More concrete language is useful when communicators don't have shared experiences and interpretations. For example, early in a friendship the suggestion to "hang out" would be more effective if it included specifics: "Let's hang out today—maybe watch the game and go out for pizza." In a new dating relationship, saying "Let's have a casual evening" would be less clear than "Let's rent a movie and fix dinner at your place tonight."

Abstract language is particularly likely to lead to misunderstandings when people talk about changes they want in one another. Concrete language and specific examples help people have similar understandings of which behaviors are unwelcome and which ones are wanted. For example, "I want you to be more helpful around the house" does not explain what would count as being more helpful. Is it vacuuming and doing laundry? Shopping for groceries? Fixing half the meals? It won't be clear what the speaker wants unless more concrete descriptions are supplied. Likewise, "I want to be closer" could mean that the speaker wants to spend more time together, to talk about the relationship, to do things together, to have a more adventurous sex life, or any number of other things.

Qualify Language Another strategy for increasing the clarity of communication is to qualify language. Two types of language should be qualified. First, we should qualify generalizations so that we don't mislead ourselves or others into mistaking a general statement for an absolute one. "Politicians are crooked" is a false statement because it overgeneralizes. A more accurate statement would be "A number of politicians have been shown to be dishonest." Qualifying reminds us of the limitations of what we say.

MindTap™

Everyday Skills To practice translating ambiguous words into concrete language, complete the activity "Communicate Clearly" at the end of the chapter or online.

We should also qualify language when describing and evaluating people. A **static evaluation** is an assessment that suggests that something is unchanging or fixed. These are particularly troublesome when applied to people: "Ann is selfish," "Don is irresponsible," "Bob is generous," "Vy is dependent." Whenever we use the word *is*, we suggest that something is inherent and fixed. In reality, we aren't static but continuously changing. A person who is selfish at one time may not be at another. A person who is irresponsible on one occasion may be responsible in other situations.

KEN

Parents are the worst for static evaluations. When I first got my license seven years ago, I had a fender bender and then got a speeding ticket. Since then, I've had a perfect record, but you'd never know it from what they say. Dad's always calling me "hot-rodder," and Mom goes through this safety spiel every time I get ready to drive somewhere. You'd think I was the same now as when I was 16.

Indexing is a technique developed by early communication scholars to remind us that our evaluations apply only to specific times and circumstances (Korzybski, 1958). To index, we would say "Ann$_{\text{June 6, 2001}}$ acted selfishly," "Don$_{\text{on the task committee}}$ was irresponsible," "Bob$_{\text{in college}}$ was generous," and "Vy$_{\text{in high school}}$ was dependent on others for self-esteem." See how indexing ties description to a specific time and circumstance? Mental indexing reminds us that we and others are able to change in remarkable ways.

CHAPTER SUMMARY

In this chapter, we discussed the world of words and meaning, the uniquely human universe that we inhabit because we are symbol users. Because symbols are arbitrary, ambiguous, and abstract, words have no inherent meanings. Instead, we actively construct meaning by interpreting symbols based on perspectives and values that are endorsed in our culture and social groups and based on interaction with others and our personal experiences. We also punctuate to create meaning in communication.

Instead of existing only in the physical world of the here and now, we use language to define, evaluate, and classify ourselves, others, and our experiences in the world. In addition, we use language to think hypothetically, so we can consider alternatives and simultaneously inhabit all three dimensions of time. Finally, language allows us to self-reflect so that we can monitor our own behaviors.

Although members of a society share a common language, we don't all use it the same way. Different groups, or speech communities, which exist both within and between countries, teach us rules for talking and for interpreting communication. Because communication rules vary between social groups, we shouldn't assume that others use words just as we do. Likewise, we shouldn't assume that others share our rules for communicating.

The final section of this chapter discussed principles for improving effectiveness in verbal communication. Because words can mean different things to various people and because different social groups instill some distinct rules for interacting, misunderstandings are always possible. To minimize them, we should engage in dual perspective, own our thoughts and feelings, respect what others say about how they think and feel, and monitor abstractness, generalizations, and static evaluations.

In Chapter 5, we will continue our discussion of the world of human communication by exploring the fascinating realm of nonverbal behavior.

Key Concepts

Practice defining the chapter's terms by using online flashcards.

FLASHCARDS...

abstract 107
ambiguous 106
arbitrary 105
communication rules 110
constitutive rules 110
hate speech 115

I language 125
indexing 128
loaded language 115
punctuation 111
regulative rules 110
speech community 120

static evaluation 128
symbols 105
totalizing 113
you language 125

Continuing the Conversation

Jason Harris © 2001 Wadsworth

When you've watched the video online, critique and analyze this encounter based on the principles you learned in this chapter. Then compare your work with the author's suggested responses. Online, even more videos will let you continue the conversation with your instructor.

Five weeks ago, Ed started a new job. He likes it a lot and sees a real future for himself with the company. Last week, Ed was invited to the annual company banquet and awards ceremony. The invitation to the banquet stated only "Hope to see you there" and had no RSVP, so Ed didn't mention to anyone that he wouldn't be attending because his daughter was in a play the same night. When he arrived at work the next Monday morning, however, his manager spoke to him.

PRACTICE ...

Manager: Hey, Ed, you missed the banquet Saturday night. I thought you were really committed to our company.

Confused, Ed tries to explain.

Ed: My daughter was in a play that night.

Manager: I don't care why you didn't come. We really pay attention to who's with us and who isn't.

When Ed talks with coworkers who have been around a few years, he discovers that top management sees the annual banquet as a "command performance" that signifies company unity and loyalty.

1. How does the concept of constitutive rules help explain the misunderstanding between Ed and his manager?

2. How might Ed learn the normative practices of the company so that he can understand the meanings longtime employees have?

3. How do the ambiguity and abstraction inherent in language explain the misunderstanding between Ed and his manager?

4. How would you suggest that Ed repair the damage done by his absence from the company banquet? What might he say to his manager? How could he use *I* language, indexing, and dual perspective to guide his communication?

Assessing Yourself

Begin the process of applying this chapter's concepts by taking a self-assessment quiz here or online—where you will find out what the results mean.

Purpose: The 10 items below allow you to measure your perception of your ability to take others' perspective.

Instructions: Rate each item for how well it describes you. Use the following scale:

5 Describes me very well
4 Mostly describes me well
3 Describes me somewhat or in some situations
2 Mostly does not describe me well
1 Does not describe me well at all

_____ 1. If another person and I see something differently, I am pretty sure the other person is wrong.

_____ 2. When talking with friends, I work hard to understand their perspectives.

_____ 3. I believe that there are many reasonable ways to look at most issues and situations.

PRACTICE...

_____ 4. I find it hard to look at an issue from another person's perspective if their perspective is very different from mine.

_____ 5. The advice to "walk a mile in another's shoes" makes sense to me.

_____ 6. Before I say anything critical to another person, I think about how I would feel if I were that person hearing me.

_____ 7. When someone says something that hurts me, I try to think about why he or she might have said that.

_____ 8. I worry that trying to understand others' perspectives might weaken my own perspective.

_____ 9. When I don't see eye to eye with others, I work to understand why they think and feel what they do.

_____ 10. I think it is possible to really understand another person's perspective without agreeing with it.

Everyday Skills

Build your communication skills further by completing the following activities here or online.

1. Communication Rules

Think about the regulative and constitutive rules you follow in your communication. For each item below, identify two rules you have learned.

Regulative Rules

List rules that regulate how you:

+ Talk with elders
+ Interact at dinnertime
+ Have first exchanges in the morning

+ Respond to criticism from your supervisor
+ Greet casual friends on campus
+ Talk with professors

Constitutive Rules

How do you communicate to show:

+ Respect
+ Love
+ Disrespect
+ Support
+ Professional ambition
+ Contempt

After you've identified your rules, talk with others in your class about the rules they follow. Are there commonalities among your rules that reflect broad cultural norms? What explains differences in people's rules?

2. Breaking the Rules of Gendered Communication

This exercise will increase your awareness of how socialization in gendered speech communities shapes your and others' perceptions of verbal communication that is and is not appropriate for each sex.

a. Select a social prescription for how your sex is supposed to communicate verbally and deliberately violate that prescription in your interactions with others for one day. (*Example:* Women might be very assertive or might interrupt others frequently; men might talk a lot about relationship issues and feelings.)

b. Describe how others responded to your violation of a gender prescription for verbal behavior.

c. Describe how you felt when you violated the prescription and when others responded to your violation.

3. Translation Guide

To increase your awareness of the specialized language used in social media, keep a list of abbreviations (*Examples:* BRB, ROFL, SRSLY) and terms (*Examples: repost, tweet*) that appear on social media sites you visit. Then provide translations for each of the abbreviations and terms. If all of the language on your social media sites is so familiar to you that you don't recognize its distinctiveness, ask someone who seldom uses social media to point out specialized terms to you.

Abbreviation	Translation	Term	Translation
_____	_____	_____	_____
_____	_____	_____	_____
_____	_____	_____	_____

4. Using *I* Language

For the next three days, whenever you use *you* language, try to rephrase what you said or thought in *I* language. How does this change how you think and feel about what's happening? How does using *I* language affect interaction with others? Are others less defensive when you own your feelings and describe, but don't evaluate, their behaviors? Does *I* language facilitate working out constructive changes?

Now that you're tuned into *I* and *you* language, monitor how you feel when others use *you* language about you. When a friend or romantic partner says, "You make me feel . . . ," do you feel defensive or guilty? Try teaching others to use *I* language so that your relationships can be more honest and open.

5. Communicate Clearly

To express yourself clearly, it's important to learn to translate ambiguous words into concrete language. Practice translating with the statements below.

Example:
Ambiguous language: "You're rude."
Clear language: "I don't like it when you interrupt me."

Ambiguous Language	Clear Language
You're conceited.	_____
I want more freedom.	_____
You text too much.	_____
I want us to be closer.	_____
Your work is sloppy.	_____

MindTap **DO ...** Additional interactive discussions, online quizzes, and activities that your instructor may assign for a grade.

Engaging with Ideas

Reflect and write about the ideas in this chapter by considering questions about personal, workplace, and ethical applications, here or online.

Personal Application Think about slang and colloquial terms that you and your peers use which aren't generally used (or understood) by people outside of your age group. How are these terms useful to you? What do they add to your communication with peers?

Workplace Application   **REFLECT ON...**
Identify constitutive rules for communicating in a job you now hold or held in the past. What counts as "being professional," "productivity," "bad attitude," "team player," and so on?

Ethical Application Compare the ethical commitments that guide using *I* language with those that guide using *you* language. Is one more ethical than the other?

Thinking Critically

Think and write critically about the ideas in this chapter, here or online.

1. To appreciate the importance of hypothetical thought enabled by symbols, try to imagine living only in the present with no memories, no anticipations of the future, and no goals for yourself. How would not having hypothetical thought affect your life?
2. Check out the graffiti on your campus. Do you see examples of loaded language, stereotyping, and hate speech? Share your findings with your classmates.

REFLECT ON...

3. What labels that you dislike have been applied to you or to groups to which you belong? Explain how the labels affect you.
4. Notice how news media describe members of different races. Do television programs, newspapers, and other media identify race when the person is not white? How often are minorities described in terms of their races (black, Asian, Hispanic, and so on)? Are people ever described as white?

© ollyy/Shutterstock.com

THE WORLD
BEYOND WORDS

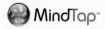
Topics Covered in this Chapter

Defining Nonverbal Communication

Principles of Nonverbal Communication

Types of Nonverbal Communication

Social Media and Nonverbal Use of Communication

Guidelines for Improving Nonverbal Communication

After studying this chapter, you should be able to . . .

Identify rules governing nonverbal communication in the context of your campus.

Assess your own nonverbal communication.

List examples of the nine types of nonverbal communication.

Engage in dual perspective regarding use of communication in social media.

Apply this chapter's guidelines to strengthen your nonverbal communication.

"It's dangerous work—one wrong move and somebody can get killed," Chris Mason told me. It was a cool morning when Chris and his crew came to my home to remove a tree that had been damaged. The top third of the tree had broken, but it was still attached to the rest of the tree and was lodged in surrounding trees.

Eric, the senior man on Chris's crew, was fitting himself into the harness as Chris and I spoke. Once secure, Eric raised his hand and Gary, the crane operator, began hoisting Eric upward. Eric secured a wire cable around the top portion of the tree, then ducked his chin slightly, and Gary lowered him 5 feet. At that level, Eric used his chainsaw to free the top portion of the tree. Just before he made the final cut, Eric braced his foot against the tree so he could kick out of the way in case the top portion ricocheted back. Gary saw this and began pulling the separated portion away from Eric. Eric rappelled down, twisted out of the harness, and joined Josh, another crew member, who had already begun cutting the downed portion of the tree into smaller parts.

Chris took the job of hauling the cut limbs to the shredder. Each time he reached for a cut limb, he first touched the back of Josh or Eric. "I have to let them know I'm behind them or they could turn and their saws could slice into me," Chris later explained to me when I interviewed him about the carefully orchestrated nonverbal communication among members of his crew. Chris told me that with cranes, saws, and shredders running, verbal language doesn't work: "Nobody can hear anything and, besides, we're wearing heavy-duty ear mufflers." He explained that he trains his crew to communicate nonverbally. "You always touch someone using a saw before you move beside or in front of them." "Gary knows to watch for head movements—if the guy in the harness moves his head up, Gary pulls him higher; down, he lowers him." "One man on the ground is always watching when someone is up in the harness."

One of the reasons that Chris has never had a worker injured in a profession where injuries are frequent is that he understands the importance of nonverbal communication, and he teaches everyone on his crew to use it effectively.

This chapter examines the fascinating world of nonverbal communication. To launch our discussion, we define nonverbal communication and note how it is similar to and different from verbal communication. Next, we identify four principles of nonverbal communication. The third section of the chapter discusses different types of nonverbal behavior, and the fourth section explores nonverbal communication in digital and online interactions. We complete the chapter with guidelines for improving personal effectiveness in nonverbal communication.

DEFINING NONVERBAL COMMUNICATION

Nonverbal communication is all aspects of communication other than words. It includes not only gestures and body language but also how we utter words: inflection, pauses, tone, volume, and accent. Nonverbal communication also includes features of environments that affect interaction, personal objects such as jewelry and clothes, and physical appearance.

Scholars estimate that nonverbal behaviors account for 65% to 93% of the total meaning of communication (Birdwhistell, 1970; Hickson, Stacks, & Moore, 2004; Mehrabian, 1981). To understand verbal and nonverbal dimensions of communication, we identify similarities as well as differences between them.

Similarities between Verbal and Nonverbal Communication

Nonverbal communication is similar to verbal communication in four respects: it is symbolic, it is rule-guided, it may be intentional or unintentional, and it reflects culture.

Nonverbal Communication Is Symbolic

Like verbal communication, much nonverbal communication is symbolic, which means that it is arbitrary, ambiguous, and abstract. Thus, people may attach different meanings to a wink. Depending on the context and the people involved, a wink might express romantic interest, signal a joke, or indicate that there is something in the person's eye.

Nonverbal Communication Is Rule-Guided

Within particular societies, we share general understandings of which nonverbal behaviors are appropriate in various situations and what they mean. Smiling generally is understood to express friendliness, and scowling normally is perceived as indicating displeasure of some type.

We follow rules (often unconsciously) to create different interaction climates. For instance, people dress differently to attend a funeral than a soccer game. Furniture in homes is generally selected and arranged to promote comfort and interaction. In business offices, however, furniture is more likely to be selected and arranged to promote efficiency and a task focus.

Nonverbal Communication May Be Intentional or Unintentional

Like verbal communication, nonverbal communication may be deliberately controlled. For example, you may carefully select clothes to create a professional impression when you are going to a job interview.

Yet nonverbal communication may also be unconscious and unplanned. Without awareness, you might wince or lower your eyes when asked a tough question by the interviewer. Thus, a nonverbal gesture is sometimes controlled and sometimes inadvertent.

Nonverbal Communication Reflects Culture

Like verbal communication, nonverbal behavior is shaped by cultural ideas, values, customs, and history. Just as we learn our culture's language, we also learn its nonverbal codes. For example, in the United States and many other countries, a handshake is the conventional way to begin and end a business meeting. Yet in some cultures, bowing or kissing both cheeks is the standard mode of greeting and bidding goodbye to business contacts. In the United States, it is common for friends and romantic partners to sample food from each other's plates, but many Germans consider this extremely rude. Although nonverbal communication reflects cultural values and understandings, there may be some universal nonverbal behaviors. Paul Eckman, a noteworthy scholar of nonverbal behavior, demonstrated that people from a range of Western and Eastern cultures agree on the meaning of facial expressions of anger, disgust, fear, happiness, sadness, and surprise (Eckman & Friesen, 1971; Eckman, Wagner, & Manstead, 1989). Next, Eckman showed that members of the Fore tribe in New Guinea, who are not

MindTap

Everyday Skills To practice identifying your own campus's rules, complete the activity "Campus Rules for Nonverbal Communication" at the end of the chapter or online.

Arthur Carlo Franco/E+/Getty Images

literate and have not been exposed to media, also agree on the meaning of those facial expressions. There is also some evidence that suggests that contempt may be another universally recognized expression (Matsumoto, 1992).

Differences between Verbal and Nonverbal Communication

There are also differences between verbal and nonverbal communication and the meanings we attach to each. We consider three distinctions between the two kinds of communication.

Nonverbal Communication Tends to Be Perceived as More Believable

Most people believe that nonverbal communication is more reliable than verbal communication in expressing true feelings (Andersen, 1999). This is especially the case when verbal and nonverbal messages are inconsistent. If you say you feel fine, but you are slumping and the corners of your mouth are turned down, others probably will not believe your verbal message.

The fact that people tend to believe nonverbal behaviors doesn't mean that nonverbal behaviors actually are honest or that we can interpret them reliably. It's possible for people to manipulate nonverbal communication, just as we manipulate our verbal communication. Politicians are coached not only in how to speak but also in how to use nonverbal communication to bolster images. Atlanta nonverbal trainer Patti Wood (Basu, 2004) analyzed nonverbal communication of the candidates in the 2004 presidential election. She concluded that George W. Bush's frequent smiles and winks established connections with voters.

Nonverbal Communication Is Multichanneled

Nonverbal communication often occurs simultaneously in two or more channels, whereas verbal communication tends to take place in a single channel. (Channels are means of transmitting messages—for instance, sound through airwaves, and facial expressions through light waves.) Nonverbal communication may be seen, felt, heard, smelled, and tasted, and we may receive nonverbal communication through several of these channels at the same time. If you touch a person while smiling and whispering an endearment, nonverbal communication occurs in three channels at once.

One implication of the multichanneled nature of nonverbal communication is that selective perception is likely to operate. If you are visually oriented, you may tune in more to visual cues than to smell or touch. On the other hand, if you are touch oriented, you may pay particular attention to tactile cues.

Nonverbal Communication Is Continuous

Finally, unlike verbal communication, nonverbal communication is continuous. Verbal symbols start and stop. We say something or write something, and then we stop talking or writing. However, we continuously adjust our posture and facial expressions. Furthermore, nonverbal features of environment, such as lighting or temperature, are ongoing influences on interaction and meaning.

PRINCIPLES OF NONVERBAL COMMUNICATION

Four principles enhance insight into how nonverbal communication influences meaning in human interaction.

Nonverbal Communication May Supplement or Replace Verbal Communication

Communication researchers have identified five ways in which nonverbal behaviors interact with verbal communication (Andersen, 1999; Guerrero & Floyd, 2006a). First, nonverbal behaviors may repeat verbal messages. For example, you might say "yes" while nodding your head. Second, nonverbal behaviors may highlight verbal communication. For instance, you can emphasize particular words by increasing your volume. Third, we use nonverbal behavior to complement or add to words. When you see a friend, you might say, "I'm glad to see you" and underline the verbal message with a warm embrace. Lyrics (verbal) often complement and reinforce music (nonverbal) as, for example, when a slow beat and soft music accompany lyrics about romantic love (Sellnow & Sellnow, 2001). Fourth, nonverbal behaviors may contradict verbal messages, such as when someone says, "Nothing's wrong!" in a hostile tone of voice. Finally, we sometimes substitute nonverbal behaviors for verbal ones. For instance, you might point to the left when asked to give directions. In all these ways, nonverbal behaviors supplement or replace verbal communication.

Nonverbal Communication May Regulate Interaction

More than verbal cues, nonverbal behaviors regulate the flow of communication between people (Guerrero & Floyd, 2006a). In conversations, we generally sense

Jose Luis Pelaez, Inc./Blend Images/Corbis

when someone else is through speaking and when it is our turn to talk. Seldom do explicit verbal cues tell us when to speak and when to keep silent. When talking, friends typically don't say, "Your turn to talk," or hold up signs saying "I have finished speaking." Instead, turn-taking in conversation usually is regulated nonverbally. We signal that we don't want to be interrupted by averting our eyes or by maintaining a speaking volume and rate that discourages interruption. When we're through talking, we look at others to signal, "Now somebody else can speak." We invite specific people to speak by looking directly at them. Although we aren't usually aware of these and other nonverbal actions that regulate interaction, we rely on them to know when to speak and when to remain silent.

Nonverbal Communication Often Establishes Relationship-Level Meanings

You'll recall that, in Chapter 1, we discussed two levels of meaning in communication. To review, the content level of meaning is the literal message. The relationship level of meaning defines communicators' identities and relationships between them. Nonverbal communication often acts as "relationship language" that expresses the overall feeling of relationships (Guerrero & Floyd, 2006a; Manusov & Patterson, 2006). Nonverbal communication can convey three dimensions of relationship-level meaning.

Responsiveness One dimension of relationship-level meaning that is often conveyed by nonverbal communication is responsiveness. Key to responsiveness is **immediacy**, which is behavior that increases perceptions of closeness between communicators. In face-to-face interaction, immediacy behaviors include smiling, making eye contact, head nodding, and attentive posture. Online, we may communicate responsiveness by using emoticons to convey feelings and by replying immediately to an instant message or to comments in a chat room. Researchers (Pogue & AhYun, 2006; Witt, Wheeless, & Allen, 2004) have demonstrated a strong, positive relationship between teacher immediacy behaviors and student motivation and affective learning.

Synchronicity, or harmony, between people's postures and facial expressions may reflect how comfortable they are with each other (Guerrero & Floyd, 2006a). Coworkers who have a long and positive history of working together often tend to mirror each other's expressions and postures when interacting. Similarly, family members also tend to share certain facial expressions and movements.

ALLAN The most useful professional development seminar I've ever taken taught me how to sit and look at people to show I am interested. Our instructor told us that a lot of times men don't show their interest with head nods and eye contact. That explained to me why some of the women I supervise complained that I never seemed interested when they came to talk to me. It wasn't that I wasn't interested. I just didn't show it with my nonverbal behavior.

Liking   A second dimension of relationship meaning is liking. Nonverbal behaviors often are keen indicators of how positively or negatively we feel toward others. Smiles and friendly touching convey positive feelings, whereas frowns and belligerent postures express antagonism.

In addition to these general rules shared in Western society, more specific rules are instilled by particular speech communities. Masculine speech communities tend to emphasize emotional control and independence, so men are less likely than women to use nonverbal behaviors to reveal how they feel. Reflecting the values of feminine socialization, women, in general, sit closer to others, smile more, and engage in greater eye contact than men (Hall et al., 2000; Reis, Senchak, & Solomon, 1985). With intimate partners, women are more likely than men to initiate hand-holding and touch (Atsuko, 2003; Knapp & Hall, 2006). Women also tend to be more nonverbally expressive of their emotions because that is encouraged in feminine speech communities.

Nonverbal behaviors also tend to reflect feelings between marriage partners. Happy couples tend to sit closer together and engage in more eye contact than unhappy couples do. Furthermore, people who like each other tend to touch often and to orient their body postures toward each other (Guerrero & Floyd, 2006a; Burgoon et al., 1995).

WILL One of the neatest things about my parents is how they are always connecting with each other. I don't mean with words. It's more like looks and touching. If Mom says something, Dad looks at her. Whenever either of them comes in a room that the other is already in, they have to touch—just brush a shoulder or scratch the other's back or whatever. It's like they're always reaching out to each other.

Power   The third dimension of relationship-level meaning is power. We use nonverbal behaviors to assert dominance and to negotiate for status and influence (Remland, 2000). Given what we have learned about gender socialization, it is not surprising that men generally assume greater amounts of space than women and use greater volume and more forceful gestures to assert themselves (Hall, 1987; Leathers, 1986; Major, Schmidlin, & Williams, 1990).

Status also affects tendencies to communicate power nonverbally. The prerogative to touch another reflects power, so people with power tend to touch those with less power. For instance, bosses touch secretaries far more often than secretaries touch bosses (Hall, Coats, & Smith-LeBeau, 2004; Spain, 1992). Time is also linked to people's status. People who are considered important can keep others waiting. How often have you waited for your appointment at a doctor's office? People with high status can also be late to appointments and events without risking serious repercussions. Yet, if someone with lower power is late, she or he may suffer disapproval, penalties, or cancellation of the appointment.

JERRY

Last summer, I had an internship with a big accounting firm in Washington, and space really told the story on status. Interns like me worked in two large rooms on the first floor with partitions to separate our desks. New employees worked on the second floor in little cubicles. The higher up you were in the hierarchy of the firm, the higher up your office was—literally. I mean, the president and vice presidents—six of them—had the whole top floor, while there were 40 or more interns crowded onto my floor.

As Jerry's observations indicate, space can express power relations. People who have power usually have more space than those who have little or no power. Most executives have large, spacious offices, whereas their secretaries often have smaller offices or workstations. As people move up the organizational ladder, they tend to have larger offices. Homes also reflect power differences among family members. Adults usually have more space than children, and men more often than women have their own rooms, chairs, or other special spaces.

Responsiveness, liking, and power are dimensions of relationship-level meanings that are often expressed through nonverbal communication.

Nonverbal Communication Reflects and Expresses Cultural Values

Like verbal communication, nonverbal patterns reflect specific cultures (Guerro & Farinelli, 2009). This implies that most nonverbal behavior is not instinctive but learned in the process of being socialized within a particular culture.

Have you ever seen the bumper sticker "If you can read this, you're too close"? That slogan proclaims North Americans' fierce territoriality. We prize private space, and we resent— and sometimes fight—anyone who trespasses on what we consider our turf. In other cultures— called *high-contact* cultures—people are less territorial. For instance, many Brazilians stand close together in shops, buses, and elevators, and when they bump into one another, they don't apologize or draw back (Andersen et. al, 2002). In many Middle Eastern countries, men often walk with their arms around other men, but in the United States affectionate touching between male friends is uncommon except during sports events.

In the hit TV series *The Sopranos*, Tony's nonverbal behaviors reflected his power as well as his cultural background.

HBO/Photofest

Iraq Culture Smart Cards, distributed to American soldiers stationed in Iraq, help the soldiers acclimate to the new culture by instructing them on nonverbal communication norms of the country. For example, Iraqis are offended by several nonverbal communications that might seem normal to an American: stepping or leaning away from a male, touching another person with your left hand, and exposing the soles of shoes or feet are all considered rude by Iraqis (Word for Word, 2005).

Patterns of eye contact also reflect cultural values. In North America, frankness and assertion are valued, so meeting another's eyes is considered appropriate and a demonstration of personal honesty. Yet, in many Asian and northern European countries, direct eye contact is considered abrasive and disrespectful (Axtell, 2007; Samovar & Porter, 2000). On the other hand, in Brazil, eye contact often is so intense that many Americans consider it rude. Imagine the confusion this causes in intercultural business negotiations.

Cultural training also influences which emotions we express and how we express them (Matsumoto, Franklin, Choi, Rogers, & Tatani, 2002). For example, many people raised in traditional Italian and Jewish communities are more emotionally expressive than people raised in English or German communities. In Japan and many other Asian cultures, it is generally considered rude to express negative feelings toward others. In the United States, the display of negative feelings is less constrained.

Cultures also differ in their orientations toward time. Some cultures have monochronic (from the root term *mono*, which means *one*) orientations toward time, whereas others have polychronic (from the root term *poly*, which means *many*) orientations. Most Western cultures are relatively monochronic, whereas many South American cultures are more polychronic. Monochronic cultures view time as a valuable commodity to be saved, scheduled, and carefully guarded. Within monochronic cultures, people do one thing at a time, and they value punctuality and efficiency. Thus, people are expected to be on time for appointments, work, and classes, and they are expected to complete work quickly (Honoré, 2004, 2005).

In contrast, polychronic cultures take a more holistic, organic view of time. Members of these cultures assume that many things are happening simultaneously. Thus, punctuality is seldom stressed. Meetings may start late, with people joining in after discussions begin. Tangential discussions and social conversations are part of normal meetings in polychronic cultures. People may even cancel meetings without the dramatic reasons expected for canceling in monochronic cultures.

JOSH Last year, my wife and I had our house painted. The company we hired had a lot of Hispanic workers. They were never on the job at 8 A.M. when the other workers were. They'd usually arrive around 8:30 or even 9, and they would take breaks and talk during the workday. But I'll have to say that they also stayed past 5. They weren't in any hurry to leave—just weren't going by the clock to do their work. The white workers were out of there at 5 on the dot.

Technology can alter our temporal rhythms and even our sense of time. The speed with which computers, phones, and tablets operate encourages us to expect things to happen at a rapid pace. Further, increasing emphasis on multitasking pushes us toward trying to do other things while we are talking with people. As a result, it's not unusual for people to interrupt a face-to-face conversation to answer a call, to text message during class discussions, or to check text messages during meetings.

In sum, four principles provide a foundation for understanding nonverbal communication. First, nonverbal behavior may supplement or replace verbal communication. Second, nonverbal behaviors may regulate interaction. Third, nonverbal behavior is more powerful than verbal behavior in expressing relationship-level meanings. Finally, nonverbal communication reflects and expresses cultural values.

Communication in Everyday Life

WORKPLACE

Cultural Differences in Workplace Nonverbal Communication
More and more companies are becoming international, but not all workers who get transferred or who do business with international colleagues find it easy to understand and adapt to the nonverbal norms of their new cultures (Axtell, 2007; Martin & Chaney, 2008; Morrison & Conaway, 2006). For instance, in Germany it is considered very rude to cough in concerts and in many other public areas. In India, whistling tunes is perceived as highly offensive, and in Ghana crossed legs are perceived as insulting (Samovar, Porter, & McDaniel, 2009). The Chinese, who tend not to use many hand movements when talking, find Americans' gestures distracting.

Gift giving is common between businesspeople, but it presents many opportunities for misunderstandings. A gift wrapped in blue and black might offend many Asians because those colors symbolize death in some Asian cultures. An American might take offense if a Japanese person does not open a presented gift. In Japan, however, it is customary not to open gifts in front of the giver. An American might bring an extravagant gift to make a good impression on a Singaporean manager with whom he hopes to do business. Unfortunately for the American, the Singaporean manager probably would view an extravagant gift as an attempt at bribery—not exactly a good impression.

Go to http://www.executiveplanet.com and read about what is appropriate in various cultures for business dress, gifts, and interaction norms.

TYPES OF NONVERBAL COMMUNICATION

We're now ready to explore the types of nonverbal behavior that we use each to establish relationships, regulate interaction, and express personal and cultural identity.

Kinesics

Kinesics refers to body position and body motions, including those of the face. Clearly, we signal a great deal about how we feel and see ourselves by how we hold our bodies. Someone who stands erect and walks confidently is likely to be perceived as self-assured, whereas someone who slouches and shuffles may be seen as lacking confidence.

Humans communicated by gesture long before they learned to communicate verbally (Corballis, 2002). Many people "talk with their hands," which psychology professor Susan Goldin-Meadow (2004) says actually helps some people think. We use gestures to emphasize verbal language and to express feelings. We use a hand gesture to indicate "okay" and a different hand gesture to communicate contempt. But gestures don't always translate across cultures. For example, the hand gesture that stands for "okay" (thumb and first finger forming a circle and the other three fingers pointing upward) in the United States is the gesture for worthlessness in France and is perceived as obscene in Iraq (Morrison & Conaway, 2006; Word for Word, 2005). It's interesting to note that the gesture of the extended middle finger, which some Westerners use to convey contempt, was used by Romans to send the same message more than 2,000 years ago (Mahany, 1997).

Our faces are intricate messengers. Our eyes can shoot daggers of anger, issue challenges, or radiate feelings of love. With our faces, we can indicate disapproval (scowls), doubt (raised eyebrows), admiration (warm gazes), and resistance (stares). Facial motions may be used to signal whether we are open to interaction. In classes, students often look downward to dissuade teachers from calling on them. To invite interaction, Westerners look at others and smile, indicating that conversation is welcome (Gueguen & De Gail, 2003). Yet, in many traditional Asian societies, direct eye contact and smiling at someone who is not an intimate might be considered disrespectful.

For good reason, poets call the eyes "the windows to the soul." Our eyes communicate some of the most important and complex messages about how we feel about others. If you watch infants, you'll notice that they focus on others' eyes. Even as adults, we tend to look at eyes to judge others' honesty, interest, friendliness, and self-confidence. Virginia Richmond and James McCroskey (2000) found supervisors who look at subordinates, smile, and incline their heads toward subordinates are perceived by subordinates as more credible and interpersonally attractive. Furthermore, these nonverbal behaviors from supervisors are positively related to subordinates' motivation and job satisfaction.

Haptics

Haptics is the sense of touch. Many scholars believe that touching and being touched are essential to a healthy life (Benjamin & Werner, 2004; Field, 2003). Babies who are held closely and tenderly tend to develop into self-confident adults who have secure attachment styles (Field, 2003; Mwakalye & DeAngelis, 1995).

Touching also communicates power and status. People with high status touch others and invade others' spaces more than people with less status do (Hall, 2006; Hall et al., 2004). Cultural views of women as more touchable than men are reflected in gendered patterns of contact. In general, parents touch sons less often and more roughly than they touch daughters. Exposure to these patterns early in life teaches the sexes different rules for using touch and interpreting touches from others. As adults, women tend to use touch to show liking and intimacy, whereas men are more likely than women to use touch to assert power and control (DiBaise & Gunnoe, 2004; Hall, 2006; Jhally & Katz, 2001).

Recent research (Schmid, 2010) shows that how things feel to us affects how we act. In one experiment, people were asked to negotiate the price of a car with a sticker price of $16,500. After their first offer was turned down by the dealer, people sitting on hard, stiff chairs raised their bid, on average, by $896.50 whereas people sitting on soft, comfortable chairs raised their bid by an average of $1,243.50. In a second experiment, people were asked to evaluate a job candidate by looking at a résumé attached to a clipboard that weighed either 3/4 of a pound or 4 1/2 pounds. People who held the heavy clipboard evaluated the job candidate as better and more serious than people reading the same résumé attached to the lighter clipboard.

Among teenagers today, hugging is a big deal. Teenagers hug to greet, say goodbye, express solidarity, and show affection. In fact, high school students have an entire vocabulary to distinguish among hugs: friend hug, bear hug, bear claw, shake and lean, and the triple (Kershaw, 2009a). Professional basketball players also rely on touch. Members of good teams tended to touch each other more than members of less successful teams in the 2008 season. And the best players were those who touched others the most: Celtics star Kevin Garnett was the touchiest of all players. Immediately after shooting a free throw, Garnett reached out to touch four teammates (Keltner, 2009).

Physical Appearance

Western culture places an extremely high value on physical appearance. For this reason, in face-to-face interactions, most of us notice how others look, and we often base our initial evaluations of others on their appearance. The emphasis Western culture places on physical attractiveness and youthful appearance contributes to eating disorders, abuse of steroids and other drugs, and the popularity of cosmetic surgery.

INSIGHT

Beauty for Sale

Increasingly, people are obsessed with having or creating the perfect body. People want larger or smaller breasts, noses, and chins. They want less fat here and more there. They want hair put on their bald heads and hair removed from their faces. They want varicose veins removed from legs and wrinkles removed from faces. They want skin tightened, eyelids lifted, tummies tucked.

Women most often have breast augmentation, tummy tucks, liposuction, eyelid surgery, and breast lifts (American Society of Aesthetic Plastic Surgeons, 2012). The most popular surgeries for men are liposuction, eyelid surgery, rhinoplasty, and face lifts (American Society of Aesthetic Plastic Surgeons, 2012). Both sexes also increasingly rely on treatments such as Botox injections—4,030,318 in 2011 at an average cost of $405 per injection (American Society of Aesthetic Plastic Surgeons, 2012).

Trends in plastic surgery tend to mirror trends in cultural views of physical attractiveness. Years ago, when a pencil-thin model named Twiggy was a supermodel, women had breast-reduction surgeries in record numbers. Larger breasts are part of the current physical ideal for women, which goes a long way toward explaining why breast-enlargement surgery has increased more than 700% since 1992 (Levy, 2005; Rives, 2005). And it's probably no coincidence that when Angelina Jolie ascended to superstar status, there was a 21% increase in lip implants, which are more lasting than the plumping injections (Barrett, 2004). In 2009, more than 21,000 people had lip augmentation (Louis, 2010). When fashions in breast and lip size change, more procedures may be needed to undo the original ones.

MindTap To what extent do you judge others by their appearance? Have you ever altered a first impression, based on appearance, once you got to know the person?

According to Daniel Hamermesh (2011), an economist, people who are above average in attractiveness are likely to make an average of 3% to 4% more than people who are below average in attractiveness. That could add up to well over $200,000 over the course of an average career. More attractive people are also more likely to be employed, obtain loan approvals, and negotiate loans with better terms.

Cultures vary in their ideals of physical beauty. Currently, Western cultural ideals emphasize thinness and youth in women (Bodey & Wood, 2009; Hesse-Biber & Leavy, 2006). By age 9, 50% to 80% of girls are trying to lose weight (Rhode, 2010). Seventy-five percent of American women say that their physical appearance is a major influence on their self-esteem, and a full 33% say it's more important than job performance or intelligence (Rhode, 2010). Current Western ideals for men emphasize buff, muscular bodies (Roosevelt, 2010).

Thinness in women is not prized or encouraged in all cultures and social communities. In traditional African societies, full-figured bodies are perceived as symbolizing health, prosperity, and wealth, which are all desirable. African Americans who embrace this value accept or prefer women who weigh more than the current ideal for Caucasians (Schooler, Ward, Merriwether, & Caruthers, 2004; Walker, 2007). Conversely, middle-class, upwardly mobile African American women are more susceptible to eating disorders and obsession with weight.

CHANDRA I don't see anything beautiful about a body like a pencil. Why do white girls want to have stick figures? I sure don't, and neither do the girls I hang out with. Guys don't like it either. The guys I know like a girl to have some curves, some substance. It's more feminine.

Artifacts

Artifacts are personal objects we use to announce our identities and heritage and to personalize our environments. Many people use avatars to symbolize online identities. In face-to-face communication, we craft our image by our hairstyles, makeup, dress, and personal objects. Nurses and physicians wear white and often drape stethoscopes around their necks; professors travel with briefcases, whereas students more often tote backpacks. White-collar professionals tend to wear tailored outfits and dress shoes, whereas blue-collar workers more often dress in jeans or uniforms and boots. The military requires uniforms that define individuals as members of a group; in addition, stripes and medals signify rank and accomplishments.

We use artifacts to define personal territories. Art lovers adorn their homes with paintings and sculptures. Religious families often express their commitments by displaying pictures of holy scenes and the Bible, the Koran, or other sacred texts. Lohmann, Arriaga, and Goodfriend (2003) found that couples who decorate their homes with objects depicting the couple as a couple rather than as individuals—wedding photos, for example—have greater closeness than couples with fewer artifacts that symbolize their couple status. People also decorate their profile pages on social networking sites to show images that matter to them and reflect their identities.

> Whenever I move, the first thing I have to do is get out the quilt that my grandmother made. Even if it is summer and I won't use the quilt, I have to unpack it first and put it out where I can see it. She brought me up, and seeing that quilt is my way of keeping her in my life.
>
> **JENETTA**

In her book *Composing a Life*, Mary Catherine Bateson (1990) observes that we turn houses into homes by filling them with what matters to us. We make impersonal spaces familiar and comfortable by adorning them with artifacts that express our experiences, relationships, values, and personalities. We use mugs given to us by special people, surround ourselves with books and magazines that announce our interests, and sprinkle our world with objects that reflect what we care about.

Although clothing has become more unisex in recent years, once you venture off campus, gendered styles are evident. Thus, women sometimes wear makeup, dresses with lace or other softening touches, skirts, high-heeled shoes, jewelry, and hosiery, all of which conform to the cultural ideal of femininity. Typically, men wear less jewelry, and their clothes and shoes tend to be more functional and less decorative. Flat shoes allow a person to walk comfortably or run if necessary; high heels don't. Men's clothing is looser and less binding, and it includes pockets for wallets, change, keys, and so forth. In contrast, women's clothing tends to be more tailored and often doesn't include pockets, making a purse necessary. Clothing is also used to reflect ethnic identity. In recent years, marketers have offered more ethnic clothing and jewelry so people can more easily acquire artifacts that express their distinctive cultural heritages. In his amusing (but also serious) book *The T-Shirt*, Scott Fresener (1995) profiles people who own thousands of T-shirts, each one important for defining some aspect of who they are or have been.

MindTap™

Everyday Skills To consider the influence of artifacts and environment in your life, complete the activity "Artifacts and Identity" at the end of the chapter or online.

DIVERSITY

Kwanzaa

Rituals allow people to acknowledge and celebrate important values (Otnes & Lowrey, 2004). One relatively new ritual is associated with Kwanzaa, which in 1966 was designated as a time for African Americans to honor their African heritage and the everyday activities of keeping a home. In this way, Kwanzaa symbolizes the centrality of home and family to African Americans historically and today (Bellamy, 1996; George, 1995).

The *kinara* is a branched candleholder that holds seven candles, one to be lit on each day of the Kwanzaa observance. Three red candles, which symbolize struggles, are placed on the left for days two, four, and six of the celebration. The day two candle symbolizes the principle of *kujichagulia*, or self-determination. The day four candle symbolizes *ujamma*, cooperative economics within communities. The day six candle represents *kuumba*, or creativity. On the right side of the kinara are placed three green candles to symbolize the future. The day three candle on the far right represents *ujima*, collective work and responsibility. The day five candle symbolizes *nio*, or purpose. The day seven candle represents *imani*, or faith. The middle candle is black, to stand for *umoja*, unity among black people.

On the sixth day of Kwanzaa, there is a feast called Karamu. During the feast, traditional African foods and family favorites are featured. Thus, Kwanzaa also celebrates foods that have been passed down through generations of Africans and African Americans.

Mark Adams/Getty Images

🔵 MindTap· What artifacts are important in your family's cultural and religious celebrations?

Tattoos, or tats, are increasingly popular. One in five Americans has at least one tat, and younger people are more likely than older people to have body art (Stancliff, 2013). The motivations for tattoos range from reminders of special people and occasions to statements of spiritual commitment to proclamations of values.

Environmental Factors

Environmental factors are elements of settings that affect how we feel and act. For instance, we respond to architecture, colors, room design, temperature, sounds, smells, and lighting (Sternberg, 2009). Rooms with comfortable chairs invite relaxation, whereas rooms with stiff chairs induce formality. Dimly lit rooms can set a romantic mood, although dark rooms can be depressing.

We tend to feel more lethargic on sultry summer days and more alert on crisp fall ones. Delicious smells can make us hungry, even if we weren't previously interested in food. Our bodies synchronize themselves to patterns of light, so we feel more alert during daylight than during the evening. In settings where people work during the night, extra lighting and even artificial skylights are used to simulate daylight so that workers stay alert.

The environments of most fast-food restaurants encourage customers to eat quickly and move on, whereas more expensive restaurants are designed to promote longer stays and extra spending on wines and desserts. In a recent study (Bakalar, 2012), one section of a Hardee's restaurant was transformed into a fine dining area—tablecloths, candles, and soundproofed walls to prevent noise from the rest of the restaurant. Although the diners in the regular and the fine dining section of Hardee's ate the same food, the people in the fine dining area spent more time eating, ate less food, and rated the food more highly.

Amount of noise may also be associated with social status. Prisons, which have low social status, are relentlessly noisy, and economically disadvantaged citizens tend to live in the most degraded soundscapes (Keizer, 2010). In business places, executives generally have private offices with doors that can be closed to keep out unwanted noise. Lower-level staff, in contrast, are often in cubicles without doors or in space shared with coworkers.

Proxemics and Personal Space

Proxemics refers to space and how we use it (Hall, 1968). Every culture has norms that prescribe how people should use space, how close people should be to one another, and how much space different people are entitled to have. In the United States, we generally interact with social acquaintances from a distance of 4 to 12 feet but are comfortable with 18 inches or less between ourselves and close friends and romantic partners (Hall, 1966). When we are angry with someone, we tend to move away and to resent it if the person approaches us. Nonverbal expectancy theory shows that societies establish norms for how closely people should come to one another and that violating those norms can negatively affect others' responses to us (Afifi & Burgoon, 2000; Burgoon & Hale, 1988; Mongeau, Carey, & Williams, 1998).

> **GARY**
>
> Part of our training for management was to learn how to manage turf. We were taught we should always try to get competitors into our offices—not to go to theirs. This gives us the advantage, just like playing on the home court gives a team an advantage. We also learned that we should go to subordinates' offices if we needed to criticize them so that they would feel less threatened and more willing to improve performance. The trainers also stressed the importance of meeting on neutral ground when we had to negotiate a deal with another company. They warned us never to meet on the other guys' turf because that would give them the advantage.

The amount of space with which people feel comfortable differs among cultures. The United States is an individualistic culture in which personal space, as well as personal rights, goals, and choices, is valued. Americans' individualism helps explain why families with sufficient finances give each child a separate bedroom. Likewise, American businesses generally have separate offices or at least cubicles so that each worker has individual space. In contrast, people in collectivist cultures place more emphasis on the group and community than individuals. Given this, it's not surprising that less personal space in homes, workplaces, and public areas is required in collectivist societies (Andersen, 2003).

A classic scene from *Office Space*, a 1999 film about overworked and dissatisfied IT workers, shows three of them crammed into the same cube for a meeting with a coworker.

20th Century Fox/Photofest

How people arrange space reflects how close they are and whether they want interaction (Guerrero & Floyd, 2006a). Couples who are very interdependent tend to have greater amounts of common space and less individual space in their homes than do couples who are more independent. Families that are less inclined to interact arrange furniture to discourage conversation. Chairs may be far apart and may face televisions instead of one another.

Chronemics

Chronemics refers to how we perceive and use time. In Western culture, there is a norm that important people with high status can keep others waiting (Hickson et al., 2004). Conversely, people with low status are expected to be punctual. It is standard practice to have to wait, sometimes a long while, to see a physician or attorney, even if you have an appointment. This conveys the message that the physician's time is more valuable than yours. Professors can be late to class and students are expected to wait, but students may be reprimanded if they appear after a class has begun. Subordinates are expected to report punctually to meetings, but bosses are allowed to be tardy.

Think about many everyday American phrases that reflect the cultural view that time is very valuable (Lakoff & Johnson, 1980): "Don't waste time," "Save time," "Spend time," "Can't spare time," "Invest time," "Run out of time," "Budget time," "Borrowed time," "Lose time," "Use time profitably." Many other cultures have more relaxed attitudes toward time and do not consider it impolite to come late to meetings or classes.

The length of time we spend with different people reflects our interpersonal priorities. When possible, we spend more time with people we like than with those we don't like or who bore us. In work settings, time is also spent with people considered more important. Bankers spend more time with clients who have large accounts, brokers spend more time with clients who have big investment portfolios, architects meet more often and for longer periods with companies that are building a series of large structures than with individuals who want to build a single home, and fund-raisers invest greater amounts of time in generous donors than in moderate contributors.

Paralanguage

Paralanguage is communication that is vocal but does not use words. It includes sounds, such as murmurs and gasps, and vocal qualities, such as volume, pitch, and inflection. Paralanguage also includes accents, pronunciation, and the complexity of sentences.

Our voices are versatile instruments that give others cues about how to interpret us. Whispering, for instance, signals secrecy and intimacy, whereas shouting conveys anger. Intonations that express ridicule are closely associated with dissatisfaction in marriage (Gottman, Markman, & Notarius, 1977). A derisive or sarcastic tone communicates scorn more emphatically than words.

To some extent, we control vocal cues that influence image. For instance, we can deliberately sound firm and sure of ourselves in job interviews when we want to project self-confidence. Yet vocal qualities we do not control as much can also influence how others perceive us. For instance, someone with a pronounced Bronx accent may be perceived as brash, and someone with a Southern drawl may be stereotyped as lazy. People with foreign accents often are falsely perceived as less intelligent than native speakers.

Paralanguage also reflects cultural heritage and may signal that we are members of specific communication communities. For example, in general African American speech has more vocal range, inflection, rhythmic variation and emphasis, and tonal quality than Caucasian speech (Garner, 1994; Ribeau et al., 1994).

Silence

A final type of nonverbal behavior is silence, which can communicate powerful messages. "I'm not speaking to you" actually speaks volumes. We use silence to communicate different meanings. For instance, it can symbolize contentment when intimates are so comfortable they don't need to talk. Silence can also communicate awkwardness, as you know if you've ever had trouble keeping conversation going on a first date. In some cultures, including many Eastern ones, silence indicates respect and thoughtfulness.

Silence soothes seriously ill babies. Hospital intensive care nurseries have found that special headphones that block noise reduce the stress caused by the sounds of respirators, ventilators, and other hospital machinery. Within the headphone is a mini-microphone that detects irritating low-frequency noises and eliminates them by generating anti-noise waves. In trials of the headphones, babies who wore them had fewer sleep disturbances and less change in blood pressure ("Cyberscope," 1996). Similarly, some hospitals are now cutting down on noises that have been shown to elevate patients' blood pressure, hinder wound healing, and otherwise harm patients (Landro, 2013).

Yet silence isn't always comforting. In some families, children are disciplined by being ignored. No matter what the child says or does, parents refuse to acknowledge his or her existence. In later life, the silencing strategy may also surface. You know how disconfirming silence can be if you've ever said "hello" to someone and gotten no reply. Even if the other person didn't deliberately ignore you, you felt slighted. We sometimes deliberately freeze out intimates and refuse to answer texts from friends with whom we're angry. In some military academies, such as West Point, silencing is a recognized method of stripping a cadet of personhood if he or she is perceived as having broken the academy code.

> Silencing is the cruelest thing you can do to a person. That was how my parents disciplined all of us. They told us we were bad and then refused to speak to us—sometimes for several hours. I can't describe how awful it felt to get no response from them, to be a nonperson. I would have preferred physical punishment. I'll never use silencing with my kids.

GINDER

MindTap

Everyday Skills To practice paralinguistics, complete the activity "Paralinguistic Cues" at the end of the chapter or online.

The complex system of nonverbal communication includes kinesics, haptics, physical appearance, artifacts, environmental features, space, chronemics, paralanguage, and silence. In the final section of this chapter, we consider guidelines for improving the effectiveness of our nonverbal communication.

SOCIAL MEDIA AND NONVERBAL COMMUNICATION

As is the case with every aspect of interpersonal communication, nonverbal behavior is connected to social media. Perhaps the most obvious issue is that nonverbal communication is more restricted in digital and online communication than in f2f interaction. Words in an email or text message don't tell us whether the person who wrote them is serious, sarcastic, or playful. The need to signal others how to interpret our words and to understand how we should interpret their words compelled invention of emoticons such as:

(::[ ]::) = band aid to symbolize comfort
;) = smile + wink to symbolize playfulness
=^.^= = cat to symbolize friskiness

But emoticons aren't expressive enough for some people, which led to the development of stickers, which are cartoon-like icons that people send to replace text messages. First used in Japan, stickers are gaining popularity among Westerners, who find words and even emoticons insufficient for what they want to express. Now that stickers have caught on, the race for super-cute is on, with startups trying to come up with the cutest stickers. Path offers Willa, a playful wombat; Facebook offers Pusheen, a cat that sometimes presents herself as a unicorn, and Napoli, a very emotional ice cream cone (Rusli, 2013). Facebook founder Mark Zuckerberg sends a blue thumbs up sign to symbolize approval. An undergraduate sends a sleepy bunny cartoon to signal that she's tired (Rusli, 2013). And stickers don't need translating when shared between users who have different languages.

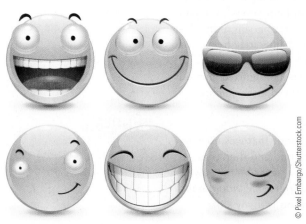

© Pixel Embargo/Shutterstock.com

A second interesting facet of nonverbal communication in social media is the size of a person's electronic footprint. Some people update their Facebook pages at least daily and sometimes more often, whereas others update their Facebook pages infrequently. Some people comment on nearly everything posted by others, whereas other people comment more selectively. There is no research to tell us what it means when people have small or large electronic footprints, but the noticeable differences in how much space people take are striking. Electronic footprints don't go away just because we delete texts or photos, so you should exercise caution in what you post online and what text messages you send.

Third, as we noted earlier in this chapter, digital communication can compete with, and sometimes interfere with, f2f communication. Do you send or check texts while talking with others f2f? (And don't think people don't notice just because you have eye contact while texting!) If so, does that convey the level of responsiveness you want to convey? Dual perspective might lead you to think about the person with whom you are in face-to-face contact. Is he or she someone who is as wired to social media as you? If not, you might want to focus on the f2f interaction.

The presence of social media in our lives has not been lost on furniture manufacturers. Traditional home offices are out and chairs and chaises specifically designed for mobile computing are in (Hrabi, 2013). Dubbed the lifestyle work-at-home collection, this furniture has wide arms for laptops and allows people to adjust them infinitely.

GUIDELINES FOR IMPROVING NONVERBAL COMMUNICATION

The following two guidelines should decrease the chance that you will misunderstand others' nonverbal behaviors or that others will misperceive yours.

Monitor Your Nonverbal Communication

Think about the previous discussion of ways we use nonverbal behaviors to announce our identities. Are you projecting the image you desire? Do friends ever tell you that you seem uninterested or far away when they are talking to you? If so, you can monitor your nonverbal actions so that you convey greater involvement and interest in conversations.

Have you set up your spaces so that they invite the kind of interaction you prefer, or are they arranged to interfere with good communication? Paying attention to nonverbal dimensions of your world can empower you to use them more effectively to achieve your interpersonal goals.

Interpret Others' Nonverbal Communication Tentatively

Although stores are filled with popular advice books that promise to show you how to read nonverbal communication, there really aren't any surefire formulas. It's naive to think we can precisely decode something as complex, ambiguous, and personal as nonverbal communication.

DIVERSITY

Policing a Multicultural Society

"Policing a Multicultural Society" is the title of a training manual given to recruits training to become New York police officers. The goal of the manual is to educate officers-to-be about customs and behaviors that they might misinterpret (Goldstein, 2013). Here's a sampling of advice included in the manual:

1. Chinese immigrants are uncomfortable asking for assistance from strangers.
2. African immigrants shake hands with a light touch of palms instead of the firm grip that is more common among Westerners.
3. Puerto Rican family members engage in eye-checking that should not be interpreted as sending signals not to speak honestly to police.
4. Immigrants from rural Mexico tend to avoid direct eye contact with authority figures.
5. New Arab immigrants are likely to get out of their car when stopped by police. This is a sign of courtesy and respect; it is not a threat.
6. Arab immigrants often speak loudly. This should not be interpreted as shouting or as fighting (for example, it does not indicate domestic violence).

But perhaps the most interesting advice in the book is not to assume that all members of any ethnic group are alike. The manual warns against stereotyping or assuming that all members of a group are bad just because a few have done bad things. The guide recommends that officers consider how they feel when a few police officers are caught engaging in a scandal and citizens assume all police are unethical.

In this chapter, we've discussed findings about the meanings people attach to nonverbal behaviors. It's important to realize that these are only generalizations. We cannot state what any particular behavior ever means to specific people in a given context. For instance, we've said that satisfied couples tend to sit closer together than unhappy couples. As a general rule, this is true in Western society. However, sometimes very contented couples prefer to keep distance between them. In work settings, people who don't look at us may be preoccupied with solving a problem and do not intend to ignore us. Different cultures teach members different rules for expressing and interpreting nonverbal behavior. Because nonverbal communication is ambiguous and personal, we should not assume we can interpret it with absolute precision. Effective communicators qualify interpretations of nonverbal communication with awareness of personal and contextual factors.

Personal Qualifications

Generalizations about nonverbal behavior tell us only what is generally the case. They may not apply to particular individuals. Although eye contact generally indicates responsiveness in Western culture, some people close their eyes to concentrate when listening. Similarly, people who cross their arms and have a rigid posture often are expressing hostility or lack of interest in interaction. However, the same behaviors might mean a person feels cold and is trying to conserve body heat. Most people use less inflection, fewer gestures, and a slack posture when they're not really interested in what they're talking about. However, we exhibit these same behaviors when we are tired.

Because nonverbal behaviors are ambiguous and vary among cultures and individuals, we need to be cautious about how we interpret others. A good practice is to rely on *I* language, not *you* language, which we discussed in Chapter 4. *You* language might lead us to inaccurately say of someone who doesn't look at us, "You're communicating lack of interest." A more responsible statement would use *I* language to say, "When you don't look at me, I feel you're not interested in what I'm saying." Using *I* language reminds us to take responsibility for our judgments and feelings. In addition, it reduces the likelihood of making others defensive by inaccurately interpreting their nonverbal behavior.

Contextual Qualifications   Our nonverbal communication also reflects the settings we inhabit. Most people are more at ease on their own turf than on someone else's, so we tend to be friendlier and more outgoing in our homes than in business meetings and public places. We also dress according to context. Students who see me in professional clothing on campus often are surprised to find me in jeans or a running suit when they come to my home or see me in town.

Immediate physical setting is not the only context that affects nonverbal communication. As we have seen, all communication, including the nonverbal dimension, reflects the values and understandings of particular cultures. We are likely to misinterpret people from other cultures when we impose on them the norms and rules of our own.

I often have been misinterpreted in this country. My first semester here, a professor told me to be more assertive and to speak up in class. I could not do that, I told him. He said I should put myself forward, but I have been brought up not to do that. In Taiwan, that is very rude and ugly, and we are taught not to speak up to teachers. Now that I have been here for 3 years, I sometimes speak in classes, but I am still more quiet than Americans. I know my professors think I am not so smart because I am quiet, but that is the teaching of my country.

Even within our own country, we have diverse speech communities, and each has its own rules for nonverbal behavior. We run the risk of misinterpreting men if we judge them by the norms of feminine speech communities. A man who doesn't make "listening noises" may well be listening intently according to the rules of masculine speech communities. Similarly, men often misperceive women as agreeing when they nod and make listening noises while another is talking. According to feminine speech communities, ongoing feedback is a way to signal interest, not necessarily approval. We should try to adopt a dual perspective when interpreting others, especially when different social groups are involved.

We can become more effective nonverbal communicators if we monitor our own nonverbal behaviors and qualify our interpretation of others by keeping personal and contextual considerations in mind.

MindTap™

Everyday Skills To practice creating responsible and clear messages about nonverbal behaviors, complete the activity "Using *I* Language about Nonverbal Behaviors" at the end of the chapter or online.

MEI-LING

CHAPTER SUMMARY

In this chapter, we've explored the world beyond words. We began by noting both the similarities and the differences between verbal and nonverbal communication. Next, we discussed how nonverbal communication functions to supplement or replace verbal messages, to regulate interaction, to reflect and establish relationship-level meanings, and to express cultural values. Because much of our communication using social media restricts the kinds of nonverbal behaviors we rely on in f2f communication, we've developed emoticons and other ways of conveying nonverbal meanings when online or on social media sites.

We discussed nine types of nonverbal communication. These are:

- kinesics (face and body motion)
- proxemics (use of space)
- physical appearance
- artifacts
- environmental features
- haptics (use of touch)
- chronemics (use of and orientations to time)
- paralanguage
- silence

Each type of nonverbal communication reflects cultural understandings and values and also expresses our personal identities and feelings toward others. In this sense, nonverbal communication has a theatrical dimension because it is a primary way we create and present images of ourselves.

Because nonverbal communication, like its verbal cousin, is symbolic, it has no inherent meaning. Instead, its meaning is something we construct as we interpret nonverbal behaviors. Effectiveness requires that we learn to monitor our own nonverbal communication and to exercise caution in interpreting that of others.

 MindTap™

Key Concepts

Practice defining the chapter's terms by using online flashcards.

FLASHCARDS...

artifacts 147	**immediacy** 139	**paralanguage** 150
chronemics 150	**kinesics** 143	**proxemics** 149
haptics 144	**nonverbal communication** 135	

Continuing the Conversation

Jason Harris © 2001 Wadsworth

When you've watched the video online, critique and analyze this encounter based on the principles you learned in this chapter. Then compare your work with the author's suggested responses. Online, even more videos will let you continue the conversation with your instructor.

> You've been hired to help doctors learn to listen more effectively when interacting with patients. You observe the following interaction between Dr. Zhug and Ms. Ryder, who came in to find out why she is so tired.

Dr. Zhug: Ms. Ryder, all the tests we did show you are normal.

Ms. Ryder: If I'm normal, why do I feel tired all the time?

Dr. Zhug: Perhaps you need to get more sleep.

Ms. Ryder: I've been getting more sleep than ever, and in the last 6 months I've felt tired no matter how many hours I sleep.

Dr. Zhug: According to the tests, you have no medical problems. Perhaps your fatigue is emotional. This is common in women your age. Would you like a referral for counseling?

Ms. Ryder: Fatigue has nothing to do with my age. I'm only 35, and I felt fine 6 months ago.

Dr. Zhug: You might try sleeping more than you used to.

Ms. Ryder: I just told you I am sleeping more, and it's not helping. What I need to know is …

Dr. Zhug: Ms. Ryder, there's no need to get hysterical. I know how to read test results, and physically you are normal.

Ms. Ryder: Doctor, this isn't normal for me. I can't do my work well. I don't have the energy I need for my family.

Dr. Zhug: I wish I could help you.

Identify nonverbal behaviors of Dr. Zhug that Ms. Ryder could interpret as a lack of attentiveness or interest in her.

1. How does Ms. Ryder's nonverbal communication change during her conversation with Dr. Zhug? To what would you attribute the changes?
2. Based on what you have learned about effective interpersonal communication from this and previous chapters, what feedback would you give Dr. Zhug so that he can communicate more effectively with patients?

Assessing Yourself

Begin the process of applying this chapter's concepts by taking a self-assessment quiz here or online—where you will find out what the results mean.

Purpose: Communication researchers (Richmond, McCroskey, & Johnson, 2003) developed a test to measure immediacy behaviors, which refer to actions that express responsiveness and liking.

Instructions: Use the following scale to indicate how much each of the 26 statements applies to you. Some of the statements may seem redundant, but you should answer each one.

5 Very often
4 Often
3 Occasionally
2 Rarely
1 Never

_____ 1. I use my hands and arms to gesture while talking to people.

_____ 2. I touch others on the shoulder or arm while talking to them.

_____ 3. I use a monotone or dull voice while talking to people.

_____ 4. I look over or away from others while talking to people.

_____ 5. I move away from others when they touch me while we are talking.

_____ 6. I have a relaxed body position when I talk to people.

_____ 7. I frown while talking to people.

_____ 8. I avoid eye contact while talking to people.

_____ 9. I have a tense body position while talking to people.

_____ 10. I sit close or stand close to people while talking with them.

_____ 11. My voice is monotonous or dull when I talk to people.

_____ 12. I use a variety of vocal expressions when I talk to people.

_____ 13. I gesture when I talk to people.

_____ 14. I am animated when I talk to people.

_____ 15. I have a bland facial expression when I talk to people.

_____ 16. I move closer to people when I talk to them.

_____ 17. I look directly at people while talking to them.

_____ 18. I am stiff when I talk to people.

_____ 19. I have a lot of vocal variety when I talk to people.

_____ 20. I avoid gesturing while I am talking to people.

_____ 21. I lean toward people when I talk to them.

_____ 22. I maintain eye contact with people when I talk to them.

_____ 23. I try not to sit or stand close to people when I talk with them.

_____ 24. I lean away from people when I talk to them.

_____ 25. I smile when I talk to people.

_____ 26. I avoid touching people when I talk to them.

Everyday Skills

Build your communication skills further by completing the following activities here or online.

1. Campus Rules for Nonverbal Communication

   To become more aware of rules governing nonverbal communication, go to a place on your campus that is central for foot traffic. Spend 15 minutes observing nonverbal rules that govern behavior in that spot. For example, who moves to the side if two people are headed directly toward each other? How often and for how long is eye contact exchanged? How often do people smile as they pass one another? Are men and women equally likely to smile?

2. Artifacts and Identity

   - How did artifacts in your childhood contribute to your gender identity? What kinds of toys did your parents give you? Did they ever discourage you from playing with particular kinds of toys? Did you ask for toys that aren't the ones society prescribes for your sex (boys asking for dolls, girls for train sets)? Did your parents let you have the toys?

   - Now, think about the clothing your parents gave you. If you're a woman, did your parents expect you to wear frilly dresses and stay clean? If you're a man, did your parents give you clothes meant for rough play and getting dirty?

- Do you have artifacts that reflect your ethnic identity? What objects are part of your celebrations and spiritual observances? Do you have any jewelry or clothes that reflect your ethnic heritage?

3. Paralinguistic Cues

Say "Oh, really" to express the following meanings:

- I don't believe what you just said.

- Wow! That's interesting.

- I find your comment boring.

- That's juicy gossip!

- I can't believe you think I can get the report done that soon.

Now, say "You love me" to convey these meanings:

- You really do? I hadn't realized that.

- That ploy won't work. I told you we're through.

- You couldn't possibly love me after what you did!

- Me? I'm the one you love?

- You? I didn't think you loved anyone.

4. Using *I* Language about Nonverbal Behaviors

I language makes communication about nonverbal behaviors more responsible and clear. Practice the skill of translating *you* language into *I* language to describe nonverbal behavior.

Example:

You Language	*I* Language
You're staring at me.	When you look at me so intensely, I feel uneasy.

You Language	*I* Language
I hate it when you give me that know-it-all look.	_____
I can tell you don't believe me by your expression.	_____
Don't crowd me.	_____
Your T-shirt is offensive.	_____

DO ... Additional interactive discussions, online quizzes, and activities that your instructor may assign for a grade.

Engaging with Ideas

Reflect and write about the ideas in this chapter by considering questions about personal, workplace, and ethical applications, here or online.

Personal Application Survey your room or apartment. Is furniture arranged to promote or discourage interaction? What's the ratio between common space (game room or living room) and individual space (study, bedroom)? What does your arrangement of space say about your identity and preferences?

Workplace Application **REFLECT ON...** Describe the typical dress for women and men in the profession you intend to pursue. Are there types of dress that would be inappropriate in this profession? If so, why?

Ethical Application Is it disrespectful to send or check text messages when you are in a f2f meeting or social interaction with others? Do the ethics of doing so vary, depending on the people with whom you are f2f? Explain your answer.

Thinking Critically

Think and write critically about the ideas in this chapter, here or online.

1. Think about the information on lawyers' nonverbal communication (in the section "Kinesics"). What ethical issues are involved in lawyers' use of nonverbal behaviors in an effort to influence jurors? What ethical issues are involved in judges' restrictions of lawyers' nonverbal communication? Is this a violation of the right to free speech?

2. Visit four restaurants near your campus. Describe the seats, lighting, music (if any), distance between tables, and colors of decor. Do you find any relationship between nonverbal communication patterns and expensiveness of restaurants?

3. Read an online journal that is devoted exclusively to research on haptic communication. Visit Haptics-E at http://www.haptics-e.org.

4. Founded in 1997, the Center for Nonverbal Studies is located in Spokane, Washington, and La Jolla, California. It publishes *The Nonverbal Dictionary of Gestures, Signs, and Body Language Cues* and presents essays on nonverbal behaviors by anthropologists, archeologists, biologists, linguists, and communication scholars. For more information, visit http://humanresources.about.com/od/interpersonalcommunicatio1/a/nonverbal_com.htm/. This is a site that offers tips for understanding nonverbal communication and includes a link to the *Dictionary of Nonverbal Gestures, Signs, and Body Language.*

REFLECT ON...

MINDFUL LISTENING

START... experiencing this chapter's topics with an online video!

Topics covered in this chapter

The Listening Process

Obstacles to Mindful Listening

Forms of Nonlistening

Adapting Listening to Communication Goals

Social Media and Listening

Guidelines for Effective Listening

After studying this chapter, you should be able to . . .

Describe six elements in the listening process.

List major external and internal obstacles to mindful listening.

Identify your own nonlistening behaviors.

Identify your reasons for listening during a typical day.

Recognize how social media can hinder mindful listening.

Apply chapter guidelines to enhance your listening skills.

READ... the complete chapter text in a rich interactive eBook!

Anna Deavere Smith is a playwright, an artist in residence at MTV, a recipient of the MacArthur Foundation "genius" award, a performance studies teacher at Tisch School of the Arts, and a professor at New York University. She's won high praise for her one-woman shows, *Fires in the Mirror*, which dealt with ethnic turmoil in Crown Heights, Brooklyn; and *Twilight: Los Angeles*, which focused on the riots that erupted following the acquittal of the police officers accused of beating Rodney King. She also played the president's secretary in *The American President* and a paralegal in *Philadelphia*, and she had a continuing role in the television series *The West Wing*.

Anna Deavere Smith lists another professional accomplishment on her résumé—teaching medical students at Yale and law students at New York University. You might wonder what qualifies her to instruct medical and law students. After all, she's not a doctor or lawyer.

Anna Deavere Smith is a virtuoso listener. That's why she was hired to teach medical and law students. Doctors and lawyers need to listen, and conventional medical and legal training doesn't teach them how to listen well. That's why the school turned to Anna Deavere Smith. She says, "Listening is not just hearing what someone tells you word for word. You have to listen with a heart. . . . It's very hard work" (Arenson, 2002, p. 35). In teaching prospective doctors and attorneys how to listen well to patients and clients, Smith emphasizes the need to be fully present with others.

Doctors and attorneys aren't the only ones who need to listen well. We all do. If you think about your normal day, you'll realize that listening—or trying to—takes up at least half your waking time (Wagner, 2001; Wolvin, 2009). You listen in classes, listen to acquaintances in casual conversation, listen to your parents during phone calls, listen to clerks in stores, listen to your supervisor and customers when you're at work, and listen to friends when they talk to you about their lives.

In this chapter, we discuss listening and how to listen effectively. First, we consider what listening involves. Next, we identify obstacles to effective listening and how we can minimize them. We also consider some common forms of nonlistening. The fourth section of the chapter explains different types of listening and the distinct skills needed for each. We then apply the ideas we have covered to digital and online environments. To wrap up the chapter, we identify guidelines for improving listening effectiveness.

THE LISTENING PROCESS

Listening is a complex process that involves far more than our ears. To listen well, we rely on our ears, minds, and hearts. The multifaceted aspects of listening are reflected in the Chinese character shown in Figure 6.1, which includes the symbols for the eyes, ears, and heart.

Although we often use the words *listening* and *hearing* as if they were synonyms, actually they are different. **Hearing** is a physiological activity that occurs when sound waves hit our eardrums. People who are deaf or hearing-impaired receive messages visually through lip reading or sign language. Listening has psychological and cognitive dimensions that mere hearing, or physically receiving messages, does not.

The International Listening Association (1995; see the ILA website at http://www.listen .org) emphasizes that listening is an active process, which means we must exert effort to listen

Communication in Everyday Life

WORKPLACE

Good Listening = Career Advancement

The costs of poor listening in the workplace can be very high. Doctors who don't listen fully to patients may misdiagnose or mistreat medical problems (Christensen, 2004; Nyquist, 1992; Scholz, 2005; Underwood & Adler, 2005). For this reason, an increasing number of medical practices hire communication specialists to provide listening workshops for medical practitioners. They'd rather pay the consultants' fees than the legal fees for malpractice suits that can result from poor listening.

Doctors aren't the only ones who need to listen well. Senior executives in a number of fields identify listening as a necessary job skill more often than they identify any other skill, including managerial ability and technical competence (Darling & Dannels, 2003; Gabric & McFadden, 2001; Landrum & Harrold, 2003).

Listening skill is ranked as the single most important feature of effective managers (Winsor et al., 1997). It's also the top-ranked communication skill for accountants (Morreale, 2004). Just as listening skill is associated with career advancement, poor listening is a leading reason that some people don't advance in their careers (Deal & Kennedy, 1999).

MindTap What purposes of listening will be most relevant to your planned career?

Eyes

Ears

Heart

Figure **6.1**

The Chinese Character for the Word "Listening"

well. We can define **listening** as an active, complex process that consists of being mindful, physically receiving messages, selecting and organizing messages, interpreting messages, responding, and remembering.

Mindfulness

The first step in listening is to make a decision to be mindful. **Mindfulness** is being fully present in the moment. It's what Anna Deavere Smith teaches medical and law students. When we are mindful, we don't check text messages, let our thoughts drift to what we plan to do this weekend, or focus on our own feelings and responses. Instead, we tune in fully to another person and try to understand what that person is communicating, without imposing our own ideas, judgments, or feelings. Mindfulness grows out of the decision to attend fully to another. Physically, this is signified by paying attention, adopting an involved posture, keeping eye contact, and indicating interest in what the other person says (Bolton, 1986).

Because mindful listening involves taking the perspective of another, it fosters dual perspective—a cornerstone of effective communication. In addition, mindfulness enhances the effectiveness of the other person's communication. When people sense we are really listening, they tend to elaborate on their ideas and express themselves in more depth.

Mindfulness is a choice. It is not a technique, nor is it a talent that some people have and others don't. No amount of skill will make you a good listener if you don't make a commitment to attend to another person fully.

MARISA   I always thought I was a good listener until I spent 2 years living in Japan. In that culture there is a much deeper meaning to listening. I realized that most of the time I was only hearing others. Often, I was thinking of my responses while they were still talking. I had not been listening with my mind and heart.

Physically Receiving Messages

The second process involved in listening is hearing, or physically receiving messages. As we noted earlier, hearing is a physiological process in which sound waves hit our eardrums so that we become aware of noises, such as music, traffic, or human voices. For people who have hearing impairments, messages are received in other ways, such as writing, lip reading, and American Sign Language.

Receiving messages is a prerequisite for listening. For most of us, hearing is automatic and unhindered. However, people with hearing impairments may have difficulty receiving oral messages. When we speak with someone who has a hearing disability, we should face the person and ask if we are coming across clearly.

Hearing impairments are not the only restriction on physically receiving messages. Hearing ability tends to decline when we are fatigued from concentrating on communication. You may have noticed that it's harder to pay attention in classes that run 75 minutes than in classes that run 50 minutes. Background noise can also interfere with hearing. It's difficult to hear well if loud music is playing, a television is blaring, cell phones are chiming, or others are talking nearby.

Women and men seem to differ somewhat in their listening. As a rule, women are more attentive than men to the whole of communication. Thus, many men tend to focus their hearing on specific content aspects of communication, whereas women generally are more likely to attend to the whole of communication, noticing details, tangents, and relationship-level meanings. Judy Pearson (1985), a prominent communication scholar, suggests that this could result from the brain's hemispheric specializations. Women usually have better-developed right lobes, which govern creative and holistic thinking, whereas men typically have better-developed left lobes, which control analytic and linear information processing. Recent research also indicates that women tend to use both lobes of their brain to listen, but men tend to engage only their more-developed left lobes ("Men Use," 2000). This doesn't mean that one sex listens better than the other, but it does mean they tend to listen somewhat differently.

Think you get more done when you multitask? Think you can absorb a class lecture while texting friends and checking eBay's latest offerings? Think again. Researchers have amassed considerable evidence that multitasking doesn't increase efficiency or productivity. In fact, it's very clear that the human brain simply isn't capable of engaging in two conceptual tasks simultaneously (Brown, 2010; Gallagher, 2009; Rubinstein, Meyer, & Evans, 2001). When you think you are multitasking, actually your brain is switching quickly from one task to another. Each time the brain switches, it has to reorient itself, which takes time and mental energy. Again and again, experiments show that people perform tasks more quickly and accurately when they do them one at a time rather than trying to do them simultaneously (Klingberg, 2008; Foerde, Knowlton, & Poldrack, 2006; Nass & Yen, 2010; Opir, Nass, & Wagner, in press; Rubinstein et al., 2001).

Many people feel they are operating at peak level when they multitask. They get a buzz from jumping in and out of tasks. That's what David Glenn (2010) calls the "illusion of competence," and he says it is particularly evident in students who often send text messages and check Facebook while in classes. They feel hyped and assume they've absorbed what happens in a class. But when it comes to recalling information or synthesizing and analyzing it, they're at a disadvantage because they didn't really grasp the information.

The human brain uses two parts of the brain for learning. When working on a single task, the hippocampus takes over helping us to acquire information in ways that we can recall and apply. When the brain is asked to work on two or more tasks at the same time, it relies more on the striatum, which controls habitual learning and is limited in its ability to apply the information (Foerde et al., 2006). Thus, when a person tries to do more than one thing at a time, he or she is relying on a part of the brain that is less able to manage information flexibly and complexly.

MindTap How often do you try to multitask? Do you ever feel the "buzz" described above?

MARK

My girlfriend amazes me. We'll have a conversation, and then later one of us will bring it up again. What I remember is what we decided in the talk. She remembers that, too, but she also remembers all the details about where we were and what was going on in the background and particular things one of us said in the conversation. I never notice all of that stuff, and I sure don't remember it later.

Selecting and Organizing Material

The third element of listening is selecting and organizing material. As we noted in Chapter 3, we don't perceive everything around us. Instead, we selectively attend to only some messages and elements of our environments. What we attend to depends on many factors, including our interests, cognitive structures, and expectations. Selective listening is also influenced by culture; even in utero, fetuses become attuned to the sounds of their language ("Babies Seem," 2013). Thus, people who learn a second language later in life may have difficulty recognizing sounds that weren't in their first language (Monastersky, 2001).

We can monitor our tendencies to attend selectively by remembering that we are more likely to notice stimuli that are intense, loud, unusual, or that otherwise stand out from the flow of communication. This implies that we may overlook communicators who speak quietly and don't call attention to themselves. Intan, an Asian American student, once told me that Americans often ignore what she says because she speaks softly and unassertively. If we're aware of the tendency not to notice people who speak quietly, we can guard against it so that we don't miss out on people and messages that may be important.

CHAD I had to have outpatient surgery on my knee last year. My doctor told me to bring an adult with me for the surgery. I said my friend Jake was going to bring me and come back to pick me up. The doctor said, "No, he must stay here with you the whole time." The doctor explained that I wouldn't be able to listen carefully to instructions because of anxiety and the anesthesia. I thought he was wrong, but he wasn't. After the surgery, I thought I was alert and normal when the doctor explained how to take care of the knee and what was normal and not normal after this surgery. By the time Jake drove me home, I couldn't remember a thing the doctor had said.

Once we've selected what to notice, we then organize the stimuli to which we've attended. We try to understand not just content but also the person speaking. Is she or he anxious or calm, open to advice or closed to it, and so on? Does she or he want to vent and may not want advice until after having had a chance to express their feelings? Finally, we decide how we should proceed in the conversation.

It's important to remember that *we construct others and their communication* when we use our schemata to make sense of situations and people. In other words, we create meaning by how we select and organize communication. Remembering this reminds us to keep perceptions tentative and open to revision. In the course of interaction, we may want to modify perceptions.

Interpreting Communication

The fourth step in listening is interpreting others' communication. The most important principle for effective interpretation is to be person-centered so that you understand another person's perspective on her or his terms. Certainly, you won't always agree with other people's ideas or how they see themselves, others, and situations. Engaging in dual perspective doesn't require you to agree with others' perspectives; however, it does require you to make an earnest effort to understand them.

To interpret someone on her or his own terms is one of the greatest gifts we can give another. Too often, we impose our meanings on others, try to correct or argue with them about what they feel, or crowd out their words with our own.

BART

I'd been married and working for years when I decided I wanted to come back to school and finish my degree. When I mentioned it to the guys I worked with, they all came down hard on me. They said I was looking for an easy life as a College Joe and trying to get above them. My dad said it would be irresponsible to quit work when I had a wife and child, and he said no self-respecting man would do that. It seemed like everyone had a view of what I was doing and why, and their views had nothing to do with mine. The only person who really listened to me was Elaine, my wife. When I told her I was thinking about going back to school, the first thing out of her mouth was, "What would that mean to you?" She didn't presume she knew my reasons, and she didn't start off arguing with me. She just asked what it meant to me, then listened for a long, long time while I talked about how I felt. She focused completely on understanding me. Maybe that's why we're married.

Responding

Effective listening also involves **responding**, which is communicating attention and interest. As we noted in Chapter 1, interpersonal communication is a transactional process in which we simultaneously listen and speak. We don't respond only when others have finished speaking; rather, we respond throughout interaction. This is what makes listening such an active process. Good listeners let others know they are interested throughout interaction by adopting attentive postures, nodding their heads, making eye contact, and giving vocal responses such as "mm-hmm" and "go on." These nonverbal behaviors demonstrate engagement. On the relationship level of meaning, responsiveness communicates that we care about the other person.

Remembering

The final aspect of listening is **remembering**, which is the process of retaining what you have heard. According to communication teachers Ron Adler and Russell Proctor (2014), we remember less than half of a message immediately after we hear it. As time goes by, retention decreases further; we recall only about 35% of a message 8 hours after hearing it.

Because we forget about two-thirds of what we hear, it's important to make sure we retain the most important third. Effective listeners let go of a lot of details to retain the more important content. Later in this chapter, we discuss strategies for retaining material.

OBSTACLES TO MINDFUL LISTENING

We've seen that a lot is involved in mindful listening. Adding to the complexity are hindrances to effective listening. There are two broad types of barriers to mindful listening: obstacles in the communication situation and obstacles in the communicators. (Did you notice that ideas to be discussed in this section were organized into two broad classes to aid your retention of the basic content?)

External Obstacles

Many barriers to mindful listening are present in communication situations. Although we can't always control external obstacles, we can be aware of them and try to compensate for the noise they create.

Message Overload The sheer amount of communication we engage in makes it difficult to listen fully all the time. Think about your typical day. You go to classes for 3 hours. How much you learn and how well you do on examinations depend on your ability to listen mindfully to material that is often difficult. After listening for 50 minutes in a history class, you listen for 50 minutes in a communication class, followed by 50 more minutes in a business class. A great deal of information comes your way in those three periods. After classes, you read three texts from friends—you need to remember them and respond before the day ends. You start doing research on the Web and find more than 300 sites for your topic—how can you possibly process all the information they offer? Then you go to work, and your supervisor informs you of a new procedure. Feeling rushed, your supervisor describes the procedure quickly, and you are expected to understand and follow it.

We often feel overwhelmed by the amount of information we are supposed to understand and retain. To deal with the overload, we often screen the talk around us, much as we screen calls on our answering machines, to decide when to listen carefully and when to attend more superficially (Todorov, Chaiken, & Henderson, 2002).

RAYMOND I've been married nearly 30 years, so I've figured out when I have to listen sharply to Edna and when I can just let her talk flow in one ear and out the other. She's a talker, but most of what she talks about isn't important. But if I hear code words, I know to listen up. If Edna says, "I'm really upset about such and such," or if she says, "We have a problem," my ears perk up.

Message Complexity The more detailed and complicated the message, the more difficult it is to follow and retain it. People for whom English is a second language often find it hard to understand English speakers who use complex sentences with multiple clauses or slang expressions. Even native speakers of English often feel overwhelmed by the complexity of some messages. It's tempting to tune out messages that are filled with technical words, detailed information, and complex sentences. If we let a message's complexity overwhelm us, however, we may perform poorly in school or on the job, and we may let down friends and intimates.

When we have to listen to messages that are dense with information, we should summon up extra energy. In addition, taking notes and asking questions for clarification may help us understand and retain difficult information. A third strategy is to group material as you listen, organizing the ideas in ways that make later recall easier.

Noise A third impediment to effective listening is physical noise. Perhaps you've been part of a crowd at a concert or a game. If so, you probably had to shout to the person next to you just to be heard. Although most noise is not as overwhelming as the roar of crowds, there is always some noise in communication situations. It might be music or television in the background, other conversations nearby, pagers that are beeping, or thunder or traffic sounds from outside.

> **GREGORY**
>
> I've been in sales for a long time, and I know when clients are really interested and when they're not. If someone answers a phone when I'm in his or her office, I know they aren't focused on what I'm saying. Taking calls or leaving the door open for people to drop in communicates that they're not interested in me or the service I represent.

Gregory reminds us that allowing distractions communicates a lack of interest on the relationship level of meaning. Good listeners do what they can to minimize environmental distractions. It's considerate to turn off a television or lower the volume of music if someone wants to talk with you. It's also appropriate to move away from a noisy area to cut down on distractions. Likewise, it is courteous to turn off the ringers on cells when attending lectures, concerts, meetings, or other events in which a ring tone could distract others who have come to listen. But others aren't the only ones who are distracted by ring tones. Cognitive psychologists report

Communication in Everyday Life

SOCIAL MEDIA

Technological Overload

Our era is dominated by digital and online communication. We can reach others faster than ever before, and we can find them even if they are in transit or on vacation. Many people feel overloaded by the relentless stream of information that technology makes possible.

You don't have to be hopelessly outdated to wonder whether communication technologies impede meaningful communication between people. Does being wired all the time diminish how we interact with people we are with in any given moment? Author Jonathan Coleman (2000) recounts a summer evening when he attended his daughter's lacrosse practice. Standing beside him was another player's father who was completely absorbed in a conversation on his cell and didn't notice that his daughter, who was on the field, kept looking toward him for approval and attention. Can we really engage others if we have a cell phone handy and we answer it if it rings? Can we listen well to any conversation—in person or on a phone—if we are actually or potentially involved in more than one conversation or activity? If we can't, then does technology, as Coleman suggests, create the illusion of intimacy with others while actually keeping us apart from them?

that the sound notifying you of the arrivals of texts, emails, and calls distracts you and your ability to give full attention to the person with you (Begley, 2009b).

Controlling distractions is also important in the workplace. Nearly one in five workers has been reprimanded for poor manners because they used electronic devices during meetings (Williams, 2009). Some organizations, including United Talent Agency and Creative Artists Agency, ban smartphones in all meetings.

Internal Obstacles

In addition to external obstacles, five barriers inside us can hinder listening: preoccupation, prejudgment, reacting to emotionally loaded language, lack of effort, and not recognizing or adapting to diverse listening styles.

Preoccupation   When we are absorbed in our own thoughts and concerns, we can't focus on what someone else is saying. Perhaps you've attended a lecture right before you had a test in another class and later realized you got almost nothing out of the lecture. That's because you were preoccupied with the upcoming test. Or maybe you've been in conversations with coworkers and realized that you weren't listening at all because you were thinking about your own concerns.

DAWN   I think my biggest problem as a listener is preoccupation. Like when my friend Marta came to me the other day and said she wanted to talk about her relationship with her boyfriend. I followed her for a few minutes, but then I started thinking about my relationship with Ted. After a while—I don't know how long—Marta said to me, "You're not listening at all. Where is your head?" She was right. My head was in a totally different place.

When we are preoccupied with our own thoughts, we aren't fully present for others; we're not being mindful. In describing how she stays mindful in intense interviews, Anna Deavere Smith says, "I empty out myself. While I'm listening, my own judgments and prejudices certainly come up. But I know I won't get anything unless I get those things out of the way" (Arenson, 2002, p. 35). It's natural for our thoughts to wander occasionally. When they do, we should note that our focus has wandered and actively call our minds back to the person who is speaking and the meaning of his or her message.

Andersen Ross/Photodisc/Getty Images

Prejudgment   Another reason we may not listen effectively is that we prejudge others or their communication (O'Keefe, 2002). Sometimes we think we already know what is going to be said, so we don't listen carefully. Recalling our earlier discussion of mind reading, you'll realize that it's unwise to assume we know what others think and feel. At other times, we decide in advance that others have nothing to offer us, so we tune them out. In a study of doctor–patient communication, doctors asked patients to describe medical problems, then interrupted the patients after an average of 23 seconds. That was how long it took doctors to decide the patients had no more information to offer (Levine, 2004).

When we prejudge, we disconfirm others because we deny them their own voices and force their words into our own preconceived mindset. This devalues them. Prejudgments also reduce what we learn in communication with others. If we decide in advance that others have nothing worthwhile to say, we foreclose the possibility of learning something new.

Communication in
Everyday Life

WORKPLACE

Cookbook Medicine

Cookbook medicine is what Doctors Leana Wen and Joshua Kosowsky (2013) think is causing a lot of misdiagnoses and unnecessary tests. In their book, *When Doctors Don't Listen*, Wen and Kosowsky point out that doctors increasingly rely on algorithms, or flow charts, to diagnose patients. A patient who has chest pain will be treated by a heart attack algorithm; a patient with fever and cough is treated by a pneumonia algorithm (Zuger, 2013). This makes sense in many cases, and it increases efficiency in treating patients.

But sometimes a rock that fell on a person caused the chest pain; sometimes fever and a cough are caused by bronchitis. The problem, say Wen and Kosowsky, is that algorithms depersonalize medicine. They urge doctors to spend more time listening to patients before prescribing diagnosis tests or assuming what the problem is. Just as good cooks don't unthinkingly follow recipes, good doctors don't let cookbook medicine substitute for listening to individual patients.

Reacting to Emotionally Loaded Language
A fourth internal obstacle to effective listening is the tendency to react to emotionally loaded language—words that evoke strong responses, positive or negative. You may find some words and phrases soothing or pleasant. Certain other words and phrases may summon up negative feelings and images for you. When we react to words that are emotionally loaded for us, we may fail to grasp another person's meaning.

Politicians often rely on voters to respond emotionally to particular words. In recent years, many politicians have referred frequently to *family values* and *environmental responsibility* because so many voters respond to those terms with strong positive emotion. Some politicians count on voters not to think critically about what they mean by *family values* or *environmental responsibility* but simply to vote for them and support their policies because the terms evoke positive feelings.

When we react to emotionally loaded language, we don't learn what another person has to say. We give up our responsibility to think critically about what others say, to consider their words carefully instead of reacting unthinkingly to particular words. One way to guard against this is to be aware of words and phrases that tend to trigger strong emotional reactions in us. If we bring these to a conscious level, then we can monitor our tendencies to respond unthinkingly.

Lack of Effort
It is hard work to listen mindfully—to focus closely on what others are saying, to grasp their meanings, to ask questions, and to give responses so that they know we are engaged. It's also hard to control situational noise and perhaps fight fatigue, hunger, or other physiological conditions that can impede listening.

Because active listening takes so much effort, we can't always do it well. We may want to listen but have trouble summoning the energy needed. When this happens, you might ask the other person to postpone interaction until a time when you will have the energy to listen mindfully. If you explain that you want to defer communication because you really are interested and want to be able to listen well, she or he is likely to appreciate your honesty and commitment to listening.

Failure to Adapt Listening Styles   A final internal hindrance to effective listening is not recognizing or adjusting to the need for different listening styles. How we listen should vary, for two reasons. First, different skills are needed when we listen for information, to support others, and for pleasure. We discuss these kinds of listening later in the chapter. A second reason for having diverse listening styles is differences between cultures and speech communities. In some cultures, listening means quietly attending to others. In other cultures, listening means participating while others are talking. In the United States, it is considered polite to make frequent, but not constant, eye contact with someone who is speaking. In other cultures, continuous eye contact is normative, and still other cultures severely restrict eye contact.

Even in the United States, there are differences in listening rules based on membership in gender, racial, and other speech communities. Because feminine socialization emphasizes conversation as a way to form and develop relationships, women tend to maintain eye contact, give substantial vocal and verbal feedback, and use nods and facial expressions to signal interest (Tannen, 1990; Wood, 1994c, 1998, 2011a). Masculine speech communities, with their focus on emotional control, teach most men to provide fewer verbal and nonverbal signs of interest and attentiveness. If you understand these general differences, you can adapt your listening style to provide appropriate responses to women and to men.

JENNIFER   I used to get irritated at my boyfriend because I thought he wasn't listening to me. I'd tell him stuff, and he'd just sit there and not say anything. He didn't react to what I was saying by showing emotions in his face or anything. Several times, I accused him of not listening, and he said back to me exactly what I'd said. He was listening, just not my way. I've learned not to expect him to show a lot of emotions or respond to what I say as I'm talking. That's just not his way, but he is listening.

Race also shapes listening style. Most Caucasians follow the communication rule that one person shouldn't speak while another is talking, especially in formal speaking situations. In some African American communities, however, talking while others are talking is a form of showing interest and active participation (Houston & Wood, 1996). Thus, some African Americans may signal that they are listening intently to a speaker by interjecting comments such as "Tell me more" or "I know that's right." Many black churches are more participatory than most white churches, with members of the congregation routinely calling out responses to what a preacher is saying. When the Reverend Martin Luther King Jr. delivered his "I Have a Dream" speech to a crowd of thousands, his words were echoed and responded to by the listeners during the speech.

Because speech communities cultivate different communication styles, we shouldn't automatically impose our rules and interpretations on others. Instead, we should try to understand and respect their styles and listen effectively to them on their terms, not ours.

FORMS OF NONLISTENING

Now that we've discussed obstacles to effective listening, let's consider forms of nonlistening. We call these patterns *nonlistening* because they don't involve real listening. We discuss six kinds of nonlistening that may seem familiar to you because most of us engage in them at times.

Pseudolistening

Pseudolistening is pretending to listen. When we pseudolisten, we appear to be attentive, but really our minds are elsewhere. We engage in pseudolistening when we want to appear conscientious, although we really aren't interested or when we are familiar with what is being said so do not need to give concentrated attention (O'Keefe, 2002). Sometimes we pseudolisten because we don't want to hurt someone who is sharing experiences.

> **OLIVIA**
>
> A lot of students pseudolisten in boring classes. I know I do. I answer emails or check my networking sites or shop, but I look up at the professor every minute or two to make him think I'm taking notes.

© Golden Pixels LLC/Shutterstock.com

Olivia might be surprised to learn that her professor probably isn't fooled. Most faculty know that many students using laptops are, at best, only partially attending to the class. Superficial social conversations and dull lectures are two communication situations in which we may consciously choose to pseudolisten so that we seem polite even though we really aren't interested. Although it may be appropriate to pseudolisten in some situations, there is a cost: We run the risk of missing information because we really aren't attending.

Pseudolisteners often give themselves away when their responses reveal that they weren't paying attention. Common indicators of pseudolistening are responses that are tangential or irrelevant to what was said. For example, if Martin talks to Valaria about his job interviews, she might respond tangentially by asking about the cities he visited: "Did you like New York or Atlanta better?" Although this is related to the topic of Martin's job interviews, it is tangential to the main issue, which she didn't grasp because she wasn't really listening. An irrelevant response would be, "Where do you want to go for dinner tonight?" That response is completely unrelated to what Martin said.

Monopolizing

Monopolizing is continuously focusing communication on ourselves instead of listening to the person who is talking. Two tactics are typical of monopolizing. One is conversational rerouting, in which a person shifts the topic back to himself or herself. For example, Ellen tells her friend Marla that she's having trouble with her roommate, and Marla reroutes the conversation with this response: "I know what you mean. My roommate is a real slob. And that's just one of her problems! Let me tell you what I have to live with. . . ." Rerouting takes the conversation away from the person who is talking and focuses it on the self.

Another monopolizing tactic is interrupting to divert attention from the speaker to ourselves or to topics that interest us. Interrupting can occur in combination with rerouting—a person interrupts and then directs the conversation to a new topic. In other cases, diversionary interrupting involves questions and challenges that disrupt the speaker. For example, Elliot says that the Social Security will be bankrupt by 2030, and Paul responds by saying, "What makes you think that? How can you be sure? The President says we're fixing the system." Having interrupted Elliot, Paul might then reroute the conversation to topics that interest him more: "Speaking of the President, do you think he'll manage to get Congress to approve the changes he wants to make in national security?" Both rerouting and diversionary interrupting are techniques for monopolizing a conversation. They are the antithesis of good listening. The following conversation illustrates monopolizing and also shows how disconfirming of others it can be:

Chuck: I'm really bummed about my Econ class. I just can't seem to get the stuff.

Sally: Well, I know what you mean. Econ was a real struggle for me too, but it's nothing compared to the Stats course I'm taking now. I mean, this one is going to destroy me totally.

Chuck: I remember how frustrated you got in Econ, but you finally did get it. I just can't seem to, and I need the course for my major. I've tried going to review sessions, but . . ..

Sally: I didn't find the review sessions helpful. Why don't you focus on your other classes and use them to pull up your average?

Chuck: That's not the point. I want to get this stuff.

Sally: You think you've got problems? Do you know that right now I have three papers and one exam hanging over my head?

Chuck: I wonder if I should hire a tutor.

Sally shows no interest in Chuck's concerns, and she pushes her own conversational agenda. Chances are good that she doesn't even understand what he is feeling because she isn't really focusing on what he says; she isn't really listening.

Monopolizing is costly not only to those who are neglected but also to the monopolizers. A person who dominates communication has much less opportunity to learn from others than does a person who listens to what others think and feel. We already know what we think and feel, so there's little we can learn from hearing ourselves!

It's important to realize that not all interruptions are attempts to monopolize. We also interrupt to show interest, to voice support, and to ask for elaboration. Interrupting for these reasons doesn't divert attention from the person speaking; instead, it affirms that person and keeps the focus on her or him. Research indicates that women are more likely than men to interrupt to show interest and support (Anderson & Leaper, 1998; Stewart, Stewart, Friedley, & Cooper, 1990).

Selective Listening

A third form of nonlistening is **selective listening**, which involves focusing only on particular parts of communication. As we've noted, all listening is selective to an extent because we can't attend to everything around us. With selective listening, however, we screen out parts of a message that don't interest us and rivet our attention to topics that do interest us. For example, students become highly attentive when a teacher says, "This will be on the test." Employees zero in on communication about raises, layoffs, and holidays. People who own beach property become highly attentive to information about hurricanes.

Selective listening also occurs when we reject communication that makes us uneasy. For instance, smokers may selectively not attend to reports on the dangers of smoking. We may also screen out communication that is critical of us. You may not take in a friend's comment that you are really judgmental; you may selectively tune out your boyfriend's or girlfriend's observation that you can be selfish. We all have subjects that bore us or disturb us, yet it's unwise to listen selectively when doing so could deprive us of information or insights that could be valuable.

Defensive Listening

After taking cooking lessons, Thelma bakes a cake for her friend Louise's birthday. When Louise sees the cake, she says, "Wow, that's so sweet. My mom always made a special cake for my birthday, and she would decorate it so elaborately." Thelma replies, "Well I'm sorry that I didn't decorate the cake extravagantly. I guess I still have a lot to learn about cooking." Thelma's response illustrates **defensive listening**, which is perceiving personal attacks, criticism, or hostility in communication that is not critical or mean-spirited. When we listen defensively, we assume others don't like, trust, or respect us, and we read these motives into whatever they say, no matter how innocent their communication may be.

It's hard *not* to be a defensive listener in Gordon Ramsay's *Hell's Kitchen*.

Fox/Photofest

Some people are generally defensive, expecting criticism from all quarters. They perceive negative judgments in almost anything said to them. In other instances, defensive listening is confined to specific topics or vulnerable times when we judge ourselves to be inadequate. A worker who fears she is not performing well may hear criticism in benign comments from coworkers; a student who fails a test may hear doubts about his intelligence in an innocent question about how school is going. Defensive listening can distort our perceptions of others' communication.

Ambushing

Ambushing is listening carefully for the purpose of attacking a speaker. Unlike the other kinds of nonlistening we've discussed, ambushing involves very careful listening, but it isn't motivated by a genuine desire to understand another. Instead, ambushers listen intently to gather ammunition they can use to attack a speaker. Krista listens very carefully to her teammate Carl as he describes a marketing campaign. When Carl finishes, Krista pounces: "You said we could get a rough draft of the whole campaign by the end of the month. You forgot that we lose 2 workdays for the annual retreat next week. Besides, your plan calls for some outsourcing. Where are you getting the funds for that?" Krista's response shows that she listened to Carl's ideas not to understand them and work with him but to identify weak spots and attack them.

KRALYN My first husband was a real ambusher. If I tried to talk to him about a dress I'd bought, he'd listen just long enough to find out what it cost and then attack me for spending money. Once, I told him about a problem I was having with one of my coworkers, and he came back at me with all of the things I'd done wrong and didn't mention any of the things the other person had done. Talking to him was like setting myself up to be assaulted.

Not surprisingly, people who engage in ambushing tend to arouse defensiveness in others. Few of us want to speak up when we feel we are going to be attacked. In Chapter 8, we look more closely at communication that fosters defensiveness in others.

Literal Listening

The final form of nonlistening is **literal listening**, which involves listening only for content and ignoring the relationship level of meaning. As we have seen, all communication includes content as well as relationship meaning. When we listen literally, we attend only to the content level and are insensitive to others' feelings and to our connections with them. Lindsay's commentary provides a good illustration of literal listening that deals only with content-level meaning.

LINDSAY When I found out I had to have wrist surgery, I told my boss and said I'd be needing some time off. He listened and then explained the policy on sick leave. He didn't say he was sorry, ask if I was worried, tell me he hoped the surgery was successful, nothing.

Literal listening may disconfirm others. When we listen literally, we don't make the effort to understand how others feel about what they say or to endorse them as people.

We have seen that there are many obstacles to effective listening. Situational obstacles include message overload, message complexity, and noise. In addition to these, there are five potential interferences inside of us: preoccupation, prejudgment, unthinking reactions to emotionally loaded language, lack of effort, and failure to adapt our style of listening. The obstacles to effective listening combine to create six types of nonlistening: pseudolistening, monopolizing, selective listening, defensive listening, ambushing, and literal listening. What you've learned prepares you to think now about how you can listen more mindfully.

ADAPTING LISTENING TO COMMUNICATION GOALS

The first requirement for listening effectively is to determine your reason for listening. We listen differently when we listen for pleasure, to gain information, and to support others. We'll discuss the particular attitudes and skills that contribute to each type of effective listening.

Listening for Pleasure

Often, we engage in **listening for pleasure**. We listen to music for pleasure. We may listen to some radio programs for enjoyment. Because listening for pleasure doesn't require us to remember or respond to communication, the only guidelines are to be mindful and control distractions. Just as being mindful in lectures allows us to gain information, being mindful when listening for pleasure allows us to derive full enjoyment from what we hear. Controlling interferences is also important when we are listening for pleasure. A beautifully rendered Mozart concerto can be wonderfully satisfying but not if a television is on in the background.

Listening for Information

When we are **listening for information**, our goal is to gain and evaluate information. We listen for information in classes, at political debates, when important news stories are reported, and when we need guidance on everything from medical treatments to directions to a new place. In each case, we listen to gain and understand information in order to act appropriately.

Be Mindful   First, it's important to choose to be mindful. Don't let your mind wander when information gets complicated or confusing. Instead, stay focused on the information, and take in as much as you can. Later, you may want to ask questions about material that wasn't clear even when you listened mindfully.

Photodisc/Digital Vision/Getty Images

Control Obstacles   You can also minimize noise in communication situations. You might shut a window to mute traffic noises or adjust a thermostat so that the room's temperature is comfortable. You should also try to minimize psychological distractions by emptying your mind of concerns and ideas that can divert your attention. Let go of preoccupations and prejudgments that can interfere with effective listening. In addition, it's important to monitor the tendency to react to emotionally loaded language. We have to make a very deliberate effort to cultivate an inner silence that allows us to listen fully to others.

Ask Questions   Asking a speaker to clarify or elaborate the message may help you understand information you didn't grasp at first; it also deepens insight into content that you did comprehend. "Could you explain what you meant by . . .?" and "Can you clarify the distinction between . . .?" are questions that allow you to extend your understanding. Questions compliment a speaker because they indicate that you are interested and want to know more.

Use Aids to Recall   To understand and remember important information, we can apply the principles of perception we discussed in Chapter 3. For instance, we learned that we tend to notice and recall stimuli that are repeated. To use this principle to enhance your retention, repeat important ideas to yourself immediately after hearing them. Repeating names of people you meet can save you the embarrassment of forgetting their names.

Another way to increase retention is to use mnemonic (pronounced "knee-MON-ic") devices, which are memory aids that create patterns. You probably already do this in studying. For instance, you could create the mnemonic MR SIRR, which is made up of the first letter of each of the six parts of listening (mindfulness, receiving, selecting and organizing, interpreting, responding, remembering). If your supervisor asks you to code and log in all incoming messages, you might remember the instruction by inventing CLAIM, a word that uses the first letter of each key word in your supervisor's instructions. If you meet someone named Kit and want to remember something about the person, you might associate something about Kit with each letter of her name: Kit from Iowa is going to be a Teacher.

Organize Information   A fifth technique for increasing retention is to organize what you hear. For example, suppose a friend tells you he's concerned about a current math course that he's finding difficult. Then he wonders what kind of jobs his history major qualifies him for and whether graduate school is necessary to get a good job, and says he needs to line up an internship for this summer. You could reduce the complexity of this message by regrouping the stream of concerns into two categories: short-term issues (the math course, setting up an internship) and long-term issues (jobs for history majors, graduate school). Remembering those two categories allows you to retain the essence of your friend's concerns even if you forget many of the specifics. Repetition, mnemonics, and regrouping are ways to enhance what we remember.

Poor listening causes mistakes and problems, which explains why many companies now require employees to attend listening workshops. Starbucks, for instance, requires employees to learn to listen to orders and rearrange customers' requests in the sequence of size, flavoring, milk, and caffeine. That's helpful when customers blurt out orders like "double-shot decaf grande," or "iced, skim, cappuccino, small."

Everyday Skills To practice remembering content that you hear, complete the activity "Improving Your Retention" at the end of the chapter or online.

Listening to Support Others

We engage in relationship listening, **listening to support others**, when we listen to a friend's worries, hear a romantic partner discuss our relationship, or help a co-worker sort through a problem (Bender & Messner, 2003; Welch, 2003). Specific attitudes and skills enhance relationship listening.

Be Mindful   The first requirement for effective relationship listening is mindfulness. You'll recall that this was also the first step in listening for information and pleasure. When we're interested in relationship-level meanings, however, a different kind of mindfulness is needed. Instead of focusing on information, we concentrate on what lies between and behind the content in order to understand what another is feeling, thinking, needing, or wanting in a conversation.

Be Careful of Expressing Judgments   When listening to help another person, it's usually wise to avoid judgmental responses, at least initially. Imposing our own judgments separates us from others and their feelings. We've inserted something between us. Yet there are times when it is appropriate and supportive to offer opinions and to make evaluative statements. Sometimes, people we care about genuinely want our judgments, and in those cases we should be honest about how we feel. Particularly when others are confronting ethical dilemmas, they may seek the judgments of people they trust.

Once, my friend Cordelia was asked to work for a presidential candidate, but she had already agreed to take a different job. She talked to me about her quandary and asked me what I thought she should do. Although it was clear to me that she wanted to join the campaign, I couldn't honestly tell her I approved of that. I told her that, for me, it would be wrong to go back on my word. I then offered to think with her about ways she might approach her future employer about starting at a later date. After a long talk, Cordelia thanked me for being honest. Part of being a real friend in this instance was making a judgment. That's appropriate only if someone invites our evaluation or if we think another person is in danger of making a serious mistake.

If someone asks our opinion, we should try to present it in a way that doesn't disconfirm the other person. I could have said to Cordelia, "How can you even think of breaking your word? That would be unethical." Whew—pretty disconfirming. Many times, people excuse cruel comments by saying, "Well, you asked me to be honest" or "I mean this as constructive criticism." Too often, however, the judgments are harsher than honesty requires. If we are committed to supporting others, we use honesty to support them, not to tear them down.

> I hate the term *constructive criticism*. Every time my dad says it, what follows is a putdown. By now, I've learned not to go to him when I have problems or when I'm worried about something in my life. He always judges what I'm feeling and tells me what I ought to feel and do. All that does is make me feel worse than I did before.

LOGAN

Understand the Other Person's Perspective   We can't respond effectively to others until we understand their perspective and meanings. To do this, we must focus on the words and nonverbal behaviors that give us clues about how others feel and think.

Paraphrasing is a method of clarifying others' meaning or needs by reflecting our interpretations of their communication back to them. For example, a friend might confide, "I think my kid brother is messing around with drugs." We could paraphrase this way: "So you're really worried that your brother's experimenting with drugs." This allows us to clarify whether the friend has any evidence of the brother's drug involvement and also whether the friend is, in fact, worried about the possibility.

The response might be, "No, I don't have any real reason to suspect him, but I just worry, because drugs are so pervasive in high schools now." This clarifies by telling us the friend's worries are more the issue than any evidence that the brother is experimenting with drugs. Paraphrasing also helps us figure out what others feel. If a friend screams, "This situation is really getting to me!" it's not clear whether your friend is angry, hurt, upset, or frustrated. We could find out which emotion prevails by saying, "You seem really angry." If anger is the emotion, your friend would agree; if not, she would clarify what she is feeling.

Another strategy for increasing understanding of others is to use **minimal encouragers**, which gently invite others to elaborate by expressing interest in hearing more. Examples of minimal encouragers are "Tell me more," "Really?" "Go on," "I'm with you," "Then what happened?" and "I see." We can also use nonverbal minimal encouragers, such as a raised eyebrow, a head nod, or widened eyes. Minimal encouragers indicate that we are listening, following, and interested. They encourage others to keep talking. Keep in mind that these are *minimal* encouragers. They should not interrupt or reroute conversation. Instead, effective minimal encouragers are brief interjections that prompt, rather than interfere with, another's talk.

Another way to enhance your understanding of another person's perspective is to ask questions that yield insight into what a speaker thinks or feels. For instance, we might ask, "How do you feel about that?" or "What do you plan to do?" Another reason we ask questions is to find out what a person wants from us. Sometimes, it isn't clear whether someone wants advice, a shoulder to cry on, or a safe place to vent feelings. If we can't figure out what's wanted, we can ask the other person, "Are you looking for advice or a sounding board?" Asking direct questions signals that we want to help and allows others to tell us how we can best do that.

Express Support   Once we understand another's meanings and perspective, it's important to communicate support. This doesn't necessarily require us to agree with the other person's perspective or feelings, but it does require that we express support for the person. We may express support in a number of ways without agreeing. For example, you can say that you appreciate the difficulty of a friend's situation, that you realize what a tough decision this is, or that you understand your friend's feelings (even if your feelings are different). Perhaps the most basic way to support another is by listening mindfully, which shows that you care enough to attend fully to him or her.

> **SHERYL**
>
> I think the greatest gift my mother ever gave me was when I told her I was going to marry Bruce. He isn't Jewish, and nobody in my family has ever married out of the faith before. I could tell my mother was disappointed, and she didn't try to hide that. She asked me if I understood how that would complicate things like family relations and rearing kids. We talked for a while, and she realized I had thought through what it means to marry out of the faith. Then she sighed and said she had hoped I would find a nice Jewish man. But then she said she supported me, whatever I did, and Bruce was welcome in our family. She told me she'd raised me to think for myself, and that's what I was doing. I just felt so loved and accepted by how she acted.

SOCIAL MEDIA AND LISTENING

How does our discussion of listening apply to social media? There are at least three ways that the ideas in this chapter are relevant to social media. First, some online communication requires listening. When you Skype or have face time with a friend or family member, you need the same listening attitude and skills that you do to listen to someone f2f.

Second, our increasing engagement with social media can be an obstacle to effective listening. Leslie Perlow, who is on the faculty of Harvard's Business School, is the author of *Sleeping with Your Smartphone* (2013), in which she asserts that our devices threaten to overtake our lives. She recommends that professional teams have blocks of time when they are entirely disconnected so that they can concentrate on listening and working together. People need to get back to talking face to face, really looking at each other and getting energy from each other. Highly creative work environments depend on listening—truly listening (Brady, 2013; Korkki, 2013).

Third, we need to exercise critical thinking when communicating online. As we have noted earlier, anyone can post anything online, so accuracy is not guaranteed. When you read blogs and tweets, you should ask critical thinking questions such as: What qualifies this person to have an informed stance on this issue?

 MindTap

Everyday Skills To increase your awareness of the extent to which social media can hinder mindful listening, complete the activity "Hindrances to Mindful Listening" at the end of the chapter or online.

Communication in Everyday Life

INSIGHT

Listener of the Year

Established in 1979, the International Listening Association is dedicated to improving listening in personal, social, political, and professional contexts. The highlight of each year's annual conference is the announcement of the Listener of the Year. Here are some of the people who have won this coveted honor:

Jimmy Carter	Alex Haley	Ann Landers	Barack Obama
Billy Graham	Michelle Obama	Jack Nicklaus	Oprah
Suzy Yehl Marta	Howard Schultz	Hugh Downs	Javier Perez du Cuellar

Does this person have any vested interest or any ties to others who have stakes in the issue? What is this person's track record of accuracy? Another way to keep your critical thinking sharp is to check other sources of information on the same issue to see if there is a consistent opinion. Consistency doesn't necessarily equal right, but it gives you one way of assessing what you read online.

GUIDELINES FOR EFFECTIVE LISTENING

Three guidelines summarize our discussion and foster effective listening.

Be Mindful

By now, you've read this suggestion many times. Because it is so central to effective listening, however, it bears repeating. Mindfulness is a choice to be wholly present in an experience. It requires that we put aside preoccupations and preconceptions to attend fully to what is happening in the moment. Mindful listening is one of the highest compliments we can pay to others because it conveys the relationship-level meaning that they matter to us. Being mindful requires discipline and commitment. We have to discipline our tendencies to judge others, to dominate the talk stage, and to let our minds wander. Mindfulness also requires commitment to another person and to the integrity of the interpersonal communication process. Being mindful is the first and most important principle of effective listening.

Adapt Listening Appropriately

Like all communication activities, listening varies according to goals, situations, and people. What's effective depends on our purpose for listening, the context in which we are listening, and the needs and circumstances of the person to whom we are listening.

When we listen for pleasure, we should be mindful and minimize distractions so that we derive as much enjoyment as possible from listening. When we listen for information, a critical attitude, evaluation of material, and a focus on the content level of meaning enhance listening. Yet when we engage in relationship listening, very different skills are needed. We want to communicate openness and caring, and the relationship level of meaning is at least as important as the content level of meaning. Thus, we need to adapt our listening styles and attitudes to different goals.

Effective listening is adapted to others. Some people need prompting and encouragement to express themselves, whereas others need us only to be silent and attentive. Paraphrasing helps some people clarify what they think or feel, whereas others don't need that kind of assistance. We need to be skilled in a variety of listening behaviors and to know when each is appropriate. Recall from Chapter 1 that the ability to use a range of skills and to exercise judgment about which ones are called for is fundamental to interpersonal communication competence.

Listen Actively

When we realize all that's involved in listening, we appreciate what an active effort it is. To listen effectively, we must be willing to focus our minds, to organize and interpret others' ideas and feelings, to express our interest on both the content level and the relationship level of meaning, and to retain what a speaker says. In some situations, we also become active partners by listening collaboratively and engaging in problem solving. Doing this is hard work!

Recognizing that mindful listening is an active process prepares us to invest the effort needed to do it effectively. To listen mindfully, you may find it useful to paraphrase and use minimal encouragers. Both of these skills signal your interest and involvement with the person to whom you are listening.

Everyday Skills To practice your paraphrasing skills, complete the activity "Learning to Paraphrase" at the end of the chapter or online.

Everyday Skills To practice incorporating minimal encouragers into your conversations, complete the activity "Using Minimal Encouragers" at the end of the chapter or online.

CHAPTER SUMMARY

In an interview with Dan Rather, Mother Teresa offered wisdom about listening (Bailey, 1998, p. C5):

Dan Rather: What do you say to God when you pray?

Mother Teresa: I listen.

Dan Rather: Well, what does God say?

Mother Teresa: He listens.

In this chapter, we've explored the complex and demanding process of mindful listening. We began by distinguishing between hearing and listening. Hearing is a physiological process that doesn't entail effort on our part. Listening, in contrast, is a complicated process involving physically receiving messages, then selecting, organizing, interpreting, responding, and remembering. To do it well takes commitment and skill.

There are many obstacles to effective listening. External obstacles include message overload, complexity of material, and external noise in communication contexts. In addition, listening can be hampered by preoccupations and prejudgments, reactions to emotionally loaded language, lack of effort, and failure to adapt our listening to fit situations. These obstacles give rise to various types of nonlistening, including pseudolistening, monopolizing, selective listening, defensive listening, ambushing, and literal listening. Also, as we noted in this chapter, social media can interfere with listening. When we are texting during meetings or taking calls when conversing with others, it's likely that we are not mindfully engaged with the people we are with.

We've identified skills and attitudes appropriate to different listening goals. Listening for pleasure is supported by mindfulness and efforts to minimize distractions and noise. Informational listening requires us to adopt a mindful attitude and to think critically, organize and evaluate information, clarify understanding by asking questions, and develop aids for retention of complex material. When we go online to get information on a topic, critical thinking is important since the ease of posting information is not matched by assurances of its quality. Relationship listening also involves mindfulness, but it calls for different listening skills. Suspending judgment, paraphrasing, giving minimal encouragers, and expressing support enhance the effectiveness of relationship listening whether communicating f2f or via social media.

The ideas we've discussed yield three guidelines for effective listening. First, we must be mindful. Second, we should adapt our listening skills and style to accommodate differences in listening purpose and individuals. Finally, we should remember that listening is an active process and be prepared to invest energy and effort in doing it skillfully. We'll revisit some of the ideas covered here as we discuss dynamics in relationships.

Key Concepts

Practice defining the chapter's terms by using online flashcards.

FLASHCARDS...

ambushing 176	listening to support others 179	pseudolistening 173
defensive listening 175	literal listening 176	remembering 167
hearing 163	mindfulness 164	responding 167
listening 164	minimal encouragers 180	selective listening 175
listening for information 177	monopolizing 174	
listening for pleasure 177	paraphrasing 180	

Continuing the Conversation

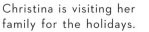

Jason Harris © 2001 Wadsworth

When you've watched the video online, critique and analyze this encounter based on the principles you learned in this chapter. Then compare your work with the author's suggested responses. Online, even more videos will let you continue the conversation with your instructor.

Christina is visiting her family for the holidays. One evening after dinner, her mother comes into her room, where Christina is typing at her computer. Her mother sits down, and the following conversation takes place.

PRACTICE...

Mom: Am I disturbing you?

Chris: No, I'm just signing off on email.

Mom: Emailing someone?

Chris: Just a guy.

Mom: Someone you've been seeing at school?

Chris: Not exactly.

Mom: [Laughs] Well, either you are seeing him or you're not, honey. Are you two dating?

Chris: Yeah, you could say we're dating.

Mom: [Laughs] What's he like?

Chris: He's funny and smart and easy to talk to. We're interested in the same things, and we share so many values. Brandon's just super. I've never met anyone like him.

Mom: When do I get to meet him?

Chris: Well, not until I do. [Laughs] We met online, and we're just starting to talk about getting together in person.

Mom: Online? And you act as if you know him!

Chris: I do know him, Mom. We've talked a lot—we've told each other lots of stuff.

Mom: How do you know what he's told you is true? For all you know, he's a 50-year-old mass murderer!

Chris: You've been watching too many movies on Lifetime, Mom. Brandon's 23, he's in college, and he comes from a family like ours.

Mom: How do you know that? He could be lying.

Chris: So? A guy I meet at school could lie, too.

Mom: Haven't you read about all the weirdos that go to these online matching sites?

Chris: Mom, Brandon's not a weirdo, and we didn't meet in a matching site. We met in a chat room where people talk about politics.

Mom: Chris, you can't be serious about someone you haven't met.

Chris: I have met him, Mom, just not face to face. I know him better than lots of guys I've dated for months.

Mom: This makes me really nervous, honey. Please don't meet him by yourself.

Chris: Mom, you're making me feel sorry I told you how we met. This is why I didn't tell you about him before. Nothing I say is going to change your mind about dating online.

Mom: [Pauses] You're right. I'm not giving him—or you—a chance. Let's start over. Tell me what you like about him.

Chris: Well, he's thoughtful.

Mom: Thoughtful? How so?

Chris: If I say something one day, he'll come back to it a day or so later, and I can tell he's thought about it, like he's really interested in what I say.

Mom: So he really pays attention to what you say?

Chris: Exactly. So many guys I've dated don't. They never return to things I've said. And when I come back to things he's said with ideas I've thought about, he really listens.

Mom: Like he values what you think and say?

Chris: Exactly! That's what's so special about him.

1. Identify examples of ineffective and effective listening on the part of Chris's mother.
2. What do you perceive as the key obstacle to listening for Chris's mom during the early part of this conversation?
3. Identify specific listening skills that Chris's mother uses once she chooses to listen mindfully.
4. Is Chris's mother being unethical by not continuing to state her concerns about Chris's safety?

Everyday Skills

Build your communication skills further by completing the following activities here or online.

1. **Developing Mindfulness**

   To develop your ability to be mindful, follow these guidelines in a situation that calls for you to listen:

   + Empty your mind of thoughts, ideas, plans, and concerns so that you are open to the other person.
   + Concentrate on the person with whom you are interacting. Say to yourself, "I want to focus on this person and on what she or he is feeling and thinking."
   + If you find yourself framing responses to the other person, try to push those aside; they interfere with your concentration on the other person's words.
   + If your mind wanders, don't criticize yourself; that's distracting. Instead, gently refocus on the person you are with and on what that person is communicating to you. It's natural for

other thoughts to intrude, so just push them away and stay focused on the other person.

- Let the other person know you are attending mindfully; give nonverbal responses (nods, facial expressions), ask questions to encourage elaboration, and keep eye contact.
- Evaluate how mindfully you listened. Did you understand the other person's thoughts and feelings? Did you feel more focused on that person than you usually do when you listen to others?

2. **Improving Your Retention**

Apply the principles we've discussed to increase your ability to remember content.

- The next time you meet someone, repeat his or her name to yourself three times in a row after you are introduced. Do you remember the name better when you do this?
- After your next interpersonal communication class, take 15 minutes to review your notes. Try reading them aloud so that you hear as well as see the main ideas. Does this increase your retention of material covered in class?
- Invent mnemonics to help you remember basic information in communication.
- Organize complex ideas by grouping them into categories. Try this first in relation to material presented in classes. To remember the main ideas of this chapter, you might use major subheadings to form categories: the listening process, obstacles to listening, forms of nonlistening, listening goals, and guidelines. The mnemonic PONGG (process, obstacles, nonlistening, goals, guidelines) could help you remember those categories.

3. **Hindrances to Mindful Listening**

To increase your awareness of extent to which social media can hinder mindful listening, focus on your listening habits over the next few days. Following the example below, identify how your use of social media impaired your ability to engage fully and actively as a listener.

Communication Goal	Situation	Effect on Ability to Listen
Example:		
Listening to support others	I was texting my sister while my friend was telling me about her current fight with her boyfriend.	Even though I used minimal encouragers like "uh-huh" and nodded my head, my friend got annoyed with me and said I wasn't listening, even though I was. By texting to my sister while I was talking face to face, I gave the impression that I wasn't listening at all.

4. **Learning to Paraphrase**

Practice effective listening by paraphrasing the following statements:

a. I've got so many pressures closing in on me right now.

_____

b. I'm worried about all the money I've borrowed to get through school.

_____

c. I'm nervous about telling my parents I'm gay when I see them next weekend.

_____

d. I don't know whether Pat and I can keep the relationship together once she moves away to her new job.

_____

5. Using Minimal Encouragers

Practice encouraging others to elaborate their thoughts and feelings by developing minimal encouragers in response to each of these comments:

a. I'm really worried about getting into grad school.

_____

b. I'm not sure whether I'm measuring up to my boss's expectations for new employees.

_____

c. I just learned that I'm a finalist for a scholarship next year.

_____

d. I think my girlfriend is cheating on me.

_____

e. I haven't gotten any job offers yet and I've been interviewing for 4 months. I'm beginning to wonder whether I'll get a job at all.

_____

f. I'm so excited about how this relationship is going! I've never been with someone as attentive and thoughtful as Chris.

_____

DO... Additional interactive discussions, online quizzes, and activities that your instructor may assign for a grade.

Engaging with Ideas

Reflect and write about the ideas in this chapter by considering questions about personal, workplace, and ethical applications, here or online.

Personal Application Which form of nonlistening do you engage in most frequently? Identify examples of when you engage in this form of nonlistening. Can you recognize a commonality that links the examples—perhaps types of situations or people? How might you reduce your tendency to engage in this form of nonlistening?

REFLECT ON...

Workplace Application Identify different types of noise that are present in a place you work now or worked in the past. To what extent does/did each type of noise interfere with effective listening?

Ethical Application Identify ethical principles involved in listening for information and listening to support others? How do ethical commitments differ for the two purposes of listening?

Thinking Critically

Think and write critically about the ideas in this chapter, here or online.

1. Who is your prototype, or model, of a listener? Describe what the person does that makes him or her effective. How do the person's behaviors fit with guidelines for effective listening discussed in this chapter?

REFLECT ON...

2. What ethical principles can you identify to guide the three kinds of listening? Are different ethical principles appropriate when listening for information and listening to support others?

3. Keep a record of your listening for the next day. How much time do you spend listening for information, listening to support others, and listening for pleasure?

4. Apply the strategies for remembering what we discussed in this chapter. Create mnemonics, organize material as you listen, and review material immediately after listening. Do you find that using these strategies increases your listening effectiveness?
5. The International Listening Association (ILA) at www.listen.org is a rich resource for learning more about listening and networking with others who recognize its importance in everyday life. Its website features exercises to test and improve listening, factoids about listening, Internet discussion groups, quotes about the nature and value of listening, and a bibliography for those who want to read more.

chapter
SEVEN

EMOTIONS AND COMMUNICATION

Topics covered in this chapter

Emotional Intelligence

Understanding Emotions

Obstacles to Communicating Emotions Effectively

Social Media and Emotions

Guidelines for Communicating Emotions Effectively

After studying this chapter, you should be able to . . .

Measure your emotional intelligence.

Distinguish among theoretical perspectives on emotions.

Recognize reasons people may not express emotions effectively.

Identify the expression of emotion on a social networking site.

Apply this chapter's guidelines to enhance your skill in communicating emotions.

My sister Carolyn and I had been very close for years when her first child, Michelle, was born. I shared Carolyn's delight in the new member of our family, yet I also felt pushed out of her life. Carolyn was so involved with her daughter that she had little time for me. Phone calls from her, which had been frequent, almost ceased. When I called Carolyn, she often cut our conversation short because it was time to feed Michelle or get her up or change her diaper. Over lunch with my friend Nancy, I complained, "Carolyn never has time for me anymore. I am so angry with her!"

"Sounds to me more like you're hurt than angry," Nancy remarked.

What was I feeling? Was it anger or hurt or both? Emotions, or feelings, are part of our lives. We feel happiness, sadness, shame, pride, embarrassment, envy, disappointment, and a host of other emotions. And we communicate to express our emotions. We may express emotions nonverbally (smiling, trembling, blushing) or verbally ("I'm excited," "I feel anxious about the interview"), or both.

Although we experience and express feelings, we don't always do so effectively. There are times when we aren't able to identify exactly what we feel, as I wasn't when trying to describe my feelings about Carolyn's reduced time for me. Even when we do recognize our emotions, we aren't always sure how to express them clearly and effectively. Do we want to vent, or do we want another person to comfort us, apologize to us, empathize with us, or behave differently toward us? To communicate well, we need to develop skill in identifying and expressing our emotions.

To open this chapter, we'll discuss *emotional intelligence*, which complements cognitive intelligence. Next, we define emotions and examine different theories that attempt to explain why and how we experience emotions. Then we explore why we sometimes fail to express our feelings and how we can learn to express them effectively. Fourth, we consider how what we have learned about emotions applies to digital and online communication. Finally, we discuss guidelines for communicating emotions in ways that foster our individual growth and the quality of our relationships with others.

EMOTIONAL INTELLIGENCE

If you have watched *The Big Bang Theory*, you know the character of Sheldon Cooper (played by Jim Parsons). Sheldon seems oblivious to others' feelings and often to his own. As a result, Sheldon routinely hurts and offends others. *The Big Bang Theory* is a comedy, and Sheldon's emotional ineptitude adds to the fun. In real life, however, people who are emotional oafs are not funny to themselves or others.

Psychologist Daniel Goleman and his colleagues have recognized a kind of intelligence distinct from the type that standard IQ tests measure. They named it **emotional intelligence**, or EQ, which is the ability to recognize feelings, to judge which feelings are appropriate in which situations, and to communicate those feelings effectively (Goleman, 1995a; Goleman, Boyatzis & McKee, 2002; Ciarrochi & Mayer, 2007; Niedenthal, Kraut-Cruber, & Ric, 2006). The concept of emotional intelligence builds on Carol Saarni's (1990) work on "emotional competence," which involves awareness of our own emotions, including multiple emotions experienced simultaneously, the ability to recognize and empathize with others' emotions, awareness of the impact of our expression of emotions on others, and sensitivity to cultural rules for expressing emotions. Although some scholars think EQ is not part of overall IQ but rather a distinct kind of intelligence, there is broad consensus that emotional intelligence is important for interpersonal effectiveness.

A concrete example will provide a clear understanding of EQ: You are driving and another driver, who has been tailgating you, whips in front of you, almost hitting the left front panel on your car. What do you feel? What do you do? You may want to scream some choice words or tailgate the other car to get revenge. It's understandable to feel and do that, but such responses don't show high emotional intelligence. A more emotionally intelligent response would be to take a deep breath and tell yourself to cool down, put on your favorite music, and think about reasons why the person in the other car might be driving this way: Perhaps there's an emergency; perhaps the driver had a flat tire and is making up time to get to a child's soccer game. This is an emotionally intelligent response because it shows awareness of your own feelings and also sensitivity to another's perspective, it calms your anger, it reflects awareness of social norms, and it doesn't lead to danger or undesirable outcomes.

Sheldon in *The Big Bang Theory*, analyzing his own emotional reactions with a Venn diagram

Emotional intelligence is linked to well-being. People who have high emotional intelligence quotients are more likely than people with lower EQs to create satisfying relationships, to be comfortable with themselves, to work effectively with others, and to have better overall health (Goleman, 1995a, 1995b, 1998; Goleman et al., 2002; Landa & López-Safra, 2010). Emotional intelligence consists of the following qualities:

- Being aware of your feelings
- Dealing with emotions without being overcome by them
- Not letting setbacks and disappointments derail you
- Channeling your feelings to assist you in achieving your goals
- Being able to understand how others feel without their spelling it out
- Listening to your feelings and those of others so you can learn from them
- Recognizing social norms for expression of emotions
- Having a strong yet realistic sense of optimism

Emotional intelligence includes more than being in touch with your feelings. You also need skill in expressing them constructively and an ability to recognize how others feel. Because humans are connected to each other, how one person expresses emotions to another affects the other person—like catching a cold, says Goleman (2006). If we express anger, others are likely to respond with anger or defiance. On the other hand, if we express love or yearning for closeness, others are likely to respond more positively. To illustrate this, let's return to my conversation with Nancy. After we had talked a while, I said, "I think I'll call Carolyn and tell her I resent being pushed out of her life."

"Well, when my friend Penny had a child and was totally preoccupied with him, I felt what I think you're feeling," Nancy disclosed.

"And what did you do?" I asked.

"I told her I missed her."

Missed her? I thought it over. I did miss Carolyn. Telling her that would be an honest and affirming way to express my feelings. Telling Carolyn I missed her might open the door to restore our closeness. Telling her I was angry or resentful probably wouldn't enhance our relationship.

Through the conversation with Nancy, I discovered that anger was a defensive reaction I was using to avoid acknowledging how vulnerable and hurt I felt. Later that day, I called Carolyn and told her I missed her. Her response was immediate and warm: "I miss you too. I'll be so glad when we get adjusted enough to Michelle that we have time for us again." I was effective in communicating my feelings to Carolyn, thanks to Nancy's insight into emotions and her skill in helping me figure out what I was feeling and how to express it effectively.

© Dubova/Shutterstock.com

UNDERSTANDING EMOTIONS

Although emotions are basic to human beings and communication, they are difficult to define precisely. Some researchers assert that humans experience two kinds of emotions: some that are based in biology and thus instinctual and universal, and others that we learn in social interaction (Kemper, 1987). Yet scholars don't agree on which emotions are basic (Izard, 1991; Shaver, Schwartz, Kirson, & O'Connor, 1987; Shaver, Wu, & Schwartz, 1992). Also, many scholars don't find it useful to distinguish between basic emotions and learned emotions (Ekman & Davidson, 1994).

Many scholars think that most or all emotions are socially constructed to a substantial degree. For example, we learn from particular others and the generalized other when to feel gratitude, embarrassment, and so forth. In her book *Anger: The Misunderstood Emotion*, Carol Tavris (1989) argues that anger is not entirely basic or instinctual. She shows that our ability to experience anger is influenced by social interaction, through which we learn whether and when we are supposed to or allowed to feel anger.

In many instances, what we feel is not a single emotion but several mingled together, as I felt in the situation with Carolyn. Paul Ekman and Richard Davidson (1994) surveyed research on emotions and concluded that blends of emotion are common. For instance, you might feel both sad and happy at your graduation or both grateful and resentful when someone helps you.

KENNETH

Last year, my daughter got married, and I've never felt so many things in one moment. As I walked her down the aisle and took her arm from mine and placed it on the arm of her future husband, I felt sadness and happiness, hope and anxiety about her future, pride in the woman she'd become and her confidence in starting a new life, and loss because we would no longer be her primary family.

Now that we have seen how important emotions are, let's define the concept. **Emotions** are our experience and interpretation of internal sensations as they are shaped by physiology, perceptions, language, and social experiences. Although researchers vary in the degree to which they emphasize each of these influences, most people who have studied emotions agree that physiology, perceptions, social experience, and language all play parts in our emotional lives.

Physiological Influences on Emotions

Have you ever felt a knot in your stomach when you got back an exam with a low grade? If so, you experienced a physiological reaction. Early theorists believed that we experience emotion when external stimuli cause physiological changes in us. This is the **organismic view of emotions**, and it is shown in Figure 7.1.

Advanced by philosopher William James and his colleague Carl Lange, the organismic view, also called the James–Lange view, asserts that when we perceive a stimulus, we first respond physiologically, and only after that do we experience emotions (James, 1890; James & Lange, 1922). This perspective assumes that emotions are reflexes that follow from physiological actions. For example, Chris Kleinke, Thomas Peterson, and Thomas Rutledge (1998) found that when people smile (physiological action), their moods (emotions) are more positive, and when people frown, their moods are more negative.

James wrote that emotional expression begins with a perception of something, perhaps seeing a gift with your name on it or noticing that someone with a weapon is running toward you. After the perception, James believed, we experience changes in our bodies: We feel a tingle of anticipation on seeing the gift; adrenaline surges when we are approached by someone with a weapon. Finally, said James, we experience emotion: We feel joy at the gift, fear at the aggressor.

The organismic view regards emotions as instinctual responses to physiological arousal caused by external stimuli. James specifically discounted what he called "intellectual mind stuff" (Finkelstein, 1980) as having nothing to do with our perceptions of stimuli and, by extension, our emotions.

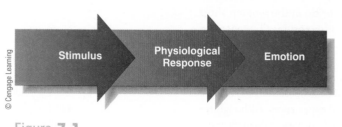

© Cengage Learning

Figure **7.1**

The Organismic View of Emotions

Perceptual Influences on Emotions

James's view of the relationship between bodily states and feelings is no longer widely accepted. Today, most researchers think the physiological influences are less important than other factors in shaping emotions.

The **perceptual view of emotions**, which is also called *appraisal theory*, asserts that subjective perceptions shape what external phenomena mean to us. External objects and events, as well as physiological reactions, have no intrinsic meaning. Instead, they gain meaning only as we attribute significance to them. We might interpret trembling hands as a symbol of fear, a raised fist as a threat, and a knot in the stomach as anxiety. Alternatively, we might interpret trembling hands as signifying joy on graduation day; a raised fist as power and racial pride, as it was during the civil rights movement of the 1960s and 1970s; and a knot in the stomach as excitement about receiving a major award. These different interpretations would lead us to define our emotions distinctly. That's the key to the perceptual view of emotions: We act on the basis of our interpretation of phenomena, not the tangible phenomena.

The ancient Greek philosopher Epictetus observed that people are disturbed not by things but by the views we take of them. Buddha observed that we are what we think; with our thoughts we make the world. In other words, how we view things leads us to feel disturbed, pleased, sad, joyous, afraid, and so forth. Thus, our perceptions filter our experiences, and it is the filtered experiences that influence what we feel and how we respond.

> **HARIHAR**
>
> Buddhism teaches us that our feelings arise not from things themselves but from what we attach to them. In my life, this is true. If I find myself upset about how a conversation is going, I ask myself, "Harihar, what is it that you were expecting to happen? Can you let go of that and enter into what is actually happening here?" That helps me realize and let go of my attachment to certain outcomes of the conversation.

We respond differently to the same phenomenon depending on the meaning we attribute to it. For example, if you earn a low score on a test, you might interpret it as evidence that you are not smart. This interpretation could lead you to feel shame or disappointment or other unpleasant emotions. Conversely, you might view the low score as the result of a tricky or overly rigorous exam, an interpretation that might lead you to feel anger at the teacher or resentment at the situation. Anger is very different from shame. Which one you feel depends on how you perceive the score and the meaning you attribute to it. The perceptual view of emotions is represented in Figure 7.2.

The perceptual view of emotions does not clearly identify the mechanism by which we interpret emotions. This problem is corrected in the **cognitive labeling view of emotions**, which is similar to the perceptual view but offers better explanation of how we move from experience to interpretation. According to the cognitive labeling view of emotions, the mechanism that allows this is language. This view claims that our labels for our physiological responses influence how we interpret those responses (Schachter, 1964; Schachter & Singer, 1962). Phrased another way, what we feel may be shaped by how we label our physiological responses. For example, if you feel a knot in your stomach when you see that you received a low grade on an exam, you might label the knot as evidence of anxiety. Thus, what you felt would not result directly from the event itself (the grade). Instead, it would be

Figure **7.2**

The Perceptual View of Emotions

© Cengage Learning

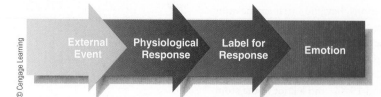

Figure **7.3**

The Cognitive Labeling View
of Emotions

shaped by how you labeled your physiological response to the event. This view of emotions is represented in Figure 7.3.

I witnessed how our labels for events and our responses to them influence what we feel. When my niece, Michelle, was 2 years old and weighed about 30 pounds, she and my sister Carolyn visited me. As they came into our home, our 65-pound dog, Madhi, ran to greet them and started licking Michelle. Immediately, Michelle started crying. I got Madhi to lie down across the room, and Michelle said, "Mommy, Mommy, I'm scared. My heart is going fast because she came after me and made me scared." Carolyn cuddled Michelle and said, "Your heart isn't going fast because you're scared, sweetheart. It's because Madhi surprised you and you were startled. Madhi was telling you how much she loves you. Dogs are our friends." Carolyn and I then petted Madhi and let her lick us and said repeatedly, "Oh, Madhi licked me because she loves me. She startled me."

Michelle quickly picked up our language and began to laugh, not cry, when Madhi bowled her over. By the end of the day, Michelle and Madhi were fast friends. Before she went to bed that night, Michelle told us, "Madhi makes my heart beat faster because I love her."

What happened here? Madhi's exuberance didn't diminish, nor did Michelle's physiological response of increased heart rate. What did change was how Michelle labeled her physiological response. Carolyn and I taught her to interpret Madhi's behavior as friendly and exciting instead of threatening. Michelle's label for her emotion also changed: *scared* became *startled*.

ARMANO

The most important lesson I learned when my family first moved to the United States was that a bad grade on a test is not a judgment that I am stupid. It is a challenge for me to do better. My ESL teacher taught me that. He said if I saw a bad grade as saying I am dumb or a failure that I would never learn English. He taught me to see grades as challenges that I could meet. That attitude made it possible for me not to give up and to keep learning.

Each of these models gives us insight into emotions. Yet none of them is complete, because none adequately accounts for the critical influence of culture in shaping emotions and how we communicate them.

Cultural Influences on Emotions

As we learned in Chapter 3, perception is influenced by the culture and the social groups to which we belong. Historian Barbara Rosenwein (1998) calls the groups we identify with "emotional communities" because they teach us how to understand and express emotions. Examples of emotional communities are families, neighborhoods, gangs, monasteries, and friends. Schools and workplaces may also be communities we identify with. The society and communities in which we live influence our beliefs about which emotions are good or bad, which emotions we should express or repress, and with whom we can appropriately communicate which emotions. For example, the emotion of shame is emphasized much more in traditional Asian societies than in Western societies. This may explain why 95% of Chinese parents report that their children understand the meaning of shame by age 3, whereas only 10% of American parents report this (Sedgwick, 1995; Shaver et al., 1987; Shaver et al., 1992).

Beginning in the 1970s, some scholars began to advance the **interactive view of emotions**, which proposes that cultural rules and understandings shape what people feel and how they do or don't express their feelings (Hochschild, 1979, 1983, 1990). The interactive view of emotions rests on three key culturally influenced concepts: framing rules, feeling rules, and emotion work.

David Silverman/Photonica World/Getty Images

Framing Rules   **Framing rules** define the emotional meaning of situations. For instance, Western culture defines funerals as sad and respectful occasions. Within any single culture, however, there are multiple social groups and resulting ways of framing events. For example, many Irish Americans hold wakes when a person dies. A wake is a festive occasion during which people tell stories about the departed person and celebrate his or her life. Other groups define funerals and the receptions following them as somber occasions at which any mirth or festivity would be perceived as disrespectful and inappropriate. During the Jewish practice of sitting *shiva*, family members do not engage others in routine ways such as talking on the phone.

Feeling Rules   **Feeling rules** tell us what we have a right to feel or what we are expected to feel in particular situations. Feeling rules reflect and perpetuate the values of cultures and social groups (Miller, 1993, 1998; Nanda & Warms, 1998). For example, some cultures view feeling and expressing anger as healthy. Yet the Semai of Malaysia think that being angry brings bad luck, and they try to avoid anger (Dentan, 1995; Robarchek & Dentan, 1987). That may be one reason that not a single murder among Semais has ever been recorded! Cultures that emphasize individuality promote the feeling rule that it is appropriate to feel pride in personal accomplishments, whereas cultures that emphasize collectivism teach members that accomplishments grow out of membership in groups and reflect well on those groups, not on individuals (Johnson, 2000). Thus, in collectivist cultures a feeling rule might be that it is appropriate for a person to feel gratitude to family and community for personal accomplishments.

A number of years ago, I read a newspaper story that shows how feeling rules differ between cultures. American teachers didn't realize that parents and students from collectivist cultures are dismayed when report cards state that students "speak up in class." Because collectivist cultures emphasize the overall community, an individual who stands out may be perceived as showing off and inappropriately calling attention to himself or herself ("Teachers' Words," 2000). All social communities have rules that specify acceptable and unacceptable ways to feel.

Feeling rules are sometimes explicated in terms of rights and duties. The following common phrases highlight the language of duty and rights that infuses feeling rules:

I'm entitled to feel sad.
She should be grateful to me for what I did.
I ought to feel happy that my friend got a job.
I have a right to be proud.
I shouldn't feel angry at my father.

There is a strong connection between feeling rules and social order. A key way that a society attempts to control people is through feeling rules that uphold broad social values and structures (1990). For example, teaching people that they should feel pride in their personal accomplishments reinforces the value that Western culture places on individualism and ambition. Teaching people to regard accomplishments as communal, not individual, upholds the value that many non-Western cultures place on groups.

A second way in which feeling rules uphold social structure is by linking the right to express feelings to social status and power. Studies of people in service industries reveal that the less power employees have, the more they tend to be targets of negative emotional communication by people who have more power (Hochschild, 1983). People who have more power may learn they have a right to express anger, offense, frustration, and so forth, whereas people who have less power may learn that it isn't acceptable for them to express such emotions. To test the validity of this idea, ask yourself who is the target of more complaints and greater hostility: servers or restaurant managers, flight attendants or pilots, receptionists or CEOs.

Everyday Skills To explore the relationship between religion and feeling rules, complete the activity "Religions and Feeling Rules" at the end of the chapter or online.

Claus Christensen/Getty Images

Parents differ in how they teach children to deal with feelings. Some parents encourage children to control their inner feelings through **deep acting**, which involves learning what they should and should not feel. For instance, children may be taught that they should feel grateful when given a gift even if they don't like the gift. Many children are taught that they should not feel angry when a friend takes a toy. Deep acting requires changing how we perceive and label events and phenomena.

Other parents emphasize **surface acting**, which involves controlling the outward expression of emotions rather than controlling feelings. Parents who emphasize surface acting teach children to control their outward behaviors, not necessarily their inner feelings. For example, children learn that they should say "thank you" when they receive a gift and that they should not hit a friend who takes a toy. Expressing gratitude is emphasized more than feeling grateful, and refraining from hitting someone who takes a toy is stressed more than feeling good about sharing toys.

Emotion Work   The final concept is **emotion work**, which is the effort to generate what we think are appropriate feelings in particular situations. Notice that emotion work concerns the process of trying to shape how we feel, not necessarily our success in doing so.

Although we do emotion work much of the time, we tend to be most aware of engaging in it when we think our feelings are inappropriate in specific situations. For example, you might think it is wrong to feel gleeful when someone you dislike is hurt. This is known as "the pinch," which is a discrepancy between what we feel and what we think we should feel (Hochschild, 1979, 1983). If you feel gleeful about another's bad luck, you might engage in emotion work in an effort to make yourself feel sad.

Typically, what we think we should feel is based on what we've learned from our social groups and the larger culture. Social groups teach us what feelings are appropriate in particular situations. For example, Clifton Scott and Karen Meyers (2005) found that firefighters engage in emotion work to manage feelings such as fear and disgust, which can interfere with controlling damage and providing medical help to victims of fires. Katherine Miller (2007) reports that human service workers engage in emotion work with clients—showing that they notice clients' lives, demonstrating empathy and person-centeredness, and responding in supportive ways.

People who have been socialized in multiple cultures or social communities with different values may be especially vulnerable to feeling "the pinch." Kimberly Gangwish (1999) describes Asian American women as "living in two worlds" in terms of their emotions and how they express them. First-generation Asian American women said they knew that, in the United States, it was acceptable to feel angry and upset, but they couldn't express those feelings because Asian cultures frown on expressing negative emotions.

> In my native country, students are supposed to be respectful of teachers and never speak out in class. It has been hard for me to learn to feel I have a right to ask questions of a professor here. Sometimes I have a question or I do not agree with a professor, but I have to work to tell myself it is okay to assert myself. To me, it still feels disrespectful to speak up.
>
> **HUANG**

We do emotion work to suppress or eliminate feelings we think are wrong (for example, feeling happy over the misfortune of someone you dislike). We also engage in emotion work to cultivate feelings we think we should have, such as prodding yourself to feel joy a friend got a job even though you did not. As Donna Vocate (1994) notes, much of our emotion work takes place through self-talk or intrapersonal communication. We try to talk ourselves into feeling what we think

Figure **7.4**

The Interactive View of Emotions

is appropriate and out of feeling what we think is inappropriate. In addition, we often talk to friends to figure out whether our feelings are appropriate—we rely on friends to help us reduce uncertainty about feelings (Heise, 1999; Milardo, 1986).

In the interactive view of emotions, framing rules, feeling rules, and emotion work are interrelated (see Figure 7.4). Framing rules that define the emotional meaning of situations lead to feeling rules that tell us what we should feel or have a right to feel in a given context. If we don't feel what our feeling rules designate we should, we may engage in emotion work to squelch inappropriate feelings or to bring about feelings that we think suit the circumstances. We then express our feelings by following rules for appropriate expression of particular emotions in specific contexts.

The interactive view of emotions emphasizes the impact of social factors on how we perceive, label, and respond emotionally to experiences in our lives. One strength of this model is that it acknowledges cultural differences in feelings and their expression.

Which of the four views of emotions you endorse has implications for how much you think you can control what you feel and how you express our feelings in everyday life. If you agree with the organismic view of emotions, then you will assume that feelings cannot be managed. Whatever you feel, you feel. That's it. On the other hand, if you accept the interactive view of emotions, you are more likely to think you can analyze your feelings and perhaps change them and your expression of them through emotion work. The interactive view assumes you have some power over what you feel and how you act. If you agree with this perspective, you are more likely to monitor your feelings and to make choices about how to communicate them.

We may not have total control over what we feel, but usually we can exert some control. Furthermore, we can exercise substantial control over how we do or don't express our feelings and to whom we express them. Taking personal responsibility for when, how, and to whom you express feelings is a cornerstone of ethical interpersonal communication (Anderson & Guerrero, 1998; Fridlund, 1994; Philippot & Feldman, 2004).

OBSTACLES TO COMMUNICATING EMOTIONS EFFECTIVELY

Skill in recognizing and expressing emotions is important to interpersonal competence, yet many of us repress feelings or express them inappropriately. Let's consider why we may not express emotions and then discuss some of the ineffective ways people express emotions.

Reasons We May Not Express Emotions

Researchers have identified four common reasons people don't communicate their emotions. As we discuss each reason, reflect on whether you rely on it in your own emotional expression.

Cultural and Social Expectations   As we have noted, what we feel and how we express it are influenced by the culture and social groups to which we belong. Gender socialization seems particularly important in shaping feelings and the expression of them. In the United States, men are expected to be more restrained than women in expressing most emotions (Burgoon & Bacue, 2003; Guerrero et al., 2006b), yet men are allowed to express anger, which is often disapproved of in women. In Italy and other countries, men routinely express a range of emotions dramatically and openly.

In societies that teach men the feeling rule that they should not feel or express a great many emotions, some men may suppress feelings or avoid expressing them. Over time, men who do this may become alienated from their feelings, unable to recognize what they do feel, because society has taught them that they shouldn't experience a great many feelings.

> Most of the time, I pretty much keep my feelings to myself like other guys do. But last spring one of my closest friends gave birth to a little girl. When I visited at the hospital and was holding the baby, she told me she wanted me to be her daughter's godfather. That blew me away and the next thing I knew I was crying and telling this little baby that I loved her. It was sort of embarrassing, but not too much. I'm glad none of the guys were with me, though.

ABE

Women face different restrictions than men on the feelings society considers it appropriate for them to express. Women are generally taught that anger is unattractive and undesirable in women (Tavris, 1989). Thus, many women are constrained by the feeling rule that they should not feel anger and that, if they do, they should not express it directly. This discourages women from acknowledging legitimate anger and expressing it constructively.

Another feeling rule that is learned by many Western women is to care about others (Eisenberg, 2002; Taylor, 2002). Thus, many women engage in emotion work in an attempt to make themselves feel caring (via deep acting) when they don't naturally feel that way.

Women may also squelch feelings of jealousy toward friends and feelings of competitiveness in personal and professional relationships. Because most Western women are taught that they should support others, they often feel that they shouldn't experience or express envy or competitiveness. Not being able to express or even acknowledge such feelings can interfere with honest communication in interpersonal relationships.

Self-Protection   A second reason we may not express our feelings is that we don't want to give others information that could affect how they perceive or act toward us. We fear that someone will like us less if we say that we feel angry with him or her. We worry that coworkers will lose respect for us if our nonverbal behaviors show that we feel weak or scared. We fear that if we disclose how deeply we feel about another person, she or he will reject us.

We may also restrain expression of feelings, particularly negative ones, because of what is known as the **chilling effect**. When we have a relationship with someone whom we perceive as more powerful than us, we may suppress complaints and expressions of dissatisfaction or anger because we fear that the more powerful person could punish us. We might fear a parent will withhold privileges, a supervisor could fire us, or a coach would sideline us. How the other person might use his or her power against us has a chilling effect on our willingness to express our feelings honestly.

We may also restrain expression of feelings, particularly negative ones, because of what is known as the **chilling effect**. When we have a relationship with someone whom we perceive as more powerful than us, we may suppress complaints and expressions of dissatisfaction or anger because we fear that the more powerful person could punish us. We might fear a parent will withhold privileges, a supervisor could fire us, or a coach would sideline us. How the other person might use his or her power against us has a chilling effect on our willingness to express our feelings honestly.

Communication in Everyday Life

DIVERSITY

Sugar and Spice and Bullying!

"Sugar and spice and everything nice" is not the whole picture about girls. Recently, scholars' tracking of adolescent girls' bullying (Simmons, 2002, 2004; Underwood, 2003) shows that many young girls engage in social aggression toward other girls, and they do so using distinctly feminine rules for expressing aggression. Unlike physical aggression, which is common among boys, social aggression is usually indirect, even covert. It takes forms such as spreading hurtful rumors, social exclusion, and encouraging others to turn against a particular girl. Why do young girls rely on indirect and social strategies of aggression? One reason appears to be that, even at young ages, girls understand that they are supposed to be nice to everyone, so they fear that being overtly mean to others would lead to disapproval or punishment. They're taught to soften their opinions and to accommodate others, particularly males (Berger, 2006; Deveny, 2009). Girls learn not to stand up to boys at school because they fear being called "bitch" (Bennett, Ellison, & Ball, 2010; Deveny, 2009). Instead of learning how to manage anger openly, young girls learn to express it indirectly.

🔵 MindTap· In your experience, do girls and women engage in more social aggression than boys and men?

Protecting Others   Another reason we often choose not to express feelings is that we fear we could hurt or upset others or cause them to lose face. Sometimes we make an ethical choice not to express emotions that would hurt another person and not achieve any positive outcome. Choosing not to express emotions in some situations or to some people can be constructive and generous, as Tara's commentary illustrates.

TARA

My best friend, Fran, is a marriage saver. When I'm really angry with my husband, I vent to her. If there's a really serious problem between me and Al, I talk with him. But a lot of times I'm upset over little stuff. I know what I'm feeling isn't going to last and isn't any serious problem in our marriage, but I may be seething anyway. Letting those feelings out to Fran gets them off my chest without hurting Al or our marriage.

The tendency to restrain emotional expression to protect others is particularly strong in many Asian cultures because they view hurting others as shameful (Johnson, 2000; Min, 1995; Ting-Toomey & Oetzel, 2002; Yamamoto, 1995). Traditional Asian cultures also view conflict as damaging to social relationships, so they discourage emotional expressions that might lead to conflict (Johnson, 2000; Ting-Toomey & Oetzel, 2002).

Yet Asians and people of Asian descent are not the only ones who want to protect relationships from tension that can arise from emotional expression. If a friend of yours behaves in ways you consider irresponsible, you may refrain from expressing your disapproval because you don't want to provoke tension between you. Totally open and unrestrained expression of feeling isn't necessarily a good idea.

Sometimes it is both wise and kind not to express feelings. It's often not productive to vent minor frustrations and annoyances. If someone we care about is already overburdened with anxiety or emotional problems, we may choose not to express our emotions so that the other person doesn't have to respond to our feelings at the moment. Thus, there can be good reasons not to show or discuss feelings, or not to show or discuss them at a given time.

> Last week, I got rejected by the law school that was my top choice. Normally, I would have gone over to Jason's apartment to hang out with him and let him boost me up. Ever since we met freshman year, we've been tight friends, and we talk about everything in our lives. But right now, Jason's struggling with his own stuff. His mother just got diagnosed with cancer, and his father is out of work. I know we'll talk about my disappointment some time, but I figured it could wait until he gets into a better place.

ISHMAEL

Ishmael's commentary provides a good example of an instance in which it is more caring not to express feelings. Yet we would be mistaken to think it's always a good idea to keep feelings to ourselves. Avoiding the expression of feelings can be harmful if those feelings directly affect our relationships with others or if doing so may threaten our own health. Susan Schmanoff (1987) found that intimacy wanes when a couple's communication consistently lacks emotional disclosures, even unpleasant ones. If not expressing feelings is likely to create barriers in relationships or to cause us serious personal distress, then we should try to find a context and mode of expression that allow us to communicate our emotions. The physical and psychological impact of denying or repressing emotions over the long term can harm you and your relationships (Pennebaker, 1997; Schmanoff, 1987).

Social and Professional Roles   A final reason we may not express some feelings is that our roles make it inappropriate. An attorney or judge who cries when hearing a sad story from a witness might be perceived as unprofessional. A doctor or nurse who expresses anger toward a patient might be regarded as unprofessional. Police officers and social workers might be judged to be out of line if they express animosity instead of objective detachment when investigating a crime.

We've identified four common reasons we may not express our emotions. Although we can understand all of them, they are not equally constructive in their consequences. There is no simple rule for when to express feelings. Instead, we must exercise judgment. We have an ethical obligation to make thoughtful choices about whether, when, and how to express our feelings. As a responsible communicator, you should strive to decide when it is necessary, appropriate, and constructive to express your feelings, keeping in mind that you, others, and relationships will be affected by your decision.

It's hard to imagine an attorney who is more professional in her demeanor than Alicia Florrick, Julianna Margulies's character in *The Good Wife.*

Eike Schroter/CBS/Photofest

The Ineffective Expression of Emotions

We don't always deny or repress our emotions. Sometimes, we are aware of having a particular feeling, and we try to express it, but our effort isn't very successful. We'll look at three of the most common forms of ineffective emotional expression.

Speaking in Generalities   "I feel bad." "I'm happy." "I'm sad." Statements such as these do express emotional states, but they do so ineffectively. Why? Because they are so general and abstract that they don't clearly communicate what the speaker feels. Does "I feel bad" mean the person feels depressed, angry, guilty, ashamed, or anxious? Does "I'm happy" mean the speaker is in love, pleased with a grade, satisfied at having received a promotion, delighted to be eating chocolate, or thrilled about an upcoming vacation? When we use general, abstract emotional language, we aren't communicating effectively about what we feel.

Also, our nonverbal repertoire for expressing emotions may be limited. Withdrawing from interaction may be an expression of sadness, anger, depression, or fear. Lowering our head and eyes may express a range of emotions, including reverence, shame, and thoughtfulness. We are capable of experiencing many, many emotions. Yet most of us recognize or express only a small number. In *Anger: The Struggle for Emotional Control in America's History* (1986), Carol Stearns and Peter Stearns report that people in the United States recognize only a few of the emotions humans can experience, and they express those emotions whenever they feel something. An acquaintance of mine says, "I'm frustrated" when he is angry, confused, hurt, anxious, disappointed, and so forth. In the example that opened this chapter, I said I felt angry when *hurt* would have more accurately described my feeling. A limited emotional vocabulary restricts our ability to communicate clearly with others (Lama & Eckman, 2009; Saarni, 1999).

Not Owning Feelings
Stating feelings in a way that disowns personal responsibility is one of the most common obstacles to effective expression of emotions (Proctor, 1991). Our discussion of *I* language and *you* language in Chapter 4 is relevant to learning to express emotions effectively.

"You make me angry" states a feeling (although the word *angry* may be overly general). Yet this statement relies on *you* language, which suggests that somebody other than the speaker is the source or cause of the angry feeling. Others certainly say and do things that affect us; they may even do things *to* us. But we—not anyone else—decide what their actions mean, and we—not anyone else—are responsible for our feelings.

How could we use *I* language to revise the statement, "You make me angry"? We could change it to this: "I feel angry when you don't call when you say you will." The statement would be even more effective—clearer and more precise—if the speaker said, "I feel hurt and insecure when you don't call when you say you will." And the statement would be still more effective if it included information about what the speaker wants from the other person: "I feel hurt and insecure when you don't call when you say you will. Would you be willing to call if we agree that it's okay for calls to be short sometimes?" This statement accepts responsibility for a feeling, communicates clearly what is felt, and offers a solution that could help the relationship.

Counterfeit Emotional Language   A third ineffective form of emotional communication is relying on **counterfeit emotional language**. This is language that seems to express emotions but does not actually describe what a person is feeling. For example, shouting "Why can't you leave me alone?" certainly indicates that the speaker is feeling something, but it doesn't describe what she or he is feeling. Is it anger at a particular person, frustration at being interrupted, stress at having to meet a deadline, or the need for time alone? We can't tell what feeling the speaker is experiencing from what he or she said.

Effective communicators provide clear descriptions of their feelings and the connection between their feelings and others' behaviors. "I feel frustrated because when I'm working and you walk in, I lose my train of thought" is a more constructive statement than "Why can't you leave me alone?" The first statement communicates what is troubling you and states that it is situation-specific.

It's also unproductive not to explain feelings. "That's just how I feel" doesn't tell a person how her or his behavior is related to your feelings or what you would like her or him to do. Sometimes, we say, "That's just how I feel" because we haven't really figured out why we feel as we do or what we want from another person. In such cases, we should take responsibility for understanding what's going on inside ourselves before we ask others to understand. Only when you can identify situations and your emotional reactions to them can you communicate clearly to others (Planalp, 1997).

MindTap

Everyday Skills To practice translating counterfeit emotional language into language that describes feelings accurately, complete the activity "Avoiding Counterfeit Emotional Language" at the end of the chapter or online.

Another form of counterfeit emotional language uses feeling words but really expresses thoughts: "I feel this discussion is getting sidetracked." The perception that a discussion is going off on a tangent is a thought, not a feeling. Maybe the speaker feels frustrated that the discussion seems to be wandering, but that feeling is not communicated by the statement.

The three types of ineffective emotional communication we've considered give us insight into some of the more common ways we may evade—consciously or not—clear and honest communication about our feelings. In the final section of this chapter, we consider specific ways to communicate our feelings effectively and constructively and to respond sensitively to others' communication about their emotions.

MindTap™

Everyday Skills To practice recognizing the expression of emotions online, complete the activity "Emotions on Social Networks" at the end of the chapter or online.

SOCIAL MEDIA AND EMOTIONS

What we have learned about emotions is relevant to digital and online communication in several ways. First, the reasons we may not express emotions in f2f interaction may also operate when we use social media. We may think it is socially unacceptable to express some feelings online, we may choose not to express them to protect ourselves or others, or we may realize that our roles make it inappropriate to express some emotions. When we are communicating with friends, coworkers, and family members any of these reasons may lead us not to express emotions. Yet we may be more likely to express emotions, including ones that are socially inappropriate, when we are communicating with people we don't know personally. The anonymity of social media emboldens some people to post rants, hate speech, and other offensive comments that they would probably never say f2f. In other words, we may be less inhibited by social norms when we are communicating online and digitally.

Second, social media may help us experience and express feelings. When something sad or shocking happens, we like to connect with people who are likely to share our feelings about what happened. After pop star Michael Jackson died, fans went online to grieve together. Research showed that fans found the content provided by YouTube helped them express their feelings and grieve (Lee, 2013). Similarly, many people find like-minded communities to celebrate happy events (the wedding of Prince Charles and Princess Kate) or make sense of violence (campus shootings).

Third, social media can become substitutes for emotional involvement with people in our f2f relationships. It can be easier to turn to an online acquaintance than your real-life friends or partners when you need emotional connection. We can say what we want and no more than we want, which is not always possible in f2f conversations. It can become easier and less emotionally threatening to turn toward online acquaintances than f2f friends. The more we share our feelings online, however, the more likely we are to feel closer to our virtual acquaintances than our f2f ones. It's a self-fulfilling prophecy. While relying on online acquaintances may satisfy immediate needs for emotional connection, there is the danger of becoming more involved with the online acquaintance than the people with whom you have f2f relationships.

GUIDELINES FOR COMMUNICATING EMOTIONS EFFECTIVELY

What we've explored so far in this chapter suggests several guidelines for becoming skilled at communicating our feelings. In this section, we extend our discussion to identify six guidelines for effective communication of emotions. This process is summarized in Figure 7.5.

Identify Your Emotions

Before you can communicate emotions effectively, you must be able to identify what you feel. As we have seen, this isn't always easy. For reasons we've discussed, people may be alienated from their emotions or unclear about what they feel, especially if they are experiencing multiple emotions at once. To become more aware of your emotions, give mindful attention to your inner self. Just as we can learn to ignore our feelings, we can teach ourselves to notice and heed them.

Sometimes, identifying our emotions requires us to sort out complex mixtures of feelings. For example, we sometimes feel both anxious and hopeful. To recognize only that you feel hopeful is to overlook the anxiety. To realize only that you feel anxious is to disregard the hope you also feel. Recognizing the existence of both feelings allows you to tune in to yourself and to communicate accurately to others what you are experiencing.

When sorting out intermingled feelings, it's useful to identify the primary or main feeling—the one that is dominant in the moment. Doing this allows you to communicate clearly to others what is most important in your emotional state. Think back to the example that opened this chapter. I had said I felt angry that Carolyn didn't seem to have time for me. I did feel anger, but that wasn't my primary emotion. Hurt was the dominant feeling, and it was the one I communicated to Carolyn. This gave her an understanding of what I felt that was more accurate than if I'd told her I felt angry.

 MindTap™

Everyday Skills To practice using emotional vocabulary effectively, complete the activity "Enlarging Your Emotional Vocabulary" at the end of the chapter or online.

Figure **7.5**

Effective Communication of Emotions

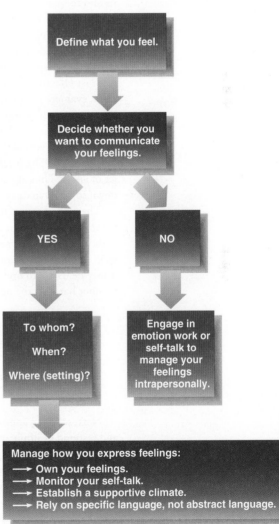

© Cengage Learning

Choose Whether and How to Express Emotions

Once you know what you feel, you can consider choices about expressing your emotions. The first choice is whether you want to communicate your emotions to particular people. As we noted in the previous section, sometimes it is both wise and compassionate not to tell someone what you feel. You may decide that expressing particular emotions would hurt others and would not accomplish anything positive. This is not the same thing as not expressing emotions just to avoid tension, because tension between people can foster growth in individuals and relationships.

We may also decide not to communicate emotions because we prefer to keep some of our feelings private. This is a reasonable choice if the feelings we keep to ourselves are not ones that other people need to know in order to understand us and to be in satisfying relationships with us. We don't have a responsibility to bare our souls to everyone, nor are we required to disclose all our feelings, even to our intimates.

If you decide you do want to communicate your emotions, then you should assess the different ways you might do that and select the one that seems likely to be most effective. Four guidelines can help you decide how to express emotions. First, evaluate your current state. If you are really upset, you may not be able to express yourself clearly and fairly. In moments of extreme emotion, our perceptions may be distorted, and we may say things we don't mean. Remember that communication is irreversible—we cannot unsay what we have said. According to Daniel Goleman (1995b), it takes about 20 minutes for us to cleanse our minds and bodies of anger. Thus, if you are really angry, you may want to wait until you've cooled down so that you can discuss your feelings more fruitfully.

The second step is to decide to whom you want to express your feelings. Often, we want to communicate our emotions to the people they concern—the person with whom we are upset or whose understanding we seek. Yet sometimes we don't want to talk to the person who is the target of our feelings. In cases such as these, it may be useful to find someone else to whom you can safely express your feelings without harming the person about whom you have them.

BOB

When I didn't get a promotion, I was ready to blow my top. But I knew better than to blow it around my boss or anyone at the company. Nope, I said I was sick and left for the day and called a friend who works at home. We met for lunch, and she let me just blow off steam with her in a place that wouldn't hurt me on the job.

Next, select an appropriate time to discuss feelings. Most of us are able to listen and respond skillfully when we are not preoccupied, defensive, stressed, rushed, or tired. Generally, it's not productive to launch a discussion of feelings when we lack the time or energy to focus on the conversation. It may be better to defer discussion until you and the other person have the psychological and physical resources to engage mindfully.

Finally, select an appropriate setting for discussing feelings. Many feelings can be expressed well in a variety of settings. For instance, it would be appropriate to tell a friend you felt happy while strolling with him through a shopping mall, walking on campus, or in a private conversation. However, it might not be constructive to tell a friend you feel angry or disappointed in her in a public setting. Doing so could make the other person feel as though she's on display, which might arouse defensiveness, making it less likely that the two of you can have a constructive, open discussion of feelings. Many people say that they feel freer to express emotions honestly online than in face-to-face communication. However, some people really dislike communicating about personal topics online. So, before choosing to discuss emotions online, make sure the other person is comfortable with that.

In her book, *How Doctors Feel* (2013), Dr. Danielle Ofri offers an honest account of feelings that doctors experience in the course of practicing medicine: grief over patients who die, shame over medical mistakes, joy at births and successful treatments, and bitterness over medical malpractice lawsuits. She writes that most doctors try to compartmentalize their feelings, but that strategy often fails as emotions flood doctors' daily lives and cause internal turmoil. Doctors fare better when they are able to identify their feelings and express them in appropriate contexts that do not upset patients or other medical staff.

Own Your Feelings

We noted the importance of owning your emotions in Chapter 4 and again in this chapter's discussion of ineffective ways of communicating feelings. Owning your feelings is so important to effective communication that the guideline bears repeating: Using *I* language to express feelings reminds us that we—not anyone else—have responsibility for our feelings. When we rely on *you* language ("You hurt me"), we risk misleading ourselves about our accountability for our emotions.

I language also reduces the potential for defensiveness by focusing on specific behaviors that we would like changed ("I feel hurt when you interrupt me") instead of criticizing another's basic self ("You are so rude"). Criticisms of specific behaviors are less likely to threaten a person's self-concept than criticisms of our personality or self (Cupach & Carlson, 2002). Thus, when we use *I* language to describe how we feel when another behaves in particular ways, the other person is more able to listen thoughtfully and respond sensitively to our expression of emotion.

Monitor Your Self-Talk

A fourth guideline is to monitor your self-talk. You'll recall from Chapter 2 that the ways we communicate with ourselves affect how we feel and act. **Self-talk** is communication with ourselves. We engage in self-talk when we do emotion work. We might say, "I shouldn't feel angry" or "I don't want to come across as a wimp by showing how much that hurt." Thus, we may talk ourselves out of or into feelings and out of or into ways of expressing feelings.

Psychologist Martin Seligman (1990) believes that "our thoughts are not merely reactions to events; they change what ensues" (p. 9). In other words, the thoughts we communicate to ourselves affect what happens in our lives. Self-talk can work for us or against us, depending on whether we manage it or it manages us. This point is stressed by Tom Rusk and Natalie Rusk in their book *Mind Traps* (1988). They point out that many people have self-defeating ideas that get in the way of their effectiveness and happiness. According to the Rusks, unless we learn to manage our feelings effectively, we cannot change patterns of behavior that leave us stuck in ruts, which can become self-fulfilling prophecies. Tuning in to your self-talk and learning to monitor it helps you manage your emotions.

Adopt a Rational–Emotive Approach to Feelings

Monitoring your self-talk allows you to appreciate the connections between thoughts and feelings. As Sally Planalp and Julie Fitness (2000) point out, "Cognition relies on emotion, emotion relies on cognition" (p. 732). Thus, how we think about feelings affects our feelings. The relationship between thoughts and feelings led a therapist named Albert Ellis to develop the **rational–emotive approach to feelings**. Ellis was known for his dramatic style and for pushing, pushing, pushing his clients. He firmly believed that people whom many clinicians diagnosed as neurotic were not neurotic but only suffering from irrational thinking. He often described this as stupid thinking on the part of smart people (Ellis, 1962; Ellis & Harper, 1975; Seligman, 1990).

The rational–emotive approach to feelings uses rational thinking and self-talk to challenge the debilitating thoughts about emotions that undermine healthy self-concepts and relationships. The rational–emotive approach to feelings proceeds through four steps.

The first step is to monitor your emotional reactions to events and experiences that distress you. Notice what's happening in your body; notice your nonverbal behavior. Does your stomach tighten? Are you clenching your teeth? Is your heart racing? Do you feel nauseated?

The second step is to identify the events and situations to which you have unpleasant responses. Look for commonalities between situations. For example, perhaps you notice that your heart races and your palms get clammy when you talk with professors, supervisors, and academic advisers, but you don't have these physiological responses when you interact with friends, coworkers, or people whom you supervise. You label your emotions as insecurity in the former cases and security in the latter ones. One commonality between the situations in which you feel insecure is the greater power of the other person. This could suggest that you feel insecure when talking with someone who has more power than you.

The third step is to tune in to your self-talk (Vocate, 1994). Listen to what's happening in your head. What is your *Me* saying? Is it telling you that you shouldn't feel certain emotions? Is it telling you to deny your feelings? Is it telling you that you have to be totally perfect all the time or that you are helpless to change matters? We need to identify and challenge debilitating ways of thinking about our emotions, and, by extension, ourselves. These irrational beliefs, or fallacies, hinder our ability to manage and express emotions effectively.

We can use our self-talk to challenge the debilitating fallacies. For example, assume that Tyronne has been working well at his job and thinks his boss should give him a raise. He tunes in to his self-talk (step 3) and hears himself saying, "Well, maybe I shouldn't ask for a raise, because, after all, I have made some mistakes. I could do better." This self-talk reflects the fallacy of perfectionism. Tyronne listens further to himself and hears this message: "If I ask him for a raise, and he gets angry, he might fire me, and then I wouldn't have a job and couldn't stay in school. Without a degree, I have no future." This self-talk exemplifies the fear of catastrophic failure.

How might Tyronne dispute these fallacies? To challenge the perfectionism fallacy, he could say, "True, I'm not perfect, but I'm doing more and better work than the other employees hired at the same time I was." To dispute the fallacy of catastrophic failure, Tyronne might say to himself, "Well, he's not likely to fire me, because I do my job well, and training someone new would be a lot of trouble. And what if he does fire me? It's not like this is the only job in the world. I could get another job pretty fast." Instead of letting debilitating fallacies defeat us, we can use our self-talk to question and challenge the irrational thinking that undermines us.

Respond Sensitively When Others Communicate Emotions

A final guideline is to respond sensitively when others express their feelings to you. Learning to communicate your emotions effectively is only half the process of communicating about emotions. You also want to become skilled in listening and responding to others when they share feelings with you. This skill is important not only in personal relationships but also in workplace relationships (Kanov, Maitlis, Worline, Dutton, Frost, & Lilus, 2004; Miller, 2007).

When others express feelings, our first tendency may be to respond with general statements, such as "Time heals all wounds," "You shouldn't feel bad," "You'll be fine," or "You'll feel better once you get this into perspective." Although such statements may be intended to provide reassurance, in effect they tell others that they aren't allowed to feel what they are feeling, or that they will be okay (right, normal) once they stop feeling what they are feeling.

Another common mistake in responding to others' expression of feelings is to try to solve the other person's problem so the feelings will go away. Research suggests that the tendency to try to solve others' problems is more common in men than women (Swain, 1989; Tannen, 1990). Helping another solve a problem may be appreciated, but usually it's not the first support a person needs when she or he is expressing strong emotions. What many people need first is just the freedom to say what they are feeling and have those feelings accepted by others. Probably because of socialization, women are generally more skilled than men at providing solace, comfort, and emotional support (Basow & Rubenfeld, 2003; MacGeorge, Gillihan, Samter, & Clark, 2003; MacGeorge, Graves, Feng, Gillihan, & Burleson, 2004).

When others express emotions to you, it's supportive to begin by showing you are willing to discuss emotional topics. Next, accept where they are as a starting place. You don't have to agree or approve to accept what another is feeling. While listening, it's helpful to interject a few minimal encouragers, which we discussed in Chapter 6. Saying "I understand" or "Go on" conveys that you accept the other person's feelings and want him or her to continue talking. It's appropriate to mention your own experiences briefly to show that you empathize. However, it's not supportive to refocus the conversation on you and your experiences.

Paraphrasing, which we discussed in Chapter 6, is another way to show that you understand what another feels. When you mirror back not just the content but the feeling of what another says, it confirms the other and what he or she feels. "So, it sounds as if you were really surprised by what happened. Is that right?" "What I'm hearing is that you are more hurt than angry. Does that sound right to you?" These examples of paraphrasing allow you to check on your perception of the speaker's feelings and also show that you are listening actively.

The guidelines we've identified may not always make emotional communication easy and comfortable. However, following them will help you understand and express your feelings and respond effectively when others discuss theirs. To practice expressing emotions effectively and to identify ineffective expressions of emotion, go to your Online Resources for *Interpersonal Communication: Everyday Encounters* and complete the activity "Express Emotions Effectively" under the resources for Chapter 7.

CHAPTER SUMMARY

In this chapter, we explored the complex world of emotions and our communications about them. We considered different views of what's involved in experiencing and expressing emotions. From our review of theories, we learned that emotions have physiological, perceptual, linguistic, and social dimensions. We also examined some of the reasons people don't express feelings or express them ineffectively both in f2f interactions and on social media. We discussed the tendency of some people to engage in emotionally inappropriate communication online and in social media, and we noted that social media provide virtual communities that may help us experience and express emotions. The final focus of our attention was on guidelines for effective communication about emotions. Because these guidelines are critical to interpersonal communication, we'll close the chapter by restating them:

1. Identify your emotions.
2. Choose how to communicate your emotions.
3. Own your feelings.
4. Monitor your self-talk.
5. Adopt a rational–emotive approach to emotions.
6. Respond sensitively when others communicate emotions.

Key Concepts

Practice defining the chapter's terms by using online flashcards.

 MindTap™

FLASHCARDS...

chilling effect 202
cognitive labeling view of emotions 195
counterfeit emotional language 205
deep acting 198

emotional intelligence 191
emotions 193
emotion work 199
feeling rules 197
framing rules 197
interactive view of emotions 197

organismic view of emotions 194
perceptual view of emotions 194
rational–emotive approach to feelings 210
self-talk 209
surface acting 199

Continuing the Conversation

Jason Harris © 2001 Wadsworth

When you've watched the video online, critique and analyze this encounter based on the principles you learned in this chapter. Then compare your work with the author's suggested responses. Online, even more videos will let you continue the conversation with your instructor.

> You work with a person who is friendly and talkative; the two of you have enjoyed casual conversation about issues related to the job as well as outside. For the past week, Chris hasn't initiated any talk and has made only minimal responses to you. You think Chris may be upset, and you decide to explore this.

You: Chris, you've been quiet lately. Is anything wrong?

Chris: Not really, not anything I know how to talk about.

You: Sounds like something is bothering you.

Chris: I guess that's life, right? I'm just down.

You: Sometimes it helps if I talk to somebody when I'm feeling down. Want to tell me what's getting to you?

Chris: It's Mr. Brewster. He's been on my case for the past 3 weeks.

You: Is he criticizing your job performance?

Chris: Yeah. He says I'm sloppy when I write reports and that I am not always nice to clients. What am I supposed to be—Little Mary Sunshine?

You: Sounds like you're angry.

Chris: I am. I come to work every day, I do my job, and I don't complain. It's not like they're paying us big bucks, so they shouldn't expect us to be all charm and cheer to every client—some of those folks are real jerks.

PRACTICE...

You: I agree. Some of them are difficult and rude. What exactly does Mr. Brewster say about how you deal with clients?

Chris: He says stuff about not being nice. I feel like he's biased against me just because I'm not as pleasant and smiley as I should be.

You: He may be biased against anyone who isn't super-nice to clients. Remember how he really drilled it into all of us when we were hired that we are supposed to be polite and smile and all that.

Chris: I don't always feel like smiling. And I don't think Mr. Brewster has any right to tie my job to whether I am a beacon of sunshine for every client who walks in! I need this job.

You: Sounds as if you may be feeling worried about the job, too. Right?

Chris: Sure, I'm worried. I need this job. I've got a child and nobody but me to support him.

You: Has Mr. Brewster said anything about your losing this job?

Chris: No, but I know I'm not perfect, and I know he can fire me any time. If he does, I'm finished. But I'm just not cheerful all the time, even if I should be. I know I should be nicer sometimes, but I can't.

1. What has happened so far in this conversation? Has Chris changed at all in terms of identifying emotions?

2. Do you perceive any examples of counterfeit emotional language in Chris's communication?

3. If you wanted to help Chris keep the job, would you advise deep acting, surface acting, or some combination of the two? Explain your reasons.

4. Does Chris seem to be operating on any irrational beliefs?

5. How would you want the conversation to progress now? What would you say next to support and help Chris?

6. Would you communicate differently if Chris were a woman or man? Do you think Chris's sex would affect how he or she communicates?

Assessing Yourself

Begin the process of applying this chapter's concepts by taking two self-assessment quizzes here or online—where you will find out what the results mean.

1. What's Your EQ?

Purpose: To determine your own emotional intelligence.

Instructions: Answer the following four questions, which are adapted from Goleman's EQ test.

1. Imagine you're on an airplane and it suddenly begins rolling dramatically from side to side. What would you do?
   a. Keep reading your book, and ignore the turbulence.
   b. Become vigilant in case there is an emergency. Notice the flight attendants and review the card with instructions for emergencies.
   c. A little of a and b.
   d. Not sure—I never notice an airplane's motion.

2. Imagine that you expect to earn an A in a course you are taking, but you get a C on your midterm exam. What would you do?
   a. Make a specific plan to improve your grade, and resolve to implement the plan.
   b. Resolve to do better in the future.
   c. Nurture your self-concept by telling yourself that the grade doesn't really matter and focus on doing well in your other courses.
   d. Go to see the professor and try to talk him or her into raising your midterm grade.

3. While riding in a friend's car, your friend becomes enraged at another driver who just cut in front of him. What would you do?
   a. Tell your friend to let it slide—that it's no big deal.
   b. Put in your friend's favorite CD and turn up the volume to distract him.
   c. Agree with him and show rapport by talking about what a jerk the other driver is.
   d. Tell him about a time when someone cut in front of you and how mad you felt, but explain you then found out that the other driver was on her way to the hospital.

PRACTICE...

4. You and your girlfriend or boyfriend have just had an argument that became a heated shouting contest. By now, you're both very upset, and each of you has started making nasty personal attacks on the other. What do you do?
   a. Suggest that the two of you take a 20-minute break to cool down and then continue the discussion.
   b. Decide to put an end to the argument by not talking anymore. Just be silent and don't speak, no matter what the other person says.
   c. Apologize to your partner, and ask him or her to say "I'm sorry," too.
   d. Pause to collect your thoughts, then explain your views and your side of the issue clearly.

2. Managing Anger

In their book *Anger Kills* (1998), Redford Williams and Virginia Williams summarize years of research and clinical studies that show that anger harms our physical and mental health. Convinced by evidence that anger is dangerous, the Williamses developed a test to measure how dangerous a person's level of anger is. Take the test, adapted from pages 5–11 of *Anger Kills*, to measure your anger level.

1. When I get stuck in a traffic jam,
   a. I am usually not particularly upset.
   b. I start to feel irritated and annoyed quickly.

2. When someone treats me unfairly,
   a. I usually forget the incident fairly quickly.
   b. I tend to keep thinking about the incident for hours.

3. When I am caught in a slow-moving line at the grocery store,
   a. I seldom notice or mind the wait.
   b. I fume at people who dawdle ahead of me.

4. When I hear or read about another terrorist attack,
   a. I wonder why some people are so cruel to others.
   b. I feel like lashing out.

Everyday Skills

Build your communication skills further by completing the following activities here or online.

1. Religions and Feeling Rules

Religions urge people to follow particular feeling rules. For example, Judeo-Christian commandments direct people to "honor thy father and thy mother" and to "not covet thy neighbor's house, nor his wife." Buddhism commands people to feel compassion for all living beings and to do what they can to alleviate suffering. Hinduism commands followers to accept their place (caste) in this life.

Make a list of all the feeling rules you can identify that are proposed by your spiritual or religious affiliation. Be sure to list both what you are supposed to feel and what you are not supposed to feel.

1. _____

2. _____

3. _____

4. _____

5. _____

6. _____

Compare your responses with those of students who have different religious or spiritual beliefs. What similarities and differences in feeling rules can you identify?

2. Avoiding Counterfeit Emotional Language

Listed here are five statements that include counterfeit emotional language. Rewrite each statement so that it describes a feeling or an emotional state. Make sure you also rely on *I* language, not *you* language, and offer precise, clear descriptions, not vague ones.

1. "Shut up! I don't want to hear anything else from you."
_____

2. "You're a wonderful person."
_____

3. "I feel like we should get started on our group project."
_____

4. "I can't believe you were here all day and didn't ever clean up this mess."
_____

5. "Can't you see I'm working now? Leave me alone."
_____

3. Emotions on Social Networks

Log onto Facebook or your preferred social networking site. Read all of the posts that have appeared in the past 24 hours. Note every instance of emotional expression—anger, joy, fear, pride, and so on. What conclusions can you draw about the extent of emotional expression and the type of emotion expressed on social networks?

4. Enlarging Your Emotional Vocabulary

A key aspect of emotional competence is adequate emotional vocabulary. Reflect on your emotional vocabulary and how and when you use particular words to describe emotions.

Listed here are some of the more common emotion words people use. For each one, write out four other emotion words that describe subtle distinctions in feeling.

Example:	Anger	resentment	outrage	offense	irritation
	Sadness	_____	_____	_____	_____
	Fear	_____	_____	_____	_____
	Anxiety	_____	_____	_____	_____
	Love	_____	_____	_____	_____
	Happiness	_____	_____	_____	_____

Extend this exercise by trying to describe your feelings more precisely for the next week. Does expanding your emotional vocabulary give you and others more understanding of what you feel?

Engaging with Ideas

Reflect and write about the ideas in this chapter by considering questions about personal, workplace, and ethical applications, here or online.

Personal Application Recall a time when you didn't feel what you thought you should feel. Describe how "the pinch" felt to you and the emotion work you did in an effort to feel what you thought you should feel in the situation.

Workplace Application Think about the profession that you intend to enter. Are there some feelings that it is in- appropriate to express (or even to have) in that profession? Ex- plain why certain feelings are inappropriate and how express- ing them would violate the professional role.

MindTap™

REFLECT ON...

Ethical Application Is honesty always the best policy? Is it ethical for one person to decide what another should know or can handle? How might ethical principles vary across cul- tures?

Thinking Critically

Think and write critically about the ideas in this chapter, here or online.

1. We discussed different perspectives on emotions. Which perspective—or which combination of sev- eral—makes the most sense to you? Why? Explain how the perspective you favor gives you insight into emotions that you don't get from other perspectives.

MindTap™

REFLECT ON...

2. How often do you in- clude emoticons or stickers in your digital communication? To what extent do you think they convey your emotions adequately?

COMMUNICATION CLIMATE: THE FOUNDATION OF PERSONAL RELATIONSHIPS

Topics covered in this chapter

Features of Satisfying Relationships

Confirming and Disconfirming Climates

Social Media and Personal Relationships

Guidelines for Creating and Sustaining Confirming Climates

After studying this chapter, you should be able to . . .

Identify features of satisfying relationships.

Distinguish communication that confirms or disconfirms in a personal relationship.

Identify rules for using social media.

Apply chapter guidelines to enhance your ability to maintain confirming climates in relationships.

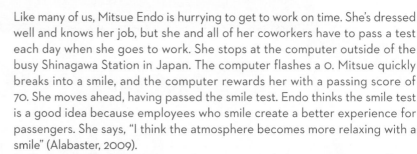

Like many of us, Mitsue Endo is hurrying to get to work on time. She's dressed well and knows her job, but she and all of her coworkers have to pass a test each day when she goes to work. She stops at the computer outside of the busy Shinagawa Station in Japan. The computer flashes a 0. Mitsue quickly breaks into a smile, and the computer rewards her with a passing score of 70. She moves ahead, having passed the smile test. Endo thinks the smile test is a good idea because employees who smile create a better experience for passengers. She says, "I think the atmosphere becomes more relaxing with a smile" (Alabaster, 2009).

Endo is insightful in realizing that our nonverbal communication affects the climate for interaction. We're more likely to feel upbeat and positive when we are around people who smile and laugh and engage in supportive communication. We tend to feel uneasy or negative when we're around people who frown and communicate about everything that is wrong.

Communication climate is the overall feeling or emotional mood between people—warm or cold, safe or anxious, accepting or rejecting, open or guarded—that is shaped by verbal and nonverbal interaction between people. Understanding communication climates will give you insight into why you feel relaxed and comfortable in some of your relationships and uneasy and defensive in others. Further, learning how communication shapes communication climates will empower you to create and sustain the climates that you want in your relationships.

This chapter explores the impact of verbal and nonverbal interaction on building and sustaining communication climates in interpersonal relationships. We begin by discussing features of satisfying interpersonal relationships. Next, we examine the kinds of communication that build confirming, supportive communication climates. Third, we consider how communication climates relate to our interaction online and in social media. Finally, we discuss guidelines for creating and sustaining healthy communication climates. In the next chapter, we'll see how confirming, supportive climates assist us in managing conflict when it arises. Although this and the next chapter focus primarily on personal or intimate relationships, the concepts and principles we discuss also apply to social and professional relationships.

FEATURES OF SATISFYING RELATIONSHIPS

As we saw in Chapter 1, we relate to others to fulfill human needs for survival, safety, belonging, esteem, and self-actualization in a diverse social world. When we are involved in satisfying relationships, we feel more positive about our lives and ourselves.

> **FIONA**
>
> The worst time in my whole life was my first semester here. I felt so lonely being away from my family and all my friends at home. Back home, there was always somebody to be with and talk to, but I didn't know anybody on this campus. I felt all alone and like nobody cared about me. I became depressed and almost left school, but then I started seeing a guy, and I made a couple of friends. Everything got better once I had some people to talk to and hang out with.

Many people feel as Fiona does. The first year of college is a lonely time for many students who have not yet made new friends. Americans rely more on friends than do Russians, Koreans, or Turks (Ryan, La Guardia, Solky-Butzel, Chirkov, & Kim, 2005). The same is true of new employees—until they form some on-the-job friendships, they are likely to feel lonely and somewhat uncomfortable. In fact, communication climate is strongly related to job satisfaction and to low turnover among employees (Anderson, Corazzini, & McDaniel, 2004).

All of our relationships are very complex and are shaped by numerous factors. Of the many influences, four are particularly critical for building and sustaining satisfying relationships: investment, commitment, trust, and comfort with relational dialectics. As we discuss each of these factors, realize that members of different cultures and speech communities may have distinct rules for what each factor includes and how it is communicated. For example, in general, many Westerners disclose personal information to casual friends and acquaintances, whereas Japanese tend to disclose only to very close friends (Seki, Matsumoto, & Imahori, 2002).

MindTap

Everyday Skills To practice assessing what you've invested in your closest relationships, complete the activity "Your Investment in Relationships" at the end of the chapter or online.

Investment

Investments are what we put into relationships that we could not retrieve if the relationship were to end. When we care about another person, we invest time, energy, thought, and feelings in interaction. We may also invest materially by spending money, giving gifts, and so forth. In workplace relationships, we also invest time, energy, thought, and feeling and often give material assistance to coworkers.

Investments cannot be recovered, so the only way to reap the benefits of your investments is to stick with a relationship. We can't get back the time, feelings, and energy we invest in a relationship. We cannot recover the material contributions we have made to a relationship. Thus, to leave is to lose the investment we've made.

Perceived equality of investment affects satisfaction with romantic relationships. The happiest dating and married partners feel that they invest equally (DeMaris, 2007). When we perceive ourselves as investing more than our partner, we tend to be dissatisfied and resentful. When we perceive our partner as investing more than we are, we may feel guilty. Thus, perceived inequity erodes satisfaction and communication (Schiebinger & Gilmartin, 2010; Sheehy, 2010; Wood, 2011b, c).

SIBBY I dated this one guy for a long time before I finally had to cut my losses. He said he loved me, but he wouldn't put anything in the relationship. I gave so much—always accommodating him, doing things for him, loving him—but there just wasn't any reciprocity. It was a one-way street with him, and I felt like he didn't value me very much at all.

© StockLite/Shutterstock.com

Commitment

Commitment is a decision to remain in a relationship. Notice that commitment is defined as a decision, not a feeling (Etcheverry & Le, 2005). The hallmark of commitment is the intention to share the future. In committed relationships, partners assume that they will continue together. Unlike passion or attraction, which arise in the present, commitment links partners together in the future. Because partners in committed relationships view their connection as continuing, they are less likely to perceive problems and tensions as reasons to end the relationship.

The decision to commit injects responsibility into relationships. When partners make a commitment, they take responsibility for continuing to invest in and care for their bond. Without responsibility, relationships are subject to the whims of feeling and fortune, which are not a stable basis for the long term.

When Denny and I decided to go out on our own, we'd worked together in a tech firm for 2 years, and neither of us felt like that was where we wanted to be for life, or even in another 3 years. So we started our own company. It was really scary because we didn't have any guarantees or any safety net. All we had was each other, and that really changed our relationship. We spent a lot more time together, talked for hours about every detail of our business, traveled together to evaluate new software and business-to-business companies. We took risks with each other, learned to trust each other to the max. And we spent a lot of time dreaming about what could happen with our company and how we could bring that about. In a way, I think the dreaming and planning together were like real cement for us. After a year of working together that closely, we were more like brothers than partners in a business.

PHILLIP

Trust

A third cornerstone of satisfying personal relationships is a high degree of trust between partners (Steiner-Pappalardo & Gurung, 2002; Veroff, 1999). **Trust** involves believing in another's reliability (that he or she will do as promised) and another's effort to look out for our welfare and our relationship. Trust doesn't come automatically in relationships. Usually, it is earned over time: We learn to trust others as they prove that they are reliable, show that they care, and make the investments to enrich the relationship. When trust is established, we feel psychologically safe in the relationship. One reason trust is so important to relationships is that it allows us to take risks with others. We open ourselves to others only if we feel we can count on them to protect our confidences and to continue caring about us.

Self-Disclosure Self-**disclosure** can both build and reflect trust between people.

© Creatista/Shutterstock.com

As we noted in Chapter 2, self-disclosure is the intentional revelation of personal information about ourselves that others are unlikely to discover in other ways. According to researchers who have studied communication between intimates, self-disclosure is a key gauge of closeness among Westerners (Hendrick & Hendrick, 2006; Samp & Palevitz, 2009; Stafford, 2009).

Self-disclosure should take place gradually and with appropriate caution (Petronio, 2000). We begin by disclosing superficial information ("I'm worried that I won't find a job," "I'm afraid of heights"). If a person responds with empathy to early and limited disclosures, we're likely to reveal progressively more intimate information ("I was fired from my last job," "I take medication for depression"). If these disclosures are also met with understanding and confidentiality, trust continues to grow.

In the early stages of relationship development, reciprocity of disclosures is important. We're willing to disclose our private feelings only as long as the other person also reveals personal information (Cunningham, Strassberg, & Haan, 1986). When a relationship is just beginning, we feel vulnerable; the other could betray a confidence or reject us because we disclose something negative. Our feeling of vulnerability is reduced if the other person is also allowing vulnerability by making self-disclosures to us. This doesn't mean that one person's self-disclosure is immediately matched by a reciprocal self-disclosure. Rather, we look for reciprocity over time so that we and our close friends share equivalent personal information over the course of a relationship (Dindia, 2000b).

Although self-disclosing is important early in the process of developing intimacy, for most relationships it is not a primary communication dynamic over the long haul. In established relationships, disclosures are less frequent than in just-forming relationships (Duck & Wood, 2006). Also, reciprocity of disclosures becomes less important as a relationship grows and stabilizes. Thus, in established relationships disclosure is more likely to be greeted with a response to what has been revealed than with an immediate, equivalent disclosure.

Although all of us disclose some personal information in close relationships, not everyone discloses equally or in the same ways. Individuals vary in how much they want to self-disclose, so an absolute amount of disclosure is not a surefire measure of trust or relationship health. Also, cultural differences shape our tendencies to self-disclose. Gender is linked to how and how much people disclose. In general, women—particularly Western women—make more verbal disclosures and place greater value on verbal disclosures than do most men (Floyd & Parks, 1995). Men generally talk less about personal feelings, especially perceived weaknesses or self-doubts (Johnson, 2000; Walker, 2004). Many men self-disclose more often with actions than with words.

When I really need some support from my girlfriend, I don't just come out and say, "I need you." What I do is go over to her place or call her to see if she wants to come to my place. Sometimes, we just sit together watching TV or something. And that helps. I know she knows that I am down and need her, but I don't have to say it. I do the same thing when I think she is feeling low. It's hard for me to say, "I love you and am sorry you feel bad." But I can be with her, and I can hug her and let her know through my actions that I care.

 RUSSELL

Comfort with Relational Dialectics

A final quality of healthy relationships is understanding and being comfortable with **relational dialectics**, which are opposing forces, or tensions, that are continuous and normal in personal relationships. Although these tensions are normal, they can be frustrating if we don't understand them and if we don't label them as normal. Table 8.1 illustrates three relational dialectics that have been identified by researchers (Baxter, 1988, 1990, 1993; Baxter & Braithwaite, 2008; Baxter & Simon, 1993; Erbert, 2000).

Autonomy/Connection All of us experience tension between the desire to be autonomous, or independent, and the desire to be close, or connected, to others. Friends and romantic partners want to spend time with each other, to have joint interests, and to talk personally. At the same time, they need to feel that their individuality is not swallowed up by relationships. Tension between the need for autonomy and the need for connection also marks relationships on the job. We may enjoy being part of teams and like the sense of community in our workplace. At the same time, we may want to do some work independently.

Relationship counselors agree that the most central and continuous friction in most close relationships arises from the opposing needs for autonomy and for connection (Beck, 1988; Scarf, 1987). When people go on vacation, they may eat all meals together, engage in shared activities, and sleep and interact in confined spaces where privacy is limited. Typically, when they return home after a vacation, they interact less than usual for several days. Having been immersed in togetherness, each person craves autonomous time and activity. Both autonomy and closeness are natural human needs. The challenge is to preserve individuality while also nurturing connection in a relationship.

KEN

Dialectics explains something that has really confused me. I've never understood how I could want so much to be with Ashley for a while and then feel suffocated and need to get away. I've worried that it means I don't love her anymore or there is something wrong between us. But now, I see how both needs are normal and okay.

Table **8.1** Relational Dialectics

AUTONOMY/CONNECTION	NOVELTY/ PREDICTABILITY	OPENNESS/CLOSEDNESS
I want to be close.	I like the familiar rhythms and routines of our relationship.	I like sharing so much with you.
I need my own space.	We need to do something new and different.	There are some things I don't want to talk about with you.

Novelty/Predictability   The second dialectic is the tension between wanting routine or familiarity and wanting novelty in a relationship. All of us like a certain amount of routine to provide security and predictability in our lives. Yet too much routine becomes boring, so we need occasional new or novel.

On-the-job relationships also feel the tension between the desire for predictability and the desire for novelty. We want enough routine at work to feel competent and familiar with our responsibilities. But we also want enough novelty, or change, to keep us stimulated. However, as Dennis points out, too much novelty in the workplace can be overwhelming.

DENNIS

Last year was extremely difficult for my wife, Katie. It seemed like everything at her job changed at once. First, the company was bought up by a large corporation. Then, the CEO Katie had worked under for 10 years was fired and a new one brought on board. The new guy implemented all kinds of changes in company policies and procedures. A lot of the staff got frustrated and quit, so that led to changes in Katie's coworkers.

Openness/Closedness   The third dialectic is a tension between wanting open communication and wanting a degree of privacy, even with intimates. With our closest partners, we self-disclose in ways we don't with coworkers and casual acquaintances. Yet we also desire some privacy, and we want our intimates to respect that. Completely unrestrained expressiveness would be intolerable (Baxter, 1993; Petronio, 1991). Wanting some privacy doesn't mean that a relationship is in trouble. It means only that we have needs for both openness and closedness.

ANDY

My girlfriend has trouble accepting the fact that I won't talk to her about my brother Jacob. He died when I was 8, and I still can't deal with all my feelings, especially with feeling guilty that he died and I'm alive. I just can't talk about that to anybody. With my girlfriend, I talk about lots of personal stuff, but Jacob is just too private and too hard.

The three dialectics create ongoing tensions in healthy relationships. This is a problem only if partners don't understand that dialectics and the tension they generate are natural parts of relational life. Once we realize that dialectical tensions are normal, we can accept and grow from them (Baxter & Braithwaite, 2008; Baxter & Montgomery, 1996; Metts, 2006b).

Negotiating Dialectical Tensions   Baxter (1990) has identified four ways partners handle the tension generated by opposing needs. One response, called *neutralization*, is to negotiate a balance between two dialectical needs. Each need is met to an extent, but neither is fully satisfied. A couple might have a fairly consistent balance between the amount of novelty and the amount of routine in their relationship.

A second response is *selection*, in which we give priority to one dialectical need and neglect the other. For example, coworkers might engage exclusively in routinized communication. Some partners cycle between dialectical needs, favoring each one alternately. A couple could be continuously together for a period and then autonomous for a time.

My folks are so funny. They plod along in the same old rut for ages and ages, and my sister and I can't get them to do anything different. Mom won't try a new recipe for chicken, because "we like ours like I always fix it." Dad won't try a new style of shirt because "that's not the kind of shirt I wear." Dynamite wouldn't blow them out of their ruts. But then, all of a sudden, they'll do a whole bunch of unusual things. Like once they went out to three movies in a day, and the next day they went for a picnic at the zoo. This kind of zaniness goes on for a while, then it's back to humdrum for months and months. I guess they get all of their novelty in occasional bursts.

A third way to manage dialectics is *separation*. When we separate dialectics, we assign one dialectical need to certain spheres of interaction and the opposing dialectical need to other aspects of interaction. For instance, employees might work independently on most tasks but operate very interactively and openly on specific teams. Many dual-career couples are autonomous professionally, relying little on each other for advice, although they are very connected about family matters.

The final method of dealing with dialectics is *reframing*. This is a complex and transformative strategy in which partners redefine contradictory needs as not in opposition. My colleagues and I found an example of this when we studied differences between intimate partners (Wood et al., 1994). Some partners transcended the opposition between autonomy and connection by defining differences and disagreements (which emphasize individuals) as enhancing intimacy (which emphasizes the relationship). For example, some partners said that disagreements added spice to their relationship. Others said disagreements were evidence that they maintained their individuality in the relationship.

Communication in Everyday Life

DIVERSITY

Dialogue and Doing: Alternate Paths to Closeness

Research indicates that women and men generally place equal value on closeness, but they tend to differ somewhat in how they create and express it. Early socialization may explain the gendered differences.

Young boys typically interact with friends by doing things in groups (playing sports or building Lego constructions). As a result, boys tend to bond with others by doing things together. Carrying the lessons of childhood play into adult friendships, many men do not regard intimate or emotional conversation and self-disclosure as the only, or even the primary, path to closeness. Instead, their preferred path to intimacy is activity (doing things with and for others). This mode is called *closeness in the doing*.

Young girls tend to interact with friends through dialogue (socializing in dyads or triads in which face-to-face communication is central). As a result, many girls learn to form intimate connections through talking. As adults, women tend to favor dialogue (sharing personal disclosures and intimate communication) as a path to intimacy. This is called *closeness in dialogue*.

Both women and men travel both paths to intimacy. What differs is the degree of emphasis that women and men, in general, place on each path. Instrumental shows of affection, or closeness in the doing, are part of most women's friendships, although they are usually not as central as in men's friendships (Floyd & Parks, 1995). Also, men sometimes express closeness through dialogue, just not as frequently as most women (Dindia & Canary, 2006; Inman, 1996; Metts, 2006a, b; Wood & Inman, 1993). Both ways of expressing and experiencing closeness are valid, and both should be respected.

Different modes of expressing closeness are not confined to personal relationships. They also show up in the workplace. Women generally rely more than men on talk to form and sustain close working relationships, whereas men generally rely more than women on doing things for and with coworkers to establish and develop close working relationships (Tannen, 1995).

To learn more about gender and other sources of diversity in workplace interactions, visit http://www.diversityinc.com.

Everyday Skills To understand the basis of satisfaction in two important relationships in your life, complete the activity "Analyzing Your Relationships" at the end of the chapter or online.

Everyday Skills To practice identifying relational dialectics in everyday situations, complete the activity "Recognizing Relational Dialectics" at the end of the chapter or online.

Research indicates that, in general, the least effective and least satisfying response is selection, in which one dialectical need is neglected (Baxter, 1990). Squelching any natural human impulse diminishes us. The challenge is to find ways to accommodate all our needs, even when they seem contradictory.

Healthy relationships exist when the people in them create a satisfying communication climate by investing, making a commitment, developing trust, and learning to understand and negotiate dialectical tensions. An important foundation for these four features is *confirmation*, which we discuss in the next section of the chapter.

CONFIRMING AND DISCONFIRMING CLIMATES

We first encountered philosopher Martin Buber in Chapter 1 when we discussed I–It, I–You, and I–Thou relationships. Buber (1957) believed that all of us need confirmation to be healthy and to grow. The essence of confirmation is feeling known and validated as an individual. Contemporary communication scholars have confirmed Buber's insight that confirmation is a critical foundation for meaningful, close relationships (Anderson, Baxter, & Cissna, 2004; Barge, 2009; Ellis, 2000; MacGeorge, 2009; Turman & Schrodt, 2006).

Communication climates exist on a continuum from confirming to disconfirming (Figure 8.1). Few relationships are exclusively confirming or disconfirming; most fall somewhere in between. Some interactions are confirming, and others are disconfirming; or communication cycles between basically confirming and basically disconfirming. The key is not whether there is negative or disconfirming interaction, but the proportion of positive to negative interactions. Marital counselor John Gottman (1994a; Gottman & Gottman, 2007) says the "magic ratio" is 5 to 1. Couples that remain satisfied and committed have at least five times as many pleasant interactions (expressions of love, appreciation, humor) as unpleasant interactions (expressions of criticism, disappointment, anger). In other words, a couple that yells and screams 10 times a day and cuddles and expresses warmth 50 times a day will be happier than a couple that fights once a day and has no pleasant interaction.

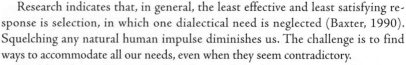

Confirming climate

Mixed climate
Cycling climate

Disconfirming climate

Figure **8.1**

The Continuum of Communication Climates

Relationships usually don't move abruptly from one level of confirmation to a different level. Usually, one level of confirmation flows into the next in a gradual way. You might not feel confirmed by a person you have just met. As the two of you talk and interact, the other person may communicate that he or she values you, so you begin to feel more confirmed. Over time, you move on to feeling that the relationship is basically confirming.

Levels of Confirmation and Disconfirmation

Building on Buber's ideas, communication scholars have identified three levels of communication that confirm or disconfirm others climates (Anderson, Baxter, & Cissna, 2004; Cissna & Sieburg, 1986). As we discuss these, you'll notice that confirming communication involves person-centeredness, which we discussed in Chapter 1. Person-centered communication recognizes another and that person's feelings and ideas as legitimate.

Recognition   The most basic form of confirmation is *recognizing that another person exists* (Reis, Sheldon, Gable, Roscoe, & Ryan, 2000). We do this with non-verbal behaviors (a smile or touch) and verbal communication ("Hello," "Good to meet you"). We disconfirm others at a fundamental level when we don't acknowledge their existence. For example, you might not look up when a coworker enters your office. A parent who punishes a child by refusing to speak to her or him disconfirms the child. Doctors who don't look at patients or introduce themselves to patients fail to recognize their patients, which is disconfirming (Kahn, 2008).

I hate it when my girlfriend gives me the silent treatment. I'd rather she shout or scream or tell me off—at least, doing that would let me know she knows I'm there. When she gives me the silent treatment, I feel totally invisible, like I'm not there at all.

RYAN

Acknowledgment   The second level of confirmation is *acknowledgment of what another feels, thinks, or says.* Nonverbally, we acknowledge others by nodding our heads or by making eye contact to show we are listening. Verbal acknowledgments are direct responses to others' communication. If a friend says, "I'm really scared that I blew the LSAT exam," you could acknowledge that by paraphrasing: "So you're worried that you didn't do well on it, huh?" This paraphrasing response acknowledges both the thoughts and the feelings of the other person. This explains why communication researcher René Dailey (2006) found that adolescents talk more openly with parents if they perceive the parents acknowledge their feelings.

We disconfirm others when we don't acknowledge their feelings or thoughts. Reponses that are tangential, irrelevant, or impersonal or that deny what another has said are disconfirming. For instance, a tangential response to your friend's statement about the LSAT would be, "Have you ever wondered what kind of person would design exams like the LSAT for a living?" "Want to go catch a movie tonight?" would be an irrelevant response that totally ignores the friend's comment. Likewise, not responding to a coworker's email or memo is ignoring their communication (Conrad & Poole, 2005). An impersonal response that fails to acknowledge your friend individually would be, "Everybody feels like that after taking the test." A denial response would be, "You did fine on the LSAT." Notice that each type of disconfirmation is not person-centered.

LORI You'd be amazed by how often people refuse to acknowledge what differently abled people say. A hundred times, I've been walking across campus, and someone has come up and offered to guide me. I tell them I know the way and don't need help, and they still put an arm under my elbow to guide me. I may be blind, but there's nothing wrong with my mind. I know if I need help. Why won't others acknowledge that?

Lori makes an important point. It is fundamentally disconfirming to have others ignore what we say. Especially when we deal with people who differ from us in important ways, we should take time to learn what they perceive as confirming and disconfirming. "Communication in Everyday Life—Diversity: Guidelines for Confirming Communication with People with Disabilities" offers advice for confirming communication with people who have disabilities.

Endorsement The strongest level of confirmation is *endorsement*. Endorsement involves accepting another's feelings or thoughts. For example, you could endorse by saying, "It's natural to be worried about the LSAT when you have so much riding on it. I know what going to law school means to you." We disconfirm others when we don't accept their thoughts and feelings. If you respond to the friend by saying, "How can you worry about the LSAT when the country is on the verge of war?" you reject the validity of the expressed feelings.

Endorsement isn't always possible if we are trying to be honest with others. Sometimes we cannot accept what another feels or thinks, so we can't give an endorsing response. A few years ago, I spent a lot of time with a 15-year-old named Bobby and continually looked for ways to confirm him. Gradually, trust between us grew, and Bobby and I shared more and more personal information. One day, he told me that he had tried acid and was looking forward to doing more acid in the future. I couldn't endorse what Bobby had done, and I couldn't support his desire to continue using acid. I told Bobby that I cared about him but couldn't approve of this behavior. I told him that, if he were caught, he could have a criminal record. I also informed Bobby of some of the long-term consequences of acid and the dangers of its being mixed with other drugs. In this situation, I was able to confirm him as a person (telling him I cared about him) without endorsing a particular behavior. The trust we had built up and the confirming climate we had established allowed us to talk honestly about the dangers of drugs.

Disconfirmation is not mere disagreement. After all, disagreements can be productive and healthy, and they imply that people matter enough to each other to argue. What is disconfirming is to be told that we are crazy, wrong, stupid, or unimportant. If you think about what we've discussed, you'll probably find that the relationships in which you feel most valued and comfortable are those with high levels of confirmation. Table 8.2 illustrates the different levels on which confirmation and disconfirmation occur.

Table **8.2** Confirming and Disconfirming Messages

Recognition	"You exist."	"You don't exist."
	"Hello."	[Silence]
Acknowledgment	"You matter to me."	"You don't matter."
	"We have a relationship."	"We are not a team."
	"I'm sorry you're hurt."	"You'll get over it."
Endorsement	"What you think is true."	"You are wrong."
	"What you feel is okay."	"You shouldn't feel what you do."
	"I feel the same way."	"Your feeling doesn't make sense."

I've gotten a lot of disconfirmation since I came out. When I told my parents I was gay, Mom said, "No, you're not." I told her I was, and she and Dad both said I was just confused, but I wasn't gay. They refuse to acknowledge I'm gay, which means they reject who I am. My older brother isn't any better. His view is that I'm sinful and headed for hell. Now, what could be more disconfirming than that?

WAYNE

Confirming and Disconfirming Communication

Communication researcher Jack Gibb (1961, 1964, 1970) studied the relationship between communication and climates in interpersonal relationships. He began by noting that with some people we feel disconfirmed and on guard, so we are unlikely to communicate openly with them. Gibb also noted that with other people we feel supported and confirmed, so we are likely to communicate freely with them. Even in the healthiest and most supportive relationships, there are usually some defensive moments and some situations in which we don't feel comfortable. Yet in most satisfying relationships, the overall climate is generally supportive and confirming.

Gibb believed that the different communication climates result largely from communication that promotes feeling confirmed or disconfirmed. Gibb identified six types of communication that promote disconfirming climates and six opposite types of communication that foster confirming climates, as shown in Table 8.3. As

Table **8.3** Communication and Climate

DISCONFIRMING COMMUNICATION	CONFIRMING COMMUNICATION
Evaluation	Description
Certainty	Provisionalism
Strategy	Spontaneity
Control	Problem orientation
Neutrality	Empathy
Superiority	Equality

you read about these, you will notice that the confirming forms of communication involve meeting one or more of the three levels of confirmation: recognition, acknowledgment, and endorsement.

DIVERSITY

Guidelines for Confirming Communication with People with Disabilities

Like all of us, people with disabilities value confirming communication that demonstrates that we respect them and their abilities. The following guidelines provide advice for communicating confirmation when interacting with people who have disabilities.

- When you talk with someone who has a disability, speak directly to the person, not to a companion or interpreter.
- When you are introduced to a person with a disability, offer to shake hands. People who have limited hand use or who have artificial limbs usually can shake.
- When you meet a person who has a visual impairment, identify yourself and anyone who is with you. If a person with a visual impairment is part of a group, preface your comments to that person with his or her name.
- You may offer assistance, but don't provide it unless your offer is accepted. Then ask the person how you can best assist (ask for instructions).
- Treat adults as adults. Don't patronize people in wheelchairs by patting them on the shoulder or head; don't use childish language when speaking to people who have no mental disability.
- Respect the personal space of people with disabilities. It is rude to lean on someone's wheelchair, because that is part of his or her personal territory.
- Listen mindfully when you talk with someone who has difficulty speaking. Don't interrupt or supply words to others. Just be patient and let them finish. Don't pretend to understand if you don't. Instead, explain what you didn't understand, and ask the person to respond.
- When you talk with people who use a wheelchair or crutches, try to position yourself at their eye level and in front of them to allow good eye contact.
- It is appropriate to wave your hand or tap the shoulder of people with hearing impairments as a way to get their attention. Look directly at the person and speak clearly, slowly, and expressively. Face those who lip-read, place yourself in a good light source, and keep hands, cigarettes, and gum away from your mouth.
- Relax. Don't be afraid to use common expressions, such as "See you later" to someone with a visual impairment, or "Did you hear the news?" to someone with a hearing difficulty. They're unlikely to be offended and may even turn the irony into a joke.

Adapted from AXIS Center for Public Awareness of People with Disabilities, 4550 Indianola Avenue, Columbus, OH 43214. For more tips on communicating with and about people who have disabilities, visit the U.S. Department of Labor website at http://www.dol.gov/odep/pubs/fact/comucate.htm.

Evaluation versus Description Few of us feel what Gibb called "psychologically safe" when we are the targets of judgments. Communication researchers report that evaluative communication evokes defensiveness (Conrad & Poole, 2005; Reis, Clark, & Holmes, 2004). We are also less likely to self-disclose to someone we think is judgmental (Caughlin, Afifi, Carpenter-Theune, & Miller, 2005; Dailey, 2006). As we noted in Chapter 6, even positive evaluations can sometimes make us defensive because they carry the relationship-level meaning that another person feels entitled to judge us (Cupach & Carlson, 2002). Here are several examples of evaluative statements: "It's dumb to feel that way," "You shouldn't have done that," "I approve of what you did."

Descriptive communication doesn't evaluate others or what they think and feel. Instead, it describes behaviors without passing judgment. *I* language, which we learned about in Chapter 4, describes what the person speaking feels or thinks, but it doesn't evaluate another. (*You* language does evaluate). Descriptive language may refer to another, but it does so by describing, not evaluating, the other's behavior: "You seem to be sleeping more lately" versus "You're sleeping too much"; "You seem to have more stuff on your desk than usual" versus "Your desk is a mess."

Certainty versus Provisionalism We communicate certainty by using language that is absolute and often dogmatic. This kind of language suggests that there is one and only one answer, valid point of view, or reasonable course of action. Because certainty proclaims one absolutely correct position, it slams the door on further discussion. There's no point in talking with people whose minds are made up and who demean any point of view other than their own.

Perhaps you've been in a conversation with someone who said, "I don't want to hear it," "You can't change my mind," or "I've already figured out what I'm going to do, so just save your breath." These comments reflect certainty and an unwillingness to consider other points of view. When confronted with such statements, we're likely to feel disconfirmed and to follow the advice to "save our breath." In the workplace, dogmatic communication discourages collaboration and the feeling of being part of a team (Wilmot & Hocker, 2006).

Communication in
Everyday Life

SOCIAL MEDIA

Online Support

If you suffer from a serious illness or other problem, it's unlikely that you have an in-person group of friends who have the same problem and understand what you are going through. That's the beauty of online support groups. They provide spaces where people who are experiencing or have been affected directly or indirectly by medical problems can talk with one another and receive support, empathy, and often sound advice.

🌐 MindTap Have you ever visited an online support group? If so, was it helpful to you?

A disabled family member: https://www.facebook.com/supportstofamilies

Cancer patients and their families: https://www.facebook.com/CancerSupportCommunity

Cancer survivors: http://csn.cancer.org/

Grieving the death of a child: http://www.compassionatefriends.org/Find_Support/Online-Community/Online_Support.aspx

Infertility: http://www.resolve.org/resources/online-support-communities.html

Heart disease: http://heart-disease.supportgroups.com

/Leukemia: http://www.lls.org/diseaseinformation/getinformationsupport/onlinechats/

One form of certainty communication is **ethnocentrism**, which is the assumption that our culture and its norms are the only right ones. For instance, someone who says, "It is just plain rude to speak out loud during a sermon" doesn't understand the meaning of the call–response pattern in African American culture. Dogmatically asserting, "It's disrespectful to be late" reveals a lack of awareness of cultures that place less value on speed and efficiency than American culture does.

MONIKA

My father is a classic case of closed-mindedness. He has his ideas, and everything else is crazy. I told him I was majoring in communication studies, and he hit the roof. He said there was no future in learning to write speeches, and he told me I should go into business so that I could get a good job. He never even asked me what communication studies is. If he had, I would have told him it's a lot more than speech writing. He starts off sure that he knows everything about whatever is being discussed. He has no interest in other points of view or learning something new. He just locks his mind and throws away the key. We've all learned just to keep our ideas to ourselves around him—there's no communication.

An alternative to certainty is provisionalism, which communicates openness to other points of view. When we speak provisionally, or tentatively, we suggest that our minds aren't sealed. We signal that we're willing to consider what others have to say, and this encourages others to voice their ideas. Provisional communication includes statements such as, "The way I tend to see the issue is…," "One way to look at this is…." Notice that each of these comments signals that the speaker realizes there could be other positions that are also reasonable, which invites continued communication.

Strategy versus Spontaneity   Most of us feel on guard when we think others are manipulating us or being less than open about what's on their minds. An example of strategic communication is this: "Would you do something for me if I told you it really mattered?" If the speaker doesn't tell us what we're expected to do, it feels like a setup. We're also likely to feel that another is trying to manipulate us with a comment such as, "Remember when I helped you with your math last term and when I did your chores last week because you were busy?" With a preamble like that, we sense a trap. When employees think supervisors are trying to manipulate them, they become defensive (Conrad & Poole, 2005).

JANA

Last year, I worked for someone who was always using strategies on me. She'd come to my workstation on Monday and ask, "How does your week look?" At first, I'd give her a straight answer, but after a few times I realized she was setting me up. If I said, "Not too bad," she'd give me another assignment. I wouldn't have minded if she'd just asked me straight up if I could do a particular thing.

Spontaneity is the counterpoint to strategy. Spontaneous communication feels open, honest, and unpremeditated. "I really need your help with this computer glitch" is a more spontaneous comment than "Would you do something for me if I told you it really mattered?" Likewise, it is more spontaneous to ask for a favor in a straightforward way ("Would you help me?") than to preface a request by reciting all we have done for someone else. Strategic communication is contrived and devious, whereas spontaneous interaction is authentic.

Control versus Problem Orientation   Like strategies, controlling communication attempts to manipulate others. Unlike strategies, controlling communication tends to be relatively overt. A common instance of controlling communication is a person's insistence that her or his solution or preference should prevail. Whether the issue is trivial

Communication in Everyday Life

WORKPLACE

Scolding Doesn't Motivate

What should a doctor do when a patient has not kicked a bad habit? Should the doctor scold the man who smokes or tell the woman who is overweight that she needs to reduce calories? Doctors have long relied on strategies such as reproaching in an effort to get patients to kick bad habits. Recent research, however, indicates that this strategy may not be effective because both tend to arouse defensiveness in patients. More effective is encouraging patients to set their own goals and then coaching the patients as they work to meet their goals (Landro, 2013b).

(what movie to see) or serious (whether to move to a new part of the country), controllers try to impose their point of view on others. This disconfirms and disrespects others.

Defensiveness arises because the relationship level of meaning is that the person exerting control thinks she or he has greater power, rights, or intelligence than others. It's disconfirming to be told that our opinions are wrong, that our preferences don't matter, or that we don't have good ideas. Supervisors who micromanage their subordinates may be perceived as communicating that they don't trust others to do the job right (Conrad & Poole, 2005). A wife who earns a higher salary might say to her husband, "Well, I like the Honda more than the Ford you want, and it's my money that's going to pay for it." The speaker not only pushes her preference but also tells her husband that she has more power than he does because she makes more money.

> My roommate freshman year was a real jerk. Her goal in life was to control me and everyone else around her. Sometimes, she'd say she felt like going out for dinner, and I'd agree, and then she'd ask me where I wanted to go. Even if I picked her favorite place, she would insist on going somewhere else. She just had to be in charge. Once I moved things around in the room, and she fussed a lot and moved them back. Later, she moved things the way I had, but then it was her choice. She didn't care about issues or working things through. All she cared about was being in control.

PAT

Problem-oriented communication tends to cultivate supportive, confirming communication climates. Problem-oriented communication focuses on finding a solution that all parties find acceptable. Here's an example of problem-oriented communication between coworkers: "It seems that we have really different ideas about how to tackle this new project. Let's talk through what each of us has in mind and see how we can connect our goals." Notice how this statement invites collaboration and emphasizes the goal of meeting both people's needs. Problem-oriented behaviors tend to reduce conflict and keep lines of communication open (Wilmot & Hocker, 2006).

One of the benefits of problem-oriented communication is that the relationship level of meaning affirms the relationship between communicators. When we convey that we want to collaborate with another person to develop a mutually satisfying solution, we let the other know that we care more about the relationship than about getting our own way. In contrast, controlling behaviors aim for one person to triumph over the other, an outcome that undercuts the other person and the relationship.

Neutrality versus Empathy   People tend to become defensive when others respond to them in a neutral or detached manner. Neutral communication is often interpreted as a lack of regard and caring for others. Consequently, it does not feel validating to most of us.

> My brother never responds to what I say. He listens, but he just gives me nothing back. Sometimes I push him and ask, "What do you think?" or "Does what I'm saying make sense to you?" All he does is shrug or say, "Whatever." He simply won't show any involvement. So I say, why bother talking to him?

NEL

Montgomery Burns of *The Simpsons*—the prototypically judgmental, supercilious boss who rarely listens to what Smithers has to say.

In contrast to neutrality, empathic communication confirms the worth of others and our concern for them. Empathic communication is illustrated by these examples: "It's an entirely reasonable way to feel like you do in your situation," and "Wow, it must have really stung when your supervisor said that to you." Empathy doesn't necessarily mean agreement; instead, it conveys acceptance of other people and respect for their perspectives. Especially when we don't agree with others, it's important to communicate that we value them as people.

Superiority versus Equality   Like many of the other communication behaviors we've discussed, the final pair of behaviors that affect climate is most pertinent to the relationship level of meaning. Communication that conveys superiority says, "I'm better." Understandably, we feel disconfirmed when people act as if they are better than we are.

Consider several messages that convey superiority: "I know a lot more about this than you," "If you had my experience, you wouldn't suggest that," "You really should go to my hairstylist." Each of these messages clearly says, "You aren't as good (smart, savvy, stylish) as I am." Predictably, the result is that we protect our self-esteem by closing up around people who belittle us.

Communication that conveys equality fosters a confirming communication climate. We feel more relaxed

Communication in Everyday Life

WORKPLACE

Mentoring Relationships

In mentoring relationships a person with greater experience or expertise helps someone with lesser experience or expertise. Supportive climates are characteristic of good mentoring relationships. According to Michael Hecht and Jennifer Warren (2006), communicating equality is especially important in mentoring relationships. Because the less experienced person may feel (and be!) subordinate, the more experienced person should try to create as much symmetry as possible—perhaps by highlighting areas in which the less experienced person has more knowledge than the mentor or by seeking the less experienced person's advice when possible.

MindTap If you have had a mentor, describe the extent to which he or she communicated equality with you.

and comfortable communicating with people who treat us as equals. At the relationship level of meaning, expressed equality communicates respect and equivalent status. We can have exceptional experience or ability in certain areas and still show regard for others and their contribution to interaction. Creating a climate of equality allows everyone to participate without fear of being judged inadequate.

We've seen that confirmation, which may include recognizing, acknowledging, and endorsing others, is the basis of healthy communication climates. Our discussion of confirming and disconfirming communication enlightens us about the specific behaviors that tend to make us feel confirmed or disconfirmed.

SOCIAL MEDIA AND COMMUNICATION CLIMATE

Climate matters when we communicate using social media just as it does in face-to-face interaction. Perhaps you have visited some sites or chat rooms that seem friendly and inviting and others that seem less so. If you now go to those sites and review the communication on them, you may discover there is more confirming communication on the sites that seem inviting.

Disclosure in online and digital environments raises particular challenges. When we disclose in a face-to-face conversation, we know to whom we are revealing personal information. The security of a specific recipient is less assured in social media. How often have you overheard people talking on cells? How often have you overheard information that was personal and that you would not intentionally disclose to a stranger? Because phones seem like a personal mode of communicating and because we get engaged in conversation, we often forget that others can hear us when we are chatting while shopping or walking on a street.

Another connection between this chapter's content and online and digital communication concerns acknowledgment, which is the most basic level of confirmation. When you say hello to someone you see, that person is likely to acknowledge your greeting with a smile, head nod, or return "hello." It's not the same with social media. When you send a text message or an email, how do you know whether and when another receives it? If a friend doesn't reply to your text message within a few minutes, it's hard to tell whether the person is ignoring you or simply hasn't received the message.

The more limited access to nonverbal cues in social media may reduce our ability to interpret others' communication. In person, we can see a wink or twinkle that indicates a friend is kidding with us. In online and digital environments, that's more difficult, even with emoticons. It's hard to tell whether a text message that says <No more needs to be said.> indicates that the sender values what you've texted and now gets your perspective; is irritated by something you texted; or is being dogmatic, saying the door to more conversation is closed. Because online and digital communication tends to be more abbreviated than face-to-face communication, offering extra cues is useful as is being tentative about how we interpret online and digital messages.

MindTap™

Everyday Skills To become more aware of your constitutive and regulative rules for communicating on social media, complete the activity "Your Rules for Social Media" at the end of the chapter or online.

GUIDELINES FOR CREATING AND SUSTAINING CONFIRMING CLIMATES

Now that we understand how communication creates communication climates, we're ready to identify five guidelines for building and sustaining healthy climates.

Actively Use Communication to Build Confirming Climates

The first principle is to use what you've learned in this chapter to enhance the communication climates in your relationships. Now that you know which types of communication fuel confirming and disconfirming climates, you can identify and curb disconfirming patterns of talk. In addition, you can actively use confirming communication.

You can also enhance communication climates by accepting and growing from the tension generated by relational dialectics. Growth in individuals and relationships depends on honoring our needs for autonomy and connection, novelty and routine, and openness and closedness. Thus, the friction between contradictory needs keeps us aware of our multiple needs and the importance of fulfilling all of them.

Accept and Confirm Others

Throughout this chapter, we've seen that confirmation is central to healthy climates and fulfilling relationships. Although we can understand how important it is, it isn't always easy to validate others. Sometimes we disagree with others or don't like certain things they do. Being honest with others is important because we expect real friends to be sources of honest feedback, even if it isn't always pleasant to hear. This implies that we should express honest misgivings about our friends and their behaviors. We can offer honest feedback within a context that assures others that we value and respect them, as Jillian's commentary explains.

JILLIAN

I owe so much to my friend Jennie. She got on my case when I started hanging out with the hookup crowd. She told me I was letting myself be used and that if I didn't respect myself, nobody else would. I tried to shake her off, but she just persisted until I listened. The amazing thing is that she kept arguing against what I was doing but always made it clear she believed in me. Nobody else cared enough to argue with me about what I now see was really stupid behavior on my part.

For a relationship to work, the people in it must feel confirmed. Confirmation begins with acknowledging others and accepting the validity of their thoughts and feelings. Perspective taking is a primary tool for accepting others because it calls on us to consider them on their own terms. Although intimate talk may be what makes you feel closest to another person, that person may experience greater closeness when you do things together. To meet the needs of both of you, you could take turns honoring each other's preferred paths to closeness. Alternatively, you might combine the two styles of intimacy by doing things together that invite conversation. For example, backpacking is an activity in which talking naturally occurs. Eleanor's commentary illustrates acknowledging another's needs.

ELEANOR

About a year after George and I married, he was offered a promotion if he'd move to Virginia. We were living in Pennsylvania at the time, and that's where our families and friends were. I didn't want to move, because I was rooted with my people, but we could both see how important the move was to George's career. The week before we moved, George gave me the greatest present of our lives. He handed me two tickets: one for a round-trip flight from Virginia to Pennsylvania so that I could visit my family, and a second ticket he'd gotten for my best friend so that she could visit me after we moved. I felt he really understood me and had found a way to take care of my needs. I still have the ticket stubs in my box of special memories.

Affirm and Assert Yourself

It is just as important to affirm yourself as it is to affirm others. You are no less valuable, your needs are no less important, and your preferences are no less valid than those of others. It is a misunderstanding to think that the interpersonal communication principles we've discussed only concern how we behave toward others. Equally, they pertain to how we should treat ourselves. Thus, the principle of confirming people's worth applies just as much to oneself as to others.

Although we can't always meet the needs of all parties in relationships, it is possible to give voice to everyone, including yourself. If your partner favors greater autonomy than you do, you need to recognize that preference and also assert your own. If you don't express your feelings, there's no way others can confirm you. Thus, you should assert your feelings and preferences while simultaneously respecting different ones in other individuals.

LAQUANDA

It took me a long time to learn to look out for myself as well as I look out for others. I was always taught to put others first, probably because I'm a girl. I mean, neither of my brothers had that drilled into them. But I did, and for years I would just muffle my needs and whatever I wanted. I concentrated on pleasing others. I thought I was taking care of relationships, but really I was hurting them, because I felt neglected, and I resented that. What I'm working on now is learning to take care of myself and others at the same time.

Unlike aggression, assertion doesn't involve putting your needs above those of others. At the same time, assertion doesn't subordinate your needs to those of

Table **8.4** Aggression, Assertion, and Deference

We're going to spend time together.	I'd like for us to spend more time together.	It's okay with me if we don't spend time with each other.
Tell me what you're feeling; I insist.	I would like to understand more about how you feel.	If you don't want to talk about how you feel, okay.
I don't care what you want; I'm not going to a movie.	I'm really not up for a movie tonight.	It's fine with me to go to a movie if you want to.

Everyday Skills To practice distinguishing among aggressive, assertive, and deferential styles of communication, complete the activity "Distinguishing Aggressive, Assertive, and Deferential Forms of Communication" at the end of the chapter or online.

others as deference does. **Assertion** is clearly and nonjudgmentally stating what you feel, need, or want (see Table 8.4). You can do this without disparaging others or what they want. You should simply state your feelings clearly in an open, descriptive manner.

Respect Diversity in Relationships

Just as individuals differ, so do relationships. There is tremendous variety in what people find comfortable, affirming, and satisfying in interpersonal interaction. For example, you might have one friend who enjoys a lot of verbal disclosure and another who prefers less. There's no reason to try to persuade the first friend to disclose less or the second one to reveal more. Differences between people create a rich variety of relationships.

DORZIUS Communication has a lot to do with climate in work relationships, too. When I first came here from Haiti, I had many job interviews. People would say to me, "We've never hired one of you," like Haitians are not normal people. They also would say I would have to work hard and was I ready to do that, which told me they assumed I was lazy. When I did get a job, my supervisor watched me much more closely than he watched American workers. He was always judging.

Even a single relationship varies over time. Because dialectics generate constant tension, people continuously shift their patterns and ways of honoring contradictory needs in their relationships. It's natural to want more closeness at some times and more distance at other times. It's also advisable to experiment with different responses to dialectical tensions. You may find that it's effective to compromise between closeness and autonomy and to satisfy your desire for openness by sharing certain topics while meeting your need for privacy by not discussing other topics.

Because people and relationships are diverse, we should strive to respect a range of communicative choices and relationship patterns. In addition, we should be cautious about imposing our meaning on others' communication. People from various cultures, including ones within the United States, have learned different communication styles. What Westerners consider openness and healthy self-disclosure may feel offensively intrusive to people from some Asian societies. The best way to understand what others' behavior means is to ask. This conveys the relational message that they matter to you, and it allows you to gain insight into the interesting diversity around us.

Respond Constructively to Criticism

A fifth guideline is to learn to respond effectively when others offer constructive criticism. Sometimes, others communicate criticism in language that fosters defensiveness: "You're selfish." We tend to react negatively to such judgmental language, and we may dismiss the criticism or just think that the other person is being mean. These are natural and understandable responses, but they deprive us of a chance to learn more about how others see us and to reevaluate our own actions. It's possible we're unaware of something we do that is irritating to others. Carol Tavris and Elliott Aronson (2007) offer this helpful analogy: "Drivers cannot avoid having blind spots in their field of vision, but good drivers are aware of them" (p. 44). Others' criticism may make us aware of our blind spots in interpersonal communication.

A constructive response to criticism is to begin by seeking more information: "Could you help me understand what I do that you see as selfish?" Asking such a question allows you to get concrete information. Remember that others may not have your understanding of how to communicate effectively. Thus, they may use abstract terms that you can help them translate into specifics to be addressed. They may also use *you* language ("You hurt me") that you can explore to determine whether there is something you do to which they respond by feeling hurt.

A second step in responding constructively to criticism is to consider it thoughtfully. Is the criticism valid? Are you selfish in some respects? If, after reflection, you don't think the criticism is accurate, offer your interpretation of the behaviors the other person perceived as inconsiderate or selfish. You might say, "I can see how you might feel it's selfish of me to go out with my friends so often, but to me it's because I care about them, just like I spend time with you because I care about you." Notice that this response not only offers an alternative interpretation of particular behavior but also affirms the other person.

If you decide that the criticism is valid, then consider whether you want to change how you act. For suggestions on how to bring about changes in yourself, you may want to review the guidelines offered at the end of Chapter 2.

I didn't appreciate it when my roommate called me a slob. But because of what I've learned in this course, I didn't just ignore what Marie said or fire back an insult to her. Instead, I asked her what she meant. She told me she hated coming home to our apartment and finding my clothes on

BETSY

the bathroom floor and dishes in the sink. Well, I could deal with that. So I resolved to pick my clothes up and wash my dishes before I left each day. Before, if this had happened, I would have felt hurt and probably wouldn't have done anything different. But I felt less hurt and more in control because of how I responded to Marie's criticism, and I know she's a lot happier living with me now!

A final suggestion is to thank the person who offered the criticism. At first, this may seem absurd. After all, criticism doesn't feel good, so it's hard to be grateful. But on second thought, you may realize that criticism is a gift. It offers us opportunities to see ourselves through others' eyes. In addition, it gives us insight into how others feel about us and what we do. Both of these effects of criticism can foster personal growth and healthy relationships that allow honest expression of feelings. Even if we disagree with a criticism, we should let others know we appreciate their willingness to share their perceptions with us. This keeps the door open for communication in the future.

The guidelines we've discussed combine respect for self, others, and relationships with communication that fosters healthy, affirming climates for connections with others. We can transform our relationships when we take responsibility for shaping communication climates and when we develop the knowledge and communication skills to do so.

CHAPTER SUMMARY

In this chapter, we've explored personal relationships, both f2f and virtual, and the communication climates that make them more or less satisfying. The four elements of healthy interpersonal relationships are investment, commitment, trust, and comfort with relational dialectics.

Perhaps the core of healthy communication climates is confirmation. Each of us wants to feel valued, especially by those who matter most to us. When partners recognize, acknowledge, and endorse each other, they communicate, "I know you are there." "You matter to me." Recognition and acknowledgement may be less immediate in online communication and social media sites because we and those with whom we are communicating are not always simultaneously present. We discussed particular kinds of communication that foster confirming and disconfirming climates in relationships. Disconfirming climates are fueled by evaluation, certainty, superiority, strategies, control, and neutrality. More confirming climates arise from communication that is descriptive, provisional, equal, spontaneous, empathic, and problem oriented.

To close the chapter, we considered five guidelines for building healthy communication climates in f2f and virtual interactions. The first is to use your communication to enhance the mood of a relationship. Second, we should accept and confirm our friends and romantic partners, communicating that we respect them, even though we may not always agree with them or feel as they do. The third guideline is a companion to the second one:

We should accept and confirm ourselves just as fully as we do others. Each of us is entitled to assert his or her own thoughts, feelings, and needs. Doing so allows us to honor ourselves and to help our partners understand us. Fourth, we should realize that diversity in relationships is a source of personal and interpersonal growth. People vary widely, as do the relationship patterns and forms they prefer. By respecting differences among us, we all expand our insights into the fascinating array of ways that humans form and sustain intimate relations. Finally, personal growth and healthy relationships are fostered by dealing constructively with criticism.

In the next four chapters, we look in greater detail at personal relationships. Chapter 9 extends our discussion of climate by examining how we can create constructive relationship contexts for dealing effectively with conflict. Chapter 10 discusses friendships, Chapter 11 considers romantic relationships, and Chapter 12 focuses on communication in families. In each chapter, we consider what these relationships are, how communication affects them, and how we might cope with some of the inevitable problems and challenges of sustaining close relationships over time. What we have learned about climate, as well as what we've learned about other facets of interpersonal communication in earlier chapters, will serve as a foundation for a deeper look at the dynamics of close relationships.

Key Concepts

Practice defining the chapter's terms by using online flashcards.

FLASHCARDS...

assertion 238	**ethnocentrism 231**	**relational dialectics 223**
commitment 220	**investments 220**	**trust 221**
communication climate 218		

Continuing the Conversation

© Wadsworth 2013

When you've watched the video online, critique and analyze this encounter based on the principles you learned in this chapter. Also online are three possible endings, each exploring different styles of handling conflict. Then compare your work with the author's suggested

responses. Online, even more videos will let you continue the conversation with your instructor.

PRACTICE...

Aoki and Esteban have met to discuss a conversation they need to have with their boss, Karl. Esteban has just told Aoki that Karl has taken away another opportunity to give an important presentation.

Aoki: This is exactly why we need to have this talk with Karl. It's like he never values our input. He can't keep treating us like we're incompetent.

Esteban: I'm not sure he treats us like we're incompetent.

Aoki: Just last Tuesday he grabbed the pictures for the Bosley project out of my office and put together the presentation after I went home. I had it all planned out and was going to put it together the next morning—it wasn't even due until the end of the week!

Esteban: He thinks he's helping. He just really cares about his work.

Aoki: But it's not his work. He needs to trust and listen to his team. I put in a whole day planning that presentation and it turned out to be wasted when he took over.

Esteban: It really irks me when that happens. We should probably talk to him.

Aoki: The only way he'll understand is if we assert ourselves.

1. How have the relationship factors of investment, commitment, trust, and comfort with relational dialectics contributed to the communication climate that exists for Aoki and Esteban at work?
2. How have Esteban and Aoki's perceptions of Karl's communication contributed to a disconfirming communication climate for Aoki and Esteban?
3. If Esteban and Aoki confront Karl with their concerns, what advice would you give Karl for how he could respond constructively to their criticism?

Everyday Skills

Build your communication skills further by completing the following activities here or online.

1. **Your Investment in Relationships**

   What have you invested in your closest friendship, romantic relationship, and workplace relationship?

   a. How much time have you spent in each relationship?

   Friend: _____ Romance: _____
   Work: _____

   b. How many decisions have you made to accommodate the other person?

   Friend: _____ Romance: _____
   Work: _____

   c. How much money have you spent?

   Friend: _____ Romance: _____
   Work: _____

   d. To what extent is your history entwined with that of the other person?

   Friend: _____ Romance: _____
   Work: _____

   e. How much trust have you given each person?

   Friend: _____ Romance: _____
   Work: _____

   f. How much support have you given each person?

   Friend: _____ Romance: _____
   Work: _____

   g. Do the other person's investments roughly equal yours?

   Friend: _____ Romance: _____
   Work: _____

   h. What would be lost if these relationships ended? Could you recover your investments?

   Friend: _____ Romance: _____
   Work: _____

2. **Distinguishing Between Love and Commitment**

   Listed below are 10 statements that friends and romantic partners might make to each other. In the blank to the left of each statement indicate whether the statement expresses commitment (C) or love (L). Answers are given online.

   _____ a. I have a really great time with you.

   _____ b. Talking with you is so helpful in sorting out my feelings.

   _____ c. I like to think about how we'll be 10 or 15 years from now.

   _____ d. I feel great when I'm with you.

_____ e. I intend to be faithful to you all of my life.

_____ f. I've never felt this way about anyone else before.

_____ g. I'm crazy about you.

_____ h. We need to be saving more in order to be ready to buy a home and start a family.

_____ i. I feel so happy with you right now.

_____ j. I've never felt so close to anyone else.

3. Analyzing Your Relationships

Think about two relationships in your life: one in which you feel good about yourself and safe in the connection, and one in which you feel disregarded or not valued. Identify instances of each level of confirmation in the satisfying relationship and instances of each level of disconfirmation in the unpleasant one. Recognizing confirming and disconfirming communication should give you insight into why these relationships are so different.

4. Recognizing Relational Dialectics

Listed below are six descriptions of common dynamics in personal relationships. Identify which relational dialectic is most prominent in each. Record your answers in the blanks to the left of the descriptions. Answers are given online.

Relational Dialectic

Example:

novelty/predictability

_____

_____

_____

_____

_____

_____

Description of Dynamics

Erin and Mike want to take a vacation and are undecided whether to return to a place they know and like or to go somewhere new and different.

a. Jennie wants to tell her friend Anne about her problems with school, but Jennie also wants to keep her academic difficulties private.

b. Tyronne and David have gotten together to watch football games every weekend for 2 years. They really enjoy this pattern in their friendship, yet they are also feeling it's getting stale.

c. Marilyn likes the fact that her boyfriend Jim respects her right not to tell him about certain aspects of her life. At the same time, she sometimes feels that what they don't know about each other creates a barrier between them.

d. Robert feels that he and Navita would be closer if they did more things together, yet he also likes the fact that each of them has independent interests.

e. Danny feels he and Kate have fallen into routines in how they spend time together. On one hand, he likes the steady rhythm they have; on the other hand, it seems boring.

f. After spending a week together on a backpacking trip, Mike and Ed get back to campus and don't call or see each other for several days.

5. Using Descriptive Language

To develop skill in supportive communication, translate the following evaluative statements into descriptive ones.

Example:

Evaluative: This report is poorly done.

Descriptive: This report doesn't include relevant background information.

Evaluative: You're lazy.

Descriptive: _____

Evaluative: I hate the way you dominate conversations with me.

Descriptive: _____

Evaluative: Stop obsessing about the problem.

Descriptive: _____

Evaluative: You're too involved.

Descriptive: _____

6. Your Rules for Social Media

To become more aware of your constitutive and regulative rules for communicating on social media, answer the following questions.

a. How quickly do you expect responses to your text messages?

b. How much self-disclosure is appropriate on public pages of network sites?

c. What counts as online support to you?

d. What counts as rude behavior on social media?

7. Distinguishing Aggressive, Assertive, and Deferential Forms of Communication

Listed below are five scenarios that describe a situation and your goal in the situation. For each scenario, write an aggressive, assertive, and deferential statement expressing your goal.

Example

Scenario: You need to study for an examination, but your boyfriend/girlfriend really wants to go out for dinner and a movie.

Aggressive response: I don't care about your preferences. I'm not going out tonight.

Assertive response: I'd like to go out tomorrow or this weekend, but I have to study tonight.

Deferential response: I guess studying isn't really that important. We can go out if you want to.

a. You think your roommate is angry with you, but you have no idea why, and she or he denied being angry when you stated your perception. But she or he is acting very distant and unfriendly.

Aggressive response: _____

Assertive response: _____

Deferential response: _____

b. One of your close friends asks to borrow your car. Normally, you wouldn't mind lending your car to a friend, but this person has a record of speeding and being careless behind the wheel. You can't afford to have your car wrecked.

Aggressive response: _____

Assertive response: _____

Deferential response: _____

c. A close friend asks you about something very personal. You want to show that you trust the friend, but you don't want to discuss this topic—even with a close friend.

Aggressive response: _____

Assertive response: _____

Deferential response: _____

d. Ten days ago you lent $20 to one of your coworkers with the understanding that the loan would be repaid within a week. The coworker has not repaid the money nor offered any explanation. You need the loan repaid.

Aggressive response: _____

Assertive response: _____

Deferential response: _____

e. One of the people in a group to which you belong tells racist and sexist jokes. You find the jokes very offensive, but you don't want to create tension in the group or make the person who tells the jokes feel bad. You just want the jokes to stop.

Aggressive response: _____

Assertive response: _____

Deferential response: _____

Engaging with Ideas

Reflect and write about the ideas in this chapter by considering questions about personal, workplace, and ethical applications, here or online.

Personal Application Practice applying this chapter's guidelines for responding to criticism. What happens when you listen to criticism without becoming angry and when you express appreciation to others for their feedback?

Workplace Application Describe the communication climate in the job you have currently or one you held

REFLECT ON...

in the past. Identify specific types of communication that cultivate a confirming or disconfirming climate in this workplace.

Ethical Application What responsibility, if any, does one person have to inform another of his or her level of commitment to a relationship? If you perceive someone as falling for you when you do not feel the same way, do you owe it to the other person to disclose your feelings?

Thinking Critically

Think and write critically about the ideas in this chapter, here or online.

1. Have you found it difficult to confirm others when you disagree with them? If so, does reading this chapter help you distinguish between recognition, acknowledgment, and endorsement? Can you distinguish between confirming others as people and endorsing particular ideas or behaviors?
2. What ethical principles are implied in communication that confirms and disconfirms others? Is it wrong to disconfirm others? All others? Intimates?
3. To what extent do you honor yourself and others in communication situations? Do you give equal

REFLECT ON...

attention to both your needs and those of others? If not, focus on balancing your efforts to confirm yourself and others in future interactions.

4. How often are you deferential, assertive, and aggressive in your communication? What are the situations and relationships in which each kind of behavior is most likely for you? Do the behaviors you select advance your own goals and your relationships?

chapter NINE

MANAGING CONFLICT IN RELATIONSHIPS

Topics covered in this chapter

Defining Interpersonal Conflict

Principles of Conflict

Orientations to Conflict

Responses to Conflict

Communication Patterns during Conflict

Social Media and Conflict Guidelines for Effective Communication during Conflict

After studying this chapter, you should be able to . . .

Define interpersonal conflict.

List six principles of conflict.

Identify your orientations to conflict.

Identify your preferred responses to conflict.

Recognize behaviors that fuel unproductive conflict in a specific interaction.

Evaluate when you can ethically exit conflict that takes place in social media.

Apply chapter guidelines to increase your ability to recognize and engage in conflict productively.

Joseph: You really made me angry when you flirted with other guys at the party last night.

Carmen: I'm surprised you could even see I was flirting, as much as you were drinking.

Joseph: Maybe I was drinking because my girlfriend was too busy dancing with other guys to pay any attention to me.

Carmen: Did it ever occur to you that maybe I'd pay more attention to you if you'd clean up your act? Why don't you get serious about graduate school and start acting responsibly?

Joseph: I'll do that right after you quit smoking and spend some time with me instead of always burying yourself in readings for your classes.

Carmen: You just say that because you're jealous that I'm in a graduate program and you're not.

START... experiencing this chapter's topics with an online video!

READ... the complete chapter text in a rich, interactive eBook!

Joseph: I wouldn't exactly call social work much of a graduate program.

Carmen: It's more than you have. At least I'm planning for a profession. Why don't you?

Joseph: You never do anything but complain, complain, complain. You really are a drag.

Carmen: It takes one to know one.

Joseph and Carmen have a problem, and it isn't just the issues they're discussing. Their larger problem is that they are not handling their conflict constructively. From previous chapters, we've learned enough to understand that negative communication fuels discord between people. For example, Joseph launched the conversation with *you* language. Instead of owning his anger, he blamed Carmen for it. In turn, she didn't own her anger. Joseph may also have misidentified what he was feeling. Is he really feeling angry at Carmen, or is he hurt or jealous that she spent more time with others than with him?

Both Joseph and Carmen disconfirmed the other with personal attacks. Furthermore, neither of them took the other's perspective: Neither acknowledged the other's point of view. Each of them listened defensively and ambushed the other. Carmen and Joseph pursued their individual agendas and failed to collaborate to resolve their issues. As a result, Carmen and Joseph's argument hurts both of them and creates a defensive climate for their relationship.

Let's start their conversation again, and see how positive communication might improve things.

Joseph: I felt hurt when you flirted with other guys at the party last night, and then I felt angry. [Joseph identifies hurt as the more basic feeling. He also owns his feelings.]

Carmen: I can understand that. I know you don't like me to pay attention to other men. [She acknowledges Joseph's feelings.] I got upset when you drank a lot, and I want you to understand how I feel about that. [Carmen owns her feelings and asserts her needs in the situation.]

Joseph: You're right about my drinking. I know you hate it when I drink too much. [He acknowledges her concern.]

Carmen: Well, I guess neither of us was at our best last night. I was really tired, so I probably got more irritated than I usually would. [She shares responsibility for what happened.]

Joseph: And I've been feeling kind of down because you're so focused on your graduate program, and I can't seem to get started. [Because an affirming climate has been created, Joseph can disclose his worries to Carmen.]

Carmen: I know you feel discouraged right now. [She again acknowledges his feelings.] I would too. [She shows empathy.] But you're so smart, and you'll do great once you settle on a course of action. [She confirms him by showing that she believes in him.] Why don't we put our heads together to sort through some of the options and try to figure out how you can proceed? [She focuses their discussion on a single issue, which may allow them to address it effectively. She offers support and shows commitment to his welfare.]

Joseph: That would really help me. I just need to talk through a lot of possibilities. [He acknowledges her offer of help.] I'd really like to get your perspective on some ideas I've got. [He shows he values her viewpoint.]

Carmen: I've got all the time you want. [She confirms his value and her commitment to the relationship. Her comment also addresses Joseph's relationship-level concern that she may not want to spend time with him.]

Joseph: (smiling) Okay, and I promise I won't drink while we're talking. [He uses humor to restore a good climate. On the relationship level of meaning, he is asking, "Are we okay now?"]

Carmen: (smiling) And I promise I won't flirt with other guys while we're talking. [She reciprocates his relationship-level message by signaling that she, too, feels friendly again.]

The conflict proceeded very differently in the second instance. Both Carmen and Joseph used *I* language to own their emotions, and each confirmed the other by acknowledging expressed feelings and concerns. The supportive climate they established enabled Joseph to reveal deeper worries that lay below his opening complaint about Carmen's flirting, and Carmen responded supportively to his disclosure. They also came up with a plan to address Joseph's worries. Especially important, they communicated effectively at the relationship level of meaning. Their relationship would be strengthened by how they managed their conflict in the second scenario.

Unlike Carmen and Joseph, we usually don't get a chance to redo a conflict we've already had. Instead, we have to live with the consequences, which may be unpleasant if we've managed conflict poorly. Because we usually don't get second chances, we should learn how to manage conflict effectively the first time around.

In this chapter, we explore communicating about conflict in interpersonal relationships. We begin by defining conflict. Next, we consider principles of conflict to add depth to our understanding of it. Third, we discuss different ways to approach conflict. The fourth section of the chapter focuses on specific communication patterns that affect the process of conflict and its impact on individuals and relationships. After applying chapter concepts to digital and online communication, we conclude by identifying guidelines for communicating effectively when engaging in conflict.

DEFINING INTERPERSONAL CONFLICT

Interpersonal conflict exists when there is expressed tension between people who are interdependent, perceive they have incompatible goals, and feel a need to resolve those differences (Wilmot & Hocker, 2006). Let's look more closely at what this definition implies.

Expressed Tension

Interpersonal conflict is expressed disagreement, struggle, or discord. Thus, it is not conflict if we don't recognize disagreement or anger or if we repress it so completely that it is not expressed directly or indirectly. Conflict exists only if disagreements or tensions are expressed.

We communicate disagreement in various ways. Shooting daggers with your eyes nonverbally communicates anger just as clearly as saying, "I'm angry with you." Walking out on a conversation and slamming the door express hostility as does refusing to talk to someone. Sometimes, we express disagreement overtly or directly, such as by saying, "I'm furious with you!" Other modes of communicating conflict are more covert or indirect, such as deliberately not responding to a text because you are angry. In each of these cases, people realize they are in conflict, and they express their conflict in some way.

Interdependence

Interpersonal conflict can occur only between people who perceive themselves as interdependent at the time of the conflict. Obviously, we are interdependent in I–Thou relationships with close friends, family members, and romantic partners. In addition, we may be temporarily interdependent with people in I–You relationships, which would include people we know only casually. For example, Russell and Brittany meet at a party and get into a boisterous argument over politics. Although they do not have a close relationship, during their conversation they do depend on each other: Russell wants to persuade Brittany to his political views, and she wants to persuade him to hers. In that moment, they are interdependent because each wants to change the other's mind, and that cannot happen without the other's cooperation. If Russell didn't have a desire to change what Brittany thinks, there would be no point in arguing with her. If Brittany didn't see a value in changing Russell's opinion, she wouldn't invest the effort in explaining her views or challenging his. You may also have expressed disagreement with a clerk who tries to overcharge you for a purchase or an individual who breaks in line in front of you at an airport.

© Martin Novak/Shutterstock.com

It's kind of strange, but you really don't fight with people who don't matter. With a lot of guys I dated, if I didn't like something they did, I'd just let it go because they weren't important enough for the hassle. But Rod and I argue a lot because we do affect each other. Maybe fighting is a sign that people care about each other. If you don't, why bother?

LENORE

Perceived Incompatible Goals

We experience conflict when we perceive that what we want is incompatible with what is wanted by a person with whom we are interdependent. The key word is *perceive*. Jeremy wants a practical car, and Alexis wants a fun car. There may be many cars that fit both of their criteria, but if they see the criteria as mutually exclusive, they're likely to clash. If we lock ourselves into a conflict script, too often we don't see mutually acceptable outcomes.

The Felt Need for Resolution

Conflict is more than just having differences. We differ with people about many things, but this doesn't invariably lead to conflict. For example, my in-laws don't like large dogs, and we don't like small ones; my best friend likes very bright paint, and I prefer more neutral tones in my home. These differences don't spark conflict: My in-laws tolerate our Shepherd mix, and we accept their Boston terrier. As my friend and I don't live together, we don't have to agree on what color to paint the walls. In these cases, differences don't result in conflict. Conflict involves tensions between goals, preferences, or decisions that we feel we need to reconcile. In other words, conflict involves two perceptions: the perception that what we want is at odds with what another person wants, and the perception that we and that other person must resolve our differences.

PRINCIPLES OF CONFLICT

Many people view conflict as inherently negative (Turner & Shutter, 2004), but that is a misunderstanding. To address this misunderstanding as well as others, we discuss five principles of conflict.

Principle 1: Conflict Is Natural in Most Western Relationships

In most Western relationships conflict is a normal, inevitable part of relating. You like to work alone, and your coworkers like to interact in teams. You think money should be enjoyed, and your partner believes in saving for a rainy day. You want to move to a place where there's a great job for you, but the location has no career prospects for your partner. Again and again, we find ourselves at odds with people who matter to us. When this happens, we have to resolve the differences, preferably in a way that doesn't harm the relationship.

The presence of conflict does not indicate that a relationship is unhealthy or in trouble, although how partners manage conflict does influence relational health (Wilmot & Hocker, 2006). Actually, engaging in conflict indicates that people care enough about each other to want to resolve differences. This is a good point to keep in mind when conflicts arise because it reminds us that a strong connection underlies even disagreement.

RON It sounds funny, but the biggest thing my fiancée and I fight about is whether it's okay to fight. I was brought up not to argue and to think that conflict is bad. In her family, people do argue a lot, and she thinks it is healthy. What I'm coming to realize is that there is a lot of conflict in my family, but it's hidden, so it never gets dealt with very well. I've seen her and her parents really go at it, but I have to admit they work through their differences, and people in my family don't.

Like Ron, some of us were taught that conflict is bad and should be avoided, whereas others learned that airing differences is healthy. Because conflict is inevitable in interpersonal relationships, we should develop constructive ways to deal with it.

Principle 2: Conflict May Be Expressed Overtly or Covertly

Conflict may be expressed either overtly or covertly. Overt conflict is out in the open and explicit. It exists when people deal with their differences in a direct, straightforward manner. They might calmly discuss their disagreement, intensely argue about ideas, or engage in a shouting match. Overt conflict can also involve physical attacks although of course that's neither healthy nor constructive.

Yet conflict isn't always overt. Covert conflict exists when people express their feelings about disagreements indirectly. When angry, a person may deliberately do something to hurt or upset another person. Knowing that Elliott hates to be kept waiting, his wife Maggie intentionally arrives 20 minutes late for a dinner date because he chose a restaurant she doesn't like. Maggie is expressing her anger covertly.

A common form of covert conflict is **passive aggression**, which is acting aggressively while denying feeling or acting aggressive. If Dedra doesn't call her mother every week, her mother "forgets" to send Dedra a check for spending money. When Arlene decides that she won't forgo studying to go out partying, Clem "coincidentally" decides to play music at high volume in the room adjacent to Arlene. Passive aggression punishes another person without accepting responsibility for inflicting the punishment.

🌐 MindTap™

Everyday Skills To practice considering the conflict script you learned in your family, complete the activity "Understanding Your Conflict Script" at the end of the chapter or online.

Much covert conflict takes place through **games**, highly patterned interactions in which the real conflicts are hidden or denied and a counterfeit excuse is created for arguing or criticizing (Berne, 1964).

The nature of games will become clear if we discuss a few specific ones. In a game called "Blemish," one person pretends to be complimentary but actually puts another down. Ann asks her friend whether she looks okay for an important interview. The friend, who is angry that Ann hasn't repaid a loan from last month, responds, "The new suit looks really great. There's just this one little thing: You seem to have gained weight. Your stomach and hips look big, and that suit doesn't hide the extra pounds." The friend is playing "Blemish": she focuses on one thing that is wrong and downplays all that is right. Her anger or resentment is expressed indirectly.

Another game is "NIGYYSOB" ("Now I've Got You, You Son of a B####"). In this one, a person deliberately sets another person up for a fall. Knowing that her coworker is not a detail-oriented person, Ellie asks him to gather some very detailed information. When the report he gives her is missing some information, she criticizes him for being careless. Ellie worked to find a way to make him fail and then pounced on him when he did.

"Mine Is Worse Than Yours" is another commonly played game. Suppose you tell a friend that you have two tests and a paper due next week, and your friend says, "You think *that's* bad? Listen to this: I have two tests, three papers, and an oral report all due in the next 2 weeks!" Your friend expressed no concern for your plight; rather, she told you that her situation is worse. In this game, people try to monopolize rather than listen and respond to each other.

> My parents specialize in games. Dad likes to set Mom up by asking her to take care of some financial business or get the car fixed. Then he explodes about what she does. I think he is just trying to find excuses for fussing at her. Mom also plays games. Her favorite is "Blemish." She always finds something wrong with an idea or a paper I've written or a vacation or whatever. Then she just harps and harps on the defect. Sometimes being around them is like being in a minefield.
>
> **CHUCK**

"Yes, But" is a game in which a person pretends to be asking for help but then refuses all help that's offered. Doing this allows the person who initiates the game to blame the other person for not helping. Lorna asks her boyfriend to help her figure out how to better manage her money. When he suggests that she should spend less, Lorna says, "Yes, but I don't buy anything I don't need." When he suggests she might work extra hours at her job, she responds, "Yes, but that would cut into my free time." When he mentions she could get a better-paying job, Lorna says, "Yes, but I really like the people where I work now." "Yes, But" continues until the person trying to help finally gives up in defeat. Then, the initiator of the game can complain, "You didn't help me."

Passive aggression, including games, is a dishonest, ineffective way to manage conflict. It is dishonest because it evades the real issues. It is ineffective because as long as conflict remains hidden or disguised, it's almost impossible for people to recognize and resolve it.

MindTap

Everyday Skills To apply what you've read about covert conflict to your own life complete the activity "Identifying Games in Your Communication" at the end of the chapter or online.

Principle 3: Social Groups Shape the Meaning of Conflict Behaviors

Our cultural membership and socialization in particular social communities affect how we view and respond to conflict.

Cultural Differences Regarding Conflict   The majority of Mediterranean cultures regard lively conflict as a normal, valuable part of everyday life. Within these cultures, people routinely argue, and nobody gets upset or angry. In France and in Arabic countries, men debate one another for the sheer fun of it. It doesn't matter who wins the debate—the argument itself is enjoyable (Copeland & Griggs, 1985). Many Hispanic cultures also regard conflict as both normal and interesting. Because Hispanic cultures tend to value emotions, conflicts are opportunities for emotional expression.

Many Asian cultures adopt the view that conflict is destructive (Gangwish, 1999; Martin & Nakayama, 2007). Yan Bing Zhang, Jake Harwood, and Mary Hummert (2005) asked Chinese adults to evaluate transcripts in which an older worker criticized a younger worker. Older participants favored an accommodating style, which focuses on relational harmony. Younger adults preferred a problem-solving style, which is assertive and cooperative to an accommodating style or perceived the two styles as equally desirable. Both older and younger participants had less positive perceptions of the avoiding style, which was perceived as disrespectful of others and the competing (driven by self-interest) style of dealing with conflict. In contrast, many Westerners prefer the competing style (Bergstrom & Nussbaum, 1996).

Mainstream culture in the United States emphasizes assertiveness and individuality, so many Americans are competitive and reluctant to give in to others. In more communal societies, people have less individualistic perspectives and are less likely to focus on winning conflicts (Ting-Toomey, 1991; Van Yperen & Buunk, 1991). In Japanese sports, the ideal is not for one team to win but for a tie to occur so that neither team loses face. When there is to be a winner, Japanese athletes try to win by only a slim margin so that the losing team is not humiliated ("American Games, Japanese Rules," cited in Ferrante, 2006).

VALAYA   One of the hardest adjustments for me has been how Americans assert themselves. I was very surprised that students argue with their teachers. We would never do that in Taiwan. It would be extremely disrespectful. I also see friends argue, sometimes very much. I understand this is a cultural difference, but I have trouble accepting it. I learned that disagreements hurt relationships.

Differences among Social Communities   Our orientations toward conflict are influenced not only by culture but also by social communities. Specific communities such as Amish and Quakers within Western culture tend to regard conflict as harmful. In addition, gender, sexual orientation, and race/ethnicity may influence orientations toward conflict. There are some general differences in how women and men respond to conflict although the generalizations don't apply to all women and men (Stafford, Dutton, & Haas, 2000; Wood, 2011a). In general, women are more likely to want to discuss conflictual issues, whereas many men tend to avoid or minimize conflict. Women are also more likely than men to defer and compromise, both of which reflect gendered prescriptions for women to accommodate others (Stafford et al., 2000).

Masculine socialization places less emphasis on expressive communication. In professional situations and athletics, men may be very vocal in dealing with conflict. Yet, in their personal lives, men often deny or minimize problems rather than deal openly with them. Long-term studies of marriage indicate that husbands are more inclined than wives to withdraw from conflict, and that husbands' refusal to address conflict is a strong predictor of divorce (Gottman & Gottman, 2007).

NICK My girlfriend drives me crazy. Any time there is the slightest thing wrong in our relationship, she wants to have a long, drawn-out analysis of it. I just don't want to spend all that time dissecting the relationship.

GINA My boyfriend is a world-class avoider. When something is wrong between us, I naturally want to talk about it and get things right again. But he will evade, tell me everything's fine when it's not, say the problem is too minor to talk about, and use any other tactic he can come up with to avoid facing the problem. He thinks if you don't deal with problems, they somehow solve themselves.

Men are more likely than women to use coercive tactics, both verbal and physical, to avoid discussing problems and to force their resolutions on others (Johnson, 2006; White, 1989). Dominating styles of handling conflict are associated with relationship dissatisfaction (Zacchillil, Hendrick, & Hendrick, 2009).

Before leaving our discussion of gender, we should note one other important finding. Psychologist John Gottman (1993; Jacobson & Gottman, 1998) reports that in general, men experience greater and longer-lasting physical responses to interpersonal conflict than women do. Compared with women, during conflict men's heart rates rise more quickly and to higher levels and stay elevated for a longer period of time. Because conflict tends to be more physically and psychologically painful to men than to women, men may be motivated to deny, avoid, or minimize issues that could cause conflict.

Sexual orientation doesn't seem to be a major influence on how people see and deal with conflict. Caryl Rusbult and her colleagues (Rusbult, Johnson, & Morrow, 1986a; Rusbult, Zembrodt, & Iwaniszek, 1986b; Wood, 1986, 1994b) report that in their responses to conflict, gay men are much like heterosexual men, and lesbians are similar to heterosexual women. Most children, regardless of sexual orientation, are socialized on the basis of their sex. Thus, boys, both gay and heterosexual, tend to learn masculine orientations toward interaction, whereas lesbian and heterosexual girls are usually socialized toward feminine styles of interaction.

Research indicates that race–ethnicity is related to conflict styles and to interpretations of them. Terri Orbuch, Joseph Veroff, and their colleagues (Orbuch & Eyster, 1997; Orbuch, Veroff, & Hunter, 1999) report that open, verbal arguing is more often destructive for white couples than black couples. They also report that black wives are more likely than white wives to believe that airing conflicts can lead to positive resolution.

Principle 4: Conflict Can Be Managed Well or Poorly

Depending on how we handle disagreements, conflict can either promote continuing closeness or tear a relationship apart. One of the main reasons conflict is handled poorly is that it often involves intense feelings, which many people do not know how to identify or express. We may feel deep disappointment, resentment, or anger toward someone we care about, and this is difficult to manage. Our discussion in Chapter 7 should help you identify your feelings and choose effective ways to communicate your emotions in conflict situations. Other skills we've discussed—such as using *I* language and monitoring the self-serving bias—will also help you manage the feelings that often accompany conflict.

Once the honeymoon was over for *The Wolf of Wall Street* high roller Jordan Belfort (Leonardo DiCaprio) and wife Naomi Lapaglia (Margot Robbie), the tension and bickering often escalated out of control.

Principle 5: Conflict Can Be Good for Individuals and Relationships

Although we tend to think of conflict negatively, it can be beneficial in a number of ways (Parker-Pope, 2010a). When managed constructively, conflict provides opportunities for us to grow as individuals and to strengthen our relationships. We deepen insight into our ideas and feelings when we express them and get responses from others. Conflict also allows us to consider points of view different from our own. Based on what we learn, we may modify our own views.

HERBERT It helped me get my own thoughts together about the primary to talk with friends. From the start I was on Obama's team, but my closest buddy just didn't like Obama. At first, we yelled a lot, but then we settled down and really talked. I began to understand why he thought Obama was an elitist, and he began to see why I didn't. He thought Obama didn't have the experience that Clinton did, and I thought Obama's judgment and philosophy trumped experience. Both of us learned from the other by really talking and listening, especially the listening part.

Conflict can also enhance relationships by enlarging partners' understandings of one another. What begins as a discussion of a particular issue usually winds up providing broader information about why partners feel as they do and what meanings they attach to the issue. In the example that opened this chapter, the original complaint about Carmen's flirting led to the discovery that Joseph felt insecure about his identity and Carmen's respect for him because she was succeeding in graduate work, and he wasn't advancing in school or a career. Once his concern emerged, the couple could address deeper issues in their relationship.

Lack of conflict isn't necessarily a symptom of a healthy relationship. Low levels of conflict could reflect limited emotional depth between partners or unwillingness to work out differences. Researchers report that there is no direct association between marital happiness and the number of arguments that spouses have (Gottman & Gottman, 2007; Muehlhoff & Wood, 2002; Wilmot & Hocker, 2006). Instead, the key is to have a greater number of positive, affirming interactions than negative ones. One group of researchers refers to this as "keeping a positive balance in the marital bank account" (Gottman & Silver, 2000).

Geoff and I have a pretty intense relationship. We fight a lot, and we fight hard. Some of my friends think this is bad, but we don't. Nothing is swept under the carpet in our relationship. If either of us is angry or upset about something, we hash it out then and there. But we are just as intense in positive ways. Geoff lets me know all the time that he loves me, and I am always hugging and kissing him. I guess you could just say our relationship is passionate—in bad moments and good ones.

JANA

To review, we've discussed five principles of interpersonal conflict. First, we noted that conflict is both natural and inevitable in most Western interpersonal relationships. Second, we discovered that conflict can be directly communicated or covertly expressed through indirect communication or games that camouflage real issues. Third, we saw that conflict styles and meanings are shaped by social location—membership in cultures and social communities. Fourth, we emphasized that how we manage conflict influences its resolution and its impact on interpersonal climates. Finally, we saw that conflict can be constructive for individuals and relationships. We can now build on these principles by discussing diverse ways that people approach and respond to conflict.

ORIENTATIONS TO CONFLICT

We now look at three basic orientations that affect how we approach conflict situations. In the next section of the chapter, we'll see how these different approaches shape our patterns of communicating during conflict. Each way of approaching conflict is appropriate in some relationships and situations; the challenge is to know when a particular approach is constructive.

Lose-Lose

A **lose–lose** orientation assumes that conflict results in losses for everyone and that it is unhealthy and destructive for relationships. A wife might feel that conflicts about money hurt her, her husband, and the marriage. Similarly, a person may refrain from arguing with a friend, believing the result would be wounded feelings for both of them. Because the lose–lose orientation assumes that conflict is inevitably negative, people who adopt it typically try to avoid conflict at all costs. Yet seeking to avoid conflict at all costs may be very costly indeed. We may have to defer our own needs or rights, and we may feel unable to give honest feedback to others.

> **THEO** I hate to fight with friends. I do just about anything to avoid an argument. But sometimes, what I have to do is sacrifice my preferences or even my rights just to avoid conflict. And sometimes, I have to go along with something I don't believe in or think is right. I'm starting to think that maybe conflict would be better than avoiding it—at least in some cases.

Although the lose–lose orientation is not usually beneficial in dealing with conflicts in close relationships, it has merit in some circumstances. Some issues—for example, where to go for dinner—aren't worth the energy and the discomfort that conflict arouses. In other cases, the potential consequences of conflict—being fired from a job, for instance—may be too great (Caughlin & Arr, 2004).

Win-Lose

Win–lose orientations assume that one person wins at the expense of the other. A person who sees conflict as a win–lose matter thinks that disagreements are battles that can have only one victor. What one person gains, the other loses; what one person loses, the other gains. Disagreements are seen as zero-sum games in which there is no possibility for everyone to benefit. The win–lose orientation is cultivated in cultures that place value on individualism, self-assertion, and competition. If you guessed that the United States emphasizes those values, you're right. A win–lose approach to conflict is not common in cultures that place priority on cooperation, keeping others from failing, and finding areas of agreement.

Partners who disagree about whether to move to a new location might adopt a win–lose orientation. In turn, this would lock them into a yes–no view in which only two alternatives are seen: move or stay put. The win–lose orientation almost guarantees that the partners won't work to find or create a mutually acceptable solution, such as moving to a third place that meets both partners' needs, or having a long-distance relationship so that each person can have the best location. The more Partner A argues for moving, the more Partner B argues for not moving. Eventually one of them "wins," but at the cost of the other and the relationship. A win–lose orientation toward conflict tends to undermine relationships because someone has to lose.

There are other potential disadvantages to a win–lose approach to conflict. The person who loses may assume the role of martyr, which often

© Monkey Business Images/Shutterstock.com

fuels resentment and dissatisfaction in the person playing martyr and frustration and anger in those around him or her (Wilmot & Hocker, 2006). Also, the person who loses may feel a need to "get even" by winning the next argument—which ensures that a sharp win–lose orientation will be present then, too (Meyer, 2004; Olson & Braithwaite, 2004).

A win–lose approach can be appropriate when we have a high desire for our position to prevail, low commitment to a relationship, and little desire to take care of the person with whom we disagree. When you're buying a car, for instance, you want the best deal you can get, and you probably have little concern for the dealer's profit and little commitment to a relationship with the salesperson.

Win–Win

Win–win orientations assume that there are usually ways to resolve differences so that everyone gains. A good solution is one that everyone finds satisfactory. When all people are committed to finding a mutually acceptable solution, a win–win resolution is possible. Sometimes, people can't

Communication in Everyday Life

WORKPLACE

Japanese and American Styles of Negotiation

The differences between Japanese and American views of conflict shape specific communication patterns during business negotiations (McDaniel & Quasha, 2000; Weiss, 1987). Consider how each of the following negotiation strategies reflects values typical of Japanese or American society.

Japanese Style
- Understate your own initial position or state it vaguely to allow the other room to state his or her position.
- Find informal ways to let the other person know your bottom line to move the agreement forward without directly confronting the other with your bottom line.
- Look for areas of agreement, and focus talk on them.
- Avoid confrontation or explicit disagreement.
- Work to make sure that neither you nor the other person fails.
- Plan to spend a long time discussing issues before even moving toward a decision.

American Style
- Overstate initial position to establish a strong image.
- Keep your bottom line secret from the other person to preserve your power and gain the most.
- Where there are differences, assert your position and attempt to win the other's assent.
- Be adversarial.
- Work to win all you can.
- Push to reach decisions as rapidly as possible.

find or create a solution that is each person's ideal. In such cases, each person may make some accommodations to build a solution that is acceptable to each person. Compromising to find a solution that is acceptable to both parties is positively associated with satisfaction, respect, and love between marital partners (Zacchillil et al., 2009).

When partners adopt win–win views of conflict, they often discover solutions that neither had thought of previously. This happens because they are committed to their own and the other's satisfaction. Sometimes, win–win attitudes result in compromises that satisfy enough of each person's needs to provide confirmation and to protect the health of the relationship.

In Chapter 3, we learned that how we perceive things has a powerful impact on what they mean to us and on the possibilities of resolution that we imagine. Remember how you couldn't solve the nine dots problem in Chapter 3 if you perceived it as a square? In a similar way, we're unlikely to find a win–win solution if we perceive conflict as win–lose or lose–lose.

RESPONSES TO CONFLICT

HANK

One thing I learned when I was serving in the military is that a fist will stop an argument a lot faster than words. You can talk all day long and never reach resolution, but a good pop in the face ends conflict real fast.

Hank is correct that physical violence can sometimes stop an argument—at least temporarily. Physical force may be an unfortunate necessity in some situations, such as combat or self-protection. In interpersonal relationships, however, it is a very poor way to deal with conflict. A great deal of research demonstrates that violence in families harms both perpetrators and victims, and it violates the trust upon which close relationships are built (Jacobson & Gottman, 1998; Johnson, 2006). In Chapter 11, we'll look more closely at the dynamics of violence between intimate partners. In this section, we'll consider ways of responding to conflict other than violence.

A series of studies identified four distinct ways North Americans respond to relational distress (Rusbult, 1987; Rusbult, Johnson, & Morrow, 1986a; Rusbult & Zembrodt, 1983; Rusbult, Zembrodt, & Iwaniszek, 1986b). These are represented in Figure 9.1. According to this model, responses to conflict can be either active or passive, depending on how overtly they address problems. Responses can also be constructive or destructive in their capacity to resolve tension and to preserve relationships.

The Exit Response

The **exit response** involves physically walking out or psychologically withdrawing. Refusing to talk about a problem is an example of psychological exit. Ending a relationship, or leaving when conflict arises are both examples of literal exit. Because exit doesn't address problems, it tends to be destructive. Because it is a forceful way to avoid conflict, it is active.

LESLIE

A friend of mine uses the exit strategy on email. Whenever we get into an argument, she stops replying to my email messages. I know she reads them because she's on email several times every day. But if we're having an argument, she just won't reply. It's like she's not there, and I can't make her talk to me.

Exit responses are associated with lose–lose and win–lose orientations toward conflict. People who have a lose–lose orientation assume that nobody can benefit if conflict takes place, so they see no point in engaging in conflict and prefer to avoid it. For different reasons, the win–lose orientation may promote the exit response. People who see conflicts as win–lose situations may exit physically or psychologically if they think they are losing an argument. Refusing to engage disagreement is generally associated with relationship dissatisfaction (Caughlin & Golish, 2002; Overall, Sibley, & Travaglia, 2010).

The Neglect Response

The **neglect response** denies or minimizes problems, disagreements, anger, tension, or other matters that could lead to overt conflict. People engaging in neglect say, "We don't really disagree" or "You're making a mountain out of a molehill." Neglect generally is destructive because it doesn't resolve tension. It is passive because it avoids discussion (Overall et al., 2010). In some situations, however, neglect may be an effective response to conflict. For instance, if an issue can't be resolved, discussing it may further harm a relationship. Also, if a conflict isn't important to a relationship's health, it may be appropriate not to deal with it.

The lose–lose and win–lose orientations may prompt the neglect response for the same reasons that each of those orientations is associated with the exit response. Either the person thinks that escalating the disagreement will harm everyone, or the person thinks that she or he will lose if the conflict is allowed to progress.

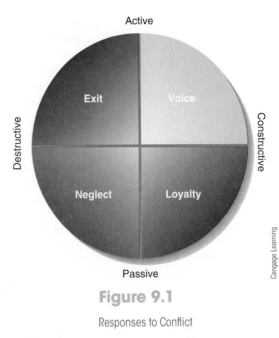

Figure 9.1

Responses to Conflict

The Loyalty Response

The **loyalty response** involves staying committed to a relationship despite differences. Loyalty may be appropriate if tolerating differences isn't too costly, but in some instances deferring your own needs and goals may be too high a price for harmony. Loyalty is silent allegiance that doesn't actively address conflict, so it is a passive response. Because it preserves the relationship, loyalty may be constructive, at least in the short term. This response, however, has the potential to result in the silently loyal partner feeling unappreciated (Overall et al., 2010).

Loyalty is most likely to spring from a lose–lose orientation toward conflict. Believing that engaging in overt disagreement only hurts everyone, people may choose to remain loyal to the relationship and not try to work through differences.

> **ZONDOMINI**
>
> In South Africa, the tradition is for women not to speak out against their husbands. Women are supposed to support whatever the husband says or does. A woman who speaks out or who disagrees with her husband or any male relative is considered bad; she is behaving inappropriately. But some of us are now challenging this custom. I disagreed with my father about my marriage, and he did not speak to me for many months after. Now he speaks to me again. I also sometimes disagree with my husband. Life is changing in South Africa.

The Voice Response

Finally, the **voice response** addresses conflict directly and attempts to resolve it. People who respond with voice identify problems or tensions and assert a desire to deal with them. Voice implies that people care enough about a relationship to notice when something is wrong and do something to improve the situation. Thus, voice is generally the most constructive way to deal with conflict in intimate relationships (Overall et al., 2010).

The voice response is fostered by a win–win orientation toward conflict. It takes belief in yourself *and* in the other person to give voice to problems and disagreements. Voicing concerns also expresses belief in the relationship. We're unlikely to voice disagreements unless we believe that a relationship can withstand our doing so. Voice may also take the form of genuine apology for behavior that has hurt another, or explicit acceptance of a partner's apology (Fincham & Beach, 2002; Vangelisti & Crumley, 1998).

Although each of us has preferred conflict responses, we can become skillful in other responses if we so choose. Constructive strategies (voice and loyalty) are advisable for relationships that matter to you and that you want to maintain. Exit may be useful as an interim strategy when partners need time to reflect or cool off before dealing with conflict directly. Loyalty may be appropriate in situations where conflict is temporary and provoked by external pressures. Developing skill in a range of responses to conflict increases your ability to communicate sensitively and effectively.

COMMUNICATION PATTERNS DURING CONFLICT

Communication skills shape the process and outcomes of conflict. Thus, we want to understand specific kinds of communication that foster or impede effective conflict.

Unproductive Conflict Communication

Unproductive communication patterns in managing conflict reflect a preoccupation with oneself and a disregard for the other. As a result, communication tends to be negative. Table 9.1 identifies behaviors that foster constructive and unproductive conflict communication (Gottman, 1993; Houts, Barnett-Walker, Paley, & Cox, 2008; Vangelisti, 1993).

The Early Stages   The first three minutes of an argument may be the most important because they tend to set the stage for how conflict will be managed (Parker-Pope, 2010a). The foundation of unproductive conflict is established by communication that fails to confirm individuals. If John says, "I want us to spend more time together," Shannon may reply, "That's unreasonable." This disconfirms John's feeling and request. Shannon could also disconfirm him by not replying at all, which would be a refusal to acknowledge him. During the early stages of conflict, people tend to listen poorly. They may listen selectively, taking in only what they expect or want to believe. They may communicate disdain nonverbally. For instance, Shannon could roll her eyes to communicate to John that she thinks his request is outrageous, or she might shrug and turn away to signal that she doesn't care what he wants.

Table 9.1 Summary of Constructive and Unproductive Communication

CONSTRUCTIVE	UNPRODUCTIVE
Validation of each other	Disconfirmation of each other
Sensitive listening	Poor listening
Dual perspective	Preoccupation with self
Expressed support of each other	Not supporting, or undercutting, each other
Recognition of other's concerns	Cross-complaining
Asking for clarification	Hostile mind reading
Infrequent interruptions	Frequent interruptions
Focus on specific issues	Kitchen-sinking
Compromises and contracts	Counterproposals
Useful metacommunication	Excessive metacommunication
Summarizing the concerns	Self-summarizing by both partners
Positive affect	Negative affect

Cross-complaining occurs when one person's complaint is met by a counter-complaint. Shannon could respond to John's request for more time by saying, "Yeah, well, what I want is a little more respect for what I do." That response doesn't address John's concern; instead it is an attempt to divert the conversation and to switch the fault from Shannon to John. Poor listening and disconfirmation establish a climate in which dual perspective is low and defensiveness is high.

Negative climates tend to build on themselves. As parties in conflict continue to talk, mind reading is likely. The negative assumptions and attributions reflect and fuel hostility and mistrust.

The Middle Stages Once a negative climate has been set, it is stoked by other unconstructive communication. People often engage in **kitchen-sinking**, in which everything except the kitchen sink is thrown into the argument. John may add to his original complaint by recalling all sorts of other real and imagined slights from Shannon. She may reciprocate by hauling out her own laundry list of gripes. The result is such a mass of grievances that John and Shannon are overwhelmed. They can't solve all the problems they've dragged into the discussion, and they may well forget what the original issue was. Kitchen-sinking is particularly likely to occur when people have a host of concerns they've repressed for some time. Once a conflict begins, everything that has been stored up is thrown in.

i love images/SuperStock

The middle stages of unproductive conflict tend to be marked by frequent interruptions that disrupt the flow of talk. Interruptions may also be attempts to derail a partner's issues and reroute discussion: "I'm not going to work on spending more time together until we discuss your responsibility for this house." Cross-complaining often continues in this middle stage of the syndrome. Because neither person is allowed to develop thoughts fully (or even to finish a sentence), discussion never focuses on any one topic long enough to make headway in resolving it.

The Later Stages   The early and middle stages didn't lay the proper groundwork for an effective discussion of solutions. As a result, each person's proposals tend to be met with counterproposals. The self-preoccupation that first surfaced in the early phase persists now, so each person is more interested in pushing his or her solution than in considering the other person's. John proposes, "Maybe we could spend two nights together each week." Shannon counterproposes, "Maybe you could assume responsibility for half the chores around here." Her counterproposal fails to acknowledge his suggestion, so her communication does not confirm him. Compounding self-preoccupation is self-summarizing, which occurs when a person keeps repeating what she or he has already said. This egocentric communication ignores the other person and simply restates the speaker's feelings and perspective.

Excessive metacommunication is also common in the later stages of unproductive conflict. Metacommunication, which we discussed in Chapter 1, is communication about communication. For example, John might say, "I think we're avoiding talking about the real issue here." This is a comment about the communication that is happening. Metacommunication is used by couples in both unproductive conflict and constructive conflict, but it is used in very different ways (Gottman et. al., 1977).

In constructive conflict communication, people use metacommunication to keep the discussion on track. For instance, during a disagreement, John might comment that Shannon doesn't seem to be expressing her feelings and invite her to do so. Then, he and Shannon would return to their discussion.

In contrast, people who manage conflict unproductively often become embroiled in metacommunication and can't get back to the issues. For example, Shannon and John might get into extended metacommunication about the way they deal with conflict and never return to the original topic of conflict. Excessive metacommunication is more likely to block partners than to resolve tensions satisfactorily.

The communication that makes up the unproductive conflict reflects and promotes egocentrism and rigid thinking because negative communication tends to be self-perpetuating. This, in turn, can trigger a domino effect of negative outcomes: Egocentrism leads to poor listening, which promotes disconfirmation, which fuels defensiveness, which stokes dogmatism, which leads to hostile mind reading and kitchen-sinking, which pave the way for self-summarizing. Each negative form of communication feeds into the overall negative system. Unproductive communication fosters a defensive, negative climate, which makes it almost impossible to resolve conflicts, confirm individuals, or nurture a relationship.

Constructive Conflict Communication

Constructive communication during conflict creates a supportive, positive climate that increases the possibility of resolving differences without harming the relationship. Let's look at how constructive communication plays out in the three phases of conflict.

The Early Stages   The foundation of constructive management of conflict is established long before a specific disagreement is aired. Climate, which is the foundation both of conflict and of the overall relationship, sets the tone for communication during conflict.

Once an argument is starting, it's critical to start it productively. Remember what we noted when discussing unproductive conflict: The first three minutes of an argument may be the most important because they establish the foundation for what will follow (Parker-Pope, 2010a). To establish a good climate, communicators confirm each other by recognizing and acknowledging each other's concerns and feelings. Returning to our example, when John says, "I want us to spend more time together," Shannon could confirm him by replying, "I wish we could, too. It's nice that you want us to have more time together." Shannon's statement communicates to John that she is listening and that she cares about his concerns and shares them. After she says that, their discussion might go like this:

John: Yeah, it just seems that we used to spend a lot more time together, and we felt closer then. I miss that.

Shannon: I do, too. It sounds as if what's really on your mind is how close we are, not specifically the amount of time we spend together. Is that right?

John: Yeah, I guess that is more what's bothering me, but I kind of think they're connected, don't you?

Shannon: To an extent, but we won't feel closer just by spending more time together. I think we also need some shared interests like we used to have.

John: I'd like that. Do you have any ideas?

Let's highlight several things in this conversation. First, notice that when Shannon responds directly to John's opening statement, he elaborates and clarifies what is troubling him. Instead of time per se, the issue is closeness. Listening sensitively, Shannon picks up on this and refocuses their conversation on closeness. We should also notice that Shannon doesn't mind read; instead, she asks John whether she has understood what he meant. When he asks Shannon whether she thinks time and closeness are related, John shows openness to her perceptions; thus, he confirms her and doesn't mind read. The openness they create clears the way for effective discussion of how to increase their closeness. Once a supportive climate is established, the couple can proceed to the middle stages of conflict knowing they are not fighting each other but working together to solve a problem.

The Middle Stages   The positive groundwork laid in the early phase of conflict supports what happens as people dig into issues. The middle stages of constructive conflict are marked by what

Gottman (1993) calls *agenda building*, which involves staying focused on the main issues. When partners keep communication on target, kitchen-sinking is unlikely to derail discussion.

Side issues may come up, as they do in unproductive conflict, but people who have learned to communicate effectively control digressions and stay with their agenda. One useful technique is **bracketing**, which is noting that an issue arising in the course of conflict should be discussed later. Bracketing allows partners to confirm each other's concerns by agreeing to deal with them later. In addition, bracketing topics peripheral to the current discussion allows partners to make progress in resolving the immediate issue. To bracket a topic, a person might say, "That's an important point, and we need to discuss it. If we deal with it now, we won't be able to stay focused on what we're discussing now. Could we agree to come back to this later?"

During the middle stage of constructive conflict, communicators continue to show respect for each other by not interrupting except to get clarification ("Before you go on, could you explain what you mean by closeness?") or to check perceptions ("So you think time together leads to closeness?"). Unlike disruptive interruptions, those that clarify ideas and check perceptions confirm the person speaking by showing that the listener wants to understand the meaning.

Parties in conflict continue to recognize and acknowledge each other's point of view. Rather than cross-complaining, they acknowledge each other's feelings, thoughts, and concerns. This doesn't mean they don't put their own concerns on the table. Constructive conflict includes asserting our own feelings and needs as part of an honest dialogue. Honoring both others *and* ourselves is central to good interpersonal communication.

The Later Stages In the culminating phase, attention shifts to resolving the tension. Whereas in unproductive conflict this involves meeting proposals with counterproposals, in constructive conflict people continue to collaborate.

Keeping in mind that they share a relationship, they continue using dual perspective to remain aware of each other's viewpoints. Instead of countering each other's proposals, they engage in **contracting**, which is building a solution through negotiation and the acceptance of parts of proposals. The difference between counterproposals and contracting is illustrated in this example:

Counterproposals

John: I want us to spend three nights a week doing things together.

Shannon: I can't do that right now because we're short-handed at work, and I am filling in nights. Get a hobby, so you aren't bored on nights.

John: Not being bored isn't the same as our being close. I want us to spend time together again.

Shannon: I told you, I can't do that. Don't be so selfish.

John: Aren't we as important as your job?

Shannon: That's a stupid question. I can't take three nights off. Let's take more vacations.

Contracting

John: I want us to spend three nights a week doing things together.

Shannon: I'm all for that, but right now we're short-handed at work. How about if we use your idea but adjust it to my job? Maybe we could start with one night each week and expand that later.

John: Okay, that's a start, but could we also reserve some weekend time for us?

Shannon: That's a good idea. Let's plan on that. I just can't be sure how much I'll have to work on weekends until we hire some new people. What if we promise to give ourselves an extra week's vacation to spend together when my office is back at full staff?

John: Okay, that's a good backup plan, but can we take weekend time when you don't work?

Shannon: Absolutely. How about a picnic this Sunday? We've haven't gone on a picnic in so long.

In the counterproposal scenario, John and Shannon were competing to get their own way. Neither tried to identify workable parts of the other's proposals or to find common ground. Because each adopts a win–lose view of the conflict, it's likely that both of them and the relationship will be losers. A very different tone shows up in the second, contracting scenario. Neither person represses personal needs, and each is committed to building on the other's proposals.

BETTINA

My son and I used to argue all the time, and we never got anywhere because we were each trying to get our own way, and we weren't paying attention to the other. Then, we went into family counseling, and we learned how to make our arguments more productive. The most important thing I learned was to be looking for ways to respond to what my son says and wants. Once I started focusing on him and trying to satisfy him, he was more willing to listen to my point of view and to think about solutions that would satisfy me. We still argue a lot—I guess we always will—but now it's more like we're working things through together instead of trying to tear each other down.

Specific differences between unproductive and productive conflict can be summarized as the difference between confirming and disconfirming communication. Communication that is characteristic of unproductive conflict disconfirms both individuals and the relationship, whereas the communication in constructive conflict consistently confirms both people and the relationship.

Conflict Management Skills

Our discussion of constructive and unproductive conflict communication highlights communication skills and attitudes we've emphasized in previous chapters. This is a good time to explain eight conflict management skills that rely on effective interpersonal communication.

"Look, instead of constantly grading one another, let's make this a simple pass/fail relationship."

Attend to the Relationship Level of Meaning

Conflict situations, like all other communication encounters, involve both the content level and the relationship level of meaning. Yet many of us tend to focus on the content level of meaning: the issues or the problem.

Focusing on the content level of meaning is understandable, but doing so neglects a major dimension of communication. We need to tune into relationship-level meanings and listen for what the other person is feeling about us and our relationship. It's equally important to monitor the relationship level of your own communication. Are you saying you care about getting your way more than you care about the relationship or other person? Are you communicating respect, attentiveness, and liking or the opposites?

Communicate Supportively From our discussion in Chapter 8, you'll recall that supportive interpersonal climates are cultivated by communication that is descriptive, provisional, spontaneous, problem oriented, empathic, and egalitarian. It's also useful to remind ourselves to avoid communication that tends to generate disconfirming climates: evaluation, certainty, strategies, control orientation, neutrality, and superiority, which we discussed in Chapter 8. In conflict situations, we may be especially likely to engage in communication that fosters defensiveness and reduces the possibilities for resolving the conflict and sustaining the relationship.

Listen Mindfully You already know that mindful listening is a very important interpersonal communication skill. This is especially true in conflict because we may not want to consider the other person's ideas or criticisms of our ideas. Even when you disagree with someone's thoughts, actions, goals, or values, you should show respect for the person by paying attention and seeking to understand him or her. That can be really difficult if the other person is not practicing effective communication skills. For example, imagine this scene: One morning as you enter your workplace, your coworker greets you by griping, "You're late again. Why can't you ever be on time?" That kind of attack tends to make us feel defensive, so a natural reply might be, "What's your problem? Don't make a big deal out of 5 minutes. Get off my case." However, this kind of retort is likely to fan the flames of discord. A more effective reply would be, "I'm sorry I kept you waiting. I didn't know that the time I get here affects you." This response acknowledges your lateness, shows respect for your coworker's feelings, and opens the door to a conversation.

Take Responsibility for Your Thoughts, Feelings, and Issues

I language is a cornerstone of effective conflict management. Own your feelings: "I feel angry when you are late" instead of "You make me angry with your lateness." It's also important to own your thoughts and your issues. "*We* need to keep this apartment cleaner" is a statement that you want the apartment cleaner. The other person may not care, in which case it's not accurate to say, "We need to keep this apartment cleaner." The issue is yours, so you should own it by saying, "I am uncomfortable with how messy this place is. Can we figure out a way to deal with this?"

Check Perceptions   Perceptions are easily distorted when conflict is afoot. You may see another person's position as more extreme than it is; you may think someone is immature or unreasonable; you may be inclined to engage in self-serving bias, which we discussed in Chapter 3. During conflict, we need to check our perceptions. Paraphrasing is one effective way to do this: "So you think we should spend every weekend cleaning our apartment?" or "Does it seem to you that I'm always late?" We can also check perceptions by asking direct questions, being careful to avoid communication that fosters defensiveness: "What would be clean enough for you?" "Is it the 5 minutes I'm late that's bothering you, or does lateness mean something else to you?"

Look for Points of Agreement   During conflict, we tend to focus on disagreements or ways we differ from another person. Although we should acknowledge and deal with real differences, we should also look for points of agreement. You and a coworker may disagree on goals, values, or courses of action, but you probably agree on other matters related to a conflict episode. Returning to the previous example, you and your coworker may disagree on whether being 5 minutes late is important. However, you may also share a belief that people who care about each other respect each other's feelings. This shared belief is common ground that may help you work out a resolution to the conflict. If we are looking for common ground, we can usually find it. When we do, we're likely to deal with conflict effectively without harming the relationship.

Look for Ways to Preserve the Other's Face   In Japan and some other Asian cultures, *face* is a central concept. Your face is the image of yourself that you want others to see and believe (McDaniel & Quasha, 2000). We are embarrassed or ashamed when we lose face. Whereas Western cultures tend to emphasize protecting one's own face, many Asian cultures emphasize the importance of protecting others' faces (Ting-Toomey, 1988; Ting-Toomey & Oetzel, 2001, 2002). The goal is for no one to feel defeated, stupid, or embarrassed.

Protecting others' faces is part of managing conflict effectively (Metts & Cupach, 2008). If your point or idea is accepted in an argument, be gracious toward the other person. He or she is likely to feel face is lost if you say, "I knew you'd come around." If you are committed to protecting the other person's face, you might say, "I appreciate your generosity in understanding how important this is to me." This statement allows the person who may have lost the argument to retain dignity and save face.

Communication in Everyday Life

WORKPLACE

Conflict in the Workplace

On-the-job conflict is common. Less common is skill in dealing with workplace conflict. Dr. Hendrie Weisinger is a therapist and consultant who has much experience in dealing with workplace conflict. His book *Anger at Work* (1996) offers two suggestions for handling workplace conflict effectively. First, try to defuse the conflict by improving the climate. Use your communication to demonstrate support, empathy, openness, and an interest in resolving the source of conflict. You might also suggest a "time out"—say you want to discuss the issue but need 10 minutes to take care of something first. This allows a cooling-off period.

Dr. Weisinger's second suggestion is to listen fully, mindfully. This can be difficult if the other person seems to be attacking you personally, yet focused listening is deeply confirming. Don't interrupt, correct, or argue. Just listen and try to understand the other person's perspective. Dealing with conflict in these two ways provides a foundation for productive conversation.

MindTap The next time you find yourself in conflict, try using Dr. Weisinger's two suggestions. Does doing so alter the course of conflict?

Imagine How You'll Feel in the Future   Recall that, in Chapter 4, we noted that one of our symbolic abilities is hypothetical thought. Among other things, this capacity allows us to imagine ourselves in the future and to respond to the future self that we imagine (Honeycutt, 2008). You can use this ability to help you manage conflict effectively. To illustrate, consider this scenario: A friend has just told you that he borrowed your car without asking and had a minor accident. You feel like shouting and attacking the friend verbally.

Before you say anything, you imagine how you would feel tomorrow or next week or next year if you launched a scathing attack on your friend. Then, you imagine how you would feel tomorrow or next week or next year if you expressed your anger calmly yet not aggressively, showed concern about whether your friend was hurt in the accident, and found a way to help your friend save face. You probably prefer the you who behaved considerately to the you who behaved combatively. Taking a moment to imagine yourself after the conflict ends can help you choose to communicate in ways that are ethical, that foster self-respect, and that support the continuation of the relationship.

The eight skills we've discussed apply general communication skills and principles into the specific context of interpersonal conflict. Developing competence in these eight skills will empower you to manage conflict competently, graciously, and effectively.

SOCIAL MEDIA AND CONFLICT

Conflict is not confined to face-to-face interaction. We also experience conflict in online and digital environments. In this section, we consider the constructive and destructive potential of communicating about conflict online and digitally.

A key advantage of social media for dealing with conflict is that it allows us to step away. Sometimes arguments get very heated. In face-to-face communication, it's difficult to call a time out because the person we are arguing with is present with us and often as engaged as we are in the conflict. With online and digital communication, by contrast, we can step aside. We can choose to delay replying or to not reply to a quarrelsome email, a provocative comment on a blog, or an insulting text message. We can give ourselves time to cool off before responding, if we choose to respond at all. In addition, social media allow us to reflect on our messages and to edit our communication before hitting the send button.

At the same time, digital and online communication can exacerbate conflict. When hostilities intensify in online environments, the result may be **flaming**, which is excessively insulting another person online, often using language that is derogatory or obscene. Someone who disagrees with a comment you post may respond with "You are ruining the gene pool." It is tempting to send a reciprocal insult, which is likely to up the ante and lead the other person to send an even more offensive insult. Because the two people are not physically in each other's presence and may not even know each other personally, it's easy to exchange messages you would never say to a person's face. Flame wars are generally unproductive.

There are several ways to respond to flaming. First, you can just ignore it. Refusing to reply deprives the flamer of knowing she or he upset you, so the flamer is not encouraged to continue. Second, if you think a flamer is offending others by engaging in hate speech or other truly harmful behavior, consider asking the system administrator or chat room moderator to intervene. A third option is to move the conversation out of a public space, such as a chat room or social network. Ask the flamer to continue the discussion privately through email or another medium.

The advice to check perceptions with others is particularly important in online communication. I recently had a conflict with colleague with whom I co-author articles. We had different ideas about how we should frame an article we were writing. After we discussed our differences, I decided her approach was better than mine so I emailed her a short message: "Okay. We'll go with your frame." She thought my short reply might signal that I was offended or angry, so she called me to ask if I really agreed with her frame or was just going along to end the conflict. When we check perceptions by paraphrasing and asking questions about another's meaning, we communicate, "You matter to me. I'm trying to understand you."

GUIDELINES FOR EFFECTIVE COMMUNICATION DURING CONFLICT

Our study of conflict, along with many of the ideas we've considered in previous chapters, suggests five guidelines for dealing with conflict constructively.

Focus on the Overall Communication System

As we noted in Chapter 1, communication is systemic, which means it occurs in contexts, and it is composed of many interacting parts. Applying the principle of systems to conflict, we can see that how we deal with conflict is shaped by the overall systems of relationships and communication.

People who have developed negative interpersonal climates cannot argue constructively simply by practicing "good conflict techniques" such as focusing talk and not interrupting. Those techniques occur within larger contexts that affect how they are interpreted. People who have learned to be generally defensive and distrustful are unlikely to respond openly to even the best conflict resolution methods. By the same reasoning, in climates that are generally supportive and confirming, even unconstructive conflict communication is unlikely to derail relationships. Conflict, like all interaction, is affected by larger contexts in which it takes place.

In other words, conflict is part of a larger whole, and we must make that whole healthy to create a context in which conflict can be resolved without jeopardizing partners or relationships. Keep in mind that conflict always has implications for three parties: you, another person, and the relationship between the two of you. Healthy conflict communication honors all three.

Time Conflict Purposefully

Timing affects how we communicate about conflicts. There are three ways to use chronemics so that conflicts are most likely to be effective.

First, try not to engage in serious conflict discussions at times when one or both people will not be fully present psychologically. Most of us are less attentive, less mindful listeners when we are tired. It's generally more productive to discuss problems in private rather than in public settings (Cupach & Carlson, 2002). If time is limited or if we are rushing, we're less likely to take the time to deal constructively with differences. It's impossible to listen well and respond thoughtfully when a stopwatch is ticking in our minds.

It's also considerate and constructive to deal with conflict when each person is ready to talk constructively about a problem. Of course, this works only if the person who isn't ready agrees to talk about the issue at a later time. Because research indicates that men are more likely than women to avoid discussing relationship conflicts, they may be especially reluctant to talk about disagreements without first gaining some distance (Beck, 1988; Rusbult, 1987). Some people prefer to tackle problems as soon as they arise, whereas others need time to percolate privately before interacting. It's generally a good idea not to discuss conflict in the heat of anger. For the same reason, it's wise to save an email reply you write when angry to see if that's what you want to send when you've cooled down. Constructive, healthy conflict communication is more likely when tempers aren't flaring.

STEPHANIE I have a really hot temper, so I can cut someone to pieces if I argue when I'm mad. I have hurt a lot of friends by attacking them before I cooled off, and I hate myself when I act like that. I have finally figured out that I can handle fights constructively if I cool down. Now when I'm hot, I tell my friends or my boyfriend that I can't discuss it right then. Later, when I'm calm, I can talk without saying things that hurt them and that I feel bad about.

A third use of chronemics to promote positive conflict is bracketing, which we discussed earlier in this chapter. It is natural for a variety of issues needing attention to come up in the course of conflict. If we try to deal with all the sideline problems that arise, however, we can't focus on the immediate problem. Bracketing other concerns for later discussion lets us keep conflict focused productively. Keep in mind, however, that bracketing works only if partners return to the issues they set aside.

Aim for Win–Win Conflict

How you approach conflict shapes what will happen in communication. When conflict exists between two people who care about each other and want to sustain a good relationship, the win–win style is usually the best choice. If you enter conflict with the assumption that you, the other person, and the relationship can all benefit from conflict, it's likely that you will bring about a resolution that benefits everyone. Adopting a win–win orientation to conflict reflects a commitment to honoring yourself, the other person, and the integrity of your shared relationship.

To maximize the chance of a win–win conflict resolution, begin by identifying your feelings and your needs or desires in the situation. You may want to review Chapter 7 to remind yourself of ways to clarify your emotions. Understanding your feelings and desires is essential to productive conflict communication. Once you figure out what you feel and need, express yourself in clear language. It's not effective to make vague or judgmental statements such as, "I don't like the way you ignore me, and I want you to be more sensitive." It would be more effective to say, "I feel hurt when you don't call, and I want us to find some way in which I can be assured of your love without making you feel handcuffed."

The second step is to figure out what the other person feels, needs, and wants. If you don't already know what the other person wants and feels, don't mind read. Instead, ask the other person what she or he is feeling and what she or he needs or wants in terms of a resolution to the conflict. When the other person expresses feelings and preferences, listen mindfully. Resist the temptation to countercomplain. Just listen, and try to understand the other person's perspective as fully as you can. Minimal encouragers and paraphrasing let the other person know you are listening closely and are committed to understanding her or his perspective.

Third, focus on language that promotes cooperation and mutual respect. To do this, rely on supportive communication, and try to avoid communication that fosters a defensive climate. You should also use *I* language to own your thoughts and feelings. Throughout conflict communication, mindful listening allows you to gain the maximum understanding of the other person's perspective and feelings.

Finally, keep reminding yourself that win–win solutions are most likely when both people balance concern for themselves and concern for each other. On the relationship level of meaning, you want to communicate this message: "I care about you and your feelings and desires, and I know you care about me and how I feel and what I want." If that message underlies your conflict communication, chances are good that you will attain a win–win resolution.

Honor Yourself, Your Partner, and the Relationship

Throughout this book, we've emphasized the importance of honoring yourself, others, and relationships. It's important to keep all three in balance especially when conflicts arise.

Constructive conflict communication is impossible if we disregard or demean the other person's needs and feelings. Doing so disconfirms the other and sets a win–lose tone for conversation. It is equally undesirable to muffle your own needs and feelings. In fairness to yourself and the other person, you should express your feelings and needs clearly.

In addition to attending to ourselves and others, we must remember that relationships are affected by how we handle conflict. For this reason, win–lose orientations toward conflict should really be called win–lose–lose because when only one person wins, both the other person and the relationship lose. Win–win orientations and constructive forms of communication make it possible for both individuals and the relationship to win.

Show Grace When Appropriate

Finally, an important principle to keep in mind during conflict is that grace is sometimes appropriate. **Grace** is granting forgiveness or putting aside our own needs when there is no standard that says we should or must do so. Grace is not the same thing as forgiving because social norms indicate we *should*. For instance, most people in Western culture believe that we should excuse inappropriate behavior from individuals who are sick or not able to control their behavior for other reasons. While this is appropriate, and often kind, this is not an act of grace; rather, it is a response to social norms.

Also, grace isn't allowing others to have their way when we have no choice. Instead, grace is unearned, unrequired kindness. For instance, two roommates agree to split chores, and one doesn't do her share because she has three tests in a week. Her roommate might do all the chores even though there is no agreement or expectation of this generosity. This is an act of grace. It's also an act of grace to defer to another person's preference when you could hold out for your own. Similarly, when someone hurts us and has no right to expect forgiveness, we may choose to forgive anyway. We do so not because we have to but because we want to. Grace is a matter of choice.

Grace involves letting go of anger, blame, and judgments about another and what she or he did. When we let go of these feelings, we release both ourselves and others from their consequences. Sometimes, we tell a friend that we forgive him for some offense, but then later we remind him of it. When we hang on to blame and judgment, we haven't really let go, so we have not

© mangostock/Shutterstock.com

really shown grace. There's no grace when we blackmail others for our kindness or hang on to hostile feelings.

Grace is given without strings. Arthur Osborne (1996) believes that grace is essential in loving relationships. He says, "The person who asks for a reward is a merchant, not a lover" (p. 6). We show kindness, defer our needs, or forgive a wrong without any expectation of reward. Grace isn't doing something nice to make a friend feel grateful or indebted to us. Nor do we act in grace when we do something with the expectation of a payback. To do a favor because you want a reciprocal favor is bargaining, not showing grace. For an act to be one of grace, it must be done without conditions or expectations of return.

Grace is not always appropriate. People can take advantage of grace and kindness. Some people repeatedly abuse and hurt others, confident that pardons will be granted. When grace is extended and then exploited, it may be unwise to extend it again to the same person. However, if you show grace in good faith, and another abuses it, you should not fault yourself. Kindness and a willingness to forgive are worthy ethical values. The richest and most enduring relationships allow room for grace occasionally.

It is important to honor and assert ourselves, as we've emphasized throughout this book. However, self-interest and self-assertion alone are insufficient ethical principles for creating rich interpersonal relationships. None of us is perfect. We all make mistakes, wound others with thoughtless acts, and occasionally do things we know are wrong and hurtful. Sometimes, there is no reason others should forgive us when we wrong them; we have no right to expect exoneration.

Reflecting on the value of granting grace for all parties, one writer (Walters, 1984) offered this moving insight: "When we have been hurt we have two alternatives: be destroyed by resentment, or forgive. Resentment is death; forgiving leads to healing and life" (p. 366). For human relationships to live and thrive, there must be some room for redemption, for forgiveness, and for grace.

Communication in Everyday Life

INSIGHT

The Communication of Forgiveness

Douglas Kelley (1998) and Vincent Waldron (Waldron & Kelley, 2007) emphasize forgiveness as a major influence on how—or whether—relationships progress. They note that transgressions, both minor and major, are inevitable in relationships, so the question becomes, "How do couples go forward after harm has been done?"

Waldron and Kelley state that one crucial dynamic in the forgiveness process is motivations of both the transgressor and the forgiver. Forgiveness is most likely to occur and to allow relationship continuity when both parties are motivated by a desire to restore the well-being of themselves, each other, and the relationship. People are more likely to grant forgiveness to a person who apologizes, expresses remorse, or takes responsibility for the wrong. Kelley and Waldron also state that the capacity to forgive is enhanced if the forgiver can reframe the hurtful event by gaining understanding into it, attributing it to factors beyond the offender's control, or viewing it as unintentional. Finally, Waldron and Kelley emphasize that forgiving is a process, not an event that occurs in a single moment. They emphasize that even after forgiveness is granted, time is needed to heal a relationship, restore trust, and return to healthy, comfortable interaction.

Adding to Waldron and Kelly's research is a study by William Cupach and Christine Carlson (2002). They found that forgiveness is more than a set of behaviors and more than efforts to overcome negative feelings, such as wanting revenge. At least as important, they report, is a desire to accept and confirm another, even—or especially—after a transgression of some sort.

Visit The Forgiveness Institute's website: http://www.forgivenessweb.com/

CHAPTER SUMMARY

Because conflicts are normal and unavoidable in any relationship of real depth, the challenge is to learn to manage conflicts effectively. Patterns of conflict are shaped by how people view conflict. We discussed lose–lose, win–lose, and win–win approaches to conflict and explored how each affects interaction. In addition, conflict patterns are influenced by how people respond to tension. Inclinations to exit, neglect, show loyalty, or voice conflict vary in how actively they deal with tension and how constructive they are for relationships. In most cases, voice is the preferred response because only voice allows partners to communicate actively and constructively when conflicts arise.

Communication is a particularly important influence on interpersonal conflict. Communication skills that promote constructive conflict management include being mindful, confirming others, showing dual perspective, listening sensitively, focusing discussion, contracting solutions, and avoiding mind reading, interrupting, self-summarizing, and cross-complaining. These skills are valuable for handling online conflict as well as face-to-face conflict.

We closed the chapter by identifying five guidelines for increasing the productivity of interpersonal conflict. First, we need to remember that conflicts occur within overall systems of communication and relationships. To be constructive, conflict must take place within supportive, confirming climates in which good interpersonal communication is practiced. Second, it's important to time conflicts so that all people have the time they need for private reflection and for productive discussion. This second guideline is particularly important when conflict arises on social media. Stepping away to get perspective can save you from posting comments you might later regret. A third principle is to aim for win–win solutions. Consistent with these three guidelines is working to balance commitments to yourself, others, and relationships when conflict arises.

Although grace can be exploited, it can also infuse relationships with kindness and make room for inevitable human errors. It's important to balance the tensions inherent in the notion of grace so that we recognize both its potential values and its dangers.

 **MindTap**™

Key Concepts

Practice defining the chapter's terms by using online flashcards.

FLASHCARDS...

Continuing the Conversation

Copyright Wadsworth 2013

When you've watched the video online, critique and analyze this encounter based on the principles you learned in this chapter. Then compare your work with the author's suggested responses. Online, even more videos will let you continue the conversation with your instructor.

Andrea and her sister Ellie.

Andrea: What are you working on?

Ellie: This book for French lit—I'm way behind.

Andrea: Can I talk to you for a few minutes?

Ellie: I'm really behind. Can it wait?

Andrea: I promise I'll be quick.

Ellie: Fine. What?

Andrea: That's part of it. The way you just said "what?" Like you're already annoyed.

Ellie: I told you I'm busy. So yeah, you're annoying me.

Andrea: You're so short with me lately.

Ellie: [trying to lighten the mood] You're my sister, you're supposed to annoy me.

Andrea: But lately it happens a lot. And sometimes you get a little out of hand. Like the other night.

Ellie: What about the other night?

Andrea: You tried to throw your alarm clock at me when we argued about whose turn it was to do the laundry.

Ellie: But I didn't throw it.

Andrea: Yeah, because it was plugged in.

Ellie: What do you want me to say?

Andrea: I want to know why you're so angry all the time over nothing.

Ellie: [angry and defensive] Nothing?! I had two exams the next day when you told me I had to do the laundry! What you call nothing is my education, my future! It's not my fault that you're too lazy or too much of a jerk to care about your classes or lift a finger around here!

Andrea: This is what I mean. You never used to call me names. You never used to yell. We would talk. I'm afraid to even try to talk to you. And sometimes I'm sorry—not to mention hurt—when I do try.

Ellie: I'm sorry. You're the only person I have to vent to and sometimes I get a little carried away.

Andrea: More than a little. It seems like we never talk anymore.

Ellie: What are we doing now?

Andrea: Sarcasm doesn't help, Ellie. I mean really talk—I think we need that. Your classes are a lot harder than mine this semester, it makes sense that you might need to release stress.

Ellie: I assume you mean in some way other than throwing objects at your head?

Andrea: Well, yeah. But also in ways that will help you feel better.

Ellie: Yeah, I did feel bad about that the other night. I'm sorry.

Andrea: I am too, for not being as understanding as I could about your schedule and stress. Maybe if we set aside a time each week to sit down and talk, we could avoid these fights.

Ellie: That makes sense. I do feel like I don't know what's going on with you anymore. Let's plan a lunch date this week.

1. Think about the different conflict orientations demonstrated by Ellie and Andrea in this scenario. What kind of conflict orientation does Ellie demonstrate? What kind of conflict orientation does Andrea demonstrate? Support your answer.
2. Identify the responses to conflict that are present in this scenario: do you see inclinations to exit, neglect, show loyalty, or voice conflict? What consequences result from the conflict responses used in this dialog?
3. Is metacommunication used constructively or unproductively in this conversation and by whom?

4. Review the eight conflict management skills discussed in this chapter. Identify examples of these skills in the dialogue between Andrea and Elle.

Assessing Yourself

Begin the process of applying this chapter's concepts by taking self-assessment quizzes here or online—where you will find out what the results mean.

1. Identifying Your Conflict Orientations

Purpose: Discover your own orientation to conflict.

Instructions: Answer the questions as honestly as you can.

1. When conflict seems about to occur, do you
   a. think of arguments that promote your solution?
   b. worry that everyone is going to get hurt?
   c. think that there's probably a way to satisfy everyone?

2. When involved in conflict, do you
   a. feel competitive urges?
   b. feel resigned that everyone will lose?
   c. feel committed to finding a mutual solution?

3. When you disagree with another person, do you
   a. assume the other person is wrong?
   b. assume neither of you is right?
   c. assume there are good reasons for what each of you thinks and feels?

2. Identifying Your Styles of Responding to Conflict

Instructions: Identify your styles of responding to conflict.

Purpose: Read the scenarios below. For each one, indicate which of the four possible responses you think it is most likely you would follow.

1. The person that you have been dating for 6 months tells you she or he is upset by your lack of interest in spending time with her or his friends. You don't want to spend time with your partner's friends, but she or he sees this as an issue that the two of you need to resolve. In this situation, you would be most likely to

5. How do you perceive the role of forgiveness in this conversation? Based on what you've learned in this chapter, can you explain why Andrea seems so quick to forgive Elle for her behavior?

MindTap™

PRACTICE...

a. walk out on the conversation.
b. tell her/him that the issue isn't important.
c. say nothing and hope the issue will go away.
d. actively work to find a resolution that satisfies both of you.

2. Last week a friend let you use his or her computer when yours crashed. Accidentally, you erased a couple of files on your friend's computer. Later, the friend confronts you about the erased files and seems really angry. In this situation, you would be most likely to
   a. tune out your friend's criticism and anger.
   b. agree that you made an error and ask how you could make it up to your friend.
   c. say nothing and hope your friend's anger blows over and the friendship continues.
   d. tell your friend that it's not a big deal since he or she always backs up the hard drive.

3. Your roommate tells you that you are a slob and that she or he wants the two of you to agree to some ground rules about cleaning and putting things up. In this situation, you would be most likely to
   a. agree to be more neat, even though you don't think it's fair that you should have to operate by your roommate's standards.
   b. tell your roommate that cleaning is not a big deal in the big picture of living together.
   c. agree that the two of you differ in how you like the place to look and offer to work out some mutually acceptable rules.
   d. leave the situation and hope that your roommate will let the matter drop.

4. The person you have been dating for a while says that you are too critical and too negative, and she or he says that she or he wants you to work on changing that aspect of your behavior. Although you realize this may be a fair criticism of you, you find it uncomfortable to hear. Further, you have no idea how

you could eliminate or improve your tendency to be judgmental. In this situation, you would be most likely to

a. agree with your dating partner's perceptions and ask if she or he has any suggestions for how you might reduce your critical, negative tendencies.

b. shrug and ignore the criticism.

c. say nothing and hope things get better.

d. point out that being critical is not really a major issue in whether two people are compatible.

5. Your parents call you to criticize you for not staying in touch. They say they want you to come home more often and call a couple of times each week. You are very involved in the campus scene and don't want to be running home all the time. In this situation, you would be most likely to

a. tell your parents they are creating a problem when none really exists.

b. agree that you haven't stayed in touch and promise to be better in the future; then follow through on your promise even though it isn't your preference.

c. tell your parents that you want to work with them to come up with ways you can stay in better touch without separating you from the campus too much.

d. hang up the phone and not return their calls in the future.

Everyday Skills

Build your communication skills further by completing the following activities here or online.

1. Understanding Your Conflict Script

What conflict script did you learn in your family? Think back to your childhood and adolescence, and try to remember rules for conflict that your family modeled implicitly and principles of conflict that your family explicitly endorsed.

+ Did people disagree openly with each other?
+ What was said when disagreements surfaced? Did your parents suggest that it was rude to argue? Did they encourage open discussion of differences? Were there any "rules" for how to argue?
+ What happened if disagreements were dealt with directly? Was the conflict resolved? What was the climate in the family like after the conflict?

+ How do you currently reflect your family's conflict script? Now that you can edit family scripts and author your own, how would you like to deal with conflict?

2. Identifying Games in Your Communication

Apply what you've read about covert conflict to your own life. Describe an instance when you or someone you have a relationship with played each of the following games. What was accomplished by playing each game? Were the real conflicts addressed?

Blemish _____

NIGYYSOB _____

Mine Is Worse Than Yours _____

Yes, But _____

MindTap **DO...** Additional interactive discussions, online quizzes, and activities that your instructor may assign for a grade.

Engaging with Ideas

Reflect and write about the ideas in this chapter by considering questions about personal, workplace, and ethical applications, here or online.

Personal Application Reflect on the ways you respond to conflict. Are you satisfied with how you manage conflict? If not, experiment with some alternative ways of responding to conflict that are described in this chapter.

REFLECT ON...

Workplace Application Recall a time when you experienced conflict with a coworker. How did the overall communication system in that workplace shape communication in that situation?

Ethical Application To what extent and under what conditions do you consider it ethical to exit conflict by refusing to reply to texts or emails? Does refusing to engage deny the other person an opportunity to resolve the conflict?

Thinking Critically

Think and write critically about the ideas in this chapter, here or online.

1. What ethical principles are implicit in lose–lose, win–lose, and win–win orientations to conflict? Some styles of conflict emphasize fairness, whereas other styles place greater value on cooperation. Do you identify more strongly with either of these value emphases?

2. Think about the ways you typically respond to conflict. Do you tend to rely on one or two of the four responses we discussed (exit, voice, loyalty, neglect)? Are your response tendencies consistent with research findings about women and men, in general?

REFLECT ON...

3. Have you ever been in a relationship in which conflict was stifled? Using the concepts you learned in this chapter, can you now describe how the conflict was repressed? Can you now think of ways you might have engaged in more effective conflict communication in that relationship?

4. Have you been in relationships in which you felt there was grace? How was grace communicated? What was the impact of grace? Have you extended grace to others?

Jeff Baker/Taxi/Getty Images

FRIENDSHIPS IN OUR LIVES

START... experiencing this chapter's topics with an online video!

Topics covered in this chapter

The Nature of Friendship

The Development of Friendship

Pressures on Friendships

Social Media and Friendships

Guidelines for Communication between Friends

After studying this chapter, you should be able to . . .

Recognize five Western expectations of friendship.

Connect the stages of friendship development to your own.

Recognize challenges to sustaining friendships.

Identify advantages and disadvantages of both face-to-face and online friendships.

Apply chapter guidelines to communicate more clearly with friends.

READ... the complete chapter text in a rich interactive eBook!

How would you like to win a $1,000 scholarship? To apply, you need to write an essay on what it means to be a friend and you need to have two of your friends confirm that you are a good friend. Believe it or not, this scholarship is for real, but you also have to be from Ames, Iowa, to apply for it. The scholarship honors Sheila Walsh, one of eleven women from the class of 1981 at Ames High School in Iowa. These 11 women were friends in high school, and 10 of them remain close friends. The 11th, Sheila Walsh, died at 22. The remaining 10 friends created the scholarship to honor the friend they lost and to honor the value of long-term friendships (Zaslow, 2009; "A Scholarship," 2009).

Like the women from Ames, most of us value friendships. We know what a comfort friends can be when we're sad and how much they multiply our happiness when life is good. In this chapter, we explore what friendships are, how they work, and how they differ among people. To launch our discussion, we identify common features of friendship and then point out variations across cultures and social communities. Second, we explore the typical developmental path of friendships and some of the common rules for friendships. Next, we consider pressures on friendship and how we can deal with them. We then consider relationships between social media and friendship. Guidelines for effective communication between friends conclude the chapter.

THE NATURE OF FRIENDSHIP

Friendship is a unique relationship. Unlike most relationships, friendship is voluntary. Biology or legal procedures establish relationships between family members, and proximity defines neighbors and coworkers. But friends come together voluntarily. Unlike marital and family relationships, friendships lack institutionalized structure or guidelines. Legal and religious ceremonies govern marriage, and social norms and laws regulate family relationships. We have no ceremonies to recognize friendships and no formal standards to guide interaction between friends.

> It's funny. Kids have ways to symbolize friendship, but adults don't. I remember when Jimmy, down the block, and I became blood brothers. It was a big, big deal for me at 8. My sister and her best friend bought matching friendship rings and wore them until their fingers turned green. But what do we have to symbolize friendships when we grow up?

WILL

Even though there are no formal standards for friendship, people within a culture hold some fairly consistent ideas about what a friend is and what happens between friends. Regardless of race, sexual orientation, gender, age, and class, most Westerners share five basic expectations of friends and friendship (Nardi & Sherrod, 1994; Parks & Floyd, 1996b).

Willingness to Invest

Friendships grow out of personal investments, which we discussed in Chapter 8 (Branje, Frijns, Finkenauer, Engles, & Meeus, 2007; Ledbetter, Griffin & Sparks, 2007). We expect to invest time, effort, thought, and feeling in our friendships, and we may also invest materially by lending or giving money, gifts, and other items of value. The investments that we make tend to stoke our commitment to friendships.

> I really count on my buddies to be there for me. Sometimes, we talk or do stuff, but a lot of times we just hang out together. That might not sound important, but it is. Hanging out with friends is a big part of my life.

DENNIS

Emotional Closeness

Emotional intimacy grows out of investments, such as time, talk, and shared experiences. As people spend time together, they tend to become more comfortable being together and to have an increased sense of bonding. Although most people agree that closeness is central to friendships, sex and gender influence how we experience and express intimacy with friends.

Closeness through Dialogue   For some people, communication is the centerpiece of friendship. This is especially true for people socialized in feminine speech communities, which emphasize talk as a primary path to intimacy. In general, women see talking and listening—face-to-face or via social media—as the main activities that create and sustain closeness (Bodey & Wood, 2009; Wood, 2015; Wright, 2006). Talk between women friends tends to be disclosive and emotionally expressive (Braithwaite & Kellas, 2006; Metts, 2006b). Women discuss not only major issues but also day-to-day activities. This "small" talk isn't unimportant because it allows friends to weave their worlds together and to understand the rhythms of each other's life (Braithwaite & Kellas, 2006; Metts, 2006b). Out of intimate conversation, friends build a deep sense of connection.

A majority of women expect to know and be known intimately by close friends. They want friends to know and understand their inner selves, and they want to know their friends at the same emotional depth. This is also true of men who have build closeness through dialogue.

LORI ANN My girlfriends and I know everything about each other. We tell all our feelings and don't hold anything back. I mean, it's total knowledge. We give updates on each new episode in our relationships, and we talk about what it means. There's just nothing I wouldn't tell my friends.

Reflecting feminine socialization, communication between women friends typically is responsive and supportive (Guerrero et al., 2006b; Mulac, 2006; Wood, 2010, 2014). Animated facial expressions and head movements convey involvement and emotional response in face-to-face encounters, and quick replies, often with emoticons, to text messages and online postings convey responsiveness in social media. In addition, women friends ask questions and give feedback to signal that they are following and want to know more. Women friends also tend to give emotional support to one another. They do this by accepting one another's feelings and by staying involved in the other's dreams, problems, and lives.

Closeness through Doing   A second way to create and express closeness is by sharing activities. Friends enjoy doing things together and doing things for one another. Closeness through doing often is the primary, but not the only, emphasis in men's friendships (Inman, 1996; Metts, 2006b; Monsour, 2006; Swain, 1989; Wood & Inman, 1993). Given the focus on doing things together, it's not surprising that male friends tend to engage in fewer verbal emotional disclosures (Burleson, Holmstrom, & Gilstrap, 2005) and spend more time engaging in activities ("You've really improved your swing.") than female friends or male and female friends (Samter & Cupach, 1998). Sharing activities and working toward common goals

© bikeriderlondon/Shutterstock.com

(winning the game, getting the contract) build a sense of camaraderie (Inman, 1996; Walker, 2004).

JOSH

The thing I like about my buddies is that we can just do stuff together without a lot of talk. Our wives expect us to talk about every feeling we have, as if that's required to be real. I'm tight with my buddies, but we don't have to talk about feelings all the time. You learn a lot about someone when you hunt together or coach Little League.

Josh has a good insight. We reveal ourselves and learn about others by doing things together. In the course of playing football or soccer, teammates learn a lot about one another's courage, reliability, willingness to take risks, and self-confidence. Soldiers who fight together also discover one another's strengths and weaknesses. Strong emotional bonds and personal knowledge can develop without verbal interaction. Intimacy through doing also involves expressing care by doing things for friends. Scott Swain (1989) says men's friendships typically involve a give-and-take of favors. Jake helps Matt move into his new apartment, and Matt later helps Jake install a new program on his computer. Perhaps because masculine socialization emphasizes instrumental activities, men are more likely than women to see doing things for others as a primary way to say they care.

It would be a mistake to conclude that women and men are radically different in how they create intimacy. They are actually more alike than we often think (Parks & Floyd, 1996b; Wright, 2006). Although women generally place a special priority on communication, men obviously talk with their friends. Like women, men disclose personal feelings, hopes, and concerns. They simply do it less, as a rule, than women. Similarly, although men's friendships may be more activity focused than women's, women also do things with and for their friends and count these activities as important in friendship.

Sometimes, different emphases on instrumental and expressive behaviors lead to misunderstandings. If Myra sees intimate talk as the crux of closeness, she may not interpret Ed's practical help in fixing her computer as indicating that he cares about her.

Yet different emphases on dialogue and doing can also enrich friendships. Many men and women enjoy friendships with members of the other sex because they find their differences stimulating. In a recent study by Aaronette White (2006), African American men said they valued close friendships with women because they could practice interpersonal communication skills with women friends, but not men friends. Men also report getting more support and attention from female than male friends (Burleson et al., 2005; Koesten, 2004).

KAYA

My husband's life centers on doing things for me and our kids. He looks for things to do for us. Like when our son came home over break, he tuned up his car and replaced a tire. I hadn't even noticed the tire was bad. When I wanted to return to school, he took a second job to make more money. One day, he came home with a microwave to make cooking easier for me. All the things he does for us are his way of expressing love.

 MindTap

Everyday Skills To practice how you might show caring by talking and doing, complete the activity "Appreciating Talking and Doing in Friendships" at the end of the chapter or online.

Acceptance

We expect friends to accept us, including our flaws. Each of us has shortcomings, and we count on friends to accept us in spite of them. With people we don't know well, we often feel we need to put on our best face to impress them. With friends, however, we don't want to put up false fronts. If we feel low, we can act that way instead of faking cheerfulness. If we are upset, we don't have to hide it. If someone dumped us, we don't have to pretend we feel fine.

As we saw with Maslow's hierarchy of human needs in Chapter 1, being accepted by others is important to our sense of self-worth. Most of us are fortunate enough to gain acceptance from family and friends. However, this is not always true. Some parents of gays, lesbians, and transpeople refuse to validate their children's basic worth.

For the late Captain Phil Harris of TV's *The Deadliest Catch,* his work friends, and sons Josh (left) and Jake (right), the often split-second tasks to be handled on a crabbing boat required an emphasis on instrumental behaviors.

MARTIN

It isn't just the homosexual who is outed. Everyone in that person's life is affected when he comes out. My ex-wife was devastated when I told her I was gay. She felt it said something about her as a woman. My father and stepmother are homophobic. They are more fearful of how friends and family will judge them than they are concerned with my issues. My coming out was all about their embarrassment and fear.

Because social and familial acceptance sometimes is lacking for them, gender-nonconforming people may count on friends for acceptance even more than heterosexuals do (Nardi & Sherrod, 1994; Roberts & Orbe, 1996). Friendships may have heightened importance because they often substitute for families as reflected in the title of Kath Weston's 1991 book, *Families We Choose.* Although lesbians, trans, bi, and gay people may depend more heavily than heterosexuals on friends for acceptance, research has not identified major differences in how their friendships operate. Gay, lesbian, and bisexual adolescents report that they are equally close to GLB and straight friends, contact them with equal frequency, and have equal hassles with them. The one difference is that GLB youth find their GLB friends are more supportive of their sexual orientation than their straight friends (Ueno, Gayman, Wright & Quantz, 2009).

Like heterosexuals, gay men and lesbians value friendship and rely on both talking and doing as paths to intimacy (Nardi & Sherrod, 1994; Parks & Floyd, 1996b).

Trust

A key component of close friendships is trust, which has two dimensions. First, trust involves confidence that others will be dependable. We count on them to do what they say they'll do and not to do what they promise they won't. Second, trust is rooted in the belief that a friend cares about us and our welfare. We count on friends to look out for us and to want the best for us. When we believe that both dimensions of trust are present, we feel safe sharing private information with friends, and secure in the knowledge that they will not hurt us.

> Trust is the bottom line for friends. It's the single most important thing. It takes me a long time to really trust someone, but when I do, it's complete. I was so hurt when a friend told another person something I told her in confidence. We still get together, but the trust is gone. I don't tell her private things, so there's no depth.

SARINI

Like most qualities of friendship, trust develops gradually and in degrees. We learn to trust people over time as we interact with them and discover that they do what they say they will, the care about our happiness, and they don't betray us. As trust develops, friends increasingly reveal themselves to one another. In turn, self-disclosures fuel feelings of intimacy and commitment to the friendship.

The level of trust that develops between friends depends on a number of factors. First, our individual histories influence our capacity to trust others. Recalling the discussion of attachment styles in Chapter 2, you'll remember that early interactions with caregivers shape our beliefs about others. For those of us who received consistently loving and nurturing care, trusting others is not especially difficult. On the other hand, some children do not get that kind of care. If caring is absent or inconsistent, the capacity to trust others is jeopardized.

> It's tough for me to really trust anybody, even my closest friends or my girlfriend. It's not that they aren't trustworthy. The problem's in me. I just have trouble putting full faith in anyone. When my parents had me, Dad was drinking, and Mom was thinking about divorce. He got in Alcoholics Anonymous, and they stayed together, but I wonder if what was happening between them meant they weren't there for me. Maybe I learned from the start that I couldn't count on others.

JAMES

Family scripts also influence how much and how quickly we trust others. Did your parents have many friends? Did you see them enjoying being with their friends? Were their friends often in your home? Basic scripts from families, although not irrevocable, often affect the ease and extent of our ability to trust and our interest in investing in friendships.

Willingness to take risks also influences trust in relationships. In this sense, trust is a leap into the unknown. To emphasize the risk in trusting, it has been said that "trust begins where knowledge ends" (Lewis & Weigert, 1985, p. 462). The risk involved may explain why we trust only selected people.

Support

We expect friends to support us. There are many ways to show support. Common to the various types of support is the relationship message, "I care about you." Often, we support friends by listening to their problems. The more mindfully

HBO/Photofest

Support is a key part of the close friendship among four very different twenty-somethings in the HBO comedy-drama series *Girls*.

we listen, the more support we provide. How we respond also shows support. For example, it's supportive to offer to help a friend with a problem or to talk through options. Another way we support friends is by letting them know they're not alone. When we say, "I've felt that way, too" or "I've had the same problem," we signal that we understand their feelings. Having the grace to accept friends when they err or hurt us is also a way to show support and validate their worth.

Another important form of support is availability. Sometimes we can't do or say much to ease a friend's unhappiness. However, we can be with friends so that at least they have company in their sadness. In one study, young adults said the essence of real friendship was "being there for each other" (Secklin, 1991). Increasingly, people rely on friends for support online—being there for them emotionally when they can't be there physically (Carl, 2006).

Women and men tend to differ somewhat in how they support friends. Because feminine socialization emphasizes personal communication, women generally provide more verbal emotional support than men do (Becker, 1987; Johnson, 2000; Monsour, 2006). They are likely to talk in detail about feelings, dimensions of emotional issues, and fears that accompany distress. By talking in depth about emotional troubles, women help one another identify and vent feelings and work out problems.

RICH If I don't want to think about some problem, I want to be with a guy friend. He'll take my mind off the hassle. If I'm with a girl, she'll want to talk about the problem and wallow in it, and that just makes it worse sometimes. But when I really need to talk or get something off my chest, I need a girl friend. Guys don't talk about personal stuff.

Men often provide support to friends through "covert intimacy," a term Swain (1989) coined to describe the indirect ways men support one another. Instead of an intimate hug, men are more likely to clasp a shoulder or playfully punch an arm. Instead of engaging in direct and sustained emotional talk, men tend to communicate support more instrumentally. This could mean giving advice on how to solve a problem, or offering assistance, such as a loan or transportation. Finally, men are more likely than women to support friends by coming up with diversions (Cancian, 1987; Walker, 2004). If you can't make a problem any better, at least you can take a friend's mind off it. "Let's go shoot some baskets" provides a diversion.

BELLINO A year ago, a friend of mine from back home called me up to ask for a loan. I said, "Sure," and asked what was up. He told me his hours had been cut back and he couldn't buy groceries for his family. I knew the problem was more than paying for groceries. I figured he also couldn't pay for lights and rent and everything else. So I talked with several of his friends in our church, and we took up a collection to help him. Then, I took it over and left it at his house without any note and without saying anything. He didn't have to ask for help, and I didn't have to say anything.

Culture also influences orientations toward friendship. In a study of Japanese and American friendships, Dean Barnlund (1989) found that both groups preferred friends who were similar to them in age and ethnic heritage. Yet Japanese respondents said togetherness, trust, and warmth were the most important qualities in friendship, whereas Americans listed understanding, respect, and sincerity as the top qualities. The differences in rankings reflect distinctions between Japanese and American culture. Interpersonal harmony and collective orientation are central values in Japan, whereas American culture emphasizes individuality, candor, and respect.

Another study (Collier, 1996) identified different priorities for friendship in four ethnic groups. European Americans give priority to sincerity and freedom to express ideas. Consistent with traditional Asian cultural values, many Asian Americans especially value courtesy, restraint, and respect for families. Among African Americans, problem solving and respect for ethnic heritage were primary criteria in selecting friends. Collier also found that Latinas and Latinos see relationship support and emotional expressiveness as priorities.

In sum, friendship grows out of investments, emotional closeness, acceptance, trust, and support. Our membership in different cultures and social communities may lead to variations in how we experience and express friendship. However, it seems that these five common expectations transcend many of the differences between us.

Rick Gayle/CORBIS

THE DEVELOPMENT OF FRIENDSHIP

Although intense bonds sometimes are formed quickly, the majority of friendships evolve through a series of stages that involve progressive investments (Mongeau & Henningsen, 2008; Rawlins, 1981, 2009). Although not every friendship follows exactly the same evolution, the general trajectory describes most Western friendships.

Growth Stages

Friendships don't start off as friendships. They begin when people meet each other. We might meet a person at work, through membership on an athletic team, in a club, or by chance in an airport, store, or class. We also might encounter new people in chat rooms or newsgroups or as friends of friends on our social networking sites (Parks & Floyd, 1996a). The initial meeting is the first stage of interaction and possibly of friendship. During this stage, we tend to rely on standard social rules and roles. We tend to be polite and to limit personal disclosures.

Because new acquaintances don't have enough personal knowledge of each other to engage in dual perspective, they tend to rely on general scripts and stereotypes. Also, early interactions are often awkward and laced with uncertainty because people haven't worked out patterns for relating to each other.

In early communication, new acquaintances usually check to see whether common ground, values, and interests exist (Weinstock & Bond, 2000). After class, Jean makes a comment to Rebekah about a new film that she saw. If Rebekah responds with her impressions of the film or by asking Jean for more details, she conveys the relationship-level message that she's interested in interacting. A businessperson may joke or mention a weekly poker game to see whether an associate wants to move beyond the acquaintance level of relating. One person in an Internet newsgroup invites another member of the group to engage in individual exchange of ideas.

If invitations to move beyond social roles are reciprocated, a fledgling friendship is launched. We might make a small self-disclosure to signal that we'd like to personalize the relationship or meet outside of contexts that naturally occur. Emily might ask her associate Sam whether he wants to get a cup of coffee after work. Ben might ask his classmate Drew to get together to study. Sometimes, we involve others to lessen the potential awkwardness of being with someone we don't yet know well. For instance, Amy might invite Stuart to a party where others will be present.

Many friendships never move beyond this phase (Knapp & Vangelisti, 2005). They stabilize as pleasant but casual friendships. The friends enjoy interacting but generally don't invest a lot of effort to arrange times together. Disclosures tend to be limited as are investments and expectations of support.

But some friendships do become closer and more important. This happens as we interact more personally with others, disclose more about ourselves, have shared experiences, and share thoughts, feelings, values, concerns, interests, and so forth.

At this point, friends begin to work out their private rules for interacting. Some friends settle into patterns of getting together for specific things (watching games, shopping, racquetball, going to movies) and never expand those boundaries. Other friends share a wider range of times and activities. Although during the nascent stage friends are working out rules for their relationship, often they aren't aware of the rules until later. The milestones of this stage are that people begin to think of themselves as friends and to work out their own patterns for interaction.

Interracial friendships often require more effort than intraracial friendships, yet the basic foundations of the friendships don't differ. Acceptance and responsiveness and revealing information about yourself and accepting information about the other are keys in same and different-race friendships (Shelton, Trail, West, & Bergsieker, 2010).

At some point, people decide they are friends, whether they vocalize that explicitly or not. The touchstone of this stage is the assumption of continuity. Whereas in earlier stages people don't count on getting together unless they make a specific plan, stabilized friends assume they'll continue to see each other even if they don't have specific dates reserved. We take future interaction for granted because we consider the relationship ongoing.

A close friendship is unlikely to stabilize until there is a mutually high level of trust. Once friends have earned each other's trust, they communicate more openly and fully. As friendships become stabilized, they are often integrated into the larger contexts of each friend's social networks (Spencer & Pahl, 2006). Thus, when we interact in our social circles, we are often nurturing multiple established friendships at the same time. Stabilized friendships may continue indefinitely, in some cases lasting a lifetime.

Online communication is an increasingly popular way to maintain established friendships (Carl, 2006). Nearly two-thirds of the people that Malcolm Parks and Kory Floyd (1996a) surveyed reported that they had a good friendship with someone they first had met on the Internet. Parks and Floyd also found that friendships maintained largely through email and Internet communication were as personal and committed as those maintained through face-to-face contact.

> **MARLENE**
>
> Martha and I go way, way back—all the way to childhood, when we lived in the same housing complex. As kids, we made mud pies and ran a lemonade stand together. In high school, we double-dated and planned our lives together. Then we both got married and stayed in touch, even when Martha moved away. We still sent each other pictures of our children, and we called a lot. When my last child entered college, I decided it was time for me to do that, too, so I enrolled in college. Before I did that, though, I had to talk to Martha and get her perspective on whether I was nuts to go to college in my thirties. She thought it was a great idea, and she's thinking about that for herself now. For nearly 40 years, we've shared everything in our lives.

Friendships generally follow rules that specify what is expected and what is not allowed (Argyle & Henderson, 1985). Most of the time, we're not consciously aware of relationship rules, even though we may be following them. Typically, **relationship rules** are unspoken understandings that regulate how people interact. For instance, most friends have a tacit understanding that they can be a little late for get-togethers but won't keep each other waiting long. A delay of 5 minutes is within the rules, but a 40-minute delay is a violation. Most friends have an unspoken understanding that private information they share is to be kept confidential. The case study at the end of Chapter 9 illustrates what can happen when friends violate the unspoken rule to keep disclosures confidential. Although friends may never explicitly discuss their rules, the rules matter, as we discover when one is violated.

Rules regulate both trivial and important aspects of interaction. Not interrupting may be a rule, but breaking it probably won't destroy a good friendship. However, stealing money, jewelry, or romantic partners may be the death knell of a friendship. Although friends often develop some very unique rules, many of our friendship rules reflect cultural perspectives, as the "Communication in Everyday Life" box above demonstrates.

Deterioration Stages

When one or both friends stop investing in a friendship, it is likely to wane. Occasionally friendships end abruptly and sometimes dramatically—a tense argument, a curt text. Such abrupt endings are generally occasioned by serious breaches in trust—a confidence aired to others, stealing, lying, and so forth.

It is more common for friendships to wane gradually. Friends may drift apart because one moves or because the two are pulled in different directions by career or family demands. In other cases, friendships deteriorate because they've run their natural course and have become boring. Many, perhaps most, friendships fade slowly rather than abruptly (Schappell, 2005).

CARY Janet and I had been friends since our first year at school. We told each other everything and trusted each other totally. When I told her that Brad had cheated on me, I knew she would not tell anyone else. She knew I felt bad about it, plus Brad and I got back together, so I didn't want anyone to know about that incident. One day, I was talking with another girl, and she asked me how I'd been able to trust Brad again after he cheated on me. I hadn't told her about that! I knew she was friends with Janet, so I figured that's how she knew. To me, that was the ultimate betrayal. I'm still on friendly terms with Janet, but she's not a close friend, and I don't tell her anything private.

When friendships deteriorate or dissolve due to serious violations, communication changes in predictable ways. Defensiveness and uncertainty rise, causing people to be more guarded, less spontaneous, and less disclosive than they were. Yet the clearest indicator that a friendship is fading may be decreased quantity and quality of communication. As former friends drift apart or are hurt by each other, they are likely to interact less often and to talk about less personal and consequential topics.

Even when serious violations occur between friends, relationships sometimes can be repaired. Sometimes, friends hurt us when they are under serious stress. If we attribute something we don't like to factors that are temporary or beyond our friends' control, we may be willing to forgive them and continue the friendship. We are usually more willing to

---

Communication in Everyday Life

DIVERSITY

Friendships around the World

Like most things, friendship is shaped by culture (Atsumi, 1980; Feig, 1989; Goodwin & Plaza, 2000; Lustig & Koester, 1999; Mochizuki, 1981). People raised in the United States may befriend people who differ from them in personal values or political allegiances. Not so in Thailand, where friendship tends to be all or nothing. Thais generally don't develop friendships with anyone of whom they disapprove in any way. Among Thais, a friend is totally accepted and approved.

The Japanese distinguish between two types of friendships. *Tsukiai* are friendships based on social obligation. These usually involve neighbors or work associates and tend to have limited life spans. However, friendships based on affection and common interests usually last a lifetime; personal friendship is serious business. The number of personal friends is very small and stable, in contrast to friendship patterns in the United States. Friendships between women and men are rare in Japan. Before marriage, only 20% of Japanese say they have close friends of the opposite sex.

In Spain, friends are important both for personal support and to anchor people in the collectivist Spanish culture. In a recent study, Spanish respondents reported that they counted on friends more than on family members to provide emotional support.

stay friends with someone who hurt us unintentionally than with someone who deliberately harmed us. To revive a friendship that has waned, however, both friends must be committed to rebuilding trust and intimacy.

PRESSURES ON FRIENDSHIPS

Like all human relationships, friendships are subject to internal tensions and external pressures.

Internal Tensions

Friendships are vulnerable to tensions inherent in being close. **Internal tensions** are relationship stresses that grow out of people and their interactions. We consider three of these.

Relational Dialectics   In Chapter 8, we discussed relational dialectics, which are opposing human needs that create tension and propel change in close relationships. The three dialectics of connection/autonomy, openness/privacy, and novelty/familiarity punctuate our friendships, prompting us to adjust continually to natural yet contradictory needs.

Friendships can be strained when people have different needs. There could be tension if Joe is bored and wants novelty but his friend Andy is overstimulated and needs calming routines. Similarly, if Andy has just broken up with a girlfriend, he may seek greater closeness with Joe at a time when Joe is very involved with family issues. When needs collide, friends should talk. It's important to be open about what you need and to be sensitive to what your friend needs. Doing this simultaneously honors yourself, your friend, and the relationship. Friends usually can work out ways to meet each person's needs or at least understand that differing needs don't reflect unequal commitment to the friendship.

> My girlfriends and I are so often in different places that it's hard to take care of each other. If one of my friends isn't seeing anyone special, she wants more time with me and wants to do things together. If I'm in a relationship with a guy, her needs feel demanding. But when I've just broken up, I really need my friends to fill time and talk with. So I try to remember how I feel and use that to help me accept it when my friends need my time.

LANA

Diverse Communication Styles   Friendships may also be strained by misunderstandings that arise from diverse cultural backgrounds. Because our communication reflects the understandings and rules of our culture, misinterpretations may arise between friends from different cultures. For instance, in many traditional Asian societies, people are socialized to be modest, whereas American culture encourages celebration of ourselves. Thus, someone born and raised in Japan might perceive an American friend as arrogant for saying, "Let's go out to celebrate my acceptance to law school."

Misunderstandings also arise from differences between social groups in the United States. Aaron, who is European American, might feel hurt if Markus, an African American friend, turns down Aaron's invitation to a concert in order to go home and care for an ailing aunt. Aaron might interpret this as a rejection by Markus because he thinks Markus is using the aunt as an excuse to avoid going out with him. Aaron would interpret Markus differently if he realized that many African Americans are more communal than European Americans, so taking care of extended family members is a priority (DeFrancisco & Chatham-Carpenter, 2000; Gaines, 1995; Orbe & Harris, 2001). Ellen may feel that her friend Jed isn't being supportive when, instead of empathizing with her problems, he suggests that they go out to take her mind off her troubles. Yet he is showing support according to masculine rules of communication. Jed, on the other hand, may feel that Ellen is intruding on his autonomy when she pushes him to talk about his feelings. According to feminine rules of communication, however, Ellen is showing interest and concern.

Differences themselves usually aren't the direct cause of problems in friendship. Instead, how we interpret and judge others' communication is the root of tension and hurt. What Jed and Ellen did wasn't the source of their frustrations. Jed interpreted Ellen according to his communication rules, not hers, and she interpreted Jed according to her communication rules, not his. Notice that the misunderstandings result from *our interpretations* of others' behaviors, not the behaviors themselves. This reminds us of the need to distinguish between facts and inferences.

Sexual Attraction Friendships between heterosexual men and women or between gay men or between lesbians often include sexual tensions. Even if

Communication in Everyday Life

INSIGHT

Just Friends?

Research suggests that being "just friends" often includes sexual activity. Walid Afifi and Sandra Faulkner (2000) surveyed 315 women and men in college about their cross-sex friendships. They found that 51% of respondents reported having had sex with a friend of the other sex at least once. A more recent study (Wyndol & Shaffer, 2011) found that nearly 60% of college students have had at least one friendship with benefits. Most people in friends-with-benefits relationships say that sexual activity increases the quality of their friendships, but a few say it harms the friendships. Perhaps most interesting is the finding that engaging in sexual activity with friends doesn't necessarily—or even usually—change a friendship into a romantic relationship.

MindTap If you have been in a friends-with-benefits relationship, what is your conclusion about the impact of sexual activity on friendship?

there is no actual sexual activity, sexual undertones may ripple beneath the surface of friendships. A recent study (Halatsis & Christakis, 2009) found that when sexual interest is expressed in a friendship, the friends need to have an explicit talk to decide if they are going to remain platonic friends, become friends with benefits, or become romantically involved. Sexual attraction or invitations become more challenging between friends who have agreed not to have a sexual relationship.

External Pressures

In addition to internal tensions, friendships may encounter pressures from outside sources. Three such pressures are competing demands, personal changes, and geographic distance.

Competing Demands   Friendships exist within larger social systems that affect how they function. Our work and our romantic relationships tend to be woven into our everyday lives, ensuring that they get daily attention. The early stages of a career require enormous amounts of energy and time. We may not have enough time or energy left to maintain friendships, even those that matter to us.

We sometimes neglect established friends because of other relationships, especially new ones. When a new romance is taking off, we may be totally immersed in it. We may also neglect friends when other important relationships in our lives are in crisis—for example, if one of our parents is ill or another friend is having trouble. To avoid hurting friends, we should let them know when we have to focus elsewhere, and assure our friends that we are still committed to them.

Personal Changes   Our friendships change as our lives do. Although a few friendships are lifelong, most are not. If you think about your experiences, you'll probably realize that you gained and lost friends as you made major transitions in your life. They'll change again when you leave college, move for career or family reasons, and perhaps have children. Similarly, unemployment can alter friendships because it takes people out of their usual social networks.

RUTH

Sandi and I had been friends for years when I had my first baby. Gradually, we saw less of each other and couldn't find much to talk about when we did get together. She was still doing the singles scene, and I was totally absorbed in mothering. I got to know other mothers in the neighborhood, and soon I thought of them as my friends. What's funny is that last year Sandi had a baby, and it was so good to get together and talk. We reconnected with each other.

Geographic Distance   Most friendships face the challenge of distance, and many don't survive it. A majority of North Americans have at least one long-distance friendship (Sahlstein, 2006). Whether distance ends friendship depends on several factors. Perhaps the most obvious influence is how much people care about continuing to be friends. The greater the commitment, the more likely a friendship is to persist despite separation.

The likelihood of sustaining a long-distance friendship also depends on other factors, such as socioeconomic class. Friendships that survive distance involve frequent emails, phone calls, texts, and visits. It takes money to finance trips, subscribe to a cell phone service, buy computers and tablets, and maintain Internet access. Thus, friends with greater economic resources are better able to maintain their relationships than are friends with less discretionary income. A second way in which socioeconomic class affects the endurance of long-distance friendships is flexibility in managing work and family. White-collar workers usually have considerable flexibility in work schedules, so they can make time to travel. Blue-collar workers tend to have less personal control over their job schedules and how much vacation time they get.

CASS

My parents are so different from each other in their approaches to friendship. When I was growing up, Dad was on a career roll, so we were always moving to better neighborhoods or new towns. Each time we moved, he'd make a whole new set of friends. Even if his old friends lived nearby, he would want to be with the people he called his new peers. Mom is 180 degrees different. She still talks with her best friend in the town where I was born. She has stayed close to all of her good friends, and they don't change with the season like Dad's do. Once, I asked him if he missed his old friends, and he said that friends were people you share common interests with, so they change as your job does. That doesn't make sense to me.

MindTap

Everyday Skills To practice strategies for maintaining long-distance friendships, complete the activity "Maintaining Friendship over Distance" at the end of the chapter or online.

Women and men differ in how likely they are to maintain long-distance friendships because they respectively see talking and activity as the nucleus of closeness. As we've seen previously, shared interests and emotional involvement are the crux of closeness for many women. Both of these are achieved primarily through communication, especially personal talk. The focus of men's friendships tends to be activities, which are difficult to share across distance. Women can sustain ties with important friends by talking on the phone, texting, emailing, and writing. Men, on the other hand, can't share activities with friends who are not present. Thus, they may be more likely to replace friends who have moved away with others who can share activities they enjoy.

Lillian Rubin (1985) distinguished between **friends of the heart**, who remain close regardless of distance and circumstances, and **friends of the road**, who change as we move along the road of life. For many people, our intimate friends tend to be friends of the heart, and our workplace and neighborhood friends tend to be friends of the road.

SOCIAL MEDIA AND FRIENDSHIPS

Social media offer us a range of ways to make friends and to maintain existing friendships. A friend's move to a new place once threatened the continuity of the friendship, but that is no longer the case. With social media, we can keep in touch with friends. Not only that; we can also make new friends in cyberspace. From texting and commenting on posts on social networking sites to playing games such as Words With Friends, many of us rely on digital and online communication for easy and ongoing contact with friends.

Yet many online friendships are not as rich and close as face-to-face friendships. William Deresiewicz (2009) questions whether social networking friendships are "real." He asks, "If we have 768 'friends,' in what sense do we have any?" And he then suggests that "once we decided to become friends with everyone, we would forget how to be friends with anyone" (p. B6). Contrasting online friendships with traditional, face-to-face ones, Deresiewicz notes that the former are less personal and less adapted to individuals. He thinks online friendships are "just broadcasting our stream of consciousness to all 500 of our friends at once" because "we're too busy to spare our friends more time than it takes to text" (p. B9). Deresiewicz may be exaggerating, but it might be worth your time to reflect on the intimacy you have with online and face-to-face friends. Think about all the friends on your social networking sites. How many of them would stay with you in the hospital if you were injured, hold you if you lost a family member, or let you live with them for 3 months if you needed lodging (Walter, 2009)?

The developmental path of friendships that we described in this chapter was developed based on research on face-to-face friendships. Research showing that people often disclose more and more quickly online than they do in person suggests that online friendships may have a distinct trajectory in which revelations occur sooner.

Social media can be used to engage in **cyberbullying**, which is text messages, online comments and rumors, embarrassing pictures posted online, and videos and fake profiles that are meant to hurt another person and are sent by email or smart phones or posted on social networking sites. Groups of friends sometimes target particular individuals for cyberbullying, and social networking sites such as Facebook have ineffectual procedures to monitor and stop cyberbullying (Bazelon, 2013).

According to a recent report (Burney, 2012), 43% of teenagers are subject to some form of cyberbullying. For LGBTQ teenagers the percentage is even higher: 53%

MindTap™

Everyday Skills To practice recognizing pros and cons of online friendships, complete the activity "Advantages and Disadvantages of Online Friendships" at the end of the chapter or online.

SOCIAL MEDIA

Cyberbullying

In 2010, 18-year-old Tyler Clementi committed suicide when he learned that his roommate Dharun Ravi had sent out Twitter and text messages inviting others to watch a sexual encounter between Clementi and another man. Ravi was tried on 15 charges, including hate crimes; he was found guilty of a bias crime and using a webcam to spy on Clementi. His sentence was 30 days in jail, 3 years on probation, and 300 hours of community service (Zernike, 2012). Clementi's is not an isolated case.

- 15-year-old Amanda threw herself in front of a bus when she could face no more of the cruel posts on her Facebook wall.

- 13-year-old Rachel hanged herself after an anonymous text saying she was a slut was circulated through her school.

- 14-year-old Jamey killed himself after an anonymous text saying he was gay became a widely spread rumor.

- 15-year-old Phoebe took the advice of a cyberbullier who told her to hang herself.

- 14-year-old Megan committed suicide when information she confided to a person who posed as a friend was turned against her online.

(Burney, 2012). Also targeted are girls and boys who do not conform to current gender ideals or, ironically, girls who conform too much to those ideals.

Girls who are victims tend to be more physically developed than others in their age cohort, are perceived as less attractive than peers, or are perceived as more attractive than peers (Anderson, 2011). Girls who are regarded as less attractive are ridiculed for not measuring up to feminine ideals while girls who are very attractive are bullied out of jealousy. One of the more common tactics for bullying girls is to spread rumors that they are sluts.

Boys, especially non-white boys, who are perceived as feminine are most likely to be victims of cyberbullying (Anderson, 2011, Burney, 2012). Collapsing distinctions between gender and sexuality, and reflecting both sexist and homophobic attitudes, bulliers belittle them for not being sufficiently masculine. In fact, posting comments that a boy is gay is a common form of cyberbullying.

Cyberbullying differs from face-to-face bullying in two important ways. First, it is often perpetrated anonymously. Through fake accounts and other online maneuvers, an individual can post hateful messages and photos without ever being accountable for her or his actions. When asked why people were so cruel online, one young boy explained, "You can be as mean as you want on Facebook" (Hoffman, 2010, p. A12). Second, cyberbullying has no necessary stopping point. The school yard bully pretty much stayed on the school yard. Thus, a victim could escape by going home or visiting a friend. Online bullying can follow the victim anywhere, 24-7. It is unremitting.

GUIDELINES FOR COMMUNICATION BETWEEN FRIENDS

Satisfying communication between friends follows the principles of good interpersonal communication that we've discussed in preceding chapters. For instance, it is important to create a confirming climate and to engage in effective verbal and nonverbal communication. Finally, managing conflict constructively is important in friendships as in all relationships. In addition to these general principles, we can identify four specific guidelines for satisfying communication between friends.

Engage in Dual Perspective

As in all interpersonal relationships, dual perspective is important in friendship. To be a good friend, we must understand our friends' perspectives, thoughts, and feelings. As we've noted before, accepting another person's perspective is not the same as agreeing with it. The point is to understand what friends feel and think and to accept that as their reality.

To exercise dual perspective, we distinguish between our judgments and perceptions and what friends say and do. Keep in mind the abstraction ladder discussed in Chapter 3. When we feel hurt or offended by something a friend says, we should remember that our perceptions and inferences do not equal their behavior. The process goes like this:

A friend acts.
We perceive the action(s) selectively.
We then interpret what happened.
We assign labels and meanings to our interpretation of what happened.
We make inferences based on the labels and meanings we chose.

Notice how far from the original act we move in the process of making sense of it. There's lots of room for slippage as we ascend the abstraction ladder. Let's consider a concrete example. Shereen tells her friend Kyle that she's upset and needs support; she shouldn't assume he's uninterested if he suggests they go out for the evening. As we have learned, men often support friends by trying to divert them from problems.

Two communication principles help us avoid misinterpreting our friends. First, it's useful to ask questions to find out what others mean. Shereen might ask Kyle, "Why would you want to go out when I said I needed support?" This would allow Kyle to explain that he was trying to support her in his own way: by coming up with an activity to distract her from her problems. Consequently, Shereen could grasp his meaning and appreciate his effort to support her.

Second, we should explain, or translate, our own feelings and needs so the friend understands what would feel supportive to us. Shereen could say, "What would help me most right now is to have a sympathetic ear. Could we just stay in and talk about the problem?" If we make our needs clear, we're more likely to get the kind of support we value.

Communicate Honestly

A few years ago, I confronted an ethical choice when my close friend Gayle asked me for advice. Several months earlier, she had agreed to give the keynote speech at a professional conference, and now she had

Everyday Skills To practice clarifying your needs, complete the activity "Communicating Needs Clearly" at the end of the chapter or online.

an opportunity to travel to Italy with her partner at the time of the conference. She wanted to accompany her partner to Italy but wondered whether it was ethical to renege on her agreement to give the keynote address. Following principles we've discussed in this book, I first asked a number of questions to find out how Gayle felt and what her perspective was. It became clear that she really wanted me to tell her it was okay to retract her agreement to give the speech.

Because I love Gayle, I wanted to support her preference and to encourage her to do what she wanted. Yet I didn't think it would be right for her to go back on her word, and I didn't think Gayle would respect herself in the long run if she didn't keep her word. Also, I knew that I wouldn't respect myself if I wasn't honest with Gayle. Ethically, I was committed both to being honest and to supporting my friend.

I took a deep breath and told her three things: First, I told her I would love her whatever she decided to do. Second, I told her that I didn't think it would be right not to give the speech. And, third, I suggested we look for more options. At first, she was quiet, clearly disappointed that I hadn't endorsed her dream. As we talked, we came up with the idea of her making the keynote speech and then joining her partner, who would already be in Italy. Even with this plan, Gayle was dejected when she left, and I felt I'd let her down by not supporting her dream. Later that night, she called to thank me for being honest with her. After we'd talked, she'd realized it went against her own values to renege on her word, and nobody else had helped her see that.

Honesty is one of the most important gifts friends can give each other. Even when honesty is less than pleasant or is not what we think we want to hear, we count on it from friends. In fact, people believe that honest feedback is what sets real friends apart from others (Burleson & Samter, 1994). Sometimes it's difficult to be honest with friends, as it was for me with Gayle. Yet if we can't count on our friends for honest feedback, then where can we turn for truthfulness?

Many people think that support means saying only nice things that others want to hear. This is not the essence of support. The key is to care enough about a person to look out for her or his welfare. Parents discipline children and set limits because they care about their children's long-term welfare. Friends who want to help each other give honest, often critical feedback so that others can improve. We can be supportive and loving while being honest about important matters. Although it may be easier to tell friends what they want to hear or only nice things, genuine friendship includes honest feedback and candid talk.

MILANDO

I can count on one hand (with three fingers left over!) the people who will really shoot straight with me. Most of my friends tell me what I want to hear. Yeah, that's kind of nice in the moment, but it doesn't wear well over the long haul. If I just want reinforcement for what I'm already feeling or doing, then why would I even talk to anyone else? Real friends tell you straight-up what's what.

Grow from Differences

A third principle for forming rich friendships is to be open to diversity in people. Western culture encourages us to think in either—or terms: Either he acts like I do, or he's wrong; either she's like me, or she's odd. The problem with either—or thinking is that it sharply limits interpersonal growth.

Most of us choose friends who are like us. We feel more immediately comfortable with friends who share our values, attitudes, backgrounds, and communication rules. But if we limit our friendships to people like us, we miss out on the fascinating variety of people who could be our friends. It does take time and effort to understand and become comfortable with people who differ from us, but the rewards of doing so can be exceptional.

Don't Sweat the Small Stuff

The 18th-century writer Samuel Johnson once remarked that most friendships die not because of major violations and problems but because of small slights and irritations that slowly destroy closeness. Johnson's point is well taken. Certainly, we can be irritated by a number of qualities and habits of others. If you are a punctual person, you might be annoyed by a friend who is chronically late. If you don't like prolonged telephone conversations, you may be irritated by a friend who likes to talk for hours on the phone. Feeling annoyance is normal; what we do with that feeling can make the difference between sustaining a friendship and suffocating it.

What we learned about perception in Chapter 3 gives us insight into how to let go of small irritations. Knowing that perceptions are subjective, you might remind yourself not to focus on aspects of a friend that you dislike or find bothersome. There's a big difference between acknowledging irritations and letting them preoccupy us. Is the lateness really more significant than all that you value in your friend? Do your friend's good qualities compensate for the long phone conversations that you dread? You can exercise some control over your perceptions and the weight you attach to them.

BERNADETTE I grew up with a single mother, but our home was always full. She had so many friends, and somebody was visiting all the time. I used to tell her that I didn't like Mrs. Jones's language or Mrs. Perry's political attitudes or the way Mr. Davis slurped his coffee. One day, when I was telling her what was wrong with one of her friends, my mother said, "Keep going like that, girl, and you won't ever have any friends. If you want to have friends, don't sweat the small stuff. Just keep your eye on what's good about them."

All of us want to be accepted and valued despite our flaws. You want that from your friends. And they want that from you. Acceptance doesn't mean you have to like everything about your friends. It does mean you accept friends and don't try to change them to suit your personal preferences.

CHAPTER SUMMARY

In this chapter, we explored how friendships form and how they function and change over time. We began by considering common expectations for friends, including investment, intimacy, acceptance, and support. Into our discussion of these common themes we wove insights about differences between us. We discovered that there are some differences in how women and men and people in different cultures and social communities create and express intimacy, invest in friendships, and show support.

Most friendships evolve gradually, moving from role-governed interactions to stable friendship and sometimes to waning friendship. Both social rules and private rules lend regularity and predictability to interaction so that friends know what to expect from one another. We also noted that friendships that develop through social media may have a different evolutionary trajectory that includes earlier disclosures of personal information.

Like all other relationships, friendships encounter challenges and tensions that stem from the relationship itself and from causes beyond it. Internal tensions of friendship include managing relational dialectics and misunderstandings and dealing with sexual attraction. External pressures on friendship are competing demands, changing personal needs and interests, and geographic distance. Principles of interpersonal communication covered throughout this book suggest how we can manage these pressures and the day-to-day dynamics of close friendships. In addition, communication between friends is especially enhanced by engaging in dual perspective, being honest, being open to diversity and the growth it can prompt in us, and not sweating the small stuff.

Key Concepts

Practice defining the chapter's terms by using online flashcards.

FLASHCARDS...

cyberbullying 297	**friends of the road** 297	**relationship rules** 291
friends of the heart 297	**internal tensions** 293	

Continuing the Conversation

Jason Harris/Cengage Learning

When you've watched the video online, critique and analyze this encounter based on the principles you learned in this chapter. Then compare your work with the author's suggested responses. Online, even more videos will let you continue the conversation with your instructor.

PRACTICE...

Bart and Sean have been friends and coworkers at Capital Bank for 10 years. They've been through a lot together, including Bart's divorce and Sean's wedding, where Bart was best man. They've kept each other informed about everyday office gossip. Both felt their friendship was solid until Sean got promoted 2 months ago. The promotion made Sean Bart's boss, though both of them try to minimize that. Now Bart feels that Sean doesn't share information with him and doesn't talk about other employees anymore. Sean feels he can't talk about work topics with Bart because it would be unfair to Bart's peers, who are also under his supervision. Sean also misses the closeness he and Bart had for so long. He wants to keep the friendship as it was but separate from their work relationship.

Bart: I heard Jack is being courted by Jefferson Financial.

Sean: I don't know the details on that.

Bart: I mean, is Capital going to match the offer, to keep Jack?... A lot of us would be upset if he got a raise and we didn't. It would be like encouraging us to go job-hunting just to get a counteroffer.

Sean: You know that it's not Capital's policy to make counteroffers to match the competition's offers.

Bart: I know the official policy. I also know Capital ignores it when they want to keep someone. I just want to know where Jack stacks up.

Sean: I can't talk to you about that, you know that.

Bart: You can trust me. Nothing you say is going any further.

Sean: Well, what about all the other managers who are not my best friend? How is it fair to them?

Bart: You could have fooled me. I thought best friends told each other things.

Sean: Because of my new job, there's just some things I can't talk to you about. For instance, this situation with Jack is creating nothing but tension between us. I can't talk to you about anything right now.

1. What relational dialectics do you see operating in the friendship between Sean and Bart?
2. Review the ways people respond to relational dialectics, which we discussed in Chapter 8. Assess how effective each response might be in this situation. How do you think separation, selection, neutralization, and reframing might affect interaction?
3. How is the trust between Bart and Sean affected by the changes in their relationship? In what ways might each man feel less able to trust the other?
4. Think about the systemic nature of relationships. Identify how the one change (Sean's promotion) affects other aspects of this relationship and interaction within it.
5. If you could rewrite the conversation between Bart and Sean, how would you revise it? What would you want to happen that isn't happening? What is happening that you would not want to happen? In revising the conversation, think about ways in which Sean and Bart might use communication to build a good interpersonal climate and express emotions effectively. How might each man listen more actively and effectively?
6. Can you envision ways in which Sean's ideal scenario might be realized, so that he and Bart could stay close friends and keep the friendship separate from their working relationship?

Assessing Yourself

Begin the process of applying this chapter's concepts by taking a self-assessment quiz here or online—where you will find out what the results mean.

Purpose: To understand your own style of friendship

Instructions: Answer the following questions about how you experience and express closeness with friends. With your closest or best friends, how often do you do the following things: very often, somewhat often, not very often?

1. Talk about family problems
   Very often   Somewhat often   Not very often

PRACTICE...

2. Exchange favors (provide transportation, lend money)
   Very often   Somewhat often   Not very often

3. Engage in sports (shoot hoops, play tennis, and so forth)
   Very often   Somewhat often   Not very often

4. Try to take their minds off problems with diversions
   Very often   Somewhat often   Not very often

5. Disclose your personal anxieties and fears
   Very often   Somewhat often   Not very often

6. Talk about your romantic relationships and family relationships
Very often   Somewhat often   Not very often

7. Do things together (camp, go to a game, shop)
Very often   Somewhat often   Not very often

8. Confide secrets you wouldn't want others to know
Very often   Somewhat often   Not very often

9. Just hang out without a lot of conversation
Very often   Somewhat often   Not very often

10. Talk about small events in your day-to-day life
Very often   Somewhat often   Not very often

11. Provide practical assistance to help friends
Very often   Somewhat often   Not very often

12. Talk explicitly about your feelings for each other
Very often   Somewhat often   Not very often

13. Discuss and work through tensions in your friendship
Very often   Somewhat often   Not very often

14. Physically embrace or touch to show affection
Very often   Somewhat often   Not very often

15. Ignore or work around problems in the friendship
Very often   Somewhat often   Not very often

Everyday Skills

Build your communication skills further by completing the following activities here or online.

1. **Appreciating Talking and Doing in Friendships**

   For each of the following scenarios, write down one thing you might say and one thing you might do to show you care about the person described.

   a. Your best friend has just broken up with his or her long-term boyfriend or girlfriend. Your friend texts you, ‹I feel so lonely.›
   You say _____
   You do _____

   b. A good friend tells you he or she has been cut from the team and won't get to play this year.
   You say _____
   You do _____

   c. Your best friend from high school calls and says she or he thinks about you often even though the two of you no longer maintain much contact.
   You say _____
   You do _____

   d. A close friend stops you on campus and excitedly says, "I just found out I've been accepted into the law school here! Can you believe it?"
   You say _____
   You do _____

2. **Maintaining Friendship over Distance**

   Do you have a long-distance friendship? If so, which of the following strategies do you use to maintain it?
   - Call or text at least once a day
   - Call or text at least once a week

   - Call at least once a month
   - Call once or twice a year
   - Email or text message at least daily
   - Email or text message at least weekly
   - Post messages on profile pages
   - Write letters
   - Visit weekly
   - Visit monthly
   - Visit occasionally
   - Have conversations in your head with the friend

   If the friendship is not staying as close as you would like, consider communicating more frequently.

3. **Advantages and Disadvantages of Online Friendships**

   Reflect on two close friendships, one of which is with someone you regularly communicate with face to face, and the other of which is with someone you communicate with mainly through social media. Identify advantages of each way of maintaining friendship. Identify disadvantages of each way.

4. **Communicating Needs Clearly**

   The three scenarios presented here describe interactions in which a friend does not initially give the desired response. For each one, write what you could say to clarify what is wanted.

   a. You've just found out that your car needs two new tires and alignment, and you don't have any extra cash. Worrying about money is the

last thing you want to do now, with everything else on your mind. You see a friend and tell him what's happened. He says, "Sit down, let's talk about it." You don't want to talk; you want to get your mind off the problem.
You say _____

b. You are unhappy because your boyfriend or girlfriend is transferring to a school 600 miles away. You think that you'll miss him or her, and you're also worried that the relationship might not survive the distance. A friend calls, and you mention your concerns. In response, she/he says, "You can handle this. Just make sure that the two of you have email accounts, and you'll be fine." Although you'd like to believe this, it seems like empty reassurance

to you. You'd rather have some help sorting through your feelings.
You say _____

c. A friend tells you that she is really worried about the job market. As she talks, you hear several things: her worry about making a living, her uncertainty about where she will be living, and her doubts about self-worth. You say to your friend, "Sounds as if you are feeling pretty overwhelmed by all of this. Maybe it would help if we took one piece of the problem at a time." Your friend lets out a frustrated sigh and replies, "I don't want to analyze every bit and piece!" You're not sure what your friend wants and how to help her.
You say _____

MindTap **DO...** Additional interactive discussions, online quizzes, and activities that your instructor may assign for a grade.

Engaging with Ideas

Reflect and write about the ideas in this chapter by considering questions about personal, workplace, and ethical applications, here or online.

Personal Application Think about how what we've discussed applies to your life. How important are talk and activities in your closest friendships? What have you invested in your closest friendships? How do you express support to your close friends? Does your membership in particular cultural groups or social communities affect what you expect of and how you behave in friendships? Do your friendships tend to follow the stages of friendship described in this chapter?

Workplace Application Do you have on-the-job friends at your current job or did you at a previous job?

If so, how does having workplace friends affect your work? Would your work be different if you didn't have friends on the job?

REFLECT ON...

Ethical Application Is it always unethical to lie to friends? If a friend asks you what you think of her new boyfriend, and you think he is a total loser, should you say that or offer a less critical comment such as "It's too soon to tell" or "You seem to be enjoying time with him." If you think your friend's boyfriend is abusing her, do you have an ethical obligation to tell her you think so? What are the rules that govern when it is appropriate to lie or shade the truth with friends?

Thinking Critically

Think and write critically about the ideas in this chapter, here or online.

1. Think about a friendship you have with a person of your own sex and a friendship you have with a person of the other sex. To what extent does each friendship conform to the gender patterns described in this chapter?

2. Write out typical topics of talk for each stage in the evolution of friendships. How do topics change as friendships wax and wane?

3. Think about someone who is a very close or best friend. Describe the investments you and your friend have made in the relationship. Describe how you build and communicate trust, acceptance, and closeness.

Are the dynamics of your friendship consistent with those identified by researchers as discussed in this chapter?

4. To learn how others view friendships and what issues arise in their friendships, visit the Friendship Page at http://www.friendship.com.au. This site offers songs, poetry, and quotes about friendship as well as chat rooms and an advice forum. To what extent do the issues raised in the advice forum reflect challenges to friendship discussed in this chapter?

chapter
ELEVEN

© Phase4Studios/Shutterstock.com

COMMITTED ROMANTIC RELATIONSHIPS

START... experiencing this chapter's topics with an online video!

Topics covered in this chapter

Committed Romantic Relationships

The Development of Romantic Relationships

Social Media and Romantic Relationships

Guidelines for Communicating in Romantic Relationships

After studying this chapter, you should be able to . . .

List features of committed romantic relationships.

Evaluate the development of a romantic relationship in your life.

Identify ways that social media affect romantic relationships.

Apply chapter guidelines to enhance the quality of your romantic relationships.

READ... the complete chapter text in a rich interactive eBook!

Ellen is upset about an issue with a colleague at work. After dinner, she tries to open a conversation with her husband Norton by saying, "Pat is still creating tension at the office." Without looking up from his laptop, Norton mumbles, "Sorry, hon." This is the third time this week that Ellen has tried to talk with Norton about an issue that is really troubling her. He always seems preoccupied.

Sighing, Ellen goes into her den, opens her laptop, and checks to see if her friend Jake is online. She met him when they were both posting comments on a political blog. Discovering much common ground, they quickly moved to one-on-one email, Skyping, and texting. Tonight, she finds him online, and they connect on Skype. She tells Jake the latest news about the problems with Pat at the office, and Jake offers empathy—he's had some difficult colleagues too. He also suggests a couple of ways she might control Pat. After 20 minutes, Ellen feels comforted and much less anxious. She says to Jake, "Sometimes you seem to understand me better than I understand myself." Jake replies, "I want to understand you because I care about you." She says, "Thanks for being there for me." Jake replies, "I'll always be here for you, Ellen."

Is Ellen being disloyal to Norton to have such a close relationship with Jake? Is there a danger that her online relationship with Jake will develop into an affair?

In this chapter, we explore communication in committed romantic relationships. We begin by defining committed romantic relationships and the different styles of loving that individuals bring to romance. Next, we discuss the developmental pattern that many romantic relationships follow as they grow, stabilize, and sometimes dissolve. The third section of the chapter considers the role of social media in committed romantic relationships. To close the chapter, we identify guidelines for communicating effectively to meet challenges that often arise in romantic relationships.

COMMITTED ROMANTIC RELATIONSHIPS

Committed romantic relationships are relationships between individuals who assume that they will be primary and continuing parts of each other's lives. These relationships are voluntary in mainstream Western culture although marriages are arranged in some cultures. We don't pick our relatives, neighbors, or work associates, but in Western countries we do choose our romantic intimates.

Committed romantic relationships are created and sustained by unique people who cannot be replaced. In many of our relationships, others are replaceable. If a colleague at work leaves, you can get another colleague, and work will go on. If your racquetball buddy moves out of town, you can find a new partner, and the games will continue. In fact, most of our social relationships are I–You connections. Committed romantic relationships, in contrast, are I–Thou bonds, in which we invest heavily of ourselves and in which each person knows the other as a completely distinct individual.

Committed romantic relationships involve romantic and sexual feelings, which are not typically part of relationships with coworkers, neighbors, family members, and most friends. Another distinctive quality of romantic relationships is that they are considered primary and enduring. We expect to move away from friends and family, but we assume we'll be connected to a romantic partner permanently or at least for a very long time.

Dimensions of Romantic Relationships

For years, researchers have struggled to define romantic commitment. As a result of their work, we now believe that romantic love consists of three dimensions: intimacy, commitment, and passion. Although we can discuss these dimensions separately, they overlap and interact (Acker & Davis, 1992; Hendrick & Hendrick, 1989). One scholar (Sternberg, 1986) arranges these three dimensions to form a triangle, representing the different facets of love (see Figure 11.1).

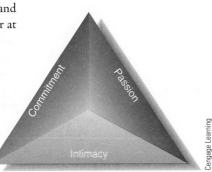

Figure 11.1

The Triangle of Love

Passion For most of us, **passion** is what first springs to mind when we think about romance. Passion describes intensely positive feelings and fervent desire for another person. Passion is not restricted to sexual or sensual feelings. In addition to sexual feelings, passion may involve powerful emotional, spiritual, and intellectual excitement. The sparks and emotional high of being in love stem from passion. It's why we refer to feeling butterflies in the stomach and falling head over heels.

Donna Day/Stone/Getty Images

As exciting as passion is, it isn't the principal foundation for most enduring romantic relationships. In fact, research consistently shows that passion is less central to our experience of love than are the dimensions of intimacy and commitment. This makes sense when we realize that passion is seldom sustained at the high levels that may be part of a new relationship. Like other intense feelings, it ebbs and flows. Because passion comes and goes and is largely beyond our will, it isn't an adequate foundation for long-term relationships. In other words, passion may set romance apart from other relationships, but typically it isn't the glue that holds romantic relationships together. To build a lasting relationship, we need something more durable.

Commitment The "something else" needed is **commitment**, the second dimension of romantic relationships. As we noted in Chapter 8, commitment is the intention to remain involved with a relationship. Although often linked to love, commitment is not the same thing as love. Love is a feeling based on the rewards of our involvement with a person. Commitment, in contrast, is a decision to remain in a relationship. There is a strong relationship between commitment and investments in a relationship—the more we invest in a relationship, the greater our commitment is likely to be (Lund, 1985; Rusbult, Drigotas, & Verette, 1994).

Researchers have identified two broad categories of reasons why people commit to relationships (Lund, 1985; Previti & Amato, 2003). First, we may stay with a relationship because we find it comfortable and pleasing—we value companionship, emotional support, financial assistance, practical benefits, and so forth. Second, we may stay with a relationship to avoid negative consequences that would accompany ending it—these barriers to leaving include violating religious values, family disapproval, and financial hardship. While both of these reasons may secure commitment, they tend to have different implications for relational happiness. Couples who stay together because of barriers to leaving tend to be less happy, less satisfied, and less likely to stay together permanently than couples who stay together because they find the relationship pleasing (Kurdek, 2006). This pattern holds true for heterosexual, gay, and lesbian couples (Kurdek, 2006).

THERESA I'm sick of guys who say they love me but run if I try to talk about the future. They're allergic to the C-word. If you truly love someone, how can you not be committed?

TED I don't know why everyone thinks that saying "I love you" means you want to plan a life together. I love my girlfriend, but I haven't even figured out what I want to do next year, much less for the rest of my life. She thinks if I really loved her, I'd want to talk about marriage. I think love and marriage can be different things.

Most Westerners want both passion and commitment in long-term romantic relationships (Bellah et al., 1985). We desire the exhilaration of passion, but we know that love alone won't allow a couple to weather rough times and won't ensure compatibility and comfort on a day-in, day-out basis. Commitment provides a sturdier foundation for a life together. Commitment is the determination to stay together despite trouble, disappointments, sporadic restlessness, and lulls in passion. Without commitment, romantic relationships are subject to the whims of transient feelings and circumstances.

Commitment involves accepting responsibility for maintaining a relationship (Swidler, 2001). Thus, it isn't surprising that commitment is positively related to willingness to sacrifice for and invest in a relationship (Rusbult et al., 1994).

> I've been married for 15 years, and we would have split a dozen times if love was all that held us together. Lucy and I have gone through spells where we were bored with each other or where we wanted to walk away from our problems. We didn't, because we made a promise to stay together "for better or for worse." Believe me, a marriage has both.

WADE

Intimacy The third dimension of romantic relationships is **intimacy**: feelings of closeness, connection, and tenderness. Intimacy is abiding affection and warm feelings for another person. It is why partners are comfortable with each other and enjoy being together even when there are no fireworks. When asked to evaluate various features of love, people consistently rate companionate features such as getting along and friendship as most important. Although passionate feelings also matter, they are less central to perceptions of love than caring, honesty, respect, friendship, and trust (Hasserbrauck & Aaron, 2001; Hasserbrauck & Fehr, 2002). Unlike passion and commitment, which are distinct dimensions of romance, intimacy seems to underlie both passion and commitment (Acker & Davis, 1992; Hasserbrauck & Fehr, 2002).

Styles of Loving

+ Does real love grow out of friendship?
+ Can you decide to love only someone who meets your criteria for a partner?
+ Would you rather suffer yourself than have someone you love suffer?
+ Is love at first sight possible?
+ Is love really a game—playful, not serious?

If you were to survey your class, you'd discover different answers to these questions. For every person who thinks love grows gradually out of friendship, someone else believes in love at first sight.

People differ in how they experience and express love (Lee, 1973, 1988). Just as there are three primary colors, there are three primary styles of loving. In addition, just as secondary colors are combinations of two primary colors, secondary love styles are combinations of two primary ones. Secondary styles are as vibrant as primary ones, just as purple (a secondary color) is as dazzling as red or blue (the primary colors that make up purple). Figure 11.2 illustrates the colors of love.

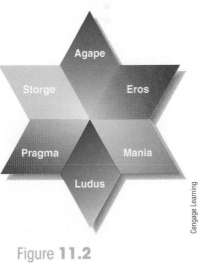

Cengage Learning

Figure **11.2**

The Colors of Love

Primary Styles of Love   The three primary styles of love are *eros*, *storge*, and *ludus*. **Eros** is a powerful, passionate style of love that blazes to life suddenly and dramatically. It is an intense kind of love that may include sexual, spiritual, intellectual, or emotional attraction or all of these. Eros is the most intuitive and spontaneous of all love styles, and it is also the fastest moving. Erotic lovers are likely to self-disclose early in a relationship, be very sentimental, and fall in love fast. Although folk wisdom claims that women are more romantic than men, research indicates that men are more likely than women to be erotic lovers (Hendrick & Hendrick, 1996).

MIKE   When I fall for someone, I fall all the way—like, I mean total and all that. I can't love halfway, and I can't go gradually though my mother is always warning me to slow down. That's just not how I love. It's fast and furious for me.

Storge (pronounced "STORE-gay") is a comfortable, even-keeled kind of love based on friendship and compatibility. Storgic love tends to develop gradually and to be peaceful and stable. In most cases, it grows out of common interests, values, and life goals (Lasswell & Lobsenz, 1980). Storgic relationships don't have the great highs of erotic ones, but neither do they have the fiery conflict and anger that may punctuate erotic relationships.

STEPHEN   Lisa and I have been together for 15 years now, and it's been easy and steady between us from the start. I don't remember even falling in love way back when. Maybe I never did fall in love with Lisa. I just gradually grew into loving her and feeling we belonged to each other.

The final primary style of love is **ludus**, which is playful love. Ludic lovers see love as a game. It's an adventure full of scheming, challenges, puzzles, and fun, but love is not to be taken seriously. For ludics, commitment is not the goal. Instead, they like to play the field and to enjoy falling in love . . . again and again. Many people go through ludic periods but are not true ludics. After ending a long-term relationship, it's natural and healthy to date casually and steer clear of serious entanglements. Ludic loving may also suit people who enjoy romance but aren't ready to settle down. Research indicates that more men than women have ludic inclinations when it comes to love (Hendrick & Hendrick, 1996).

VIJAY   I'm not ready to settle down, and I may not ever be. I really like dating and seeing if I can get a girl to fall for me, but I'm not out for anything permanent. To me, the fun is in the chase. Once somebody falls for me, I kind of lose interest. It's just not challenging anymore.

Secondary Styles of Love   The three secondary styles of love are *pragma*, *mania*, and *agape*. **Pragma**, as the word suggests, is pragmatic or practical love. Pragma blends the calculated planning of ludus with the stable security of storge. Pragmatic lovers have clear criteria for partners, such as religious affiliation, career, and family background. Although many people dismiss pragma as coldly practical, pragmatic lovers aren't necessarily unfeeling or unloving. For them, though, practical considerations are the foundation of enduring commitment, so these must be satisfied before they allow themselves to fall in love. Pragmas are likely to like online matching services that allow them to specify their criteria for a desirable mate. Pragmatic considerations also guide arranged marriages, in which families match children based on economic and social criteria.

> **RANCHANA**
>
> I have to think carefully about who to marry. I must go to graduate school, and I must support my family with what I earn when I finish. I cannot marry someone who is poor, who will not help me get through school, or who won't support my family. For me, these are very basic matters.

Mania derives its name from the Greek term *theia mania*, which means "madness from the gods" (Lee, 1973). Manic lovers have the passion of eros, but they play by ludic rules—a combination that can be perilous. Typically unsure that others really love them, manics may devise tests and games (that's the ludic streak in mania) to evaluate a partner's commitment. They often experience emotional extremes, ranging from euphoria to despair (that's the erotic streak). In addition, manics may obsess about a relationship and be unable to think about anyone or anything else.

> **PAT**
>
> I never feel sure of myself when I'm in love. I always wonder when it will end, when my boyfriend will walk away, when he will lose interest. Sometimes I play games to see how interested a guy is, but then I get all upset if the game doesn't work out right. Then I just wallow in my insecurities, and they get worse the more I think about them.

The final style of love is **agape** (pronounced "ah-GAH-pay"), which is a blend of storge and eros. The term *agape* comes from Saint Paul's admonition that we should love others without expectation of personal gain or return. People who love agapically feel the intense passion of eros and the constancy of storge. Generous and selfless, they put a loved one's happiness ahead of their own without any expectation of reciprocity. For them, loving and giving to another are their own rewards. Although the original studies of love styles found no people who were purely agapic, many people have agapic tendencies.

> **KEENAN**
>
> My mother is agapic. She has moved more times than I can count because my father needed to relocate to advance. She agreed to the house he wanted and went on the vacations he wanted, even when she had other ideas. There's nothing she wouldn't do for him. I used to think she was a patsy, but I've come to see her way of loving as very strong.

If you are trying to figure out your love style, you should keep in mind five issues related to identifying your love style. First, most of us have a combination of styles (Hendrick, Hendrick, Foote, & Slapion-Foote, 1984). So you might be primarily storgic with strong agapic inclinations, or mainly erotic with an undertone of ludic mischief. Second, styles of love are not necessarily permanent.

Warner Bros/Photofest

Is it unrealistic to think that someone could experience mania about a computerized voice, as Theodore Twombly (Joaquin Phoenix) does for "Samantha" (Scarlett Johansson) in *Her*?

We learn how to love (Maugh, 1994), so our style of loving may change as we have more experiences in loving. Third, a love style is part of an overall interpersonal system, so it is affected by all other aspects of a relationship (Hendrick & Hendrick, 1996). Your partner's style of love may influence your own. For instance, even if you don't tend toward mania, being with a strongly ludic partner could foster manic tendencies in you. Fourth, individual styles of love are not good or bad in an absolute sense; what matters is how partners' styles fit together.

A final issue related to love styles is that their perceived appropriateness, or desirability, varies across cultures. In the United States and other cultures that are highly individualistic, passionate love (eros) is culturally endorsed. In more collectivist cultures such as China, India, and Korea, however, passionate love is not culturally endorsed because it can threaten familial values and kin relations (Kim & Hatfield, 2004). Storgic love is more the ideal in collectivist cultures.

THE DEVELOPMENT OF ROMANTIC RELATIONSHIPS

Like friendships, romantic relationships tend to follow a developmental course. Irwin Altman and Dalmas Taylor (1973, 1987) developed social penetration theory to explain how romantic intimacy progresses in Western cultures. The key idea in social penetration theory is that intimacy grows as interaction between people penetrates from the outer to inner layers of each person's personality. In other words, we have to move beyond the surface of another person to know him or her well enough to develop an I–Thou relationship. In more collectivist cultures, however, the American tendency to bare one's soul to intimates is not culturally valued or expected (Kito, 2005).

Some years after Altman and Taylor introduced social penetration theory, James Honeycutt (1993) amended it to note that intimacy progresses based on our perceptions of interaction, not on interaction itself. For example, if Terry discloses personal information to Janet, and if Janet and Terry both interpret self-disclosure as a move toward greater intimacy, the relationship is likely to escalate. If Janet doesn't perceive disclosure as linked to intimacy, however, then she's unlikely to feel closer to Terry. It is the meaning they assign to self-disclosing, not the actual act of self-disclosing, that determines how they perceive their level of intimacy.

The meanings we assign to behavior in romantic relationships are not entirely individualistic. They also reflect broad cultural views, which we learn and often internalize. For this reason, there are strong consistencies in how people social-ized in the same culture and social groups attribute meaning to communication in romantic relationships. Research shows that college students in the United States agree on the goals and script for initial get togethers (Metts, 2006a; Mongeau, Serewicz, & Therrien, 2004; Pryor & Merluzzi, 1985). Both women and men per-ceive getting to know the new person and having fun as parts of a first-encounter script. Women are more likely than men to perceive companionship as a goal, and men are more likely than women to perceive sexual activity as a goal (Mongeau et al., 2004).

Members of a culture also tend to have similar ideas about how men and women should act. The majority of college students in the United States think that men should initiate and plan get togethers and make decisions about most activities, but that women control sexual activity (Laner & Ventrone, 2002; Metts, 2006a). However, women tend to be more egalitarian than men in their ratings of who is responsible for paying the first time a couple hangs out. While only 9% of men think either partner could pay, 22% of women think either person could (Laner & Ventrone, 2002). In other cultures, different rules prevail for ini-tial get togethers and the whole process of courting. For example, in parts of India, marriages are often arranged by parents; love is understood to be something that develops after marriage. In Nepal, ritualistic dancing and celebrations are an im-portant part of courtship.

Research on the evolution of romantic relationships has focused on Western society, so we know the most about the developmental course of romance in the West. Investigations show that Westerners typically perceive romantic relation-ships as evolving through three broad phases: growth, navigation, and deterioration (Mongeau & Henningsen, 2008). Within these three broad categories, we distin-guish a number of more specific stages.

Growth

Researchers have identified six growth stages through which romance typically, but not always, progresses. The first is *individuality*: each of us is an individual with particular needs, goals, love styles, perceptual tendencies, and qualities that affect what we look for in relationships. Our choices of people with whom to begin a romance are influenced by our personal histories and our identities, including our attachment styles (Mikulincer & Shaver, 2005) and whether we give to others con-ditionally or unconditionally (Clark & Finkel, 2005).

> **EDNA**
>
> It's funny how things change as we age. When I was first dating in my teens, the topics for small talk early in the relationship were your major, career plans, and background. Now I'm 47, divorced, and dating again, and the opening topics tend to be about career achievements, past mar-riages, and finances.

The second growth stage is *invitational communication*, in which people signal that they are interested in interacting; during this stage they also respond to invitations

DIVERSITY

Development of Interracial Relationships

The number of interracial marriages tripled between 1970 and 2002, and interracial dating grew at an even higher rate (Troy & Laurenceau, 2006). In addition to the stages generally followed in developing intimacy, partners in interracial relationships often deal simultaneously with four distinct developmental stages (Foeman & Nance, 1999).

1. **Racial awareness**—Each partner becomes conscious of his or her race and his or her views of the partner's race. In addition, partners become more aware of broad social perspectives on their own and each other's racial group.
2. **Coping**—The couple struggles with external pressures, including disapproval from family and friends, and develops strategies to protect their relationship from external damage.
3. **Identity emergence**—Partners declare their couple identity to themselves and others.
4. **Relationship maintenance**—The couple works at preserving the relationship as it incorporates new challenges, such as having children, moving to new areas, and entering new social circles.

from others. "I love this kind of music," "Where are you from?" and "Hi, my name's Shelby" are examples of bids for interaction. We may also invite interaction in chat rooms or websites that are designed for meeting new people. The most important meaning of invitational communication is found on the relationship level, not the content level. "I love this kind of music" literally means that a person likes the music. On the relationship level of meaning, however, the message is, "I'm interested in interacting. Are you?"

Hooking up, which is engaging in some degree of sexual activity with a person with no expectation of seeing that person again, is an increasingly popular form of initial get-together. Broad surveys of college students report that 72% of both sexes have hooked up (40% intercourse; 35% kissing and touching; 12% hand and genital contact; 12% oral sex) (Blackstrom, Armstrong, & Puentes, 2012). African Americans are less likely to hook up (35%) than are Caucasian Americans (60%) (Jayson, 2011). Hooking up has become an alternative to dating for several reasons. One is that women students outnumber men students so heterosexual women have fewer choices and heterosexual men have more choices. A second reason is that individuals want freedom from commitments that might interfere with summer internships and jobs or early career focus (Taylor, 2013; Uecker & Regnerus, 2011). Although both sexes engage in hooks ups, women are more likely than men to regret hooking up, to feel guilty, and to be depressed (Bradshaw, Kahn, & Saville, 2010).

Of all the people we meet, we find only a few sufficiently attractive to warrant further get togethers. Three of the greatest influences on initial attraction are attractiveness, proximity, and similarity. Among members of each sexual orientation, there tend to be somewhat consistent criteria for selecting dating partners. Many gay men place priority on physical characteristics, including slimness, body conditioning, and grooming (Huston & Schwartz, 1995). Heterosexual men also place importance on physical attractiveness; many prefer women who are slim and beautiful (Sprecher & Regan, 2002). Heterosexual women and lesbians tend to emphasize qualities of personality, such as kindness, honesty, and integrity (Huston & Schwartz, 1995).

Yet the bases of attraction we just discussed are not universal but are shaped by culture. In other words, what we look for in partners varies across cultures. A recent study (Riela, Rodriguez, Aron, Xu, & Acevedo, 2010) found that Americans place more emphasis on appearance than Chinese, and Chinese place more emphasis on personality, fulfilling needs, and social influence.

Proximity and similarity are major influences on initial attraction. We can interact only with people we meet in person or in social media, so where we live, work, and socialize and the social media we use constrain the possibilities for relationships. Nearness to others doesn't necessarily increase liking. The term **environmental spoiling** denotes situations in which proximity breeds ill will. This happens when we're forced to be around others whose values, lifestyles, or behaviors conflict with our own.

Similarity is also important in romantic relationships. In the realm of romance, "birds of a feather flock together" seems truer than "opposites attract" (Levin, Taylor, & Caudle, 2007; Samp & Palevitz, 2009). The hypothesis that the United States is classless has been disproved by the fact that most people seek romantic partners of their own social class or above it (Sprecher & Regan, 2002; Whitbeck & Hoyt, 1994).

Most people seek romantic partners whose values, attitudes, and lifestyles are similar to their own (Amodio & Showers, 2005; Buston & Emlen, 2003; Lutz-Zois, Bradley, Mihalik, & Moorman-Eavers, 2006). Similarity of personality is also linked to the fit between people and to long-term satisfaction in relationships (Gonzaga, Carter & Buckwalter, 2010).

People increasingly rely on online sites to meet potential partners. Over 16 million Americans say they have gone online to look for dating partners (Rosen, Cheever, Cummings, & Felt, 2008). Online dating services may be especially helpful to people who are shy about launching romantic relationships (Scharlott & Christ, 1995).

Explorational communication is the third stage in the escalation of romance, and it focuses on learning about each other. In this stage, people fish for common interests and grounds for interaction: "Do you like jazz?" "Where have you traveled?" "Have you been following the political debates?" In this stage, we continue trying to reduce our uncertainty about the other person so that we can evaluate the possibility of a more serious relationship. We may make self-disclosures, which can increase trust and feelings of intimacy (Laurenceau, Barrett, & Rovinne, 2005; Sprecher & Hendrick, 2004). It's also possible for this phase to be where a relationship settles—that is, stabilizes as a casual hook-up or hang out-relationship (Knapp & Vangelisti, 2005).

What we tell each other during these early stages of relationships isn't necessarily entirely truthful. Many people "put their best foot forward" in new relationships. Beyond that, some people misrepresent themselves in more significant ways—for example, claiming degrees they haven't earned or abilities they don't have. This is equally true in online relationships. In online dating, men are more likely than women to misrepresent their personal assets (e.g., financial worth), relationship goals (e.g., to claim interest in a long-term relationship when they are actually interested in shorter-term connection), personal attributes (e.g., height), and personal interests. Women are more likely than men to misrepresent their weight (Hall, Park, Song, & Cody, 2010).

The fourth growth stage is *intensifying communication*, which my students nicknamed euphoria to emphasize its intensity and happiness. During this stage, partners spend more time together, and they rely less on external structures such as films or parties. They may immerse themselves in the relationship and may feel

INSIGHT

Valentine's Day

Valentine's Day means love, romance, and passion. It's a time for sweethearts, a time to be mushy. If that's how you think of Valentine's Day, think again. In A.D. 498, the Roman Catholic Church declared February 14 to be St. Valentine's Feast Day, meant to recognize that marriage was a necessary institution but certainly not a romantic one. Prior to the Church's decision, however, on February 14, girls' names were put into a container and each boy drew out one name. For the next year, the boy and the girl whose name he had drawn would be sexual partners. The Church thought this practice should be stopped because, at that time, the Church had little use for passion, love, or even marriage (Coontz, 2005b).

Of course, young people disagreed and continued to think that passion and love were central to romance. By the Middle Ages, St. Valentine had become associated with romance in popular culture, but even then, romance was not assumed to lead to or to be part of marriage. Only in the 18th century did the idea that love and marriage go together begin to gain popular acceptance in the West.

And just who was St. Valentine? He was a Christian priest who, in the 3rd century, was jailed (the reason is a matter of controversy). Awaiting execution, he wrote a sentimental goodbye letter to his jailer's daughter, with whom he had fallen in love. He signed the letter, "from your Valentine."

that they can't be together enough. Further disclosures occur, personal biographies are filled in, and partners increasingly learn how the other feels and thinks. As partners increase the depth of their knowledge of each other, they begin to develop dual perspective and begin thinking and talking of themselves as a couple. During this stage, couples usually agree to make their relationship exclusive. In Japan, couples commit to *tsukiau* relationships; *tsukiau* roughly translates into "going steady" (Farrer, Tsuchiya, & Bagrowicz, 2008).

Also characteristic of the intensifying stage are idealizing and personalized communication. Idealizing involves seeing the relationship and the partner as more wonderful, exciting, and perfect than they really are (Hendrick & Hendrick, 1988; Murray, Holmes, & Griffin, 1996a, 1996b). During euphoria, partners often exaggerate each other's virtues, downplay or fail to perceive vices, and overlook problems in the relationship. It is also during euphoria that partners begin to develop private nicknames and language.

Revising communication, although not a stage in the development of all romantic relationships, is important when it does occur. During this stage, partners come out of the clouds to look at their relationship more realistically. Problems are recognized, and partners evaluate whether they want to work through them. Many people fall in love and move through the intensifying stage yet do not choose to stay together. A student of mine had a long-term love relationship with a man she loved, but she never let her parents know of the relationship because he is African American and she is Indian and expected to marry within her ethnicity. It is entirely possible to love a person with whom we don't choose to share our life.

Susan Piver (2008) advises couples who are considering long-term commitment to answer 100 questions to assess their compatibility and readiness to commit. Here's a sampling of the questions:

+ What proportion of our time do you expect to spend maintaining our home?
+ How many couple friends do you expect us to have?
+ How often do you expect us to get together with joint friends?
+ How do you feel about saving money versus enjoying spending it?
+ How do you want our home to look and feel?
+ Do you want children? How many? When?

As important as answers to the questions are the conversations that are prompted by asking them. In dealing with questions such as these, many couples discover that they have serious differences that could jeopardize the relationship's stability.

Breaking up with Ted was the hardest thing I ever did. I really loved him, and he loved me, but I just couldn't see myself living with a Christian. My whole heritage is Jewish—it's who I am. I celebrate Hanukkah, not Christmas. Seder, Passover, and Yom Kippur are very important to me. Those aren't part of Ted's heritage, and he wouldn't convert. I loved him, but we couldn't have made a life together.

The final growth stage is *commitment*, which is the decision to stay with the relationship. Before commitment, partners don't assume that the relationship will continue forever. With commitment, the relationship becomes a given, around which they arrange other aspects of their lives. Commitment also leads partners to invest more in a relationship, especially in terms of communication to maintain satisfaction. Not surprisingly, partners in on-again, off-again relationships, in which commitment has not been made, engage in fewer maintenance behaviors when a relationship is on than partners in stable relationships. Specifically, partners in on-again, off-again relationships report that when a relationship is on, they are less cooperative, patient, and polite in communicating with their partners and involve their partners less in their social circles than do partners in stable relationships (Dailey, Hampel, & Roberts, 2010).

EMILY

A lot of people my age don't really date that much. We're more likely to hook up with people. What sounds like the intensifying stage in the model is more like explorational stage for us. Sometimes after physical intimacy with a hookup, something else develops.

Navigation

Navigation is the ongoing process of staying committed and living a life together despite ups and downs, and pleasant and unpleasant surprises. Couples continually adjust, work through new problems, revisit old ones, and accommodate changes in their individual and relational lives. During navigation, partners also continually experience tension from relational dialectics, which are never resolved once and for all. As partners respond to dialectical tensions, they revise and refine the nature of the relationship itself.

To use an automotive analogy, navigating involves both preventive maintenance and periodic repairs (Canary & Stafford, 1994; Dindia, 2000; Parker-Pope,

Onscreen and off, Brad Pitt and Angelina Jolie are a solid, established couple.

WORKPLACE

Workplace Romance

It's hardly surprising that workplace romances are common. When 40% of employees spend more than 50 hours a week on the job (Losee & Olen, 2007), the workplace is the most likely place to find romantic partners. But is it a good idea to get involved with a coworker? As long as the relationship sails along, all may be fine. However, most workplace romances don't last, just like most non-workplace romances don't last. 53% of workplace romances end within 1 year, and 84% end within 5 years (Clark, 2006). When they end, the fallout may include hostility, retaliation, poor teamwork, and even sexual harassment suits. All of these are reasons why many employers discourage or even prohibit sexual and romantic relationships between employees. However, Paul Abramson (2007) argues that every adult has a right to free choices about relationships. Abramson believes we have a constitutional right to consensual adult relationships as long as we don't harm others.

MindTap If you have had a relationship with a co-worker, how much of the fallout mentioned above did you experience?

2010a). The goals are to keep intimacy satisfying and healthy and to deal with any serious problems that arise. To understand the navigation stage, we'll discuss relational culture, placemaking, and everyday interaction.

The nucleus of intimacy is **relational culture**, which is a private world of rules, understandings, meanings, and patterns of acting and interpreting that partners create for their relationship (Bruess, 2011; Bruess & Hoefs, 2006; Wood, 1982, 2000a). Relational culture includes the ways in which a couple manages their relational dialectics. Jan and Byron may negotiate a lot of autonomy and little togetherness, whereas Louise and Kim emphasize connectedness and minimize autonomy. Bob and Cassandra are very open, whereas Mike and Zelda preserve more individual privacy in their marriage. Satisfied couples tend to agree on how to deal with dialectical tensions (Fitzpatrick & Best, 1970).

Relational culture also includes rules and rituals. Couples develop rules, usually unspoken, about how to communicate anger, sexual interest, and so forth. Couples also develop rules about everyday thoughtfulness and kindness. A recent study (Algoe, Gable, & Maisel, 2010) found that when one partner does something thoughtful, the other partner is likely to feel grateful and that gratitude acts as a "booster shot" for romantic relationships. Both women and men felt more satisfied with relationships when they also felt grateful to their partners. In addition, couples develop rules for commemorating special times such as birthdays and holidays and create rituals for couple time (Duck, 2006; Wood, 2006a), celebrations and play, and so forth (Bruess & Pearson, 1997). The rules and rituals that partners develop and follow provide a predictable rhythm for intimate interaction.

Placemaking is the process of creating a comfortable personal environment that reflects the values, experiences, and tastes of the couple (Bateson, 1990; Werner, Altman, Brown, & Ginat, 1993). In our home, Robbie and I have symbols of our travels: Tibetan carpets, a batik from Thailand, ancient masks from Nepal, marble dishes from Turkey, wooden bowls from Belize, and a wood carving from Mexico. Photographs of friends and family members who matter to us are scattered throughout our home, and we have built-in bookshelves, all overloaded, in most rooms. The books, photos, and travel souvenirs make the house into a home that reflects who we are and what we've done together.

An especially important dimension of relational culture is everyday interaction (Parker-Pope, 2010a; Wood & Duck, 2006a, 2006b). The importance of everyday interaction for couples becomes most obvious when it's not possible. People in long-distance relationships say that being together for big moments is not what they miss most; instead, they miss sharing small talk and the trivial details of their days with each other.

Deterioration

Some relationships end abruptly. A person moves or dies or simply quits making contact. Most relationships that have reached the level of commitment, however, deteriorate through a series of stages. Steve Duck (2007; Duck & Wood, 2006) describes relational deterioration as happening through a five-stage sequence: intrapsychic processes, dyadic processes, social support, grave-dressing processes, and resurrection processes.

First, there are *intrapsychic processes*, during which one or both partners begin to feel dissatisfied with the relationship and to focus their thoughts on its problems or shortcomings. As gloomy thoughts snowball, partners may actually bring about the failure of their relationship. During the intrapsychic phase, partners may begin to think about alternatives to the relationship.

Usually we know if we have lost someone we love. The person dies or leaves in a clear-cut way. But what happens if a loved one's departure isn't definite? That's what interests Dr. Pauline Boss. She studies what she calls *ambiguous loss*—the experience in which a person seems both present and absent simultaneously (Boss, 2007). Physical absence happens when someone leaves without goodbye. For instance, the person abruptly disappears with no explanation or is a soldier reported as missing in action. The people left behind know the person is gone, but they have no certainty that the person is dead or forever gone. Psychological absence occurs when someone is physically present but emotionally and mentally absent. For example, a person who is in a coma or who has amnesia or dementia is psychologically absent (Sherman & Boss, 2007).

There are other forms of ambiguous loss in which a person seems to be both present and absent. Children with some forms of autism may be physically present but not psychologically accessible (O'Brien, 2007), and military families often experience ambiguous loss when family members are deployed and contact is difficult (Faber, Willerton, Clymer, MacDermid, & Weiss, 2008). Kristen Norwood (2010) found that many families with a transgender member experienced ambiguous loss. Family members grieved for the loss of a son or brother or father or husband but also recognized the new presence of a daughter or sister or mother or wife.

MindTap Have you experienced ambiguous loss? If so, how did it differ from unambiguous loss?

If not reversed, the intrapsychic phase generally leads to *dyadic processes*, which involve the breakdown of established patterns, rules, and rituals that make up the relational culture. Partners may stop talking over dinner, no longer text when they are running late, and in other ways neglect rules that have operated in their relationship. As the fabric of intimacy weakens, dissatisfaction intensifies.

There are general sex differences in the causes of dyadic breakdown (Duck & Wood, 2006). For many women, unhappiness with a relationship tends to arise when communication declines in quality, quantity, or both. Men, in general, are more likely to be dissatisfied when specific behaviors or activities change (Riessman, 1990). Many women regard a relationship as breaking down if "we don't really communicate with each other anymore," whereas men tend to be dissatisfied if "we don't do fun things together anymore." Women also tend to be more concerned with relationship equity than men. Marital quality diminishes for women as they contribute more whereas men's marital quality increases when they contribute more to domestic labor (DeMaris, 2010).

Another sex difference lies in who notices the problems in a relationship. As a rule, women are more likely than men to notice tensions and early symptoms of problems (Canary & Wahba, 2006; Cancian, 1989).

There are also sex differences in sources of jealousy. In general, women are more jealous of emotional commitments and men are more jealous of sexual involvements. These gender differences also show up in reactions to online relationships. Women are more jealous of a partner's emotional investment in another relationship whereas men are more jealous of a partner's sexual infidelity (cybersex) (Groothof, Dijkstra, & Bareids, 2009).

Dyadic processes may also include discussion of problems and dissatisfaction. This doesn't always occur (Duck, 2007) because many people avoid talking about problems (Baxter, 1984; Metts, Cupach, & Bejlovec, 1989). Although it is painful to talk about the decline of intimacy, avoiding discussion does nothing to resolve problems and may make them worse. The outcome of dyadic processes depends on how committed the partners are, whether they perceive attractive alternatives to the relationship, and whether they have the communication skills to work through problems. If partners lack commitment or the communication skills needed to resuscitate intimacy, they must decide how to tell outsiders that they are parting.

Social support is a phase in which partners look to friends and family for support. Partners may give self-serving accounts of the breakup to save face and to secure sympathy and support from others. Thus, Beth may portray Janine as at fault and herself as the innocent party in a breakup. During this phase, partners often criticize their exes and expect friends to take their side (Duck, 2007; La Gaipa, 1982). Although self-serving explanations of breakups are common, they aren't necessarily constructive. It's a good idea to monitor communication during this period so that we don't say things we'll later regret. When relationships end because of the death of one partner, the surviving person may rely on social networks for sympathy and support.

Grave-dressing processes involve burying the relationship and accepting its end. During grave dressing, we work to make sense of the relationship: what it meant, why it failed, and how it affected us. Usually, people need to mourn intimacy that has died. Even if we initiate a breakup, we are sad about the failure to realize what once seemed possible. Grave-dressing processes also include explaining to others why the relationship ended.

Although some rumination is inevitable and probably healthy, excessive thoughts about an ended relationship tend to hurt us more than they help us. Specifically, people who brood extensively or engage in "what if" thinking are more likely to experience depression and lack of motivation and to adjust less well to breakups than people who ruminate for a short while and then move on (Honeycutt, 2003; Saffrey & Ehrenberg, 2007).

The final part of relationship deterioration involves *resurrection processes*, during which the two people move on with their lives without the other as an intimate. We conceive of ourselves as single again, and we reorganize our lives to break the synchrony that we had with our ex-partner.

The stages we have discussed describe how many romantic relationships evolve. However, not all people follow these stages in this order. For example, people with pragmatic love styles might not allow themselves to enter into euphoria until they have engaged in the very practical considerations of the revising stage. Other couples skip one or more stages in the typical sequences of escalation or deterioration, and many of us cycle more than once through certain stages. For example, a couple might soar through euphoria, work out some tough issues in revising, then go through euphoria a second time. It's also normal for long-term partners to depart from navigation periodically to experience both euphoric seasons and intervals of dyadic breakdown and then move back to navigating. Furthermore, because relationships are embedded in larger systems, romantic intimacy follows different developmental paths in other cultures.

© CandyBox Images/Shutterstock.com

Everyday Skills To gauge the strength of your romantic relationship, complete the activity "Measuring the Strength of Your Relationship" at the end of the chapter or online.

SOCIAL MEDIA AND ROMANTIC RELATIONSHIPS

In the foregoing pages, we have already noted some of the ways in which social media affect romantic relationships. Before social media existed, our choices of relationship partners were largely limited to the people we encountered face to face. In addition, the primary way to check out potential partners was through dating, which requires some expense and time to learn what we can now learn quickly through online profiles. Once couples in long-distance relationships relied on letters and expensive plane tickets and long-distance calls to maintain contact, whereas today we can Skype and text to stay in touch (Tong & Walther, 2011). Even intimates who live together rely on social media to stay in close contact throughout each day (Walther & Ramirez, 2010). In many ways, social media have made it far easier to form and maintain romantic relationships.

At the same time, social media have introduced new challenges for people seeking romance. As noted in this chapter, deception is perhaps more easily accomplished online than face to face. Both sexes tend to misrepresent themselves when posting online profiles (Hall et al., 2010). People may give false information about their physical attractiveness, and people who are less attractive are more likely to embellish their photographs and self-descriptions (Toma & Hancock, 2010).

Another concern about social media is the potential for cyberstalking. Former boyfriends and girlfriends may monitor your online communication and harass you or interfere with your communication with other people. In addition, someone you meet online can become obsessed with you and, in extreme cases, can engage in stalking you online, following your every move and imposing himself or herself into your life.

Social media also offer opportunities for infidelity as the scenario that opened this chapter suggested. While there is nothing new about cheating on a partner, social media increase the opportunities to be unfaithful and perhaps the likelihood of doing so without discovery. When asked how they would feel if they learned their partner had been involved in an online romantic relationship, college students responded that online infidelity was just as wrong and hurtful as in-person betrayal (Henline, Lamke & Howard, 2007).

GUIDELINES FOR COMMUNICATING IN ROMANTIC RELATIONSHIPS

Romantic relationships often experience unique challenges. We'll now discuss four guidelines for communicating to meet such challenges and to build and maintain a healthy, satisfying relationship.

Engage in Dual Perspective

In Chapter 10, we offered the same guideline—engage in dual perspective—for maintaining friendships. It's equally important to engage in dual perspective in romantic relationships (Parker-Pope, 2010a). When we love someone, we want to know and be known by that person. We want to understand and to be understood by that person. And we want to feel that she or he takes our perspective into account when interacting with us. Engaging in dual perspective requires us to get to know the other person really well, and then to use that knowledge to guide our communicative choices.

AUSTIN Mandy's the first girlfriend I've ever had who understands that I need time to think things through when we have a difference of opinion. All of the girls before her pressured me to talk when they wanted to, with no respect for when *I* wanted to. If I refused, they accused me of avoiding conflict or something like that. Mandy gets it that I really need to work things out before I can talk about issues, and she respects that.

Austin gives a good example of what it feels like to have someone you care about take your perspective into consideration. It feels like—and it is—a very special gift. In I–Thou relationships, dual perspective is especially important.

Practice Safe Sex

We usually think of sexual activity in terms of pleasure. In addition to its pleasures, sexual activity can pose serious, even deadly, threats. Engaging in safer sex is a communication issue for two reasons. First, cultural views, often mistaken, about who is likely and not likely to have sexually transmitted diseases are communicated to us through everyday conversations as well as media. Second, engaging in safer sex requires communication between partners. They must talk about their sexual histories, medical checkups, and what each of them requires in terms of protections to feel safe.

Committing to communication about safer sex is a matter of health and survival. Each year, about 2 million people die of AIDS (Collins & Fauci, 2010). Each year 56,000 people in the United States are diagnosed with AIDS (Collins & Fauci, 2010), and more than one and a quarter million people in the United States are living with HIV today (Altman, 2008). Many of them contracted the virus through sex with a hook-up, casual date, or serious romantic partner. New HIV and AIDS cases have actually increased since 1999 (Altman, 2008; Carey & O'Connor, 2004; Schott, 2008). Every single day, worldwide, 6,800 people are infected with HIV (Schott, 2008).

HIV is not the only sexually transmitted disease (STD). In fact, one in four girls ages 14–19 is infected with a common STD ("One in Four," 2008). In 2008, 1,210,523 cases of sexually transmitted chlamydia were reported to CDC. This is the largest number of cases ever reported to CDC

Facts about Sexually Transmitted Diseases

Many people hold dangerous misunderstandings about sexually transmitted diseases (STDs). Let's check the facts. (American Social Health Association, 2005; Cates, Herndon, Schulz, & Darroch, 2004; Collins & Fauci, 2010; Cowley & Murr, 2004; Dennis & Wood, 2012; "One in Four," 2008; http://www.cdc.gov/ncidod/diseases/hepatitis/b/fact.htm).

Misconception: If I'm tested for HIV, and I make sure my sexual partner is, then I'm safe.

The Facts: HIV is not the only STD, and it's not the most common. Other STDs include genital warts, genital herpes, hepatitis B, human papillomavirus (HPV), chlamydia, gonorrhea, syphilis, and trichomoniasis. One in 20 people will get hepatitis B in his or her lifetime, and 15% to 25% of those who do will die of liver disease.

Misconception: I'm heterosexual, so I'm not at risk for HIV.

The Facts: Seventy percent of women who are HIV positive contracted the disease through heterosexual sexual contact.

Misconception: I don't think I'm being too risky because only a few people have STDs.

The Facts: One in two sexually active youths will contract an STD by age 25. Over 65 million Americans are currently living with an STD, and 15 million new cases are diagnosed each year.

Misconception: STDs only affect older people.

The Facts: Half of all new STDs occur in people 15 to 24 years old. Each year, one in four teens contracts an STD. Among blacks, 50% of 14- to 19-year-olds contract an STD.

Misconception: The incidence of STDs is declining.

The Facts: Some STDs, such as genital warts, chlamydia, and gonorrhea, are actually increasing.

Misconception: I can't catch an STD if I have only oral sex.

The Facts: You can contract STDs from oral, anal, or vaginal sexual activity.

Misconception: I could tell if someone had an STD because there are symptoms.

The Facts: Some STDs have no visible symptoms. For instance, HPV, which 50% of sexually active people will contract at some point, often has no symptoms.

Misconception: STDs can be treated, so there aren't serious consequences even if I do get one.

The Facts: Some can be treated. Some are resistant to treatment. And for some, such as HIV, we do not have a cure. Also, because some have no symptoms, people may not seek treatment until it's too late. In all cases, it's best to be treated as early as possible.

for any condition and is a 9.2% increased over the prior year. Rates of reported chlamydia among women have increasing annually since the late 1980s. In 2008, the chlamydia rate in black men was 12 times higher than in white men; the chlamydia rate in black women was 8 times higher than in white women (Centers for Disease Control, 2010).

One reason people sometimes fail to practice safe sex is that they are impaired by alcohol or other drugs, so they don't use their usual good sense and caution. College students often neglect precautions when they drink heavily (Bowen & Michal-Johnson, 1995).

A second reason for not exercising care when engaging in sex is the belief that you are not at risk. Many people rely on talk with friends instead of health professionals for their information about sexual health. This is especially true for young men. Less than 25% of boys aged 15 to 19 have received counseling about STDs whereas nearly 66% of sexually active girls have received some counseling about STDs (Grady, 2010). Based on communication with friends, many people hold dangerous misconceptions such as, "Nice people don't have STDs," "AIDS only affects gays," "You can't get an STD by having oral sex," and "As long as you're monogamous, you're safe." Many people believe that it's sufficient to ask a potential sexual partner if he or she has any sexual diseases, but that assumes people know if they have a disease and will be truthful. One in five people with HIV do not know they have it (Collins & Fauci, 2010). Kara's commentary illustrates the risks of being misinformed.

KARA When I had a medical exam, the doctor told me I had herpes. "What? Me? That's impossible," I said. I only have oral sex because I don't want to risk getting diseases. Turns out you can get them from oral sex, too. Now I have oral herpes, and I will have it for the rest of my life.

A final reason people don't practice safer sex is that they find it difficult and embarrassing to talk about it with an intimate. They find it awkward to ask direct questions of partners ("Have you been tested for HIV?" "Are you having sex with anyone else?") or to make direct requests of partners ("I want you to wear a condom," "I would like us to be tested for STDs before we have sex"). Naturally, it's difficult to communicate explicitly about sex and the dangers of STDs. However, it is far more difficult to live with an STD or the knowledge that you have infected someone else.

The principles of effective interpersonal communication we've discussed can help ease the discomfort of negotiating safer sex. *I* language that owns your feelings is especially important. It is more constructive to say, "I feel unsafe having unprotected sex" than to say, "Without a condom, you could give me an STD." A positive interpersonal climate is fostered by using relational language, such as "we," "us," and "our relationship."

Your health and perhaps your life depend on your willingness to engage in talk about sex. Think about the fact that choosing to practice safe sex is an act of respect toward yourself and your partner: People who care about themselves and their partners are honest about their sexual histories and careful in their sex practices. Before you decide it's too hard to talk about safer sex with your partner, carefully consider the dangers of silence.

Manage Conflict Constructively

Chapter 9 was devoted to managing conflict in relationships. Doing so is important for all kinds of relationships. Yet there are two reasons romantic relationships require special attention to effective conflict management. First, romantic bonds, particularly serious ones, are important to us, and they are fragile. Lack of skill in handling conflicts can end a relationship that really matters.

The second reason for giving special attention to managing conflict in romantic relationships is one we'll discuss in depth. Although we like to think of romantic relationships as loving, many are not. Violence and abuse are unfortunately common between romantic partners, and they cut across lines of class, race, and ethnicity (Jacobson & Gottman, 1998; Johnson, 2006; Spitzberg & Cupach, 1998, 2009; West, 1995; Wood, 2000b, 2001). Researchers (Cahn, 2009) have shown that many people who engage in violence against romantic partners lack the communicative skills to constructively manage emotions and conflicts.

Intimate partner violence, which is sometimes also called domestic violence, occurs not only in marriage but also in dating and cohabiting relationships of both heterosexuals and gays (Johnson, 2006, 2008; Spitzberg & Cupach, 1998, 2009). The Centers for Disease Control's 2011 report states that 1 in 4 U.S. women have been violently attacked by husbands or boyfriends, and 1 in 7 men have been violently attacked by wives or girlfriends. Intimate partner violence is also on the rise in dating relationships, including those of very young people. Nearly 10% of high school students report being physically hurt by a girlfriend or boyfriend, and 1 in 3 high school students report psychological violence from a girlfriend or boyfriend (Hoffman, 2012).

Women and men alike can be targets of violence from intimates. Women exceed men in social aggression, which is intentionally designed to hurt romantic partners by manipulating social relationships (Goldstein, 2011). Yet the majority of reported physical violence is committed by men against women: 95% of cases involve male abusers and female victims (Johnson, 2006). Furthermore, male abusers are far more likely than female abusers to inflict physical injuries, sometimes severe ones (Johnson, 2006). In fact, intimate partner violence is the most common form of violence committed against women in the United States (Haynes, 2009).

It's important to remember that the statistics on violence between intimates are based on reported incidents and are therefore significantly underrepresented: Many people do not report incidents to the police at all. Women may not report assaults by intimate partners because they are afraid that the consequences might be even worse violence, because they want to protect their partners from punishment, or because they want to spare their children or themselves from the abuser's ensuing anger or vengeance. Men abused by women may not report assaults by intimate partners because they feel ashamed or embarrassed that a woman is assaulting them.

Stalking is repeated, intrusive behavior that is uninvited and unwanted, that seems obsessive, and that makes the target afraid or concerned for her or his safety. In studies conducted on college campuses (Spitzberg & Cupach, 2009), 13% to 21% of students report having been stalked (Spitzberg & Cupach, 2009). About half of female victims are stalked by ex-partners and another 25% by men they have dated at least once (Meloy, 2006). Stalking is particularly common on campuses because it is easy to monitor and learn others' routines. Further, IMing and social networking sites such as MySpace and Facebook give stalkers more ways to learn about (potential) victims' habits and patterns.

Relationships in which men abuse women often reflect traditional power dynamics that structure relationships between women and men. Some men are taught to use power to assert themselves and to dominate others (Coan, Gottman, Babcock, & Jacobson, 1997; Sugarman & Frankel, 1996; Truman, Tokar, & Fischer, 1996; Wood, 2004), and some women are socialized to defer and preserve relationships (Ellington & Marshall, 1997; Wood, 2001). When these internalized patterns combine in heterosexual relationships, a foundation exists for men to abuse women and for women to tolerate it rather than to be assertive.

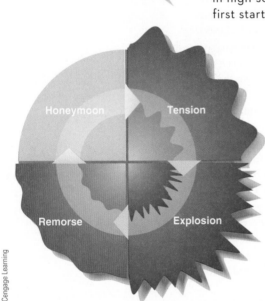

Cengage Learning

Figure 11.3

The Cycle of Abuse

MARLA

Looking back, I can't believe I stayed with Sean for so long, but at the time, I couldn't imagine leaving him. We started hanging out together in high school, and then we both came to this university. When we first started seeing each other, he was so nice to me—flowers sometimes, lots of phone calls, and all the stuff. But the summer after we graduated from high school, he hit me for the first time. I was shocked. He was really sorry and said he was just so stressed about the whole college thing. A little while later, it happened again, and he apologized again, and I forgave him again. But it didn't stop. It got worse. Whenever he was in a bad mood, he took it out on me—really hitting hard, even beating me at times. Finally, my roommate saw bruises and put two and two together and walked me to a counselor at student health. That was the start of getting out of the relationship.

Violence seldom stops without intervention (Clements, Holtzworth-Munroe, Schweinle, & Ickes, 2007). Instead, it usually follows a predictable cycle, just as Marla described: Tension mounts in the abuser; the abuser explodes, becoming violent; the abuser then is remorseful and loving; the victim feels loved and believes the relationship will improve; and then tension mounts, and the cycle begins again (see Figure 11.3).

People who engage in dual perspective (Clements et al., 2007) and who develop skills in identifying and expressing their emotions and in managing conflict are less likely to resort to violence in their romantic relationships.

Adapt Communication to Maintain Long-Distance Relationships

A majority of college students are or have been in long-distance romances (Sahlstein, 2006; Stafford, 2005). Three problems, or tensions, are commonly experienced in long-distance relationships, and each can be addressed with communication. Perhaps the greatest problems are the lack of daily sharing of small events, and unrealistic expectations about time together. As we have seen, sharing ordinary comings and goings helps partners keep their lives interwoven. Routine conversations form and continually reform the basic fabric of our relationships (Wood & Duck, 2006a, 2006b). Technology allows us to engage in more sharing of everyday things, even if not via face-to-face conversation.

The lack of routine contact leads to the second problem faced by long-distance couples: unrealistic expectations for time together. Because partners have limited time together, they often think that every moment must be perfect and that they should be together all of the time. Yet this is an unrealistic expectation. Conflict and needs for autonomy are natural and inevitable in all romantic relationships. They may be even more likely in reunions of long-distance couples because partners are used to living alone and have established independent rhythms that may not mesh well. Laura Stafford, Andy Merolla, and Janessa Castle (2006) studied couples who united in the same place after being in long-distance relationships. One-third of the couples broke up not long after they were in the same place. The key reasons were that being physically together denied the couples what they most valued in the long-distance relationship: novelty and autonomy.

A third common problem in long-distance relationships is unequal effort invested by the two partners. The inequity in investment creates resentment in the person who is assuming the majority of the work to keep the relationship alive and may create guilt in the partner who is investing less.

George Shelley/Media Bakery

The good news is that these problems don't have to sabotage long-distance romance. Many people maintain satisfying commitments despite geographic separation (Stafford, 2005). In fact, there are some noteworthy advantages of long-distance relationships. Because couples aren't together continually, they tend to be more loving and passionate when they are together (Blake, 1996; Reske & Stafford, 1990).

In sum, four guidelines for communication in romantic relationships are to engage in dual perspective, to practice safe sex, to manage conflict effectively to avoid intimate partner violence, and to maintain communication in long-distance relationships. Commitment, flexibility, and effective interpersonal communication help partners meet the challenges of keeping romance healthy and satisfying over the life of the relationship.

CHAPTER SUMMARY

In this chapter, we focused on romantic relationships. Although passion may be the most dramatic dimension of romantic relationships, it is not as central as commitment (the intention to stay together) and intimacy (feelings of warmth and connection). Love comes in many forms; we considered six distinct styles of loving and how they might combine in romantic relationships.

Relationship partners are no longer limited to those people in our immediate physical environment. Social media allow us to meet people who live miles or even continents away. We can get to know others online, and we can also use social media to stay in touch with long-distance partners.

The typical developmental course of romance, whether online or face to face , begins with an escalation phase, in which communication is concentrated on gaining personal knowledge and building a private culture for the relationship. If partners decide to stay together permanently, they commit to a future of intimacy. At that point, they enter the extended phase of navigation, in which they continually adjust to small and large changes in their individual and joint lives. If a romantic bond falters, partners may enter into deterioration and eventually lay their relationship to rest.

Romantic relationships are subject to unique challenges. We discussed three guidelines for communicating to meet these challenges. Engaging in dual perspective, negotiating safer sex, and managing conflict constructively are vital to healthy, satisfying romantic relationships.

Key Concepts

Practice defining the chapter's terms by using online flashcards.

FLASHCARDS...

agape 313
commitment 310
**committed romantic
   relationships** 309
environmental spoiling 317

eros 312
hooking up 316
intimacy 217
ludus 312
mania 313

passion 310
placemaking 320
pragma 312
relational culture 320
storge 312

Continuing the Conversation

MindTap

Copyright Wadsworth 2013

When you've watched the video online, critique and analyze this encounter based on the principles you learned in

PRACTICE...

this chapter. Then compare your work with the author's suggested responses. Online, even more videos will let you continue the conversation with your instructor.

Max and Tara are preparing dinner together. Max has just finished a certificate program at college and informed Tara that he's thinking about continuing coursework in the fall for a bachelor's degree in engineering.

Tara: If you're keeping your project management job, why would you need a bachelor's in engineering? You're not an engineer.

Max: Not now anyway. But I think I might like to be one.

Tara: When did this happen?

Max: Since taking these classes. I didn't realize how interesting it is. Sometimes I get really bored at my job and I think about trying something else.

Tara: So our life is boring now?

Max: I didn't say that. I said my job can be boring.

Tara: Mine can too—do you think I enjoy updating charts all day? That's how jobs are. But *I* still want to see *you* at night.

Max: It's not about us.

Tara: How is this not about us if you're deciding to spend four nights a week in classes instead of with me? And how are we going to afford classes? Your job isn't going to pay for this.

Max: No, it won't. The money will be an issue to discuss. But I'm pretty sure I can get some grants. And we'll figure out how to make more time for us—maybe do more lunches together during the week? Our jobs aren't that far apart.

Tara: I'm just confused. I thought we liked our life the way it is. Now it seems like you want to be someone else. Is this not enough for you anymore? Now you need to be some big man on campus?

Max: I love our life. And I'd hardly be the big man on campus. I know this was a lot for me to throw at you. I just wanted to tell you what I was thinking—we can keep talking about it. I'm not doing anything without you. And I certainly don't want to be someone new. Maybe just someone with a new job. Ok?

Tara: Ok. I guess there are ways to make this work if it's what you really want. I just hope you won't think less of me once you're a big college man.

Max: You're better at your job than any college man or woman could ever be. I respect that.

1. What love styles do you think Max and Tara have? What cues in the dialogue lead you to identify each person's love style?
2. Based on the dialogue, how would you judge Tara and Max's levels of commitment to the relationship?
3. If Max is gone four nights a week, would Tara's lack of contact mean that she would experience "ambiguous loss?"
4. If Max decides to pursue college classes in the fall, what suggestions for maintaining contact in long-distance relationships might be applied to this couple?

Assessing Yourself

Begin the process of applying this chapter's concepts by taking a self-assessment quiz here or online—where you will find out what the results mean.

Purpose: Evaluate your love styles.

Instructions: Below are 12 statements adapted from an instrument for measuring love styles (Hendrick, Hendrick, Foote, & Slapion-Foote, 1984). After each statement, indicate whether you basically agree or disagree.

1. I believe that love at first sight is possible. Agree _____ Disagree _____

PRACTICE...

2. At the first touch, I know if love is a possibility. Agree _____ Disagree _____

3. The best kind of love grows out of a long friendship. Agree _____ Disagree _____

4. Kissing, cuddling, and sex shouldn't be rushed; they will happen naturally when love grows. Agree _____ Disagree _____

5. Part of the fun of being in love is testing your skill at keeping it going to get what you want from the relationship. Agree _____ Disagree _____

6. It is fun to see if I can get somebody to want to date me even if I don't want to date that person. Agree _____ Disagree _____

7. It's best to love someone with a similar background. Agree _____ Disagree _____

8. I couldn't truly love someone I wouldn't be willing to marry. Agree _____ Disagree _____

9. When things aren't going right in a love relationship, my stomach gets upset. Agree _____ Disagree _____

10. When I am in love, I can't think of anything else. Agree _____ Disagree _____

11. I would rather suffer myself than let somebody I love suffer. Agree _____ Disagree _____

12. I would rather break up with someone I love than stand in the way of what she or he needs or wants. Agree _____ Disagree _____

Everyday Skills

Build your communication skills further by completing the following activities here or online.

1. Measuring the Strength of Your Relationship

Ask yourself he following questions, which marriage researcher John Gottman (Gottman & Silver, 2000; Kantowitz & Wingert, 1999) uses to gauge the strength of relationships, based on his assumption that in strong relationships, partners know each other well and share a deep understanding of the other's life, feelings, thoughts, and perceptions.

+ I can name my partner's best friends.
+ I can tell you what stresses my partner is currently facing.
+ I know the names of some of the people who have been irritating my partner lately.
+ I can tell you some of my partner's life dreams.
+ I can list the relatives my partner likes least.
+ At the end of the day, my partner is glad to see me.
+ My partner is one of my best friends.
+ We just love to talk to each other.
+ I feel that my partner knows me pretty well.
+ My partner appreciates the things I do in this relationship.

2. Gendered Personals Ads

Read personals ads that are posted on an online matching site such as match.com or eharmony. Notice how members of each sex present themselves. For instance, do women describe their attractiveness more than men? Do men describe their financial security more than women?

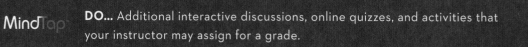
DO... Additional interactive discussions, online quizzes, and activities that your instructor may assign for a grade.

Engaging with Ideas

Reflect and write about the ideas in this chapter by considering questions about personal, workplace, and ethical applications, here or online.

Personal Application Apply the model of romantic relationship development to a romantic relationship that you are in or one you were in. Did you go through all of the stages if the relationship ended, or through navigation if you are still in the relationship? Was your communication during each stage consistent with that described in the model? Did you go through stages that aren't in the model? Are there ways you would modify the model to describe your relationship more accurately?

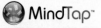

REFLECT ON...

Workplace Application Have you ever had a romantic relationship with a coworker or supervisor? If so, describe ways in which the romance affected your workplace and ways the workplace affected the romance.

Ethical Application What ethical guidelines would you propose for virtual relationships for a person who is in a committed face-to-face relationship? How, if at all, are the guidelines different from those you would propose for a face to face relationship for a person in a committed relationship?

Thinking Critically

Think and write critically about the ideas in this chapter, here or online.

1. If you have a current romantic partner, can you identify her or his love style? How does it fit with your own love style? Does understanding love styles give you any new insights into your relationship?
2. Have you been or are you currently involved in a long-distance relationship? If so, have you experienced one or more of the three special problems of long-distance relationships discussed in this chapter? Did you or do you follow the suggestions for maintaining contact that were presented in this chapter?
3. Have you experienced relationships in which love or commitment, but not both, was present? Describe relationships in which there was love

REFLECT ON...

but not commitment. Describe relationships in which there was commitment but not love. What can you conclude about the impact of each?
4. Do you think that deception is more likely in online than in face-to-face interaction, or are different kinds of deception equally likely in the two kinds of interaction?
5. The U.S. government's Violence Against Women office describes its mission, activities, and resources at http://www.ovw.usdoj.gov/. Research the latest information and statistics on violence at http://www.ncadv.org. Learn about men's commitment to stopping violence against women by visiting the Men Stopping Violence website at http://www.-menstoppingviolence.org.

COMMUNICATION IN FAMILIES

Topics covered in this chapter

Diversity in Family Life

Communication in Families

The Family Life Cycle

Social Media and Family Communication

Guidelines for Effective Communication in Families

After studying this chapter, you should be able to . . .

Describe different definitions of family.

Identify family communication patterns in a particular familial interaction.

Recognize different stages in your family's life cycle.

Assess ways that social media affect families.

Apply chapter guidelines to improve communication in your family.

START... experiencing this chapter's topics with an online video!

READ... the complete chapter text in a rich interactive eBook!

In their mid-twenties, Pat and Chris decide to share their lives. They buy a home and share the responsibilities of mortgage payments, maintenance, and housekeeping. They also pool their financial resources and provide each other with emotional support and care during sickness. After 7 years, Pat's unmarried sibling dies, leaving an 8-year-old child, Jamie, who moves in with Pat and Chris. During the 10 years that follow, Pat and Chris share the emotional and financial responsibilities of raising Jamie as well as typical parental responsibilities, such as taking Jamie to the doctor and the dentist and attending PTA meetings, games, and school concerts. Later, Pat and Chris accompany Jamie to visit college campuses, and the three of them decide which college Jamie will attend.

Are Pat, Chris, and Jamie a family?

Does your answer depend on whether Pat and Chris are a male and a female? Does your answer depend on whether Pat and Chris are legally married and Jamie is legally adopted? Does your answer depend on whether Pat, Chris, and Jamie live in the United States or in France, which grants legal status to unions between any two people who live together?

If this example had appeared in a textbook in 1980, most people in the United States would have counted Pat, Chris, and Jamie a family only if either Pat or Chris was male and the other female, if they were married, and if Jamie was legally adopted. In 1980, most people in the United States viewed "family" as a legally married man and woman who had children. Many people considered a married man and woman who did not have children a "couple" but not a "family."

Today there is less agreement about what a family is. A majority of Americans still conceive of family as involving children, marriage (rather than cohabitation), and blood or legal ties (Baxter, 2011). Also, a majority of Americans today believe that same-sex marriages should be legal. In the past 25 years, views of family have changed a great deal and so have families themselves. For that reason, the first section of this chapter elaborates on the opening theme by noting the diversity of families in our era. The second section of the chapter discusses elements and patterns of family communication. Next, we consider a model of the family life cycle and explore the kinds of families it does and doesn't describe. After discussing the roles of social media in contemporary families, we close the chapter with guidelines for communicating effectively to meet the challenges of family life in our era.

DIVERSITY IN FAMILY LIFE

Before we begin discussing families, we should note that not everyone lives with others. Approximately 25% of households in the United States consist of one person—the greatest number of people living alone in this country's history (Olds & Schwartz, 2010).

The other 75% of Americans have formed diverse types of families. Think for a minute about your friends and acquaintances. How many different family forms do they embody? When I did this exercise myself, I came up with 14 different kinds of families in my social circle:

- A heterosexual African American man and woman who have been married for 12 years, who have two children, and who both work outside the home.
- A heterosexual Caucasian woman and man who have cohabited for 2 years, who are child free, and who both work outside the home.
- Two gay men, both Caucasian, who have cohabited for 20 years, who both work outside the home, and who have an adopted son from another country.
- A heterosexual Caucasian man and Latina woman who are married and have three children; he works outside the home, and she is a stay-at-home mom.
- A single Vietnamese man who has built close relationships with friends whom he considers his family.
- Two lesbians, one Caucasian, one African American, who married last year after cohabiting for 26 years and who have two adopted teenaged sons of a race different from theirs.
- A single Caucasian woman who adopted a daughter from Russia and who works outside the home.
- A widowed African American grandmother who is raising her granddaughter.

- A child-free marriage between a Caucasian man who lives in Pennsylvania and a Chinese-American woman who lives in North Carolina.
- A man and a woman of different races, both in their second marriage, who have five children from their previous marriages and who both work outside the home.
- A stay-at-home Caucasian dad who is married to a Caucasian woman who works outside the home.
- A heterosexual Caucasian man and woman who live as a couple, having raised two children, both of whom have moved across the country.
- A 27-year-old single Hispanic mom whose mother just moved in with her.

If we look beyond mainstream culture in the United States, we discover even more diversity in family forms.

- In some countries, marriages are arranged by families, and spouses may get to know each other only *after* the wedding ceremony. In some arranged marriages, the preferred match is between first cousins (Strong, DeVault, & Cohen, 2011).
- Polygamy is practiced in some societies (Regan, 2008).
- Some cultures regard marriage as so sacred that divorce is allowed only if a spouse denounces ancestors or kills someone in his or her mate's family (WuDunn, 1991).
- In the Vanatinai of the South Pacific, dining together without others defines marriage more than sleeping together (Coontz, 2005b).
- In parts of India, Africa, and Asia, children as young as six may marry, although they may not live with a spouse until later. In many other societies, however, marriage joins two families, and couples are intricately connected to both families, including cousins, grandparents, and great-grandparents. It is not unusual for multiple generations of family to live in the same home (Strong, et al., 2011).
- Traditional Native Americans consider the clan, a group of related families, as the family unit (Yellowbird & Snipp, 2002).
- Many Latinas and Latinos consider *compadres* (godparents) members of the family (Strong et al., 2011).

MANSOORA

I find it very odd that Americans marry only each other and not whole families. In South Africa, people marry into families. The parents must approve of the choice, or marriage does not happen. After marriage, the wife moves in with the husband's family. To me, this is stronger than a marriage of only two people.

Diverse Forms of Families

The most common family form in the United States continues to be marriage although fewer Americans are married today than in the past. Currently, 51% of all Americans are married ("Fraying Knot," 2013). However, this percentage is significantly less than the 72% of Americans who were married in 1960 ("Fraying Knot,"

2013). Despite the decline in marriage, a majority of 18- to 34-year-old men and women of all races regard having a happy marriage as a top priority (Knox & Hall, 2010), and 81% of high school students expect to get married (Blow, 2013; "Fraying Knot," 2013). In fact, only 6% of whites and 12% of non-whites say they have never been married and never want to be (Blow, 2013).

Contemporary Americans are marrying at later ages than previous generations, which partially accounts for the decline in the percentage of married people. Whereas the typical bride in 1960 was not even 21, today the average age of first marriage in about 27 for women and 29 for men (Coontz, 2013).

No longer is marriage in the United States defined as one man and one woman. In 2013, the Supreme Court ruled that same-sex couples are entitled to the same Federal rights as mixed-sex couples, thereby echoing majority sentiment in America. Many states have passed laws recognizing same-sex marriages. As a result, increasing numbers of gays and lesbians are choosing to marry.

PEGGY My mom and Adrienne have lived together since she and Daddy divorced when I was two. We've always been a family. We eat together, work out problems together, vacation together, make decisions together—everything a heterosexual family does. But my mom and Adrienne aren't accepted as a legitimate couple. We've had to move several times because they were "queers," which is what a neighbor called them. Mom's insurance company won't cover Adrienne, so they have to pay for two policies. It goes on and on. I'll tell you, though, I don't know many heterosexual couples as close or stable as Adrienne and Mom.

Yet not everyone marries, and not everyone who marries stays married. Of adults in the United States, 28% have never married, and the number of unmarried people in the United States has doubled since 1960 (Coontz, 2013; "Fraying Knot," 2013). By the age of 35, 10% of American women have lived with three or more husbands or domestic partners, showing that commitments don't necessarily last (Cherlin, 2010).

Not being married doesn't necessarily mean not having children. Approximately one-third of American families consist of a single parent and a child or children ("Fraying Knot," 2013). More than 40% of births in America are to unmarried parents (Coontz, 2007, "Fraying Knot," 2013). Single women and single men who adopt children increase the number of single-parent families. Also adding to the number of single-parent families are widows, widowers, and divorced parents who have custody of children.

Cohabitation is a popular family form for some couples cannot marry or choose not to marry. There are many reasons why some people choose not to marry: Some don't marry because state laws prohibit them from marrying. Others don't marry because they don't want to, or aren't ready for a total commitment. And some people don't marry because they reject the institution of marriage and see it as incompatible with their values and identities. Although cohabitation before marriage was once linked to a higher divorce rate, this is no longer the case. Since the 1990s, people who cohabit before marriage are no more or less likely to divorce than those who don't (Manning & Cohen, 2012; Smock & Manning, 2010).

> **DIMITRI**
>
> I'm crazy about Bridgette, but I'm not ready for marriage now—not even ready to think about that! There's a lot I want to do on my own before I think about settling down permanently and having a family. But I do love Bridgette, and I want to be with her now and in more than a casual way.

Some cohabitors view living together as a "trial marriage" that allows them to assess whether they truly want to be together for the long term (Regan, 2008). For other people, cohabitation is a preferred permanent alternative, not just a precursor to marriage. They care enough about each other to want to live together and perhaps raise children, but they dislike the institution of marriage or they don't want to marry for practical, often financial, reasons. For them, cohabitation is a way to make a permanent commitment on their own terms. Audrey, who has cohabited for 15 years, explains why she chooses not to marry.

> **AUDREY**
>
> What I feel for Don isn't a matter of what's on a piece of paper or what could be said before a preacher. We don't need those formalities to know we love each other and want to spend our lives with each other. Both of us prefer to know we stay together because we love each other, not because of some legal contract.

Diverse Goals for Families

Families are diverse not only in the people who belong to them but also in their goals—the reasons people want to be involved in long-term relationships. Yet the reasons for families have varied over time, and there continue to be a range of reasons today.

Historically, marriage has been regarded as a means to other goals. In hunting and gathering societies, unions were strategic arrangements to preserve peace between tribes (Rosenblum, 2006). For ancient Greeks, the

Communication in Everyday Life

INSIGHT

Voluntary Kin

Families are no longer defined exclusively by blood and kin. People are increasingly creating social networks that function as families. Communication scholars have identified four types of voluntary kin (Braithwaite, Bach, Baxter, Diverniero, Hammonds, Hosek, Willer, & Wolf, 2010). Substitute family replace biological and legal family. For instance, if families of origin reject someone who is gay or trans, that person may form close familial ties with friends. Supplemental family fulfills needs and desires not met by biological and legal family. For instance, you might have a friend with whom you are closer than you are to siblings. Convenience family grows out of a particular context such as a workplace, a particular time period such as people on a study abroad program, or a stage of life such as hallmates in the first year of college. Finally, extended family are people considered part of biological and legal families, for instance the neighbor who becomes the godfather of your children or an aunt whom you consider a sister.

From The WallStreet Journal, Nov. 6, 1996. Reprinted by permission of Cartoon Features Syndicate

"And the prince and princess lived happily ever after, but not with each other."

purpose of marriage was to produce offspring—passion and pleasure were found with lovers outside the marriage (Rosenblum, 2006). During the Middle Ages, marriages functioned to forge political alliances, link families, and cement property transactions. The idea that passion and love are reasons to marry was not widely accepted until the 18th century. Prior to that time, the wedding day often marked the end of the bride's and groom's romances with other people and their entry into the purely practical, unemotional institution of marriage.

Beginning in the late 1700s or early 1800s, most people in the United States started choosing mates based on love and companionship. In times and places where marriage served other purposes, the waning of love—or the absence of it from the start—was not a reason to consider ending the marriage (Coontz, 2005b). If stable families are a goal, then love may not be the ideal basis for forming a family.

Historically, Americans also have viewed raising children as a primary objective of marriage (Coontz, 2005a, 2005b). Raising children is no longer seen as the only goal of marriage. In 1990, 65% of Americans said children were very important to successful marriage, but two decades later only 41% believe that (Parker-Pope, 2010a). Increasing in popularity are individualized relationships, which enhance each partner's personal accomplishments and satisfaction.

JOANNA I'd be miserable without my job. I love the sense of accomplishment that I get from teaching first graders. When a child finally catches on to reading, it's magic. Being part of that magic for so many children over the years gives me a sense of purpose in life.

As Joanna points out, many people of both sexes define their work not just as a source of income but as central to who they are. They find work personally fulfilling. As we will see later in the chapter, balancing work and family responsibilities and opportunities is one of the greatest challenges facing families today.

As work increasingly provides personal fulfillment and economic support, women are becoming less dependent on men for financial support. Men are also less dependent on wives to take care of children and homemaking. Day care and live-in babysitters are available today, and labor-saving appliances make home maintenance much less time- and labor-intensive than it was even 20 years ago. What was a full-time job in the 1950s can be done in far less time today. In other words, for both women and men today, marriage is more a choice than a necessity (Coontz, 2005a, 2005b; Galvin, 2006).

There are reasons other than the ones we've discussed that motivate people to marry. Some people see marriage as a route to financial security or a co-parent for existing children or a child on the way. A Kaiser Family Foundation poll reported that 7% of Americans marry to gain access to health care coverage (Sack, 2008).

Cultural Diversity of Family Forms

Our choices of whom to marry have also grown. In the 1900s an overwhelming majority of Americans married people of their own race. Today, marriage between members of different races is more popular and accepted. Also increasing is the number of Americans who marry someone who was born in a different country. Today, approximately 5 million Americans are married to someone from another country: That's double the number of these marriages since 1960 (Palmar, 2013). Interfaith marriages have also increased in America. In her book, *'Til Faith Do Us Part*, Naomi Riley (2013) describes enduring and happy marriages between an evangelical Christian and a Muslim, a Jew and a Catholic, a Jew and a lapsed Jehovah's Witness, and others.

Diverse Family Types

Given the diversity in family forms and goals that we have discussed, you won't be surprised to learn that researchers have identified varied ways that people organize their families. Communication scholar Mary Ann Fitzpatrick (1988) and her colleagues (Fitzpatrick & Best, 1970; Koener & Fitzpartrick, 2002a, b, 2006; Noller & Fitzpatrick, 1992) identified three distinct types of relationships: traditional, independent, and separate. Couples who fit into the traditional category are highly interdependent and emotionally expressive with each other. Traditional couples also share conventional views of marriage and family life, and they engage in conflict regularly.

Independents made up 22% of the couples in Fitzpatrick's study. Independents hold less conventional views of marriage and family life. Compared to traditionals, independents are less interdependent, more emotionally expressive, and they engage in conflict more often. Autonomy is moderately high for independents, so this couple type is likely to have fewer common interests and activities than traditional couples. If Fitzpatrick were to repeat her study today, she would likely find a far greater number of independents because greater emphasis is now placed on individual fulfillment and personal happiness.

© ArrowStudio/Shutterstock.com

The third marital type is separates, who made up 17% of the couples Fitzpatrick studied. As the term implies, separates are highly autonomous. Partners give each other plenty of room, and they share less emotionally than the other two types. Separates also try to avoid conflict, perhaps because it often involves emotional expressiveness and pushes them to negotiate to reach a common decision rather than to operate separately.

In Fitzpatrick's research, almost 60% of couples fit into one of these three types of marriage, but 40% did not. In these couples, which Fitzpatrick termed "mixed marriages," the husband and wife subscribe to different perspectives on marriage. The most common form of mixed marriage is the separate–traditional couple. In the couples Fitzpatrick studied, it was typically the wife who held a traditional view of marriage and wanted high interdependence and emotional closeness. Generally, husbands in mixed marriages fit the separate category. They wanted a high degree of autonomy, and a number of them felt emotionally divorced from the marriage.

At the time of Fitzpatrick's research, the highest levels of marital satisfaction were reported by traditional and separate–traditional couples. At first, it seems surprising that separate–traditional couples would have high satisfaction. However, it makes sense when we realize that this kind of couple embodies conventional gender roles. The traditional partner, who wants closeness and emotional expressiveness, is generally a woman, and the separate partner, who wants high independence and little emotional expressiveness, is generally a man. Because their preferences are consistent with conventional feminine and masculine roles, they may see the relationship as complementary, with each partner contributing something the other values. The traditional partner may meet her or his needs for connection and intimacy through relationships with friends, children, and other family members. The separate partner is not expected to provide emotional intimacy and can derive his or her satisfaction from independent activities such as career or hobbies.

Since Fitzpatrick conducted her research, Western values have changed markedly. Egalitarian values have become much more central in relationship satisfaction and durability (Coontz, 2013), which suggests that there might be fewer couples who fit the traditional category today, and non-traditional couples might have higher satisfaction than they did in the 1970s.

COMMUNICATION IN FAMILIES

All families communicate, but not all families communicate in the same ways. Each family has its own norms and patterns of communicating. The communication that characterizes a family shapes the closeness, openness, and satisfaction of family members.

Elements in Family Communication

Clifford Notarius (1996) identifies three key elements, as shown in Figure 12.1, that influence satisfaction with long-term relationships: words, thoughts, and emotions.

MindTap

Everyday Skills To explore communication patterns used by married couples, complete the activity "Identifying Marital Types" at the end of the chapter or online.

Words refer to how family members talk and behave toward each other. Communication influences self-esteem and feelings about the relationship. In happier relationships, members tend to communicate more support, agreement, understanding, and interest than in less happy couples. In contrast, unhappy families include frequent criticism, negative statements, mind reading, and egocentric communication, in which family members do not engage in dual perspective (Gottman & Carrère, 1994; Gottman & Silver, 2000; Notarius, 1996).

The differences in the communication of happy and unhappy families echo the material on climate and conflict that we discussed in Chapters 8 and 9. The differences also suggest the importance of forgiveness, at least of minor transgressions. Lorig Kachadourian, Frank Fincham, and Joanne Davila (2004) found that willingness to forgive was positively related to satisfaction with the relationship.

The second element in family communication is *thoughts*, which is how family members think about each other and family. Our thoughts shape our emotions and words. From Chapter 3 you'll recall that, in satisfying relationships, people tend to attribute nice actions by others to stable, internal qualities that are within individual control (Fincham, Bradbury, & Scott, 1990). For example, a mother might think, "My son came home for the weekend because he is a thoughtful person who makes time to show me he cares." Likewise, in satisfying relationships, people tend to attribute negative actions and communication to unstable, external factors that are beyond individual control. If a daughter forgets to call on her parents' anniversary, the father might explain it by telling himself, "She forgot because she is overwhelmed with final exams."

A third key to family communication is *emotions*, which we discussed in detail in Chapter 7. As we saw in that chapter, emotions are affected by words and thoughts. How we feel is affected by what we say to others and what we communicate to ourselves through self-talk. For example, the attributions we make for our partners' behaviors affect how we feel about those behaviors. If a wife sees her husband's gift of flowers as evidence of his thoughtfulness and caring, she will feel closer to him than if she sees the flowers as something he bought because they were on sale.

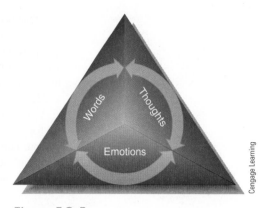

Figure 12.1

The Circle of Words, Thoughts, and Emotions

Cengage Learning

Communication in Everyday Life

DIVERSITY

Love Languages

How do you communicate love to family members? How do people in your family express their love to you? Gary Chapman (2010) has identified five distinct ways that we communicate love, which he calls the five love languages.

Affirming words: Written or oral compliments, support, and expressions of valuing another communicate love.

Quality time: Being mindfully present with another and giving another your total attention for an extended amount of time are loving behaviors.

Gifts: Small or large, expensive or not, gifts are tokens of affection and thoughtfulness.

Service: Doing chores or unrequested favors such as tuning up a car tells another that you care about her or him.

Touch: Physical contact, sexual or otherwise, is an important way of expressing affection and intimacy.

Most of us have one or two primary languages of love—perhaps words and touch are most meaningful to you—and other love languages mean less to us. However, there is no guarantee that people you love will have the same language preferences that you do. It's important to engage in dual perspective to learn what another counts as loving.

Obviously, the words, thoughts, and actions that family members find satisfying depend on many factors, including family type. For example, we would expect separate partners to communicate less than traditional partners. However, we would still expect that separates who are happy together and satisfied with their shared life would communicate supportively, make relationship-enhancing attributions, and feel positive about each other and the relationship.

Words, thoughts, and emotions affect each other in overlapping ways: What we feel affects how we communicate and how we think about ourselves, others, and our family. What we think influences how we feel and communicate. How we communicate shapes how we and our partners think and feel about relationships, ourselves, and each other.

Communication Patterns

Building on Notarius's views of the three keys to family communication, we can now consider overall communication patterns in families. Communication researchers (Fitzpatrick & Ritchie, 1994; Koerner & Fitzpatrick, 2002a, b, 2006; Keating, Russell, Cornacchione & Smith, 2013) have identified two key dimensions of communication that define a family's communication style. The first dimension, **conversation orientation**, refers to how open or closed communication is. In families with high conversation orientation, members feel free to openly express their thoughts and feelings about a range of topics, including ones that are personal or private. Families that are low in conversation orientation tend to talk mainly about superficial topics, and members tend not to disclose personal feelings and thoughts.

The second dimension of family communication style is **conformity orientation**, which refers to the extent to which family members are expected to adhere to a family hierarchy and conform in beliefs. Families differ in how much they expect members to respect hierarchy, particularly parental authority and in how much they expect family members to avoid conflict by agreeing (or acting as if they agree). In families that have high conformity orientation, there is little overt conflict and lines of authority are respected. Families with low conformity orientation experience more disagreement and conflict, and children are more or less likely to adhere to all of their parents' beliefs and values.

These two dimensions of family communication, conversation orientation and conformity orientation, combine to create four basic types of family communication patterns.

Figure 12.2

Family Communication Patterns

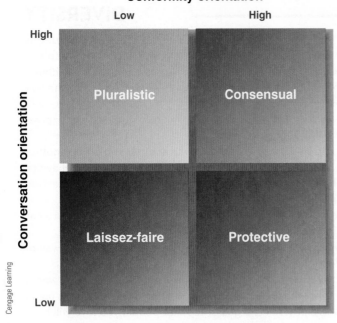

Consensual families have high conversation orientation and high conformity orientation. In consensual families, communication tends to have substantial depth and breadth. Parents encourage children to express their ideas and feelings, yet once everyone has had their say, parents expect and encourage children to adhere to the parents' values and beliefs.

Pluralistic families are high on the dimension of conversation and low on conformity. Communication is open, all family members are encouraged to express their thoughts and feelings, and agreement among family members is not required or compelled. Parents respect their children's views and decisions, even if they do not agree with them.

Low conversation and high conformity define **protective families**' communication. Conflict is avoided, and children are expected to adhere to parents' values, beliefs, and decisions, which may undermine open and honest communication between parents and children (Keating et al., 2013).

The final type of family communication pattern is laissez-faire. As the name implies, there is limited connection among members of **laissez-faire families**. Parents and children have limited interaction, children are inclined to be relatively independent of parents, and family members may not feel close bonds. Both conversation and conformity orientations are low.

As you might imagine, these basic communication patterns shape what happens in families as well as how close family members are. Easy topics might be discussed in families with any of the four communication patterns, but dealing with difficult topics might be more challenging and less likely in families that have protective or consensual patterns where agreement is expected.

THE FAMILY LIFE CYCLE

Many families follow a general pattern of evolution (Olson & McCubbin, 1983). Although these stages are experienced by many families, they may not apply, for instance, to the developmental paths of many cohabiting, gay, single parent, and lesbian couples. Nor do all the stages apply to child-free marriages. Couples who do not have children would not go through Stages 2, 3, 4, or 5 because raising and launching children would not be part of their relationship.

Stage 1: Establishing a Family

During this phase, a couple settles into a committed relationship and works out expectations, interaction patterns, and daily routines for their shared life. Partners get accustomed to living together. For couples who are married, spouses get used to the labels "wife" and "husband" and to the social and legal recognition of their union.

Stage 2: Enlarging a Family

A major change in many families' lives is the addition of children. The transition to parenthood typically brings a whole array of joys, problems, challenges, and new constraints for the couple. It also introduces new roles. In addition to her identities as wife or partner and probably a worker, a woman also becomes a mother. A man becomes a father in addition to his identities as a husband or partner and probably a worker.

Furthermore, children decrease the amount of couple time and change the focus of a couple's communication. For most parents, children are a primary focus of conversation: "How are they doing?" "Which of us is taking Susie to the doctor tomorrow?" "When you had the conference with Bobby's teacher, did she have any suggestions for dealing with his behavior problems?" "How do we save money for their college education?"

STAN

Just about everything in our lives changed when Dina was born. We had to sell our little two-door sports car because we couldn't use Dina's car seat in it. We used to enjoy a glass of wine before dinner, but now one of us fixes the dinner while the other feeds and bathes Dina. We used to sometimes decide on the spur of the moment to drive to the beach for a day trip, but now we either have to plan ahead and hire a babysitter or pack everything Dina will need, from diapers to food to toys. We're both so tired from ragged sleep because Dina wakes up several times each night. When we go to bed, neither of us is interested in sex—sleep is far more appealing.

Stan's reflection on becoming a parent is not unusual. Mari Clements and Howard Markman (1996) note that a baby can be both a bundle of joy and a home wrecker. A great deal of research shows that marital satisfaction declines after the birth of a child or children (Belsky & Rovine, 1990; Clements & Markman, 1996; Cowan, Cowan, Heming, & Miller, 1991; Segrin & Flora, 2005). For many years, researchers assumed that the decline resulted from the presence of children and the demands they make. Yet that may not be true.

A research team headed by Howard Markman (Markman, Clements, & Wright, 1991) followed 135 couples from engagement through 10 or more years of marriage. The team discovered that marital satisfaction declines after children arrive, which usually occurs after a few years of marriage. However, they also found that marital satisfaction declines after the first few years for couples who do not have children. In other words, after the first few married years, most couples experience a dip in marital satisfaction *regardless of whether they have children*.

Parents whose ethnicity is not the privileged one in their culture tend to invest more energy in instilling ethnic pride in children than do parents who belong to privileged ethnic groups. African American parents were more likely to act as cultural advisors and to use more stringent discipline than European American parents (Socha, Sanchez-Hucles, Bromley, & Kelly, 1995). African American mothers were more likely than European American mothers to characterize adolescent daughters as "best friends." They also tend to set more hard-and-fast rules and to engage in more sarcasm than European American mothers (Pennington & Turner, 2004). In African American families headed by single women, daughters frequently exhibit greater self-reliance and self-esteem than their European American counterparts (McAdoo, 2006). African American parents also place significantly more emphasis on teaching children racial identity, history, and pride—as well as awareness of prejudice and sarcasm in the world.

Thus, the second stage of family life may be a time of adjusting expectations and experiencing some disappointments. It may also be that this period in family life is prone to a phenomenon known as *pileup* (Boss, 1987). Pileup occurs when many negative events occur in a short period of time and strain a family's ability to cope. A baby arrives, an older child is having problems in school, one partner's father is diagnosed with a serious heart condition, one partner gets a promotion that requires moving across the country. That's a lot of change and a lot of stress to handle in a short span of time.

Everyday Skills To consider the impact of children on committed relationships, complete the activity "Bundles of Joy and Change" at the end of the chapter or online.

Stage 3: Developing a Family

Parent–child relationships are critical influences on children's identities (Socha & Stamp, 2009; Socha & Yingling, 2010). Recall from Chapter 2 that attachment styles develop in a child's first human relationship, which is usually with a parent, and that parent is more often the mother than the father. A consistently loving, attentive parent cultivates a secure attachment style in the child. Other attachment styles are fostered by other patterns of caregiving. Parents also shape children's self-concepts through labels ("such a sweet little girl," "such a big, strong boy") and identity scripts that make it clear who children are and are supposed to be.

Although fathers spend less time than mothers with children, today's fathers are more active parents than fathers of previous generations. Today, college-educated mothers spend an average of 21.2 hours a week with children and mothers with less education spend an average of 15.9 hours a week with children. By comparison, college-educated fathers average 9.6 hours and less educated fathers average 6.8 hours in an average week (Parker-Pope, 2010b). A recent study was based on taping the daily lives of 32 dual-career families from 2002 until 2005. Among the findings were that housework claims 27% of mothers' time and 18% of fathers' time. Mothers give themselves less time for breaks from housework and child care: Leisure breaks account for 11% of mothers' time and 23% of fathers' time (Carey, 2010).

Stage 4: Encouraging Independence

As children enter adolescence, they tend to seek greater autonomy. This is a natural part of their effort to establish identities distinct from those of their parents. Often, this stage involves some tension between parents and children. Parents may feel hurt by the children's reduced interest in being with the family. Also, parents may not approve of some of their children's interests, activities, and friends. Children may feel that parents are overly protective or intrusive.

For children, this is a very important phase in personal development. They are learning to be less dependent on their families, which is essential to becoming a healthy adult. Ideally, parents realize that their children need to try their wings, and they encourage progressive independence—while keeping a watchful eye.

MAGGIE After Annie arrived, Rick and I decided we wanted to attend a parenting class. It was really helpful in preparing us for the stages Annie would go through. But one thing that the teacher emphasized was that our primary job as parents was to "prepare your children not to need you." Those were her exact words. I still remember them. It just crushed me to think my job was to prepare our baby not to need me, but I knew that was good advice. Hard but good.

Stage 5: Launching Children

Launching is a time of vital change for most families. Children leave home to go to college, marry, or live on their own. When the last child leaves home, parents, who for 18 years or more have centered their lives around children, now find themselves a couple again. For parents, this can be an abrupt change. For instance, if there is only one child (or twins or triplets) in the family, when that child leaves, the parents become a couple. For parents who have more than one child, the children tend to leave home at different times, so the adjustment to a smaller family is more gradual. For the children, who are now young adults, this is a time of increased independence and self-discovery.

MARK When you have a child with special needs, the launching phase doesn't happen. We'll never have an empty nest, because Josh will never be able to live on his own. When he was born, we thought he was the most perfect baby in the world. By the time he was 1, we knew he wasn't, knew something was wrong. He is brain-damaged and somewhat autistic. He's 32 and still lives in our home. I retired last year, but our nest isn't empty.

Mark makes a good point. Some parents never experience the so-called empty nest. Although some special needs children are able to live relatively independent lives, many are not. In addition to having a child with special needs, parents may feel responsible for raising grandchildren or for letting their children live at home if they are unable to support themselves.

The recession that began in 2008 made it very difficult for new college graduates to find jobs. Often called "boomerang children," they often return to parents' home for financial reasons: high debt, a need to save money, or inability to find a job. When adult children move in with parents, family roles have to be renegotiated (Vogl-Bauer, 2009). Unlike when they lived at home earlier, the adult children have become accustomed to freedom from parental rules and supervision. Parents, too, may have come to enjoy greater space and freedom that comes with not having children in the home. Individual families have to figure out logistical issues and how financial responsibilities and contributions to the household will be managed. If the boomerang children have their own children, that adds to the complexity of family dynamics. Mark's reflection also reminds us that the stage model of family life cycles doesn't describe all families. Tracy makes the same point with her story.

> It would be a real challenge to try to fit my family into the model of the family life cycle. My parents divorced when I was 6 years old. My sister and I lived with Mom until we went to college, her 4 years ago and me 2 years ago. Then, Mom started seeing this man who transferred to our town. He was a widower with 3-year-old twin boys. Last year, they got married, so my family is in the postlaunching and developing-a-family phases!

TRACY

Stage 6: Postlaunching of Children

After the departure of children from the home, partners have to redefine their marriage. This period can be a time of lower satisfaction between partners if the couple is out of practice in engaging each other outside of their roles as parents. The partners have more time for each other but that may be a blessing, a curse, or both.

For some couples, this is a time of renewed love—a second honeymoon—as they enjoy being able to focus on their paired relationship and not having to plan around children's schedules. Many couples find the "empty nest years" the happiest in their marriages because there are fewer stresses and more couple time (Parker-Pope, 2009; Scarf, 2008).

For other couples, the absence of children makes obvious the distance that has arisen between them, and dissatisfaction grows. Children can often be the glue that holds couples together: Some couples divorce after the last child has left home. Gretchen points out that many partners find that they have to relearn how to be together with just each other and how to enjoy activities that don't involve their children.

> When our last child left home for college, Brant and I realized how little we had in common as a couple. We'd centered our lives around the three children and family activities. Without any of them in the home anymore, it was like Brant and I didn't know what to do with each other. At first, it was really awkward. If we weren't Christians, maybe we would have divorced, but both of us feel marriage is forever. That meant we had to rediscover each other. We went to a weekend workshop sponsored by our church. It was called "Rediscovering Love in Your Marriage." That workshop got us started in finding our way back to each other.

GRETCHEN

349

Communication in Families

Stage 7: Retirement

Retirement brings about further changes in family life. Like other changes, those ushered in by retirement can be positive or negative. For many people, retirement is a time to do what they want instead of focusing on earning a living. Many people who retire are highly active, often volunteering in community groups, traveling, and taking up new hobbies or interests.

For other people, retirement may evoke feelings of boredom and lack of identity. Individuals whose sense of self-worth is strongly tied to their work may feel unanchored when they retire. Naturally, this discontent can foster tension in the marriage.

STUART I looked forward to retiring for years, and I finally did it 2 years ago. For about 6 months, it was everything I had dreamed of—sleeping as late as I wanted, no pressures or deadlines, golfing anytime I felt like it. Then, I got kind of bored with nothing I had to do and nobody who was counting on me for ideas or work. Every day seemed like every other day—long and empty. You can only sleep and golf for so long.

HOWARD I retired 4 years ago, and the last 4 years have been the best years of my life! I'd always loved woodworking, but I had little time for it when I was punching the time clock. Now, I can spend as much time as I want working in my shop. I've even started selling things at the local co-op. When I was working, I always felt guilty that I didn't give anything back through civic or volunteer work. Now, I have time to contribute to my community—the Lions Club is my main volunteer activity. We raise a lot of money to help people who have vision problems and other kinds of things where they need some help. My life is more satisfying now than it has ever been.

During retirement years, the family may grow again, this time through the addition of grandchildren (Mares, 1995). Grandchildren can be welcome new members of the family who provide interest and an additional focus for grandparents' lives. The coming of grandchildren may also foster new kinds of connection and communication as grandparents talk with their children about raising grandchildren and as they interact with children for whom they don't have primary responsibility.

The later years in parents' lives can also be difficult medically. It

---

Communication in Everyday Life

SOCIAL MEDIA

Connecting Generations

How do social media change the ways that families communicate? To find out, AARP and Microsoft conducted a joint research project to examine how computers, mobile devices, and the Internet affect frequency and quality of communication among family members (Connecting Generations, 2013). Here are the results:

83%, including at least 80% in every age group, regards online communication as a helpful way to stay in touch with family members.

More than two-thirds of teenagers think computer contact increases both the quantity and quality of their communication with family members who live a substantial distance from them.

Only slightly fewer people aged 39 and older think computer contact increases the frequency (63%) and quality (57%) of contact with family members.

is not unusual for age to be accompanied by health problems. In addition to physical challenges, there may be cognitive impairments ranging from forgetfulness to Alzheimer's. Such physical and mental changes are difficult both for the people experiencing them and for loved ones who witness the changes.

As we noted when introducing this discussion of family life cycle, the model doesn't apply to all families. Mark and Tracy wrote of their family experiences, which do not fit well into the sequence of stages in the generic model of the family life cycle. This is another reminder of how diverse families are in our era: No single model represents all of them.

SOCIAL MEDIA AND FAMILY COMMUNICATION

Social media have changed family communication many ways. One obvious change is that social media increase the ways that family members can interact. In addition, cell phones and email allow family members to be in touch frequently through the exchange of very brief messages. Smart phones allow contact between young children and parents, between parents, among siblings, and so forth.

As children grow older and need more independence from family, social media have complex influences. On the one hand, social media make it very easy for adolescents to stay in minute-by-minute contact with peers and, thus, to establish relationships outside of the family. Yet those same media make it easy for adolescents to stay in touch with parents. Some teenagers text their mothers 15 times a day, asking their moms' opinions on shoes they are thinking about buying, course registration, and so forth. That makes it harder for adolescents to achieve a healthy degree of separation from parents (Hafner, 2009; Turkle, 2008).

Social media also enable a degree of monitoring or tracking that parents did not have before the era of information technologies. Parents may use phones and other devices to require children to maintain contact and even to monitor children who are out of the home.

Social media facilitate communication when family members no longer live together or even in close proximity. Parents and children can video chat when children are engaged in study abroad programs or when they move a significant distance from their parents' home. Siblings stay in touch by texting and posting on social network sites. Grandparents are able to see photos of grandchildren and to talk with them via Skype and other VOIP systems. Games also allow ongoing connection. Each day, I play Words With Friends with my sister and my niece, and we sometimes chat while playing.

Social media also augment family communication by providing opportunities for social support beyond family members and face-to-face friends. Many people belong to online communities that provide social stimulation, advice, and support.

GUIDELINES FOR EFFECTIVE COMMUNICATION IN FAMILIES

Throughout this chapter, we've noted how varied families are: They come in all sorts of shapes and sizes, and they adopt a wide range of interaction styles and communication patterns. For that reason, families face different challenges and find different ways to meet them. Despite this diversity, four guidelines apply to effective communication in most, if not all, families.

Maintain Equity in Family Relationships

One of the most important guidelines for sustaining healthy families is to make fairness a high priority. The responsibilities of maintaining a family should not fall just or primarily on one person. Likewise, the benefits of family life should not be substantially greater for one person than for another.

Social exchange theory (Kelley & Thiabaut, 1978; Rusbult & Buunk, 1993; Sayer & Nicholson, 2006; Thiabaut & Kelley, 1959) states that people apply economic principles to evaluate their relationships: They conduct cost–benefit analyses. Costs are the undesirable elements that stem from being in a relationship. Perhaps a relationship costs you time, effort, and money. Rewards are the desirable elements that come from being in a relationship. You may value the companionship, support, and affection that come from a relationship. According to social exchange theory, as long as your rewards outweigh your costs, the net outcome of the relationship is positive, so you are satisfied. If costs exceed rewards, however, we're dissatisfied and may move on.

Yet most of us are probably not as coldly calculating about relationships as social exchange theory suggests: few people spend their time tallying the rewards and costs of being in a family to make sure that they are getting a "good deal." At the same time, most of us do want relationships that are equitable, or fair, in a general sense (Wood, 2011c). **Equity** is fairness, based on the perception that both people invest equally in a relationship and benefit similarly from their investments.

© Goodluz/Shutterstock.com

Equity theory does not accept social exchange theory's assumptions that people demand equality and measure the rewards and costs to decide whether to stay in a relationship. Instead, it says that whether a relationship is satisfying and enduring depends on whether the people in it perceive the relationship as relatively equitable over time. In other words, people are generally satisfied if they are in relationships with people who contribute about as much as they do to the aspects of family life that matter to them. This is a more flexible explanation for why relationships do or do not endure.

There may be times, sometimes prolonged times, when one member of a family invests more than other members of the family. According to equity theory, this would not necessarily mean that the greater investor feels dissatisfied. He or she might not, if, in the past, he or she invested less, or if, in the past, others in the family had given more than their fair share. As long as the relationship is perceived as relatively equitable over time, we're likely to be satisfied.

We want our family relationships to be equitable over time. Inequity tends to breed unhappiness, which lessens satisfaction and commitment and sometimes precedes affairs or other threats to a family's survival (Anderson & Guerrero, 1998; DeMaris, 2007, 2010; Sprecher, 2001; Sprecher & Felmlee, 1997; Wood, 2011b).

Equity has multiple dimensions. We may evaluate the fairness of financial, emotional, physical, and other contributions to a relationship. Couple satisfaction seems especially affected by equity in housework and child care. Inequitable division of domestic labor fuels dissatisfaction and resentment, both of which harm intimacy (DeMaris, 2007; Helms, Proulx, Klute, McHale, & Crouter, 2006).

One of the biggest issues related to equity is the division of domestic labor. Egalitarian values are more central to relationships today than ever before. Today 62% of Americans rank sharing chores as very important to marital success; that percentage is higher than the importance attributed to having an adequate income (53%) or having shared religious beliefs (49%) (Coontz, 2013).

An equitable division of labor requires more than agreeing that each partner will do a fair share of chores. Partners must also agree on a standard of housekeeping. Many couples argue because one person wants floors vacuumed and beds changed more often than the other person. The person with the higher standard may feel frustrated that her or his partner doesn't do more, while the person with the lower standard resents being nagged to do work he or she considers unimportant (Wood, 2011b). There's no right or wrong standard for domestic labor, but family members, at least adult members, need to agree on the standard they will use.

Even when both partners in heterosexual relationships work outside the home, women do the majority of child care and homemaking (Baxter, Hewitt, & Western, 2005; Tichenor, 2005; Wood, 2011b). In fact, men who don't have jobs in the

Communication in Everyday Life

WORKPLACE

The Second Shift

In the majority of dual-worker families, women leave work and come home to what is considered a **second shift**, which is work that one partner—usually, but not always, a woman—does after coming home from a shift in the paid labor force outside the home (DeMaris, 2007, 2010; Wood, 2011b). Many women who work outside the home assume primary responsibility for fixing meals each night, fitting in housework in the evenings, and caring for children. Women tend to do the day-in, day-out jobs, such as cooking, shopping, and helping children with homework. Men more often do domestic work that can be scheduled flexibly. Mowing the lawn can be done morning or evening any day of the week, whereas preparing meals must be done on a tight timetable. Men also are likely to participate actively in playing with children and in fun activities, such as visiting the zoo, whereas women are more likely to take care of the routine, daily tasks, such as bathing, dressing, and feeding children.

As a rule, women assume most of the **psychological responsibility**, which involves remembering, planning, and scheduling family matters. Parents may alternate who takes children to the doctor, but it is usually the mother who remembers when checkups are needed, makes appointments, and reminds the father to take the child. Birthday cards and gifts are signed by both partners, but women often assume psychological responsibility for remembering birthdays of all family members and for buying cards and gifts.

paid labor force and whose female partners work outside the home engage in *less* child care and home maintenance than men who have jobs in the paid labor force (Dokoupil, 2009). As a point of comparison, unemployed women spend twice as much time on child care and housework as employed women (Dokoupil, 2009).

Although most men in dual-worker families don't do half of the work involved in running a home and raising children, today most men assume more of those responsibilities than they did 20 or even 10 years ago.

How are domestic responsibilities managed in same-sex relationships? A majority of gay and lesbian couples create more egalitarian relationships than do heterosexuals (Huston & Schwartz, 1995; Parker-Pope, 2013). This may be because gay and lesbian relationships are less likely to divide work along traditional sex and gender lines. A recent study sponsored by the National Institutes of Health tracked gay and straight couples over 10 years. The results were not ambiguous. Compared to heterosexual partners, same-sex couples had more egalitarian relationships in which partners contributed relatively equally to homemaking and child care, when children were present. Gay couples also reported greater happiness, intimacy, and sharing of confidences and less conflict than heterosexual couples (Parker-Pope, 2013).

Make Daily Choices That Enhance Intimacy

A second important guideline is to pay attention to daily opportunities to enrich family relationships. Although we are not always aware that we are making choices, we continuously choose who we will be and what kind of relationships we will fashion. Intimate partners choose to sustain closeness or let it wither, to build defensive or supportive climates, to rely on constructive or destructive communication to deal with conflict, to fulfill or betray trust, and to enhance or diminish each other's self-concepts.

JACKSON One of the things I love most about Meleika is the way she starts each day. Before getting out of bed, she reaches over and kisses my cheek. Then, she gets up and showers while I sneak a little more shut-eye. When I get up, the first thing she always says is "Morning, love." That is such a great way to start each day. Even after 5 years of marriage, she starts each day by letting me know I matter.

Typically, we focus on large choices, such as whether to commit or how to manage a serious conflict. As important as major choices are, they don't make up the basic fabric of family life. Instead, it is the undramatic, small choices that create or destroy families (Totten, 2006; Wood & Duck, 2006b). Do you listen mindfully to your child when you are tired? Do you buy flowers or a card for a parent when there is no special reason? Do you find the energy to go to your child's game even when you've had a rough day? Do you engage in dual perspective so that you can understand your parents on their terms? Do you stay in touch with your partner's concerns and dreams?

Seemingly small choices weave the basic fabric of our families. Reflecting on his own long marriage, former president Jimmy Carter (1996) wrote, "What makes a marriage? Is a personal union built or strengthened by dramatic events? I would say no. It's the year-by-year, dozen-times-a-day demonstration of the little things that can destroy a marriage or make it successful" (p. 76). Through awareness of the impact of the "small" choices we make a dozen times a day, we can make choices that continuously enhance the quality of our families.

Show Respect and Consideration

For families to remain healthy and satisfying, family members need to demonstrate continuously that they value and respect each other. As obvious as this guideline seems, many families don't follow it. Sometimes we treat strangers with more respect and kindness than we offer our romantic partners or our children (Emmers-Sommer, 2003). It's easy to take for granted the people who are continuing parts of our lives and to be less loving, respectful, and considerate than we should be.

It's especially important to communicate respect when discussing problems and complaints. Satisfied couples assert grievances and express anger and disagreement, but they do so in ways that don't demean each other (Hendrick & Hendrick, 2006). Respectful, open communication between parents and adolescent children is also associated with satisfying relationships (Dailey, 2006; Guerrero, Jones, & Boburka, 2006). Because communication is irreversible, we need to be mindful of our ethical choices when communicating with family members.

Don't Sweat the Small Stuff

We first discussed this guideline in Chapter 10 as a way to maintain healthy friendships. The advice not to sweat the small stuff also pertains to family relationships. If we want a healthy, vibrant family life, we must be willing to overlook many minor irritations and frustrations that are inevitable in living with others (Carlson & Carlson, 1999; Christensen & Jacobson, 2002; White, 1998).

We all have quirks, habits, and mannerisms that irritate others: the toothpaste cap left off the tube, the clinking of a coffee spoon, the loud music played late at night, or watching football every Sunday. In addition, family members frequently constrain one another's schedules and preferences. For instance, when one child in the family becomes vegan, that creates new challenges for shopping and preparing meals. At times, families seem like nothing but a hassle! And yet most of us would never consider giving up our families. We love our family members, and we want them in our lives.

To reduce the tendency to make mountains out of molehills, we can take responsibility for our perceptions and our responses to them. My partner, Robbie, is hopelessly forgetful, and that isn't going to change. If I focus on that (the keys he misplaces, the errands he forgets to run), I make myself unhappy with him and with our marriage. Notice that I am owning responsibility for how I choose to focus my perceptions and how that choice affects how I feel and act.

When her children were young, my sister Carolyn sometimes said to me that she found it frustrating that her children were so well behaved with others but sometimes spoiled brats at home. She interpreted their misbehavior at home as evidence that they respected her and her partner less than they respected people outside of the family. Another mother offered Carolyn the insight that children act up where they feel most safe, secure that they can do so without losing others' affection and love. Once Carolyn interpreted her children's occasional misbehavior at home as evidence that they felt secure and loved, she was less frustrated by the behavior. She still corrected them, but she no longer interpreted their misconduct as a sign that they disrespected her and her partner.

We can also monitor the self-serving attribution that may lead us to overestimate our good qualities and behaviors and underestimate those of our partner. When I used to get angry at Robbie for being forgetful, I conveniently overlooked my own failings and his grace in accepting them. I am not as punctual as Robbie is, so he's often ready and waiting for me. Yet he seldom criticizes me when I'm a few minutes late. Realizing that he accepts qualities in me that he doesn't like makes it easier for me to return the favor.

In their book *Don't Sweat the Small Stuff in Love*, Richard Carlson and Kristine Carlson (1999) advise us to take charge of our own happiness. When we say, "I'd be happy if only she would stop doing A" or "I'd be happy if only he would do B," we're assuming that another has control of our happiness. Of course, your happiness is affected by others, particularly intimates. However, the fact that others affect how you feel doesn't mean they are responsible for your feelings or your happiness.

When we take charge of our happiness, we can also take ownership of our issues. Ask yourself whether the issue is the other person's behavior or your own feeling about it. For years, I fussed at Robbie for not keeping our home neat. When I saw newspapers left on the table or bath towels not folded on the rack, I grumbled, "Why can't you be neater?" Robbie's gentle response was, "Why does it matter?" He had a good point. The desire for neatness was *my* issue. My own desire for neatness—not Robbie's leaving newspapers or towels around—made me displeased when things were not arranged as I wanted them to be. I couldn't and still can't control Robbie (thank goodness!), but I can control how I respond to stray newspapers and unfolded towels.

CHAPTER SUMMARY

In this chapter, we focused on communication in families. We first examined many forms that families take and the goals they serve in our era. We then focused on long-term commitments, including marriage and cohabitation. Once again, we noted the variety in long-term relationships. In the third section of the chapter, we considered a model of the family life cycle. In our discussion, we noted ways in which the model is limited to certain kinds of families, and we considered how it might be adapted to fit other sorts of families. Social media have greatly increased family members' ability to stay in touch, share photos, and interact.

The final section of the chapter identified guidelines for communicating effectively to meet the challenges of family life. First, building and maintaining equitable relationships is critical to family satisfaction and stability. Second, ongoing, daily choices enhance family relationships. Small choices can matter as much as or more than big ones in weaving the fabric of family life. Third, we pointed out the value of showing respect and consideration to family members. Too often, we save our good manners for social relationships and behave less respectfully and considerately with our partners and children. Finally, we repeated the guideline first offered in Chapter 10: Don't sweat the small stuff. Irritations are inevitable in family relationships; focusing on them is not. Save your energy for working on big stuff.

Key Concepts

Practice defining the chapter's terms by using online flashcards.

FLASHCARDS...

conformity orientation 344
consensual family 345
conversation orientation 344
equity 352

laissez-faire family 345
pluralistic family 345
protective family 345
second shift 353

psychological responsibility 353
social exchange theory 352

Continuing the Conversation

MindTap™

Jason Harris © 2001 Wadsworth

When you've watched the video online, critique and analyze this encounter based on the principles you learned in this chapter. Then compare your work with the author's suggested responses. Online, even more videos will let you continue the conversation with your instructor.

Dan and Charlotte have been married almost 5 years. They both have great careers and are very comfortable in their life and relationship. Dan is talking to his mom on the phone while Charlotte sits in the living room working on her laptop.

Dan: That sounds good. We'll swing by after dinner. . . . No, Mom, we're still not sure. . . . We're still thinking whether we're even going to have kids! I really don't want to get into that right now. Yeah, we'll see you then. Bye.

Charlotte: How's Mom?

Dan: Oh, fine. Wondering when her grandkids are on the way!

Charlotte: Your mom's funny. She's really got a one-track mind.

PRACTICE...

Dan: We really should figure out if we're going to do it or not.

Charlotte: Have kids?

Dan: Yeah, we've been married 5 years. It's now or never.

Charlotte: What do you think?

Dan: It's the ultimate commitment. If we're going to do it, we have to do it right. I know so many people who jumped right into it and resent their kids for being a burden. I don't want to be one of those parents.

Charlotte: Absolutely. And there are our careers to think about. We're both doing great now, and we're really happy as a couple. I'd have to cut back to part-time, and I'd need help from you. Having a child would mean less time, money, energy for ourselves.

Dan: But do we really want to have kids?

Charlotte: I'm not against it. What about you?

Dan: I feel the same. I'm not against it, but do we really want to give up what we have now?

Ending 1

A few months later, Dan and Charlotte attend a friend's dinner party. A lot of their friends have brought their children. As Charlotte mingles, Dan plays with the younger kids. Charlotte's friend Maggie is talking about her own child.

Maggie: It's hard work, but it's so much fun. I really don't know what my family did before we had a child. We all just sit and watch her do her thing. She'll dance and sing, tell us stories. It's so funny!. . . So when are you two going start trying?

Dan approaches and hands Charlotte a drink.

Charlotte: We really aren't planning on having kids.

Maggie: Haven't you guys been married for a long time? If you wait any longer, it could get complicated. There's something to be said about having kids young because the older you get, the less energy you'll have.

Dan: We're not planning on having kids at all.

Maggie: What about your parents? Aren't they expecting grandkids?

Dan: It's not up to them. We decided what's best for us.

Later that night at home, Dan and Charlotte discuss the party.

Charlotte: Did everyone there have kids? It felt like the Inquisition, you know?

Dan: Yeah, that was weird. I actually felt a bit left out. I love playing with everyone's kids, but it seems like the only topic of conversation was when we're going to have one.

Charlotte: Do you still feel okay about our decision? You seemed to be having a lot of fun with the kids.

Dan: I love playing with them! But I love where we are and what we do, and I don't want to change it. I stand by our decision. What about you?

Charlotte: Definitely. We'll just have to deal with the fact that things have changed. Our relationships with our friends are going to be different since everyone else has kids.

Ending 2

A year and a half later, Dan and Charlotte have had their own child. One night, Dan is putting the baby to bed in her crib. He tickles her and smiles at her before he turns off the light and goes into the living room to sit on the couch across from Charlotte.

Dan: Tired?

Charlotte: Exhausted. She was up four times last night and wouldn't go back to sleep. I think she has a new tooth coming in.

Dan: I have tomorrow off. I'll get up with her, and you can sleep in.

Charlotte: Thanks.

Dan: You seem a little distant tonight.

Charlotte: There's just a lot happening at work that I'm missing—things I'd like to be involved with, but since I'm part-time now, I can't really take them on.

Dan: Man, we really need to watch our spending this month. We're pretty tight. *The baby begins to cry. Dan starts to get up, but Charlotte stops him.*

Charlotte: Dan, didn't we agree to let her cry for a while? She has to get used to the crib sometime, right?

Dan: Isn't it hard for you to hear her cry like that?

Charlotte: Of course, but she has to learn to calm herself down. This is what Maggie and John did with Katie, and it worked. . . . Did you think it would be this hard?

Dan: It's harder than I expected. I do miss just the two of us hanging out. And the tight budget is something to get used to.

Charlotte: Today, she was eating her oatmeal in her chair. I went outside for a second, and when I came back in, the entire bowl was on her head! I wouldn't change any of this. I don't care how tight our budget is or how exhausted we are. I love her so much.

Dan: Yeah, me too. I really love being a dad. There's nothing more important than that.

1. In their conversation about whether to have a child, to what extent do Charlotte and Dan engage in person centered communication?

2. Dan responds somewhat defensively to Maggie's questions. Based on what you have learned about communication that fosters defensiveness, explain why Dan might have felt this when talking with Maggie.

3. Identify some of the "little things" that Dan and Charlotte do to strengthen their relationship.

Everyday Skills

Build your communication skills further by completing the following activities here or online.

1. **Identifying Marital Types**

   Think about married or cohabiting couples you know fairly well—perhaps relatives and long-time friends of your family. They may have children or not. Using Fitzpatrick and Best's typology, how would you classify each of the couples? Now, describe the communication patterns you notice in each couple. Note differences among couples in communication patterns. Explain why particular communication patterns might be more and less prominent in different types of couples.

2. **Bundles of Joy and Change**

   Talk with three parents. Ask the following questions of each parent:

   a. What change was the least expected after your first baby was born?

   b. How did communication with your partner and others change after the baby was born?

   c. How did having a child affect your marriage or relationship (if the parent was in a committed relationship at the time that the baby arrived)?

   How does the information you gathered from parents compare with this chapter's discussion of the impact of children on committed relationships?

3. **Your Parents' Stage in Family Life**

   At what stage in the family life cycle would you place your parents as a couple? Alternately, if they are divorced or separated, at which stage is each of your parents? How do you perceive this stage and their happiness in it?

MindTap **DO...** Additional interactive discussions, online quizzes, and activities that your instructor may assign for a grade.

Engaging with Ideas

MindTap™

Reflect and write about the ideas in this chapter by considering questions about personal, workplace, and ethical applications, here or online.

Personal Application How would you modify the model presented here to make it more descriptive of your family's developmental pattern? Which stages would not be in a model for your family? Which stages would you have to add to represent how your family has evolved?

Workplace Application   **REFLECT ON...**
Talk with people who are in dual-worker families to learn about how they balance commitments to careers and families and how they work out the responsibilities of caring for homes and children.

Ethical Application: Is it ethical for parents to track their children electronically so that the parents know where the children are at all times? Is it ethical until a child is 16 or 18?

Thinking Critically

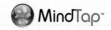

Think and write critically about the ideas in this chapter, here or online.

1. How do you define *family*? What do family members do for each other? Which types of relationships discussed in this chapter do and do not fit your definition?

2. In this chapter, you read about some of the ways in which marriage has changed over time. Based on cultural trends and evolving values of your generation, what changes in marriage would you predict over the next 50 years?

REFLECT ON...

3. In your romantic relationships, who has had psychological responsibility for various facets of the relationship? How have you felt about the way that psychological responsibility was allocated?

© Dudarev Mikhail/Shutterstock.com

CONTINUING THE CONVERSATION

Although this book is drawing to a close, the conversation we've launched in these pages will continue. Interpersonal communication will be vital to your life in the years ahead. As I reflect on what we've discussed since the Introduction, I notice three threads that weave through the entire book.

COMMUNICATION CREATES AND REFLECTS IDENTITY

Communication is both an important influence that shapes personal identity and a primary means by which we express who we are. Our sense of personal identity grows directly out of interpersonal communication. We enter the world without any clear sense of self, and we look to others to tell us who we are. Parents, grandparents, siblings, and others who are significant in the first years of our lives express how they see us and how they value us. In turn, our own sense of self reflects our perceptions of their appraisals of us.

As we venture beyond the confines of family, we continue to learn from others and to see ourselves through the eyes of others. Peers, teachers, friends, neighbors, coworkers, mentors, and romantic partners communicate their views of us, and they become part of how we see ourselves and how we define our goals for personal growth.

How we communicate expresses who we are. Verbally and nonverbally, we present our faces to others. We use communication to present ourselves as competent to coworkers and supervisors, friendly and helpful with neighbors, caring with friends and family, and informed and civic-minded with volunteer groups. Throughout our everyday lives, we use communication to define ourselves to others.

INTERPERSONAL COMMUNICATION IS CENTRAL TO RELATIONSHIPS

Communication is the heart of personal relationships. The health and endurance of personal relationships depend in large measure on our ability to communicate effectively. For relationships to be satisfying, we need to know how to express our feelings, needs, and ideas in ways that others can understand. We also need to know how to listen sensitively and responsively to people in our lives so that they feel safe being open and honest with us.

Interpersonal communication skills also allow us to create climates that are supportive and affirming. When we need to work through issues in our relationships, we can do so more effectively if we have built a supportive, trusting climate. Communication is the basis of meaning in human relationships, and it is the primary way we build, refine, sustain, and transform our connections with others.

INTERPERSONAL COMMUNICATION TAKES PLACE IN A DIVERSE WORLD

Social diversity shapes and is reflected in communication. We've seen that the social communities to which we belong affect how we communicate and how we interpret the communication of others. What is normal or desirable in one social group may be offensive or odd in other communities. Our ways of communicating, then, reflect not just our individual identities but also perspectives that are shaped by the social groups to which we belong.

Diverse cultures and the communication styles they cultivate offer rich opportunities to learn about ourselves and others. The more we interact with people whose backgrounds, beliefs, and communication styles differ from our own, the more we will grow as individuals and as members of a shared world.

Upon reflection, you will discern how each of these themes resonates in your current life. Now let's consider how they pertain to our personal and collective futures.

THE ROAD AHEAD

Interpersonal communication will be as important for your future as it is today, although it may assume different forms and functions in the years ahead. The skills and perspectives we've discussed in this book will serve you well in meeting the challenges that will accompany changes in yourself, relationships, and society.

In the coming years, your interpersonal relationships will change in both anticipated and surprising ways. Some of the friends you have today will still remain close, whereas others will fade away, and new people will assume importance in your life. Some romances of the moment will flourish and endure, and others will wither. New people will come into your life, and familiar ones will leave. Each person who enters or exits your life will affect your personal identity just as you will affect the identity of each of them.

There will also be changes and surprises in how people go about the process of forming and sustaining relationships. The trend toward long-distance romances and friendships will grow as more people who care about each other find that they cannot live and work in the same location. Technology will also change how we communicate with friends and romantic partners. Increasingly, we will rely upon electronic forms of communication to sustain important personal relationships.

Currently, I use e-mail to stay in daily contact with a man who has been my friend for 20 years, and I am looking forward to meeting, in person, a woman with whom I've developed an online friendship. Many of my students rely on text-messaging to communicate daily with parents, friends, and siblings. In the future, friends, romantic partners, and family members will make even greater use of social media to stay in touch.

Finally, interpersonal communication and relationships will evolve in response to changes in the larger society. Medical advances will stretch the average lifespan further, so that a promise to stay together "'til death do us part" will involve a greater time commitment than it does today. Longer lives will also increase the number of older people in society and the opportunities for them to be part of our friendships and families.

Relationship forms that are not recognized or approved today may be accepted in the future. Interaction with an increasing diversity of people will change our perspective on what relationships are and how to sustain them. In addition, the horizons that diversity fosters will broaden the options we recognize for creating our own relationships.

Neither you nor I can foresee what lies ahead for us and for our world. However, we can predict confidently that there will be changes in us, others, and cultural life in general. Whatever changes we experience, we can be sure that interpersonal communication will continue to be central to our happiness and effectiveness.

From this book and the course it accompanies, you have learned a good deal about interpersonal communication. I hope that the understandings and skills you've acquired will be valuable to you in the years ahead. If you are committed to practicing these skills in your everyday life and to building on this knowledge, then you are on the threshold of a lifelong journey that will enrich you and your relationships with others. I wish all of that and more for you.

Julia T Wood

GLOSSARY

A

abstract Removed from concrete reality. Symbols are abstract because they are inferences and generalizations abstracted from a total reality.

agape A secondary style of loving that is selfless and based on giving to others, not on receiving rewards or returns from them. A blend of *eros* and *storge*.

ambiguous Subject to multiple meanings. Symbols are ambiguous because their meanings vary from person to person and context to context.

ambushing Listening carefully to an exchange for the purpose of attacking the speaker.

anxious/ambivalent attachment style A mode of relating/attachment style characterized by preoccupation with relationships and inconsistent behavior toward the partner. Develops in childhood when a caregiver behaves inconsistently toward a child, sometimes loving and sometimes rejecting or neglectful.

arbitrary Random or not constrained by necessity. Symbols are arbitrary because there is no necessary reason for a particular symbol to stand for a particular referent.

artifacts Personal objects that we use to announce our identity and personalize our environment.

assertion A clear, nonjudgmental statement of what we feel, need, or want. Not synonymous with aggression, which involves putting our needs ahead of others' needs, sometimes at cost to them.

attachment style A pattern of relating instilled by the way a caregiver teaches the child who he or she is, who others are, and how to approach relationships.

B

attribution Subjective account of why something happens or why someone acted a certain way.

bracketing Noting an important issue that comes up in the course of discussing other matters and agreeing to discuss it at a later time. By acknowledging and agreeing to deal with the bracketed issue later, this technique allows people to stay effectively focused on the specific issue at hand.

C

chilling effect Occurs when we suppress complaints and expressions of dissatisfaction or anger from someone we perceive as more powerful than us, because we fear that the more powerful person could punish us.

chronemics The aspect of nonverbal communication that involves our perceptions and use of time to define identities and interaction.

cognitive complexity In our interpretation of experience, the number of constructs used, how abstract they are, and how elaborately they interact to create perceptions.

cognitive labeling view of emotions The theory that our feelings are shaped by the labels we apply to our physiological responses.

commitment A decision to remain with a relationship. One of three dimensions of enduring romantic relationships, commitment has greater influence on relationship continuity than does love alone. Also refers to an advanced stage in the escalation of a romantic relationship.

committed romantic relationship A voluntary relationship between individuals who assume they will be primary and continuing parts of each other's life. Committed romantic relationships include three dimensions: intimacy, passion, and commitment.

communication climate The overall feeling, or emotional mood, of a relationship. Shaped by verbal and nonverbal interaction between people.

communication rules Shared understandings of what communication means and what behaviors are appropriate in various situations.

conformity orientation The extent to which family members are expected to adhere to a family hierarchy and conform in beliefs.

consensual family Type of family that has high conversation orientation and high conformity orientation.

constitutive rules Rules that define what communication means by specifying how certain communicative acts are to be counted.

constructivism The theory that we organize and interpret experience by applying cognitive structures called *schemata*.

content meaning The content of, or denotative information in, communication. Content-level meanings are literal.

contracting Building a solution through negotiation and acceptance of parts of proposals for resolution. Contracting usually is present in the later stages of constructive conflict.

conversation orientation The degree to which communication within a family is open or closed.

counterfeit emotional language Communication that seems to express feelings but doesn't actually describe what a person is feeling.

culture Beliefs, understandings, practices, and ways to interpret experience that are shared by a group of people.

cyberbullying Text messages, comments, rumors, embarrassing pictures, videos, and fake profiles that are meant to hurt another person and are sent by e-mail or smartphone or posted on social networking sites.

D

deep acting Management of inner feelings.

defensive listening Perceiving personal attacks, criticisms, or hostile undertones in communication when none are intended.

direct definition Communication that explicitly tells us who we are by specifically labeling us and reacting to our behaviors. Usually first occurs in families, then in interaction with peers and others.

dismissive attachment style A mode of relating instilled typically early in life by a disinterested, rejecting, or abusive caregiver, in which the individual later tends to dismiss others as unworthy and thus does not seek close relationships. Unlike people with fearful attachment styles, those with a dismissive style do not accept the caregiver's view of them as unlovable.

dual perspective The ability to understand both your own and another's perspective, beliefs, thoughts, and feelings.

E

emotional intelligence The ability to recognize which feelings are appropriate in which situations, and the skill to communicate those feelings effectively.

emotions Our experience and interpretation of internal sensations as they are shaped by physiology, perceptions, language, and social experiences.

emotion work The effort we invest to make ourselves feel what our culture defines as appropriate and not to feel what our culture defines as inappropriate in particular situations.

empathy The ability to feel with another person, to feel what she or he feels.

environmental spoiling The process by which proximity breeds ill will, when we are forced to be around others whose values, attitudes, and lifestyles conflict with our own.

equity Fairness based on the perception that both partners should invest roughly equally in a relationship and benefit similarly from their investments. Perceived equity is a primary influence on relationship satisfaction.

eros One of the three primary styles of loving, a powerful, passionate style of love that blazes to life suddenly and dramatically.

ethics The branch of philosophy that deals with moral principles and codes of conduct. Because interpersonal communication affects people, sometimes profoundly, it always has ethical implications.

ethnocentrism The assumption that one's own culture and its norms are the only right ones. Ethnocentric communication reflects certainty, which tends to create defensive communication climates.

exit response To leave conflict, either psychologically (by tuning out disagreement) or physically (by walking away from an argument, or even leaving the relationship). One of four ways of responding to conflict, the exit response is active and generally destructive.

F

Face The impression of self that we want others to accept when we are interacting in social situations.

fearful attachment style A mode of relating instilled by a caregiver in the first relationship (usually parent–child) who communicates to the child in consistently negative, rejecting, or even abusive ways. People with fearful attachment styles are inclined to feel apprehensive and insecure about relationships.

feedback Responses to messages. Feedback is continuous, and it may be verbal, nonverbal, or both; it may be intentional or unintentional.

feeling rules Culturally based guidelines that tell us what we have a right to feel or are expected to feel in specific situations.

flaming Excessively insulting another person online, often using language that is derogatory or obscene.

framing rules Culturally based guidelines that define the emotional meaning of situations and events.

friends of the heart Friends who remain close regardless of distance and life changes.

friends of the road Temporary friends with whom intimacy is not sustained when one of the friends moves or other life changes occur.

fundamental attribution error Overestimating the internal causes of others' behavior and underestimating the external causes.

G

games Interactions in which the real conflicts are hidden or denied and a counterfeit excuse is created for arguments or put-downs.

generalized other One source of social perspectives that people use to define themselves and guide how they think, act, and feel; our perception of the views, values, and perspectives that are endorsed by society as a whole.

grace Granting forgiveness or putting aside our personal need in favor of someone else's when it is not required or expected. Grace reflects generosity of spirit.

H

haptics The sense of touch and what it means. Haptics are part of nonverbal communication.

hate speech Language that dehumanizes others and that reflects and often motivates hostility toward the target of the speech.

hearing The physiological result of sound waves hitting our eardrums. Unlike listening, hearing is a passive process.

hooking up Engaging in some degree of sexual experience with no expectation of seeing a person again.

I

identity script A guide to action based on rules for living and identity. Initially communicated in families, identity scripts define our roles, how we are to play them, and basic elements in the plots of our lives. Not the same as a script, which is one of the four cognitive schemata.

I-It communication Impersonal communication in which people are treated as objects or as instrumental to our purposes.

I language Language in which one takes personal responsibility for feelings with words that own the feelings and do not project responsibility for the feelings onto others.

immediacy Behavior that increases perceptions of closeness between communicators.

implicit personality theory Our often unconscious assumptions about what qualities fit together in human personalities.

impression management Management of communication in an effort to persuade others to believe in the face we present.

inattention blindness The tendency, after concentrating on a task, not to see what is right in front of one

indexing A technique of linking our evaluations of speech and events to specific times or circumstances, to remind ourselves that evaluations are not static or unchanging.

interactive model A model that represents communication as a feedback process, in which listeners and speakers both simultaneously send and receive messages.

interactive view of emotions The theory that social rules and understandings shape what people feel and how they express and withhold feelings.

internal tensions Relationship stresses that grow out of people's needs and people's interactions.

interpersonal communication A selective, systemic process that allows people to reflect and build personal knowledge of one another and create shared meanings.

interpersonal communication competence Proficiency in communication that is interpersonally effective and appropriate. Competence includes the abilities to monitor oneself, to engage in dual perspective, to enact a range of communication skills, and to adapt communication appropriately.

interpersonal conflict Expressed tension between people who are interdependent, perceive they have incompatible goals, and feel a need to resolve those differences

interpretation The subjective process of evaluating and explaining perceptions.

intimacy One of three dimensions of enduring, committed romantic relationships. Intimacy refers to feelings of closeness, connection, and tenderness between lovers.

investments Elements (such as energy, time, money, and emotion) put into a relationship that cannot be recovered should the relationship end. Investments, more than rewards and love, increase commitment.

I-Thou communication Fully interpersonal communication in which people acknowledge and deal with each other as unique individuals who meet fully in dialogue.

I-You communication Communication midway between impersonal and interpersonal communication, in which the other is acknowledged as a human being but not fully engaged as a unique individual.

J

Johari Window Developed in 1969 by Joseph Luft and Harry Ingham, this is a model of the different types of knowledge that affect self-development.

K

kinesics Body position and body motions, including those of the face.

kitchen-sinking An unproductive form of conflict communication in which "everything but the kitchen sink"—irrelevant reasons, insults, and excuses—is thrown into the argument.

L

laissez-faire family Type of family that has low conversation orientation and conformity orientation.

linear model A model that represents communication as a one-way process that flows in one direction, from sender to receiver. Linear models do not capture the dynamism of communication or the active participation of all communicators.

linguistic determinism The theory that language determines what we can perceive and think. This theory has been largely discredited, although the less strong claim that language shapes thought is widely accepted.

listening A complex process that consists of being mindful, hearing, selecting and organizing information, interpreting communication, responding, and remembering. Listening is a very different process from hearing, which is simply a physiological action.

listening for information One of the three goals of listening; focuses on gaining and evaluating ideas, facts, opinions, reasons, and so forth.

listening for pleasure One of the three goals of listening; motivated by the desire to enjoy rather than to gain information or to support others.

listening to support others One of the three goals of listening; focuses more on the relationship level of meaning than on the content level of meaning. Aims to understand and respond to others' feelings, thoughts, and perceptions in affirming ways.

literal listening Listening only to the content level of meaning and ignoring the relationship level of meaning.

loaded language An extreme form of evaluative language that relies on words that strongly slant perceptions and thus meanings.

lose–lose An orientation toward conflict that assumes that nobody can win and everyone loses from engaging in conflict.

loyalty response Silent allegiance to a relationship and a person when conflict exists. One of the four ways of responding to conflict, loyalty is passive and tends to be constructive.

ludus One of the three primary styles of love, in which the goal is not commitment but to have fun at love as a game or a series of challenges and maneuvers.

M

mania Passionate, sometimes obsessive love that includes emotional extremes. One of the three secondary styles of love; made up of *eros* and *ludus*.

metacommunication Communication about communication. When excessive, as in unproductive conflict interaction, metacommunication becomes self-absorbing and diverts partners from the issues causing conflict.

mindfulness Being fully present in the moment. A concept from Zen Buddhism;

the first step of listening and the foundation of all the other steps.

mind reading Assuming that we understand what another person thinks or how another person perceives something. Often a harmful practice, because mind reading denies the other person the chance to explain their own thoughts or feelings.

minimal encourager A brief phrase ("Go on") or sound ("Um-hm") that gently invites another person to elaborate by expressing our interest in hearing more.

models Representations of what something is and how it works.

monitoring Observing and regulating your own communication.

monopolizing Continually focusing communication on ourselves instead of on the person who is talking.

Müller-Lyer illusion Perceptual illusion in which lines that are actually identical in length appear to be of different lengths.

N

neglect response Denial or minimization of problems. One of the four ways of responding to conflict, neglect is passive and tends to be destructive.

noise Anything that distorts communication such that it is harder for people to understand each other. Noise can be physical, psychological, semantic, and so forth.

nonverbal communication All forms of communication other than words themselves. Includes inflection and other vocal qualities, haptics, and several other behaviors.

O

organismic view of emotions The theory that external phenomena cause physiological changes that lead us to experience emotions. Also called the James–Lange view of emotions.

P

paralanguage Vocal communication, such as accents and inflection, that does not use words.

paraphrasing A method of clarifying another's meaning by reflecting our interpretations of his or her communication back to him or her.

particular others One source of social perspectives that people use to define themselves and guide how they think, act, and feel; people who are especially important to the self.

passion Intensely positive feelings and desires for another person. One of the three dimensions of enduring romantic relationships, passion is based on the rewards of involvement and is not equivalent to commitment.

passive aggression Attacking while denying doing so; a means of covertly expressing conflict, anger, or both.

perception The active process of selecting, organizing, and interpreting people, objects, events, situations, and activities.

perceptual view of emotions The theory that subjective perceptions shape the meanings of external phenomena and the emotions we associate with them. Also called appraisal theory.

personal constructs Bipolar mental yardsticks by which we measure people and situations along specific dimensions of judgment.

person-centeredness The ability to perceive people as unique and to differentiate them from social roles and generalizations based on their membership in social groups.

placemaking The process of creating a physical environment that is comfortable and reflects one's values, experiences, and tastes. Physical environment is part of relational culture, which is the nucleus of intimacy.

pluralistic family Type of family that has high conversation orientation and low conformity orientation.

pragma Pragmatic or practical love. One of the secondary styles of loving, *pragma* is a blend of *storge* and *ludus*.

process An ongoing, continuous, dynamic flow that has no clear-cut beginning or ending and is always evolving and changing. Interpersonal communication is a process.

protective family Type of family that has low conversation orientation and high conformity orientation.

prototypes Knowledge structures that define the clearest or most representative examples of some category.

proxemics An aspect of nonverbal communication that includes space and our uses of it.

pseudolistening Pretending to listen.

psychological responsibility The responsibility for remembering, planning, and coordinating domestic work and child care. In general, women assume psychological responsibility for child care and housework, even though both partners may share the actual tasks.

punctuation Defines the beginning and ending of interaction or interaction episodes. Punctuation is subjective.

R

rational-emotive approach to feelings Using rational thinking to challenge and change debilitating emotions that undermine self-concept and self-esteem.

reflected appraisal The process of seeing and thinking about ourselves in terms of the appraisals of us that others reflect.

regulative rules Communication rules that regulate interaction by specifying when, how, where, and with whom to talk about certain things.

relational culture A private world of rules, understandings, and patterns of acting and interpreting that partners create to give meaning to their relationship; the nucleus of intimacy.

relational dialectics Opposing forces, or tensions, that are normal parts of all relationships. The three relational dialectics are autonomy/intimacy, novelty/routine, and openness/closedness.

relationship meaning What communication expresses about the relationship between communicators. The three dimensions of relationship-level meanings are liking or disliking, responsiveness, and power (control).

relationship rules Guidelines that friends or romantic partners have for their relationships. Usually, relationship rules are tacit, not explicit, understandings.

remembering The process of recalling what you have heard; the sixth element of listening.

responding Symbolizing your interest in what is being said with observable feedback to speakers during the process of interaction; the fifth of the six elements of listening.

S

script A definition of expected or appropriate sequences of action in a particular setting. Scripts are one of the four cognitive schemata; not the same as an identity script.

second shift Work that a person, usually a woman, does after coming home from working in the paid labor force outside the home, such as fixing meals, doing housework, shopping, and caring for children.

secure attachment style A mode of relating that involves confidence in oneself and in relationships. Like other attachment styles, the secure mode is instilled by a caregiver who responds in a consistently attentive, loving way to a child; the most common and most positive of the four attachment styles. People with secure attachment styles tend to be comfortable forming close bonds with others.

selective listening Focusing only on selected parts of communication. We

listen selectively when we screen out parts of a message that don't interest us or with which we disagree and when we rivet attention on parts of communication that do interest us or with which we agree.

self A constantly evolving, processual understanding of oneself that grows out of the processes of interacting with others and society and internalizing values and views of our identity that others reflect to us.

self-disclosure The act of revealing personal information about ourselves that others are unlikely to discover in other ways.

self-fulfilling prophecy Acting in a way that embodies expectations or judgments about us.

self-sabotage Self-talk that communicates that we are no good, that we can't do something, that we can't change, and so forth. Self-sabotage undermines our belief in ourselves and our motivation to change and grow.

self-serving bias The tendency to attribute our positive actions and successes to stable, global, internal influences under our control, and to attribute our negative actions and failures to unstable, specific, external influences beyond our control.

self-talk Intrapersonal communication that affects our feelings and behaviors.

social comparison Comparing ourselves with others in order to form judgments of our own talents, abilities, qualities, and so forth.

social exchange theory The theory that people apply economic principles to evaluate their relationships in terms of costs and benefits, and that people are satisfied only in relationships in which the benefits outweigh the costs.

speech community A group of people who share norms, regulative rules, and constitutive rules for communicating and interpreting the communication of others.

standpoint The knowledge and perspective shaped by the material, symbolic, and social conditions common to members of a social group.

static evaluation Assessments that suggest that something is unchanging. "Bob is impatient" is a static evaluation.

stereotypes Predictive generalizations about people and situations.

storge A comfortable, friendly kind of love, often likened to friendship. One of the three primary styles of loving.

surface acting Controlling outward expression of inner feelings.

symbol An abstract, arbitrary, and ambiguous representation of a phenomenon.

systemic Taking place within multiple systems that influence what is communicated and what meanings are constructed; a quality of interpersonal communication. Examples of systems affecting communication include physical context, culture, personal histories, and previous interactions between people.

T

totalizing Responding to a person as if one aspect of his or her life were the totality of the person.

transactional model A model of communication as a dynamic process that changes over time and in which participants assume multiple roles.

trust Belief in another's reliability (that he or she will do what is promised) and emotional reliance on the other to care about and protect our welfare; the belief that our private information is safe with the other person.

V

voice response Communicating about differences, tensions, and disagreements. One of the four responses to conflict, the voice response is active and can be constructive for people and relationships.

W

win-lose An orientation toward conflict that assumes that one person wins at the expense of another person.

win-win An orientation toward conflict that assumes that everyone can win, or benefit, from engaging in conflict and that it is possible to generate resolutions that satisfy everyone.

Y

you language Language that projects responsibility for one's own feelings or actions onto other people. Not recommended for interpersonal communication.

Aakers, J., & Smith, A. (2010). *The dragonfly effect*. San Francisco: Jossey Bass.

Abramson, P. (2007). *Romance in the ivory tower: The rights and liberty of conscience*. Cambridge, MA: MIT Press.

Acitelli, L. (1988). When spouses talk to each other about their relationship. *Journal of Social and Personal Relationships, 5*, 185–199.

Acitelli, L. (1993). You, me, and us: Perspectives on relationship awareness. In S. W. Duck (Ed.), *Understanding relationship processes: 1: Individuals in relationships* (pp. 144–174). Newbury Park, CA: Sage.

Acker, J. (2013). Is capitalism gendered and racialized? In M. Andersen & P. H. Collins (Eds.), *Race, class and gender: An anthology* (8th ed., pp. 125–133). Boston: Cengage.

Acker, M., & Davis, M. H. (1992). Intimacy, passion and commitment in adult romantic relationships: A test of the triangular theory of love. *Journal of Social and Personal Relationships, 9*, 21–51.

Adler, R., & Proctor, R. (2014). *Looking out/looking in* (14th ed.). Boston, MA: Belmont.

Afifi, W., & Burgoon, J. (2000). The impact of violations on uncertainty and the consequences for attractiveness. *Human Communication Research, 26*, 203–233.

Afifi, W., & Faulkner, S. (2000). On being "just friends": The frequency and impact of sexual activity in cross-sex friendships. *Journal of Social and Personal Relationships, 17*, 205–222.

Ainsworth, M. D. S., Blehar, M. C., Waters, E., & Wall, S. (1978). *Patterns of attachment: A psychological study of the strange situation*. Hillsdale, NJ: Erlbaum.

Alabaster, J. (2009, July 24). *Japanese train workers told to pass "smile test."* Retrieved May 25, 2010, from http://abcnews.go.com/International/wireStory?id=8162152

Algoe, S., Gable, S., & Maisel, N. (2010). It's the little things: Everyday gratitude as a booster shot for romantic relationships. *Journal of Personal Relationships, 17*, 217–233.

Allen, B. (2006). Communicating race at WeighCo. In J. T. Wood & S. W. Duck (Eds.), *Composing relationships: Communication in everyday life* (pp. 146–155). Belmont, CA: Wadsworth.

Alpert, E. (2013, May 30). More U.S. women than ever are breadwinners, study finds. *Raleigh News & Observer*, pp. 1A, 5A.

Altman, I., & Taylor, D. (1973). *Social penetration: The development of interpersonal relationships*. New York: Holt.

Altman, I., & Taylor, D. (1987). Communication in interpersonal relationships: Social penetration processes. In M. Roloff & G. Miller (Eds.), *Interpersonal processes: New directions in communication research* (pp. 257–277). Newbury Park, CA: Sage.

Altman, L. (2008, August 3). HIV estimates low, CDC study shows. *Raleigh News & Observer*, p. 4A.

American Social Health Association. (2005). *State of the Nation 2005: Challenges facing STD prevention in youth*. Research Triangle Park, NC: Author.

Amodio, D., & Showers, C. (2005). "Similarity breeds liking" revisited: The moderating role of commitment. *Journal of Social and Personal Relationships, 22*, 817–836.

Andersen, M. L., & Collins, P. H. (Eds.). (2013). *Race, class, and gender: An anthology* (8th ed.). Belmont, CA: Wadsworth.

Andersen, P. (1999). *Nonverbal communication: Forms and functions*. Mountain View, CA: Mayfield.

Andersen, P. (2003). In different dimensions: Nonverbal communication and culture. In L. A. Samovar & R. E. Porter (Eds.), *Intercultural communication: A reader* (10th ed., pp. 239–252). Belmont, CA: Wadsworth.

Andersen, P., Hecht, M., Hoobler, G., & Smallwood, M. (2002). Nonverbal communication across cultures. In W. Gudykunst & B. Mody (Eds.), *The handbook of international and intercultural communication* (2nd ed., pp. 89–106). Thousand Oaks, CA: Sage.

Anderson, J. (2011, November 7). National study finds widespread sexual harassment of students in grades 7 to 12. *New York Times*, p. A10.

Anderson, K., & Leaper, C. (1998). Meta-analyses of gender effects on conversational interruption: Who, when, where, and how? *Sex Roles, 39*, 225–252.

Anderson, P., & Guerrero, L. (Eds.). (1998). *Handbook of communication and emotion*. San Diego, CA: Academic Press.

Anderson, R., Baxter, L., & Cissna, K. (Eds.). (2004). *Dialogue: Theorizing difference in communication*. Thousand Oaks, CA: Sage.

Anderson, R., Corazzini, K., & McDaniel, R., Jr. (2004). Complexity science and the dynamics of climate and communication: Reducing nursing home turnover. *Gerontologist, 44,* 378–388.

Arenson, K. (2002, January 13). The fine art of listening. *Education Life,* pp. 34–35.

Argyle, M., & Henderson, M. (1985). The rules of relationships. In S. W. Duck & D. Perlman (Eds.), *Understanding personal relationships: An interdisciplinary approach* (pp. 63–84). Beverly Hills, CA: Sage.

Arroyo, A., & Harwood, J. (2012). Exploring the causes and consequences of engaging in fat talk. *Journal of Applied Communication Research, 40,* 167–187.

Atsuko, A. (2003). Gender differences in interpersonal distance: From the viewpoint of oppression hypothesis. *Japanese Journal of Experimental Social Psychology, 42,* 201–218.

Atsumi, R. (1980). Patterns of personal relationships. *Social Analysis, 5,* 63–78.

Axtell, R. (2007). *Essential do's and taboos: The complete guide to international business and leisure travel.* New York: Wiley.

Babies seem to pick up language in utero. (2013, January 8). *New York Times,* p. D6.

Bachen, C., & Illouz, E. (1996). Imagining romance: Young people's cultural models of romance and love. *Critical Studies of Mass Communication, 13,* 279–308.

Bailey, P. (1998, September 29). Daily bread. *Durham Herald Sun,* p. C5.

Bakalar, N. (2012, September 4). Setting the mood to enjoy a smaller meal. *New York Times,* p. D6.

Balcetis, E., & Dunning, D. (2013). Wishful seeing: Desirable objects are seen as closer. *Current Directions in Psychological Science, 22,* 33–37.

Bargh, J. (1999, January 29). The most powerful manipulative messages are hiding in plain sight. *Chronicle of Higher Education,* p. B6.

Barge, K. (2009). Social groups, workgroups, and teams. In W. F. Eadie (Ed.), *21st century communication: A reference handbook* (pp. 340–348). Thousand Oaks, CA: Sage.

Barnlund, D. (1989). *Communication styles of Japanese and Americans: Images and reality.* Belmont, CA: Wadsworth.

Barrett, J. (2004, May 10). No time for wrinkles. *Newsweek,* pp. 82–85.

Bartholomew, K., & Horowitz, L. M. (1991). Attachment styles among young adults: A test of a four-category model. *Journal of Personality and Social Psychology, 61,* 226–244.

Basow, S. I., & Rubenfeld, K. (2003). "Troubles talk": Effects of gender and gender-typing. *Sex Roles, 48,* 183–187.

Basu, M. (2004, September 27). Experts interpret the body politic. *Raleigh News & Observer,* p. 4A.

Bates, S. (2005). *Speak like a CEO.* New York: McGraw-Hill.

Bateson, M. C. (1990). *Composing a life.* New York: Penguin/Plume.

Baxter, J., Hewitt, B., & Western, M. (2005). Post-familial families and the domestic division of labor. *Journal of Comparative Family Studies, 36,* 583–600.

Baxter, L. A. (1984). Trajectories of relationship disengagement. *Journal of Social and Personal Relationships, 7,* 141–178.

Baxter, L. A. (1988). A dialectical perspective on communication strategies in relationship development. In S. W. Duck, D. F. Hay, S. E. Hobfoll, W. Iches, & B. Montgomery (Eds.), *Handbook of personal relationships* (pp. 257–273). London: Wiley.

Baxter, L. A. (1990). Dialectical contradictions in relational development. *Journal of Social and Personal Relationships, 7,* 69–88.

Baxter, L. A. (1993). The social side of personal relationships: A dialectical perspective. In S. W. Duck (Ed.), *Understanding relationship processes: 3: Social context and relationships* (pp. 139–165). Newbury Park, CA: Sage.

Baxter, L. A. (2011). *Voicing relationships.* Thousand Oaks, CA: Sage.

Baxter, L. A., & Braithwaite, D. O. (2008). Relational dialectics theory: Crafting meaning from competing discourses. In L. A. Baxter & D. O. Braithwaite (Eds.), *Engaging theories in interpersonal communication: Multiple perspectives* (pp. 349–361). Thousand Oaks, CA: Sage.

Baxter, L. A., & Montgomery, B. M. (1996). *Relating: Dialogues and dialectics.* New York: Guilford.

Baxter, L. A., & Simon, E. P. (1993). Relationship maintenance strategies and dialectical contradictions in personal relationships. *Journal of Social and Personal Relationships, 10,* 225–242.

Bazelon, E. (2013). *Sticks and stones: Defeating the culture of bullying and recovering the power of character and empathy.* New York: Random House.

Beck, A. (1988). *Love is never enough.* New York: Harper & Row.

Begley, S. (2009, July 9). What's in a word? *Newsweek,* p. 31.

Beil, L. (2011, November 29). The certainty of memory has its day in court. *New York Times,* pp. D1, D6.

Bellah, R., Madsen, R., Sullivan, W., Swindler, A., & Tipton, S. (1985). *Habits of the heart: Individualism and commitment in American life.* Berkeley: University of California Press.

Bellamy, L. (1996, December 18). Kwanzaa cultivates cultural and culinary connections. *Raleigh News & Observer,* pp. 1F, 9F.

Belsky, J., & Pensky, E. (1988). Developmental history, personality, and family relationships: Toward an emergent family system. In R. A. Hinde & J. Stevenson-Hinde (Eds.), *Relationships within families: Mutual influences* (pp. 193–217). Oxford, UK: Clarendon.

Belsky, J., & Rovine, M. (1990). Patterns of marital change across the transition to parenthood: Pregnancy to three years postpartum. *Journal of Marriage and the Family, 52,* 5–19.

Bender, S., & Messner, E. (2003). *Becoming a therapist: What do I say, and why?* New York: Guilford.

Benjamin, B., & Werner, R. (2004). Touch in the Western world. *Massage Therapy Journal, 43,* 28–32.

Bennett, J., Ellison, J., & Ball, S. (2010). Are we there yet? *Newsweek,* pp. 42–46.

Bergen, K., & Braithwaite, D. O. (2009). Identity as constituted in communication. In W. F. Eadie (Ed.), *21st century communication: A reference handbook* (pp. 166–173). Thousand Oaks, CA: Sage.

Berger, C. (1987). Communicating under uncertainty. In M. Roloff & G. Miller (Eds.), *Interpersonal processes: New directions in communication research* (pp. 39–62). Newbury Park, CA: Sage.

Berger, E. (2006). *Raising kids with character.* New York: Rowman & Littlefield.

Bergner, R. M., & Bergner, L. L. (1990). Sexual misunderstanding: A descriptive and pragmatic formulation. *Psychotherapy, 27,* 464–467.

Bergstrom, M., & Nussbaum, J. (1996). Cohort differences in interpersonal conflict: Implications for older patient-younger care provider interaction. *Health Communication, 8,* 233–248.

Berne, E. (1964). *Games people play.* New York: Grove.

Bernstein, B. (1974). *Class, codes, and control: Theoretical studies toward a sociology of language* (Rev. ed.). New York: Shocken.

Berrett, D. (2011, November 18). What spurs students to stay in college and learn? Good teaching and diversity. *Chronicle of Higher Education,* p. A27.

Berrett, D. (2012, November 30). Diversity aids in critical thinking, 4 studies find. *Chronicle of Higher Education,* p. A3.

Bianchi, S., Robinson, J., & Milkie, M. (2006). *Changing rhythms of American family life.* New York: Russell Sage Foundation.

Bilton, N. (2013, March 18). Digital era is redefining etiquette. *Raleigh News & Observer,* pp. 1D, 2D.

Bippus, A., & Young, S. (2005). Owning your emotions: Reactions to expressions of self-versus other-attributed positive and negative emotions. *Journal of Applied Communication Research, 33,* 26–45.

Birdwhistell, R. (1970). *Kinesics and context.* Philadelphia: University of Pennsylvania Press.

Blackstrom, L., Armstrong, E., & Puentes, J. (2012). Women's negotiation of cunnilingus in college hookups and relationships. *Journal of Sex Research, 49,* 1–12.

Blake, S. (1996). *Loving your long-distance relationship.* New York: Anton.

Blieszner, R., & Adams, R. (1992). *Adult friendship.* Newbury Park, CA: Sage.

Blow, C. (2013, August 3). Marriage and minorities. *New York Times,* p. A19.

Bodey, K. (2009). *Exploring the possibilities of self work: Girls speak about their lives.* Ph.D. Dissertation Department of Communication Studies, University of North Carolina, Chapel Hill.

Bodey, K., & Wood, J. T. (2009). Grrrl power: Whose voices count and who does the counting? *Southern Communication Journal, 74,* 325–337.

Bond, J., Thompson, C., Galinsky, E., & Prottas, D. (2002). *Highlights of the national study of the changing workforce: Executive summary* (No. 3, pp. 1–4). Washington, DC: Families and Work Institute. Retrieved July 14, 2013, from http://familiesandwork.org/site/research/summary/nscw2002summ.pdf

Bonnett, C. (2007, May 13). What's up with mom? *Raleigh News & Observer,* pp. 1E, 3E.

Boss, P. (1987). Family stress. In M. B. Sussman & S. K. Steinmerz (Eds.), *Handbook of marriage and the family* (pp. 695–723). New York: Plenum.

Boss, P. (2007). Ambiguous loss theory: Challenges for scholars and practitioners. *Family Relations, 56,* 105–111.

Bowen, S. P., & Michal-Johnson, P. (1995). Sexuality in the AIDS era. In S. W. Duck & J. T. Wood (Eds.), *Understanding relationship processes: 5: Relationship challenges* (pp. 150–180). Thousand Oaks, CA: Sage.

Bowlby, J. (1973). *Separation: Attachment and loss* (Vol. 2). New York: Basic.

Bowlby, J. (1988). *A secure base: Parent-child attachment and healthy human development.* New York: Basic.

Bradbury, T. N., & Fincham, F. D. (1990). Attributions in marriage: Review and critique. *Psychological Bulletin, 107,* 3–33.

Bradshaw, C., Kahn, A., & Saville, B. (2010). To hook up or date: Which gender benefits? *Sex Roles, 62,* 661–669.

Brady, J. (2013, May 22). Some companies foster creativity, others fake it. *Wall Street Journal,* p. A15.

Braithwaite, D. W. (1996). "Persons first": Exploring different perspectives on the communication of persons with disabilities. In E. B. Ray (Ed.), *Communication and disenfranchisement: Social health issues and implications* (pp. 449–464). Hillsdale, NJ: Erlbaum.

Braithwaite, D. W., Bach, B. W., Baxter, L. A., Diverniero, R., Hammonds, J. R., Hosek, A. M., et al. (2010). Constructing family: A typology of voluntary kin. *Journal of Social and Personal Relationships, 27,* 388–407.

Braithwaite, D. W., & Kellas, J. K. (2006). Shopping for and with friends: Everyday communication at the shopping mall. In J. T. Wood & S. W. Duck (Eds.), *Composing relationships: Communication in everyday life* (pp. 86–95). Belmont, CA: Wadsworth.

Braithwaite, S. R., Delevi, R., & Fincham, F. D. (2010). Romantic relationships and the physical and mental health of college students. *Personal Relationships, 17,* 1–12.

Branje, S., Frijns, T., Finkenauer, C., Engles, R., & Meeus, W. (2007). You are my best friend: Commitment and stability in adolescents' same-sex friendships. *Personal Relationships, 14,* 587–603.

Brenning, K., Soenens, B., Braet, C., & Bosmans, G. (2011). An adaptation of the experiences in close relationships scale-revised for use with children and adolescents. *Journal of Personal and Social Relationships, 28,* 1048–1072.

Brody, J. (2013, May 14). Shaking off loneliness. *New York Times,* p. D5.

Brooks, D. (2009, May 29). The empathy issue. *New York Times,* p. A23.

Brooks, D. (2010, February 16). The lean years. *New York Times,* p. A23.

Brooks, D. (2013, May 21). What our words tell us. *New York Times,* p. A21.

Brown, A. B. (2010, February 5). Attention, please! Your book is calling. *Chronicle of Higher Education,* pp. B13–B14.

Bruess, C. (2011). Yard sales and yellow roses. In D. O. Braithwaite & J. T. Wood (Eds.), *Casing interpersonal communication: Case studies in personal and social relationships* (pp. 131–138). Dubuque, IA: Kendall Hunt.

Bruess, C., & Hoefs, A. (2006). The cat puzzle recovered: Composing relationships through family ritual. In J. T. Wood & S. W. Duck (Eds.), *Composing relationships: Communication in everyday life* (pp. 65–75). Belmont, CA: Wadsworth.

Bruess, C., & Pearson, J. (1997). Interpersonal rituals in marriage and adult friendship. *Communication Monographs, 64,* 25–46.

Buber, M. (1957). Distance and relation. *Psychiatry, 20,* 97–104.

Buber, M. (1970). *I and thou* (W. Kaufmann, Trans.). New York: Scribner.

Burgoon, J. K., & Bacue, A. E. (2003). Nonverbal communication skills. In B. Burleson & J. O. Greene (Eds.), *Handbook of communication and social interaction skills* (pp. 179–219). Mahwah, NJ: Erlbaum.

Burgoon, J. K., & Hale, J. (1988). Nonverbal expectancy violations: Model, elaboration and application to immediacy behaviors. *Communication Monographs, 55,* 58–79.

Burleson, B. R. (1984). Comforting communication. In H. E. Sypher & J. L. Applegate (Eds.), *Communication by children and adults: Social cognitive and strategic processes* (pp. 63–104). Beverly Hills, CA: Sage.

Burleson, B. R. (1987). Cognitive complexity. In J. C. McCroskey & J. A. Daly (Eds.), *Personality and interpersonal communication* (pp. 305–349). Newbury Park, CA: Sage.

Burleson, B. R., Holmstrom, A. J., & Gilstrap, C. M. (2005). "Guys can't say that to guys": Four experiments assessing the normative motivation account for deficiencies in the emotional support provided by men. *Communication Monographs, 72,* 468–501.

Burleson, B. R., & Rack, J. (2008). Constructivism theory. In L. A. Baxter & D. O. Braithwaite (Eds.), *Engaging theories in interpersonal communication: Multiple perspectives* (pp. 51–63). Thousand Oaks, CA: Sage.

Burleson, B. R., & Samter, W. (1994). A social skills approach to relationship maintenance: How individual differences in communication skills affect the achievement of relationship functions. In D. J. Canary & L. Stafford (Eds.), *Communication and relational maintenance.* Orlando, FL: Academic Press.

Burney, M. (2012, March 15). Standing up to bullies. *Chronicle of Higher Education* [Supplement: Diverse: Issues in Higher Education], pp. 50–53.

Buston, P. M., & Emlen, S. T. (2003). Cognitive processes underlying human mate choice: The relationship between self-perception and mate preference in Western society. *Proceedings of the National Academy of Sciences, 100,* 8805–8810.

Butzer, B., & Campbell, L. (2008). Adult attachment, sexual satisfaction, and relationship satisfaction: A study of married couples. *Personal Relationships, 15,* 141–154.

Cacioppo, J., & Patrick, W. (2009). *Loneliness.* New York: Norton.

Cahn, D. (Ed.). (2009). *Family violence: Communication processes.* Albany, NY: State University of New York Press.

Camara, S. K., & Orbe, M. P. (2010). Analyzing strategic responses to discriminatory acts: A co-cultural communicative investigation. *Journal of International and Intercultural Communication, 3,* 83–113.

Canary, D., & Stafford, L. (Eds.). (1994). *Communication and relational maintenance.* New York: Academic Press.

Canary, D., & Wahba, J. (2006). Do women work harder than men at maintaining relationships? In K. Dindia & D. Canary (Eds.), *Sex differences and similarities in communication* (2nd ed., pp. 359–377). Mahwah, NJ: Erlbaum.

Cancer. (2009, September 1). *New York Times*, p. D6.

Cancian, F. (1987). *Love in America*. New York: Cambridge University Press.

Cancian, F. (1989). Love and the rise of capitalism. In B. Risman & P. Schwartz (Eds.), *Gender in intimate relationships* (pp. 12–25). Belmont, CA: Wadsworth.

Carey, B. (2009, May 12). Judging honesty by words, not fidgets. *New York Times*, pp. D1, D4.

Carey, B. (2010, April 6). Seeking emotional clues without facial cues. *New York Times*, pp. D1, D6.

Carey, B., & O'Connor, A. (2004, February 15). How to get those at risk to avoid risky sex? *New York Times*, pp. D1, D7.

Carlson, R., & Carlson, K. (1999). *Don't sweat the small stuff in love*. New York: Hyperion.

Carnes, J. (1994, Spring). An uncommon language. *Teaching Tolerance*, pp. 56–63.

Carter, J. (1996). *Living faith*. New York: Times Books/Random House.

Cassirer, E. (1944). *An essay on man*. New Haven, CT: Yale University Press.

Cates, J. R., Herndon, N. L., Schulz, S. L., & Darroch, J. E. (2004). *Our voices, our lives, our futures: Youth and sexually transmitted diseases*. Chapel Hill: University of North Carolina at Chapel Hill School of Journalism and Mass Communication.

Caughlin, J., Afifi, W., Carpenter-Theune, K., & Miller, L. (2005). Reasons for, and consequences of, revealing personal secrets in close relationships: A longitudinal study. *Personal Relationships*, 12, 43–59.

Caughlin, J., & Arr, T. (2004). When is topic avoidance unsatisfying? Examining moderators of the association between avoidance and dissatisfaction. *Human Communication Research*, 30, 479–513.

Caughlin, J., & Ramey, M. (2005). The demand/withdraw pattern of communication in parent-adolescent dyads. *Personal Relationships*, 12, 337–355.

Caughlin, J., & Vangelisti, A. (2000). An individual difference explanation of why married couples engage in the demand/withdraw pattern of conflict. *Journal of Social and Personal Relationships*, 17, 523–551.

Centers for Disease Control. (2010). *National overview of Sexually Transmitted Diseases (STDs), 2008*. Retrieved May 20, 2010, from http://www.cdc.gov/std/stats08/natoverview.htm

Chapman, G. (2010). *The 5 love languages*. Chicago: Northfield.

Cherlin, A. J. (2010). *The marriage go-round: The state of marriage and the family in America today*. New York: Vintage.

Christensen, A. (2004). *Patient adherence to medical treatment regimens: Bridging the gap between behavioral science and biomedicine*. New Haven, CT: Yale University Press.

Christensen, A., & Heavey, C. (1990). Gender and social structure in the demand/withdraw pattern in marital conflict. *Journal of Personality and Social Psychology*, 59, 73–81.

Christensen, A., & Jacobson, N. (2002). *Reconcilable differences*. New York: Guilford.

Ciarrochi, J., & Mayer, J. (2007). *Applying emotional intelligence*. Florence, KY: Psychology Press.

Cissna, K. N. L., & Sieburg, E. (1986). Patterns of interactional confirmation and disconfirmation. In J. Stewart (Ed.), *Bridges, not walls* (4th ed., pp. 230–239). New York: Random House.

Clark, M. S., & Finkel, E. J. (2005). Willingness to express emotion: The impact of relationship type, communication orientation, and their interaction. *Personal Relationships*, 12, 169–180.

Clark, R. A. (1998). A comparison of topics and objectives in a cross section of young men's and women's everyday conversations. In D. Canary & K. Dindia (Eds.), *Sex differences and similarities in communication: Critical essays and empirical investigations of sex and gender interaction* (pp. 303–319). Mahwah, NJ: Erlbaum.

Clark, S. (2006, March 31). Workplace romance creates trouble for many companies. *Austin Business Journal*, p. 3.

Clements, K., Holtzworth-Munroe, A., Schweinle, W., & Ickes, W. (2007). Empathic accuracy of intimate partners in violent versus nonviolent relationships. *Personal Relationships*, 14, 369–388.

Clements, M., & Markman, H. (1996). The transition to parenthood: Is having children hazardous to marriage? In N. Vanzetti & S. W. Duck (Eds.), *A lifetime of relationships* (pp. 290–310). Pacific Grove, CA: Brooks/Cole.

Cloven, D. H., & Roloff, M. E. (1991). Sense-making activities and interpersonal conflict: Communicative cures for the mulling blues. *Western Journal of Speech Communication*, 55, 134–158.

Coan, J., Gottman, J., Babcock, J., & Jacobson, N. (1997). Battering and the male rejection of influence from women. *Aggressive Behavior*, 23, 375–388.

Colapinto, J. (2000). *As nature made him*. New York: HarperCollins.

Coleman, J. (2000, March 27). My turn: Is technology making us intimate strangers? *Newsweek*, p. 12.

Collier, M. J. (1996). Communication competence problematics in ethnic friendships. *Communication Monographs*, 63, 314–336.

Collins, F. S., & Fauci, A. S. (2010, May 23). AIDS in 2010: How we're living with HIV. *Parade*, pp. 10–12.

Collins, P. H. (1998). *Fighting words: Black women and the search for justice*. Minneapolis: University of Minnesota Press.

Colwell, K., Hiscock-Anisman, C. K., Memon, A., Colwell, L., Taylor, L., & Woods, D. (2009). Training in Assessment Criteria Indicative of Deception (ACID) to improve credibility assessments. *Forensic Psychology Practice, 9*, 99–107.

Connecting Generations. (2013, July 8). *Collaborative research sponsored by AARP and Microsoft*. Retrieved July 8, 2013, from http://www.dhs.gov/sites/default/files/publications/Connecting%20Generations_0.pdf

Conrad, C., & Poole, M. S. (2005). *Strategic organizational communication* (6th ed.). Fort Worth, TX: Harcourt.

Cooley, C. H. (1961). The social self. In T. Parsons, E. Shils, K. D. Naegele, & J. R. Pitts (Eds.), *Theories of society* (pp. 822–828). New York: Free Press.

Coontz, S. (2005a, February 14). Historically incorrect canoodling. *New York Times*, p. A23.

Coontz, S. (2005b). *Marriage, a history*. New York: Viking Adult.

Coontz, S. (2007, November 26). Taking marriage private. *New York Times*, p. A27.

Coontz, S. (2013, June 23). The disestablishment of marriage. *New York Times*, p. SR12.

Cooper, M. (2012, December 13). Census: U.S. to have no majority by 2043. *Raleigh News & Observer*, p. 3A.

Copeland, L., & Griggs, L. (1985). *Going international*. New York: Random House.

Corballis, M. C. (2002). *From hand to mouth: The origins of language*. Princeton, NJ: Princeton University Press.

Cowan, C., Cowan, P., Heming, G., & Miller, N. (1991). Becoming a family: Marriage, parenting, and child development. In P. A. Cowan & M. Hetherington (Eds.), *Family transitions* (pp. 79–109). Hillsdale, NJ: Erlbaum.

Cowley, G., & Murr, A. (2004, December 8). The new face of AIDS. *Newsweek*, pp. 76–79.

Cox, R. (2010). *Environmental communication and the public sphere* (2nd ed.). Thousand Oaks, CA: Sage.

Crockett, W. (1965). Cognitive complexity and impression formation. In B. A. Maher (Ed.), *Progress in experimental personality research* (Vol. 2, pp. 47–90). New York: Academic Press.

Cronen, V., Pearce, W. B., & Snavely, L. (1979). A theory of rule-structure and types of episodes and a study of perceived enmeshment in undesired repetitive patterns ("URPs"). In D. Nimmo (Ed.), *Communication yearbook* (Vol. 3, pp. 121–145). New Brunswick, NJ: Transaction.

Cunningham, J. A., Strassberg, D. S., & Haan, B. (1986). Effects of intimacy and sex-role congruency on self-disclosure. *Journal of Social and Clinical Psychology, 4*, 393–401.

Cupach, W. R., & Carlson, C. (2002). Characteristics and consequences of interpersonal complaints associated with perceived face threat. *Journal of Social and Personal Relationships, 19*, 443–462.

Cyberscope. (1996, December 23). *Newsweek*, p. 10.

Dailey, R. (2006). Confirmation in parent-adolescent relationships and adolescent openness: Toward extending conformation theory. *Communication Monographs, 73*, 434–458.

Dailey, R., Hampel, A. D., & Roberts, J. B. (2010). Relational maintenance in on-again/off-again relationships: An assessment of how relational maintenance, uncertainty, and commitment vary by relationship type and status. *Communication Monographs, 77*, 75–101.

Dainton, M. (2006). Cat walk conversations: Everyday communication in dating relationships. In J. T. Wood & S. W. Duck (Eds.), *Composing relationships: Communication in everyday life* (pp. 36–45). Thousand Oaks, CA: Sage.

Darling, A., & Dannels, D. (2003). Practicing engineers talk about the importance of talk: A report on the role of oral communication in the workplace. *Communication Education, 52*, 1–16.

Davies, D. (2006, March). The happiness factor. *Business Leader*, p. 6.

Davis, K. (1940). Extreme isolation of a child. *American Journal of Sociology, 45*, 554–565.

Davis, K. (1947). A final note on a case of extreme isolation. *American Journal of Sociology, 52*, 432–437.

DeFrancisco, V. (1991). The sounds of silence: How men silence women in marital relations. *Discourse and Society, 2*, 413–423.

DeFrancisco, V., & Chatham-Carpenter, A. (2000). Self in community: African American women's views of self-esteem. *Howard Journal of Communication, 11*, 73–92.

Delia, J., Clark, R. A., & Switzer, D. (1974). Cognitive complexity and impression formation in informal social interaction. *Speech Monographs, 41*, 299–308.

DeMaris, A. (2007). The role of relationship inequity in marital disruption. *Journal of Social and Personal Relationships, 24*, 177–195.

DeMaris, A. (2010). The 20-year trajectory of marital quality in enduring marriages: Does equity matter? *Journal of Social and Personal Relationships, 27*, 449–471.

Dennis, A., & Wood, J. T. (2012). "We're not going to have this conversation, but you get it": Black mother-daughter communication about sexual relations. *Women's Studies in Communication, 35*, 204–223.

Dentan, R. (1995). Bad day at Bukit Pekan. *American Anthropologist, 97,* 225–231.

Deresiewicz, W. (2009, December 11). Faux friendship. *Chronicle of Higher Education,* pp. B6–B9.

Deveny, K. (2009, June 30). We're bossy—and proud of it. *Newsweek,* p. 58.

DiBaise, R., & Gunnoe, J. (2004). Gender and culture differences in touching behavior. *Journal of Social Psychology, 144,* 49–62.

Dickson, P. (2007). *Family words: A dictionary of the secret language of families.* Oak Park, IL: Marion.

Diggs, N. (1998). *Steel butterflies: Japanese women and the American experience.* New York: State University of New York Press.

Diggs, N. (2001). *Looking beyond the mask: When American women marry Japanese men.* New York: State University of New York Press.

Dindia, K. (2000a). Relational maintenance. In C. Hendrick & S. Hendrick (Eds.), *Close relationships: A sourcebook* (pp. 287–300). Thousand Oaks, CA: Sage.

Dindia, K. (2000b). Sex differences in self-disclosure, reciprocity of self-disclosure, and self-disclosure and liking: Three meta-analyses reviewed. In S. Petronio (Ed.), *Balancing the secrets of private disclosures* (pp. 21–35). Mahwah, NJ: Lawrence Erlbaum.

Dindia, K., & Canary, D. (Eds.). (2006). *Sex differences and similarities in communication* (2nd ed.). Mahwah, NJ: Erlbaum.

Dokoupil, T. (2009, March 2). Men will be men. *Newsweek,* p. 50.

Domingue, R., & Mollen, D. (2009). Attachment and conflict communication in adult romantic relationships. *Journal of Social and Personal Relationships, 26,* 678–696.

Douthwaite, J. (2002). *The wild girl, natural man, and the monster.* Chicago: University of Chicago Press.

Dreifus, C. (2009, May 26). A conversation with Pauline Wiessner. *New York Times,* p. D2.

Duck, S. W. (2006). The play, playfulness, and the players: Everyday interaction as improvised rehearsal of relationships. In J. T. Wood & S. W. Duck (Eds.), *Composing relationships: Communication in everyday life* (pp. 15–23). Belmont, CA: Wadsworth.

Duck, S. W. (2007). *Human relationships* (4th ed.). London: Sage.

Duck, S. W., & Wood, J. T. (2006). What goes up may come down: Gendered dynamics in relational dissolution. In M. Fine & J. Harvey (Eds.), *Relational dissolution* (pp. 169–187). Mahwah, NJ: Erlbaum.

Eckman, P. (1989). Universal facial expressions. In H. Wagner & A. Manstead (Eds.), *Handbook of social psychophysiology* (pp. 143–164). Chichester, England: Wiley.

Ekman, P., & Friesen, W. V. (1971). Constants across cultures in the face and emotion. *Journal of Personality and Social Psychology, 17,* 124–129.

Eisenberg, N. (2002). Empathy-related emotional responses, altruism, and their socialization. In R. J. Davidson & A. Harrington (Eds.), *Voices of compassion: Western scientists and Tibetan Buddhists examine human nature* (pp. 131–164). London: Oxford University Press.

Ellington, J., & Marshall, L. (1997). Gender role perceptions of women in abusive relationships. *Sex Roles, 36,* 349–369.

Ellis, A. (1962). *Reason and emotion in psychotherapy.* New York: Lyle Stuart.

Ellis, A., & Harper, R. (1975). *A new guide to rational living.* Englewood Cliffs, NJ: Prentice Hall.

Ellis, K. (2000). Perceived teacher confirmation: The development and validation of an instrument and two studies of the relationship to cognitive and affective learning. *Human Communication Research, 26,* 264–291.

Emmers-Sommer, T. (2003). When partners falter: Repair after a transgression. In D. J. Canary & M. Dainton (Eds.), *Maintaining relationships through communication: Relational, contextual, and cultural variations* (pp. 185–205). Mahwah, NJ: Erlbaum.

Erbert, L. (2000). Conflict and dialectics: Perceptions of dialectical contradictions in marital conflict. *Journal of Social and Personal Relationships, 17,* 638–659.

Etcheverry, P. E., & Le, B. (2005). Thinking about commitment: Accessibility of commitment and prediction of relationship persistence, accommodation, and willingness to sacrifice. *Personal Relationships, 12,* 103–123.

Faber, A. J., Willerton, E., Clymer, S. R., MacDermid, S. M., & Weiss, H. M. (2008). Ambiguous absence, ambiguous presence: A qualitative study of military reserve families in wartime. *Journal of Family Psychology, 2,* 222–230.

Farrer, J., Tsuchiya, H., & Bagrowicz, B. (2008). Emotional expression in tsukiau dating relationships in Japan. *Journal of Social and Personal Relationships, 25,* 169–188.

Feeley, T., Hwang, J., & Barnett, G. (2008). Predicting employee turnover from friendship networks. *Journal of Applied Communication Research, 36,* 56–73.

Feeley, T., Moon, S., Kozey, R., & Slowe, A. (2010). An erosion model of employee turnover based on network centrality. *Journal of Applied Communication Research, 38,* 167–188.

Fehr, B. (1993). How do I love thee: Let me consult my prototype. In S. W. Duck (Ed.), *Understanding relationship processes: 1: Individuals in relationships* (pp. 87–122). Newbury Park, CA: Sage.

Fehr, B., & Russell, J. A. (1991). Concept of love viewed from a prototype perspective. *Journal of Personality and Social Psychology, 60,* 425–438.

Feig, J. (1989). *A common core: Thais and Americans*. Yarmouth, ME: Intercultural Press.

Feigenson, N. (2000). *Legal blame: How jurors think and talk about accidents*. Washington, DC: American Psychological Association.

Ferrante, J. (2013). *Sociology: A global perspective* (8th ed.). Belmont, CA: Wadsworth.

Field, T. (2003). *Touch*. Cambridge, MA: MIT Press.

Fincham, F. D. (2000). The kiss of the porcupines: From attributing responsibility to forgiving. *Personal Relationships, 7*, 1–23.

Fincham, F. D., & Beach, S. (2002). Forgiveness in marriage: Implications for psychological aggression and constructive communication. *Personal Relationships, 9*, 239–251.

Fincham, F. D., & Bradbury, T. N. (1987). The impact of attributions in marriage: A longitudinal analysis. *Journal of Personality and Social Psychology, 53*, 510–517.

Fincham, F. D., Bradbury, T. N., & Scott, C. K. (1990). Cognition in marriage. In F. D. Fincham & T. N. Bradbury (Eds.), *The psychology of marriage: Basic issues and applications* (pp. 118–119). New York: Guilford.

Fincham, F. D., Paleari, G., & Regalia, C. (2002). Forgiveness in marriage: The role of relationship quality, attributions, and empathy. *Personal Relationships, 9*, 27–37.

Finkel, E., Rusbult, C. E., Kumashiro, M., & Hannon, P. (2002). Dealing with betrayal in close relationships: Does commitment promote forgiveness? *Journal of Personality and Social Psychology, 82*, 956–974.

Finkelstein, J. (1980). Considerations for a sociology of emotions. *Studies in Symbolic Interaction, 3*, 111–121.

Fitzpatrick, M. A. (1988). *Between husbands and wives: Communication in marriage*. Newbury Park, CA: Sage.

Fitzpatrick, M. A., & Best, P. (1970). Dyadic adjustment in relational types: Consensus, cohesion, affectional expression and satisfaction in enduring relationships. *Communication Monographs, 46*, 167–178.

Fitzpatrick, M., & Ritchie, L. (1994). Communication schemata within the family: Multiple perspectives on family interaction. *Human Communication Research, 20*, 275–301.

Fleishman, J., Sherbourne, C., & Crystal, S. (2000). Coping, conflictual social interactions, social support, and mood among HIV-infected persons. *American Journal of Community Psychology, 28*, 421–453.

Fletcher, G. J., & Fincham, F. D. (1991). Attribution in close relationships. In G. J. Fletcher & F. D. Fincham (Eds.), *Cognition in close relationships* (pp. 7–35). Hillsdale, NJ: Erlbaum.

Floyd, K., & Parks, M. (1995). Manifesting closeness in the interactions of peers: A look at siblings and friends. *Communication Reports, 8*, 69–76.

Foeman, A., & Nance, T. (1999). From miscegenation to multiculturalism: Perceptions and stages of interracial relationship development. *Journal of Black Studies, 29*, 540–557.

Foerde, K., Knowlton, B., & Poldrack, R. (2006). Modulation of competing memory systems by distraction. *Proceedings of the National Academy of Sciences, 103*(31), 11778–11783.

Fox, L., & Frankel, H. (2005). *Breaking the code: Two teens reveal the secrets of better parent-child communication*. New York: Penguin/New American Library.

The fraying knot. (2013, January). *The Economist*, pp. 27–28.

Fresener, S. (1995). *The T-shirt*. Layton, UT: Gibbs Smith Publishers.

Fridlund, A. J. (1994). *Human facial expression*. San Diego, CA: Academic Press.

Friedman, M., Rholes, W. S., Simpson, J., Bond, M., Diaz-Loving, R., & Chan, C. (2010). Attachment avoidance and the cultural fit hypothesis. *Journal of Personal Relationships, 17*, 107–126.

Friesen, M., Fletcher, G., & Overall, N. (2005). A dyadic assessment of forgiveness in intimate relationships. *Personal Relationships, 12*, 61–77.

Frijda, N. H. (2006). *The laws of emotion*. Mahwah, NJ: Erlbaum.

Fryberg, S. A., & Markus, H. R. (2003). On being American Indian: Current and possible selves. *Self and Identity, 2*, 325–344.

Gabric, D., & McFadden, K. (2001). Student and employer perceptions of desirable entry-level operations management skills. *Mid-American Journal of Business, 16*, 51–59.

Gaines, S., Jr. (1995). Relationships among members of cultural minorities. In J. T. Wood & S. W. Duck (Eds.), *Understanding relationship processes: 6: Off the beaten track: Understudied relationships* (pp. 51–88). Thousand Oaks, CA: Sage.

Gallagher, C. (2012). Color-blind privilege. In E. Higginbotham & M. Andersen (Eds.), *Race and ethnicity in society* (3rd ed., pp. 57–61). Boston: Cengage.

Gallagher, W. (2009). *Rapt: Attention and the focused life*. New York: Penguin.

Galvin, K. (2006). Gender and family interaction: Dress rehearsal for an improvisation? In B. Dow & J. T. Wood (Eds.), *Handbook of gender and communication* (pp. 41–55). Thousand Oaks, CA: Sage.

Gangwish, K. (1999). *Living in two worlds: Asian-American women and emotion*. Paper presented at the National Communication Convention, Chicago.

Garcia, G. (2008). *The decline of men: How the American male is tuning out, giving up, and flipping off his future*. New York: Harper.

Garner, T. (1994). Oral rhetorical practice in African American culture. In A. González, M. Houston, & V. Chen (Eds.), *Our voices: Essays in culture, ethnicity, and communication* (pp. 81–91). Los Angeles: Roxbury.

Gentner, D., & Boroditsky, L. (2009). Early acquisition of nouns and verbs: Evidence from the Navajo. In V. Gathercole (Ed.), *Routes to language* (pp. 5–36). New York: Taylor & Francis.

George, L. (1995, December 26). Holiday's traditions are being formed. *Raleigh News & Observer*, pp. C1, C3.

Gerstein, M. (1998). *Victor: A novel based on the life of Victor, the savage of Aveyron*. New York: Farrar & Straus.

Gibb, J. R. (1961). Defensive communication. *Journal of Communication, 11,* 141–148.

Gibb, J. R. (1964). Climate for trust formation. In L. Bradford, J. Gibb, & K. Benne (Eds.), *T-group theory and laboratory method* (pp. 279–309). New York: Wiley.

Gibb, J. R. (1970). Sensitivity training as a medium for personal growth and improved interpersonal relationships. *Interpersonal Development, 1,* 6–31.

Glascock, N. (1998, February 22). Diversity within Latino arrivals. *Raleigh News & Observer*, p. 9A.

Glenn, D. (2010, February 5). Divided attention. *Chronicle of Higher Education*, pp. B6–B8.

Goffman, E. (1959). *The presentation of self in everyday life*. New York: Doubleday.

Goffman, E. (1967). *Interaction ritual*. New York: Pantheon.

Goldin-Meadow, S. (2004). *Hearing gesture: How our hands help us think*. Cambridge, MA: Harvard University Press.

Goldstein, J. (2013, June 11). A not-for-tourists guide to navigating a multicultural city (It's for the police). *Wall Street Journal*, pp. A18, A19.

Goldstein, S. (2011). Relational aggression in young adults' friendships and romantic relationships. *Journal of Personal Relationships, 18,* 645–656.

Goleman, D. (1995a). *Emotional intelligence*. New York: Bantam.

Goleman, D. (1995b, November–December). What's your emotional intelligence? *Utne Reader*, pp. 74–76.

Goleman, D. (1998). *Working with emotional intelligence*. New York: Bantam.

Goleman, D. (2006). *Social intelligence*. New York: Bantam.

Goleman, D., Boyatzis, R., & McKee, A. (2002). *Primal leadership: Realizing the power of emotional intelligence*. Cambridge, MA: Harvard Business School Press.

Gonzaga, G., Carter, S., & Buckwalter, G. (2010). Assortative mating, convergence, and satisfaction in married couples. *Journal of Personal Relationships, 17,* 634–644.

Goodwin, R., & Plaza, S. (2000). Perceived and received social support in two cultures: Collectivism and support among British and Spanish students. *Journal of Social and Personal Relationships, 17,* 282–291.

Gottman, J. (1993). The roles of conflict engagement, escalation or avoidance in marital interaction: A longitudinal view of five types of couples. *Journal of Consulting and Clinical Psychology, 61,* 6–15.

Gottman, J. (1994a). *What predicts divorce? The relationship between marital processes and marital outcomes*. Hillsdale, NJ: Erlbaum.

Gottman, J. (1994b). Why marriages fail. *The Family Therapy Newsletter, 27,* 41–48.

Gottman, J. (1997, May). *Findings from 25 years of studying marriage*. Paper presented at the Conference of the Coalition of Marriage, Family, and Couples Education, Arlington, VA.

Gottman, J., & Carrère, S. (1994). Why can't men and women get along? Developmental roots and marital inequities. In D. J. Canary & L. Stafford (Eds.), *Communication and relational maintenance* (pp. 203–229). New York: Academic Press.

Gottman, J., & Gottman, J. (2007). *Ten lessons to transform your marriage: America's love lab experts share their strategies for strengthening your relationship*. New York: Three Rivers Press.

Gottman, J., Markman, H. J., & Notarius, C. (1977). The topography of marital conflict: A sequential analysis of verbal and nonverbal behavior. *Journal of Marriage and the Family, 39,* 461–477.

Gottman, J., & Silver, N. (2000). *The seven principles for making marriage work*. Three Rivers, MI: Three Rivers Press.

Grady, D. (2010, April 20). Global update: Few boys counseled on sexual health. *New York Times*, p. D6.

Gravois, J. (2005, April 8). Teach impediment. *Chronicle of Higher Education*, pp. A10–A12.

Gray, P., & Anderson, K. (2010). *Fatherhood: Evolution and human behavior*. Cambridge: Harvard University Press.

Greenberg, S. (1997, Spring/Summer). The loving ties that bind. *Newsweek* [Special Issue], pp. 68–72.

Greene, J., & Burleson, B. (Eds.). (2003). *Handbook of communication and social interaction skills*. Mahwah, NJ: Erlbaum.

Greene, K., Derlega, V. J., & Mathews, A. (2006). Self-disclosure in personal relationships. In A. L. Vangelisti & D. Perlman (Eds.), *Cambridge handbook of personal relationships* (pp. 89–104). Cambridge: Cambridge University Press.

Groopman, J. (2007). *How doctors think*. Boston: Houghton Mifflin.

Groothof, H. A. K., Dijkstra, P., & Bareids, D. P. H. (2009). Differences in jealousy: The case of Internet infidelity. *Journal of Social and Personal Relationships, 26,* 1119–1129.

Gudykunst, W., & Lee, C. (2002). Cross-cultural communication theories. In W. Gudykunst & B. Mody (Eds.), *The handbook of international and intercultural communication* (2nd ed., pp. 25–50). Thousand Oaks, CA: Sage.

Gueguen, N., & De Gail, M. (2003). The effect of smiling on helping behavior: Smiling and good Samaritan behavior. *Communication Reports, 16,* 133–140.

Guerrero, L. (1996). Attachment style differences in intimacy and involvement: A test of the four-category model. *Communication Monographs, 63,* 269–292.

Guerrero, L. (2008). Attachment theory. In L. A. Baxter & D. O. Braithwaite (Eds.), *Engaging theories in interpersonal communication: Multiple perspectives* (pp. 295–307). Thousand Oaks, CA: Sage.

Guerrero, L., & Farinelli, L. (2009). The interplay of verbal and nonverbal codes. In W. F. Eadie (Ed.), *21st century communication: A reference handbook* (pp. 239–248). Thousand Oaks, CA: Sage.

Guerrero, L., & Floyd, K. (2006). *Nonverbal communication in close relationships.* Mahwah, NJ: Erlbaum.

Guerrero, L., Jones, S., & Boburka, R. (2006). Sex differences in emotional communication. In K. Dindia & D. Canary (Eds.), *Sex differences and similarities in communication* (pp. 242–261). Mahwah, NJ: Erlbaum.

Hafner, K. (2009, May 26). Texting may be taking toll. *New York Times,* pp. D1, D6.

Halatsis, P., & Christakis, N. (2009). The challenge of sexual attraction within heterosexuals' cross-sex friendship.

Journal of Social and Personal Relationships, 26, 919–937.

Hall, E. T. (1966). *The hidden dimension.* New York: Anchor.

Hall, E. T. (1968). Proxemics. *Current Anthropology, 9,* 83–108.

Hall, J. A. (1987). On explaining gender differences: The case of nonverbal communication. In P. Shaver & C. Hendricks (Eds.), *Sex and gender* (pp. 177–200). Newbury Park, CA: Sage.

Hall, J. A. (2006). How big are nonverbal sex differences? The case of smiling and nonverbal sensitivity. In K. Dindia & D. Canary (Eds.), *Sex differences and similarities in communication* (pp. 59–81). Mahwah, NJ: Erlbaum.

Hall, J. A., Carter, J. D., & Horgan, T. G. (2000). Gender differences in nonverbal communication of emotion. In A. H. Fischer (Ed.), *Gender and emotion: Social psychological perspectives* (pp. 97–117). Cambridge, UK: Cambridge University Press.

Hall, J. A., Coates, E., & Smith-LeBeau, L. (2004). Nonverbal behavior and the vertical dimension of social relations: A meta-analysis. *Psychological Bulletin, 131,* 898–924. Cited in M. L. Knapp & J. A. Hall (2006). *Nonverbal communication in human interaction.* Belmont, CA: Thomson/Wadsworth.

Hall, J., Park, N., Song, H., & Cody, J. (2010). Strategic misrepresentation in online dating: The effects of gender, self-monitoring, and personality traits. *Journal of Social and Personal Relationships, 27,* 117–135.

Hallstein, L. (2000). Where standpoint stands now: An introduction and commentary. *Women's Studies in Communication, 23,* 1–15.

Hamachek, D. (1992). *Encounters with the self* (3rd ed.). Fort Worth, TX: Harcourt Brace Jovanovich.

Hamermesh, D. (2011). *Beauty pays: Why attractive people are more*

successful. Princeton, NJ: Princeton University Press.

Hamlet, J. D. (2004). The reason why we sing: Understanding traditional African American worship. In A. González, M. Houston, & V. Chen (Eds.), *Our voices: Essays in culture, ethnicity, and communication* (4th ed., pp. 113–118). Los Angeles: Roxbury.

Haraway, D. (1988). Situated knowledges: The science question in feminism and the privilege of partial perspective. *Signs, 14,* 575–599.

Harding, S. (1991). *Whose science? Whose knowledge? Thinking from women's lives.* Ithaca, New York: Cornell University Press.

Harris, T. J. (1969). *I'm OK, you're OK.* New York: Harper & Row.

Hart Research Associates. (2013). *It takes more than a major: Employer priorities for college learning and student success.* Washington, DC: Author.

Hasserbrauck, M., & Aaron, A. (2001). Prototype matching in close relationships. *Personality and Social Psychology Bulletin, 27,* 1111–1122.

Hasserbrauck, M., & Fehr, B. (2002). Dimensions of relationship quality. *Personal Relationships, 9,* 253–270.

Hayakawa, S. I. (1962). *The use and misuse of language.* New York: Fawcett.

Hayakawa, S. I. (1964). *Language in thought and action* (2nd ed.). New York: Harcourt, Brace & World.

Haynes, J. (2009). Exposing domestic violence in country music videos. In L. Cuklanz & S. Moorti (Eds.), *Local violence, global media* (pp. 201–221). New York: Peter Lang.

Hecht, M. L., & Warren, J. (2006). Helpful professional relating: Constructing mentoring relationships through everyday talk. In J. T. Wood & S. W. Duck (Eds.), *Composing relationships: Communication in everyday life* (pp. 156–165). Belmont, CA: Wadsworth.

Heider, F. (1958). *The psychology of interpersonal relations*. New York: Wiley.

Heine, S. J., & Hamamura, T. (2007). In search of East Asian self-enhancement. *Personality and Social Psychology Review, 11*, 1–24.

Heine, S. J., & Raineri, A. (2009). Self-improving motivations and culture: The case of Chileans. *Journal of Cross-Cultural Psychology, 40*, 158–163.

Heise, D. (1999). Controlling affective experience interpersonally. *Social Psychology Quarterly, 62*, 4–11.

Helms, H., Proulx, C., Klute, M., McHale, S., & Crouter, A. (2006). Spouses' gender-typed attributes and their links with marital quality: A pattern analytic approach. *Journal of Social and Personal Relationships, 23*, 843–864.

Hendrick, C., & Hendrick, S. (1988). Lovers wear rose colored glasses. *Journal of Social and Personal Relationships, 5*, 161–184.

Hendrick, C., & Hendrick, S. (1989). Research on love: Does it measure up? *Journal of Personality and Social Psychology, 56*, 784–794.

Hendrick, C., & Hendrick, S. (1996). Gender and the experience of heterosexual love. In J. T. Wood (Ed.), *Gendered relationships* (pp. 131–148). Mountain View, CA: Mayfield.

Hendrick, C., Hendrick, S., Foote, F. H., & Slapion-Foote, M. J. (1984). Do men and women love differently? *Journal of Social and Personal Relationships, 2*, 177–196.

Hendrick, S., & Hendrick, C. (2006). Measuring respect in close relationships. *Journal of Social and Personal Relationships, 23*, 881–899.

Henline, B., Lamke, L., & Howard, M. (2007). Exploring perceptions of online infidelity. *Personal Relationships, 14*, 113–128.

Henrich, J., & Norenzayan, A. (2010). The weirdest people in the world? *Behavioral and Brain Sciences, 33*, 61–135.

Hesse-Biber, S. N., & Leavy, P. (2006). *The cult of thinness* (2nd ed.). New York: Oxford University Press.

Hewes, D. (Ed.). (1995). *The cognitive bases of interpersonal perception*. Mahwah, NJ: Erlbaum.

Hickson, M., Stacks, D., & Moore, N. (2004). *Nonverbal communication: Studies and applications*. Los Angeles: Roxbury.

Higginbotham, E., & Andersen, M. (2012). *Race and ethnicity: An anthology* (3rd ed.). Boston: Cengage.

Hochschild, A. (1979). Emotion work, feeling rules, and social structure. *American Journal of Sociology, 85*, 551–575.

Hochschild, A. (1983). *The managed heart*. Berkeley: University of California Press.

Hochschild, A. (1990). Ideology and emotion management: A perspective and path for future research. In T. Kemper (Ed.), *Research agendas in the sociology of emotions* (pp. 117–142). New York: State University of New York Press.

Hoffman, J. (2010, June 28). Online bullies pull schools into the fray. *New York Times*, pp. A13, A14, A15.

Hoffman, J. (2012, June 4). A warning to teenagers before they start dating. *New York Times*, pp. A12, A13.

Hoijer, H. (1994). The Sapir-Whorf hypothesis. In L. Samovar & R. Porter (Eds.), *Intercultural communication: A reader* (7th ed., pp. 38–49). Belmont, CA: Wadsworth.

Holt-Lunstad, J., Smith, T., & Layton, J. (2010). Social relationships and mortality risk: A meta-analytic review. *PLoS Med, 7*, e1000316. Retrieved June 4, 2013, from http://www.plosmedicine.org/article/info%3Adoi%2F10.1371%2Fjournal.pmed.1000316

Honeycutt, J. M. (1993). Memory structures for the rise and fall of personal relationships. In S. W. Duck (Ed.), *Understanding relationship processes: 1: Individuals in relationships* (pp. 30–59). Newbury Park, CA: Sage.

Honeycutt, J. M. (2003). *Imagined interactions*. Cresskill, NJ: Hampton.

Honeycutt, J. M. (2008). Imagined interaction theory. In L. A. Baxter & D. O. Braithwaite (Eds.), *Engaging theories in interpersonal communication: Multiple perspectives* (pp. 77–87). Thousand Oaks, CA: Sage.

Honoré, C. (2004). *In praise of slowness*. San Francisco: Harper.

Honoré, C. (2005). *In praise of slowness: Challenging the cult of speed*. San Francisco: HarperCollins.

Hoover, E. (2010, January 29). An immigrant learns 2 new languages. *Chronicle of Higher Education*, p. A22.

Houston, M. (2004). When black women talk with white women: Why dialogues are difficult. In A. González, M. Houston, & V. Chen (Eds.), *Our voices: Essays in culture, ethnicity, and communication* (4th ed., pp. 119–125). Los Angeles: Roxbury.

Houston, M., & Wood, J. T. (1996). Difficult dialogues, expanded horizons: Communicating across race and class. In J. T. Wood (Ed.), *Gendered relationships* (pp. 39–56). Mountain View, CA: Mayfield.

Houts, R. M., Barnett-Walker, K. C., Paley, B., & Cox, M. J. (2008). Patterns of couple interaction during the transition to parenthood. *Personal Relationships, 15*, 103–122.

Hrabi, D. (2013, June 22–23). Nestle while you work. *Wall Street Journal*, pp. D1, D8.

Huston, M., & Schwartz, P. (1995). Relationships of lesbians and gay men. In J. T. Wood & S. W. Duck (Eds.), *Understanding relationship* processes: 6: Off the beaten track: Understudied relationships (pp. 89–121). Thousand Oaks, CA: Sage.

Ijzerman, H., & Saddlemyer, J. (2012, December 9). Getting the cold shoulder. *New York Times*, p. SR12.

Inman, C. (1996). Friendships among men: Closeness in the doing. In J. T. Wood (Ed.), *Gendered relationships* (pp. 95–110). Mountain View, CA: Mayfield.

International Listening Association. (1995, April). An ILA definition of listening. *ILA Listening Post, 53,* 4.

Izard, C. E. (1991). *The psychology of emotions.* New York: Plenum.

Jacobs, T. (2010). *Cyberbullying investigated.* Minneapolis, MN: Free Spirit Publishing.

Jacobson, N., & Gottman, J. (1998). *When men batter women.* New York: Simon & Schuster.

James, W. (1890). *Principles of psychology.* New York: Henry Holt.

James, W., & Lange, C. B. (1922). *The emotions.* Baltimore: Williams & Wilkins.

Jayson, S. (2011, March 30). Is dating dead? *USA Today,* p. A1.

Jhally, S., & Katz, J. (2001, Winter). Big trouble, little pond. *Umass,* pp. 26–31.

Johnson, F. L. (1989). Women's culture and communication: An analytic perspective. In C. M. Lont & S. A. Friedley (Eds.), *Beyond the boundaries: Sex and gender diversity in communication* (pp. 301–316). Fairfax, VA: George Mason University Press.

Johnson, F. L. (2000). *Speaking culturally: Language diversity in the United States.* Thousand Oaks, CA: Sage.

Johnson, M. (2006). Gendered communication and intimate partner violence. In B. Dow & J. T. Wood (Eds.), *Handbook of gender and communication* (pp. 71–87). Thousand Oaks, CA: Sage.

Kachadourian, L., Fincham, F., & Davila, J. (2004). The tendency to forgive in dating and married couples: The role of attachment and relationship satisfaction. *Personal Relationships, 11,* 373–393.

Kahn, M. (2008, December 2). The six habits of highly respectful physicians. *New York Times,* p. D6.

Kanov, J. M., Maitlis, S., Worline, M., Dutton, J., Frost, P., & Lilius, J. (2004). Compassion in organizational life. *American Behavioral Scientist, 47,* 808–827.

Kantowitz, B., & Wingert, P. (1999, April 19). The science of a good marriage. *Newsweek,* pp. 52–57.

Kaufman, L. (2013, May 21). For the word on the street, courts call up an online witness. *New York Times,* pp. A1, A3.

Keating, D., Russell, J., Cornacchione, J., & Smith, S. (2013). Family communication patterns and difficult family conversations. *Journal of Applied Communication Research, 41,* 160–180.

Keizer, G. (2010). *The unwanted sound of everything we want: A book about noise.* New York: Perseus-Public Affairs.

Kelley, D. (1998). The communication of forgiveness. *Communication Studies, 49,* 1–17.

Kelley, H. H. (1967). Attribution theory in social psychology. In D. Levine (Ed.), *Nebraska symposium on motivation* (Vol. 15, pp. 192–238). Lincoln: University of Nebraska Press.

Kelley, H. H., & Thiabaut, J. (1978). *The social psychology of groups.* New York: Wiley.

Kelley, R. (1997). *Yo' mama's disFUNKtional!* Boston: Beacon.

Kelly, C., Huston, T. L., & Cate, R. M. (1985). Premarital relationship correlates of the erosion of satisfaction in marriage. *Journal of Social and Personal Relationships, 2,* 167–178.

Kelly, G. A. (1955). *The psychology of personal constructs.* New York: W. W. Norton.

Keltner, D. (2009). *Born to be good: The science of a meaningful life.* New York: W. W. Norton.

Kemper, T. (1987). How many emotions are there? Wedding the social and autonomic components. *American Journal of Sociology, 93,* 263–289.

Kendall, D. (2011). *Framing class.* Landham, MD: Rowman & Littlefield.

Kershaw, S. (2009a, May 28). For teenagers, hello means 'how about a hug?' *New York Times,* pp. A1, A3.

Kesebir, P., & Kesebir, S. (2012). The cultural salience of moral character and virtue declined in twentieth century America. *Journal of Positive Psychology, 7,* 471–480.

Kilbourne, J. (2010, summer). Sexist advertising, then & now. *Ms.,* pp. 34–35.

Kim, J., & Hatfield, E. (2004). Love types and subjective well-being: A cross-cultural study. *Social Behavior and Personality, 32,* 173–182.

Kirshenbaum, & Sheril. (2011). *The science of kissing.* New York: Grand Central Publishing.

Kito, M. (2005). Self-disclosure in romantic relationships and friendships among American and Japanese college students. *Journal of Social Psychology, 145,* 127–140.

Kleinke, C., Peterson, T., & Rutledge, T. (1998). Effects of self-generated facial expressions on mood. *Journal of Personality and Social Psychology, 74,* 272–279.

Klingberg, T. (2008). *The overflowing brain: Information overload and the limits of working memory.* New York: Oxford University Press.

Knapp, M. L., & Hall, J. A. (2006). *Nonverbal communication in human interaction.* Belmont, CA: Thomson/Wadsworth.

Knapp, M. L., & Vangelisti, A. (2005). *Interpersonal communication and human relationships* (5th ed.). Boston: Allyn and Bacon.

Knox, D., & Hall, S. (2010). *Relationship and sexual behaviors of a sample of 2,922 university students*. Unpublished data collected for D. Knox, M & F: Marriage and family, Cengage, Boston.

Koerner, A., & Fitzpatrick, M. (2002a). Toward a theory of family communication. *Communication Theory, 12*, 70–91.

Koerner, A., & Fitzpatrick, M. (2002b). Understanding family communication patterns and family functioning: The roles of conversation orientation and conformity orientation. *Communication Yearbook, 26*, 37–69.

Koerner, A., & Fitzpatrick, M. (2006). Family communication patterns theory: A social cognitive approach. In D. Braithwaite & L. Baxter (Eds.), *Engaging theories in family communication* (pp. 50–65). Thousand Oaks, CA: Sage.

Koesten, J. (2004). Family communication patterns, sex of subject, and communication competence. *Communication Monographs, 71*, 226–244.

Korkki, P. (2013, June 16). Messagets galore, but no time to think. *New York Times*, p. BU7.

Korn, M. (2013, May 2). Business schools know how you think, but how do you feel? *Wall Street Journal*, p. B1.

Krasnova, H., Wenninger, H., Widaja, T., & Buxmann, P. (2013, 27th February–1st March). *Envy on Facebook: A hidden threat to users' life satisfaction*. 11th International Conference on Wirtschaftsinformatik, Leipzig, Germany. Retrieved March 5, 2013, from http://warhol.wiwi.hu-berlin.de/~hkrasnova/Ongoing_Research_files/WI%202013%20Final%20Submission%20Krasnova.pdf

Kurdek, L. (2006). The nature and correlates of deterrents to leaving a relationship. *Personal Relationships, 13*, 521–535.

Labov, W. (1972). *Sociolinguistic patterns*. Philadelphia: University of Pennsylvania Press.

La Gaipa, J. J. (1982). Rituals of disengagement. In S. W. Duck (Ed.), *Personal relationships: 4: Dissolving personal relationships*. Newbury Park, CA: Sage.

Lakoff, G., & Johnson, M. (1980). *Metaphors we live by*. Chicago: University of Chicago Press.

Lama, D., & Eckman, P. (2009). *Emotional awareness: Overcoming the obstacles to psychological balance*. New York: Henry Holt.

Landa, J., & López-Zafra, E. (2010). The impact of emotional intelligence on nursing: An overview. *Psychology, 1*, 50–58.

Landro, L. (2013a, April 30). To motivate patients to change, doctors stop scolding. *Wall Street Journal*, pp. D1, D2.

Landro, L. (2013b, June 11). Hospitals work on the most frequent complaint: Noise. *Wall Street Journal*, p. D1.

Landrum, R., & Harrold, R. (2003). What employers want from psychology graduates. *Teaching of Psychology, 30*, 131–133.

Laner, M. R., & Ventrone, N. A. (2002). Dating scripts revisited. *Journal of Family Issues, 21*, 488–500.

Langer, S. (1953). *Feeling and form: A theory of art*. New York: Scribner.

Langer, S. (1979). *Philosophy in a new key: A study in the symbolism of reason, rite, and art* (3rd ed.). Cambridge, MA: Harvard University Press.

Langston, D. (2007). Tired of playing monopoly? In M. L. Andersen & P. H. Collins (Eds.), *Race, class, and gender: An anthology* (pp. 118–127). Belmont, CA: Wadsworth.

Lasswell, H. D. (1948). The structure and function of communication in society. In L. Bryson (Ed.), *The communication of ideas* (pp. 37–51). New York: Harper & Row.

Lasswell, M., & Lobsenz, N. M. (1980). *Styles of loving*. New York: Doubleday.

Laurenceau, J. P., Barrett, L. F., & Rovine, M. J. (2005). The interpersonal process model of intimacy in marriage: A daily-diary and multilevel modeling approach. *Journal of Family Psychology, 19*, 314–323.

Leaper, C. (Ed.). (1994). *Childhood gender segregation: Causes and consequences*. San Francisco: Jossey-Bass.

Leaper, C. (1996). The relationship of play activity and gender to parent and child sex-typed communication. *International Journal of Behavioral Development, 19*, 689–703.

Leaper, N. (1999). How communicators lead at the best global companies. *Communication World, 16*, 33–36.

Ledbetter, A., Griffin, E., & Sparks, G. (2007). Forecasting "friends forever": A longitudinal investigation of sustained closeness between best friends. *Personal Relationships, 14*, 343–350.

Lee, C. S. (2012). Exploring emotional expressions on YouTube through the lens of media system dependency theory. *New Media & Society, 14*, 457–475.

Lee, J. A. (1973). *The colours of love: An exploration of the ways of loving*. Don Mills, Ontario, Canada: New Press.

Lee, J. A. (1988). Love styles. In R. J. Sternberg & M. L. Barnes (Eds.), *The psychology of love* (pp. 38–67). New Haven, CT: Yale University Press.

Le Poire, B. A., Shepard, C., & Duggan, A. (1999). Nonverbal involvement, expressiveness, and pleasantness as predicted by parental and partner attachment style. *Communication Monographs, 66*, 293–311.

Levin, S., Taylor, P., & Caudle, E. (2007). Interethnic and interracial dating in college: A longitudinal study. *Journal of Social and Personal Relationships, 24,* 323–341.

Levy, A. (2005). *Female chauvinist pigs.* New York: Free Press.

Lewin, T. (2008, April 25). Informal style of electronic messages is showing up in schoolwork, study finds. *New York Times,* p. A12.

Lewin, T. (2010, January 20). Children awake? Then they're probably online. *New York Times,* pp. A1, A3.

Lewis, J. D., & Weigert, A. J. (1985). Social atomism, holism and trust. *Sociological Quarterly, 26,* 455–471.

Li, J. (2012). *Cultural foundations of learning: East and West.* New York: Cambridge University Press.

Lim, T. (2002). Language and verbal communication across cultures. In W. Gudykunst & B. Mody (Eds.), *The handbook of international and intercultural communication* (2nd ed., pp. 69–88). Thousand Oaks, CA: Sage.

Lofland, L. (1985). The social shaping of emotion: The case of grief. *Symbolic Interaction, 8,* 171–190.

Lohmann, A., Arriaga, X., & Goodfriend, W. (2003). Close relationships and placemaking: Do objects in a couple's home reflect couplehood? *Personal Relationships, 10,* 437–449.

Losee, S., & Olen, H. (2007). *Office mate: Your employee handbook for romance on the job.* Cincinnati, OH: Adams Media.

Louis, C. S. (2010, April 29). Cosmetic surgery gets a nip and tuck. *New York Times,* p. E3.

Lowry, J. (2013, June 13). Hands-free devices not risk-free, study says. *Raleigh News & Observer,* p. 5A.

Luft, J. (1969). *Of human interaction.* Palo Alto, CA: National Press Books.

Lund, M. (1985). The development of investment and commitment scales for predicting continuity of personal relationships. *Journal of Social and Personal Relationships, 2,* 3–23.

Luster, T., & Okagaki, L. (Eds.). (2005). *Parenting: An ecological perspective* (2nd ed.). Mahwah, NJ: Erlbaum.

Lustig, M., & Koester, J. (1999). *Intercultural competence: Interpersonal communication across cultures.* New York: Longman.

Lutz-Zois, C., Bradley, A., Mihalik, A., & Moorman-Eavers, E. (2006). Perceived similarity and relationship success among dating couples: An idiographic approach. *Journal of Social and Personal Relationships, 23,* 865–880.

MacGeorge, E. L. (2009). Social support. In W. F. Eadie (Ed.), *21st century communication: A reference handbook* (pp. 283–291). Thousand Oaks, CA: Sage.

MacGeorge, E. L., Gillihan, S. J., Samter, W., & Clark, R. A. (2003). Skill deficit or differential motivation? Accounting for sex differences in the provision of emotional support. *Communication Research, 30,* 272–303.

MacGeorge, E. L., Graves, A. R., Feng, B., Gillihan, S. J., & Burleson, B. R. (2004). The myth of gender cultures: Similarities outweigh differences in men's and women's provision of and responses to supportive communication. *Sex Roles, 50,* 143–175.

MacNeil, S., & Byers, E. S. (2005). Dyadic assessment of sexual self-disclosure and sexual satisfaction in heterosexual dating couples. *Journal of Social and Personal Relationships, 22,* 169–181.

Mahany, B. (1997, August 7). A hands-on study of language. *Raleigh News & Observer,* pp. 1E, 3E.

Major, B., Schmidlin, A. M., & Williams, L. (1990). Gender patterns in social touch: The impact of setting and age.

In C. Mayo & N. M. Henley (Eds.), *Gender and nonverbal behavior* (pp. 3–37). New York: Springer-Verlag.

Maltz, D. N., & Borker, R. (1982). A cultural approach to male-female miscommunication. In J. J. Gumperz (Ed.), *Language and social identity* (pp. 196–216). Cambridge, UK: Cambridge University Press.

Manning, W., & Cohen, J. (2012). Premarital cohabitation and marital dissolution: An examination of recent marriages. *Journal of Marriage and Family, 74,* 377–387.

Manusov, V., & Patterson, M. L. (2006). *The Sage handbook of nonverbal communication.* Thousand Oaks, CA: Sage.

Manusov, V., & Spitzberg, B. (2008). Attribution theory. In L. A. Baxter & D. O. Braithwaite (Eds.), *Engaging theories in interpersonal communication: Multiple perspectives* (pp. 37–49). Thousand Oaks, CA: Sage.

Mares, M. (1995). The aging family. In M. Fitzpatrick & A. Vangelisti (Eds.), *Explaining family interactions* (pp. 237–251). Thousand Oaks, CA: Sage.

Markman, H. (1990). *Advances in understanding marital distress.* Unpublished doctoral dissertation, University of Denver, Denver, CO.

Markman, H., Clements, M., & Wright, R. (1991, April). *Why father's prebirth negativity and a first-born daughter predict marital problems: Results from a ten-year investigation.* Paper presented at a symposium at the biennial meeting of the Society for Research in Child Development, Seattle, WA.

Martin, J., & Chaney, L. (2008). *Passport to success: The essential guide to business culture and customs in America's largest trading partners.* Santa Barbara, CA: Praeger.

Martin, J., & Nakayama, T. (2007). *Intercultural communication in context* (4th ed.). New York: McGraw-Hill.

Martz, D., Petroff, A., Curtin, L., & Bazzini, D. (2009). Gender differences in fat talk among American adults. *Sex Roles*, 61, 34–41.

Maslow, A. H. (1954/1970). *Motivation and personality* (3rd ed.). New York: Harper & Row.

Maslow, A. H. (1959/1970). *New knowledge in human values*. Chicago: H. Regnery.

Maslow, A. H. (1968). *Toward a psychology of being*. New York: Van Nostrand Reinhold.

Matsumoto, D. (1992). More evidence for the universality of a contempt expression. *Motivation and Emotion*, 16, 363–368.

Matsumoto, D., Franklin, B., Choi, J., Rogers, D., & Tatani, H. (2002). Cultural influences on the expression and perception of emotion. In W. Gudykunst & B. Mody (Eds.), *The handbook of international and intercultural communication* (2nd ed., pp. 107–126). Thousand Oaks, CA: Sage.

Maugh, T., II. (1994, November 26). Romantics seem to be bred, not born. *Raleigh News & Observer*, pp. 1A, 4A.

McAdoo, H. P. (Ed.). (2006). *Black families* (4th ed.). Thousand Oaks, CA: Sage.

McClellan, C. (2004, May 14). Man raised as a girl commits suicide at 38. *Raleigh News & Observer*, p. 9B.

McCullough, M., & Hoyt, W. (2002). Transgression-related motivational dispositions: Personality substrates of forgiveness and their links to the big five. *Personality and Social Psychology Bulletin*, 28, 1556–1573.

McDaniel, E., & Quasha, S. (2000). The communicative aspects of doing business in Japan. In L. Samovar & R. Porter (Eds.), *Intercultural communication: A reader* (9th ed., pp. 312–324). Belmont, CA: Wadsworth.

McGuffey, S., & Rich, L. (2004). Playing in the gender transgression zone: Race, class, and hegemonic masculinity in middle school. In J. Spade & C. Valentine (Eds.), *The Kaleidoscope of gender: Prisms, patterns, and possibilities* (pp. 172–183). Belmont, CA: Wadsworth.

McIntosh, P. (1995). White privilege and male privilege: A personal account of coming to see correspondences through work in women's studies. In M. L. Andersen & P. H. Collins (Eds.), *Race, class, and gender: An anthology* (2nd ed., pp. 94–105). Belmont, CA: Wadsworth.

McKay, V. (2000). Understanding the co-culture of the elderly. In L. Samovar & R. Porter (Eds.), *Intercultural communication: A reader* (9th ed., pp. 180–189). Belmont, CA: Wadsworth.

Mead, G. H. (1934). *Mind, self, and society*. Chicago: University of Chicago Press.

Mehrabian, A. (1981). *Silent messages: Implicit communication of emotion and attitudes* (2nd ed.). Belmont, CA: Wadsworth.

Meloy, R. (2006). *The psychology of stalking: Clinical and forensic perspectives* (2nd ed.). New York: Academic Press.

Men use half a brain to listen, study finds. (2000, November 29). *The Raleigh News & Observer*, p. 8A.

Metts, S. (2006a). Gendered communication in dating relationships. In B. Dow & J. T. Wood (Eds.), *Handbook of gender and communication research* (pp. 25–40). Thousand Oaks, CA: Sage.

Metts, S. (2006b). Hanging out and doing lunch: Enacting friendship closeness. In J. T. Wood & S. W. Duck (Eds.), *Composing relationships: Communication in everyday life* (pp. 76–85). Belmont, CA: Wadsworth.

Metts, S., & Cupach, W. R. (2008). Face theory. In L. A. Baxter & D. O. Braithwaite (Eds.), *Engaging theories in interpersonal communication: Multiple perspectives* (pp. 203–214). Thousand Oaks, CA: Sage.

Metts, S., Cupach, W. R., & Bejlovec, R. A. (1989). "I love you too much to ever start liking you": Redefining romantic relationships. *Journal of Social and Personal Relationships*, 6, 259–274.

Meyer, J. (2004). Effect of verbal aggressiveness on the perceived importance of secondary goals in messages. *Communication Studies*, 55, 168–184.

Mikulincer, M., & Shaver, P. (2005). Attachment theory and emotions in close relationships: Exploring the attachment-related dynamics of emotional reactions to relational events. *Personal Relationships*, 12, 149–168.

Milardo, R. (1986). Personal choice and social constraint in close relationships: Applications of network analysis. In V. Derlega & B. Winstead (Eds.), *Friendship and social interaction* (pp. 145–166). New York: Springer-Verlag.

Miller, D. W. (2000, February 25). Looking askance at eyewitness testimony. *Chronicle of Higher Education*, pp. A19–A20.

Miller, J. B. (1993). Learning from early relationship experience. In S. W. Duck (Ed.), *Understanding relationship processes, 2: Learning about relationships* (pp. 1–29). Newbury Park, CA: Sage.

Miller, K. (2007). Compassionate communication in the workplace: Exploring processes of noticing, connecting, and responding. *Journal of Applied Communication Research*, 35, 223–245.

Miller, W. I. (1993). *Humiliation*. Ithaca, NY: Cornell University Press.

Miller, W. I. (1998). *The anatomy of disgust*. Cambridge, MA: Harvard University Press.

Min, P. (Ed.). (1995). *Asian Americans: Contemporary trends and issues.* Thousand Oaks, CA: Sage.

Mochizuki, T. (1981). Changing patterns of mate selection. *Journal of Comparative Family Studies, 12,* 318–328.

Monastersky, R. (2001, July 6). Look who's listening. *Chronicle of Higher Education,* pp. A14–A16.

Mongeau, P., Carey, C., & Williams, M. (1998). First date initiation and enactment: An expectancy violation approach. In D. Canary & K. Dindia (Eds.), *Sex differences and similarities in communication* (pp. 413–426). Mahwah, NJ: Erlbaum.

Mongeau, P., & Henningsen, M. (2008). Stage theories of relationship development. In L. A. Baxter & D. O. Braithwaite (Eds.), *Engaging theories in interpersonal communication: Multiple perspectives* (pp. 363–375). Thousand Oaks, CA: Sage.

Mongeau, P., Serewicz, M., & Therrien, L. (2004). Goals for cross-sex first dates: Identification, measurement, and the influence of contextual factors. *Communication Monographs, 71,* 121–147.

Monkerud, D. (1990, October). Blurring the lines. Androgyny on trial. *Omni,* pp. 81–86.

Monsour, M. (1997). Communication and cross-sex friendships across the life cycle: A review of the literature. In B. Burleson (Ed.), *Communication yearbook* (Vol. 20, pp. 375–414). Thousand Oaks, CA: Sage.

Monsour, M. (2006). Communication and gender among adult friends. In B. Dow & J. T. Wood (Eds.), *Handbook of gender and communication* (pp. 57–89). Thousand Oaks, CA: Sage.

Morgan, L. (1996). When does life begin? A cross-cultural perspective on the personhood of fetuses and young children. In W. Haviland & R. Gordon (Eds.), *Talking about people: Readings in contemporary cultural anthropology* (pp. 24–34). Mountain View, CA: Mayfield.

Morreale, S. (2001, May). Communication important to employers. *Spectra,* p. 8.

Morreale, S. (2004, December). Accounting graduates need better listening skills and correct grammar. *Spectra,* p. 7.

Morrison, T., & Conaway, W. (2006). *Kiss, bow, or shake hands?* Avon, MA: Adams Media.

Muehlhoff, T. (2006). "He started it!": Communication in parenting. In J. T. Wood & S. W. Duck (Eds.), *Composing relationships: Communication in everyday life* (pp. 46–54). Belmont, CA: Wadsworth Thompson.

Muehlhoff, T., & Wood, J. T. (2002). Speaking of marriage: The marriage between theory and practice. *Journal of Social and Personal Relationships, 19,* 613–619.

Mulac, A. (2006). The gender-linked language effect: Do language differences make a difference? In K. Dindia & D. Canary (Eds.), *Sex differences and similarities in communication* (pp. 219–239). Mahwah, NJ: Erlbaum.

Murphy, K. (Ed.). (2006). *A critique of emotional intelligence.* Mahwah, NJ: Erlbaum.

Murray, S., Holmes, J., & Griffin, D. (1996a). The benefits of positive illusions: Idealization and the construction of satisfaction in close relationships. *Journal of Personality and Social Psychology, 70,* 79–98.

Murray, S., Holmes, J., & Griffin, D. (1996b). The self-fulfilling nature of positive illusions in romantic relationships: Love is not blind, but prescient. *Journal of Personality and Social Psychology, 71,* 1155–1180.

Mwakalye, N., & DeAngelis, T. (1995, October). The power of touch helps vulnerable babies survive. *APA Monitor,* p. 25.

Nanda, S., & Warms, R. (1998). *Cultural anthropology* (6th ed.). Belmont, CA: West/Wadsworth.

Nass, C. I., with Yen, C. (2010). *The man who lied to his lap top: What computers can teach us about human relationships.* New York: Penguin.

Nasser, H. E., & Overberg, P. (2010, June 11–13). Diversity grows as majority dwindles. *USA Today,* p. 1A.

Negra, D. (Ed.). (2006). *The Irish in us: Irishness, performativity, and popular culture.* Durham, NC: Duke University Press.

Nettle, D., & Romaine, S. (2000). *Vanishing voices: The extinction of the world's languages.* Oxford, UK: Oxford University Press.

Neyer, F. (2002). The dyadic interdependence of attachment security and dependency: A conceptual replication across older twin pairs and younger couples. *Journal of Social and Personal Relationships, 19,* 483–503.

Nicholson, J. (2006). "Them's fightin' words": Naming in everyday talk between siblings. In J. T. Wood & S. W. Duck (Eds.), *Composing relationships: Communication in everyday life* (pp. 55–64). Belmont, CA: Wadsworth.

Niedenthal, P. M., Krauth-Gruber, S., & Ric, F. (2006). *Psychology of emotion.* Thousand Oaks, CA: Sage.

Noller, P., & Fitzpatrick, M. (1992). *Communication in family relationships.* New York: Allyn and Bacon.

Norwood, K. (2010). *Here and gone: Competing discourses in the communication of families with a transgender member.* Ph.D. Dissertation, Department of Communication Studies, University of Iowa, Iowa City, IA.

Nosek, B., & Hansen, J. (2008). The associations in our heads belong to us: Searching for attitudes and knowledge in implicit evaluation. *Cognition & Emotion, 22,* 553–594.

Notarius, C. I. (1996). Marriage: Will I be happy or will I be sad? In N. Vanzetti & S. W. Duck (Eds.), *A lifetime of relationships* (pp. 265–289). Pacific Grove, CA: Brooks/Cole.

Nunberg, G. (2003, May 29). Fresh air [Radio interview]. Cited in R. West & L. Turner, (2006). In *Understanding interpersonal communication* (p. 164). Belmont, CA: Wadsworth.

Nyquist, M. (1992, Fall). Learning to listen. *Ward Rounds,* 11–15.

O'Brien, M. (2007). Ambiguous loss in families of children with Autism spectrum disorders. *Family Relations, 56,* 135–146.

Ofri, D. (2013). *What doctors feel.* Boston: Beacon Press.

O'Hair, D., & Eadie, W. F. (2009). Communication as an idea and an ideal. In W. F. Eadie (Ed.), *21st century communication: A reference handbook* (pp. 3–11). Thousand Oaks, CA: Sage.

O'Keefe, D. (2002). *Persuasion: Theory and research* (2nd ed.). Newbury Park, CA: Sage.

Olds, J., & Schwartz, R. (2010). *The lonely American: Drifting apart in the twenty-first century.* Boston: Beacon.

Olson, D., & McCubbin, H. (1983). *Families: What makes them work?* Thousand Oaks, CA: Sage.

Olson, L. N., & Braithwaite, D. O. (2004). "If you hit me again, I'll hit you back": Conflict management strategies of individuals experiencing aggression during conflicts. *Communication Studies, 55,* 271–285.

One in four girls. (2008, March 17). *New York Times,* p. A22.

Opir, E., Nass, C. I., & Wagner, A. D. (2009). Cognitive control in media multitaskers. *Proceedings of the National Academy of Sciences (Washington, DC), 106,* 15583–15587.

Orbuch, T., & Eyster, S. (1997). Division of household labor among black couples and white couples. *Social Forces, 76,* 301–322.

Orbuch, T., Veroff, J., & Hunter, A. (1999). Black couples, white couples: The early years of marriage. In E. Hetherington (Ed.), *Coping with divorce, single parenting, and remarriage* (pp. 23–43). Mahwah, NJ: Erlbaum.

Orloff, J. (2009). *Emotional freedom.* New York: Three Rivers.

Osborne, A. (1996, Summer). The paradox of effort and grace. *Inner Directions,* pp. 4–6.

Otnes, C., & Lowrey, T. (Eds.). (2004). *Contemporary consumption rituals.* Mahwah, NJ: Erlbaum.

Overall, N., Sibley, C., & Travaglia, L. (2010). Loyal but ignored: The benefits and costs of constructive communication behavior. *Journal of Personal Relationships, 17,* 127–148.

Painter, N. (2010). *White people's history.* New York: W. W. Norton.

Parker-Pope, T. (2009, January 20). Your nest is empty? Enjoy each other. *New York Times,* p. D5.

Parker-Pope, T. (2010a). *For better: The science of a good marriage.* New York: Dutton.

Parker-Pope, T. (2010b, April 6). Surprisingly, family time has grown. *New York Times,* p. D5.

Parker-Pope, T. (2013, July 2). Same, but different. *New York Times,* pp. D1, D6.

Parks, M., & Floyd, K. (1996a). Making friends in cyberspace. *Journal of Communication, 46,* 80–97.

Parks, M., & Floyd, K. (1996b). Meanings for closeness and intimacy in friendship. *Journal of Social and Personal Relationships, 13,* 85–107.

Parmer, N. (2013, May 21). A global love affair. *WSJ.Money,* p. 12.

Pataki, S., Shapiro, C., & Clark, M. (1994). Children's acquisition of appropriate norms for friendships and acquaintances. *Journal of Social and Personal Relationships, 11,* 427–442.

Pearce, W. B., Cronen, V. E., & Conklin, F. (1979). On what to look at when analyzing communication: A hierarchical model of actors' meanings. *Communication, 4,* 195–220.

Pearson, J. C. (1985). *Gender and communication.* Dubuque, IA: Brown.

Pennebaker, J. W. (1997). *Opening up: The healing power of expressing emotions* (Rev. ed.). New York: Guilford.

Pennington, B. A., & Turner, L. H. (2004). Playground or training ground? The function of talk in African American and European American mother-adolescent daughter dyads. In P. M. Buzzanell, H. Sterk, & L. H. Turner (Eds.), *Gender in applied contexts* (pp. 275–294). Thousand Oaks, CA: Sage.

Perlow, L. (2012). *Sleeping with your smartphone.* Boston: Harvard Business Review Press.

Petronio, S. (1991). Communication boundary management: A theoretical model of managing disclosure of private information between married couples. *Communication Theory, 1,* 311–335.

Petronio, S. (2000). *Balancing the secrets of private disclosure.* Mahwah, NJ: Erlbaum.

Pettigrew, T. F. (1967). Social evaluation theory: Consequences and applications. In D. Levine (Ed.), *Nebraska symposium on motivation* (pp. 241–311). Lincoln: University of Nebraska Press.

Philippot, P., & Feldman, R. (Eds.). (2004). *The regulation of emotion.* Mahwah, NJ: Erlbaum.

Phillips, G. M., & Wood, J. T. (1983). *Communication and human relationships.* New York: Macmillan.

Pinker, S. (2008). *The stuff of thought: Language as a window to human nature.* New York: Penguin.

Pitt-Catsouphes, M., Kossek, E., & Sweet, S. (Eds.). (2006). *The work and family handbook*. Mahwah, NJ: Erlbaum.

Piver, S. (2007). *The hard questions: 100 questions to ask before you say "I do."* New York: Tarcher/Penguin.

Planalp, S. (1997, September). Personal correspondence.

Planalp, S., & Fitness, J. (2000). Thinking/feeling about social and personal relationships. *Journal of Social and Personal Relationships, 16*, 731–750.

Pogue, L., & AhYun, K. (2006). The effect of teacher nonverbal immediacy and credibility on student motivation and affective learning. *Communication Education, 55*, 331–344.

Politically correct monikers are labeled incorrect. (1995, November 7). *Wall Street Journal*, p. A1.

Previti, D., & Amato, P. R. (2003). Why stay married? Rewards, barriers, and marital stability. *Journal of Marriage and Family, 65*, 561–573.

Proctor, R. (1991). *An exploratory analysis of responses to owned messages in interpersonal communication*. Doctoral dissertation Bowling Green University, Bowling Green, OH.

Pryor, J. B., & Merluzzi, T. V. (1985). The role of expertise in processing social interaction scripts. *Journal of Experimental Social Psychology, 21*, 362–379.

Rawlins, W. K. (1981). *Friendship as a communicative achievement: A theory and an interpretive analysis of verbal reports*. Unpublished doctoral dissertation, Temple University, Philadelphia.

Rawlins, W. K. (2009). *The compass of friendship*. Thousand Oaks, CA: Sage.

Reis, H. T., Clark, M. S., & Holmes, J. G. (2004). Perceived partner responsiveness as an organizing construct in the study of intimacy and closeness. In D. J. Mashek & A. P. Aron (Eds.), *Handbook of closeness and intimacy* (pp. 201–225). Mahwah, NJ: Erlbaum.

Reis, H. T., Senchak, M., & Solomon, B. (1985). Sex differences in the intimacy of social interaction: Further examination of potential explanations. *Journal of Personality and Social Psychology, 48*, 1204–1217.

Reis, H. T., Sheldon, K. M., Gable, S. L., Roscoe, J., & Ryan, R. M. (2000). Daily well-being: The role of autonomy, competence, and relatedness. *Personality and Social Psychology Bulletin, 26*, 419–435.

Remland, M. (2000). *Nonverbal communication in everyday life*. Boston: Houghton Mifflin.

Reske, J., & Stafford, L. (1990). Idealization and communication in long-distance premarital relationships. *Family Relations, 39*, 274–290.

Rhode, D. (2010). *The beauty bias*. New York: Oxford University Press.

Rhodes, T. (2010, November). Learning across the curriculum. *Spectra*, pp. 12–15.

Ribeau, S. A., Baldwin, J. R., & Hecht, M. L. (1994). An African-American communication perspective. In L. Samovar & R. Porter (Eds.), *Intercultural communication: A reader* (7th ed., pp. 140–147). Belmont, CA: Wadsworth.

Richmond, V., & McCroskey, J. (2000). The impact of supervisor and subordinate immediacy on relational and organizational outcomes. *Communication Monographs, 67*, 85–95.

Richmond, V., McCroskey, J., & Johnson, A. (2003). Development of the Nonverbal Immediacy Scale (NIS): Measures of self- and other-perceived nonverbal immediacy. *Communication Quarterly, 51*, 504–517.

Richtel, M. (2010, January 17). Phones drive us to distraction, even when we walk. *New York Times*, p. 4A.

Riela, S., Rodriguez, G., Aron, A., Xu, X., & Acevedo, B. (2010). Experiences of falling in love: Investigating culture ethnicity, gender, and speed. *Journal of Social and Personal Relationships, 27*, 473–493.

Riessman, C. (1990). *Divorce talk: Women and men make sense of personal relationships*. New Brunswick, NJ: Rutgers University Press.

Riley, N. (2013). *'Til faith do us part: How interfaith marriage is transforming America*. New York: Oxford University Press.

Rives, K. (2005, May 22). Keep up appearances. *Raleigh News & Observer*, p. 1A.

Robarchek, C., & Dentan, R. (1987). Blood drunkenness and the bloodthirsty Semai: Unmaking another anthropological myth. *American Anthropologist, 89*, 356–363.

Roberts, G., & Orbe, M. (1996, May). *Creating that safe place: Descriptions of intergenerational gay male communication*. Paper presented at the annual meeting of the International Communication Association, Chicago.

Rogers, E. (2008). Relational communication theory. In L. A. Baxter & D. O. Braithwaite (Eds.), *Engaging theories in interpersonal communication: Multiple perspectives* (pp. 335–347). Thousand Oaks, CA: Sage.

Roosevelt, M. (2010, January 14). When the gym isn't enough. *New York Times*, pp. E1, E8.

Roper poll. (1999). *How Americans communicate*. Retrieved January 8, 2000, from http://www.natcom.org/research/Roper/how_americans_communicate.htm

Rosen, L., Cheever, N., Cummings, C., & Felt, J. (2008). The impact of emotionality and self-disclosure on online dating versus traditional dating. *Computers in Human Behavior, 24*, 2124–2157.

Rosenbaum, L. (2011, November 22). The doctor feels your pain. *Raleigh News & Observer*, pp. 1D–2D.

Rosenblum, G. (2006, June 27). Changes in marriage always unsettling. *Raleigh News & Observer*, pp. 1E, 3E.

Rosenwein, B. (1998). *Anger's past: The sacred uses of emotion in the Middle Ages*. Ithaca, New York: Cornell University Press.

Roux, A. (2001). Rethinking official measures of poverty: Consideration of race, ethnicity, and gender. In D. Vannoy (Ed.), *Gender mosaics* (pp. 290–299). Los Angeles: Roxbury.

Rubin, L. (1985). *Just friends: The role of friendship in our lives*. New York: Harper & Row.

Rubinstein, J., Meyer, D., & Evans, J. (2001). Executive control of cognitive processes in task switching. *Journal of Experimental Psychology, 27*, 763–797.

Rusbult, C. (1987). Responses to dissatisfaction in close relationships: The exit-voice-loyalty-neglect model. In D. Perlman & S. W. Duck (Eds.), *Intimate relationships: Development, dynamics, and deterioration* (pp. 109–238). London: Sage.

Rusbult, C. E., & Buunk, B. (1993). Commitment processes in close relationships: An interdependence analysis. *Journal of Social and Personal Relationships, 19*, 175–204.

Rusbult, C. E., Drigotas, S., & Verette, J. (1994). The investment model: An interdependence analysis of commitment processes and relationship maintenance phenomena. In D. Canary & L. Stafford (Eds.), *Communication and relational maintenance* (pp. 115–140). San Diego, CA: Academic Press.

Rusbult, C. E., Johnson, D. J., & Morrow, G. D. (1986). Impact of couple patterns of problem solving on distress and nondistress in dating relationships. *Journal of*

Personality and Social Psychology, 50, 744–753.

Rusbult, C. E., & Zembrodt, I. M. (1983). Responses to dissatisfaction in romantic involvement: A multidimensional scaling analysis. *Journal of Experimental Social Psychology, 19*, 274–293.

Rusbult, C. E., Zembrodt, I. M., & Iwaniszek, J. (1986). The impact of gender and sex-role orientation on responses to dissatisfaction in close relationships. *Sex Roles, 15*, 1–20.

Rusk, T., & Rusk, N. (1988). *Mind traps: Change your mind, change your life*. Los Angeles: Price, Stern, Sloan.

Rusli, E. (2013, June 12). When words just aren't enough some turn to flatulent bunnies. *Wall Street Journal*, pp. A1, A14.

Ryan, R., La Guardia, J., Solky-Butzel, J., Chirkov, V., & Kim, Y. (2005). On the interpersonal regulation of emotions: Emotional reliance across gender, relationships, and cultures. *Personal Relationships, 12*, 145–163.

Saarni, C. (1990). Emotional competence: How emotions and relationships become integrated. In R. A. Thompson (Ed.), *Socioemotional development: Nebraska symposium on motivation* (pp. 115–182). Lincoln: University of Nebraska Press.

Saarni, C. (1999). *The development of emotional competence*. New York: Guilford.

Sack, K. (2008, August 12). Health benefits inspire rush to marry, or divorce. *New York Times*. Retrieved August 10, 2008, from http://www.nytimes.com/2008/08/13/us/13marriage.html?pagewanted=all&_r=0

Saffrey, C., & Ehrenberg, M. (2007). When thinking hurts: Attachment, rumination, and postrelationship adjustment. *Personal Relationships, 14*, 351–368.

Sahlstein, E. M. (2006). Relational life in the 21st century: Managing people, time, and distance. In J. T. Wood & S. W. Duck (Eds.), *Composing relationships: Communication in everyday life* (pp. 110–118). Belmont, CA: Thomson/Wadsworth.

Samovar, L., & Porter, R. (Eds.). (2000). *Intercultural communication: A reader* (9th ed.). Belmont, CA: Wadsworth.

Samovar, L., Porter, R., & McDaniel, E. R. (2009). *Communication between cultures* (12th ed.). Belmont, CA: Thomson.

Samp, J. A., & Palevitz, C. E. (2009). Dating and romantic partners. In W. F. Eadie (Ed.), *21st century communication: A reference handbook* (pp. 322–330). Thousand Oaks, CA: Sage.

Samter, W., & Cupach, W. (1998). Friendly fire: Topical variations in conflict among same- and cross-sex friends. *Communication Studies, 49*, 121–138.

Sanchanta, M. (2010, June 7). Cultivating multiculturalism. *Wall Street Journal*, p. B6.

Sayer, L. C., & Nicholson, L. L. (2006, March). *Economic resources, marital bargains, and marital quality*. Paper presented at the Annual Meeting of the Population Society of America, Silver Spring, MD.

Scarf, M. (1987). *Intimate partners*. New York: Random House.

Scarf, M. (2008). *September song: The good news about marriage in the later years*. New York: Riverhead.

Schachter, S. (1964). The interaction of cognitive and physiological determinants of emotion states. In P. Leiderman & D. Shapiro (Eds.), *Psychobiological approaches to social behavior* (pp. 138–173). Stanford, CA: Stanford University Press.

Schachter, S., & Singer, J. (1962). Cognitive, social, and physiological determinants of emotional state. *Psychological Review, 69,* 379–399.

Schaller, S. (1991). *A man without words.* New York: Summit Books.

Schappell, E. (2005). *The friend who got away.* New York: Doubleday.

Scharlott, B., & Christ, W. (1995). Overcoming relationship-initiation barriers: The impact of a computer-dating system on sex role, shyness, and appearance inhibition. *Computers in Human Behavior, 11,* 191–204.

Schiebinger, L., & Gilmartin, S. K. (2010, January–February). Housework is an academic issue. *Academe,* 39–34.

Schiminoff, S. B. (1980). *Communication rules: Theory and research.* Newbury Park, CA: Sage.

Schmanoff, S. (1987). Types of emotional disclosures and request compliance between spouses. *Communication Monographs, 54,* 85–100.

Schmid, R. (2010, July 5). Sense of touch affects behavior in startling ways. *Raleigh News & Observer,* p. 4B.

A scholarship for friendship. (2009, December 4). *Chronicle of Higher Education,* p. A6.

Scholz, M. (2005, June). A "simple" way to improve adherence. *RN, 68,* 82.

Schott, B. (2008, May 16). Minute waltz. *New York Times,* p. A23.

Schooler, D., Ward, M., Merriwether, A., & Caruthers, A. (2004). Who's that girl: Television's role in the body image of young white and black women. *Psychology of Women Quarterly, 28,* 38–47.

Schramm, W. (1955). *The process and effects of mass communication.* Urbana: University of Illinois Press.

Schutz, A. (1999). It was your fault! Self-serving bias in the autobiographical accounts of conflicts in married couples. *Journal of Social and Personal Relationships, 16,* 193–208.

Schutz, W. (1966). *The interpersonal underworld.* Palo Alto, CA: Science and Behavior Books.

Scott, C., & Meyers, K. (2005). The socialization of emotion: Learning emotion management at the fire station. *Journal of Applied Communication Research, 33,* 67–92.

Scott, J., & Leonhardt, D. (2013). Shadowy lines that still divide. In M. Andersen & P. H. Collins (Eds.), *Race, class and gender: An anthology* (8th ed., pp. 117–124). Boston: Cengage.

Seay, E. (2004, February 11). Lost city, lost languages. *Princeton Alumni Weekly,* pp. 17, 43.

Secklin, P. (1991, November). *Being there: A qualitative study of young adults' descriptions of friendship.* Paper presented at the Speech Communication Association Convention, Atlanta, GA.

Sedgwick, E. K. (1995). *Shame and its sisters: A Silvan Tomkins reader.* Durham, NC: Duke University Press.

Sedikides, C., Campbell, W., Reeder, G., & Elliott, A. (1998). The self-serving bias in relational context. *Journal of Personality and Social Psychology, 74,* 378–386.

Segrin, C., & Flora, F. J. (2005). *Family communication.* Mahwah, NJ: Erlbaum.

Seki, K., Matsumoto, D., & Imahori, T. (2002). The conceptualization and expression of intimacy in Japan and the United States. *Journal of Cross-Cultural Psychology, 33,* 303–319.

Seligman, M. E. P. (1990). *Learned optimism: How to change your mind and your life.* New York: Simon & Schuster/Pocket Books.

Seligman, M. E. P. (2002). *The authentic self.* New York: Free Press.

Seligson, H. (2009, December 24). For American workers in China, a culture clash. *New York Times,* pp. B1, B2.

Selingo, J. (2012, September 28). Colleges and employers point fingers over skills gap. *Chronicle of Higher Education,* p. A20.

Sellnow, D., & Sellnow, T. (2001). The "illusion of life" rhetorical perspective: An integrated approach to the study of music as communication. *Critical Studies in Media Communication, 18,* 295–415.

Shannon, C., & Weaver, W. (1949). *The mathematical theory of communication.* Urbana: University of Illinois Press.

Shattuck, T. R. (1994). *The forbidden experiment.* New York: Farrar, Straus & Giroux.

Shaver, P., Schwartz, J., Kirson, D., & O'Connor, C. (1987). Further explorations of a prototype approach. *Journal of Personality and Social Psychology, 52,* 1061–1086.

Shaver, P., Wu, S., & Schwartz, J. (1992). Cross-cultural similarities and differences in emotion and its representation: A prototype approach. In M. S. Clark (Ed.), *Emotion* (pp. 175–212). Newbury Park, CA: Sage.

Sheehy, G. (2010). *Passages in caregiving.* New York: William Morrow.

Shellenbarger, S. (2013, May 29). Just look me in the eye already. *Wall Street Journal,* pp. D1, D2.

Shelton, J. N., Trail, T., West, T., & Bergsieker, H. (2010). From strangers to friends: The interpersonal process of intimacy in development of interracial friendships. *Journal of Social and Personal Relationships, 27,* 71–90.

Sherman, C. W., & Boss, P. (2007). Spousal dementia caregiving in the context of late-life remarriage. *Dementia: The International Journal of Social Research and Practice, 6,* 245–270.

Simmons, L. (2002). *Odd girl out: The hidden culture of aggression in girls.* Orlando, FL: Harvest Books.

Simmons, L. (2004). *Odd girl speaks out: Girls write about bullies, cliques, popularity, and jealousy.* Orlando, FL: Harvest Books.

Simon, S. B. (1977). *Vulture: A modern allegory on the art of putting oneself down.* Niles, IL: Argus Communications.

Smock, P. J., & Manning, W. D. (2010). New couples, new families: The cohabitation revolution in the United States. In B. Risman (Ed.), *Families as they really are* (pp. 131–139). New York: Norton.

Socha, T. J., Sanchez-Hucles, J., Bromley, J., & Kelly, B. (1995). Invisible parents and children: Exploring African-American parent-child communication. In T. J. Socha & G. H. Stamp (Eds.), *Parents, children and communication: Frontiers of theory and research* (pp. 127–145). Mahwah, NJ: Erlbaum.

Socha, T. J., & Stamp, G. (Eds.). (2009). *Parents and children communicating with society.* New York: Routledge.

Socha, T. J., & Yingling, J. (2010). *Families communicating with children.* Malden, MA: Polity.

The social scene. (2013, June 3). *Wall Street Journal*, p. D2.

Solebello, N., & Elliott, S. (2011). "We want them to be as heterosexual as possible": Fathers talk about their teen children's sexuality. *Gender & Society, 25*, 293–315.

Spencer, L., & Pahl, R. (2006). *Rethinking friendship: Hidden solidarities today.* Princeton, NJ: Princeton University Press.

Spitzberg, B., & Cupach, W. (Eds.). (1998). *The dark side of close relationships.* Mahwah, NJ: Erlbaum.

Spitzberg, B., & Cupach, W. (2009). Unwanted communication, aggression and abuse. In W. F. Eadie (Ed.), *21st century communication: A*

reference handbook (pp. 444–453). Thousand Oaks, CA: Sage.

Sprecher, S. (2001). A comparison of emotional consequences of and changes in equity over time using global and domain-specific measures of equity. *Journal of Social and Personal Relationships, 18*, 477–501.

Sprecher, S., & Felmlee, D. (1997). The balance of power in romantic heterosexual couples over time from "his" and "her" perspectives. *Sex Roles, 37*, 363–379.

Sprecher, S., & Hendrick, S. (2004). Self-disclosure in intimate relationships: Associations with individual and relationship characteristics over time. *Journal of Social and Clinical Psychology, 23*, 857–877.

Sprecher, S., & Regan, P. (2002). Liking some things (in some people) more than others: Partner preferences in romantic relationships and friendships. *Journal of Social and Personal Relationships, 19*, 463–481.

Stafford, D. (2009, May 31). Workers cuss a blue streak. *Raleigh News & Observer*, pp. 1E, 6E.

Stafford, L. (2005). *Maintaining long-distance and cross-residential relationships.* Mahwah, NJ: Erlbaum.

Stafford, L. (2009). Spouses and other intimate partnerships. In W. F. Eadie (Ed.), *21st century communication: A reference handbook* (pp. 296–302). Thousand Oaks, CA: Sage.

Stafford, L., Dutton, M., & Haas, S. (2000). Measuring routine maintenance: Scale revision, sex versus gender roles, and the prediction of relational characteristics. *Communication Monographs, 67*, 306–323.

Stafford, L., & Merolla, A. (2007). Idealization, reunions, and stability in long-distance dating relationships. *Journal of Social and Personal Relationships, 24*, 37–54.

Stafford, L., Merolla, A., & Castle, J. (2006). When long-distance dating partners become geographically close. *Journal of Social and Personal Relationships, 23*, 901–919.

Stancliff, D. (2013, May 19). Tattoo you! New meaning to corporate branding, addiction Retrieved May 22, 2013, from http://www.times-standard.com/opinion/ci_23277780/tattoo-you-new-meaning-corporate-branding-addiction

Stearns, C., & Stearns, P. (1986). *Anger: The struggle for emotional control in America's history.* Chicago: University of Chicago Press.

Stepp, L. S. (2007). *Unhooked.* New York: Penguin/Riverhead.

Sternberg, E. (2009). *The silence of place and well-being.* Cambridge, MA: Harvard University Press.

Sternberg, R. J. (1986). A triangular theory of love. *Psychological Review, 93*, 119–135.

Stewart, J. (1986). *Bridges, not walls* (4th ed.). New York: Random House.

Stewart, L. P., Stewart, A. D., Friedley, S. A., & Cooper, P. J. (1990). *Communication between the sexes: Sex differences and sex role stereotypes* (2nd ed.). Scottsdale, AZ: Gorsuch Scarisbrick.

Strong, B., DeVault, C., & Cohen, T. (2011). *The marriage and family experience* (11th ed.). Boston: Cengage.

Sugarman, D., & Frankel, S. (1996). Patriarchal ideology and wife assault: A meta-analytic review. *Journal of Family Violence, 1*, 11–40.

Swain, S. (1989). Covert intimacy: Closeness in men's friendships. In B. Risman & P. Schwartz (Eds.), *Gender and intimate relationships* (pp. 71–86). Belmont, CA: Wadsworth.

Swidler, A. (2001). *Talk of love.* Chicago: University of Chicago Press.

Swift, M. (2010, May 9). Social media ease into the workplace. *Raleigh News & Observer*, p. 3E.

Tannen, D. (1990). *You just don't understand: Women and men in conversation*. New York: William Morrow.

Tannen, D. (1995). *Talking nine to five*. New York: William Morrow.

Tavris, C. (1989). *Anger: The misunderstood emotion*. New York: Simon & Schuster.

Tavris, C., & Aronson, E. (2007). *Mistakes were made (but not by me)*. New York: Harcourt.

Taylor, K. (2013, July 14). She can play that game, too. *New York Times*, p. ST1, 6.

Taylor, S. (2002). *The tending instinct: How nurturing is essential for who we are and how we live*. New York: Times Books.

Teachers' words may clash with cultures. (2000, February 23). *Raleigh News & Observer*, p. 4E.

Thiabaut, J., & Kelley, H. H. (1959). *The social psychology of groups*. New York: Wiley.

This year's freshmen. (2010, January 29). *Chronicle of Higher Education*, p. A23.

Tichenor, V. (2005). Maintaining men's dominance: Negotiating identity and power when she earns more. *Sex Roles, 53*, 191–205.

Tierney, J. (2009, May 5). Ear plugs to lasers: The science of concentration. *New York Times*, p. D2.

Tierney, J. (2013, March 19). Good news beats bad on social networks. *New York Times*, p. D3.

Ting-Toomey, S. (1988). Intercultural conflict styles: A face-negotiation theory. In Y. Kim & W. Gudykunst (Eds.), *Theories in intercultural communication* (pp. 213–235). Newbury Park, CA: Sage.

Ting-Toomey, S. (1991). Intimacy expressions in three cultures: France, Japan, and the United States. *International Journal of Intercultural Relations, 15*, 29–46.

Ting-Toomey, S. (2005). The matrix of face: An updated face-negotiation theory. In W. B. Gudykunst (Ed.), *Theorizing about intercultural communication* (pp. 71–92). Thousand Oaks, CA: Sage.

Ting-Toomey, S. (2009). Facework collision in intercultural communication. In F. Bargiela-Chiappini & M. Haugh (Eds.), *Face, communication, and social interaction* (pp. 227–249). Oakville, CT: Equinox.

Ting-Toomey, S., & Oetzel, J. (2001). *Managing intercultural conflict effectively*. Thousand Oaks, CA: Sage.

Ting-Toomey, S., & Oetzel, J. (2002). Cross-cultural face concerns and conflict styles. In W. Gudykunst & B. Mody (Eds.), *Handbook of international and intercultural communication* (2nd ed., pp. 143–163). Thousand Oaks, CA: Sage.

Tjalling, J., Deege, D., Beekman, A., van Tilburg, T., Stek, M., Jonker, C., et al. (2012). Feelings of loneliness, but not social isolation, predict dementia onset: Results from the Amsterdam study of the elderly. *Journal of Neurology, Neurosurgery, & Psychiatry*. Retrieved May 15, 2013, from http://jnnp.bmj.com/content/early/2012/11/06/jnnp-2012-302755

Todorov, A., Chaiken, S., & Henderson, M. (2002). The heuristic-systemic model of social information processing. In J. P. Dillard & M. Pfau (Eds.), *The persuasion handbook: Developments in theory and practice* (pp. 195–211). Thousand Oaks, CA: Sage.

Toma, C., & Hancock, J. (2011). Looks and lies: The role of physical attractiveness in online dating self-presentation and deception. *Communication Research, 37*, 335–351.

Tomasello, M. (2009). *Why we cooperate*. Boston: MIT Press.

Tong, S., & Walther, J. (2011). Just say "no thanks": The effects of romantic rejection across computer-mediated communication. *Journal of Personal and Social Relationships, 28*, 488–506.

Totten, L. D. (2006). Who am I right now? Negotiating familial and professional roles. In J. T. Wood & S. W. Duck (Eds.), *Composing relationships: Communication in everyday life* (pp. 186–193). Belmont, CA: Wadsworth.

Trees, A. (2006). Attachment theory: The reciprocal relationship between family communication and attachment patterns. In D. Braithwaite & L. Baxter (Eds.), *Family communication: Multiple perspectives* (pp. 165–180). Thousand Oaks, CA: Sage.

Tropp, L. R., & Wright, S. C. (2003). Evaluations and perceptions of self, in-group, and out-group: Comparisons between Mexican-American and European-American children. *Self and Identity, 2*, 203–221.

Trotter, R. J. (1975, October 25). The truth, the whole truth, and nothing but. . . . *Science News, 108*, 269.

Troy, A., & Laurenceau, J. (2006). Interracial and intraracial romantic relationships: The search for differences in satisfaction, conflict, and attachment style. *Journal of Social and Personal Relationships, 23*, 65–80.

Truman, D., Tokar, D., & Fischer, A. (1996). Dimensions of masculinity: Relations to date rape supportive attitudes and sexual aggression in dating situations. *Journal of Counseling and Development, 74*, 555–562.

Turkle, S. (2008). Always-on/always-on-you: The tethered self. In J. Katz (Ed.), *Handbook of mobile communication studies* (pp. 121–137). Cambridge, MA: MIT Press.

Turman, P. D., & Schrodt, P. (2006). Student perceptions of teacher power as a function of perceived teacher confirmation. *Communication Education, 55,* 265–279.

Turner, L. H., & Shutter, R. (2004). African American and European American women's visions of workplace conflict: A metaphorical analysis. *Howard Journal of Communication, 15,* 169–183.

TVB Research Central. (2010). *Media Trends Track.* Retrieved April 22, 2010, from http://www.tvb.org/ rcentral/mediatrendstrack/tvbasics/02_TVHouseholds.asp

Twenge, J. M., Campbell, W. K., & Freeman, E. C. (2012). Generational differences in young adults' life goals, concern for others, and civic orientation, 1966–2009. *Journal of Personality and Social Psychology, 102,* 1045–1062.

Twenge, J. M., Campbell, W. K., & Gentile, B. (2012). Generational increases in agentic self-evaluations among American college students, 1966–2009. *Self and Identity, 11,* 409–427.

Uecker, J., & Regnerus, M. (2011). *Premarital sex in America: How young Americans meet, mate, and think about marrying.* Oxford, UK: Oxford University Press.

Ueno, K., Gayman, M. D., Wright, E. R., & Quantz, S. D. (2009). Friends' sexual orientation, relational quality, and mental health among gay, lesbian and bisexual youth. *Personal Relationships, 16,* 659–670.

Underwood, A., & Adler, J. (2005, April 25). When cultures clash. *Newsweek,* pp. 68–72.

U.S. Census Bureau. (2007). Table 1312: Marriage and divorce rates by country, 1980 to 2003. *Statistical Abstract of the United States, 2007.* Retrieved April 8, 2008, from http://census.gov/compendia/statab/tables/07s1312.xls

U.S. Census Bureau. (2008). *United States population.* Retrieved February 25, 2005, from http://www.census.gov/population/estimates/nation/intfile1-3

U.S. Census Bureau. (2008). *2008 American Community Survey Table S1101. Households and families.* Retrieved May 10, 2010, from http://factfinder.census.gov

U.S. Department of Justice. (1999, October). *Eyewitness evidence: A guide for law enforcement.* Washington, DC: Author.

Vachss, A. (1994, August 28). You carry the cure in your own heart. *Parade,* pp. 4–6.

Vangelisti, A. (1993). Couples' communication problems: The counselor's perspective. *Journal of Applied Communication Research, 22,* 106–126.

Van Yperen, N. W., & Buunk, B. P. (1991). Equity theory and exchange and communal orientation from a cross-national perspective. *Journal of Social Psychology, 131,* 5–20.

Veroff, J. (1999). Marital commitment in the early years of marriage. In W. Jones & J. Adams (Eds.), *Handbook of interpersonal commitment and relationship stability* (pp. 149–162). New York: Plenum Press.

Vickers, S. (1999). *Native American identities: From stereotype to archetype in art and literature.* Albuquerque: University of New Mexico Press.

Vilhauer, R. (2009). Perceived benefits of online support groups for women with metastic breast cancer. *Women & Health, 49,* 381–404.

Vivian, J. (2011). *The media of mass communication* (10th ed.). Boston: Allyn & Bacon.

Vocate, D. (Ed.). (1994). *Intrapersonal communication: Different voices, different minds.* Hillsdale, NJ: Erlbaum.

Vogl-Bauer, S. (2009). When the world comes home. In T. Socha & G. Stamp (Eds.), *Parents and children communicating with society* (pp. 285–304). New York: Routledge.

Wade, N. (2009, December 1). We may be born with an urge to help. *New York Times,* pp. D1, D6.

Waldron, V., & Kelley, D. (2007). *Communicating forgiveness.* Thousand Oaks, CA: Sage.

Walker, K. (2004). Men, women, and friendship: What they say, what they do. In J. Spade & C. Valentine (Eds.), *The kaleidoscope of gender: Prisms, patterns, and possibilities* (pp. 403–413). Belmont, CA: Thomson/Wadsworth.

Walker, S. (2007). *Style and status: Selling beauty to African American women.* Lexington, KY: University of Kentucky Press.

Walter, T. J. (2009, April 24–26). Ties that bind—especially now. *Parade,* pp. 14–15.

Walters, R. (1984). Forgiving: An essential element in effective living. *Studies in Formative Spirituality, 5,* 365–374.

Walther, J., & Ramirez, A., Jr. (2010). New technologies and new directions in online relating. In N. S. W. Smith & S. R. Wilson (Eds.), *New direction in interpersonal communication research* (pp. 274–284). Thousand Oaks, CA: Sage.

Waltman, M. (2003). Strategems and heuristics in the recruitment of children into communities of hate: The fabric of our future nightmares. *Southern Journal of Communication, 69,* 22–36.

Wann, D., & Schrader, M. (2000). Controllability and stability in the self-serving attributions of sports spectators. *Journal of Social Psychology, 140,* 160–176.

Watters, E. (2013, March/April). We aren't the world. *Pacific Standard,* pp. 46–53.

Watzlawick, P. (2005). Self-fulfilling prophecies. In J. O'Brien & P. Kollock (Eds.), *The production of reality* (4th ed., pp. 87–109). Thousand Oaks, CA: Sage.

Watzlawick, P., Beavin, J., & Jackson, D. D. (1967). *Pragmatics of human communication*. New York: W. W. Norton.

Wegner, H., Jr. (2005). Disconfirming communication and self-verification in marriage: Associations among the demand/withdraw interaction pattern, feeling understood, and marital satisfaction. *Journal of Social and Personal Relationships, 22*, 19–31.

Weinstock, J., & Bond, L. (2000). Conceptions of conflict in close friendships and ways of knowing among young college women: A developmental framework. *Journal of Social and Personal Relationships, 17*, 687–696.

Weisinger, H. (1996). *Anger at work*. New York: William Morrow.

Weiss, S. E. (1987). The changing logic of a former minor power. In H. Binnendijk (Ed.), *National negotiating styles* (pp. 44–74). Washington, DC: U.S. Department of State.

Welch, I. (2003). *The therapeutic relationship: Listening and responding in a multicultural world*. Westport, CT: Praeger/Greenwood.

Welch, R. D., & Houser, M. E. (2010). Extending the four-category model of adult attachment: An interpersonal model of friendship attachment. *Journal of Social and Personal Relationships, 27*, 351–366.

Wen, L., & Kosowsky, J. (2013). *When doctors don't listen*. New York: St. Martin's/Thomas Dunne.

Werking, K. (1997). *We're just good friends: Women and men in nonromantic relationships*. New York: Guilford.

Werner, C. M., Altman, I., Brown, B. B., & Ginat, J. (1993). Celebrations in personal relationships: A transactional/dialectical perspective. In S. W. Duck (Ed.), *Understanding relational processes: 3: Social context and relationships* (pp. 109–138). Newbury Park, CA: Sage.

West, J. (1995). Understanding how the dynamics of ideology influence violence between intimates. In S. W. Duck & J. T. Wood (Eds.), *Understanding relationship processes: 5: Confronting relationship challenges* (pp. 129–149). Thousand Oaks, CA: Sage.

Weston, K. (1991). *Families we choose: Lesbians, gays, kinship*. New York: Columbia University Press.

Whaley, K., & Rubenstein, T. (1994). How toddlers "do" friendship: A descriptive analysis of naturally occurring friendships in a group child care setting. *Journal of Social and Personal Relationships, 11*, 383–400.

Whitbeck, L. B., & Hoyt, D. R. (1994). Social prestige and assortive mating: A comparison of students from 1956 and 1988. *Journal of Social and Personal Relationships, 11*, 137–145.

White, A. M. (2006). "You've got a friend:" African American men's cross-sex feminist friendships and their influence on perceptions of masculinity and women. *Journal of Social and Personal Relationships, 23*, 523–542.

White, B. (1989). Gender differences in marital communication patterns. *Family Process, 28*, 89–106.

Whorf, B. (1956). *Language, thought, and reality*. New York: MIT Press/Wiley.

Williams, A. (2009, June 22). At meetings, it's mind your BlackBerry or mind your manners. *New York Times*, pp. A1, A3.

Williams, R., & Williams, V. (1998). *Anger kills*. New York: HarperPerennial.

Williams-Baucom, K. J., Atkins, D. C., Sevier, M., Eldridge, K. A., & Christensen, A. (2010). "You" and "I" need to talk about "us": Linguistic patterns in marital interactions. *Personal Relationships, 17*, 41–56.

Wilmot, W., & Hocker, J. (2006). *Interpersonal conflict* (7th ed.). New York: McGraw-Hill.

Witt, P. L., Wheeless, L. R., & Allen, M. (2004). A meta-analytical review of the relationship between teacher immediacy and students learning. *Communication Monographs, 71*, 184–207.

Wolvin, A. (2009). Listening, understanding and misunderstanding. In W. F. Eadie (Ed.), *21st century communication: A reference handbook* (pp. 137–146). Thousand Oaks, CA: Sage.

Wood, J. T. (1982). Communication and relational culture: Bases for the study of human relationships. *Communication Quarterly, 30*, 75–84.

Wood, J. T. (1986). Different voices in relationship crises: An extension of Gilligan's theory. *American Behavioral Scientist, 29*, 273–301.

Wood, J. T. (1992). Telling our stories: Narratives as a basis for theorizing sexual harassment. *Journal of Applied Communication Research, 4*, 349–363.

Wood, J. T. (1993). Engendered relations: Interaction, caring, power, and responsibility in intimacy. In S. W. Duck (Ed.), *Understanding relationship processes: 3: Social context and relationships* (pp. 26–54). Newbury Park, CA: Sage.

Wood, J. T. (1994a). Gender and relationship crises: Contrasting reasons, responses, and relational orientations. In J. Ringer (Ed.), *Queer words, queer images: The construction of homosexuality* (pp. 238–265). New York: New York University Press.

Wood, J. T. (1994b). Gender, communication, and culture. In L. Samovar & R. Porter (Eds.), *Intercultural communication: A reader* (7th ed., pp. 155–164). Belmont, CA: Wadsworth.

Wood, J. T. (1994c). *Who cares? Women, care, and culture.* Carbondale: University of Southern Illinois Press.

Wood, J. T. (Ed.). (1996). *Gendered relationships.* Mountain View, CA: Mayfield.

Wood, J. T. (1997). Clarifying the issues. *Personal Relationships, 4,* 221–228.

Wood, J. T. (1998). *But I thought you meant …: Misunderstandings in human communication.* Mountain View, CA: Mayfield.

Wood, J. T. (2000). That wasn't the real him: Women's dissociation of violence from the men who enact it. *Qualitative Research in Review, 1,* 1–7.

Wood, J. T. (2001). The normalization of violence in heterosexual romantic relationships: Women's narratives of love and violence. *Journal of Social and Personal Relationships, 18,* 239–261.

Wood, J. T. (2004). Monsters and victims: Male felons' accounts of intimate partner violence. *Journal of Social and Personal Relationships, 21,* 555–576.

Wood, J. T. (2005). Feminist standpoint theory and muted group theory: Commonalities and divergences. *Women & Language, 28,* 61–64.

Wood, J. T. (2006a). Chopping the carrots: Creating intimacy moment by moment. In J. T. Wood & S. W. Duck (Eds.), *Composing relationships: Communication in everyday life* (pp. 24–35). Belmont, CA: Thomson/Wadsworth.

Wood, J. T. (2006b). Feminist, critical theories of the family. In D. Braithwaite & L. Baxter (Eds.), *Engaging theories in family communication: Multiple perspectives* (pp. 197–212). Thousand, Oaks, CA: Sage.

Wood, J. T. (2010a). The can-do discourse and young women's anticipations of future. *Women and Language, 33,* 103–107.

Wood, J. T. (2010b). He says, she says: Misunderstandings between men and women. In D. O. Braithwaite & J. T. Wood (Eds.), *Casing communication: Case studies in interpersonal communication* (pp. 59–65). Dubuque, IA: Kendall-Hunt.

Wood, J. T. (2011). Which ruler? What are we measuring? Thoughts on theorizing the division of domestic labor. *Journal of Family Communication, 11,* 39–49.

Wood, J. T. (2014). *Gendered lives: Communication, gender, and culture* (11th ed.). Stamford, CT: Cengage Learning.

Wood, J. T. (in press). He says/she says: Misunderstandings in communication between women and men. In D. O. Braithwaite & J. T. Wood (Eds.), *Casing interpersonal communication* (2nd ed.). Dubuque, IA: Kendall-Hunt.

Wood, J. T., Dendy, L., Dordek, E., Germany, M., & Varallo, S. (1994). Dialectic of difference: A thematic analysis of intimates' meanings for differences. In K. Carter & M. Presnell (Eds.), *Interpretive approaches to interpersonal communication* (pp. 115–136). New York: State University of New York Press.

Wood, J. T., & Duck, S. W. (Eds.). (2006a). *Composing relationships: Communication in everyday life.* Belmont, CA: Thomson/Wadsworth.

Wood, J. T., & Duck, S. W. (2006b). Introduction: Composing relationships: Communication in everyday life. In J. T. Wood & S. Duck (Eds.), *Composing relationships: Communication in everyday life* (pp. 1–13). Belmont, CA: Thomson/Wadsworth.

Wood, J. T., & Inman, C. C. (1993). In a different mode: Masculine styles of communicating closeness. *Journal of Applied Communication Research, 21,* 279–295.

Word for word. (2005, March 6). *New York Times,* p. WK7.

Words. (2013, May 19). *NPR Radio Lab.* First broadcast August 9, 2010.

Wright, P. H. (2006). Toward an expanded orientation to the comparative study of women's and men's same-sex friendships. In K. Dindia & D. Canary (Eds.), *Sex differences and similarities in communication* (pp. 37–57). Mahwah, NJ: Erlbaum.

WuDunn, S. (1991, April 17). Romance, a novel idea, rocks marriages in China. *New York Times,* pp. B1, B12.

Wydo, F., & Shaffer, L. (2011). Romantic partners, friends, friends with benefits, and casual acquaintances as sexual partners. *Journal of Sex Research, 48,* 554–564.

Yamamoto, T. (1995). Different silence(s): The poetics and politics of location. In W. L. Ng, S. Chin, J. Moy, & G. Okihiro (Eds.), *Reviewing Asian America: Locating diversity* (pp. 132–145). Pullman: Washington State University Press.

Yao, M., Mahood, C., & Linz, D. (2010). Sexual priming, gender stereotyping, and likelihood to sexually harass: Examining the cognitive effects of playing a sexually-explicit video game. *Sex Roles, 62,* 77–94.

Yellowbird, M., & Snipp, C. (2002). American Indian families. In R. Taylor (Ed.), *Minority families in the United States: A multicultural perspective* (3rd ed., pp. 226–249). Englewood Cliffs, NJ: Prentice-Hall.

Yen, H. (2010, January 16). More moms become breadwinners. *Raleigh News & Observer,* p. 3A.

Yen, H. (2012, May 17). Minority birthrate now surpasses whites in US, census shows. *Huffinington Post.* Retrieved May 28, 2012, from http://www.huffingtonpost.com/2012/05/17/minorities-birth-rate-now-surpass-whites-in-us-census_n_1523230.html

Yum, J. (2000). The impact of Confucianism on interpersonal relationships and communication patterns in East Asia. In L. Samovar & R. Porter (Eds.), *Intercultural communication: A reader* (9th ed., pp. 63–73). Belmont, CA: Wadsworth.

Zacchillil, T. L., Hendrick, C., & Hendrick, S. (2009). The romantic partner conflict scale: A new scale to measure relationship conflict. *Journal of Social and Personal Relationships, 26*, 1073–1096.

Zaslow, J. (2009). *The girls from Ames: A story of women & a forty-year friendship.* New York: Gotham.

Zenco, M. (2013, January 23). Ask the experts: Social media and conflict prevention. *Politics, Power, and Preventive Action.* Retrieved January 25, 2013, from http://blogs.cfr.org/zenko/2013/01/23/ask-the-experts-social-media-and-conflict-prevention/

Zernike, K. (2012, March 17). Jury finds spying in Rutgers dorm was a hate crime. *New York Times,* pp. A1, A16.

Zhang, Y. B., Harwood, J., & Hummert, M. L. (2005). Perceptions of conflict management styles in Chinese intergenerational dyads. *Communication Monographs, 72*, 71–91.

Zuger, A. (2013, April 1). A prescription for frustration. *New York Times,* p. B7.